Metropolis
1890–1940

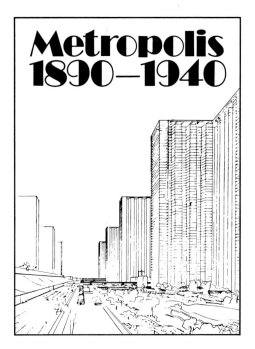

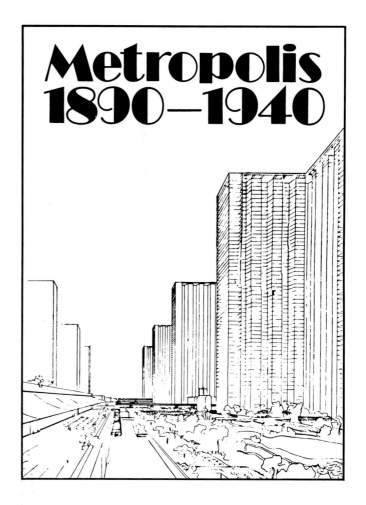

Metropolis 1890–1940

edited by
ANTHONY SUTCLIFFE
An Alexandrine Press Book

MANSELL · LONDON

This book is part of the series
Studies in History, Planning and the Environment
edited by Professor Gordon E. Cherry and Professor Anthony Sutcliffe

Mansell Publishing Limited, 6 All Saints Street, London N1 9RL

First published 1984

This book was commissioned, edited and designed by
Alexandrine Press, Oxford

British Library Cataloguing in Publication Data

Metropolis, 1890–1940.—(Studies in history, planning
    and the environment).—(An Alexandrine Press book)
    1. Sociology, Urban
    I. Sutcliffe, Anthony   II. Series
    307.7′6   HT151
    ISBN 0-7201-1616-3

Art production and text set in 10/12 pt Palatino by Katerprint Co Ltd, Oxford.
Printed and bound in Great Britain at the University Press, Cambridge.

Contents

The Contributors

DAVID HAROLD COX is Senior Lecturer in the Department of Music, University of Sheffield. He is a composer of vocal, chamber, orchestral and choral music, and a musicologist whose interests include the works of Edgard Varèse and the development of Electronic Music.

NORMA EVENSON is Professor of Architectural History at the University of California, Berkeley. She specializes in the history of modern architecture and urbanism. Her principal publications include *Chandigarh* (1966); *Le Corbusier: The Machine and the Grand Design* (1969); and *Two Brazilian Capitals: Architecture and Urbanism in Rio de Janeiro and Brasilia* (1973). Her most recent book, *Paris: A Century of Change 1878–1978*, was awarded the 1980 Hitchcock Prize by the American Society of Architectural Historians. Her current research is on the impact of Western architecture in India.

R.A. FRENCH is Senior Lecturer in the Geography of the USSR, jointly at University College London and the School of Slavonic and East European Studies. He is co-editor, with F.E. Ian Hamilton, of *The Socialist City* (1979), and is currently working on the urban and historical geography of Russia and the Soviet Union.

PATRICIA L. GARSIDE is Lecturer in Housing Administration, Department of Civil Engineering, University of Salford. She has worked extensively on the political and planning history of nineteenth- and twentieth-century London, and her publications include *Metropolitan London: Politics and Urban Change, 1837–1981* (1982) (with Ken Young).

PETER HALL is Professor of City and Regional Planning and of Geography in the University of California, Berkeley, and Professor of Geography, University of Reading. He has worked extensively on the comparative analysis of the planning problems of large metropolitan areas; his book *The World Cities* (1966), which helped to inspire this conference, is to appear in its third edition in 1984.

KENNETH T. JACKSON is Professor of History at Columbia University, where he has taught since 1968. His books include *The Ku Klux Klan in the City, 1915–1930* (1967); *American Vistas* (1971); *Cities in American History* (1972); and *Atlas of American History* (1978). Currently completing a broad analysis of suburbanization in the United States, he has recently been named General Editor of the Columbian History of Urban Life.

PETER KEATING is Reader in English Literature at the University of Edinburgh. His publications include *The Working Class in Victorian Fiction* (1971); *Into Unknown England* (1976); and *The Victorian Prophets* (1981). He is at present working on a social history of the late Victorian and early modern novel.

LARS OLOF LARSSON is Professor of the History of Art at the Christian-Albrechts-Universität,

Kiel. He has published a book on Speer's plans for Berlin, *Die Neugestaltung der Reichshauptstadt* (1978), and several articles on twentieth-century architecture in Scandinavia and Germany.

ANDREW LEES is Associate Professor of History at Rutgers University in Camden, New Jersey. He has written *Revolution and Reflection: Intellectual Change in Germany during the 1850s* (1974) and several articles on German attitudes towards cities. He co-edited *The Urbanization of European Society in the Nineteenth Century* (1976). He is working on the city as a theme in European thought between the early nineteenth century and the Second World War.

HORST MATZERATH is an economic and social historian with special interests in urban administration. A *Privatdozent* of the Free University of Berlin, he has recently taken up a post at the Historical Archives of the City of Cologne. Since 1970 he has been co-editor of *Informationen zur modernen Stadtgeschichte*. His publications include *Nationalsozialismus und kommunale Selbstverwaltung* (1970).

MICHAEL NASLAS, sometime Lecturer in the Department of Town and Regional Planning, University of Sheffield, is an architect and planner. He is working on a study of the influence of William Morris on British town planning.

JÜRGEN REULECKE is a *Privatdozent* of the University of Bochum, where he lectures in the Department of Historical Studies. His publications include *Die wirtschaftliche Entwicklung der Stadt Barmen von 1910 bis 1925* (1973), and two edited volumes, *Die deutsche Stadt im Industriezeitalter* (2nd edn., 1980), and *Alltag im Nationalsozialismus* (1981) (with Detlev Peukert). He is currently working on the middle-class contribution to social reform in nineteenth-century Germany.

THEDA SHAPIRO is Associate Professor in French Studies in the Department of Literatures and Languages at the University of California, Riverside. She is author of *Painters and Politics: The European Avant-Garde and Society, 1900–1925* (1976) and is currently working on a study of the artistic profession in Paris in the seventeenth and eighteenth centuries. In the longer term, she is planning a book on artists and the city.

ANTHONY SUTCLIFFE is Professor in the Department of Economic and Social History, University of Sheffield. As co-founder and meetings secretary of the Planning History Group, he organized the conference from which this volume has emerged. He recently completed a comparative study of the pre-1914 origins of urban planning, *Towards the Planned City: Germany, Britain, the United States, and France* (1981).

SHUN-ICHI J. WATANABE is Head of the Research Planning Division of the Building Research Institute, Ministry of Construction, Japan. A book, based upon his dissertation on American urban planning and the 'community ideal', won the annual award of the City Planning Institute of Japan in 1978. He is working on comparative studies of urban planning from American, British and Japanese perspectives as well as planning in developing countries. He is presently interested in Japanese planning history and is active in the Planning History Group in Japan. He is also an active member of the Academic Committee of the City Planning Institute of Japan.

Acknowledgements

First and foremost, the Planning History Group wishes to express its gratitude to the Social Science Research Council in general, and to its Human Geography and Planning Committee in particular, for the generous financial support which allowed the conference on which this volume is based to take place. Crucial additional support was provided by the Nuffield Foundation and the British Academy, to which our grateful thanks are also due. We are grateful to the Royal Town Planning Institute for its friendly interest and hospitality during the conference, and to the domestic and administrative staff of the University of Sussex for their affable and efficient attention.

Our individual debts of gratitude are as follows. Theda Shapiro wishes to thank the Academic Senate Committee on Research of the University of California, Riverside, for its support for the research on which her chapter is based, and her research assistant, Mark Sherman Simpson, for invaluable help in locating hundreds of images of the metropolis. Peter Hall wishes to thank Carmen Hass-Klau for a bibliographical search in connection with the German sections of his chapter. Jürgen Reulecke's German text has been translated by the editor. Horst Matzerath wishes to thank Dolorez L. Pérez for her help in translating his chapter into English. Anthony Sutcliffe wishes to thank the National Film Archive Stills Library and its staff for providing copies of a number of still photographs. Editor's thanks for additional typing are due to Kath Langstaff, Beverley Eaton and Beryl Moore. Finally, the editor wishes to thank his own editor, Ann Drybrough-Smith of the Alexandrine Press, for the support, attention, and design flair without which this volume would not have appeared in its present form.

Finally, acknowledgement for permission to reproduce copyright material is gratefully made to: Bibliothèque Nationale, Paris; Busch-Reisinger Museum, Harvard University; Chappell Music Ltd.; *Evening News*; Galerie der Stadt Stuttgart; Greater London Council Photo Library; Greater London Record Office; International Museum of Photography, George Eastman House, Rochester, N.Y.; Kunsthistorisch Institut der Rijksuniversiteit te Leiden; Kunstsammlung Nordrhein-Westfalen, Düsseldorf; Landesarchiv Berlin; Landessbildstelle Berlin; Los Angeles County Museum of Art; Macmillan Publishing Co.; Metro-Goldwyn-Mayer Film Co.; Metropolitan Museum of Art, New York; Municipal Archives of the City of New York; Musée National d'Art Moderne; Museen der Stadt Wien; Museum of Modern Art, New York; National Film Archive, London; Nationalgalerie, Berlin (West); New School for Social Research, New York City; Newark Museum; Préfecture de Paris; Préfecture de la Seine; Princeton University Press; Régie Autonome des Transports Parisiens; H. Roger-Viollet; The Samuel Goldwyn Company; Tass; Ville de Paris; Whitney Museum of American Art, New York.

A.S.

Chapter 1

Introduction: Urbanization, Planning, and the Giant City

ANTHONY SUTCLIFFE

My baby takes the morning train
He works from 9 to 5 and then
He takes another home again
To find me waiting for him.
'9 to 5', [1]

THE rhythms of the giant cities dominate our globe. Sheena Easton's hymn to the commuter reached the top of the British hit parade at the end of August, 1980, just as the Planning History Group was holding its second international conference, at the University of Sussex. In its nagging way, the song confirmed the immediacy of the conference theme – the giant city phenomenon. This book emerges from the conference, into a world in which the great metropolitan areas are even more a focus of interest than in 1980. In the newly-industrializing areas of the South, cities of unheard-of size are coming to the fore. A population of more than thirty-one millions is predicted for Mexico City by the end of the century [2]. In Britain and the United States, meanwhile, the largest urban centres are declining in population [3]. Both phenomena are high on the world's agenda of social problems. The teeming shanty suburbs of the Third World, and the partially demoralized denizens of the North Atlantic inner cities, each call the idea of progress into question, and pose a sullen threat to social and political stability [4]. Meanwhile, the great cities of the socialist world, Moscow and Peking at their head, offer an implicit critique and alternative which may yet become a prophecy, should Western society not withstand these mounting pressures [5].

The institution most directly involved in facing these problems is that product of industrial urbanization, urban and regional planning. The early 1980s find it at a low ebb. Pessimism and loss of direction have succeeded that vigorous optimism which reigned for a quarter of a century after the Second World War [6]. During that period, the evolution of the urban environment had appeared at last to be under enlightened public control. That control was crowned by mastery, or near-mastery, of the most intractable problem of all, the giant city. Renewed and reordered, its growth moderated and redistributed, the giant city had apparently been allotted an entirely efficient and socially desirable function within the settlement network. No longer would even a Paris – creator of a 'French desert', in Gravier's memorable phrase – be allowed to devour and blight. No longer would London's East End degrade and destroy its human contents while, ten miles distant, sprawling suburbs consumed thousands of agricultural acres and, two hundred miles away, men stood on street corners waiting for work which could never return. Planning had relegated all this to history. But then, from around 1970, this confidence began to crumble. Great mistakes, it seemed, had been made in urban reconstruction [7]. Urbanization was no more under control than it had been in the past, and in some respects intervention had undermined highly desirable processes of social and economic development [8]. The planners lost the confidence of the public to such an extent that even their own self-respect was undermined. New perceptions of planning, questioning its progressive potential, emerged on the Left, while it was eroded from the Right by a renewed advocacy of a beneficent market [9]. How, then, could planning respond to the metropolitan challenge of the 1980s?

In a recent analysis of the evolution of planning theory and practice, Peter Hall has pointed to a dialectical process, partially linked to economic and political cycles, whereby today's orthodoxy can become tomorrow's anathema [10]. The post-war vision of the ideal city has faded, but we patently have little with which to replace it. In a striking analogy, James Read has recently pointed to the utility of history at such a depressing and confusing time [11]. If the ship of planning is lost and awash on a storm-tossed ocean, its navigators should look back over their course. In so doing, they will both come to understand what combination of forces and decisions produced that course, and locate well-charted landmarks from which a new course can more confidently be plotted. The historians are those navigators. In this book, they seek the origins of post-1945 planning in the struggle with the giant city which went on for half a century before the Second World War, a period in which planning's emergence as a coherent expertise coincided with a distinctive phase in the much longer history of gargantuan urbanization.

The Giant City: Its Function and Historical Context

The idea of a modern world dominated by outsize cities has been given its most insistent form by Lewis Mumford. Mumford's apocalyptic vision of a progress from a dominating 'Metropolis', through a devouring 'Megalopolis', to a wasted 'Necropolis', has greater poetic than analytical qualities [12]. However, Mumford has not been alone in drawing attention to the distinctive qualities of the exceptionally large cities generated within industrial society. In the modern world, most national states sustain one city which is markedly larger – and sometimes several times larger – than any other city within its boundaries [13]. Some geographers have tried to explain the phenomenon in terms of a 'law of the primate city' [14]. Such centres clearly act as the focal points of national settlement systems, performing certain specialized domestic functions which are most efficiently concentrated at one location. However, in doing so, they participate more fully than smaller places in an international system of commodity and information flows within which they can achieve a further specialization of function. In this way, they become part of a worldwide urban network which is partially independent of the national networks. This is the sense of the German coinage, *Weltstadt* (world city), which came into common use in the nineteenth century and was adopted by Patrick Geddes in 1915 [15]. The high-order functions which this privileged status implies are also high-earning functions, so these cities can sustain very large populations. However, great size carries the additional benefit of external economies of scale in processing, so an important manufacturing function tends to develop alongside the higher-order, tertiary activities which provide the main dynamic of the city [16]. This amalgam of functions allows each city to exercise a considerable influence over its vicinity, stretching from its immediate hinterland to the country in which it is located, and sometimes even over adjoining national territories. It consequently tends to function as more than just a 'central place', *serving* the inhabitants of smaller settlements. As a market, a centre of information, and often a locus of political power, it tends to *dominate* activities taking place within its sphere of influence.

The phenomenon of the metropolis can be traced back to the Ancient world. There, in the context of a low level of economic activity, political factors were paramount in calling forth and sustaining these outstanding cities, most of which rose and fell with the great empires which were ruled from them. In the Mediterranean area, Thebes, Memphis, Babylon, Athens and Rome were successively the most reputed examples. In India and China, and possibly in the southern and central Americas as well, equivalent centres were to be found [17]. The idea of spatial dominance exercised from a large urban centre was summed up in the Greek coinage 'metropolis', meaning a mother city from which smaller cities (colonies) have been settled.

The largest of the giant cities of the Ancient world was Rome, with a population of between half a million and one million people at its apogee in the first and second centuries AD. After the dissolution of the Roman Empire, however, the fragmentation of political authority discouraged the giant city. Even Constantinople, at the height of its power in the seventh century, probably did not exceed half a million people. Subsequently, the capital of the Byzantine Empire was rivalled in size by the big centres of Islamic might, Baghdad in the east and Cordoba in the west. Charlemagne's Holy Roman Empire, meanwhile, was too dispersed to sustain a large imperial centre. Economic development within feudal Europe generated a dispersed system of trading and manufacturing towns, and it was not until large kingdoms and city states began to emerge from the twelfth century that giant cities comparable to the imperial centres of North Africa and the

East came onto the scene. Outstanding was Paris, capital of the precociously powerful kingdom of France, which had a population of well over two hundred thousand in the early fourteenth century, over twice the size of the biggest Italian trading cities, Venice, Milan and Genoa. Depopulation in late medieval Europe discouraged large cities and it was not until the sixteenth century, when renewed population growth was combined with a shift of Europe's centre of economic gravity towards the north as contacts with the New World were extended, that progress towards the emergence of very large cities was renewed.

Especially notable at this time was the rise of London. London confirmed what the growth of the big Italian trading cities had suggested earlier, that the new, mercantile economy of Western Europe was generating a new primary *raison d'être* for giant cities, that of coordinator of a long distance network of exchange. However, the distinction between London and the giant cities of Antiquity was not clear-cut, for trading outside Europe tended to lead to the acquisition of colonial territories, so that London eventually became an imperial capital in its turn. By the mid-seventeenth century, London's population of over four hundred thousand approached that of Paris. During the eighteenth century, London overtook the French capital and in 1801, the year of the first British census, London's population of over 850,000 ranked it among the two or three largest cities in the world – Peking, Canton, and, possibly, Edo (Tokyo) being its peers. By this time, a further stimulus to London's growth had been provided by the industrialization process, which had begun in Britain in the middle decades of the eighteenth century. As an important centre of trade and finance, with substantial manufacturing activities as well, London participated in and to a large extent coordinated British industrialization. As the nineteenth century wore on, London grew into the largest city the world had ever known, with a population of over five and a half million people by 1890 [18]. However, its pre-eminence within Britain had been undermined by the growth of centres of manufacturing and communications nearer the British coalfields. In 1801, London had been ten times the size of the next largest British city, Glasgow. Towards the end of the century, it was only five times larger than the two biggest provincial agglomerations, Merseyside and Manchester/Salford.

Paris grew at much the same rate as London during the nineteenth century, and so was constantly about half as populous as the British capital. However, it was able to maintain and even enhance its role as France's leading industrial city. It had also become, by the end of the century, the leading commercial and financial centre on the continent of Europe and the capital of a large overseas empire. On this basis, it reinforced its pre-eminence within France. In 1800, Paris had been five times the size of the largest provincial city, Lyons. Lyons grew fast enough to retain its position as France's second city, but by the end of the century it had fallen back to be only one-seventh the size of the capital.

The economic and political success of the United Kingdom and France encouraged the reorganization of much of the rest of Europe on national lines during the nineteenth century. The strongest of the new nation states was Germany, and the capital of the German Empire, Berlin, rose from relative obscurity in 1800, when it had a population of around 170,000, to reach over two million inhabitants, in city and suburbs, by the early 1890s. Like Paris, Berlin grew on the basis of its expanding manufacturing function as an important railway centre and source of demand, as well as of its political, administrative, financial and commercial roles. The German tradition of decentralization, which was reflected in the federal constitution of the German Empire after 1871, was too strong for Berlin to establish a numerical predominance comparable to that of Paris, or even of London. By the end of the century, Berlin was only three times the size of Germany's second city, Hamburg. However, Berlin's spatial influence put it on a par with Paris and London. By 1890 it was the capital of a small overseas empire, but even more important was its role as the dominant urban centre in central Europe.

Elsewhere in Europe the capitals of the new or strengthened nation states lagged well behind the three giants of London, Paris and Berlin in terms of population. Rome and Madrid had only half a million inhabitants each at the end of the century. Vienna was three times their size, and still the sixth-largest city in the world in 1900, but its growth had slowed since Austria's defeat by Prussia in 1866. Meanwhile, St. Petersburg and Moscow were growing faster and approaching Vienna's size, foreshadowing the important changes in the urban pattern of eastern Europe which would follow the collapse of the Habsburg Empire and the creation of a system of socialist republics in Russia at the end of the First World War.

The emergence of a new generation of giant cities on the fringes of Europe reflected the spread of industrialization from its heartlands in Britain, Belgium, France and Germany. However, the urban implications of this diffusion, in terms of the creation of giant cities, were even greater outside Europe. The incorporation of the Americas into a dynamic Atlantic economy had promoted New York to the rank of second-largest city in the world, with over four million inhabitants, by 1900. The great area, and the federal system, of the United States restricted New York's domestic pre-eminence, however. Chicago's population was two-fifths that of New York in 1900 and Philadelphia and Boston each had more than one million inhabitants. In accordance with Jeffersonian principles, New York was not even the capital of the Empire State, let alone of the Union, and its primacy in North America was based almost exclusively on its economic and cultural power. South and Central America, and Canada, less developed industrially than the United States, generated a number of regional nodes, but the largest of them, Buenos Aires, still had less than a million inhabitants towards the end of the century.

In the East, which had maintained some of the world's largest cities during Europe's medieval and early modern period of adjustment, the pattern of urbanization was transformed by the rapid industrialization of Japan after the Meiji restoration in 1868. With China now relatively remote from the main currents of Western trade, Tokyo (previously Edo) overtook Peking as the largest city in the Orient, reaching a population of one and a half million by 1900. Tokyo was only half as large again as Japan's second city, Osaka, at the end of the nineteenth century. However, its status as the imperial capital gave it an unquestioned predominance within Japan and throughout the growing Japanese sphere of influence on the Chinese mainland and in the Pacific. This political importance reinforced Tokyo's superiority to Calcutta and Bombay which, though very populous, exercised virtually no influence outside India because of their subservient position within the British imperial trading system.

The Giant City: 1890–1940

It had thus become clear, by the end of the nineteenth century, that the giant city throve on industrialization. Table 1.1, in which the giant cities chosen as representative in this study are compared with the next-largest cities in their territories, is far from a formal demonstration of this point, but it goes some way to suggest that the giant cities tended to maintain or even enhance their relative position at the head of their respective national urban networks during most of the nineteenth century. Some faltering can be detected in the last quarter of the century, but the effect visible in the table is partly due to the opening up of the American Mid-West and the consequent rise of Chicago at the relative expense of New York.

More suggestive, in the long term, is the relative decline of London towards the end of the century, consequent upon the shedding of industry after the 1860s; the marked decline in the rate of population growth in the world's largest city in the 1880s was seriously discussed by contemporaries as a climacteric [19]. Indeed, there was much interest in the 1890s in the possibility of a long-term shift away from large cities as a consequence of new means of communication and the adoption of electric power in manufacturing. Paul Meuriot, the French demographer and specialist in urban statistics, epitomized this tendency when he mused, in 1897:

> Cheap and speedy transport, unknown to our predecessors, is already permitting the partial removal of an overcrowded population from our cities. However, another innovation, the transmission of energy by electricity, may yet produce effects of quite a different order. The most important of them would be to liberate the industrial worker and abolish those concentrations of human population which today's equipment requires. The implications of a revolutionary technical change of this order are boundless. We can sum it up in this way: just as the extreme development of urban centres sprang from one scientific revolution, so may a second revolution cure the evils which are inseparable from that extreme development [20].

Table 1.1. Comparison of population growth of selected giant cities and their next largest cities, 1825–1950.

| | | (Population in thousands) | | | | | Multiple of growth | |
		Giant cities			Next-largest cities		Giant cities	Next-largest cities
(a) 1825–50		*1825*	*1850*		*1825*	*1850*	*1825–50*	*1825–50*
	London	1335	2320	Liverpool	170	422	1.7	2.5
	Paris	855	1314	Lyons	141	254	1.5	1.8
	New York	170	682	Philadelphia	138	426	4.0	3.1
	Edo (Tokyo)	530	567	Kyoto	350	323	1.1	0.9
	Berlin	222	446	Hamburg	130	193	2.0	1.5
	Total	3112	5329	Total	929	1618	1.7	1.7
(b) 1850–75		*1850*	*1875*		*1850*	*1875*	*1850–75*	*1850–75*
	London	2320	4241	Liverpool	422	650	1.8	1.5
	Paris	1314	2250	Lyons	254	331	1.7	1.3
	New York	682	1900	Philadelphia	426	791	2.8	1.9
	Berlin	446	1045	Hamburg	193	348	2.3	1.8
	Tokyo	567	780	Osaka	300	320	1.4	1.1
	Total	5329	10216	Total	1595	2440	1.9	1.5
(c) 1875–1900		*1875*	*1900*		*1875*	*1900*	*1875–1900*	*1875–1900*
	London	4241	6480	Manchester	590	1255	1.5	2.1
	New York	1900	4242	Chicago	405	1717	2.2	4.2
	Paris	2250	3330	Lyons	331	487	1.5	1.5
	Berlin	1045	2424	Hamburg	348	895	2.3	2.6
	Tokyo	780	1497	Osaka	320	931	1.9	2.9
	Total	10216	17973	Total	1994	5285	1.8	2.7
(d) 1900–1925		*1900*	*1925*		*1900*	*1925*	*1900–25*	*1900–25*
	New York	4242	7774	Chicago	1717	3564	1.8	2.1
	London	6480	7742	Manchester	1255	1725	1.2	1.4
	Tokyo	1497	5300	Osaka	931	2219	3.5	2.4
	Paris	3330	4800	Lyons	487	653	1.4	1.3
	Berlin	2424	4013	Hamburg	895	1369	1.7	1.5
	Moscow	1120	1764	Leningrad	1439	1430	1.6	1.0
	Total	19093	31393	Total	6724	10960	1.6	1.6
(e) 1925–50		*1925*	*1950*		*1925*	*1950*	*1925–50*	*1925–50*
	New York	7774	12300	Chicago	3564	4906	1.6	1.4
	London	7742	8860	Manchester	1725	2382	1.1	1.4
	Tokyo	5300	7547	Osaka	2219	3480	1.4	1.6
	Paris	4800	5900	Lyons	653	650	1.2	1.0
	Moscow	1764	5100	Leningrad	1430	2700	2.9	1.9
	Berlin	4013	3707	Hamburg	1369	1580	0.9	1.2
	Total	31393	43414	Total	10960	15698	1.4	1.4

Notes
The Ruhr, as a multi-nodal conurbation rather than a concentric urban area, is omitted throughout. The Moscow–St. Petersburg comparison is omitted from the 1825–50, 1850–75, and 1875–1900 tables as St.Petersburg was the larger throughout those periods.

Source: Calculated from Chandler and Fox (1974) pp. 323–37 (see note 17).

The context of Meuriot's reflections was the world economic revival which, after a period of generally low investment since the early 1870s – sometimes referred to as the Great Depression – was well under way by the mid-1890s. That revival accelerated the development and adoption of transport innovations, and the application of new sources of power to industry. The immediate effect of these changes was to accelerate the growth of towns, and especially of large towns, giving further encouragement to the crude anti-urban sentiments to which so many critics of late-nineteenth-century social conditions were prone. However, the innovations seemed to hold out the hope to such people of an eventual deconcentration or even dissolution of the large city. Ebenezer Howard's Garden City idea, elaborated in the 1890s, was a typical product of this conjuncture.

As rapid economic growth continued into the early twentieth century, and a new transport innovation, petrol motor traction, came into wider use, it became clear that the built-up area of cities was expanding faster than ever before. However, there were few signs of a *dissolution* of the city. Technical advances seemed only to enhance the efficiency of the large cities so that they attracted even *more* employment. The giant cities, as table 1.1 suggests, shared fully in this new phase of accelerated urban growth. As early as 1899, Adna F. Weber, the American statistician whose comprehensive analysis of urbanization deservedly eclipsed Meuriot's, dismissed the prophets of disurbanization as 'literary critics and *dilettantes* in political economy' [21]. He predicted precisely the opposite: the continued growth of the largest cities. Indeed, urban growth, for Weber, was 'essentially a great-city growth' [22]. Large cities offered important economies of scale in manufacturing together with access to the market under conditions of easy transport [23]. The growth of industrial productivity thus reinforced the existing central-place function of large cities as centres of exchange and high-order functions of all types. Weber paid due regard to the possibility that the largest cities might be beginning to lose their comparative advantage in manufacturing, owing mainly to congestion costs, but he inclined to the view that decentralization within the concentric urban area would normally overcome this disadvantage [24].

Down to 1940 (and indeed until around 1970), Weber's analysis remained the purest orthodoxy. The revolution in intra-urban transport spread the city and minimized congestion costs, allowing enterprise to take full advantage of the economies of agglomeration and scale offered by the largest urban areas. Meanwhile, the giant cities were favoured by changes in the structure of the world economy. Now that the essentials of the industrial infrastructure were in place, a big growth of consumer industries occurred. It was largely based on mass-production techniques appropriate to the employment of large quantities of unskilled and semi-skilled labour. The giant cities were a prominent source of such labour, particularly among females. Moreover, the growing consumer-orientation of industry encouraged firms to locate near to their markets, among which the giant cities were, of course, particularly important. Manufacturing growth in the giant cities thus tended to be self-reinforcing. Secondly, the big growth in services which accompanied the expansion of mass consumption took a distinctively labour-intensive form. The giant cities retained their historic role as favoured locations for high-order tertiary functions, so they built up huge armies of white-collar labour. This relatively high-earning labour chose to reside in the outer districts, beyond the inter-mingled factories and workers' housing of the inner cities. As a result, the emergence of a specialized central business district, accessible to both clientele and employee, was accelerated. Consequently, although the giant cities decentralized their populations much further than they had done before 1890, they were more focused than ever on their central and inner districts. The result was a strongly concentric form of growth, with predominantly radial traffic movements [25]. It was no coincidence, therefore, that the main descriptive model of this type of city should have been developed, in Chicago, as early as the second decade of the twentieth century [26].

This revitalization of the giant cities from the 1890s was not, however, purely the product of private enterprise. The internal transport on which the new growth depended was increasingly regulated, or even provided, by public authority. The extremes of environmental conditions which the giant cities tended to generate were brought increasingly under public control. Around the turn of the century there emerged, on the basis of growing municipal enterprise, a new administrative mechanism which was considered capable of dealing more effectively than ever with urban physical problems. This mechanism was the developing expertise, backed by an even grander ideal, of urban and regional planning. Progress towards the realization of an effective town planning had been made, before about 1900, principally in the big provincial cities. By the time the First World War broke out, however, the giant cities had begun to incorporate these provincial institutions and methods. There thus sprang up a debate in which planning directly confronted the giant city, its greatest challenge [27].

It is this combination of rapid giant-city growth and prolific planning thought that makes the 1890–1940 period so interesting. The planning *achievement* of the period is, frankly, restricted in comparison with that of the quarter-century which followed the Second World War. The context of this lack of achievement was the general downturn of the world economy to which the First World War contributed, and which lasted throughout the 1920s and 1930s. However, the frustrations of the period made a major contribution to the vision of a comprehensively planned giant city, and to the will to bring it to pass, which were unleashed by a Second World War which reduced some of the world's largest cities to ruins. New ideas proliferated and interacted – the Garden City idea (and its derivative, the satellite town), the linear city, public housing, the regional city, neighbourhood planning, disurbanism and de-urbanism, the Modern Movement in architecture, the Athens Charter, neo-classicism, the city of towers, anti-urbanism – it was the most exciting of times. And many – if not most – of those ideas sprang from the dialogue with the giant city, now more effectively studied by a new breed of urban scientists than ever in the past, now, in a society of mass consumption and mass communications, more influential than ever – economically, politically and culturally. If most of the effective transformation of the giant city took place after 1945, most of the thinking had been done by 1940.

Metropolis 1890–1940: Plan and Themes

This volume falls into three parts. Its core consists of case studies of seven of the world's largest urban areas, echoing the formula of Peter Hall's pioneering study of contemporary big-city planning, *The World Cities* [28]. The main criterion for the selection was size; New York, London, Tokyo, Paris and Berlin were, in 1925, the largest cities in the world. Moscow was much smaller at that time, lying thirteenth, behind cities such as Chicago, Buenos Aires and Vienna. It has been included, however, as the leading example of the coming 'socialist metropolis', the testbed and standard-bearer of an alternative metropolitan planning. The Ruhr, with its 3,400,000 inhabitants in 1925, did not lack in size, but as a region of cities it was not strictly comparable to the other six. It was chosen as the leading pre-1940 example of a conurbation planned by a federation of urban and rural administrations, and as a forerunner of the multi-centric areas of metropolitan government which began to be perceived more clearly after the Second World War. In short, we have fixed our size threshold just above Chicago, but included two smaller agglomerations for qualitative reasons, Moscow for its planning interest alone, and the Ruhr for its combination of structural and planning interest. The case studies are preceded by thematic essays on aspects of the giant-city phenomenon. The main aim here is to assess the role and influence of the great metropolis, and to suggest ways in which broad perceptions and attitudes affected its planning. Finally, a key contributor looks backwards and forwards on the metropolitan phenomenon from a vantage point in the early 1980s. The intention here is to evaluate the significance of the 1890–1940 period and to relate it to longer-term concerns. 'How does the giant city stand?' is the central theme of this epilogue.

The main intention of this volume is to generate debate and no rigid uniformity of treatment or interpretation has been imposed on the contributors. Some, indeed, have their doubts about the theme, the periodization, and the choice of cities. Lars Olof Larsson, for instance, in his study of architectural developments, detects a distinctively metropolitan architecture but maintains that it is not generated to any significant extent by the giant cities. Some of the leading Modern Movement architects were associated with, and inspired by, quite small national capitals, such as Amsterdam, or provincial cities like Frankfurt. Peter Hall's survey of planning theories and techniques also allots considerable importance to Frankfurt, which arguably carried into the 1920s the role of German planning pioneer which it had played before 1914. Berlin clearly took over the leadership in the 1930s, but only under the aegis of a National Socialist regime which had no place for the socialist sympathies of Ernst May and other leading Frankfurt planners and architects. Most of the leading German urbanist refugees of the 1930s, of course, gravitated towards the United States, but the focus of their interest there, at any rate as far as big-city architecture was concerned, was perhaps Chicago rather than New York. Peter Keating's study of metropolitan images in literature makes a similar point; Dublin was as much a source of a new view of the city as was London or New York. These differences of emphasis extend into the case studies. Jürgen Reulecke questions the Ruhr's metropolitan credentials and R. A. French points out that the period 1890–1940 is not a coherent one as far as Moscow is concerned. Similarly, whereas Kenneth T. Jackson sees 1890–1940 as New York's 'most important period of change and development', for Norma Evenson's Paris it is 'a relative lull between two storms'.

The Paris–New York contrast helps provide a partial resolution of these contradictions, however. The years 1890–1940 marked the apotheosis of New York as the world metropolis *par excellence*. The urban design paradigm of Haussmann's Paris, which had dominated the late nineteenth and early twentieth centuries, was eclipsed after 1918 by the city of towers, of which Manhattan was the most persuasive physical expression. This implicit dialogue *between* the giant cities lies at the heart of the processes this volume seeks to investigate.

It should not be assumed, however, that we are seeking to impose a rigid structural determinism on changes in planning thought. The rise of the ideal of verticality as a symbol of modernity was substantially influenced by developments in the perception of the city, in particular through the prism of art. The growing appeal of the clean and angular lines of the skyscraper was partly due to the Cubist revolution in the graphic arts around the turn of the century. Yet Cubism, as portrayed by Theda Shapiro, springs directly from the artists' confrontation with a new, and disturbing, urban experience encountered mainly in the giant cities. Indeed, all the thematic contributors are agreed that a revolution in the perception of the urban phenomenon occurred from the 1890s. This 'crisis' of perception produced a 'modern movement' in a number of areas of intellectual production (and not just in architecture). It was from this ferment that the fascination with 'cities of the future', so ably exploited by H. G. Wells, sprang up. However, the futuristic image of the 'domed city' was more an attempt to synthesize and simplify conflicting forces than a disturbing vision of a real future. The disturbance was seen to lie in the contemporary city, and it was no coincidence that it produced, from around 1900, two artistic symptoms of alienation, abstract art and atonal music. These new artistic idioms did not sweep all before them. Many artists tried to maintain representational techniques even in their portrayals of giant cities. Among the composers, for instance, Aaron Copland and Ralph Vaughan-Williams wrote descriptive music which portrayed New York and London as lively, stimulating, and, occasionally, even restful places. George Gershwin and Eric Coates went so far as to develop a giant-city genre of light orchestral music which presented an illusion of coherence. However, Copland and Vaughan-Williams, like the more thoughtful representatives of traditional idioms in the graphic arts, were patently happier in portraying rural scenes. Where explicit comments could not be avoided, as in the cinema or theatre, the disturbing impact of the big city was brought clearly to the fore, especially in Germany where reactions to the urban phenomenon had frightening political implications. In both the Expressionist portrayal of the big city in the cinema of the 1920s and Kurt Weill's sardonic operatic and orchestral music, reflecting the grotesque expressionism of German inter-war painting, the sense of forces out of human control is clearly expressed.

In such a ferment of ideas, any attempt to distinguish dominant tendencies is bound to involve over-simplification. However, there is little doubt that, after 1890, existing fears of the city and pessimism about the future of urbanism were reinforced, largely as a result of gloomy perceptions of the giant cities and their impact on individuals [29]. This pessimism sprang in part from the general decline of the liberalism, optimism and rationalism which had flourished in the nineteenth century. The defeat of these older industrial values was confirmed by the First World War which, in giving rise to the Soviet political system and an atavistic Fascist authoritarianism, created political forces which, initially at least, distrusted the giant city and fostered the discussion of alternatives. This fear or hatred of the large city was based on the great importance accorded to *culture* as a force in human development in the late nineteenth and early twentieth centuries, and reflected in the thinking of figures as different as Patrick Geddes, Oswald Spengler, Lewis Mumford, and Louis Wirth. This belief in an independent urban culture, flourishing in a distinctive urban environment, was partially derived from the application to society of biological analogies in the aftermath of the Darwinian revolution. It was closely associated, therefore, with the idea that the functioning and the physical form of human settlements were essentially *organic*. This organic image could be either comforting or disconcerting. When applied to small towns or villages which were not subject to massive change, it was likely to suggest continuity and equilibrium. However, if the renewed rapid growth of the giant cities, with its attendant core congestion and peripheral spread, was seen as an organic process, a sense of loss of control was likely to result. Thus we find Frank Lloyd Wright referring to the large city as a 'fibrous tumour' and Le Corbusier describing Paris as a 'cancer'.

Architects, of course, were prone to such analogies, but their persuasiveness becomes clearer when we find them used by social scientists. In 1939, for instance, we discover William A. Robson, the authority on public administration, writing of a British capital which he regarded as both over-grown and poorly planned: '. . . London is not a healthy organism at present for the very reason that it has grown to so excessive a size; and the more it is permitted to grow the more unhealthy it will become' [30]. Even the friends of the giant cities were influenced by these parallels. Frank Pick, for instance, the main creator of London's inter-war transport system, was afraid of a continuing process of layered growth in which housing and industry moved outwards alternately into more and more distant suburban rings to produce 'a confluent pox'. Thus pseudo-scientific perceptions reinforced the idea, which had a very wide currency by the 1930s, that the growth of the giant cities was both harmful and out of control.

The main weakness of the organic analogy of city functioning was that it did not to any great extent correspond to reality. It saw service in the absence of a full understanding of the economics of cities, and was reinforced by the cultural theories built upon it. Thus a tension was created between the theory – and the norms derived from it – and the reality of urban development. Revolutionary Russia generated strong 'de-urbanist' and 'disurbanist' tendencies in the 1920s, only to find that the industrialization decreed by Stalin required large cities, within a classic urban network, to function efficiently. The result was the planning for growth in Moscow in the 1930s according to a conventional, concentric pattern which differed little from Western solutions. In Germany, the arid ideology of National Socialism was, in principle, utterly opposed to cities but grounds were soon found to bow to the requirements of big business and to plan for their further growth. However, these victories for economic realism were not won without curious design distortions, the product of efforts to obscure the contradiction between ideology and reality. These distortions are most obvious in the case of Berlin, for instance in the pressing into service of neo-classical styles for putative skyscrapers. However, similar stylistic contortions in New York reflect less explicit tensions in the United States between deeply rooted naturist ideals and the extreme urbanization of the New York agglomeration. Only in Tokyo, for historic reasons less subject than the Western cities to anti-urban opinion, were these pressures not apparent, and Tokyo's sprawling, largely uncontrolled growth conformed more to nineteenth-century Western patterns than to the emerging ideal of the planned city.

The unrealistic premises of the anti-urbanists condemned them to a check which was more likely to produce confusion than positive planning ideas. Consequently, the main forward-looking thinking came from those who sought to maintain the giant cities at a high level of efficiency, like Frank Pick in London, and Thomas Adams in New York. The idea of *restricting* growth in order to *maintain* the existing giant city achieved its greatest currency in London. This inclination sprang partly from considerations of national planning, reflected in the Barlow Report in 1940, according to which some redistribution of employment and population towards the depressed regions of the North was desirable on grounds of national economic efficiency, social justice, and security from air attack. Additionally, however, it was encouraged by London's strongly concentric form and the incapacity of its transport system to provide a mass commuter service beyond a radius of ten or fifteen miles from the centre without very heavy new investment. From as early as the 1880s, London's immense size and incipient economic problems, viewed by informed opinion in a partially Henry-Georgeite perspective, had stimulated ideas of deconcentration, decentralization, and even dispersal, to an extent unparalleled among the other giant cities. The most revolutionary of these proposals, Ebenezer Howard's Garden City idea, was formulated in direct response to the circumstances of London. Put into effect in two prototype garden cities, Letchworth and Welwyn, founded by Howard and his supporters shortly before, and immediately after, the First World War, and advocated by an influential and well-organized pressure group, the Garden Cities and Town Planning Association, the Garden City idea dominated the inter-war London planning debate. Associated with it was the idea of the London green belt, also first suggested around the turn of the century. Largely through Raymond Unwin's advocacy of satellite towns, a potential compromise was increasingly perceived between the obvious utility of London and the complete dispersal of large urban concentrations which Howard favoured. After the Second World War this compromise was to be put into effect in the form of the London green belt and new towns strategy, which was subsequently to be applied through a national planning system to other British cities and, thanks to the immense prestige of the planning system forged in Britain during and after the war, to other parts of the world. Thus London played a key part, with New York, in securing respect for the idea of a dispersal of part of the population of the giant city into satellites within an overall regional plan. It was also through London that the relationship between the planning of the capital city and national economic planning was first clearly perceived.

However, in helping to generate this apparently practical solution, London was also among the first to encounter the associated difficulties. One of the main problems faced by the giant cities between 1890 and 1940 was that their renewed overall population growth, combined with better transport, tended to drive their built-up areas out well beyond their administrative boundaries. Moreover, the political obstacles to boundary extensions were much more serious than those faced by smaller cities, partly because of regional and national objections to the further reinforcement of the influence of the giant city which they implied, and partly because of conflicts within the cities themselves between the interests of the inner areas and those of the suburbs. Berlin and Moscow were spared this difficulty during the later part of the period. In the case of Berlin, the adventurous political attitudes prevailing after the First World War permitted the creation of a Greater Berlin authority in 1920. In Moscow, a continuity of autocracy between the Czarist and Bolshevik regimes overrode all objections to the creation of a unified authority for the whole Moscow area. In London, on the other hand, the London County Council, restrained behind boundaries dating back to the mid-nineteenth century, became increasingly cautious and even isolationist between the wars, especially after Labour's accession to power in 1934 formalized the conflicts of interest between the inner districts and the middle-class suburbs on both sides of the county boundary. London thus followed in the footsteps of Paris, where a city-suburb conflict had discouraged the effective planning of the whole agglomeration since the turn of the century.

At the other end of the spectrum stood the Ruhr. As a collection of cities, towns, and amorphous, semi-rural settlements standing on a rich coalfield, it had no dominant centre, nor indeed any tradition of enterprising administration. This weakness came to be its strength when regional perspectives began to supersede the purely local view. As Jürgen Reulecke demonstrates, the idea of a regional organization for the Ruhr conurbation took shape in the last years before the First World War, and was given an institutional expression shortly after the return of peace with the creation of the *Siedlungsverband Ruhrkohlenbezirk*. Admittedly, as in Berlin, exceptional post-war difficulties were the occasion for so radical a step, but whereas Berlin saw a reinforcement of the dominance of a central urban authority which was likely in due course to generate further tensions between inner and outer areas, there was established in the Ruhr a federal structure which minimized internal disagreements, and permitted easy extensions of the planned area as exploitation of the coalfield spread. This cooperation between urban authorities within a regional system was a rare achievement before 1940, despite all the talk of regional planning which went on in the 1920s and 1930s. Admittedly, a variant of it was achieved in Tokyo, where inter-municipal coordination was effectively encouraged by the central government, but, here again, the forward-looking solution was to some extent the product of a nineteenth-century retardation of urban government. This general retardation of effective regional planning around some of the big capitals foreshadowed the national imposition of regional organization upon them after 1945.

The most interesting focus of the regional debate was, however, New York. Without capital city status, New York was spared some of the conflicts of local and national interest which afflicted the primate cities of Europe. Its accession to the status of the world's largest city coincided with the publication of the most wide-ranging and ambitious regional plan the world had ever seen. The plan, however, implied the continuing centrality and dominance of New York City. Moreover, it was purely advisory. It thus acted as a partial stimulus to the interactions of myriad local and private interests, rather than as a blueprint for coordinated action. Significantly, New York, like London, generated an unofficial planner who, through his influence over transport, managed to integrate the region more effectively than explicit mechanisms were able to do. Equally significantly, whereas Frank Pick's area of activity in London was public transport within a tight radius of 10 to 15 miles, Robert Moses made his biggest impact on the New York region through the building of roads over a much wider area, thus reinforcing a decentralization which precluded green-belt solutions. The experiences of both London and New York were thus already diverging before the Second World War reinforced the differences between them. If London was incorporated, willy-nilly, into a regional and even national planning system after 1945, New York continued to combine rapid growth with a lack of overall control which contributed to the decentralization identified by Jean Gottmann as the new form of 'Megalopolis' in 1961 [31].

As the giant cities grew, the main expression of their outward spread and the growing densification of their centres was *tension*. The tension could be dynamic and creative, or it could be negative, disturbing and disruptive. Clearly, the tensions had not been resolved by 1940. They were expressed in design terms in the opposition of two extremes – regionalist deurbanism, as advocated by Mumford, and the ultra-urbanism of the futurist tendency within the Modern Movement in architecture. Between the two lay the compromise of the garden suburb, the combination of town and country which economic forces tended to produce irrespective of the intervention of planners and architects. The compromise of the suburb, however, generated its own reaction in favour of the reassertion of urbanity which infused the reconstruction of the giant cities after 1945. In 1940, the skyscraper was still restricted almost entirely to the United States; twenty years later it had swept the world and spread to even the smallest of towns. That vision of the vertical city sums up the period 1890–1940, a period in which debate was accompanied by a frustration which was partially removed by the Second World War.

The Significance of the Giant City, 1890–1940

How much, then, of the initial hypothesis survives these detailed studies? It is clear that the giant city, as a focal point for economic, social and cultural forces, did play an important part in the formation of attitudes towards urbanism between 1890 and 1940, and that it was the source of most of the more innovative planning ideas for much of that period. On the other hand, it can be seen that the national influence of the giant cities tended to vary according to their degree of primateness and their political status. London and Paris undoubtedly generated a perception of urban problems, and a brand of planning, which were diffused throughout Britain and France before and after the Second World War. Berlin and New York, important cities within federal states, with a more limited superiority of size in relation to their next-largest cities, were much less dominant within Germany and the United States. Where the giant cities had most in common was in their role as concentrated symbols of the future. In a world economy switching from the production of capital goods to a stronger emphasis on consumer goods and services, the giant cities were able to influence lifestyles throughout their spheres of influence. Their problems, and the solutions appropriate to them, came to dominate the planning systems and strategies of the countries in which they were located. At the same time, we have suggested an accumulation of frustration, particularly in the 1920s and 1930s, when a world-wide economic deceleration coincided with, and partly encouraged, the survival of political and administrative obstacles to energetic action, except in an increasingly autocratic Soviet Union and Germany. The Second World War thus let loose a pent-up wave of ideas and ambition which led to a substantial transformation of the giant cities during a period of unprecedented economic growth centred on the 1950s and 1960s. That episode was more spectacular than the one we examine in this volume. Its roots, however, were firmly fixed in the phenomenon of Metropolis 1890–1940.

NOTES

1. '9 to 5', words and music by Florrie Palmer © 1979 Pendulum Music Ltd., administered throughout the world by Chappell Music Ltd.
2. Barney, Gerald O. *et al.* (1982) *The Global 2000 Report to the President, Vol. 2: The Technical Report.* Harmondsworth: Penguin, p. 242.
3. See Hall, Peter (1981) The inner city worldwide, in Hall, Peter (ed.) *The Inner City in Context.* London: Heinemann, pp. 64–70.
4. The relationship between urbanization, exploitation and political tensions is fully explored in Roberts, Bryan (1978) *Cities of Peasants: The Political Economy of Urbanization in the Third World.* London: Edward Arnold. For the rise of the British 'inner city' problem, see the recent discussion in Lawless, Paul (1981) *Britain's Inner Cities: Problems and Policies.* London: Harper and Row, especially pp. 3–16.
5. The pithiest introduction to the socialist city in English is Bater, J. (1980) *The Soviet City.* London: Edward Arnold. For a wide-ranging, multi-author discussion of the Soviet Union and the East European socialist states, see French, R.A. and Hamilton, F.E.I. (eds.) (1979) *The Socialist City: Spatial Structure and Urban Policy.* Chichester: John Wiley.
6. See, for example, *The Planner*, **67** (1), January–February 1981, which contains a number of articles on the role of British planning in the 1980s. Gloom and uncertainty are only partially overlain by a veneer of traditional optimism in these pieces.
7. As far as British planning was concerned, a decade of growing doubts was crowned by the withering critique of Ravetz, Alison (1980) *Remaking Cities.* London: Croom Helm.
8. For a discussion of one aspect of this effect – the diversion of new industrial development from South-East England to the Continent of Europe, see Hall, Peter *et al.* (1973) *The Containment of Urban England.* London: Allen and Unwin, Vol. II, pp. 375–7.
9. The Marxist critique of planning has recently been encapsulated in Dear, Michael and Scott, Allen J. (1981) *Urbanization and Planning in Capitalist Society.* London/New York: Methuen.
10. The existence of this process forms part of the more complex argument presented in Hall, Peter (1980) *Great Planning Disasters.* London: Weidenfeld and Nicolson.
11. Read, J. (1982) Looking backward? *Built Environment*, **7** (2), pp. 68–81.
12. See Mumford, L. (new edn, 1940) *The Culture of Cities.* London: Secker and Warburg, pp. 223–99.
13. See, for example, the treatment in Florence, P. Sargant (1955) Economic efficiency in the metropolis, in Fisher, Robert M. (ed.) *The Metropolis in Modern Life.* Garden City, NY: Doubleday, pp. 85–91.
14. An early, though unscientific, exposition of the theory was Jefferson, Mark (1939) The law of the primate city. *Geographical Review*, **29**, pp. 226–32. Jefferson's formulation of the law (p. 231) was: 'A country's leading city is always disproportionately large and exceptionally expressive of national capacity and feeling'. For a later exposition, see Linsky, A.S. (1965) Some generalizations concerning primate cities. *Annals of the Association of American Geographers*, **55**, pp. 506–13.
15. See Hall, Peter (1977) *The World Cities* (2nd

edn). London: Weidenfeld and Nicolson, p.1.

16. The self-sustaining interaction of tertiary and secondary functions within very large cities, producing a 'top-heavy' structure of city size, is discussed in Morrill, Richard L. (1970) *The Spatial Organization of Society.* Belmont, Ca: Wadsworth, pp. 156–7.

17. The most consistently reliable inter-millennial source of information on urban populations, on which the inferences set out in this section are based, is Chandler, Tertius and Fox, Gerald (1974) *3000 Years of Urban Growth.* New York/London: Academic Press.

18. Census of England and Wales 1911, Vol. I, p. xxiv.

19. See, for example, *London Statistics, 7,* 1896–7, p. x.

20. Meuriot, Paul (1897) *Des agglomérations urbaines dans l'Europe contemporaine: essai sur les causes, les conditions, les conséquences de leur développement.* Paris: Belin Frères, pp. 452–3 (author's translation).

21. Weber, Adna F. (1899) *The Growth of Cities in the Nineteenth Century: A Study in Statistics.* New York: Macmillan, p. 158.

22. *Ibid.,* p. 448.

23. *Ibid.,* pp. 198–9.

24. Weber's discussion of this point is somewhat dispersed, but see especially pp. 158, 202, 204–6, and 222–9.

25. For the United States, see, for example, Harris, C.D. (1943) Suburbs. *American Journal of Sociology, 49,* pp. 1–13.

26. For an early exposition of the concentric zone model of urban structure, see Park, Robert E. and Burgess, Ernest W. (1925) *The City.* Chicago: University of Chicago Press.

27. This interpretation of the emergence of planning is set out at greater length in Sutcliffe, A. (1981) *Towards the Planned City: Germany, Britain, the United States, and France.* Oxford: Basil Blackwell.

28. Hall (1977) *op. cit.* (see note 15).

29. See, for example, Weber's discussion of this view, already widespread in the 1890s, in Weber, *op. cit.,* pp. 368–70 (see note 21).

30. Robson, W.A. (1948, 1st edn, 1939) *The Government and Misgovernment of London.* London: Allen and Unwin, p. 441.

31. Gottmann, J. (1961) *Megalopolis: The Urbanized Northeastern Seaboard of the United States.* Cambridge, Mass: MIT Press.

Chapter 2

Metropolis 1890–1940: Challenges and Responses

PETER HALL

THE early twentieth century might be labelled the first age of the giant metropolis. Between 1890 and 1940, the Greater London agglomeration grew from 5,638,000 to 8,700,000; the three *départements* making up the *Région Parisienne* from 4,128,000 to 6,598,000; Greater Berlin from 1,579,000 to 4,332,000; Moscow from 799,000 to 4,137,000 [1]; the Ruhr coalfield agglomeration from 1,500,000 to 4,300,000 [2]; between 1889 and 1942, the Tokyo region expanded from 1,370,000 to 7,358,000 [3]. From 1900 to 1940 the Metropolitan District of New York grew from 4,608,000 to 11,691,000 [4]. In Europe alone, the number of 'million cities' grew from five in 1890 to fourteen in 1940 [5]; in the shorter period from 1910 to 1940, in the United States, the number of Metropolitan Districts with one million and more inhabitants grew from five to eleven [6]. These figures cannot claim any rigorous comparability; they are based on a mixture of administrative, physical and functional definitions [7]. But they can perhaps serve to give an impressionistic picture of the growth of the metropolis during the period when it first came of age.

The Metropolis as Problem: Two Stages of Perception

With remarkable consistency over time and between nations, in this period the great metropolis came to be seen as a major problem requiring action at the highest national level. Two stages in the perception of this problem must however be distinguished. The first stemmed from the raw facts of poverty, poor housing and social malaise in the congested metropolis of the first industrial revolution. The second came only as and when the problems of the first stage began to be overcome – as, in the United States and in Britain, they began to be in the 1920s and 1930s. It took the form of a reaction against the physical spread of the metropolis and the associated problems of traffic, commuting, social isolation and loss of agricultural land. But, such were the failures of some countries in meeting the problems of the first stage, that we still find some of them grappling with them down to 1940.

Responses to the Classic Slum
It would be difficult to make a comparative quantitative analysis of the horrors of the early industrial metropolis. Each city, producing its own version of the classic

slum [8], seemed to have suffered in its own way; each became convinced, at some stage, that its problems were uniquely horrendous. The most obvious aspects, linked together in an unhappy logic, were low incomes and overcrowded housing. Even in London, hailed by its most perceptive foreign observer as the Unique Metropolis on the ground of its low-density single-family home pattern of growth [9], observers came to be obsessed by the poor quality and simple scarcity of housing. In 1901, more than one-third of families in many of London's inner boroughs were living in one or two rooms; in Finsbury the proportion rose to over 45 per cent [10]. The simple reason, despite the fact that even then London was spreading and thinning out, was poverty: according to Charles Booth's classic early social survey of the 1890s, in most inner boroughs more than 40 per cent were in poverty, in the sense of having less than £1.05 a week to support a moderate family [11]. In the climate of social turmoil of the 1880s, this had aroused a real fear among prosperous middle-class opinion: 'the pages of the reviews and the daily press were as preoccupied with bad housing as a cause of possible revolution as they had earlier been with bad drainage as a cause of epidemics' [12]. That concern had led to the Royal Commission on the Housing of the Working Classes of 1884–85 and, indirectly, to an Act of 1890 that increased the power of local authorities – previously very limited – to build housing [13]. In London, the newly-created London County Council concentrated at first on limited slum reconstruction, and only after the Act was amended in 1900, to encourage building outside the County area, did the LCC begin to build on a large scale, particularly in out-county estates at Tooting, Norbury, Tottenham and White City [14]. The programme accelerated massively with the aid of government subsidies under the 1919 Housing Act, culminating in the great schemes for 40,000 people at St. Helier and 116,000 at Becontree [15].

But these efforts did not necessarily improve conditions near the centre of London, where the increasing pace of demolition for commercial development began to lead to worsening conditions after 1900 [16]. It was at that time that recruitment to the South African War exposed another fear: of 11,000 Manchester men trying to enlist, only 3000 were accepted – and only 1000 were fit for regular army service [17]. During World War One, the Verney committee reiterated the fear that 'the physique of those portions of our nation who live in crowded streets rapidly deteriorates, and would deteriorate still further if they were not to some extent reinforced by men in the country districts' [18]. From this it was a short step to the notion that the city dweller was also psychologically unstable:

> The England of the past has been an England of reserved, silent men, dispersed in small towns, villages and country houses . . . The problem of the coming years is just the problem of this New Town type . . . a characteristic *physical* type of town dweller: stunted, narrow-chested, easily wearied; yet voluble, excitable, with little ballast, stamina, or endurance – seeking stimulus in drink, in betting, in any unaccustomed conflicts at home or abroad [19].

Small wonder that Masterman feared for the 'future progress of the Anglo-Saxon race, and the policy of the British Empire in the world' [20]. The same thought came from the lawyer Ralph Neville, who provided powerful support for Ebenezer Howard's ideas on the ground that in large cities 'nothing could prevent the ultimate decadence and destruction of the race' [21].

Across the German Ocean, almost identical thoughts were being expressed in almost identical language; and the origin was the same. Berlin – a city of close on two million in 1890, of over four million in 1913 – grew from 1870 on at the same pace as an American city [22]. As it did so, inadequate building regulations [23] helped stimulate an orgy of land speculation, making Berlin 'die grösste Mietskasernenstadt der Welt' [24]. The 'rental barracks', a characteristic Berlin building form, had their origin in Frederick the Great's mortgage regulations of 1748, which made it highly profitable to mortgage building land and thus to speculate on it [25], and behind which some observers have seen a desire to impose collectivized military styles of life on a civilian population [26]. The famous 1858–62 plan by James Hobrecht drew some of its inspiration from Haussmann's Paris; but by accepting the inadequate building regulations of 1853, it gave a charter for speculation [27]. The result, by the early twentieth century, was 'the most compact city in Europe; as she grows she does not struggle out with small roads and peddling suburban houses, but slowly pushes her wide town streets and colossal tenement blocks over the open country, turning it at one stroke into a full-blown city' [28]. But, as Abercrombie admitted, this was also one of the most densely built and overcrowded cities in Europe if not in the world: 45.9 per cent of all building lots contained more than twenty dwellings, another 13.6 per cent between sixteen and twenty; 723 people lived on each hectare of built-up land, compared with 380 in Hamburg and only 275 in Frankfurt; 41.1 per cent of dwellings had two rooms or less, compared with 4.6 per cent in Hamburg; 79.4 per cent of dwellings had two heatable rooms or less, compared with 52.2 per cent in Hamburg [29]; rents were the highest in Germany [30]. Horsfall in 1904, despite his admiration for German planning, had to admit that in Berlin (in 1890) an average of 52.6 people inhabited each lot, compared with 7.6 in London [31].

The most obvious result of these conditions, as with the rather different form of overcrowding in London, was an unfit population. Of the army service draft of 1913, an average of 63.6 per cent of young German men passed their physical examination; for rural districts the figure was 66.3 per cent, for Berlin 42.3 per cent [32]. From this developed another fear, that the lower birth rate in the cities would lead to a failure of the whole nation to reproduce; an argument first used by Georg Hansen in his influential book *Die drei Bevölkerungsstufen* in the 1890s, and later developed by Otto Amman into the theory that the agrarian 'Nordic' race declined in the cities [33]. By 1918 Oswald Spengler had made this one of the main themes of his study of the *Decline of the West*: 'Now the giant city sucks the country dry, insatiably and incessantly demanding and devouring fresh streams of men, till it wearies and dies in the midst of an almost uninhabited waste of country' [34]. But, just as in Britain, other concerns fuelled *'die Angst vor der Stadt'* [35]; the fear of social decomposition, as instanced by rates of suicide, alcoholism and venereal disease; a lack of spiritual qualities, due to 'excessive rationality'; and a resulting lack of political security. Logically, and increasingly through the Weimar years, the result was a demand for a return to simpler forms of life in smaller-scale settlements [36].

Paris had an equally melancholy record in congestion and overcrowding. Within the city limits as extended under Haussmann, the population rose from 2.45 million in 1891 to 2.89 million in 1911 and to a peak of 2.91 million in 1921 [37]. The population density at that time, close on 37,000 people to the square kilometre, was more than double the figure for London and some six times the average for New York City, where the high densities of Manhattan were outweighed by the sprawling suburban boroughs [38]. As the population grew, so housing conditions worsened; it was estimated that in 1911 there were 216,000 overcrowded families living at two persons and more per room in the city and another 85,000 in the suburbs, plus 925,000 in the city and 422,000 in the suburbs living in 'insufficient' dwellings at between one and two persons per room; by 1921 these figures had swelled [39]. Perhaps mercifully, the great Haussmannesque roadworks – which, as studies in the 1920s showed, actually exacerbated the problem – diminished greatly after 1871 [40]. But not only were many of the inner *arrondissements* grossly overcrowded; they were also highly insanitary. As late as 1925, almost half the houses in Paris were not connected to a sewer; cholera attacked in 1892, typhoid in 1882 and 1894; deaths from tuberculosis rose during the 1880s and 1890s [41] and again after World War One [42]; bubonic plague attacked one slum during the 1920s [43].

To make matters worse, after World War One something like paralysis descended on the Parisian building industry. A combination of rent control, which made it uneconomic to build or improve, and of inflated building costs, brought building within the city almost to a stop. Though clearance powers had been strengthened on paper, compensation problems made it almost impossible to proceed. *Îlots insalubres*, first defined in 1905–6, were redefined in 1919 when seventeen of them – with a total of 187,000 people – were designated for early clearance. Yet the worst of these, Îlot 1, was not demolished even in part until 1932 and then lay empty for forty years, until the Centre Pompidou was erected on it in the late 1970s [44]; clearance of the rest of the area was not complete even by 1939 [45].

If conditions in Berlin and Paris were bad, in Moscow they almost beggared description. With a population that rose from 753,000 in 1885 to 1,039,000 in 1897 and 1,806,000 in 1915 [46], it remained 'a big village, a one- and two-storey bastion of patriarchical provincialism' [47]. Its housing conditions, like those of other pre-revolutionary Russian cities, 'was one of the worst in the modern world' [48]. In 1912, the average Moscow apartment had between eight and nine inhabitants, compared with four in Berlin and 2.7 in Paris; 70 per cent of the population were estimated to live in extremely overcrowded conditions; more than 100,000 lived in basements; more than 300,000 had no home of their own, and lived in wretched dormitories attached to their factories; the total urban living space was estimated at seven square metres per head, compared with a generally accepted minimum standard of nine square metres [49]. But, incredibly enough, after the revolution conditions actually worsened – a result of chaotic policies towards the private landlord, rapid in-migration from the countryside, and the low priority given to housing in the early five-year plans from 1928 onwards [50]. It is suggested that poor housing conditions in both Moscow and St. Petersburg may have contributed directly to the revolutionary upheaval of 1917 [51]; how people felt by 1940 has gone unrecorded.

In addition to its housing deficiencies, pre-revolutionary Moscow suffered from a chronic lack of modern urban services. Water was so short that it was rationed to institutions; central Moscow did not receive a sewerage system until the end of the nineteenth century, and even by 1914 only 30 per cent of houses were connected; only 40 per cent had running water, and 30 per cent had electricity [52]. In St. Petersburg, still the capital down to the Revolution, matters were as bad: typhus and cholera deaths were greatly in excess of other European cities, because of the poor quality of the water supply [53]. In Moscow the electric tram network for the city was completed only in 1912, and did not extend to the suburbs; a Metro project was cancelled, not to be revived until the 1930s [54]. In both Moscow and St. Petersburg, civic revenues were chronically inadequate; during World War One the St. Petersburg government spent 32 roubles per head of population, compared with Paris's 60 and Berlin's 70 [55]. Then, because of the crises of the 1920s, the Soviet authorities could do very little to make matters better. As late as 1931 only 42 per cent of the houses in Moscow had running water, and 37 per cent of streets had no main drainage [56].

These conditions were without parallel in other major Western cities. But many Russians, who extricated themselves by making the long journey across the Atlantic, found little comfort in their new urban home. And not just Russians: 'New York–Brooklyn was the greatest centre of immigrants in the world, having half as many Italians as Naples, as many Germans as Hamburg, twice as many Irish as Dublin and two and a half times as many Jews as Warsaw' [57]. Between 1900 and 1910, the greatest decade for new arrivals, there occurred a net immigration of 220,000 Italians, 161,000 Russians and 324,000 Austro-Hungarians into New York City [58]. By this time, 80 per cent or more of the population of New York and other big cities was foreign-born [59]. Between 1881 and 1914, more than one-third of the Jews of Eastern Europe left their homelands in one of the greatest migrations of modern history: 'America was in everyone's mouth' [60].

There was a predictably heavy price to pay. Already in 1890, the Jews – together with the other major group of recent arrivals, the Italians – were more heavily 'ghettoized' than other groups. Almost 75 per cent of those with Russian and Polish origin were packed into only three city wards: the 7th, the 10th and the 13th. Ward 10 contained a majority of people born in, or having parents from, those countries [61]. Between 1880 and 1893, the population density of the 10th Ward increased from 432 to 702 to the acre; by the latter date, most of its 75,000 people lived in only 1200 apartment blocks [62]. Such congestion was a product of poverty coupled with extreme linguistic and cultural barriers to assimilation; one-quarter of the foreign population could not speak English [63]. It rapidly reached extra-ordinary proportions: 'From every available source – contemporary journalism, memoirs, government reports, sociological studies – the evidence seems conclusive: living conditions in the Jewish quarter during the last decades of the nineteenth century were quite as ghastly as early nineteenth-century London' [64]. The Tenement House Commission of 1894 found that the 10th Ward in 1890, with 626 to the acre, was 30 per cent more crowded than the most congested district of Prague, believed to be the worst in Europe. One part of the adjacent 11th Ward had 986 to the acre, much in excess of the most congested district of Bombay [65]. Paradoxically, the root of the problem – just as in Berlin – was a superficially reformist, but actually perverse, building design. The notorious dumbbell tene-ment, the result of a competition in 1879, allowed twenty-four apartments to be packed on to six floors of a narrow 24 by 100 foot building lot, by dint of giving ten out of the fourteen rooms on each floor access only to an almost lightless and airless 'air well' [66]. Usually, because of the extreme poverty of the immigrants, each of these wretched apartments soon filled up with two or more families [67]. In 1908, a census of 250 typical East Side families showed that less than a quarter slept two to a room or better; about half slept three to four to a room; and nearly a quarter slept at five and more to a room. Water facilities were restricted to communal taps and fixed baths were virtually non-existent. Small wonder that tuberculosis affected twelve in every thousand of East Side Jews []8].

The challenge produced a response very similar to that in London. Jacob Riis's classic *How the Other Half Lives* (1890) was the equivalent of *The Bitter Cry of Outcast London* (1883); it was followed by the Tenement House Commission of 1894 (the parallel to the Royal Commission of 1884–85) by the widely publicized Charity Organization Society exhibition of 1900, which graphically showed how disease and poverty were concentrated in the worst tenements [69], and by another Tenement House Commission of the same year, that succeeded in outlawing the further construction of dumbbells and in compelling the modification of existing ones [70]. Its leading light and the most effective American housing improver of that era, Lawrence Veiller, was strongly committed to solutions based on restrictive legislation and strong centralized management; he was opposed to model tenements or model housing schemes, and still more to public housing solutions which he thought would sound the death knell for private housing [71]. Though he began to encounter opposition by 1914, his influence ensured that New York would not follow the London example of decentralization through public housing schemes on garden suburb lines.

Behind these moves toward reform, just as in London and Berlin, lay a deep middle-class fear of the new generation of urbanites. The new ghetto districts 'came to symbolize both material and social failure in urban America and were often erroneously identified with high rates of infant mortality, crime, prostitution, drunkenness, and various other symptoms of social ills' [72]. These rumours fuelled a much older tradition of 'adverse metaphysical reaction and bad dreams about urban life, of esthetic and moral recoil from the American city's ugliness, commercialism, and crime' [73]. Jefferson's view of great cities 'as pestilential to the morals, the health and the liberties of men' [74] was certainly echoed a century later by writers such as Adams, James and Howells [75]. They, and many others, shared with Jefferson the view of the city as 'a malignant social form . . . a cancer or a tumour' [76]. Alfred E. Smith, a pioneer private-enterprise housing reformer, was already writing in 1879 of the tenement districts as 'nurseries of the epidemics which spread with certain destructiveness into the fairest homes . . . hiding-places of the local banditti . . . cradles of the insane who fill the asylums and of the paupers who throng the alm-houses'; he was echoed by Jacob Riis in 1893, who warned that 'as we mould the children of the toiling masses, so we shape the destiny of the State' [77]. Behind Riis's concern lay his explicit fear of social violence: the tenement dwellers 'hold within their clutch the wealth and business of New York and hold them at their mercy in the day of mob-rule and wrath. The bullet-proof shutters, the stacks of hand-grenades, and the Gatling guns in the Treasury are tacit admissions of the quality of the mercy expected' [78]. The 'masses of ignorant foreigners congregated in many cities', Americans were warned by another authority, were 'the magazines of explosives to which these fiends continually try to apply the torch' [79]. This fear extended even to a notion of racial pollution; even the *New York Times* was complaining in 1892 of an invasion of 'the physical, moral and mental wrecks' of Europe, 'of a kind which we are better without' [80].

The reaction to this fear took complex forms. One obvious and immediate one, as in London, was the development of individual attempts at moral reformation through religious missions and the Charity Organization Society. A second, seen in muted form in Britain but much more influential in America, was moral coercion, particularly through attacks on the liquor traffic, culminating in the passage of the historic Eighteenth Amendment in 1919. Yet a third, very influential for the subsequent history of the metropolis not only in the United States but also in Europe, was an emphasis on positive environmental improvement, first through the development of local parks and playgrounds and then – inspired by Frederick Law Olmsted and other pioneers of landscape planning – a stress on urban park systems which, in Olmsted's words, could exert on the urban masses a 'harmonizing and refining influence . . . favourable to courtesy, self-control and temperance' [81]. Naturally, this developed into the idea that the city itself could engender civic loyalty, thus to 'provide the foundation stone of an even more close-knit and harmonious moral order' [82]. Here, in the environmentally-determinist notion that a close link existed between the city's physical appearance and its moral or spiritual state, lay the philosophical core of the City Beautiful movement [83].

Responses to Decentralization

Some metropolitan cities, around the time of World War One, began in different ways – part public action, part market forces – to mitigate the worst horrors of the early industrial city. But as they did so, critics began to accuse them of trying to solve the problem in the wrong way, and thereby of creating an entirely new set of problems. As opposed to mere palliatives in the form of improved housing and transport, these critics advocated solutions in the form of more comprehensive urban planning. These solutions provide the theme of the second half of this chapter, but in order to appreciate them, we need to look more closely at the partial solutions which they aimed to supersede.

The most extreme example of such 'palliatives' is surely London. Greater London's population rose from 7.5 million in 1921 to 8.7 million in 1939 – some one-third of the net population increase in all England and Wales. But during the same period the population of the inner (London County Council) area fell by over 446,000; the net increase in the out-county was thus over 1.6 million. To house them, and provide better conditions for those already there, well over one and a quarter million new houses were built in Greater London, virtually all of them in the suburban ring outside the LCC area [84]. A whole host of factors contributed: they included the development of the Building Society movement, the generally low rate of interest, declining to 4¼–4½ per cent in the mid-1930s, coupled with a low down payment that brought owner-occupation within the reach of skilled manual workers [85]; and, above all, the great increase in the supply of building land through the rapid extension of the suburban railway system. Though almost all these extensions were assisted by government, to the extent that they carried little or no interest [86], they were expensive and required rapid suburban development to make them break even; the 1935–39 extension plan of London Transport was posited on a population growth of 650,000 people in the areas that were newly served [87].

The whole programme, and the integration of London's buses and trams and underground lines, represented the vision of one extraordinary man, who had perhaps as much influence on London's development in the twentieth century as Haussmann had on that of Paris in the nineteenth: its commercial manager and finally chief executive officer, Frank Pick [88]. But Pick, who possessed an enormous theoretical and practical understanding of city growth, well understood the dangers in the process he had set in train. First, there was a limit to outward growth, set by the limits of a 6d (2½p) fare and a journey of approximately 30 minutes; this set the outer extent of London's growth at about 12 miles (20 km) from the centre [89]. But car ownership was the real villain; it was 'planting villas sporadically all over the countryside without any regard for a reasonable economy in the employment of land, so that the distinction between town and country around London is almost wholly breaking down' [90]. Such developments were 'almost analogous to cancerous growth' [91]; a disciple of D'Arcy Thompson's classic *On Growth and Form*, Pick believed that cities had analogies to the alimentary, respiratory, and circulatory systems of the body but that a brain, in the form of a planning system, was lacking [92]. Questioned by Abercrombie before the Royal Commission on the Distribution of the Industrial Population in 1938, Pick said 'There comes a point when the size of London becomes its undoing'; if the expansion went on, London might go into decline [93]. What Pick most feared, he told the Commission, was further decentralization of industry, 'layering first industry and then residences . . . indefinitely, but that would not be London'; rather, the development of a 'confluent pox' [94].

Pick here already demonstrated his vision of London. Like the Stockholm planners after 1945 or the Parisian planners of 1965, he saw transport planning and effective physical planning as two parts of the same process. Functionally, London should remain a compact conurbation dependent upon centralized employment and a radial public transport system. The rapid decentralization of industrial employment in the 1920s and 1930s, to places like the Lea Valley, Park Royal and Slough, which had created some 140,000 jobs by the early 1930s [95], was for Pick a real threat to this vision, since it could mean a disjuncture between the functional and the physical London [96]. Hence he put his influential voice on the side of those who maintained that London's growth should be physically restricted.

He had plenty of allies. Traditionalists, ranging from Clough Williams-Ellis to George Orwell, bemoaned the submergence of the traditional English countryside under a rash of bungalows: 'As the Joneses fly from town, so does the country fly from the pink bungalow that they have perched so hopefully on its eligible site' [97]. Orwell's Tubby Bowling, revisiting the country town of his boyhood at the end of the 1930s, found the result: 'But where was Lower Binfield? Where was the town I used to know? It might have been anywhere. All I knew was that it was buried somewhere in the middle of that sea of bricks' [98]. Significantly, Bowling – himself a London suburbanite – is driving one of the 1,847,000 additional cars that came on to the roads of Britain between the two world wars, a large proportion of them in the Home Counties [99]. In 1937, the geographer Dudley Stamp showed for the first time just how great a loss of good agricultural land the process of suburban growth had involved, above all in the intensive market-gardening areas west of London [100]. Geographers and others pointed out the sharp contrast in the 1930s between the prosperity and continued sprawl of London, and the depressed areas of the North, Scotland and Wales. Before the Barlow Commission, this made an impressively coordinated chorus. But the key role in orchestrating it was played by the Town and Country Planning Association – above all by its leading light Frederic Osborn, who, as he later confessed, drafted key sections of the main report and of the influential minor report calling for national controls over industrial development [101]. Thus it was Osborn, manipulating the Commission from outside, who was truly responsible for its radical recommendations to curb London's growth.

Over the water in Paris, the process of suburban growth took a radically different form. There too, as the inner area – the city of Paris – began to decline in population after 1921, the *banlieue* massively gained; its population rising from 1.5 million to 2.0 million between 1921 and 1931 alone [102]. But the basis was very different. In the first place, there was a much weaker transport base, since Paris had no Frank Pick. When the city won a long fight with the central government to build the Metro – the first section of which was opened in 1900 – it deliberately terminated the system at the city limits in order to guard against the loss of its tax base by suburban outmigration [103]. For a time, this strategy worked in keeping Paris a relatively high-density city, served by a very dense network of public transport. Only after 1929 was the Metro extended out into the *proche banlieue* [104]. Thus, as the suburbs grew the main weight of commuting fell upon the nineteenth-century main railway lines, which had been built between 1837 and 1890 and had only belatedly developed a suburban function [105] Many of these lines, particularly the important network into the Gare St. Lazare, made an indirect journey to the centre and, because of an almost pathological distrust of the city of a possible takeover of the Metro by the main lines, no direct communication was made with the Metro system as occurred in the London suburbs in Pick's extensions [106]. Within Paris, there was no overall organization equivalent to London Transport until after World War Two [107]. Although by 1936 some 400,000 workers a day were commuting to the city from the *banlieue,* they did so under conditions which must have seriously discouraged further suburban growth [108].

There was, however, another critical difference. London between the wars had the benefit at least of elementary planning legislation under Acts of 1909, 1919, 1932, and 1935; the Parisian *banlieue* did not even have effective building regulations. Coupled with a grievous shortage of housing in the city caused by the virtual cessation of building there during and after World War One, massive in-migration into the city, and low interest rates in the 1920s, this failure left the door wide open to rampant speculative development. Between 1920 and 1939, some 8700 hectares – an area equal to the City of Paris – were laid out in speculative *lotissements*. By 1939 it was estimated that in the entire *banlieue* there were some 250,000 *lotissements,* housing perhaps 700,000 people – nearly three-quarters of the total growth of the agglomeration during the inter-war period [109]. Most of the buyers, it appears, were people of modest means; the registered offices of the companies which sold the lots were mostly in the working-class eastern quarters of Paris [110]. The results were predictably squalid; at the edge of Paris, vast shanty towns sprang up. Elementary services were lacking; in winter, the roads were seas of mud; the water supply, drawn from wells, was liable to contamination and often failed in summer; tuberculosis and diarrhoea were rife; commuting often started and finished with a 2–4 kilometre walk over unpaved roads [111]. After the mid-1920s the *mal-lotis* began to organize, and the Communist Party started to win a substantial share of the vote. It took three legal attempts – in 1919, 1924 and 1928 – to get the lots effectively serviced, and even then the cost fell disproportionately on the unfortunate residents [112]. And, though the majority of the lots were serviced between 1928 and 1933, many were still without services well after World War Two [113].

In comparison with London, Paris did relatively little to make amends by public housing. A programme for the voluntary building of subsidized units (*Habitations à bon marché*, or HBM) developed as a result of laws of 1894 and 1906, and in 1912 a further law allowed local authorities to establish HBM agencies [114]. But the powers were very weakly used. In all France only 300,000 HBM units were built between the two wars, compared with 1,785,000 public housing units in Britain [115]. The Seine *Département* HBM agency, established in 1915 [116], and one of the most active in France, built only 85,000 units in this period – sufficient to house only one-quarter of the population increase [117].

Berlin suburbanized even more weakly between the two wars. Those who could afford to do so had already begun to move out and away from the *Mietskasernen* in the late nineteenth century [118]. By 1900, there had been extensive suburban development in the south-west, the east and south-east, and (to a lesser extent) the north, stretching as far as 30–40 kilometres [119]. Much of this development was influenced by English architectural models [120]. But, though the suburban railway lines gave relatively good connections into the mainline termini, and a surface *Stadtbahn* existed from 1882, the underground network (started in 1902) remained much more skeletal than in Paris or in London, and an essential north-south link was never built [121]. Only in 1929 were the bus, tram and underground systems brought under common management [122]. At that time, two-thirds of individual journeys by public transport were still being made by bus or tram on the congested street system [123]. Only cheap and rapid transit could allow true garden suburbs to develop in Berlin – and, well into the 1930s, it was lacking [124]. Frank Pick, visiting the city at that time, commented on the city's still highly compact form, with five million people crammed within a six-mile radius; despite this the public transport system still lost money, since the average Berliner took only 330 rides a year, as against 430 in London [125]. The far-flung suburbs along the rail lines thus catered only for the fortunate few.

At the same time, industry was moving out – and Berlin, despite its administrative role, was primarily a city of manual workers. Thanks to its good market location and good transport, as well as its large pool of labour drawn from the backward eastern provinces, Berlin had shared fully in the rapid industrialization of Germany after 1871. But after the turn of the century, the bigger and more successful works tended to move out from the congested inner city in search of space and cheaper land [126]. The result was the characteristic industrial *Siedlungen* of the 1920s, which won the approval of *Stadtbaurat* Wagner. These formed large, homogeneous developments at moderate density at the edge of the city, particularly towards the west and north-west. Their form and overall density reflected the authorities' attempt to reduce building height and bulk and to introduce more green space into the city [127] – an attempt made easier, perhaps, by a massive extension of Berlin's boundaries in 1920, which had no parallel in the other great cities.

In Moscow the suburbanization process can hardly be said to have taken place before the 1930s. As early as 1897, it is true, as against 978,500 people in the city (at the 1897 Census), a further 59,500 lived beyond the boundaries. These areas were very poor, and the City *Duma* was unwilling to incorporate them because of the extra tax burdens they would doubtless bring [128]. When the City did take in these neighbouring areas, immediately after the Revolution, it extended its area almost three times, from 80 to 228 square kilometres [129]. But, after 1917, conditions in the extended city were so bad that the population actually fell sharply, from 1,806,000 in 1915 to 1,028,000 in 1920, recovering to 2,026,000 only in 1926 [130]. From that point, some independent towns beyond the city boundaries did begin to develop as satellites of Moscow; the surrounding region increased in population by nearly one million, from 472,300 in 1926 to 1,428,800 in 1939 [131] and five second-order agglomerations began to grow, threatening the green belt (established by the 1935 Plan) through linear extensions outward from the city [132].

In contrast New York shares with London a history of very marked suburbanization, especially after the end of World War One. Generally throughout the United States, as the Committee on Urbanization noted in 1937, 'the urbanite is steadily becoming the suburbanite. The motives leading to this type of existence are to be sought in the urge to escape the obnoxious aspects of urban life without at the same time losing access to its economic and social advantages' [133]. Notably, the second generation immigrants began to de-ghettoize – though many, such as the Jews, remained firmly locked into the city [134]. A new black wave of immigrants, more highly segregated than even any previous group, began to take their places on Manhattan Island [135]. Technological developments – the telephone, the skyscraper, the elevator, central heating – encouraged the steady takeover of central districts by offices [136]. Particularly, development of a rapid transit system allowed the city to spread. New York's first elevated line was in 1869, six years after London's first underground railway; the subway was to wait until 1904 [137]. The result, in the 1920s and 1930s, was a sea of cheaply-built wooden-frame houses along the subway lines of Brooklyn, the Bronx and Queens – the area today appropriately known as the grey area of New York City [138].

Additionally, as car ownership rose ten-fold nationally between 1915 and 1941, increasing numbers migrated beyond the reach of public transport systems [139].

The figures tell the story. Warren S. Thompson in 1947 made the first of many analyses of American urban change using the framework of the Metropolitan District (later Metropolitan Area). He showed that while the population of New York City had continued to increase in every decade from 1900 to 1940, it had done so at a decreasing rate; against an average of more than a million a decade from 1900 to 1930, the increase for the 1930s had been only about half that number. The 'satellite areas', or suburban ring, had gained only about 300,000 people in the 1930s, but – just as in every previous decade – their percentage growth rate had been faster than that of the city itself. What was most remarkable about the 1930s was the sharp brake that had been put on the growth of the city and its surrounding area; the metropolitan district had grown by 28 per cent during the 1920s, but by only 7 per cent in the 1930s [140]. This, Thompson pointed out, was part of a general trend; metropolitan growth generally was slow compared with previous decades, and the largest size-group in particular was growing less rapidly than the national average [141]. It demonstrated the fact, Thompson argued, that larger cities and their metropolitan districts were 'slowly but rather steadily losing their industrial pre-eminence to peripheral areas' and were 'more and more becoming trade and service centers and centers of financial and industrial control in an increasingly complex economic system' [142]. For the future, it was 'highly plausible' that metropolitan districts in the south and west of the country would grow, even more rapidly than in the 1930s, because of a favourable climate and a basis of defence industries [143]. But, as Thompson so rightly surmised, the heyday of the great eastern metropolis was past.

Planners' Responses: Ideology and the Metropolis

Faced with these twin challenges, the infant art of planning developed very different responses. They ranged across the spectrum, from a desire to abolish the metropolis, to a determination to assure its position as a centralized node of activity. Central to them were the Garden City movement in its varied manifestations as its gospel spread through the urbanized world – and, in some cases, the rejoinder to it.

The Battle of Extremes: Urbanists vs. Deurbanists
It is easiest to start at the ideological extremes – if only because, in the Soviet Union of the 1920s, they were locked in acrimonious embrace. One party to that debate, the *deurbanists,* have curious parallels with the extreme anti-urbanist of American planning philosophy, Frank Lloyd Wright. The other side, the *urbanists,* have a more direct link to the arch-urbanist of French planning, Le Corbusier.

The deurbanist approach can be traced, in an indirect line, from the writings of Geddes in Scotland, Vandervelde in Belgium, and Kropotkin in England, around the turn of the century. All in different ways stressed the liberating effect of the new technologies – above all electricity and the internal combustion engine – on urban life and work. For Geddes the twentieth century would be 'the period of the great exodus, the return to the land' [144]. For Wells, the 'new forces, at present still so potently centripetal in their influence, bring with them, nevertheless, the distinct promise of a centrifugal application that may be finally equal to the complete reduction of our present congestions' [145]. Thus 'old "town" and "city" will be . . . terms as obsolete as "mail coach", to be replaced by "an urban region", laced all together not only by road and railway and telegraph but by novel roads . . . and by a dense network of telephones, parcels delivery tubes, and like nervous and arterial connections' [146]. Vandervelde, similarly, foresaw the progressive decongestion of cities and the urbanization of the countryside, to the point when eventually, perhaps, they would completely interpenetrate [147]. Kropotkin was writing in almost identical terms: 'the scattering of industries amidst all civilised nations will be necessarily followed by a further scattering of factories over the territories of each nation', allowing the combination of agriculture and industry [148].

For the Russian deurbanists, such ideas united with the traditional Russian love of nature [149] and with the notion in Marx's earlier writings of the eventual elimination of differences between town and country [150]. Electricity and new forms of transport would allow complete dispersion of the population into linear zones running across the country and creating an environment that was neither town nor country [151]. Within these zones, every adult would have his own lightweight and even transportable small house, but all activities except sleeping and repose would be collectivized [151]. This was the vision ridiculed by Le Corbusier:

> The cities will be part of the country; I shall live 30 miles away from my office under a pine tree; my secretary will live 30 miles away from it too, in the other direction, under another pine tree. We shall both have our own car. We shall use up tires, wear out road surfaces and gears, consume oil and gasoline. All of which will necessitate a great deal of work . . . enough for all [153].

But the vision went further still: in the celebrated 'Green Plan' of 1930 by M. Ginsburg and M. Brashch, two of the movement's leaders, Moscow's industries and administrative functions and scientific institutes were progressively to be transferred throughout the USSR, allowing the city eventually to be razed to the ground to form a huge park and urban museum [154].

The deurbanists' vision seems literally fantastic; and before long it was officially condemned, not least because of its enormous resource costs [155]. It also ignored the fact that the logic of Stalin's five-year plans, from 1928 onwards, was concentrating development in new towns – an irony, since the deurbanists thought that theirs was the logical way of meeting the demands of the plans [156]. But it needs stressing that in one respect the idea was less fantastic than it seems: Moscow in 1930, a city where some 62 per cent of the housing stock consisted of outmoded wooden structures [157], was in any event due for almost total reconstruction during the next thirty years.

Curiously, the rival camp – the urbanists – were equally utopian, and also anti-urban. Their preferred solution was to build new cities – in units of about 50,000 – in open countryside, outside the existing agglomerations [158]. The critical difference, in theological terms, lay in the urbanists' insistence on an even more heavily collectivized form of living. People would live in gigantic collective apartment blocks, with individual space reduced to the absolute minimum required for a bed – and, in one version by the notable designer Leonidov, with glass walls [159]. Marriages and divorces could be effected by opening or closing doors. There were to be no individual or family kitchens or bathrooms; all activities, save sleep, were to be ruthlessly collectivized [160]. In Kuzmin's house commune, life was to be regulated by the minute, from reveille at 6 a.m. to the departure to the mine at 7 a.m. [161]; while Melnikov envisaged a unit in which huge orchestras would induce sleep for insomniacs, simultaneously drowning the snores of those already asleep [162]. But, given the grim reality of actual Soviet housing at the time – the average house space per person dropped from 6.45 square metres in 1923 to 5.7 square metres in 1928 and to 4.09 square metres in 1940 [163] – perhaps some of these notions seem slightly less fantastic.

The relationship between the deurbanists in the USSR, and Frank Lloyd Wright in the USA, is certainly an indirect one. Around 1930, both were developing their ideas apparently in independence; the first sketch for Wright's Broadacre City came in 1932 [164]. The philosophic basis of Wright's city is very different from that of the deurbanists; it is a return to the individual life of the American home-steaders, which he knew in his Wisconsin boyhood. His characterization of the existing city as a 'fibrous tumour' [165] belongs to an anti-urban tradition in American thinking that – as already seen – goes back to Jefferson [166]; his alternative city is based on universal individual ownership [167], eschewing even the collective ownership of Howard – though for both the objective was to rid society of landlord's rent; and his city is seen as the means to a reassertion of democracy [168]. Thus, while the technical means of deurbanization – electricity, universal car ownership – are identical, the basis and the objective are quite opposed.

In contrast, the links between the Russian urbanists and Le Corbusier are both clear and direct. Le Corbusier was invited to Moscow in the 1920s and worked there on one important building. More significantly still, he intervened in the great debate on the side of the urbanists. And the plans of the urbanists for communal house blocks – such as those by Ivanov, Terekhin and Smolin in Leningrad, and by Barshch, Vladimirov, Alexander and Vesnin in Moscow – bear the clearest possible resemblance, even to the details of the high ceilings, to Le Corbusier's 1946 *Unité* at

Marseilles [169]. Ironically, before Le Corbusier could intervene effectively, both the urbanists and the deurbanists were routed by the traditionalists [170]. One reason for their victory was the clear fact that communal living – despite the collective traditions of the peasants who made up so much of the Moscow and Leningrad populations at that time – was so greatly disliked [171]. Possibly, indeed, in any country *La Ville Radieuse* could have been achieved only through a dictatorship. Indeed, its author accepted that 'the design of cities was too important to be left to the citizens' [172]; the city was to be run by cadres of industrialists, scientists and artists who would know what was best [173].

At first, Le Corbusier thought that the architect-planner – the leader of his intellectual élite – could achieve his aims in association with private industry: the Voisin plan of 1922 refers not to the neighbourhood of Central Paris that was to be razed, but to the motor company that financed the preparation of the plan. But, in the depression of the 1930s, such hopes failed; the political basis of *La Ville Radieuse* is an all-embracing syndicalism where planning is the function of an expert élite [174]. From that, it was a short step to a version of Fascism; the centre of the Radiant City is a stadium for 'spontaneous' public demonstrations in front of the 'leader' [175]. And, in World War Two, Le Corbusier believed that the Vichy government would at last provide the political leverage that would allow him to achieve his natural role as supreme planner of France – a hope that, like so many others in his career, was frustrated [176]. The truth is that Le Corbusier was supremely blinkered as to the real problems of city planning – that arise from the variety of problems and the conflict of interests that affect all cities [177]. His ideal was a simple-minded return to the age of absolutism; the final illustration of his book *L'urbanisme* shows Louis XIV directing the construction of the Invalides, with the caption:

> Homage to a great town planner. This despot conceived great projects and realised them. Over all the country his noble works still fill us with admiration. He was capable of saying 'We wish it', or 'Such is our pleasure' [178].

Ironically, Le Corbusier never found his *Roi Soleil*.

All this is well known, as is Le Corbusier's machine-age prescription: to free people by super-urbanization, with traffic and trees on the ground and people in the air. What is perhaps less well appreciated is that Le Corbusier – perhaps following his Russian experience – became a deurbanist. After 1930 he lost his previous optimism about the future of cities. Echoing Frank Lloyd Wright, he even came to see Paris as a 'cancer' [179]. The 'sickness of great cities' applied not merely to their structures, but to their people: Le Corbusier had joined the intellectual revolt against the metropolis [180]. He now believed that Paris should lose two-thirds of its three million people. Manufacturing should relocate out of the city, into linear industrial cities along national transportation corridors – a reflection again of the Russian experience. Administration might remain in the nodes where these corridors met [181]. Of course, the greatest of these would be Paris; Le Corbusier's metropolis was to be inhabited by élite people like himself [182].

Between the urbanist and deurbanist extremes, a narrow spectrum of related ideologies can be traced. The central and the most important of these is undoubtedly the Garden City movement which, beginning in Britain at the very end of the nineteenth century, rapidly spread to France, Germany, Russia and the United States. In the last-named country, it had a complex development. It merged into regional planning of the metropolis, but in turn this immediately divided into two separate – and often warring – camps. One, the more conservative, derived as much from the City Beautiful movement – a distinctively American planning tradition, albeit clearly deriving its inspiration from Europe – as from the Garden City tradition. The other represented a radical extension of the Garden City movement, and in particular of the idea of the Social City. The clash between the two centred upon the planning of New York, and there upon the practicable limits of decentralization. In contrast the regional planning debate in London and in Paris appears relatively weak.

The Garden City Movement in Europe and America
The most important in retrospect of all these reactions to metropolis, the Garden City movement, naturally shared some antecedents with the movements already discussed. Howard's classic [183] is clearly written against the background of continued metropolitan growth and rural depopulation, which had been especially marked in free-trade Britain after a flood of cheap food had driven many British farmers out of business during the 1880s and 1890s [184]. But, interestingly, it appeared in the same year as Kropotkin's book and before the contributions of Wells or Geddes; so it does not owe a direct debt to the Geddesian view of a neotechnic future. Indeed, Osborn doubts that it owes much directly to the sources most said to have influenced it – Wakefield, Marshall, Spencer and Buckingham; they were probably written in afterwards as justifications for views that Howard had independently developed [185]. What was most important to Howard was the urgent debate among London intellectuals in the 1880s and 1890s about living and working conditions in the metropolis. Howard's argument is essentially the same as that of Alfred Marshall, in his classic paper of 1884 on the housing of the London poor:

> For a committee, whether specially formed for the purpose or not, to interest themselves in the formation of a colony in some place well beyond the range of the London smoke. After seeing their way to building or buying suitable cottages there, they would enter into communication with some of the employers of low-waged labour . . . then mere self interest would induce employers to bring down their main workshops, and even to start factories in the colony [186].

But Howard gave vivid practical expression to this idea.

In comparison with the excesses of the urbanists and the deurbanists, the Garden City movement seemed to have its feet on the ground and its eyes fixed firmly on practical objectives. Of all reactions to the fact of the great metropolis, it was surely the one most likely to succeed. Yet in fact, in the period down to 1940, its practical outcomes were meagre. They were of course greatest in its original homeland. By 1940 Howard's two original garden cities at Letchworth (1903) and Welwyn (1920) were partly completed while the satellite city of Wythenshawe outside Manchester – a development with a fair right to the title of Third Garden City – was under construction. Yet, during the 1920s and 1930s, the mood of the Garden City movement was a combination of failure and indignation. For its leader after Howard's death in 1928, Frederic Osborn, an 'advance along the wrong track has brought London to a visible crisis, and the fate of London may give pause to those responsible for the great towns and town-conglomerations of the North and Midlands' [187]. After Howard's impulsive purchase of the land for Welwyn, in 1920, the movement itself had split over the critical question: should garden city building be primarily a natural, governmental responsibility or a private, charitable one? Howard's view, expressed forcibly to Osborn, was that the movement had better help itself: 'If you wait for the authorities to build new towns you will be older than Methusaleh before they start'. But 'to the rest of us that was unacceptable' [188]. In a new preface to his book published at the end of the war in 1918, and reprinted in 1942, Osborn recalled:

> I had put very clearly . . . that unless (new towns) were applied as a national policy, the great housing endeavour would go all wrong – we should just get vast new suburban additions to cities already far too large. And that, of course, is what actually happened [189].

That paragraph, Osborn notes, had been in the future tense in the original edition; he had rewritten it 'with melancholy recollection of my own foresight' [190].

The movement had split in yet another way, however. In the definition produced in 1919 by the Garden Cities and Town Planning Association:

> A Garden City is a town planned for industry and healthy living; of a size that makes possible a full measure of social life, but not larger; surrounded by a permanent belt of rural land; the whole of the land being in public ownership or held in trust for the city' [191].

But, starting with the construction of Hampstead Garden Suburb in 1906, vast numbers of developments had been begun that had some of these features but not all – in particular, lacking the essential feature of self-containment. Purdom complained in 1921 of these so-called garden cities:

> There is hardly a district in which the local council does not claim to be building one, and unscrupulous builders everywhere display the name on their advertisements . . . The thing itself is nowhere to be seen at the present time, but in Hertfordshire, at Letchworth and Welwyn [192].

Raymond Unwin, the architect who had given physical form to the first garden city, had powerfully aided this confusion of identity. For, first as architect of Hampstead and planner of the less well-known second garden suburb at Ealing [193], and later, after World War One, as chief architect at the Ministry of Health, he had given expression to these suburban parodies of the pure Garden City ideal. In this, he may have simply been compromising with political forces too powerful to overcome. Shortly after his arrival at the Ministry of Health, he had acquired a powerful political ally in the form of his newly-elected Minister, the ex-mayor of Birmingham, Neville Chamberlain; Chamberlain had almost immediately chaired a committee 'to consider and advise on principles to be followed in dealing with unhealthy cities', which had duly advocated a Garden City solution; but Chamberlain, apparently, had found few allies. Significantly, almost Chamberlain's first act on becoming Prime Minister in 1937 was to appoint the Barlow Commission on the Distribution of the Industrial Population: the body whose recommendations were to lead indirectly to the creation of the whole British post-war planning system and thus to the New Towns programme [194]. It followed that even the leading advocates of the Garden City movement occasionally seemed confused as to what was a garden city and what was not. Purdom himself extended the definition to include 'satellite towns', such as the London County Council estate at Becontree, which had no independent employment and was a pure dormitory settlement [195].

The Garden City movement soon spread abroad; but there, it became subject to similar definitional confusions. Tony Garnier, remarkably, had conceived his *Cité Industrielle* in 1898 – the same year as Howard's book appeared – though his full plan was not to be published until 1918. Though he may have seen Howard's book, it seems more likely that his was an independent notion, developed in response to the notions of the French regionalist school as expounded by Le Play and others [196]. Essentially the *Cité* was a regional centre, which would use local resources and teach local crafts. While Howard's idea was a response to his experience of the metropolis of London, Garnier's arose from his life and work in the provincial city of Lyon [197]. So it was the Howard rather than the Garnier version of the garden city that later came to influence Parisian planning. From 1916 onwards the *Office Public des Habitations à Bon Marché du Département de la Seine*, under the direction of Henri Sellier, designed a series of new settlements that were consciously based on English models. Unwin's book, *Town Planning in Practice*, was employed as a design guide, while in 1919 a party of architects from the *Office* went to England on a planning study tour [198]. The resulting moderately low-density developments, planned at between 95 and 150 persons to the hectare, are however garden suburbs in the Hampstead mould rather than true garden cities; they tend to be of fairly small size, ranging from 1040 up to a maximum of 5500 dwellings [199], and they clearly lack any element of self-containment [200]. Later, as rising land costs forced replacement of houses by flats, they departed even further from the pure gospel of Howard or Unwin [201].

The Germans, too, had their independent claim to have invented the garden city. Their Garnier was in some ways oddly cast for the role; the rabid propagandist Theodor Fritsch, whose *Die Stadt der Zukunft* (1896) had many features in common with Howard's model: the geometrical form, the ring-like distributions of land uses, the stress on low-rise houses at moderately low densities, the surrounding green belt and industrial zone, and the communal land ownership [202]. But there were differences too: Fritsch's city is not seen as a satellite of a bigger city, rather it is a big city in itself; in its second version, it is an extension of an existing city, not a new one. Fritsch's city extends indefinitely, Howard's is finite; Fritsch's city is specifically class-segregated, while Howard's is not [203]. For nationalistic reasons, Fritsch was later at pains to claim that he had truly invented the garden city, and indeed accused Howard of plagiarism [204]; but in truth it appears impossible to discover what if any influence each had on the other [205] and indeed it seems likely that Howard wrote his crucial conclusions as early as 1893, about the same time as Fritsch [206]. Whatever the truth, the spirit animating the two concepts is in important ways similar. Both rejected the conventional, overcrowded, polluted city of their time. And both to some degree regarded people as objects to be controlled – as emerges from Howard's famous diagram of the three magnets, where 'the people' play the role of the iron filings [207]. Both saw the new city as the key to a regulated, conflict-free, socially harmonious order.

These principles certainly appealed to the founders of the *Deutsche Gartenstadt-gesellschaft,* founded in 1902 after a German salesman, Heinrich Krebs, had brought back Howard's book from England [208]. It rapidly grew in membership during the first decade of the century, not least because of its appeal to two quite different and even contradictory strands of thought: on the one hand the left-liberal Life Reform Movement that stressed radical changes in food, clothing, housing and total lifestyle; on the other the more conservative elements in Wilhelmine Germany [209]. Thus Hans Kampffmeyer, the movement's chief ideologue, was already recommending by 1908 the establishment of garden cities as a way of promoting better labour relations, for which Germans of the time so admired Great Britain: 'the feeling that workers and employers in many cases have the same interests, is better developed there than with us', and that surely owed something to the paternal settlements of Bournville and Port Sunlight and to the new town at Letchworth [210].

This proved a potent appeal; as with the parallel movement in Britain, it seemed to promise a cooperative path to reform that might appeal to social democrats and liberal conservatives alike. During the pre-1914 period, the movement had one major success: the construction of a German Letchworth in the form of Gartenstadt Hellerau, outside Dresden. Heavily influenced by the Life Reform Movement, it was based on a cooperative furniture factory, the German Workshops for Craft Work, and contained a Centre for Applied Rhythmics [211]. The large development at Falkenberg near Grünau, south-east of Berlin, was only a garden suburb [212].

Overall, by 1915 the movement had produced some fifteen developments with a combined eventual population target of only 13,000; most were very small, and deserving of the label garden suburb rather than garden city [213]. The greatest practical triumphs of the German movement were to come later, however, during the Weimar Republic – and not in the national metropolis, but in the regional centre of Frankfurt-am-Main. Furthermore, they took the form of public interventions close to the city; a progressive Social Democratic administration, faced with a serious housing shortage, was in the fortunate position of owning extensive stretches of open land that had been incorporated into the city in 1910. It brought in Ernst May as *Stadtbaurat,* with an already considerable reputation as planner of Breslau (Wrocław). Working with enormous energy, May developed his celebrated plan for *Trabantenstädte* (satellite cities) of between 10,000 and 20,000 people, loosely clustered in a semi-circle around the compact inner city. Influenced both by the existing examples of Hellerau and the Krupp settlement at Margaretenhöhe outside Essen, and also by his work in England on Letchworth and Hampstead with Unwin, May strove to make the *Trabanten* true garden cities. They were individual small towns set against the open landscape of the Main and Nidda valleys. Some, inevitably, were dormitory towns; others contained some local industry and local services, though for higher-level services they were connected by highway and tramway with the centre of Frankfurt, as Howard had suggested in his celebrated diagram of the Social City [214]; thus they could be regarded as semi-garden cities, rather like Wythenshawe in Manchester [215]. But May also injected his own contribution, in the form of new housing designed uncomprisingly in the new international style, and carefully oriented to give maximum exposure to sun and minimum exposure to traffic [216]. This was good technical planning, but it was designed to be more; its aim – as it had been for the left wing of movement from its origins – was to create a new kind of socialist-cooperative lifestyle [217].

After World War One, Berlin, curiously, went in a quite different direction – but one that was of distinctively German provenance, borrowed from the Ruhr coalfield. As the *Ruhrgebiet* grew massively after the achievement of German unification in 1871, its coal owners and steel magnates had faced an unprecedented problem of housing the hundreds of thousands of migrants who poured into the burgeoning industrial cities for work. They solved it by a device already used by Owen and Salt in Britain and in even earlier experiments in France, but here on a much larger scale: the construction of *Arbeiterkolonien*, usually of single-family houses with gardens, close by the mines and factories. By the early twentieth century the mining companies alone were building between 3500 and 4000 houses a year, around one-quarter of all new housing in the *Ruhrgebiet*; by 1914 there were some 52,900 such houses [218]. Some cities, such as the mining town of Bottrop, consist almost exclusively of such colonies [219]; even the older-established cities, such as Essen, contain large areas of such uniform workers' housing [220]. Too often monotonous and uninspired, they nevertheless offered housing of a standard quite unimaginable to the average Berliner of that time. And in at least one case they eventually produced major pieces of design. Alfred Krupp, influenced by English town design and especially by the early garden suburb of Bedford Park, began to improve the designs; and after 1900 the Krupp family began to develop big self-contained satellites of Garden City type, notably Alfredshof and Margaretenhöhe, both completed in the early twentieth century [221].

The motives of the industrialists were not in much doubt, and they provide a field day for the Marxist commentators; the settlements were restricted to skilled workers of long service, and were clearly designed to reduce class consciousness and to *embourgeoiser* the workers [222]. But such sentiments seem to have been better developed in the Ruhr area than in Berlin, where the patriarchal tradition was weak and the relations between employers and employees were more distant [223]. However, after 1895 came a major change with the outward movement of Berlin's major engineering and electrical plants to new sites beyond the ring railway, till then the outer boundary of development. By moving to relatively distant locations – as far as 50 kilometres from the centre – and by then building company housing, the big firms could attract key workers and monopolize their local labour on the Ruhr model [224]. Thus 'enlightened capitalism' could go hand in hand with self-interest [225].

During the Weimar years, this tradition of large *Siedlungen* continued; Siemensstadt (1929), developed by the company's own building society, achieved local fame by employing international architects including Walter Gropius. But the new tradition had already been set by other non-profit-making building societies, notably the *GEHAG* which developed big projects such as Berlin-Britz and Berlin-Zehlendorf in outlying areas as individual – but in no way self-contained – garden suburb units. Though various architects worked on these schemes – including Muthesius, who had taken a large part in the garden city of Hellerau [226] – the dominant influence was that of *Stadtbaurat* Martin Wagner. In deliberate contradistinction to the Garden City theorists, he held that industries determined urban character [227]. A city should develop not through self-contained satellites, as at Frankfurt, but through large settlements that were an integral part of the city [228]. May's plans, and by implication Howard's, represented for Wagner a misguided attempt to deny the essential contradiction between town and country, and represented a path toward conceptual as well as economic bankruptcy [229].

There was of course an obvious difference between Frankfurt and Berlin in those days: one of size. Frankfurt in the 1920s was a typical German provincial city of some 500,000 people; Berlin was a vast metropolis of four million. In some ways May's solution for Frankfurt resembles Parker's plans for the satellite of Wythenshawe outside Manchester, a city of similar size, in 1927. Unless powers could be seized to create a bold plan of long-distance decentralization as urged by the Garden City movement, Berlin – like London – was doomed to develop through more or less contiguous accretion. But the form of the Berlin *Siedlungen*, with their stress on very large developments of apartment houses, reflects perhaps also an ideological tendency on the part of the many distinguished architects who designed them, including Gropius, Scharoun, Häring and others [230]. For them, economic and political autonomy – the keynote of the garden city – was simply not worth fighting for [231].

What is most interesting about this ultra-urban tendency in Berlin is the reaction to it. As we have already seen, the *Gartenstadtbewegung* had almost from the start attracted strong conservative support. Even by 1908 Hans Kampffmeyer was commending the notion of establishing garden cities in the thinly-populated agricultural districts of eastern Germany as an 'imposing monument to German culture' [232]. Coming at a time when conservative Germans were already becoming alarmed by the 'biological decline' of urban populations, the idea proved irresistible; as developed by the propagandist Erich Keup the movement was already using the word *'Lebensraum'* by 1917, and was calling for planned colonization with the removal of 'population that is harmful to our national character' [233]. It was a short step to the anti-urbanism of the early Nazi theorists of the mid-1920s, Richard Walter Darré and Paul Schultze-Naumburg, with its contrast between the 'Jewish-capitalist' metropolis and the 'Nordic' agrarian tradition [234]. By 1929 the Nazi official organ, the *Völkischer Beobachter*, was condemning the metropolis – by implication Berlin – as the 'melting-pot of all evil . . . of prostitution, bars, illness, movies, Marxism, Jews, strippers, Negro dances, and all the disgusting offspring of so-called "modern art" '; Berlin was the 'most infertile city in the world' [235]. By 1931, it was calling for repatriation to the soil [236].

Though deurbanization never became official policy after Hitler's seizure of power, the first emphasis of Nazi planning was a straight takeover of social democratic policies from the Weimar era: the building of small settlements at the edge of the city and the development of *Kleinsiedlungen* at some distance from it, with an agricultural basis, for the relief of the urban unemployed [237]. Later though, the housing effort weakened because of the competition of rearmament, and the emphasis shifted even more heavily to rural colonization [238]. At the very end of the 1930s Gottfried Feder, the leading Nazi planning theorist, called in his book *Die neue Stadt* for planned settlements of small towns in the agricultural districts of East Prussia [239]. These country towns, with their self-sufficiency and their small houses with gardens, indeed have some superficial resemblance to the notions of Fritsch – and of Howard. But they differ from both models in their stress on individual occupation of the land, a key Nazi ideological concept [240]. However, in practice very little of this actually got done – as with the rest of Nazi planning theory. And, as will shortly be seen, the original opposition to the big city underwent drastic modification in the hands of Hitler and his architect-planner, Albert Speer.

In pre-revolutionary Russia, too, the Garden City movement flourished.

Howard's book was first publicized in 1908 and translated in 1911; in 1912 the garden city of Prozorovka, 40 kilometres east of Moscow, was started as the main service town of the new Moscow-Kazan railway: 'it appears even today as a page out of Howard's notebook' [241]. By 1913 there were Garden City associations in every major city; at the 1914 congress in London, the Russians made up one-fifth of the total foreign and colonial delegates [242]. The mood of the movement, as elsewhere, tended to be moderately socialist, but it was also felt that garden cities were especially suited to Russian conditions, because of the opening-up of Siberia and Central Asia [243].

After the Revolution, many of the movement's leading theorists found themselves in leading professional positions: V. N. Semionov, who had designed Prozorovka garden city and had written the most important Russian book on planning theory, *Public Servicing of Towns*, in 1912, became head of the town planning department of the Central Administration of Communal Economics of the Commissariat of the Interior. It was small wonder that among the first regulations produced by the new administration was a requirement for minimum open space and for a green belt around every town [244]. But, in the chaotic conditions of Russian planning in the 1920s, it is almost certain that these regulations came to almost nothing. So did the ambitious Greater Moscow Plan of 1925, according to which the towns outside the city – but close to it – would have been extended into garden cities which would then have been incorporated administratively into Moscow [245].

In the 1920s, however, the pure Garden City gospel was heavily overshadowed by the debate between the urbanists and the deurbanists. Some industrial garden cities were actually started, such as Krasnyi and Bogatyr outside Moscow [246], but the total outcome was disappointing. Finally, when Ernst May left Frankfurt in 1929, he was invited to produce a further plan for Moscow, which he duly did in the form of a central administrative city surrounded by twenty-four satellites, connected up by fast electric trains. The authorities gave the plan a cold reception; and – after a similar discouraging experience at the new steel town of Magnitogorsk – May left with most of his German collaborators after only three years' stay [247]. It took, May notes wryly, a further generation before the Russian official machine was ready for the satellite concept [248]. But this was because, already by the time May was producing his plan, an older and more conservative planning tradition was gaining the ascendancy.

Two Regional Ideologies:
The New York Regional Plan vs. the RPAA
In order to understand better that process, it is useful first to go back to the United States; for here, perhaps, was the greatest ideological debate of all. It took place between two wings of the Garden City movement. One, represented by the authors of the massive Regional Plan for New York, can be termed the

metropolitan planning movement. The other, represented by the Regional Planning Association of America, can be called the regional planning movement. As with any such debate, at a distance of time, what united the protagonists might seem more important than what divided them. But the dispute was pursued for many years, with vigour and even with ferocity.

The metropolitan planning movement, in essence, was Garden City planning grafted on to a distinctly American movement of almost the same period, the City Beautiful movement. The greatest achievement of the latter, Daniel Burnham's 1909 plan for Chicago, was 'to restore to the city a lost visual and aesthetic harmony, thereby creating the physical prerequisite for the emergence of a harmonious social order' [249]. The physical means to that end were highly reminiscent of classical European planning in the Haussmannesque mode: big new arteries, a vast new park, and classical public buildings grouped round new central squares, which would represent 'what the Acropolis is to Athens, or the Forum to Rome, and what St Mark's Square is to Venice, the very embodiment of civic life' [250].

Unsurprisingly, New York City also produced a City Beautiful plan – and even scooped Chicago by two years [251]. However, it lacked the dynamic approach of Burnham's Chicago plan, with its emphasis on new radial and orbital connections. For New York, the standard City Beautiful approach was too static: 'any attempt at planning of urban growth in New York required something far more flexible than the plaster models that had stirred their imagination at Chicago's fair in 1893' [252]. To achieve that flexibility, a new strain of thought was needed.

So New York tried again – with a direct link back to Chicago. Charles Dyer Norton, a key figure in commissioning the Burnham plan, moved to New York in 1911 and soon began to campaign with the President of the Borough of Manhattan, George McAneny, for a regional plan. In this he failed after McAneny's resignation in 1916; so he turned to the Russell Sage Foundation, becoming its trustee and treasurer in 1918. In 1921 the Foundation announced its support for a major planning study; Thomas Adams, a British emigré who had been first President of the Town Planning Institute (in 1914), was made its director. After nearly a decade of work and the expenditure of over $1 million, the ten volumes of survey and two volumes of the plan were published between 1928 and 1931 [253].

Even its most severe critics had to admit that the New York plan broke new ground. First, it was one of the first plans to consider the development of a large city in relation to its surrounding region. Adams, even before taking over the task, had emphasized the new approach in a talk in 1919 that was almost Geddesian: '. . . the artificial boundaries of the city are becoming more and more meaningless . . . no city planning scheme can be satisfactory which is not prepared with due regard to the regional development surrounding the city, and no local plan of means of communication by rail or road can be adequate or efficient' [254]. So the plan covered an extremely broad sweep, as already outlined by Norton in 1915. 'From the City Hall a circle must be swung which will include the Atlantic Heights and Princeton; the lovely Jersey hills back of Morristown and Tuxedo; the incomparable Hudson as far as Newburg; the Westchester lakes and ridges, to Bridgeport and beyond, and all of Long Island' [225]. Secondly, the plan was equally faithful to Geddes in being founded on regional survey. Indeed, it is doubtful if any subsequent planning survey has ever equalled it in comprehensiveness. It covered the economic base of the region, land use and transportation, land values and housing. And in several of these fields – as in Robert Murray Haig's classic analysis of patterns of location of economic activities – it virtually created new traditions of academic analysis [256]. Haig starts out by asserting that the job of planning is less to create a City Beautiful than to develop a 'productive piece of economic machinery' [257]. The key was to understand the competition for space, which caused some activities to displace others according to their relative need for a central location [258]. This is a natural and healthy process, but it is the task of the planner – through zoning – to take account of what the economist would now call negative externalities: '. . . unless zoning is fully and skillfully applied, it is entirely possible for an individual to make for himself a dollar of profit, but at the same time cause a loss of many dollars to his neighbors and to the community as a whole, so that the social result is a net loss . . . Zoning finds its economic justification in . . . forcing each individual to bear his own expenses' [259].

The general philosophy of the plan came to follow this analysis. Neither concentration of activities, nor deconcentration were good or bad in themselves; but congestion was unambiguously bad [260]. Deconcentration in itself could achieve nothing. What was needed was a 'reorientation of centralization on the basis of making all its centers and sub-centers healthy, efficient and free from congestion' [261]. From this emerged one main stress of the plan: 'the dispersal of industry over wider areas, the more stringent control over building densities, and restraint of gambling in land' [262]. The main evil of the present organization of the region, the plan argued, was the congestion at its heart. But this itself was a simple function of the permitted height and bulk of buildings, coupled with subsidies to rapid transit [263]. The ideal way to limit congestion might have been to build upwards, if part of the space so liberated had actually been left free, 'if the skyscrapers had been spaced five-hunded feet apart . . . the American metropolis would have comprised a series of towers surrounded by vast areas of parks, gardens and drives' [264]. Harvey W. Corbett, the designer of the heavily neoclassical Bush House in London, produced for the plan a positively Corbusian vision of this kind – whether in knowledge or ignorance of the *Plan Voisin* is unknown [265]. But, whatever the formula, some restriction on building height and bulk was vital; and the most important was reduction of the coverage [266].

The plan was less clear when it came to the other main element: transport. Though subsidized rapid transit was a cause of congestion at the centre, it might also be a means of building new sub-centres elsewhere. The trick was to produce one without the other, but the plan does not exactly suggest how this should be done. It was clear that there was a need for 'by-passes or belt lines . . . to permit free circulation between the major subdivisions' [267]. But on the other hand, to the ire of its critics, it gave to Garden City solutions only a limited role, for 'experiments have proved that this did not prove a complete remedy, except for the very small part of industry and population that could be made to move to new centres, while for the greater part that remained in the large cities it was only a palliative' [268].

This caution was combined with extreme scepticism as to the value of State intervention in housing. Even if public housing had achieved some good results in Britain and elsewhere in Europe, nevertheless much public aid had been given in the wrong way, wastefully, to people who did not need it [269]. Here, doubtless, Adams was expressing the deep financial conservatism of his business sponsors [270]. But equally, and perhaps more fundamentally, he was expressing his profound pessimism about the limits of planning. True, 'to the extent that it is practicable to secure it, the migration of population from the large cities into well-planned and comparatively small city units will lead to the ideal form of distribution'; but experience showed that most people would still go on living – and increasing – in the existing urban regions. Though, even here, it was right to get as many people into garden cities as possible, nevertheless, 'the Garden City movement has had such a strong influence in correcting the evils of existing communities and in making parts of urban regions more attractive that, to some extent, it is lessening the need for Garden Cities' [271]. But, by seeking 'an ideal based on realities' Adams recognized that he laid himself open to attack by 'either the practical man who thinks mainly of the immediate present or the idealist who dreams of a perfect future' [272]. The central feature of the plan – the outward movement of population and economic activity, to be then recentralized in clusters – was bound to seem hopelessly inadequate to dedicated Garden City activists [273].

The counter-attack was not slow in coming. In his celebrated review of the plan, the leading Garden City polemicist, Lewis Mumford, condemned it in almost every particular. Its spatial frame was too narrow; it accepted growth as inevitable, ignoring the potential of planning and the fact that the growth had slowed in recent years; it considered no alternatives; it continued to allow overbuilding of central areas; it condemned the last remaining close-in open space, the Hackensack Meadows, to be built over; it condemned garden cities to the realm of the utopia; it condoned the filling-up of suburban areas; through its rejection of public housing, it condemned the poor to continue to live in poor housing; it favoured yet more subsidization of Manhattan rapid transit, thus engendering yet more of the very congestion it condemned [274]. Its central defect was that it appeared to support everything – concentration and dispersal, social control versus speculation, subsidization versus the market – but, all appearances to the contrary, its fundamental general drift was towards centralization, Mumford concluded:

> In sum: the 'Plan for New York and its Environs' is a badly conceived pudding into which a great many ingredients, some sound, many dubious, have been poured and mixed: the cooks tried to satisfy every appetite and taste, and the guiding thought in selecting the pudding-dish was that it should 'sell' one pudding to the diners, especially to those who paid the cooks. The mixture as a whole is indigestible and tasteless: but here and there is a raisin or a large piece of citron that can be extracted and eaten with relish. In the long run, let us hope, this is how the pudding will be remembered [275].

Adams, naturally, came back in his own defence:

> This is the main point on which Mr Mumford and I, as well as Mr Mumford and Geddes, differ – that is, whether we stand still and talk ideals or move forward and get as much realization of our ideals as possible in a necessarily imperfect society, capable only of imperfect solutions to its problems [276].

This, in essence, was the difference in philosophy between the Regional Plan Association – formed in 1929 to promote the plan through business leadership [277] – and the Regional Plan Association of America: a body of idealists, founded already as long ago as 1923 and dominated by Lewis Mumford, Clarence Stein, and Henry Wright [278]. The philosophy and objectives of the RPAA are complex, but they are well summarized in the 1925 Special Issue of the magazine, *Survey Graphic*, which represents a kind of credo of the movement. Drawing from Geddes, Mumford argued there that new technologies were promoting a fourth migration that, in the words of Stein, would demonstrate the total obsolescence of the present 'Dinosaur Cities' [279]. Although this movement would soon occur of its own accord, it was the job of the planner to recognize it, speed it up – and guide it. For, once the fact of movement was faced, a proper social accounting system would show the economic superiority of a new regional basis for planning. In the same issue, Stuart Chase, the movement's economist, anticipated the economics of the 1980s in his stress on an energy-frugal framework for planning:

> The regional planning of communities would wipe out unnecessary national marketing, wipe out city congestion and terminal wastes, balance the power load, take the bulk of coal off the railroad, eliminate the duplication of milk and other local deliveries, short circuit . . . unnecessary practices . . . Gone the necessity for the skyscraper, the subway and the lonely country-side! [280].

From these stands came the central feature that distinguished the RPAA from its metropolitan planning counterparts: the development of the region, not as a subsidiary backdrop to the giant city, but as a whole concept of which the city was only one of the parts:

> Regional planning asks not how wide an area can be brought under the aegis of the metropolis, but how the population and civic facilities can be distributed so as to promote and stimulate a vivid, creative life throughout the whole region – a region being any geographical area that possesses a certain unity of climate, soil, vegetation, industry and culture [281].

This concept, of course, leant heavily on Geddes, to whom Mumford – then as afterwards – proclaimed his debt. It was essentially a concept of a rural region unsullied by the complications of metropolitan life, as Geddes had honestly admitted in a key passage a quarter-century before:

> Coming to concrete Civic Survey, where shall we begin? . . . London may naturally claim pre-eminence. Yet even at best, does not this vastness of world cities present a more or less foggy labyrinth, . . . from which surrounding regions with their smaller cities can be but dimly descried . . . For our more general and comparative study, then, simpler beginnings are preferable . . . the clearer outlook, the more panoramic view of a definite geographic region such, for instance, as lies before us on a mountain holiday [282].

It was such a region, for Mumford, that required planning: the 'comprehensive ordering of the natural resources of a community, its material equipment and its population for the purpose of laying a sound physical basis for the "good life" ' [283]. But the key to this planning, as Geddes had also seen, was to distribute metropolitan advantages throughout the regions of the land by means of modern technology [284]. With this dispersal would go the decentralization of power and the development of planning by the local community at each geographical scale [285].

The RPAA philosophy, then, forms a complete – and also a massive – extension of the Garden City idea. It accepted garden cities – but only as a relatively small part of a much wider planning package, representing a fundamental reconstitution of society. In essence, it wanted the progressive realization of Howard's Social City, which it renamed the regional city: a symbiotic town-country relationship, without predefined size or form [286]. Its philosophical origins went back both through Geddes to the French regionalist movement of the late nineteenth century, and to early American concepts of balance and harmony between man and nature [287]. It thus represented an enormous extension of the whole area of planning, from the purely physical, through the socio-economic, to embrace also natural resource planning and conservation [288]. Further, it came to see planning as a replacement for the market, not as its handmaiden. And here, perhaps, was the cleanest break with the business conservatism of the New York Plan. Stuart Chase was quite specific:

> We were mildly socialist, though not all communist; liberal but willing to abandon large areas of the free market in favor of a planned economy. So we were not doctrinaire socialists. We were open-minded; kind of Fabian Socialists [289].

Thus the views of the RPAA were certainly out of line with those of most Americans – and certainly most American leaders – in the 1920s and 1930s. So it is small wonder that their contribution was theoretical and critical rather than practical or constructive. Stein, one of their leading lights, did provide the plan for what was intended as a full-blooded new town experiment at Radburn, New Jersey (some fifteen miles from Manhattan), developed between 1929 and 1933. Stein was clear that he and his co-designers 'still had the theme that Ebenezer Howard had created so vividly in his book *Garden Cities of Tomorrow*. We believed thoroughly in green belts, and towns of a limited size planned for work as well as living' [290]. Tragically, the town got into financial difficulties and was never completed. The original social ideas were soon abandoned and today the town, still distinct by reason of its radical pedestrian-vehicle segregation, has been swallowed up in the endless New Jersey suburbs.

The New Deal and the Metropolis

It was, however, a national phenomenon, the New Deal, ushered in by Franklin Delano Roosevelt's presidential victory of 1932, that gave the RPAA its greatest potential chance to carry some of its ideas into practical action. For Roosevelt had an abiding interest in planning, which – as he recalled in 1931 – was stimulated by the work of his uncle Frederic Delano on the Regional Plan of New York; he felt that 'perhaps the day is not far distant when planning will become a part of the national policy of this country' [291]. But Roosevelt's instincts and interests were profoundly rural; he was, as the planner Rexford Tugwell said, 'a child of the country' [292]. His earliest policy decisions, under the New Deal, emphasized that fact. The Public Works bill of June 1933 was an abortive attempt to resettle the urban unemployed in subsistence homesteads on the land, so as to 'redress the overbalance of population in our industrial centers' and 'to secure through the good earth the permanent jobs they have lost in the overcrowded, industrial cities and towns' [293]. This policy, with its curious parallels to the *Kleinsiedlungen* in Nazi Germany at the same time, was soon overtaken by events; political pressures, in particular FDR's keen perception of the need to win the cities for the Democrats, soon had the tide of money flowing their way [294].

For planning, however, the most interesting of Roosevelt's early decisions was the creation – in April 1935 – of the Resettlement Administration under the direction of Rexford Tugwell. Tugwell was an unrepentant ideologue and RPAA sympathizer, who believed that capitalism was about to be replaced by a planned economy [295]. Almost immediately he had persuaded the President to make a first appropriation of money for one of his central ideas: a massive programme of new town building, in the suburban fringes of big urban areas [296]. He argued on the basis of actual trends; already, at that time, central cities were static or declining while suburban rings were growing, so that the programme 'accepted a trend instead of trying to reverse it' [297]. Further, Tugwell asserted, along lines that derived directly from Ebenezer Howard, that fringe areas uniquely combined the advantages of metropolitan employment and rural environment [298]. Already convinced that a radical back-to-the-land movement was doomed to failure, Roosevelt approved the project, but characteristically – for he liked to bet a little on a whole series of horses – on a small scale. Instead of the 3000 towns Tugwell had hoped to build, the $31 million vote allowed only for a list of twenty-five which was whittled down to five and then – because of threats of legal action – to three [299]. Ironically, one of the towns that disappeared at that point was the only one that would have served the New York region: Greenbrook in New Jersey. Of the remaining three, only Greenbelt in Maryland served a large metropolis – Washington DC [300]. The others, Greendale in Wisconsin (for Milwaukee) and Greenhills in Ohio (for Cincinnati) were both related to medium-sized cities [301].

In retrospect the green-belt cities were a curious combination of audacious success and abject failure. On the one hand they represent a quite extraordinary, radical break with past American policies; they were built under total Federal control, without consultation with local government; the land was compulsorily purchased; Tugwell had a free choice of cities and sites [302]. In these respects, the green-belt towns anticipated the British legislation of 1946. But on the other hand, the total achievement was in quantitative terms very puny: 'providing an attractive environment for only 2267 familes can hardly be considered significant' [303]. Further, the towns lacked both local employment and – at first – adequate public transport into the city [304]. The unit costs were high and the modern architectural style was unpopular [305]. Lastly – perhaps most extraordinary of all in such a radical programme – black people were excluded, probably because of a fear of local opposition [306]. But this did not prevent Tugwell being branded as a communist 'shifting people around from where they are to where Dr Tugwell thinks they ought to be' [307]. Building and real estate interests, finance and the media were all against the programme on the ground that it was opposed to the free market; Unwin, lecturing at Columbia University in 1937, felt that the 'rugged individualism' of America was a serious obstacle to any serious planning [308]. After the virtual completion of the truncated programme in June 1938, Congressional opposition precluded its continuation; and after World War Two the towns were sold off [309].

But even more significant for the ideals of the RPAA, in a larger sense, was yet another New Deal experiment. The National Resources Planning Board, created under the chairmanship of Roosevelt's uncle Frederic Delano, was one of the incoming President's earliest institutional inventions. Vaguely committed to the notion of planning the entire resources of the nation in the communal interest, its guiding philosophy at first appeared to be close to that of the RPAA. After a sudden diversion by Roosevelt into natural resource planning (in 1934), it turned to the problem of the cities. Its Committee on Urbanism, which was appointed in 1935 and reported in 1937, was a group with major ambitions to restructure urban government. It rejected wholesale urban decentralization, arguing instead for a moderately decentralized yet integrated urban structure – thus recalling the recommendations of the Regional Plan for New York [310]. It called for a rationalization of local government powers in such vast metropolitan areas as the Northeastern Seaboard, through Congressional permission to establish interstate compacts within metropolitan districts for planning and related purposes [311]. It wanted to see a permanent National Planning Board with powers to improve the pattern of distribution of industry and transportation [312]. It was also in favour of Federal intervention in housing, public works and law enforcement [313]. Its report was predictably received with enthusiasm by the advocates of planning, and was promptly ignored both by the President and Congress [314]. During World War Two an urban section of the Board was brought into being; but only two years later the Board was killed off by Congress, and the establishment of a Department of Housing and Urban Development had to await the Johnson administration of 1965 [315].

Thus ended a major experiment that promised much more than it ever delivered. As Friedmann and Weaver have pointed out, the work of the National Resources Planning Board combined, in a highly eclectic synthesis, a whole skein of different planning ideas and philosophies. One of the earliest was natural resource planning under a permanent national planning board, in which the distinction between metropolitan and regional planning virtually disappeared. A second and related theme was regionalism based on a river basin unit, as classically demonstrated by the Tennessee Valley Authority. But in thus taking over a central RPAA idea, the Board somehow inverted it; the original anti-metropolitan bias all but disappeared. Thus the way was opened to a third main strain: urban planning for metropolitan areas through greater local cooperation under Federal guidance. In these ways, Friedmann and Weaver argue, the original RPAA philosophy became modified almost to the point of extinction [316]. But perhaps it was truer to say that to the very end, the various strands were never properly integrated. As was true of FDR's policies as a whole, the Board was capable of pursuing different, even contradictory aims at almost the same time.

Planning the Metropolitan Region in Europe

Perhaps the supreme irony of the inter-war period is that the most comprehensive and radical philosophy of anti-metropolitan regional planning emerged in the United States – the one country least likely to be able to carry it to fruition. Certainly, apart from the Russian deurbanists of the 1920s, nothing quite as sweeping was to be seen elsewhere. In Britain, regional planning theory took the form of a logical and limited extension of Howard's original concept of the Social City, where garden cities multiplied by a kind of cellular division once they had reached a certain size, each being separated from its neighbour by being set in a green-belt background. Arthur Crow's plan of 1910 provided for ten new 'cities of health', at the termini of new express rapid transit lines some 14 miles from central London, each occupying 25,000 acres and housing 500,000 people, set against a green belt background [317]. George Pepler in the same year called for a 'great girdle' around London, ten miles from the centre, with a parkway to connect new suburban developments [318]. C. B. Purdom in 1921 was emphasizing the critical distinction between the fully self-contained and separate garden city, and the imitation garden suburb; he proposed the creation of a whole series of garden cities in the ring roughly between 15 and 30 miles from central London [319]. Raymond Unwin, appointed as technical adviser to a group of local authorities to produce a regional plan for the area around London, suggested in his final 1933 report that steps be taken to secure a 'supply of playing fields and other recreation areas, and of open spaces, in the form of a girdle of open space round London'; outside this, 'every effort should be made by full use of the powers in the Town and Country Planning Act to define the areas in this outer region which may be allowed to building development, and secure the background of open lands from which public open spaces may be obtained as and when needed' [320]. Powers should be sought in the new Town and Country Planning Bill, going through Parliament as Unwin wrote, to give new powers to build garden cities and promote industrial development in them [321]. The key diagram in the 1933 report shows a scheme akin to Pepler's of 1921, with many garden cities and other satellite developments against a continuous background of open country [322]. But the necessary powers were not taken, and London continued to sprawl in all directions. It was to take until 1944 for Abercrombie to recycle the ideas of Howard, Pepler and Unwin, and at last to produce the sketch that proved decisive for action [323].

In Paris there was a similar lack of effective regional intervention. Alarmed by the uncontrolled spread of the *lotissements*, in 1928 the Poincaré Government set up the *Comité supérieur de l'Aménagement et de l'Organisation générale de la Région Parisienne* (CARP). Poincaré was frank about the government's motives: '. . . *si la population parisienne augmente encore il en resulterait un grand danger social'* [324]. The new committee was to oversee a region stretching some 35 kilometres from central Paris and embracing all or part of the *départements* of the Seine, Seine-et-Oise, Seine-et-Marne and Oise, with a total area of 5120 square kilometres and a population of 6.4 million, and including representatives of all these and of the central government [325]. In 1932 came a law that empowered the committee to prepare a planning project for the whole region, the existence of which was thus confirmed [326]. Expected to take a year to produce, the plan was constantly delayed by local objections and in fact was agreed only in 1939. The 'Plan Prost-Dausset' was highly unadventurous; eschewing Garden City solutions [327], it contented itself by trying to draw limits to urban expansion through a *zone non-affectée*, in which no development could take place without the committee's decision [328] and in which a rural character could be maintained [329]. In this way it hoped to combat the expansion of the *lotissements*; but the limits to development were so widely drawn that it could hardly have been successful [330]. The plan also called for the reservation of park space, and the regulation of building heights in an effort to bring some form to the chaotic expansion of the Parisian *banlieue* [331].

Perhaps most surprisingly, for a Paris still having few cars, the Prost plan proposed a gigantic programme of some 3300 kilometres of new roads, while giving virtually no attention to public transport [332]. Of the roads, only the *Autoroute de l'Ouest* had been finished by the start of the war; the other radial motorways were finished only well after World War Two, and the proposed *rocades* are not even now complete [333]. Worst of all, the authors of the Prost Plan were not empowered to consider the city of Paris itself, a fact that made a virtual nonsense of any concept of regional planning; it was not remedied until wartime laws of 1941 and 1943 integrated the city in the region and virtually necessitated a new plan [334]. But the biggest sin of the plan, in the eyes of suburban people, was that 'it was seen not as a plan for growth, but as a plan for non-growth, and as such it was opposed. . .' [335].

Neither Paris nor London, then, succeeded in producing an effective regional plan even for the continuously built-up metropolitan agglomeration, still less for its surrounding sphere of influence. That was because in both areas the planning process was left to loose and – in the case of London – impermanent advisory organizations, while effective executive power still remained with a multitude of local authorities. In both cases, the densely built-up inner area was under the control of one authority, representing a purely historical definition of the agglomeration, while the outer suburban ring was under divided responsibility. For London, William Robson scathingly denounced the resultant absurdities in a brilliant piece of academic polemic, concluding with a call for the establishment of a Greater London Council [336]; but implementation was to wait until well after World War Two.

Germany, as early as the 1920s, did better; Greater Berlin came under unified control in 1920. In the same year, a unique experiment began in Germany's second greatest agglomeration. The *Ruhrgebiet* was unusual among Europe's major aggregations of population in being polycentric [337]; it was dominated by a string of major cities of roughly equal rank, some with long histories, others recent creations of the industrial revolution [338]. By the early twentieth century, the mushroom growth of these cities – from 1.5 to 2.5 million between 1895 and 1905 alone [339] was causing problems beyond the capacity of any one of them to solve. In 1912 the *Stadtbaurat* of Essen, Robert Schmidt, suggested the need for a general settlement plan dealing with all aspects of the life of the agglomeration: housing, recreation, work, transport, pollution and aesthetic aspects. Such a plan would need to be much more than the traditional building plan: Schmidt called it an economic plan, but it was equally a social and cultural plan [340].

The establishment in the same year of a loose planning federation for the Greater Berlin area – itself a prelude for the formation of Greater Berlin in 1920 – gave an impetus to Schmidt's proposals. But the final spur came from the unprecedented in-migration, immediately after World War One, of some 150,000 miners and their families – a total of some 600,000 people to be housed almost instantly [341]. In 1920 the eighteen cities and 310 *Landgemeinden*, organized in eleven *Kreise* and three *Regierungsbezirke*, agreed to surrender their planning powers to a new special purpose agency, the *Siedlungsverband Ruhrkohlenbezirk* (SVR). The SVR was unusual in its organization: decision-making organs – the Council and Committee – consisted only one half of local government representatives, the other half representing organizations of employers and workers [342]. With an area of 3690 square kilometres and a population of 3.58 million – extended in the late 1920s to cover 4591 square kilometres and a (1939) population of 4.20 million – it formed a unique, and soon highly effective, experiment in regional planning and the coordination of public transport [343].

Planning under Totalitarianism:
The Return to the City Beautiful
In the democratic countries, then, metropolitan regional planning during the 1920s and 1930s was fitful and weak. In totalitarian countries, by way of contrast, it took on a new lease of life during the 1930s – but in a wayward direction. In both Stalin's Russia and Hitler's Germany, there occurred a strange and spectacular flowering of the City Beautiful movement.

At the June 1931 Plenum of the Central Committee of the All-Union Communist Party, the great debate over Moscow's future came to an abrupt end. The urbanists and deurbanists were told that their excesses must stop. Moscow was to remain where and what it was; but a limit was to be placed on its growth. There was to be a ban on new industrial enterprises, though not on the extension of existing concerns. 'Insanitary' factories were to move out. (A year later, an internal passport system was designed to limit the inflow of workers into the capital [344].) And, expressing surprise that the development of the city was subject to no general plan at all, the conference called for one to be prepared [345].

The planners went to work. At first, distinguished foreign planners – Le Corbusier, May, Wright – were invited to give their views. May, as already noted, proposed a satellite plan. Le Corbusier suggested leaving the city as an urban museum, creating a new city of towers on another site. Unsurprisingly, the Soviet planners found these suggestions less than helpful. After 1933 they worked alone, in ten workshops, to produce a more indigenous plan which was approved in 1935 [346].

The basic principles of the 1935 plan were thoroughly conservative. Moscow was to remain a single, unitary, centralized city without satellites. It was to grow to a rigidly determined limit: from 28 square kilometres to 52 square kilometres, accommodating a maximum population of five million, mainly through a major extension of 16 square kilometres in the Lenin Hills district in the south-west sector. Beyond this, there was to be a 10-kilometre forest belt, to stop the city's further growth. Virtually the entire existing city, apart from a few new buildings and some outstanding historic structures, was to be torn down and rebuilt. Instead of the old one- and two-storey village city of wooden structures, there would arise a new high-density city in which the minimum normal building height would be six storeys, rising in places to fourteen storeys, and with an average density of some 400 people per hectare. The existing structure of the city, with radial streets intersected by rings, was to be retained and reinforced by rebuilding all the principal streets, which were to be greatly widened to 30 or 40 metres; some new streets would be built to complete the ring and radial pattern. There was to be a new Metro system, plus new tram and bus routes, and extensive electrification of the main-line commuter rail system [347].

The plan seemed grandiose, almost foolhardy. But it must be remembered that its authors were starting almost from scratch. The previous plan of 1925 had proved utopian and had almost immediately been shelved. The whole infrastructure of the city was still unbelievably primitive, with an almost pre-industrial lack of basic urban services [348]. The shortage of housing was grievous and was worsening, so that the plan had to provide a housing programme equal to the entire building stock of the then city [349]. So in some ways the plan was a genuine attempt to bring order, for the first time, out of chaos. What was, however, most significant was that the plan was completely monumental in character. The streets were to be widened to become some of the widest in Europe, though car traffic was negligible and seemed destined to remain so virtually for ever. Further, the architectural treatment was deliberately designed to fortify the impression of immense vistas and imposing structures. Architectural styles were no longer to represent a great social transformation, as the debaters of the 1920s had naively thought, but instead were to serve as an ideological tool representing the might of the Soviet State: 'Henceforth architecture had to be expressive, representational, oratorical. Every building, however modest its function, had henceforth to be a monument' [350]. Stalin personally approved the designs for the major buildings; once, offered two alternatives, he approved both and the frightened designers produced a structure in which the left side did not match the right [351]. The culmination of the plan was the 1300-foot Palace of the Soviets, to be crowned by a gigantic statue of Lenin; perhaps mercifully, it ran into major structural problems and was never built [352].

The new emphasis on the rhetorical and the grandiose may have reflected a growing element of fantasy in the whole planning process. Whatever the case, the plan was massively under-fulfilled. Between 1935 and 1939, the population rose to 4,137,000 – that is, to more than 80 per cent of the 'absolute' eventual limit, without sign of cessation. Yet the area had grown by slightly less than half the increase planned to the year 1945, because the housing programme was 80 per cent below its planned schedule over the first five years of the plan [353]. So housing space standards actually deteriorated further [354]. Further, significantly, about half of the actual building programme was concentrated on only thirteen major radial highways and three concentric boulevards. The same emphasis on prestige, on immediate display, clearly lay behind the enormous public buildings, the subway, the statues and the parks [355].

Worse than this, it was clear that the whole work was very inadequately coordinated. Ministries and industries had their own construction plans and building departments, and pursued their own designs. There were few site plans. Industrial permits tended to be given contrary to the plan. Plans were prepared for facades only. In the judgement of a Soviet geographer, the plan was more of an architectural than a town-planning plan and lacked the necessary economic grounding. Instead of the systematic development of one district at a time, housing was built in strips along the roads; many sites were chosen at random, with no economic justification; and dwellings were scattered over wide areas [356]. Nevertheless, the plan was capable of exciting the admiration of some disting- uished foreign visitors. Lord Simon, coming from Manchester, concluded in 1937 that 'It seems to us undemocratic; it may have what we should regard as very serious results; but for getting on with the job of the reconstruction of Moscow it is magnificent' [357]. He felt that Manchester could benefit from something similar, though his own Wythenshawe did have 'something approaching the advantages of Moscow in town planning' [358]. Curiously, Simon had to admit that the almost universal housing standards in Moscow were so bad that in Manchester only 1 or 2 per cent of the population lived that way; and that Manchester was even then demolishing slums that in Moscow would represent an improvement for nine in ten families [359]. Nevertheless 'everybody I spoke to was most emphatic that the old two-storey houses must go, that Moscow must be a real city with buildings worthy of the capital of the greatest country in the world' [360]. Maybe, Stalin gave Moscow the buildings appropriate to his ruling style. At least, that is what a later generation of Muscovites came to think.

If Stalin's plan had the quality of a Potemkin village, a facade of buildings set up to impress and placate the ruling autocrat, the plans of the other Great Dictator somewhat resembled a set for some unfinished Hollywood epic. Perhaps it was no accident that Hitler appointed Albert Speer to the post of director of the *Generalbebauungsplan* for Berlin in 1937, after Speer's successes in producing a suitably theatrical background for the Nuremburg rallies. But Speer, like Stalin's planners, soon discovered that his master was determined to play a positive role in the design of the new capital. Hitler, who had dreamt of becoming an architect, had carefully studied the plans of Vienna and Paris, and was a particular admirer of Haussmann [361]. He knew the exact measurements of the Champs-Elysées, and promptly set Speer to work on a Berlin equivalent two and a half times the length [362]. The Berlin plan, it was made clear, was to be based on two huge processional axes: one, partially existing in the Unter den Linden and the Heerstrasse, running east-west; the other, running north-south [363]. But these were only the begin- nings of a plan for an almost exclusively monumental remodelling of the Reich capital. There were in all to be seventeen radial highways and four rings, each 200 feet in width – recalling the Moscow plan. Outside an *Autobahn* ring, the city was to be bounded by a replanting of Frederick the Great's forest belt [364]. In the final version of the plan, the monumental streets were lined with quite separate monumental buildings separated by wide open spaces. At the convergence of the two major axes, where an inflexion occurs in the east-west line, Hitler and Speer planned a great domed hall with an 825-foot-diameter cupola, 726 feet high: an essentially mystical or pseudo-religious temple that would hold up to 180,000 people at one time [365].

There is no doubt about the direct inspirations for the Hitler plan. The most important was central Paris, above all the Champs-Elysées and the Arc de Triomphe. Second was Hitler's recollection of Vienna, where the Ringstrasse provided the model for the disposition of the massive public buildings. But more generally, as Larsson points out, the inspiration was the City Beautiful movement. The Berlin plan in essence is a rediscovery of Burnham's plan for Chicago, with its massive domed town hall, which before World War One Kaiser Wilhelm had so much admired as a model for Berlin. The plan also recalls Lutyens's New Delhi, an expression in stone of imperial power [366].

But, Larsson also emphasizes, there is a stranger parallel still. In many important respects – the separation of land uses, the total renewal approach, the massive traffic streets, the emphasis on sun and green space for housing – the Hitler-Speer plan is in total agreement with the ideologues of the architectural modern movement, in the CIAM Charter of Athens (1934). But Le Corbusier, perhaps the most important figure in that movement, was another admirer of Haussmann – and indeed of the *Roi Soleil*. Perhaps, the difference between the *Plan Voisin* and the *Generalbebauungsplan* is only skin deep. Both, in essence, represented the totalitarian approach to metropolitan reconstruction – as did Stalin's plan for Moscow, in so many ways uncannily mimicking its Nazi counterpart.

Even in detail the parallels persist. Stalin's development of the South-West District finds its equivalent in Berlin's Südstadt, a residential district for 210,000 residents and an industrial zone for 100,000 workers, stretching along a major radial for 16 kilometres inward from the Autobahnring. The last version of the Südstadt plan shows closed apartment blocks around big garden yards – a strange contrast with the Nazi ideology and its stress on *Kleinsiedlungen* and single-family homes. But perhaps in essence there was no contradiction. Hitler's Berlin, like Stalin's Moscow, occupied a special place in the settlement hierarchy; this was to be the special exception to the rule of metropolitan decadence, which Nazi propaganda had so sedulously propagated. Berlin was the Nazi Rome [367]; it was less a real city than a symbol of unity and national greatness [368]. The ring roads would have served little purpose for traffic, but that was beside the point; they were there to provide monumental and symbolic form for the city [369]. Cities were to be not so much places for living – that function was to be provided by villages and small towns – as religious and magical centres of world power [370].

In a sense, then, there was no contradiction in Nazi attitudes to the city; as it stood it was the source of evil, but by destroying and rebuilding it in a monumental mould, it could be purged and made to serve the purposes of the totalitarian State [371]. The only problem was the economics of the operation; to have reconstructed all major German cities in this way would have cost more than 100 billion marks, at a time when rearmament had already become first priority [372]. Small wonder that little of the plan for Berlin, and even less of those for other cities, was ever completed. Speer did achieve something of the creation of the processional axes in the very centre of Berlin, but the Great Hall – like its Moscow equivalent – remained a fantasy. By a supremely appropriate irony, the east-west axis was completed after World War Two by the Russians, who named it Stalinallee [373].

Conclusions

Thus, by 1940 the great metropolitan cities were still at very different stages of evolution. While some were still struggling with some of the primal problems of industrialization, others were reacting to the fact of rapid suburbanization. Reactions to these facts had taken different forms, with different intensity of feeling. In particular, the Garden City movement had scored modest triumphs in Britain, in France and in Germany, had promised a revolution in the United States but had then broken against the resistance of market forces, and had been ousted in the Soviet Union.

The organization of the metropolis took very varied forms. London, Moscow and Berlin had achieved partial integration of their transport systems – though in all cases the national railway suburban lines were excluded. Paris and New York had not. New York City had achieved civic unity as early as 1898 in an early form of metropolitan government [374]; but state boundaries made it impossible to encompass the whole of the sprawling metropolitan district. Berlin had followed the same path in 1920, and had effective control of its physical built-up area; Moscow, enlarged in 1917, similarly had a unified administration and a plan, albeit raggedly implemented. Paris in contrast had no administrative unity, though the newly recognized *Région Parisienne* provided a loose coordinating agency for the planning of a wide area. London suffered from a plethora of local government units and from the lack of any overall strategic planning authority; and William Robson's call for such an authority, in the form of a Greater London Council [375], was still more than two decades away from implementation. The *Siedlungsverein Ruhrkohlenbezirk* was a unique example of an executive plan authority to which existing local government units surrendered their powers over planning and transport.

Equally varied, lastly, were the attitudes of different nations to the future of their giant metropolitan regions. The Soviet Union had committed itself to a plan that placed an absolute limit on Moscow's further growth, reinforced by a green belt. Britain had just received a Royal Commission report concluding that the growth of London presented a 'social, economic and strategic problem which demands immediate attention' [376]; the government's response was to lead directly to the historic Abercrombie Plan of 1944, with its proposal similarly to limit London's growth. But in Paris the Prost Plan of 1939 had represented a weak compromise that allowed most of the growth that was likely to happen, while in Berlin the Nazi planners worked on plans for a grander *Reichshauptstadt*. New York continued to grow through market forces, modified lightly by local Planning Commissions that took some heed of the recommendations of the Regional Plan [377]. Most significantly, perhaps, the American equivalent of the Barlow Commission [378] had remained firmly on the fence on this critical issue: 'The concentration of so large a proportion of the urban population in extremely limited areas is wasteful of resources, time and energy. The same would be true of undue dispersion. The Committee believes that the most desirable environment for the urban dweller and for the most effective use of human and material resources lies somewhere between these extremes'; the right course lay in the 'judicious reshaping of the urban community and region . . . taking advantage of trends to decentralization of industry and people, and easier movement . . . to create a more decentralized urban pattern' [379].

It was for that kind of compromise that Mumford and his fellow idealists had attacked the Regional Plan of New York. Soviet communists, and the social democrats in Britain's Barlow Commission, might agree with Mumford and his colleagues on the arguments for limiting the growth of the giant metropolis. But for the conservative business leaders of New York, as for the suburban politicians of the Paris region, these arguments were unpersuasive. There was no agreement on the case against the metropolis, and consequently no accord on the right principles which should guide the planning of the metropolitan region.

NOTES

1. Mitchell, B.R. (1975) *European Historical Statistics, 1750–1970*. London: Macmillan, pp. 76–78.
2. Schnur, R. (1970) Entwicklung der Rechtsgrundlagen und der Organisation des SVR, in *Siedlungsverband Ruhrkoklenbezirk 1920–1970* (*Schriftenreihe Siedlungsverband Ruhrkohlenbezirk*, 29). Essen: SVR, p. 9; Hall, P. (1977) *The World Cities* (2nd edn). London: Weidenfeld and Nicolson, p. 123.
3. Hall (1977), *op.cit.*, pp. 222–3 (see note 2).
4. Thompson, W.S. (1947) *Population: The Growth of Metropolitan Districts in the United States: 1900–1940* (U.S. Department of Commerce, Bureau of the Census). Washington DC: US Government Printing Office, p. 40.
5. Mitchell, *op. cit.*, pp 76-8 (see note 1).
6. Thompson, *op. cit*, p. 26 (see note 4).
7. Hall, P. (1971) Spatial structure of Metropolitan England and Wales, in Chisholm, M. and Manners, G. (eds) *Spatial Policy Problems of the British Economy*. Cambridge: Cambridge University Press, pp. 96–101.
8. Roberts, R. (1971) *The Classic Slum*. Manchester: Manchester University Press, *passim*.
9. Rasmussen, S.E. (1937) *London: The Unique City*. London: Jonathan Cape, pp. 23, 386–7.
10. Wohl, A.S. (1977) *The Eternal Slum: Housing and Social Policy in Victorian London*. London: Edward Arnold, p. 310.
11. *Ibid.*, p. 315.

12 *Ibid.*, p. 218.

13 Wohl, *op. cit.*, 252–3 (see note 10); Tarn, J.N. (1973) *Five Per Cent Philanthropy: An Account of Housing in Urban Areas Between 1840 and 1914.* Cambridge: Cambridge University Press, pp. 115, 122.

14. Tarn, *op. cit.*, pp. 137–42 (see note 13); Wohl, *op. cit.*, p. 256 (see note 10).

15. Jackson, A.A. (1973) *Semi-Detached London: Suburban Development, Life and Transport, 1900–39.* London: George Allen and Unwin, pp. 291, 309.

16. Wohl, *op. cit.*, p. 303 (see note 10).

17. Bauer, C. (1935) *Modern Housing.* London: George Allen and Unwin, p. 21.

18. Purdom, C.B. (ed.) (1921) *Town Theory and Practice.* London: Benn, p. 111.

19. Masterman, C.F.G. *et al.* (1901) *The Heart of the Empire: Discussions on Problems of Modern City Life in England with an Essay on Imperialism.* London: T. Fisher Unwin, pp. 7–8.

20. *Ibid.*, p. 7.

21. Fishman, R. (1977) *Urban Utopias in the Twentieth Century: Ebenezer Howard, Frank Lloyd Wright and Le Corbusier.* New York: Basic Books, p. 58.

22. Krause, R. (1958) *Der Berliner City: frühere Entwicklung/gegenwärtige Situation, mögliche Perspectiven.* Berlin: Duncker and Humblot, p. 25; Hegemann, W. (1930) *Das steinerne Berlin: Geschichte der grössten Mietskasernenstadt der Welt.* Berlin: Gustav Kiepenheues, p. 409.

23. Ehrlich, H. (1933) *Die Berliner Bauordungen, ihre wichtigsten Bauvorschriften und deren Einfluss auf den Wohnhausbau der Stadt Berlin.* Jena: G. Neuenhahn, *passim*; Thienel, I. (1973) *Städtewachstum im Industrialisierungsprozess der 19. Jahrhundert; der Berliner Beispiel.* Berlin/New York: Walter du Gruyter, pp. 35–40.

24 Hegemann, *op. cit.*, title page (see note 22); Voigt, P. (1901) *Grundrente und Wohnungsfrage in Berlin und seinen Vororten,* Erster Teil. Jena: Gustav Fischer, pp. 127–40; Hecker, M. (1974) Die Berliner Mietskaserne, in Grote, L. (ed.) *Die deutsche Stadt im 19. Jahrhundert: Stadtplanung und Baugestaltung im Industriellen Zeitalter.* Munich: Prestel Verlag, p. 274.

25. Hegemann, *op. cit.*, p. 170 (see note 22).

26. Eberstadt, R. (1909, 1917) *Handbuch des Wohnungswesens und der Wohnungsfrage.* Jena: Gustav Fischer, p. 285; Peltz-Dreckmann, U. (1978) *Nationalsozialistischer Siedlungsbau.* Munich: Minerva, p. 170.

27 Hegemann, *op. cit.*, p. 281 (see note 22); Grote, L. *op. cit.*, p. 14 (see note 24).

28. Abercrombie, P. (1914) Berlin: its growth and present state. *Town Planning Review,* **4**, p. 219.

29. Eberstadt, *op. cit.*, pp. 172, 181 (see note 26).

30. *Ibid.*, p. 192.

31. Horsfall, T.C. (1904) *The Improvement of the Dwellings and Surroundings of the People: The Example of Germany.* Manchester: Manchester University Press, pp. 2–3.

32. Eberstadt, *op. cit.*, p. 214 (see note 26).

33. Lees, A. (1979) Critics of urban society in Germany, 1854–1914. *Journal of the History of Ideas,* **40**, pp. 65–66.

34. Spengler, O. (1934) *The Decline of the West,* Vol. II. London: George Allen and Unwin, p. 102.

35. Peltz-Dreckmann, *op. cit.*, p. 63 (see note 26).

36. Lees, *loc. cit.*, pp. 68–74 (see note 33); Peltz-Dreckmann, *op. cit.*, pp. 62–63 (see note 26).

37. Morizet, A. (1932) *Du vieux Paris au Paris moderne: Haussmann et ses prédécesseurs.* Paris: Hachette, p. 342.

38. *Ibid.*, p. 353.

39. Sellier, H. and Bruggeman, A. (1927) *Le problème du logement, son influence sur les conditions de l'habitation et l'aménagement des villes.* Paris and New Haven: Presses Universitaires de France and Yale University Press, pp. 1–2.

40. Sutcliffe, A. (1970) *The Autumn of Central Paris: The Defeat of Town Planning 1850–1970.* London: Edward Arnold, p. 241; Lavedan, P. (1975) *Histoire de l'urbanisme à Paris.* Paris: Hachette, pp. 492–3.

41. Evenson, N. (1979) *Paris: A Century of Change, 1878–1978.* New Haven/London: Yale University Press, pp. 208–10.

42. Sutcliffe, *op. cit.*, p. 241 (see note 40).

43. Evenson, *op. cit.*, p. 216 (see note 41).

44. Lavedan, *op. cit.*, pp. 497–500 (see note 40); Evenson, *op. cit.*, pp. 211-6 (see note 41).

45. Sutcliffe, *op. cit.*, p. 257 (see note 40).

46. Harris, C.D. (1970) *Cities of the Soviet Union.* Chicago: Rand McNally, p. 244.

47. Hamm, M.F. (ed) (1976) *The City in Russian History.* Lexington: University of Kentucky Press, p. 40.

48. Dimaio, A.J. (1974) *Soviet Urban Housing: Problems and Politics.* New York: Praeger, p. 6.
49. Saushkin, Yu. G. (1966) *Moscow.* Moscow: Progress Publishers, p. 122; Dimaio, *op. cit.,* pp. 6–7. (see note 48).
50. Dimaio, *op. cit.,* p. 15 (see note 48).
51. Hamm (1976), *op. cit.,* pp. 48–49 (see note 47).
52. Frolic, B.M. (1975) Moscow: the socialist alternative, in Eldredge, H.W. (ed.) *World Capitals: Toward Guided Urbanization.* New York: Anchor Press/Doubleday, p. 306.
53. Bater, J.H. (1979) The legacy of autocracy: environmental quality in St. Petersburg, in French, R.A. and Hamilton, F.E.I. (eds.) *The Socialist City: Spatial Structure and Urban Policy.* Chichester: John Wiley, pp. 40–43.
54. Hamm, M.F. (1976) The breakdown of urban modernization: a prelude to the Revolutions of 1917, in Hamm (1976) *op. cit.,* p. 191 (see note 48).
55. *Ibid.,* pp. 185–6.
56. Simon, R. and Hookman, M. (1954) Moscow, in Robson, W.A. (ed.) *Great Cities of the World.* London: George Allen and Unwin, pp. 400–1.
57. Schlesinger, A.M. (1933) *The Rise of the City, 1878–1898* (A History of American Life, Vol. X). New York: Macmillan, p. 73.
58. Rosenwaike, I. (1972) *Population History of New York City.* Syracuse: Syracuse University Press, p. 95.
59. Boyer, P.S. (1978) *Urban Masses and Moral Order in America, 1820–1920.* Cambridge, Mass: Harvard University Press, pp. 123–4.
60. Howe, I. (1976) *The Immigrant Jews of New York: 1881 to the Present.* London: Routledge and Kegan Paul, p. 27.
61. Rosenwaike, *op. cit.,* p. 84 (see note 58).
62. Chudacoff, H.P. (1975) *The Evolution of American Urban Society.* Englewood Cliffs, NJ: Prentice Hall, p. 105.
63. Cook, A., Gittell, M. and Mack, H. (eds.) (1973) *City Life, 1865–1900: Views of Urban America.* New York: Praeger, p. 67.
64. Howe, *op. cit.,* p. 88 (see note 60).
65. Scott, M. (1969) *American City Planning Since 1890: A History Commemorating the Fiftieth Anniversary of the American Institute of Planners.* Berkeley: University of California Press, p. 10.
66. Lubove, R. (1962) *The Progressives and the Slums: Tenement House Reform in New York City, 1890–1917.* Pittsburgh University Press, pp. 30–31.
67. *Ibid.,* pp. 95–96.
68. Howe, *op. cit.,* pp. 148–9 (see note 60).
69. Lubove (1962), *op. cit.,* p. 123 (see note 66).
70. *Ibid.,* chapter 5 *passim.*
71. Lubove (1962), *op. cit.,* pp. 132, 175–80 (see note 66); Lubove, R. (1967) *The Urban Community: Housing and Planning in the Progressive Era.* Englewood Cliffs, NJ: Prentice Hall, pp. 7-8.
72. Ward, D. (1971) *Cities and Immigrants.* New York: Oxford University Press, p. 106.
73. White, M.G. and White, L. (1962) *The Intellectual versus the City: From Thomas Jefferson to Frank Lloyd Wright.* Cambridge, Mass.: Harvard University Press and MIT Press, p. 75.
74. *Ibid.,* p. 17.
75. *Ibid.,* p. 97.
76. *Ibid.,* p. 218.
77. Glaab, C.N. and Brown, A.T. (1976) *A History of Urban America* (2nd edn). New York: Macmillan, p. 222.
78. Dorsett, L.W. (1968) *The Challenge of the City, 1860–1910.* Lexington: D.C. Heath, p. 11.
79. Boyer, *op. cit.,* p. 126 (see note 59).
80. Lubove (1962), *op. cit.,* pp. 53–54 (see note 66).
81. Boyer, *op. cit.,* p. 239 (see note 59).
82. *Ibid.,* p. 252.
83. *Ibid.,* p. 262.
84. Johnson, J.H. (1964) The suburban expansion of housing in Greater London 1918–1939, in Coppock, J.T. and Prince, H. (eds.) *Greater London.* London: Faber and Faber, pp. 142, 153–6.
85. Jackson, *op. cit.,* pp. 190–3 (see note 15).
86. Jackson, *op. cit.,* p. 220 (see note 15); Barman, C. (1979) *The Man Who Built London Transport: A Biography of Frank Pick.* Newton Abbot: David & Charles, pp. 78, 88, 147–8.
87. Jackson, *op. cit.,* p. 241 (see note 15).
88. Barker, T.C. and Robbins, M. (1974) *A History of London Transport. Vol. II, The Twentieth Century to 1970.* London: George Allen and Unwin, p. 140.
89. Pick, F. (1936) The organization of transport with special reference to the London Passenger Transport Board. *Journal of the Royal Society of Arts,* **84**, pp. 215–6; Barman, *op. cit.,* pp. 246–7 (see note 86).
90. Pick, *loc. cit.,* pp. 213 (see note 89).

91. *Ibid.*, p. 213.
92. Barman, *op. cit.*, pp. 248–9 (see note 86).
93. *Ibid.*, p. 248.
94. Royal Commission on the Geographical Distribution of the Industrial Population (1938) *Minutes of Evidence*, Q. 3107. London: HMSO.
95 Smith, D.H. (1933) *The Industries of Greater London*. London: P.S. King, p. 173.
96. Hall, P., Thomas, R., Gracey, H. and Drewett, R. (1973) *The Containment of Urban England*. London: George Allen and Unwin. Vol. II, pp. 380–1.
97. Williams-Ellis, C. (1928) *England and the Octopus*. London: Geoffrey Bles, p. 40.
98. Orwell, G. (1939) *Coming Up for Air*. London: Secker and Warburg, p. 180.
99. Cherry, G.E. (1974) *The Evolution of British Town Planning*. London: Leonard Hill, p. 81.
100. Hall, *et al.*, *op. cit.*, Vol. II, p. 49 (see note 96); Stamp, L.D. (1962) *The Land of Britain: Its Use and Misuse*. London: Longman, p. 431.
101. Mumford, L., and Osborn, F.J. (ed. by Hughes, M.R.) (1971) *The Letters of Lewis Mumford and Frederick J. Osborn: A Transatlantic Dialogue 1938–70*. Bath: Adams and Dart, p. 271.
102. Morizet, *op. cit.*, p. 342 (see note 37).
103. Bastié, J. (1964) *La croissance de le banlieue parisienne*. Paris: Presses Universitaires de France, pp. 134–5; Lavedan, *op. cit.*, p. 512.
104. Lavedan (1975), *op. cit.*, p. 517 (see note 40).
105. Bastié, *op. cit.*, pp. 107-8, 124–6 (see note 103).
106. Lavedan (1975), *op. cit.*, p. 511 (see note 40).
107. Evenson, *op. cit.*, p. 114 (see note 41).
108. *Ibid.*, p. 502.
109. Bastié, *op. cit.*, pp. 229–32 (see note 103).
110. *Ibid.*, p. 257.
111. *Ibid.*, pp. 265-6.
112. *Ibid.*, pp. 322–3.
113. *Ibid.*, pp. 296, 322.
114. Sutcliffe, *op. cit.*, pp. 228–9 (see note 40).
115. Bastié, *op. cit.*, p. 258 (see note 103).
116. Lavedan (1975), *op. cit.*, p. 501 (see note 40).
117. Sutcliffe, *op. cit.*, p. 258 (see note 40).
118. Voigt, *op. cit.*, p. 123 (see note 24); Fassbinder, H. (1975) *Berliner Arbeiterviertel, 1800-1918*. Berlin: Verlag für das Studium der Arbeiterbewegung, p. 105.
119. Voigt, *op. cit.*, pp. 154–5 (see note 24).
120. Hofmeister, B. (1975) *Bundesrepublik Deutschland und Berlin* (Wissenschaftliche Länderkunde, 8). Berlin: Wissenschaftliche Buchgesellschaft, p. 403.
121. Larsson, L.O. (1978) *Die Neugestaltung der Reichshauptstadt: Albert Speers Generalbebauungsplan*. Stockholm: Almkvist and Wiksell, pp. 14–16.
122. Werner, F. (1976) *Stadtplanung Berlin: Theorie und Realität, Teil 1: 1900–1960*. Berlin: Verlag Kiepert, p. 26.
123. Hegemann, *op. cit.*, p. 444 (see note 22).
124. *Ibid.*, p. 448.
125. Pick, *op. cit.*, pp. 220–1 (see note 89).
126. Thienel, I. (1973), *op. cit.*, pp. 49–53, 78–80 (see note 23).
127. Werner, *op. cit.*, p. 33 (see note 122).
128. Saushkin, *op. cit.*, p. 60 (see note 49).
129. *Ibid.*, p. 60; Dimaio, *op. cit.*, pp. 6–7 (see note 48).
130. Harris, *op. cit.*, p. 257 (see note 46).
131. Lappo, G.M. (1973) Trends in the evolution of settlement patterns in the Moscow Region. *Soviet Geography: Review and Translation*, **14**, pp. 13–14.
132. Lappo, G.M., Chikishev, A. and Bekker, A. (1976) *Mocow – Capital of the Soviet Union*. Moscow: Progress Publishers, p. 15.
133. National Resources Planning Board (United States) (1937) *Our Cities: Their Role in the National Economy*. Washington, DC: U.S. Government Printing Office, p. 35.
134. McKelvey, B. (1973) *American Urbanization: A Comparative History*. Glenview, Ill.: Scott Foresman, p. 115; Wilson, W.H. (1974) *Coming of Age: Urban America, 1915–1945*. New York: John Wiley, p. 30.
135. Glaab and Brown, *op. cit.*, pp. 258–9 (see note 77).
136. *Ibid.*, pp. 138–47; Tunnard, C. and Reed, H.H. (1955) *American Skyline: The Growth and Form of Our Cities and Towns*. Boston: Houghton Mifflin, pp. 160-1; Banham, R. (1969) *The Architecture of the Well-Tempered Environment*. London: Architectural Press, *passim*.
137. Tunnard and Reed, *op. cit.*, pp. 153–5 (see note 136).
138. Warner, S.B. (1972) The Urban Wilderness: A History of the American City. New York: Harper Row, fig. 9; Hall (1977), *op. cit.*, p. 191 (see note 2).

139. Wilson, *op. cit.*, p. 49 (see note 134).
140. Thompson, *op. cit.*, p. 40 (see note 4).
141. *Ibid.*, p. 14.
142. *Ibid.*, p. 24.
143. *Ibid.*, p. 23.
144. Geddes, P. (1905) Civics: as applied sociology. *Sociological Papers*, **1**, p. 120.
145. Wells, H.G. (1902) *Anticipations of the Reaction of Mechanical and Scientfic Progress Upon Human Life and Thought*. London: Chapman and Hall, p. 44.
146. *Ibid.*, p. 61.
147. Vandervelde, E. (1903) *L'exode rural et le retour aux champs*. Paris: Félix Alcan, pp. 291–2.
148. Kropotkin, P.A. (1908) (1899) *Fields, Factories, and Workshops*. London: Nelson (orig. Hutchinson), pp. 357, 361; Fishman, *op. cit.*, pp. 36–37 (see note 21).
149. Kopp, A. (1970) *Town and Revolution: Soviet Architecture and City Planning, 1917–1935*. London: Thames and Hudson, p. 181.
150. Parkins, M.F. (1953) *City Planning in Soviet Russia: With an Interpretative Bibliography*. Chicago: University of Chicago Press, p. 24.
151. Lubetkin, B. (1933) Town and landscape planning in Soviet Russia. *Journal of the Town Planning Institute*, **19**, p. 70.
152. Starr, S.F. (1977) L'urbanisme utopique pendant la révolution culturelle soviétique. *Annales E.S.C.*, **32**, p. 91; Bliznakov, M. (1976) Urban planning in the USSR: integrative theories, in Hamm (1976) *op. cit.*, p. 251 (see note 47); Kopp, *op. cit.*, p. 177 (see note 149).
153. Le Corbusier (1967) (1933) *The Radiant City*. London: Faber and Faber, p. 74.
154. Kopp, *op. cit.*, p. 179 (see note 149); Thomas, M.J. (1978) City planning in Soviet Russia (1917–1932). *Geoforum*, **9**, p. 275.
155. Lubetkin, *op. cit.*, p. 70 (see note 151); Frampton, K. (1968) Notes on Soviet urbanism, 1917–32. *Architect's Yearbook*, **12**, p. 238; Starr, *op. cit.*, p. 98 (see note 152).
156. Starr, *op. cit.*, p. 96 (see note 152).
157. *Ibid.*
158 Frampton, *op. cit.*, p. 238 (see note 155); Starr, *op. cit.*, p. 89 (see note 152).
159. Hamm, M.F. (1977) The Modern Russian City: An Historiographical Analysis. *Journal of Urban History*, **4**, p. 63.
160. Kopp, *op. cit.*, pp. 171–2 (see note 149).
161. Hamm (1977), *op. cit.*, pp. 62–63 (see note 159).
162. Berton, K. (1977) *Moscow: An Architectural History*. London: Studio Vista, p. 210.
163. Lubetkin, *op. cit.*, p. 73 (see note 151); Dimaio, *op. cit.*, p. 15 (see note 48).
164. Fishman, *op. cit.*, p. 123 (see note 21).
165. Wright, F.L. (1945) *When Democracy Builds*. Chicago: University of Chicago Press, p. 10.
166. White and White, *op. cit.*, p. 193 (see note 73).
167. Fishman, *op. cit.*, pp. 126–7 (see note 21).
168. Wright, *op. cit.*, pp. 45–46 (see note 165).
169. Kopp, *op. cit.*, pp. 146–7, 169, 171 (see note 149).
170. Bliznakov, *op. cit.*, p. 252 (see note 152); Hamm (1977) *op. cit.*, p. 63 (see note 159).
171. Hamm (1977), *op. cit.*, p. 73 (see note 159); Kopp, *op. cit.*, p. 144 (see note 149).
172. Fishman, *op. cit.*, p. 190 (see note 21).
173. *Ibid.*, p. 195.
174. Fishman, *op. cit.*, pp. 211, 228–9 (see note 21).
175. *Ibid.*, p. 241.
176. *Ibid.*, p. 248.
177. Sutcliffe, A. (1977) A vision of utopia: optimistic foundations of Le Corbusier's *doctrine d'urbanisme*, in Walden, R. (1977) *The Open Hand: Essays on Le Corbusier*. Cambridge, Mass., and London: MIT Press, p. 233.
178. Banham, R. (1960) *Theory and Design in the First Machine Age*, London: Architectural Press, p. 176.
179. Sutcliffe (1977), *loc. cit.*, p. 227 (see note 177).
180. *Ibid.*, p. 227.
181. *Ibid.*, p. 221.
182. Fishman, *op. cit.*, pp. 192–3, 200 (see note 21).
183. Howard, Ebenezer (1946) (1898) *Garden Cities of Tomorrow*. London: Faber and Faber (originally published under the title *Tomorrow: A Peaceful Path to Real Reform*).
184. Hall, P. (1973) England in 1900, in Darby, H.C. (ed.) *A New Historical Geography of England*. Cambridge: Cambridge University Press, pp. 379–88.
185. Osborn, F.J. (1950) Sir Ebenezer Howard: the evolution of his ideas. *Town Planning Review*, **21**, p. 230.
186. Marshall, A. (1884) The housing of the

London poor. *Contemporary Review*, **45**, pp. 233–30.

187. Osborn, F.J. (1934) *Transport, Town Development and Territorial Planning of Industry*. London: Fabian Society, p. 5.

188. Osborn, F.J. (1942) *New Towns after the War*. London: J. M. Dent, p. 8.

189. *Ibid.*

190. *Ibid.*, p. 36, footnote.

191. Purdom, *op. cit.*, p. 34 (see note 18).

192. *Ibid.*, p. 33.

193. Co-Partnership Tenants' Housing Council (1906?) *Garden Suburbs, Villages and Homes: All About Co-Partnership Houses*. London: The Council, p. 71.

194. Hall *et al.*, *op. cit.*, Vol. II, p. 46 (see note 96).

195. Purdom, C.B. (1925) *The Building of Satellite Towns: A Contribution to the Study of Town Development and Regional Planning*. London: J. M. Dent, pp. 32–34.

196. Wiebenson, D. (1969) *Tony Garnier: The Cité Industrielle*. London: Studio Vista, p. 17.

197. Pawlowski, C. (1967) *Tony Garnier et les débuts de l'urbanisme fonctionnel en France*. Paris: Centre de Recherche d'Urbanisme, p. 79.

198. Read, J. (1978) The Garden City and the growth of Paris. *Architectural Review*, **113**, pp. 349–50.

199. Evenson, *op. cit.*, pp. 222–3 (see note 41).

200. Read, *op. cit.*, p. 352 (see note 198).

201. *Ibid.*, p. 351.

202. Fritsch, E.T. (1912) (1896) *Die Stadt der Zukunft*. Leipzig: Hammer Verlag, p. 28; Reiner, T.A. (1963) *The Place of the Ideal Community in Urban Planning*. Philadelphia: University of Pennsylvania Press, pp. 36–38; Hartmann, K. (1976) *Deutsche Gartenstadtbewegung: Kulturpolitik und Gesellschaftsreform*. Munich: Heinz Moos Verlag, p. 33.

203. Kampffmeyer, H. (1908) Die Gartenstadtbewegung. *Jahrbücher fur Nationalökonomie und Statistik, III*. Series III, p. 594; Peltz-Dreckmann, *op. cit.*, pp. 46–47 (see note 26).

204. Bergmann, K. (1970) *Agrarromantik und Grossstadtfeindschaft* (Marburger Abhandlungen zur Politischen Wissenschaft, 20). Meisenheim: Verlag Anton Heim, p. 148.

205. Peltz-Dreckmann, *op. cit.*, p. 44 (see note 26).

206. Hartmann, *op. cit.*, p. 33 (see note 202).

207. Bergmann, *op. cit.*, p. 149 (see note 204).

208. Kampffmeyer, *op. cit.*, p. 594 (see note 203).

209. Bergmann, *op. cit.*, pp. 153–4, 162 (see note 204).

210. Kampffmeyer, *op. cit.*, p. 598 (see note 203).

211. Bergmann, *op. cit.*, p. 160 (see note 204).

212. Kampffmeyer, *op. cit.*, p. 607 (see note 203).

213. Kampffmeyer, H. (1918) Die Gartenstadtbewegung, in Fuchs, C.J. (ed.) *Die Wohnungs- und Siedlungsfrage nach dem Kriege*. Stuttgart (Munich): Callwey, pp. 336–7.

214. Bangert, W. (1936) *Baupolitik und Stadtgestaltung in Frankfurt-am-Main*. Würzburg: K. Triltsch, pp. 88–89, 91, 101; Brükschmidt, J. (1962) *Ernst May. Bauen und Planungen*, **1**, pp. 36–38; Bullock, N. (1978) Housing in Frankfurt 1925 to 1931 and the New Wohnkultur. *Architectural Review*, **113**, pp. 335–6.

215. Cherry, G.E. (1972) *Urban Change and Planning: A History of Urban Development in Britain since 1750*. Henley: Foulis, p. 133.

216. Bauer, *op. cit.*, pp. 180–1 (see note 17); Gallion, A.B. and Eisner, S. (1963) *The Urban Pattern*. Princeton: D. van Nostrand, p. 108; Bullock, *loc. cit.*, p. 218 (see note 214).

217. Brükschmitt, *op. cit.*, p. 38 (see note 214).

218. Peltz-Dreckmann, *op. cit.*, pp. 26–29, 50–51 (see note 26).

219. Vogel, I. (1959) *Bottrop: eine Bergbaustadt in der Emscherzone des Ruhrgebietes* (Forschungen zur Deutschen Landeskunde, 114). Remagen: Bundesanstalt für Landeskunde, pp. 73–74.

220. Weis, D. (1951) *Die Grossstadt Essen: die Siedlungs-, Verkehrs- und Wirtschaftliche Enwicklung des heutigen Stadtgebietes von der Stiftsgründung bis zur Gegenwart* (Bonner Geographische Abhandlungen, 7). Bonn: Geographische Institut, p. 61.

221. Klapheck, R. (1930) *Siedlungswerk Krupp*. Berlin: Wasmuth, p. 127; Gallion and Eisner, *op. cit.*, p. 103 (see note 216).

222. Brandenburg, A. and Materna, J. (1980) Zum Aufbruch in die Fabrikgesellschaft: Arbeiterkolonien. *Archiv für die Geschichte des Widerstandes und der Arbeit*, **1**, pp. 37–39.

223. Neumeyer, F. (1978) Zum Werkwohnungsbau in Deutschland um 1900, in Siepmann, E. (ed.) *Kunstt und Alltag um 1900*. Giessen/Lahn: Anabas Verlag, p. 243.

224. *Ibid.*, pp. 251–2.

225. *Ibid.*, p. 246.

226. Bergmann, *op. cit.*, p. 160 (see note 204).
227. Uhlig, G. (1977) Stadtplanung in der Weimarer Republik: sozialistische Reformaspekte, in Neue Gesellschaft für Bildende Kunst (ed.) *Wem gehört die Welt? Kunst und Gesellschaft in der Weimarer Republik.* Berlin: Gesellschaft, p. 52.
228. *Ibid.*, p. 56.
229. *Ibid.*, p. 55.
230. *Ibid.*, p. 57.
231. Harmann, *op. cit.*, p. 44 (see note 202).
232. Kampffmeyer, *op. cit.*, p. 608 (see note 203).
233. Bergmann, *op. cit.*, pp. 169–71 (see note 204).
234. Lane, B.M. (1968) *Architecture and Politics in Germany, 1918–1945.* Cambridge, Mass.: Harvard University Press, p. 405; Bergmann, *op. cit.*, p. 358 (see note 204); Peltz-Dreckmann, *op. cit.*, p. 405 (see note 26).
235. Lane, *op. cit.*, p. 155 (see note 234).
236. *Ibid.*, p. 156.
237. Peltz-Dreckmann, *op. cit.*, pp. 102, 123–4 (see note 26).
238. Peltz-Dreckmann, *op. cit.*, p. 405 (see note 26); Werner, *op. cit.*, p. 38 (see note 122).
239. Peltz-Dreckmann, *op. cit.*, p. 198 (see note 26).
240. *Ibid.*, p. 205.
241. Starr, S.F. (1976) The revival and schism of urban planning in twentieth-century Russia, in Hamm, *op. cit.*, p. 234 (see note 47); Cooke, C. (1977) Activities of the Garden City Movement in Russia. *Transactions of the Martin Centre for Architectural and Urban Studies,* **1**, pp. 229–31; Cooke, C. (1978) Russian responses to the Garden City idea. *Architectural Review,* **163**, pp. 356–7.
242. Cooke (1977), *op. cit.*, pp. 229, 239 (see note 241).
243. *Ibid.*, p. 237.
244. *Ibid.*, p. 246.
245. Cooke (1978), *op. cit.*, p. 358 (see note 241).
246. Starr (1976), *op. cit.*, p. 236 (see note 241).
247. May, E. (1961) Cities of the future. *Survey,* **38**, pp. 181–2.
248. *Ibid.*, p. 181.
249. Boyer, *op. cit.*, p. 272 (see note 59).
250. Condit, C.W. (1973) *Chicago, 1910–29: Building, Planning, and Urban Technology.* Chicago and London: University of Chicago Press, p. 79.
251. Kantor, H.A. (1973) The City Beautiful in New York. *New York Historical Society Quarterly,* **57**, pp. 164–5.
252. *Ibid.*, p. 171.
253. Conkin, P.K. (1959) *Tomorrow a New World: The New Deal Community Program.* Ithaca: Cornell University Press, p. 68; Hays, F.B. (1965) *Community Leadership: The Regional Plan Association of New York.* New York/London: Columbia University Press, pp. 7–11; Scott, *op. cit.*, p. 177 (see note 65); Wilson, *op. cit.*, p. 136 (see note 134).
254. Scott, *op. cit.*, pp. 178–9 (see note 65).
255. *Ibid.*, p. 177.
256. Regional Plan of New York and its Environs (1927–31) *Regional Survey of New York and its Environs,* 8 vols (in 10). New York: The Regional Plan. Vol. I. *Major Economic Factors in Metropolitan Growth and Development,* pp. 19–44.
257. *Ibid.*, p. 19.
258. *Ibid.*, p. 40.
259. *Ibid.*, p. 44.
260. *Ibid.*, Vol. II, *Population, Land Values and Government,* p. 31.
261. *Ibid.*, p. 31.
262. *Ibid.*, p. 141.
263. *Ibid.*, Vol. VI, *Buildings: Their Uses and the Spaces About Them,* pp. 71, 102-3.
264. *Ibid.*, p. 105.
265. *Ibid.*, p. 107.
266. *Ibid.*, p. 66.
267. *Ibid.*, Vol. IV, *Transit and Transportation,* 1929, p. 129.
268. *Ibid.*, Vol. VI, *Buildings: Their Uses and the Spaces About Them,* p. 25.
269. *Ibid.*, p. 281.
270. Wilson, *op. cit.*, p. 136 (see note 134).
271. Adams, T. (1930) The need for a broader conception of town planning and decentralization, in Warren, H. and Davidge, W.R. (eds.) (1930) *Decentralisation of Population and Industry: A New Principle of Town Planning.* London: P. S. King, pp. 142–5.
272. Scott, *op. cit.*, p. 262 (see note 65).
273. Hays, *op. cit.*, pp. 20, 29 (see note 253).
274. Sussman, C. (ed.) (1976) *Planning the Fourth Migration: The Neglected Vision of the Regional Planning Association of America.* Cambridge, Mass.: MIT Press, pp. 228–46.
275. *Ibid.*, p. 259.

276. *Ibid.*, p. 263.
277. Hays, *op. cit.*, pp. 25–26, 36–40 (see note 253).
278. Lubove, R. (1963) *Community Planning in the 1920s: The Contribution of the Regional Planning Association of America.* Pittsburgh: Pittsburgh University Press, pp. 1–2, 31, 117–9.
279. Sussman, *op. cit.*, pp. 61–64, 66–69 (see note 274).
280. *Ibid.*, p. 88.
281. *Ibid.*, p. 90.
282. Geddes, *op. cit.*, pp. 104–5 (see note 144).
283. Friedmann, J. and Weaver, C. (1979) *Territory and Function.* London: Edward Arnold, p. 32.
284. *Ibid.*, p. 34.
285. Sussman, *op. cit.*, pp. 120, 126–7 (see note 274).
286. Lubove (1963), *op. cit.*, p. 90 (see note 278); Lubove (1967), *op. cit.*, p. 21 (see note 71).
287. Lubove (1967), *op. cit.*, pp. 84–96 (see note 71).
288. Lubove (1963), *op. cit.*, pp. 91–96 (see note 278).
289. Sussman, *op. cit.*, p. 23 (see note 274).
290. Stein C. (1958) *Toward New Towns for America.* Liverpool: Liverpool University Press.
291 Lepawsky, A. (1976) The planning apparatus: A vignette of the New Deal. *Journal of the American Institute of Planners*, **42**, p. 22.
292. Gelfand, M.I. (1975) *A Nation of Cities: The Federal Government and Urban America, 1933–1965.* New York: Oxford University Press, p. 24.
293. Gelfand, *op. cit.*, p. 25 (see note 292); Conkin, *op. cit.*, pp. 111–2 (see note 253).
294. Gelfand, *op. cit.*, pp. 67–68 (see note 292); Wilson, *op. cit.*, pp. 191–4 (see note 134).
295. Conkin, *op. cit.*, pp. 149–51 (see note 253).
296. Arnold, J.L. (1971) *The New Deal in the Suburbs: A History of the Greenbelt Town Program 1935–1954.* Columbus, Ohio: Ohio State University Press, pp. 24–26.
297. Arnold, *ibid.*, p. 201; Glaab and Brown, *op. cit.*, p. 279 (see note 77).
298. Arnold, *ibid.*, p. 26.
299. Arnold, *ibid.*, p. 43; Glaab and Brown, *op. cit.*, p. 277 (see note 77).
300. McFarland, J.R. (1960) The administration of the New Deal Greenbelt Towns. *Journal of the American Institute of Planners*, **32**, pp. 221–2.
301. Stein, *op. cit.*, p. 121 (see note 290).
302. McFarland, *op. cit.*, 219–22 (see note 300).
303. Glaab and Brown, *op. cit.*, p. 278 (see note 77).
304. Gelfand, *op. cit.*, p. 133 (see note 292); Arnold, *op. cit.*, p. 153 (see note 296).
305. Wilson, *op. cit.*, p. 160 (see note 134).
306. Arnold, op. cit., pp. 143–4 (see note 296).
307. *Ibid.*, p. 197.
308. *Ibid.*, p. 209.
309. Conkin, *op. cit.*, pp. 322–5 (see note 253).
310. National Resources Planning Board, *op. cit.*, p. xiii (see note 133); Scott, *op. cit.*, p. 345 (see note 65).
311. National Resources Planning Board, *op. cit.*, pp. 67–69, 80 (see note 133).
312. *Ibid.*, pp. 77–79.
313. *Ibid.*, p. 11.
314. Gelfand, *op. cit.*, p. 97 (see note 292).
315. *Ibid.*, pp. 100–2.
316. Friedmann and Weaver, *op. cit.*, pp. 65–71 (see note 283).
317. Crow, A. (1911) Town planning in old and congested areas, with special reference to London, in Royal Institute of British Architects, *Town Planning Conference – Transactions.* London: RIBA, pp. 411–12.
318. Pepler, G.L. (1911) Greater London, in Royal Institute of British Architects, *Town Planning Conference – Transactions.* London: RIBA, pp. 614–5.
319. Purdom, *op. cit.*, pp. 32–34 (see note 195).
320. Greater London Regional Planning Committee (1933) *Second Report* (includes *Interim Reports*). London: Knapp, Drewett, p. 83.
321. *Ibid.*, p. 109.
322. *Ibid.*, p. 32.
323. Abercrombie, P. (1945) *Greater London Plan 1944.* London: HMSO, *passim.*
324. Bastié, *op. cit.*, p. 325 (see note 103).
325. Morizet, *op. cit.*, p. 357 (see note 37); Evenson, *op. cit.*, p. 332 (see note 41).
326. Morizet, *op. cit.*, p. 358 (see note 37); Lavedan, *op. cit.*, p. 114 (see note 40); Bastié, *op. cit.*, p. 327 (see note 103).
327. Evenson, *op. cit.*, p. 334 (see note 41).
328. Bastié, *op. cit.*, p. 327 (see note 103).
329. Lavedan, *op. cit.*, p. 520 (see note 40).
330. Bastié, *op. cit.*, p. 327 (see note 103);

Delouvrier, P. (1972) Paris, in Robson, W.A. and Regan, D.E. (eds.) (1972) *Great Cities of the World*. Third Edition. Two volumes. London: George Allen and Unwin, p. 746.

331. Bastié, *op. cit.*, p. 327 (see note 103).

332. *Ibid.*, pp. 327–9.

333. Lavedan (1975), *op. cit.*, pp. 519–20 (see note 40).

334. Lavedan, P. (1960) *Histoire de Paris*. Paris: Presses Universitaires de France, p. 114.

335. Evenson, *op. cit.*, pp. 335–6 (see note 41).

336. Robson, W.A. (1939) *The Government and Misgovernment of London*. London: George Allen and Unwin, p. 388.

337. Hall (1977), *op. cit.*, chapter 5 (see note 2).

338. Weis, *op. cit.*, pp. 63–64 (see note 220).

339. Schnur, *op. cit.*, p. 9 (see note 2).

340. Umlauf, J. (1960) Die Entwicklung der Planungsarbeit des Siedlungsverband Ruhrkohlenbezirks, in *Siedlungsverband Ruhrkohlenbezirk, Tätigkeitsbericht 1958–60*. Essen: SVR, pp. 15–17; Neufang, H. (1963) Die Siedlungsverband Ruhrkohlenbezirk (1920–1963). *Die Öffentliche Verwaltung*, **16**, p. 812.

341. Schnur, *op. cit.*, pp. 11–12 (see note 2).

342. *Ibid.*, pp. 13–14.

343. *Ibid.*, p. 16.

344. Simon, E.D. *et al.* (1937) *Moscow in the Making*. London: Longmans, pp. 199–200; Simon, E.D. (1937) Town planning: Moscow or Manchester. *Journal of the Town Planning Institute*, **23**, p. 381.

345. Machler, M. (1932) Town development in Soviet Russia. *Journal of the Town Planning Institute*, **18**, p. 96.

346. Simon (1937), *loc. cit.*, p. 382 (see note 344); Parkins, *op. cit.*, p. 36 (see note 150).

347. Simon *et al.* (1937) *op. cit.*, pp. 186–90 (see note 344); Simon (1937), *loc. cit.*, p. 382 (see note 344); Raffé, W.G. (1936) The reconstruction of Moscow: the Ten Year Plan. *Town and Country Planning*, **4**, pp. 54–59; Parkins, *op cit.*, pp. 32–41 (see note 150).

348. Parkins, *op. cit.*, pp. 31–33 (see note 150).

349. *Ibid.*, p. 40.

350 Kopp, *op. cit.*, p. 227 (see note 149).

351. Berton, *op. cit.*, pp. 228–9 (see note 162).

352. Kopp, *op. cit.*, p. 223 (see note 149); Berton, *op. cit.*, pp. 223–4 (see note 162).

353. Parkins, *op. cit.*, pp. 42–44 (see note 150).

354. Blackwell, W.L. (1976) Modernization and urbanization in Russia: A comparative view, in Hamm, *op. cit.*, p. 324 (see note 47).

355. Parkins, *op. cit.*, pp. 44–45 (see note 150); Berton, *op. cit.*, p. 235 (see note 162).

356. Saushkin, *op. cit.*, p. 121 (see note 49).

357. Simon (1937), *loc. cit.*, pp. 383 (see note 344).

358. *Ibid.*, p. 385.

359. Simon *et al.* (1937), *op. cit.*, pp. 154–5 (see note 344).

360. *Ibid.*, p. 160.

361. Speer, A. (1970) *Inside the Third Reich*. London: Weidenfeld and Nicolson, p. 75.

362. *Ibid.*, p. 77.

363. *Ibid.*, pp. 77–79.

364. *Ibid.*, pp. 78–79.

365. Speer, *op. cit.*, pp. 152–3 (see note 361); Werner, *op. cit.*, p. 68 (see note 122); Larsson, *op. cit.*, pp. 33–36 (see note 121).

366. Larsson, *op. cit.*, p. 116 (see note 121).

367. Lane, *op. cit.*, p. 189 (see note 234).

368. *Ibid.*, p. 188.

369. Werner, *op. cit.*, p. 72 (see note 122).

370. Thies, J. (1978) Hitler's European building programme. *Journal of Contemporary History*, **13**, pp. 413–31.

371. *Ibid.*, p. 417.

372. *Ibid.*, p. 418.

373. Speer, *op. cit.*, p. 77 (see note 361).

374. Scott, *op. cit.*, p. 26 (see note 65).

375. Robson, *op. cit.*, chapter 14 (see note 336).

376. Royal Commission on the Distribution of the Industrial Population (Great Britain) (1940). *Report*. Cmd. 6153. London: HMSO, p. 195.

377. Hays, *op. cit.*, pp. 30–31, 68–69 (see note 253).

378. National Resources Planning Board, *op. cit.* (see note 133).

379. *Ibid.*, 84.

Chapter 3

The Metropolis and the Intellectual

ANDREW LEES

HOW did men perceive and evaluate very large cities in Western Europe and America during our period? Before we can answer this question we must consider briefly the origins and some of the meanings of the words they used to denote generically the phenomena they were discussing. 'Metropolis' was first used by the ancient Greeks. Derived from the combination of 'mater' and 'polis', it literally meant 'mother city'. For the Greeks, and later for the Romans, it served primarily to designate cities that had founded colonies. In this sense the word implied nothing with regard to size, some of the Greek metropolises having numbered only a few thousand inhabitants. Secondarily, in Greek, it meant the home town of an individual. In this sense, a particular city would be a metropolis for some people but not for others. The ancients also used 'metropolis' to refer to a capital city or the chief city of a province, but even this usage did not necessarily imply great magnitude. In English usage from the early sixteenth century through to the late nineteenth, a metropolis was usually the seat of an archbishop, a capital, or the chief centre of a particular sort of activity. 'Metropolis' was often used interchangeably with 'London' (frequently referred to not as 'a' but as 'the' metropolis), but only rarely was metropolitan status accorded to other big cities simply by virtue of their great size. By about 1900 'metropolis' (and 'métropole', in French) seems to have taken on something like the broader meaning we attach to it today. One must bear in mind, however, that other terms were also available. The Greek 'megalopolis', which had meant literally 'giant city' in antiquity, had precisely the same meaning for a small but growing number of British and American authors who felt the need for a term that would connote great size without any of the ambiguity that still surrounded 'metropolis'. Germans increasingly distinguished between merely big and very big cities by referring to the former as *Grossstadt* and to the latter as *Weltstadt*. Whereas any city with 100,000 or more inhabitants was considered to be 'big', it qualified as a 'world' city only if it was a 'modern big city of international importance', preferably with a population in excess of 1,000,000 [1].

In the literature of urban analysis and description that was produced in steadily growing abundance during the nineteenth century – first in Britain and the United States, then in France and Germany – there was more and more emphasis on 'big cities', 'grandes villes', and 'Grossstädte' [2]. Writers perceived these places as the crucially important urban phenomena of their time, and they regarded them quite differently than the smaller towns that had characterized pre-industrial society. When men talked about the problems posed and the possibilities offered by cities, they were usually referring either explicitly or implicitly to the various aspects of life in towns whose populations numbered at least 100,000, and they lumped all such places under a common heading. This habit continued throughout the first four decades of the twentieth century. As a consequence, even though the words 'metropolis', 'megalopolis', and 'Weltstadt' stood ready to hand, commentators on the urban scene did not make much effort to separate out for sustained analysis the handful of really big cities from the much more numerous group of moderately big cities. The deepest fault line on the scale of urban settlements ran between places such as Bradford and York, Bochum and Rothenburg, Lille and Bourges, or Worcester and Salem, rather than between Manchester and London, Frankfurt and Berlin, Marseilles and Paris, or Boston and New York. As we shall see, a few writers did address themselves more specifically to the giant city as such. (One thinks especially of Oswald Spengler and Lewis Mumford.) But for the most part general views about the metropolis appeared only in works whose authors wrote not about the metropolis in particular but about big cities in general. These writers, however, at least implied that the qualities which could be discerned in most large cities in contrast to small towns and villages became more and more evident as one moved up the population ladder. Their propositions about modern urban life in general were deemed to enjoy greater and greater validity as they were applied to larger and larger settlements. In a sense, the metropolis was the extreme embodiment of an ideal type, providing an ultimate standard against which to measure other places that were tending either to assume metropolitan dimensions or to be sucked into the orbit of an existing metropolis. Fortunately for my purposes, in addition to these general writings we also have a vast number of books and articles about individual metropolises. These works are by and large much more descriptive than theoretical, but many contain reflections that rise well above the level of minute detail, and collectively they tell us a good deal about perceptions of metropolitan life by men who were located in the middle and lower ranks of the intellectual hierarchy. In the rest of this chapter, I shall examine a selection of writings of both sorts, which I shall consider in terms of the basic intellectual approaches and purposes of the men who produced them [3].

Social Scientists and the Metropolis as an Object of Research

With very few exceptions, the most systematic and coherent efforts to assess the significance of the metropolis and the quality of metropolitan life were undertaken by men who approached urban phenomena as professional social scientists. This was a great age in the maturation of the academic social sciences, especially sociology, an age in which their representatives gained ever greater strength in universities and research institutes, and a great deal of their energy was expended upon the urban milieu. These men sought in the first instance neither to praise nor to condemn the big city but rather to comprehend its constituent elements and the processes at work not only within it but also between it and the less densely populated areas of settlement that surrounded it. While providing ample ammunition to men who sought to build a case against the metropolis, they themselves usually accepted it as at least a necessity if not a positive good. Social scientists approached the metropolis from many directions. Some were concerned primarily with demography, others with economic well-being, urban mentalities, or the relationships among social groups. Some were rigorous empiricists who packed their writings with statistical data and maps, while others preferred to follow the path of theoretical speculation. The range of possible modes of discourse about the metropolis within the social-scientific tradition, as well as the social scientists' even-handed and ambivalent evaluations of what they were analysing, will become clearer as we look in more detail at some of the work of four clusters of men from France, Germany, Britain, and the United States.

Two Frenchmen writing in the 1890s offered broad statistical perspectives on urban life in general and on the metropolis in particular. Their works summarized much of what was known at the time by quantitative social scientists not only about big cities in France but also about their counterparts elsewhere in Europe, and they provided basic data of the sort that others would be unable to ignore in formulating their own judgments throughout the rest of our period. The better known of these authors was Émile Levasseur, an economist, geographer, and statistician, who held a number of prestigious positions in the French academic world. In his work on the population of the cities, Levasseur sought primarily to delineate the course of urban growth in France during the nineteenth century, giving special attention to the phenomenal increase in the size of Paris, which amounted to over 300 per cent between 1801 and 1886, without counting the inhabitants of the territory that was added by a boundary extension in 1860. The absorption by Paris of an ever larger percentage of the overall French population, which had been growing very slowly for some time, could be seen as an illustration of a law of nature that held good in human affairs just as it did in the world described by the physicists: '. . . the force of attraction of human groups, like that of matter, is in general proportional to mass'. But there were more specific reasons for the growth of the French metropolis: its centuries-old status as the national capital, the educational institutions and the recreational opportunities associated with the presence of literature, the sciences, and the arts, and the economic developments that had made the city a 'hive' of light industry and attracted much heavy industry as well, caused it to become the centre of the national network of railroads, and made it 'the principal warehouse of French commerce'. Levasseur placed even more emphasis on Paris in his account of urban demographic behaviour, showing that Parisian adults were less inclined to marry than their non-Parisian compatriots, that (especially among the upper classes) they produced fewer children, that they died far more rapidly, and that they suffered from much higher rates of poverty and illness. In view of the fact that big cities were plagued by prostitution and that 'the working masses' furnished 'easily inflammable material which tempt[ed] the eloquence and the ambition of the tribunes', it was clear to Levasseur that Paris and the other 'great agglomerations' were 'insalubrious both for the body and for morals'. Nonetheless, he concluded his analysis in the same vein in which he had begun, insisting that Paris was not 'a monstrous wart that had sprouted accidentally on the face of France' but rather 'an essential organ of the nation', comparable to a head or a heart, whose prosperity was intimately linked to that of the whole country. Like other large cities, it was to be viewed not as a necessary evil but rather as a basically good thing that contained regrettable admixtures of evil. 'If one consider[ed] a nation as a living organism', many of these evils could be seen in a perspective that seemed to render them almost harmless: '. . . the countryside', he wrote, 'produces more human beings than it can use . . . [and] the cities absorb and consume a part of the excess and return to the nation in exchange considerable value in wealth and civilization' [4].

The urban themes that Levasseur had treated within the general context of the history of population received much fuller consideration a few years later in a major work of synthesis written by one of his students. Paul Meuriot sought to elucidate the growth of 'urban agglomerations' as a European-wide phenomenon. Like his teacher, he gave special attention to metropolitan developments, including a separate chapter on 'The Metropolises of Europe' in his account of urban growth and referring continually not only to Paris but also to London, Berlin, Vienna, and St. Petersburg in his discussion of the consequences of this growth. Much of what he had to say – particularly about the crucial importance of economic change and about marriages, births, deaths, and disease – buttressed the positions taken by Levasseur, leading him to suggest that without the influx of new blood as a result of immigration the population of Paris would disappear in about five centuries [5]. His data on urban crime, illegitimacy, suicide, and alcoholism and his remarks on the rising political power enjoyed by the growing masses of urban workers similarly elaborated upon a general idea already advanced by his teacher: namely, that the big cities threatened both moral order and social stability [6]. But at the same time that he was demonstrating all of these demographic, moral, and social ills, he insisted strongly on the benefits that accrued from urban growth in general. In this connection, he pointed not simply to urban economic productivity, but also to the stimulating effect of urban economic demand on agricultural output, the salaries of rural workers, and the prices of agricultural land. One other point, which was not apparent in Levasseur's work, deserves special emphasis. Meuriot argued that, far from contributing to general depopulation, the growth of cities helped to maintain the number of people living in the nation as a whole by providing an alternative for migrants from the countryside to leaving the State altogether. 'Indeed', he wrote, 'these internal migrations do not represent depopulation but rather a transformation of the fashion in which a country is populated; the essential thing for a state is to conserve and augment its human capital, whether this capital . . . lives more or less in the countryside or in the city'. For this reason, as well as for reasons having to do with political prestige and national culture, urban decline would be an unmistakable 'symptom of stagnation or retrogression of civilization in general' [7].

Shortly after the turn of the century, a group of German academics signalled a marked upsurge of concern with urban problems in their country in a major work about big cities that spoke less to the community of scholars than to the general educated public [8]. Their collective endeavour took shape in Dresden in the winter of 1902–3 as a series of lectures sponsored by a local foundation in conjunction with a wide-ranging exhibition on city life at which 128 German municipalities and more than 400 manufacturers displayed their wares. The exhibitors used not only the printed word but also charts, models, pictures, and other artifacts in order to convey their sense of the enormous progress their communities had made since the establishment of the Second Reich in providing a physically salubrious environment for their inhabitants [9]. But the scholars' purpose was neither to bestow praise nor to assign blame. They sought rather to provide general understanding of what lay behind and beneath the phenomena that others had gathered to celebrate. In contrast to Levasseur and Meuriot, they tended, with few exceptions, to eschew statistics. They relied instead on qualitative analysis and interpretation, in part because of the nature of their audience, in part also because most of them did not work in areas that required expertise in quantitative methods. Nonetheless, they all approached the metropolis as social scientists, striving to delineate the conditions of its existence and its inner workings without passion or prejudice.

Several of the contributors set their sights on aspects of urban life that lay well within the parameters marked out by Levasseur and Meuriot, and they arrived at conclusions that echoed the judgments pronounced earlier by the Frenchmen. Karl Bücher, a distinguished economist and economic historian, offered an introductory overview of modern urban growth in which he emphasized the central importance of material considerations in the minds of men who migrated to the city of their own free will because that was the place where they felt they could most effectively assert themselves in the competitive struggle for a better standard of living. Despite the regrettable social and moral conditions that often accompanied 'the frantic pace of the acquisitive life', the big city had 'liberated undreamed of national energies in the areas of technology, science, art, and social welfare', and it thus constituted 'a higher form of social existence than all earlier types of cities, not excluding the Greek polis'. Friedrich Ratzel pursued the topic of urban growth from a geographer's perspective, showing how cities increased in size as a result of their access to the means of transportation; with regard to consequences, he argued that cities had contributed greatly to the stability and permanence of the civilizations in which they were located. 'States could no longer be completely uprooted, peoples could not be scattered; even after a severe defeat something of the nation remained'. Georg von Mayr, a statistician, provided the one heavily quantitative contribution, a careful assessment of urban demographic trends. While he refused to accept the contention by theorists such as Otto Ammon that the big city would ultimately disappear without the infusion of new blood from the countryside, he pointed out that birth rates in German cities were clearly lower than the rates for the country as a whole, despite the relative over-representation of men and women who were of an age to produce children. Urban death rates appeared to be relatively favourable, but once again, he observed, the urban deficit *vis-à-vis* the countryside was disguised by the age structure of the urban population, with its disproportionate contingent of men and women in the prime of life. H. Waentig elaborated upon Bücher's remarks on economics primarily by providing detailed information on the urban workforce, but also by outlining the great variety of public facilities upon which city governments were spending their constantly increasing revenues. In the concluding essay, the historian Dietrich Schäfer reflected on political and military problems, emphasizing the possibilities in the past of conquering whole countries by taking their capitals and the prevalence among city-dwellers in the present of 'a special predilection for extreme views, particularly of a radical sort'. Like Levasseur and Meuriot, he was obviously mindful of the threat of popular mobilization and perhaps insurrection [10].

The most distinctive aspect of these essays was their authors' interest in the effects of urban life on popular mentality. For Waentig, urban man's outstanding traits were his 'extreme alertness . . . [and] intensity at work and at play'. For Schaefer, the big city produced 'heightened esteem for intelligence' and 'a note of superiority . . . wit, and sarcasm' [11]. But it was two other authors, Theodor Petermann and Georg Simmel, who explored the cultural and emotional dimensions of the metropolis in the greatest depth. Petermann offered a broad overview of the big city's role in the life of intellect from antiquity to the present. The book trade, newspapers, universities, and theatres – all of which had become heavily dependent upon densely populated areas of settlement – had induced 'an excess of intelligence' to crowd into the big cities. As a result, individuals who might have made a worthy contribution in small towns or in the countryside were overwhelmed and their talents were wasted. The urban milieu did help some men to develop their capacities, but at the same time it tended to reduce them to a common level of mediocrity. For Petermann, the metropolis was a 'sounding board' that enabled men to disseminate their ideas, but it was 'more an enemy than a friend of great originality' [12]. These gloomy forebodings stood in marked contrast to the brief but generally optimistic remarks about urban civilization made by Levasseur and Meuriot, but they were quite consistent with much of what was being written at the time by other Germans about the pressures exerted on the individual by the rise of a mass society [13]. Much more original was a speculative essay by Simmel, a philosopher and one of the founders of German sociology [14]. Simmel was concerned not with urban culture but with the urban psyche. Like Petermann, he discerned powerful forces in the metropolis that impinged upon the personalities of its inhabitants and threatened to deprive them of their individual autonomy. Constant changes in the physical and social environment, oppressively close contacts with fellow urbanites, the division of labour, and the 'crystallized and impersonalized spirit' that had taken shape in cultural and political institutions all bore in and down upon urban man [15]. But Simmel's main interest lay not in the pressures themselves. It lay rather in how men adjusted to the circumstances in which they found themselves. Men coped with nervous stimulation by reacting with their heads rather than their hearts, by developing their conscious intellectual capacities in place of their emotions, and by displaying a veneer of blasé sophistication. They defended themselves against the personal demands they might make upon one another by developing protective layers of reserve, indifference, and aversion, 'a mental strangeness and repulsion'. And in order to assert their differentness, men were 'tempted to adopt the most tendentious peculiarities, that is, the specifically metropolitan extravagances of mannerism, caprice, and preciousness'. The individual summoned 'the utmost in uniqueness and particularization, in order to preserve his most personal core'. Ultimately, the metropolis was thus to be viewed as a stimulus to psychic development and psychic freedom [16]. Simmel admitted that his freedom might be felt by many as a dubious blessing. 'It is,' he wrote, 'only the obverse of this freedom if, under certain circumstances, one nowhere feels as lonely and lost as in the metropolitan crowd. For here as elsewhere it is by no means necessary that the freedom of man be reflected in his emotional life as comfort'. But he was not bothered by this ambiguity. It was not his task, as he wrote in conclusion, 'either to accuse or to pardon, but only to understand' [17].

In the 1920s, a cluster of American urbanists, several of whom had been strongly influenced by German sociological traditions, began to establish a collective reputation of enormous power not only in their own country but also in many other parts of the world. They were known as 'the Chicago school' because most of them either taught or studied at the University of Chicago, but the label was doubly appropriate inasmuch as they devoted much of their scholarly attention to the city in which they worked. Here, at the university where the nation's first academic department of sociology had been established in 1892 and at the centre of a vast metropolitan agglomeration that had expanded more rapidly during the preceding century than any other in the world, was the perfect setting for a new science of metropolitan society. The founder of the Chicago school and the *doyen* of American urban sociology was Robert Park. Having begun his study of society informally as a newspaperman before starting graduate study at Harvard in psychology and philosophy and then listening to Simmel at the University of Berlin, Park first attracted attention as a scholar with an influential essay titled 'the city: suggestions for the investigation of human behaviour in the urban environment'. First published in the *American Journal of Sociology* in 1915 and later reprinted as the introductory piece in a famous collaborative work that was simply titled *The City* [18], Park's essay set forth not only an agenda for research but also a systematic set of generalizations for others to test. Subsequently, Ernest Burgess, Ellsworth Faris, William Ogburn, and Louis Wirth, among others, collaborated with Park and followed through on many of his suggestions [19].

Park and his colleagues regarded the metropolis as an ideal place in which to observe not only collective behaviour but also many other aspects of human life. Because of the freedom it offered to individuals to develop in exceptional and abnormal ways, it tended 'to spread out and lay bare to the public view in a massive manner all the human characters and traits which are ordinarily obscured and suppressed in smaller communities. The city, in short, shows the good and evil in human nature in excess. It is this fact, perhaps more than any other, which justifies the view that would make of the city a laboratory or clinic in which human nature and social processes may be conveniently and profitably studied' [20]. Urban freedom, intimately linked as it was with the breakdown of primary groups as agents of social control, unquestionably led to increased vice and crime [21], but it also gave men the chance to develop their potentialities in ways that would have remained quite beyond them in smaller communities, and the result was a marvellous research opportunity for the social scientist. T. V. Smith articulated a similar outlook a few years later when he wrote: 'In the modern city more perhaps than anywhere else on earth . . . is present in condensed, rapid, observable form the social mobility that makes fruitful research possible'. He went on to depict study of the city as an enterprise that yielded a kind of aesthetic delight, comparable to 'the fascination that captivates the onlooker at a horse race or a partisan at a football game as the senses feast upon the colours and scents and expectancies fused into a complex whole'. But beyond this, he expected the social scientists' insights to lead men to a view of the city as 'an object of sensitive appreciation and moral devotion'. Scientific knowledge was thus to culminate in an enhanced sense of belonging to the community the social scientist was studying [22].

Most members of the Chicago school and other urban sociologists evinced little in the way of such lyricism, viewing their task more prosaically and focusing heavily on the problems of social disorganization and deviance that were the unattractive counterparts to the freedom so eloquently described by Park. E. S. Bogardus emphasized the prevalence of 'the lack of fellow-feeling and understanding which characterizes social distance . . . everywhere . . . in cities'. Nicholas Spykman regarded the city as a 'pluralistic social universe with a plurality of social standards' whose inhabitants displayed 'individualism and self-assertion, rationalism and relativism'. Louis Wirth, in his classic essay on 'urbanism as a way of life', argued that the mode of life prevalent in cities – especially in metropolises – was conducive to 'anomie', 'mutual exploitation', 'loneliness', 'the acceptance of instability and insecurity in the world at large as a norm', and 'personal disorganization, mental breakdown, suicide, delinquency, crime, corruption, and disorder' [23]. But the sociologists of the Chicago school, unlike their German forebears, were not content to analyse the various aspects of metropolitan life in such a way that the city appeared to be a unified entity, cut from whole cloth. While they believed strongly in the existence of uniformities *among* cities they pointed repeatedly to the fact of variety *within* cities. Although, to be sure, it was possible to discern certain characteristics that attached to big cities as such, it was ultimately more important to specify the ways in which these and other attributes were distributed geographically among the city's 'natural areas'. As Park put it: 'Natural areas are the habitats of natural groups. Every typical urban area is likely to contain a characteristic selection of the population as a whole. In great cities the divergence in manners, in standards of living, and in general outlook on life in different urban areas is often astonishing'. Burgess developed this idea by using charts that schematically divided the city into five concentric zones that took shape in the course of urban expansion: a central business district (named 'The Loop' after the downtown area of Chicago), a transitional zone of older housing that was being invaded by business and light industry, a more stable zone of workingmen's homes, a residential zone characterized by high-class apartments and single-family homes, and a suburban commuters' zone. Finally, numerous other authors made use of this model in their studies of social pathology, showing how disorganization and vice were linked to the instability that was most evident in the transitional zone adjacent to the urban core [24].

British social scientists provided little during our period in the way of broad reflections on the big city comparable to the ones we have discussed up to this point. With few exceptions, they failed to analyse metropolitan life as a general problem in anything like the depth achieved by the Germans and the Americans [25]. But they certainly did not ignore the metropolis. In fact, they displayed singular vigour in surveying what at the start of the period was still far and away the largest of all the world cities, namely their own city of London. Their collective efforts to comprehend the social, economic, and cultural life of the British capital resulted in two of the outstanding monuments of modern urbanology.

The first of these works was Charles Booth's famous *Life and Labour of the People in London,* which appeared in seventeen volumes between 1889 and 1903 [26]. Having devoted his young adulthood to business, Booth turned to social investigation in middle age without the benefit of any formal academic training. Motivated in large part by a desire to refute what he felt were wildly exaggerated assertions by socialists about the extent of urban poverty, he embarked with a team of assistants (including the young Beatrice Potter, later to become Beatrice Webb) upon an exceedingly ambitious effort to reveal the quality of life as it was experienced by all elements of the London population. Using census data, sampling techniques, studies of individuals and institutions, and personal observations and impressions, he assembled a sprawling compendium of urban data that bore primarily on the questions of economic and social well-being. The final product was not in any sense a work of theory but rather an outstanding example of the potential fruits of dogged empiricism. The survey was divided into three separately titled but overlapping series: one on *Poverty*, another on *Industry*, and a third on *Religious Influences*. The first series employed two approaches, 'dividing the people by districts and again by trades, so as to show at once the manner of their life and of their work'. Using numerous maps as well as tables, Booth and his co-workers showed how eight social groupings (listed in ascending order from 'A. the lowest class of occasional labourers, loafers, and semi-criminals' to 'H. upper middle class') were distributed both among the city's various regions and among some of its occupational groups. The second series focused on the relations between poverty, occupational distribution, and crowding. The third, arranged geographically, dealt with 'the action of organized religion in all its forms', with that of 'other organized social and philanthropic influences', with the public authorities, and with a number of social conditions that had received insufficient attention in the first two series (providing information 'on housing and health, on drink, prostitution and crime, on marriage and on thrift'). One basic fact emerged from the mass of information contained in these volumes and quickly imprinted itself on the consciousness of many men who never looked at any of what Booth had written. Contrary to Booth's initial expectations, it turned out that 30.7 per cent of London's population lived below the poverty line, 'receiving less than a decent income'. Although poverty was most severe in East London, it was a serious problem in vast reaches of the rest of the city as well. This was a finding of cardinal importance for social reformers, who were also able to draw on Booth's numerous specific suggestions regarding possible remedies for poverty, but the larger significance of Booth's work lay in its inspirational value for other social scientists.

Four decades after Booth's findings had begun to appear in print, another collaborative work started to appear under the title *The New Survey of London Life and Labour*. Published in nine volumes between 1930 and 1935 under the editorship of Hubert Llewellyn Smith, one of Booth's erstwhile assistants, it brought to light the results of a vast investigation undertaken in 1928 at the London School of Economics. Structurally, this survey resembled Booth's quite closely. Three volumes constituted a *Survey of Social Conditions* that served to update the *Poverty* series, the volumes on *London Industries* corresponded to the earlier *Industry* series, and a volume on *Life and Leisure* dealt with many of the topics discussed in the series on *Religious Influences*. In contrast to the earlier survey, this one treated areas that lay beyond the boundaries of the county of London (the total area being about 50 per cent larger than the territory surveyed by Booth), but its range of vision with regard to social groups was considerably narrower, focusing primarily on the working class. Smith and his collaborators used more sophisticated sampling techniques than those available to Booth, and their chapters, though more cogently organized than Booth's, were more heavily statistical and less vivid to read. Another difference was that whereas Booth looked only at the present, the researchers at the LSE sought to assess the extent of social and economic change over time. They showed not only how things were but also how they differed from the conditions that had prevailed forty years earlier. Their basic questions were: 'In what direction are we moving? Is poverty diminishing or increasing? Are the conditions of life and labour in London becoming better or worse?' Their answers to these questions gave the work an upbeat tone that contrasted markedly with the sombre mood that pervaded Booth's survey. They found that the percentage of the population living in poverty (adjusting Booth's standards only for inflation) was between one-third and one-quarter of what it had been earlier, that crime rates and death rates had declined, and that there had been a vast improvement in the quality as well as the quantity of leisure. As Smith wrote in the concluding volume: 'Of all the manifold impressions left upon my mind by the Survey, the deepest and most abiding is not the gravity and multiplicity of the still unsolved problems of London life and labour, but the energy and vitality of the human response to each new need as it has arisen. And so far there is no sign that the sources of this vital energy are running dry' [27].

The Cultural Critic and the Metropolis as an Object of Aesthetic Contemplation

There is an unmistakable parallel between the way in which many social scientists were coming to understand metropolitan life and an attitude toward the metropolises evinced by certain non-academic intellectuals whose primary interests lay in culture and the arts. This is not the place to treat the multifarious perceptions of these places that were afforded by painters, novelists, and poets, whose works are discussed at length by other contributors to this volume. But some of the assumptions that underlay their growing interest in the metropolis, assumptions articulated by a number of cultural critics, do deserve mention as counterparts to views expressed by men such as Robert Park and T. V. Smith. Like these sociologists, commentators on the contemporary cultural scene regarded the metropolis as a powerful stimulus to men's powers of perception and understanding. Whatever one might say about its social problems or its moral failings, it provided a marvellous vehicle by means of which the contemplative aesthete could enrich his sensibilities and abundant raw material that creative artists could use to great advantage in their works of art.

August Endell, an art critic and architect who lived in Berlin, proclaimed this attitude lyrically and unreservedly in an early twentieth-century work on 'the beauty of the big city'. Endell rejected the romantic paean to the beauties of nature and charms of the past. He admitted that urban life was beset by all sorts of drawbacks, but he still insisted that the big city was a beautiful and joyful place in which to live. 'The big city', he wrote, 'despite all the ugly buildings, despite the noise, despite everything in it that one can criticize, is a marvel of beauty and poetry to anyone who is willing to look, a fairy-tale, brighter, more colourful, more diverse than anything ever invented by a poet, a home [*Heimat*], a mother, who daily bestows new happiness in great abundance upon her children'. Urban beauty could be seen first and foremost in the realm of labour – in workshops and factories, in tools and machines, all of which embodied 'an abundance of imaginative power, phantasy, cleverness, and consistency'. Moreover, there was a beauty in the institutions that regulated and directed labour. Writing of big businesses, he compared them to 'crystalline forms' because of what he regarded as their clear and streamlined organizational structures. Outside the workplace, in city streets, the great variety of noises and sights, which continually changed in appearance depending upon whether they were viewed in the bright sun, through fog and mist, or with the aid of lights at night, all provided a rich aesthetic experience. So, too, did the brilliant panorama of different types of human beings whom one might encounter on a streetcar, even – indeed especially – when some of their faces were marked by sickness and despair. 'There is', he wrote, 'hardly anything prettier than sitting quietly in the tram . . . and contemplatively experiencing and enjoying strange human beings. How much beauty there is to discover, often quite imperceptible . . . enveloped in old age, in sickness, in grief, in severe anguish . . . How fine the sick complexions of big-city children are, and see how often their features take on a marvellously severe beauty precisely as a result of need and deprivation. Even depravity and insolence can possess beauty, energy, indeed greatness' [28].

A strikingly similar viewpoint was discernible in a piece titled 'Metropolis' by the reigning American cultural critic of the inter-war years, the editor and essayist H. L. Mencken. Mencken complained about what he felt was the absence of New York from the best American novels of his time. This situation, he asserted, resulted from the city's numerous distractions and its 'machinery of dissipation', which provided writers with unending temptations to indulge in pleasure instead of doing their work. But Mencken went beyond these strictures to insist that the omnipresence of 'organized badness' ought to spur the artist to seek new heights of creativity. What seemed to stand in his way could in fact be regarded as offering an enormous opportunity, if only the writer approached the urban milieu from the proper angle. It was crawling with 'frauds and scoundrels . . . quacks and cony-catchers . . . suckers and visionaries', none of whom might be admirable but all of whom were interesting. New York had 'passed beyond all fear of Hell or hope of Heaven', but nobody could accuse it of being dull. 'The gorgeous, voluptuous colour of this greatest of world capitals' meant that, 'if only as a spectacle', the city was 'superb', and Mencken argued that 'this spectacle, lush and barbaric in its every detail, offer[ed] the material for a great imaginative literature'. He made it quite clear that he felt little love for New York. 'It is', he concluded, 'immensely amusing, but I see nothing in it to inspire the fragile and shy thing called affection . . . But I am speaking now of spectacles, not of love affairs. The spectacle of New York remains – infinitely grand and gorgeous, stimulating like the best that comes out of goblets, and none the worse for its sinister smack. It is immensely trashy – but it remains immense' [29].

Political Intellectuals and the Metropolis as an Object of Reform

We encounter a very different outlook on the metropolis when we turn to a number of intellectuals who had close ties with organized political movements. These men were not content simply to analyse urban life scientifically or to contemplate it aesthetically. Armed with data provided by social investigators and morally energized by the portrayals of social distress contained in works of poetry and fiction, as well as by their own first-hand experiences, they sought both to understand the metropolis and to change it. These thinkers, for the most part adherents of liberalism, saw the metropolitan milieu as the place in which modern social problems had become most acute, and they approached this milieu as an object of reform. Among the many urban reformers active during this period – most of whom remained at the lowly level of particular remedies for particular ills – two groups of thinkers stand out as critics of existing cities and advocates of better ones.

We begin with a remarkable group of young Englishmen who pooled their efforts shortly after the turn of the century to produce a penetrating volume of essays that was titled *The Heart of the Empire: Discussions of Problems of Modern City Life in England* [30]. The editor of the volume and the man who had the most to say about cities in other publications was Charles F. G. Masterman. A fellow of Christ's College, Cambridge, he lived in Camberwell, was active in settlement house work, and served as a member of the local Board of Guardians. In 1904, he was to become a Liberal MP, and subsequently he held several ministerial positions in the reforming governments of Henry Campbell-Bannerman and Herbert Asquith. The other contributors – Frederick W. Lawrence, Reginald A. Bray, Noel Buxton, Walter Hoare, P.W. Wilson, A. C. Pigou, Frederick W. Head, G. P. Gooch, and George M. Trevelyan – for the most part displayed the same combination of intellectuality, personal involvement with the poor, and active commitment to political life, the central purposes of which were indicated in their early writings [31]. Together, they challenged the Liberal Party to renew its moral authority by coming to grips with the ills of metropolitan society.

Although these men were ostensibly writing about British urban life in general, they focused particularly on London. As Masterman explained: 'The problem, in effect the same in all these gigantic aggregations, has reached its fullest development in London; and we shall do well to concentrate our attention upon this enormous mass of population, where we shall be able to trace most clearly the lines of progress and the change from the old conditions to the new' [32]. The urban 'problem' to which Masterman referred comprised a wide range of separate problems. They were perhaps less obvious than the primitive sanitary conditions, the crime, and the wretched housing that had plagued London half a century earlier but no less fateful in their implications for the physical and moral vigour of the nation. Alluding to recent popular demonstrations in connection with the Boer War, he recalled 'turbulent rioting over military successes, hooliganism and a certain temper of fickle excitability'. A new type of Englishman was emerging among a second generation of town-dwellers who had not migrated from the countryside but had lived in the metropolis from the time of their birth. These men and women were not only 'stunted, narrow-chested, easily wearied' but also 'voluble, excitable, with little ballast, stamina, or endurance'. Avid readers of 'the new sensational press', they were oblivious of 'any form of spiritual religion' [33]. Masterman's view of London as a threat to order and stability was vividly conveyed in his grim forebodings concerning 'the turmoil of the coming flood and the tramp of many footsteps'. London's streets, he wrote, had 'suddenly become congested with a weird and uncanny people . . . emerging like rats from a drain, blinking in the sunshine'. But Masterman did not simply fear the upheaval that might result from continuing deprivation and diminished self-control. He wrote just as eloquently about a quite different but equally dismal possibility: the danger that men would succumb to a drab, dull, colourless uniformity, learning to adjust to lives that were devoid of idealism and individuality. He feared that the result of metropolitan living would be 'the elimination of the highest and lowest elements of human nature'. In the city, man was 'rubbing his social angles down'. In the future, everything would be 'ordered, smooth, clean, similar'. The typical urbanite would be 'a sort of polished, whitewashed variety of man, with life reduced to its simplest dimensions' who would 'pass from the great deep to the great deep, industrious, vacant, cheerful, untroubled by envy, aspiration or desire' [34].

Such statements seemed to indicate a deep feeling of despair, a belief that the metropolis was almost beyond redemption, but Masterman was not a total pessimist, and as time went on his hopes began to rise. The point of his writing and of the essays written by the men who were associated with him was not simply to malign the metropolis but rather to impress upon their fellow liberals the need for a host of measures that would lead to its amelioration. In his early writing, Masterman devoted much of his attention to organized religion, which provided 'the most hopeful machinery for the warfare against the degenerating influences of town life'. The established Church was far too conservative and had failed to reach out effectively to the urban masses, but it still had a vital role to play in the area of social reform as an agent of moral revitalization in opposition to the forces of individual selfishness [35]. Subsequently, Masterman placed less emphasis on religious renewal and more on the specific steps that ought to be taken by men in positions of political power. Summarizing many of the suggestions made by other contributors to *The Heart of the Empire* – who had dealt in detail with housing, education, temperance reform, the distribution of industry, and charity, among other topics – he helped to clarify a reformist agenda that would provide a set of objectives for his party when it returned to power. He called for various measures that would strengthen the economic position of yeomen farmers and break up large landed estates in the hope of keeping more men in the countryside. He advocated harsh treatment of slumlords, housing construction by the municipality, and the development of mass transit as ways of alleviating crowded living conditions. 'Better homes', he wrote, 'fresh air, the spreading of the town into something approaching the garden cities of our dreams, will help to break up the congestions which at present are creating impenetrable lumps of poverty'. He also pointed to the need for further educational reform, efforts to combat unemployment, old-age pensions, and better working conditions and higher remuneration for public employees. He cautioned his readers against the belief 'that political or social change, effected by legislature or council, has power of itself to create the world of our desire, and bring that better day for which all are longing'. For most men, life would 'never be a victorious business'. And yet, he wrote: 'So much can be done, so much demands doing; in the days of the life of a man, as all the past witnesses, a world may perish, a world be born' [36].

The period around the turn of the century witnessed a comparable outburst of reformism in the United States by men who were counted among the increasingly influential forces of Progressivism. They were less specifically interested in any particular metropolis than their British contemporaries and less oppressed by the sheer size of urban agglomerations. But their views must be considered in any account of efforts to articulate constructive criticisms of the big city. Social reformism had begun to gather momentum in the 1890s, with the publication of works such as Jacob Riis's *How the Other Half Lives* (1890; an account of immigrant neighbourhoods in New York), *The Hull-House Maps and Papers* (1895; an outgrowth of settlement-house work in Chicago); W. E. B. Dubois' *The Philadelphia Negro* (1899), and Robert Woods's *The City Wilderness* (1899; a description of poor neighbourhoods in Boston). But the distinctive thrust of Progressivism *vis-à-vis* the city emerged from a growing concern with the quality of American urban government. In 1902, the journalist Lincoln Steffens published a widely read book, consisting of previously printed magazine articles, under the title *The Shame of the Cities*. This work, which excoriated corrupt politicians in half a dozen cities, was symptomatic of rising upper middle-class revulsion at the greed and incompetence that had become ensconced in American city halls, and it was followed by many others whose authors propagandized in favour of good government at the local level [37].

Among the municipal reformers who attempted to gain a general view of the urban scene, none was more energetic or influential than Frederic C. Howe. Howe obtained first-hand knowledge of urban affairs via service on the city council and as a financial official in Cleveland, whose mayor between 1901 and 1909, Thomas L. Johnson, made that city one of the best governed in the nation. He was thus in a position not only to call for improvement but also to record it, in the hope of encouraging others to adopt policies that had already been tested in practice. His first work, *The City: The Hope of Democracy* (1905), proclaimed his optimism clearly in its title. Later, he wrote books on British and European municipalities, holding up their achievements as a reproach and an example to his countrymen. His thinking is conveniently summarized in a work titled *The Modern City and Its Problems* (1915), which he dedicated appropriately to Steffens. Howe's fundamental urbanity was evident from the outset. 'The great epochs of civilization', he stated in his introduction, 'have always coincided with a highly developed urban life . . . With the city came education, culture, and a love of the fine arts . . . Science, invention, industry, are also urban'. The city was 'the greatest machine of all' and (in a mixture of the mechanical metaphor with organic ones) 'the brain of a cosmic machine . . . the heart and sensory system of the world as well'. He rejected the dream of a return to the land, asserting that the city was here to stay and arguing that whatever was wrong with cities could be remedied by restructuring their political institutions. He admitted that in the very large 'metropolitan city' more and more problems presented themselves. Men no longer knew their neighbours, and their health was endangered by vice and crime, by impure food, by bad working conditions, and by crowded housing. Official wrong-doing was widespread in dealings between city governments and business interests. But Howe was convinced that all of these ills could be corrected if only the municipalities had more power to control their own affairs and made vigorous use of that power in the interests of their citizens. In fact, more municipal ownership of public utilities, in line with the example set by German cities, would lead not only to better and cheaper services for the public but also to a reduction of corrupt behaviour by public officials. Enhanced virtue among the members of the governing élite and a broader range of benefits for ordinary city-dwellers (including, in addition to public utilities, more health inspection, public markets, and public housing) were thus seen as mutually reinforcing aspects of a programme of reform that would enable cities to enjoy unbroken progress in years to come [38].

Freelance Prophets of Metropolitan Doom

Another, much smaller, group of men saw the metropolis less as an object of reform than as a harbinger of inevitable catastrophe. Located for the most part only on the fringes of formal academic institutions or organized political movements, these men descended far more deeply into despair than any of the reformers, Masterman included. They spoke of decay and decline, of disaster and doom, as the end products of metropolitan growth. The paucity of their numbers might appear to deprive their ideas of much significance. But the fact remains that two of them, Oswald Spengler and Lewis Mumford, sought in their works more directly and explicitly than any other writers active in our period to assess the metropolis as a specific form of modern social and cultural life, and their influence was (and in Mumford's case remains) enormous. Others contributed arresting images of particular places, helping to exert a powerful and enduring influence on men's intellectual conceptions of the metropolis and their emotional attitudes toward it.

The man who did more than anyone else to propagate pessimism about the role of the metropolis in the life of modern civilization was Oswald Spengler. Having worked for several years as a teacher in German secondary schools, he resigned from his position in Hamburg and moved to Munich in 1911 in order to devote himself to a lonely exploration of the basic forces at work in the course of world history. The first volume of his *magnum opus*, titled *Der Untergang des Abendlandes*, was largely finished by 1914, but it was not published until 1918, when its counsels of despair quickly found a receptive audience in a country that had just experienced a shattering defeat. The volume was strewn with gloomy remarks on cities that echoed the conservative anti-urbanism which had formed a powerful current in German thought during the pre-war decades. But it was not until the appearance in 1922 of the eagerly awaited second volume, which contained a long chapter on 'The Soul of the City', that Spengler's views about the metropolis were expressed in more or less systematic fashion. The phrase 'more or less' is appropriate here, because Spengler was not a rigorous thinker. Having decided that he would not permit his search for large-scale insights to be hindered by adherence to the canons of academic respectability, he wrote intuitively and often confusingly. Nonetheless, the main thrust of what he had to say was unmistakable. The metropolis was the supreme symbol and the final cause of the decay of culture and the death of civilization [39].

In Spengler's view, the growth of cities was intimately linked with the cycles of development and decline in world history. 'World history,' he wrote, 'is the history of civic man. Peoples, states, politics, religion, all arts, and all sciences rest upon one prime phenomenon of human being, the town'. Such a statement seemed to suggest a positive recognition of some of the city's virtues, but Spengler quickly changed this one. As cities grew larger and larger, ultimately becoming giant *Welstädte*, their inhabitants lost their sense of national identity. 'Today', he wrote, 'a Brandenburg peasant is closer to a Sicilian peasant than he is to a Berliner'. Modern cities conformed to 'a more and more uniform type', which cut across national boundaries. It was only 'the small number of genuine megalopolitans at the top' who were 'at home wherever their spiritual postulates [were] satisfied', but these 'spiritual postulates' were becoming more and more widespread in the thinking of metropolitan man in general. 'Man', he asserted, 'becomes intellect, "free" like the nomads, whom he comes to resemble, but narrower and colder than they'. The cold, unfeeling rationality of the modern urbanite was, for Spengler, as different from the mentality of the peasant as water was from blood. It found expression in the abstractions of political democracy and a money-based economy, in chess-board layouts of streets, and in reluctance to have children, as well as in the realm of high culture. The world cities themselves, with their 'deep, long gorges between high, stony houses filled with coloured dust and strange uproar', were becoming more and more remote from unspoiled nature. In the end, 'the stone Colossus' turned the man whose culture had been formed in the countryside 'into its creature, its executive organ, and finally its victim'. The *Weltstadt*, 'insatiably and incessantly demanding and devouring fresh streams of men', would 'suck the country dry' until it grew weary and died 'in the midst of an almost uninhabited waste'. After sacrificing 'the blood and soul of its creators to the needs of its majestic evolution and then the last flower of that growth to the spirit of Civilization', the giant city of the future, like the giant cities of the past, would bring about its own destruction and thereby the destruction of civilization itself. This was the unavoidable destiny of metropolitan civilization, the inevitable fate of men who were 'committed to stone and to intellectualism'. Biological sterility and spiritual petrifaction would bring the cycle of historical development back to the point at which it had begun, and no reforms could forestall this outcome [40].

The political overtones of such jeremiads were obviously conservative (and it should be noted that Spengler himself became an increasingly active as well as popular figure in the intellectual movement known as the 'new conservatism' in the Weimar Republic), but the note of hopeless despair could be sounded on the left as well as on the right. One example of this possibility presents itself in an article by the journalist (and later governor and senator from Alaska) Ernest H. Gruening on New York, which appeared in the left-liberal weekly *The Nation* in the same year that saw the publication of the second volume of *Der Untergang des Abendlandes*. Too early to have been directly influenced by Spengler, Gruening's essay nevertheless offers some striking parallels to much of what Spengler had to say. In words that suggested Spengler's view of the metropolis in general, Gruening described New York as 'the ultimate of human gregariousness, the culmination of twentieth-century civilization . . . a great synthetic monolith of steel and cement and stone, an ordered macrocosm to house man and his works'. As it 'tunneled through rock, buried rods beneath the surface [of] the rebelling springs and streams it could not annihilate, flattening every undulation, straightening every variation, squeezing itself into endless rows of rectangles, as impersonal as pig iron', the city had 'forecast the regimentation that is America'. In Gruening's view, this regimentation was spiritual as well as physical. As a result of densely crowded living conditions there was 'limitation not only for the eye, but for every sense', and men's souls were the prisoners of their environment. 'New York', he wrote, 'is hard, cynical, ruthless, even beyond other cities. From their early repression, its children emerge sophisticated, both stunted and overdeveloped, perverted, premature, forced by the artificiality of their environment'. Consequently, 'love, friendship, and human contacts' were 'harassed and trammeled', and men ceased to become neighbours. And finally, evoking the Spenglerian sense of the metropolis as a consumer of men and women, he referred to the city as a 'Moloch [that] demands and gets its victims. Countless moths and butterflies are singed at its flame, countless brave swimmers dragged down into its maelstrom, sunk without a trace' [41].

When we turn to another American, Lewis Mumford, we encounter a man whose criticisms of the metropolis displayed unrivalled breadth and detail, as well as extraordinary insight and intensity of feeling. Mumford was an independent cultural historian and cultural critic, who finished his sixth book while still under the age of forty. His seventh book, *The Culture of Cities,* which appeared in 1938, has become a classic of urban history and urban analysis, only partially superseded by his later volume on *The City in History* (1961). The book offers extensive reflections on the medieval town, on Baroque capitals, and on 'the insensate industrial town', portraying the latter two city types as deformations of the first, which, with all its imperfections, had possessed a degree of humanity that was later to be undermined and overwhelmed. For our purposes, however, the crucial section of the book is the chapter that treats the 'Rise and Fall of Megalopolis'. This chapter, which is far more readily intelligible than its counterpart in *The Decline of the West,* deserves to be regarded as the single most solid as well as suggestive piece of writing about the giant cities of the twentieth century produced by anyone during the entire period we have been considering.

Much of what Mumford had to say constituted an eloquent summary and reworking of accusations that had frequently been levelled against big cities in general as well as metropolises in particular by others before him. Like many another critic of modern urban life, he saw the metropolis as the chief enemy of the natural environment. 'Nature', he wrote, 'except in a surviving landscape park, is scarcely to be found near the metropolis; if at all, one must look overhead, at the clouds, the sun, the moon, when they appear through the jutting towers and building blocks'. Similarly, he indicted the metropolis on biological grounds. 'For all its boasted medical research, for all its real triumphs in lessening the incidence of disease and prolonging life, the city must bow to the countryside in the essentials of health: almost universally the expectation of life is greater in the latter, and the effect of deteriorative disease is less'. Marked by 'sprawl and shapelessness as an inevitable by-product of its physical immensity', the metropolis was deficient in social as well as physical cohesion. Social control based on effective association was sorely lacking in places where the density of settlement was so great that men remained strangers even to their immediate neighbours. As a result, the metropolis offered 'positive encouragement to a-social or anti-social actions', including crime as well as vice [42].

The great force of Mumford's attack, however, stemmed from a much more intensive analysis of the relations between metropolitanism and threats to individual liberty than was contained in any of the works we have discussed so far.

Mumford was not alone in expressing greater fear of regimentation than of the loss of social control. We have already seen indications of such a shift of opinion in Charles Masterman's remarks on London and in some of what Ernest Gruening had to say about New York. The growing concern about the big city as a threat to men's personal autonomy was similarly evident in the remark, in a textbook published in 1931 by the American sociologist, Niles Carpenter, that in the city the forces of social conditioning 'attend the city dweller's life from his arrival into the urban community and dog his every footstep while he remains within it' [43]. Indeed, Paul Boyer has argued that during the 1920s and 1930s, after a century in which American social thinkers had repeatedly denounced the city as a cause of social disintegration, there was a growing tendency to view it as 'the dwelling place of millions of conformists' [44]. The idea that the metropolis was a great levelling force was thus already in the air well before Mumford adopted it, but it received far fuller treatment in his work than in anyone else's. In order to push along the process of metropolitan concentration, and thus to reap the profits that accrued to them from the metropolitan economy, monopoly capitalists, Mumford argued, worked to establish a monopoly of opinion. By means of advertising, news reporting, and periodical literature, they sought 'to give the stamp of authenticity and value to the style of life that emanates from the metropolis'. The effect of such efforts was to drain outlying areas not only of many of their inhabitants but also of much of their peculiar character and identity. Even people who stayed at home came under the homogenizing influence of metropolitan civilization. 'Though the physical radius of the metropolis may be only twenty or thirty miles, its effective radius is much greater: its blight is carried in the air, like the spores of a mold, the outcome is a world whose immense potential variety . . . has been sacrificed to a low metropolitan standardization'. But in order to maintain the grip of the metropolis on the life of the country, there were other necessities as well: a powerful political bureaucracy and a war machine that would protect the life-lines between the giant city and the markets it exploited, both at home and abroad. The bureaucrats and the soldiers sought to strengthen their own positions by fomenting 'the demented cult of "patriotism": coercive group unanimity: blind support of the rulers of the state: maudlin national egoism: an imbecile willingness to commit collective atrocities for the sake of "national glory"'. They used the physical structure of the city itself to serve these ends. 'The buildings of the imperial metropolis', wrote Mumford, 'serve as an appropriate background for these war-ceremonies and reinforce these pretensions'. Not only Tokyo, Berlin, and Rome, but also Washington provided 'a monotonous reflection of the military-bureaucratic mind'. The end result of the action of these forces, which Mumford sketched in a section titled 'A Brief Outline of Hell', was 'the paralysis of all the higher activities of society: truth shorn or defaced to fit the needs of propaganda: the organs of cooperation stiffened into a reflex system of obedience: the order of the drill sergeant and the bureaucrat . . . a regime . . . deeply antagonistic to every valuable manifestation of life' [45].

Mumford was nowhere near as gloomy as Spengler about the prospects of modern civilization as a whole. He offered an alternative to the processes of further metropolitan concentration and encroachment upon the life of the hinterlands. Conscious planning and construction of much smaller regional cities – containing something in the order of 50,000 inhabitants – was not only a theoretical possibility but also a real one, indicated, among other tendencies, by the Garden City movement [46]. But he left little doubt that the metropolis itself was doomed. The basic question regarding its future was not whether it would survive and prosper but whether its ultimate disappearance would occur in conjunction with a renewal of more humane forms of urban life or in an orgy of destruction.

Boosters of Metropolitan Pride

Despite the power of Mumford's writing and its singular stature as an attempt to analyse the metropolitan phenomenon in depth, it would be a mistake to let him have the last word. The fact is that when we look at the many, admittedly much less well known, authors who wrote descriptively and historically about particular cities, we discover an attitude toward metropolitan life that was overwhelmingly favourable. These men were not academically trained social scientists. Some, like the prophets of doom, were freelance writers – journalists and other authors who made at least part of their living by producing books and essays for the general public – and in coming to their conclusions they were very much their own men. Others worked, at least when writing about the city, either under the supervision or under the influence of institutions that had an obvious interest in seeing to it that the metropolis got a good press. Whatever their varying motivations, they all helped to boost metropolitan pride. Let us now consider their views of Paris, London, Berlin, New York, and Chicago.

No metropolis enjoyed as many devoted admirers as Paris, and the numerous works that describe the city and recount its history are almost wholly laudatory. Many themes pervade the writings that appeared in our period: the administrative and technological advances that occurred after the debacle of the Commune, the physical beauty of the city, and its quasi-erotic attractiveness to the people who lived there, to name only a few. But perhaps the most distinctive note in the celebration of the French capital was an insistence on its central place not only in the life of the nation but also in the life of the world. As Charles Delon put it in 1888: 'Whoever loves France loves Paris. Whoever does not know Paris is ignorant of France. Why? Because Paris *is* France'. He continued: 'If France has made Paris, Paris has also helped France to create itself. It has forged its national spirit and its language. It has thought and acted, it has fought, and it has suffered for her. In the history of France, Paris is the hero, Paris is the martyr'. But the stature of Paris far transcended the national level. Because it was so rich culturally, offering in abundance 'the noble pleasures of the mind', the city was 'a salon, a museum, so to speak, a school, and the foremost in the world'. As Charles Simond put it at the turn of the century: 'Modern life will become cosmopolitan in the twentieth century, but Paris will remain the hearth of this cosmopolitanism, and all attention, all dreams, and all desires for approval will converge on this home of light and enlightenment'. Writing in the aftermath of the First World War, Gustave Rodrigues proclaimed that Paris was 'not the capital of a nation but the chief city of the universe'. It was 'Athens . . .but an enlarged, international Athens'. Finally, in 1930, André Warnod described the city as 'the spiritual capital of the civilized world'. He regarded Paris as 'the crucible where the civilization and the arts of the entire world have been blended'. In these and in many comparable passages by other authors, the metropolitan internationalism that Spengler found so ominous was held up for admiration as the great glory of a great city [47].

When we turn to descriptions of London, a city in which the problem of poverty generated great concern among social investigators and reformers in the 1880s and 1890s, we encounter a good deal less in the way of such ecstasy and enchantment. The pictures were painted with fewer bright colours, and the hymns of praise were marred by more discordant notes. Nonetheless, there remained a powerful current of admiration and affection for the first of the modern metropolises. Little was said about London's role as a force for national unity, but a great deal was said about its world-wide significance. As one writer put it at the start of our period: 'London sits enthroned at the gates of the sea, the mighty centre – commercial, financial, political, social, and intellectual – of a vast realm where English laws, English institutions, the English tongue, and all the treasures of English literature reign and govern . . . with a sovereignty that seems imperishable and destined never to pass away'. Like ancient Rome, London was great in large part because of its position at the heart of a mighty empire, an empire far more imposing than that governed from Paris. Even more than Paris, London impressed as a cultural centre to which men came from the far corners of the world and in which they rubbed shoulders with one another. In the words of Ford Madox Hueffer (alias Ford Madox Ford): 'It is . . . the meeting place of all Occidentals and of such of the Easterns as can come, however remotely, into touch with the Western spirit . . . In it may be found, as it were "on show", the best of all music. And it has at odd moments "on show" the best products of the cook, of the painter, of the flower-gardener, of the engineer, of the religious and of the scientists . . . It is . . . a perennial Nijni Novgorod bazaar, a permanent world's fair'. Observations such as these formed part of a more general perception of London as a city whose attractiveness lay in large measure in its unending complexity and variety. Not only because of its world role but also because of its long history and its sheer size, the city could never be fully understood, and its ultimate incomprehensibility was perhaps the main source of its fascination for the many intellectuals who loved it. Paul Cohen-Portheim, an emigré from Germany in the 1930s, observed that

London consisted of a whole series of 'small towns with a character of their own', and that it possessed an enormous variety of social classes as well as ethnic groups. It was 'the most complex city in the world', and this complexity endowed it with a character all its own. 'Paris with the addition of Marseilles, Berlin with that of Hamburg, New York with that of Washington would yet not attain its completeness; but London resembles none of them, and is like nothing in the world except itself'. He wrote that 'in a world growing more uniform every day . . . its fascination will grow on you; you will never tire of it, because you will never feel you really know it; it is too vast for that, and too complex' [48].

When we turn to writings about Berlin, the international dimension is much less in evidence. The *Hauptstadt* of the empire created by Otto von Bismarck, of the Weimar Republic, and of the Third Reich, Berlin was unquestionably a *Weltstadt* as well as a capital, but it lacked the cosmopolitanism of Paris and London, and most German observers saw its significance within a primarily national context. Among the recurrent themes in much of their writing, one is struck by an emphasis on the city's dynamic energy. A publicist describing the city in the 1890s remarked on its 'fresh diligence and buoyant spirit of enterprise . . . [and its] earnest struggling and restless striving upward – ever more conscious of the goal, more independent, more deserving of respect'. Shortly thereafter, a historian of the city wrote: 'Berlin is a city of labour. In no other big city on the European continent can one find the joy in productivity, the restless activity, which manifest themselves in Berlin wherever one looks'. All branches of the economy, of the city administration, and of cultural life could take pride in their many accomplishments. During and after the First World War, the critic and art historian Max Osborn was similarly impressed by the city's 'iron energy, concentrated desire and ability to work, and indomitable urge to create new values', which clearly were making a major contribution to the war effort and thus to national strength. An important part of this general line of argument had to do with the benefits bestowed upon Berlin's citizenry by the energetic administrators who had given the city a reputation as the best-governed metropolis in the world. According to Ernst Kaeber, the city archivist in the 1920s, Berlin was laying claim with ever-growing justification to its inhabitants' devotion as its governors provided them with more and more for which to be grateful. It was no longer simply their place of residence but increasingly their *Heimat*, or 'home town', as well. Even the Nazis, despite their repeated attacks against big cities as sources of moral corruption, found occasions for portraying Berlin as a community that had earned the devotion of its citizens. According to the preface to a history of the city written under the auspices of the city administration in the 1930s, 'each Berlin child should feel itself to be the member of a large family', that family being the city in which he lived [49].

Men who celebrated the metropolis American-style, including foreigners as well as American citizens, saw many but not all of the qualities attributed to the great cities of Europe, and they discerned others that were scarcely noticed at all on the other side of the Atlantic. In their remarks about New York and Chicago, they had rather little to say either about the glories of the past or about national power and prestige. Both of these omissions were quite understandable. In comparison with Paris, London, and Berlin, New York and especially Chicago (first settled in 1833) had been in existence for only a relatively short period, and neither enjoyed the status of a national capital. We do, however, find a growing awareness of the cosmopolitanism of these cities. Charles Whibley, a British journalist, wrote of New York in 1907 that it was not 'a city' but 'a collection of cities. Here, on the narrow rock which sustains the real metropolis of the United States, is room for men and women of every faith and every race. The advertisements which glitter in the windows or are plastered upon the hoardings suggest that all nationalities meet with an equal and flattering acceptance'. Edward Hungerford, like many others, described Chicago in 1913 as 'a great crucible into which the people of all nations and all corners of one of the greatest nations are being poured'. By the 1920s at the latest, New York had acquired a reputation as an international city not only because of its obvious ethnic diversity but also because of its sophisticated culture. Ford Madox Ford wrote: 'New York differs from London in having a keener intellectual life . . . New York is becoming more of an intellectual center as the days go on – and that adds enormously to the world . . . The artistic life of New York is assimilating itself more to that of Paris – and I do not know that it does not carry the process of international fusion further than Paris allows it to be carried'. Another element that we have so far encountered primarily in writings about Berlin was awe at the tremendous energy and the restless innovativeness that seemed to leap forth from every corner of these cities. As the American journalist Morris Markey wrote in 1932: 'The whole of Chicago seems organized for toil, a breathless outpouring of energy with all goals obscured in the clamor of labor for its own sake'. Finally – and here we broach a theme that was relatively infrequent in all the writing about European metropolises – both cities stood out physically by virtue of the spectacular changes that had been wrought as a result of the purposeful channelling of this energy into the construction of modern buildings. 'New York', wrote the French historian Bernard Faÿ in 1929, 'overwhelms us with its incongruous magnificence, its power and voluptuousness. Buildings fifty storeys high, covered with marble . . . Straight lines everywhere, horizontal and vertical, which affirm the will to . . . act directly, to make room for millions of people . . . New York is . . . a city of rectangles, harsh and brilliant, the center of an intense life which it sends out in all directions'. A year later, Mary Borden, a novelist who had been born in Chicago and had later moved to England, returned to her native city for a visit. In her report on her trip, she described Chicago as 'the city of magic'. 'Genii had risen out of the lake and ogres out of the prairie land. They had woven monstrous spells above this spot where I stood, and the earth had opened, and towers of steel had spurted into the air like geysers, like fountains, and great blocks of marble had gone hurtling through space and had been planted in stone gardens and clustered, tapering groves of stone, and a great energy had poured through the bodies of these stones, galvanizing them into life'. In this view, in contrast to Spengler's, stone was not a harbinger of death but a proof of vitality [50].

Conclusion

After surveying the analyses and descriptions of the metropolis in general, and of individual metropolises in particular, published between 1890 and 1940, one is inevitably struck by the pervasiveness of many themes that appeared in the writing of all or almost all of the groups of authors discussed in this chapter. There was the recognition that because of comparatively low birth rates and high death rates metropolises consumed more human beings than they produced. On the other hand, men saw these cities as enormously dynamic economic and cultural powerhouses, whether for good or for evil. There was widespread awareness that the metropolis played a crucial part in the functioning of industrial capitalism. There was also a sense that the metropolis acted as a powerful stimulus to men's mental development, sometimes producing over-intellectuality and nervousness. Most thinkers were struck by the freedom the metropolis permitted, although this freedom was often regarded negatively as a symptom of social disorganization and a cause of loneliness. As time went on, there was growing emphasis on the ways in which the metropolis could reduce men's autonomy by forcing them to conform to the standards of a mass society, but by and large freedom remained the keynote. Finally, even though individual metropolises were still seen as cities that possessed separate personalities, there was a growing agreement that they were becoming increasingly similar throughout the world.

Much of the best thinking about metropolitan life cannot be stretched to fit the procrustean bed that consists of the categories of approval and hostility. The views of the social scientists in particular were marked by considerable ambivalence. Among non-professionals who were writing for a mass audience, there were of course many extreme views: denunciations of the metropolis *à la* Spengler versus the hymns of praise, but many of these men cannot be placed clearly in one camp or the other. Insofar as it is possible to total up opponents of the metropolis on one side and defenders on the other, I am struck more by the latter than by the former. Some influential thinkers did hurl thunderbolts against the metropolis as a prime source of physical and cultural decay, but many more writers evoked a sense of the great cities as places that were indispensable to the life of their times. When one thinks about it, this situation was not all that surprising. The world cities were, after all, places of freedom and stimuli to thought, both because of their inner variety and because of their cultural institutions. For these reasons, among others, they were bound to exert a powerful attraction on men of ideas.

NOTES

1. Liddell, H.G. and Scott, R. (1940) *Greek–English–Lexicon*, 9th ed. Oxford: The Clarendon Press, pp. 1130–1, 1087; Lewis and Short (1879) *A Latin Dictionary*. Oxford: The Clarendon Press, p. 1141; *The Oxford English Dictionary* (1933) Oxford: The Clarendon Press, Vol. VI, p. 400; Burchfield, R. W. (ed.) (1976) *A Supplement to the Oxford English Dictionary*. Oxford: The Clarendon Press, Vol. II, p. 880; *Deutsches Wörterbuch von Jacob Grimm und Wilhelm Grimm* (1955). Leipzig: S. Hirzel, Vol. XIV, I. Abteilung, 1. Teil, pp. 1699–1701.

2. For developments in Europe, see the following: Pfeil, E. (1950) *Grossstadtforschung*. Bremen-Horn: W. Dorn, pp. 13–87; Coleman, B.I. (ed.) (1973) *The Idea of the City in Nineteenth-Century Britain*. London and Boston: Routledge and Kegan Paul; Bergmann, K. (1970) *Grossstadtfeindschaft und Agrarromantik*. Meisenheim am Glan: Verlag Anton Hain; Lees, A. (1979) Critics of urban society in Germany, 1854–1914. *Journal of the History of Ideas*, **40** (1), pp. 61–83; and Glaab, C.N. and Brown, A.T. (1976) *A History of Urban America* (2nd edn) New York and London: Macmillan, pp. 45–65, 209–29. For Japan, see Smith, H.D. (1978) Tokyo as an Idea: an exploration of Japanese urban thought until 1945. *Journal of Japanese Studies*, **4** (1), pp. 45–80.

3. This study is based of a survey of works listed under the headings 'cities' and 'towns' in the card catalogue of the Library of Congress, in the printed catalogue of the British Museum, in the *English Catalogue of Books*, in Poole's *Index to Periodical Literature*, and in *The Subject Index to Periodical Literature* and the *International Index to Periodical Literature*. For German publications, I have also looked at works listed under the headings 'Grossstadt' and 'Stadt' in the major libraries in Munich and Berlin, in Kayser's *Vollständiges Bücherverzeichniss*, and in the *Bibliographie der deutschen Zeitschriftenliteratur*. I have also looked at a large number of works listed in the catalogues of the Library of Congress and the British Museum under headings for London, Paris, and Berlin. For New York, I have used Bayrd Still, *Mirror for Gotham: New York as Seen by Contemporaries from Dutch Days to the Present*. New York: New York University Press, 1956), which contains an excellent bibliography as well as excerpts from numerous primary sources.

4. Levasseur, E. (1891) *La population française*. Paris: Rousseau, Vol. II, pp. 355, 359, 397–407, 410–15.

5. Meuriot, P. (1897) *Des agglomérations urbaines dans l'Europe contemporaine: essai sur les causes, les conditions, les conséquences de leur développement*. Paris, pp. 29, 367–73, 377–87.

6. *Ibid.*, pp. 347–55, 417–18.

7. *Ibid.*, pp. 409–12, 451–2. See Weber, A.F. (1899) *The Growth of Cities in the Nineteenth Century: A Study in Statistics*. New York: Macmillan, for a slightly later work by an American investigator who dealt with much the same subject matter within a world-wide geographic framework. Weber, however, did not dwell as heavily as Meuriot on the very largest cities.

8. *Die Grossstadt: Vorträge und Aufsätze zur Städteausstellung*. (1903). Dresden: Zahn und Jaensch.

9. On the exhibition, see Wuttke, R. (ed.) (1904), *Die deutschen Städte: geschildert nach den Ergebnissen der ersten deutschen Städteausstellung zu Dresden 1903*. Leipzig: Friedrich Brandstetter.

10. *Die Grossstadt*, *op cit.*, pp. 8–9, 29–30, 38, 72, 104, 129–33, 175–6, 231ff., 264–75 (see note 8).

11. *Ibid.*, pp. 182, 277-8.

12. *Ibid.*, pp. 213–14, 221-3, 226–30.

13. For academic opinion, see Ringer, F.K. (1969) *The Decline of the German Mandarins: The German Academic Community, 1890–1933*. Cambridge, Mass: Harvard University Press, pp. 253–304.

14. Simmel's essay, titled 'Die Grossstädte und das Geistesleben', has been translated and reprinted several times under the title 'The metropolis and mental life'. See Wolff, K. (ed.) (1950) *The Sociology of Georg Simmel*. Glencoe: The Free Press, pp. 409–24.

15. *Ibid.*, pp. 409–10, 415, 420, 422.

16. *Ibid.*, pp. 410–11, 413–14, 415–16, 421–3.

17. *Ibid.*, pp. 418, 424.

18. Park, R.E., Burgess, E.W. and McKenzie, R.D. (1925) *The City*. Chicago: The University of Chicago Press.

19. For general treatments, see Faris, R.E.L. (1970) *Chicago Sociology, 1920-1932* (revised edn). Chicago: The University of Chicago Press; also, Short, J.F. (1971) Introduction, in Short, J.F. (ed.) *The Social Fabric of the Metropolis: Contributions of the Chicago School of Sociology*. Chicago and London: The University of Chicago Press. Smith remarks on the influence of Park and Burgess on Okui Fukutaro, one of the first academic students of urban society in modern Japan (Smith, *op. cit.*, p. 72 (see note 2)).

20. Park, *et al., op. cit.*, pp. 22, 45–46 (see note 18). See also Park, R.E. (1929) The city as a social laboratory, in Smith, T.V. and White, L.D. (eds.) *Chicago: An Experiment in Social Science Research*. Chicago: The University of Chicago Press, pp. 1–19.

21. Park, *et al., op. cit.*, pp. 23–25 (see note 18).

22. Smith, T.V. (1929) Social science research and the community, in Smith and White, *op. cit.*, pp. 221, 243, 245–6 (see note 20).

23. Bogardus, E.S. (1926) Social distance in the city, in Burgess, E.W. (ed.) *The Urban Community*. Chicago: The University of Chicago Press, p. 48; Spykman, N.J. (1926) A social philosophy of the city, in Burgess, *op. cit.*, pp. 58, 64; Wirth, L. (1938) Urbanism as a way of life, reprinted (1969) in Sennett, R. (ed.) *Classic Essays on the Culture of Cities*. New York: Appleton-Century-Croft, pp. 153, 156, 157.

24. Park, R.E. (1926) The urban community as a spacial pattern and a moral order, in Burgess, *op. cit.*, p. 11 (see note 23); Burgess, E.W. (1925) The growth of the city, in Park *et al., op. cit.*, pp. 50–51 (see note 18); for discussion of some of the specific studies of 'natural areas', see Park (1929) *loc. cit.*, p. 8 (see note 20).

25. One of the few I have been able to find was Glass, D.V. (1935) *The Town and a Changing Civilization*. London: John Lane. This book is not without merit, but it is derivative rather than original, relying heavily on the work of Americans.

26. For a cogent outline of the bases and structure of the survey, see Glass, R. (1955) Urban sociology in Great Britain: a trend report. *Current Sociology*, **4** (4), pp. 45–47. For a more extended analysis and some representative selections, see Pfautz, H.W. (ed.) (1967) *Charles Booth on the City: Physical Pattern and Social Structure*. Chicago and London: The University of Chicago Press. My quotations are drawn from these works.

27. Glass, *loc. cit.*, pp. 47–48 (see note 26); Smith, H.L. (ed.) (1934) *The New Survey of London Life and Labour*, Vol. I. London: P. S. King and Son, pp.. 4, 7, 17, 22, 31, 35–36, 48; Smith (1935) *The New Survey of London Life and Labour*, Vol. IX, pp. 3ff., 40.

28. Endell, A. (1908) *Die Schönheit der grossen Stadt*. Stuttgart: Strecker und Schröder, pp. 23, 26, 29, 31, 49, 60, 67–8.

29. Mencken, H.L. (1927) *Prejudices: Sixth Series*. New York: Alfred A. Knopf, pp. 209–15.

30. First published in 1901 in London by T. Fisher Unwin; reprinted in 1973 by The Harvester Press, with an introduction by Bentley B. Gilbert (now available only from Harper and Row, in New York).

31. See Gilbert, *op. cit.*, pp. xxvi–xxxiii (see note 30).

32. Masterman, C.F.G. (1901) Realities at home, in Masterman, *op. cit.*, p. 9 (see note 30).

33. *Ibid.*, pp. 7–8.

34. Masterman, C.F.G. (1902) (anon.) *From the Abyss: Of its Inhabitants by One of Them*. London: Johnson, pp. 2, 35, 37.

35. Masterman, *The Heart of the Empire, op. cit.*, pp. 34, 45, 50–51 (see note 30).

36. Masterman, C.F.G. (1904) The English city, in Oldershaw, L. (ed.) *England: A Nation, Being the Papers of the Patriot's Club*. London and Edinburgh: R. Brimley Johnson, pp. 66, 72, 77, 78, 83, 85, 86, 92-93.

37. On the Progressives and the city, see Glaab and Brown, *op. cit.*, pp. 196–223 (see note 2); Boyer, P. (1978) *Urban Masses and Moral Order in America, 1820–1920*. Cambridge, Mass and London: Harvard University Press, pp. 191–292; and Schiesl, M.J. (1977) *The Politics of Efficiency: Municipal Administration and Reform in America, 1880–1920*. Berkeley and Los Angeles: University of California Press.

38. Howe, F.C. (1915) *The Modern City and Its Problems*. New York: Charles Scribner's Sons, pp. 1, 4–6, 38–40, 59–60, 165ff., 252ff., 289ff.

39. See Hughes, H.S. (1962) *Oswald Spengler: A Critical Estimate*, 2nd edn. Boston: Scribner's; also, Bergmann, *op. cit.*, pp. 179–83 (see note 2).

40. Spengler, O. (1928) *The Decline of the West*,

Vol. II. *Perspectives on World History* (trans. Atkinson, C.F.) New York: Alfred A. Knopf, pp. 90, 91, 108, 98, 92, 97, 100, 103–4, 94, 107.

41. Gruening, E.H. (1922) New York: I. the city – work of man. *The Nation*, **115**, pp. 571–5.

42. Mumford, L. (1938) *The Culture of Cities*. New York: Harcourt Brace Jovanovich, pp. 252, 253, 234, 239, 250–1, 266.

43. Quoted in Boyer, *op. cit.*, p. 290 (see note 37).

44. *Ibid.*, pp. 290–2.

45. Mumford, *op. cit.*, pp. 228–30, 255, 232, 273, 278 (see note 42).

46. *Ibid.*, pp. 300–401.

47. Delon, C. (1888) *Notre capitale: Paris*. Paris Maurice, pp. 1–2, 5; Simond, C. (ed.) (1901) *Paris de 1800 à 1900*, Vol. III. Paris: Plon, p. 619; Rodrigues, G. (1919) *La France éternelle*. Paris, pp. 50, 59; Warnod, A. (1930) *Visages de Paris*. Paris: Firmin-Didot, p. 323.

48. Hodder, E. (ca. 1889) *Cities of the World: Their Origin, Progress, and Present Aspect*, Vol. IV. London: Cassell, p. 226; Hueffer, F.M. (1905) *The Soul of London*. London: A. Rivers, p. 13; Cohen-Portheim, P. (1935) *The Spirit of London*. London: B. T. Batsford, pp. 13, 36, 107, 112.

49. Lindenberg, P. (1895) *Berlin in Wort und Bild*. Berlin: F. Dümmler, pp. 6–8; Streckfuss, A. and Fernbach, L. (1900) *500 Jahre Berliner Geschichte*. Berlin: A. Goldschmidt, pp. 764–94, esp. pp. 776–7; Osborn, M. (1915) Das Antlitz der Grossstadt, *Der Kunstfreund*, **2**, p. 99; Kaeber, E. (1926) Die Weltstadt als Heimat, in Brennert, H. and Stein, E. (eds.) *Probleme der neuen Stadt Berlin: Darstellungen der Zukunftsaufgaben einer Viermillionenstadt*. Berlin: Deutscher Kommunalverlag, p. 206; Grantzow, H. (1937) *700 Jahre Berlin*. Berlin: im Auftrage der Stadtverwaltung.

50. Quotations on New York from Still, *op. cit.*, pp. 281, 294–5,. 298 (see note 3); quotations on Chicago from Pierce, B. (ed.) (1933) *As Others See Chicago: Impressions of Visitors, 1673–1933*. Chicago: The University of Chicago Press, pp. 431, 511, 496–7.

Chapter 4

The Metropolis in the Visual Arts: Paris, Berlin, New York, 1890–1940

THEDA SHAPIRO

THE visual arts of the period 1890–1940 are filled with reflections of the bustling urban life of a time when the population of most Western countries first became more urban than rural and major cities grew to gigantic proportions. The metropolis regularly appears in documentary and *avant-garde* photography, and realist, expressionist and abstract painting of the time; it is of less importance in modern sculpture. But while the artist-inhabitants of the metropolis – that is, almost all 'modern' artists of our century – willingly depicted their urban surroundings, few of them ever verbally expressed their feelings about the big city, or based their depictions on a firm view of the metropolis as a distinctly modern phenomenon. So their attitudes to the city must be gleaned almost entirely from their works, and one cannot expect those attitudes to be highly precise.

I am going to describe here what I see as the major modes of artistic response to the metropolis between 1890 and 1940 with reference to the images depicting, and the artists living in, the three cities which were the most important art centres of the period: Paris, Berlin, and New York. I have chosen Paris because it had a long tradition of urban concentration and was the international art capital up to 1940; from the early nineteenth to the mid-twentieth century, it was the art mecca to which all innovations – many originating elsewhere – were referred for comparison and criticism. Berlin was relatively new as a big city; it rapidly became an important cultural centre after 1870 and just as rapidly lost its international status after the Nazi takeover in 1933. Its artists before 1933 have some unusual contributions to make to our subject. New York, finally, represents the most extreme metropolitan modernity and stood, in the eyes of all Western artists, for the metropolis *par excellence*; and it inherited the international art leadership when many artists emigrated to the United States in flight from fascism and when the European cities became inaccessible during the Second World War. Moreover, New York art represents an extraordinary multiplicity of styles and an ultimate blending of indigenous American attitudes with the European modernism imported through exhibitions and immigration.

Artists' responses to the metropolis were affected by a variety of factors other than each individual artist's personality, philosophy and urban experience. These, of course, play an important role but cannot be fully dealt with here because my purpose is to identify general categories of response rather than to catalogue individual reactions. The broader influences acting on artists I take to be the following: first of all, stylistic preference, which often determines the artist's degree of receptivity to the city as a subject, the urban aspects he chooses to depict, and the 'committed' or 'uncommitted' way in which he looks at the city; second, economic and social conditions in the metropolis at different times, which affect artists along with all residents; and third, the various *national* responses to industrialization and metropolitan growth, which affect artists along with their fellow nationals. Without proceeding didactically from artist to artist or from city to city, I will try to show the impact of these interlocking influences on the visually-stated responses to the metropolis in modern art [1].

The City in Art

Up to the second half of the nineteenth century, when the cityscape definitively became a frequent subject for artists, there were only two major types of urban views in Western art. The first, beginning in the early Renaissance in both Italy and Northern Europe, features a general view of a European city, often represented in minute detail, as a historical or symbolic background-setting for a religious scene taking place in the foreground. In medieval theology the earthly city had come to stand as a pale, impure yet philosophically and visually meaningful analogy for the heavenly Jerusalem to which all Christians were to direct their earthly lives and daily prayers. Artists accordingly often set religious scenes within European cities, which served both to stand in for the biblical settings, which the artists had never seen, and to represent the ideal heavenly city.

The second major type of early urban view is the realistic cityscape, pioneered in El Greco's 'View of Toledo', and popularized by Dutch seventeenth-century painters, who established the city as a subject worthy of representation in its own right. Here the emphasis is on accurate reproduction of the 'look' of a specific city, with its streets, waterways and buildings, its monumental churches and palaces, and the daily activities of its population. The artists most famous for these urban scenes are the *vedutista*, view-painters, of eighteenth-century Venice, who painted their own city and many European capitals often with almost obsessive accuracy. Out of this dual Dutch and Italian realist tradition grew both the cityscape as glorification piece for the ruler or memento for the world traveller, in either case featuring buildings above all; and the urban genre scene recording the daily activities of commoners out-of-doors. Both the cityscape and the open-air genre scene were to have considerable long-term success and were greatly to influence later urban art, especially that of realism and Impressionism, but in their own time they were regarded as minor art forms as opposed to the historical, classical and religious subjects considered by art academies as the only worthy material for art.

With the triumph of realism after 1850, coupled to the rapid urbanization then taking place in the West, the city view was revalorized as an important subject in art. The invention and rapid refinement of photography, and the introduction of the photographic postcard toward the end of the century, made straightforward view-painting obsolete. But a market for 'hand-painted' urban views has continued to exist, and modernist artists began to choose the big city as the subject of more abstract works.

Artists in the City

Art-making, as well as art exhibition and sale, has always been localized to some degree in the largest European cities, but a very high degree of centralization came about only in the nineteenth century, with the decline in art patronage by the Catholic church and old aristocracy and the rise of a large urban middle-class public avid for exhibitions and interested in buying 'ready-to-hang' small pieces. Until the late nineteenth century, however, landscape painting – now stressing open-air work – constituted a large share of the art market; and thus many artists had dealers in the large cities but lived in smaller towns. The Postimpressionists in France and the Expressionists in Germany were the last such major groups, although landscape painting, like urban view painting, has remained an active field in popular, if not 'high', art. The classical and historical works still in vogue among the academically-minded until well after the mid-nineteenth century were often painted in urban studios, but they betray no signs of their big-city origins.

With the French Impressionists of the 1870s, who were, of course, also great landscape painters, the metropolis came into its own as a subject. The Impressionists' concern with representing the ordinary moment in daily life and the changing effects of climate and atmosphere on objects led them to close inspection of the environment and activities of the city. They divided their time between Paris and various rural localities. Since the Impressionists and the Postimpressionists, most artists have been by predilection city-dwellers.

What did the metropolis represent to these artists, apart from the images of it that they have given us? To many, from the Impressionists to the present, however great its discomforts, it was the only acceptable place to live – because of its centrality to buyers and dealers, because of their need for continual dialogue with other artists, writers and critics, because of the unparalleled visual stimulation offered by the urban scene, and because of the privacy that the big city afforded. In Baudelaire's highly influential formulation, the metropolis represents 'solitude' and 'the multitude' all at once, which meant for artists freedom from social, moral and creative constraints, abundance of subject matter, and anonymity for work purposes (with the simultaneous possibility of gaining notoriety) [2]. Until the Second World War all the big cities offered inexpensive lodgings to those willing to make do with little; urban artists usually congregated in inelegant neighbourhoods, creating villages for daily living while having the whole city at their disposal when needed. It is important to remember that they were *artisans*, not factory workers, and that their daily lives were virtually untouched by industrialization until they themselves chose to acknowledge technology as a visual element of their surroundings and as a possible innovative force in their techniques. They did not have to accept the metropolis wholesale, as did those tied to daily routine, industrial or commercial labour, commuting, and family life in a small space. They took from the metropolis what served their needs for personal independence and visual stimulation, and the urban visions they created in return are often utopian dreams, sometimes realistic depictions, and always highly selective fragments of urban life.

Before the First World War: Representational Art

The major common denominator in the urban views by most French and American painters and photographers who retained a fully representational style between 1890 and 1914 is that they are all considerably influenced by Impressionism, in particular by its modernity of subject matter and its 'soft-focus' treatment of objects. Not all artists retained the Impressionist disintegration of the image into a blur of highly-coloured brushstrokes; some retained a more visually exact mode of representation, while others further heightened their colour and figural distortion with the intention of replacing Impressionism's seeming insipidity by a deeper investigation of emotion. Nevertheless, most city paintings of this period retain the Impressionists' luminous light, their preoccupation with subjects of leisure or the pleasanter aspects of work, and their tendency to prettify the cityscape.

It must be noted, however, that many Postimpressionist artists were uninterested in the city as a subject, either because, like Van Gogh and Gauguin [3], they were absorbed in defining their personal responses to nature and to folk culture, or because they were concerned with mysticism or symbolism, like Odilon Redon and Gustave Moreau. So those who might have found the metropolis an uncongenial environment give us no visual clues to their feelings about it – and this is a non-response we will encounter again later on.

The Paris of the *Belle Époque* was a prosperous and comfortable city whose centre had been scarcely affected – visually, at least – by industrialization, except for the iron-and-glass architecture of markets, railway stations and exhibition halls, the Eiffel Tower, the newly-constructed underground and newly-mechanized trams. Due to the exceedingly centralized administrative structure of France, Paris had been the hub of the country and a very large city for the last three hundred years. Its monumental architectural complexes built since the beginning of the Bourbon monarchy, its many public parks, and its broad tree-lined nineteenth-century boulevards cutting through the centre and along the river banks were enormously attractive to artists, as were the numerous pleasure-spots, high and low, that filled the boulevards and the still village-like Montmartre to the north.

Paris was, among other things, a great public open-air theatre, and that is how

FIGURE 4.1. Pierre Bonnard, 'The Boulevard' (lithograph),
from *Quelques aspects de la vie de Paris*, c.1895 (Bibliothèque
Nationale, Cabinet des Estampes).

the urban-minded Postimpressionists, the Fauves, and many photographers
showed it. The paintings of the time, by such artists as Pissarro, Vuillard, Bonnard,
the young Picasso just after his arrival from Spain in 1900, the early Matisse, Albert
Marquet and others of the Fauves, show pleasant scenes along the river; sweeping
views of public monuments, parks, squares and boulevards, often seen from above
and alive with strollers, vendors and playing children (figure 4.1); scenes of
rejoicing crowds in the Montmartre dancehalls, *à la* Toulouse-Lautrec. The
photographers of the period also emphasized the historic neighbourhoods and
picturesque inhabitants: Eugène Atget took views of old streets and buildings, and
of vendors, entertainers and prostitutes: the young Jacques Henri Lartigue chose to
represent mainly his own upper bourgeois family and the outings of the
fashionables of the day to the Bois du Boulogne or Longchamp; when in Paris,
Alfred Stieglitz, more interested in the accidental effects of climate, traffic and
pedestrians, photographed the boulevards wet with rain or clothed in fog and
traversed by workers and pedestrians.

Of course, Toulouse-Lautrec and the early Picasso dwelt with melancholy on
the lonely world of the Paris prostitutes, entertainers and clowns, expressing
thereby their own sense of being misfits, far from home; and Utrillo's placid scenes
of Montmarte streets are also often melancholic – but these depictions do not
often refer to the metropolis as such, but rather to a particular outcast milieu. The

FIGURE 4.2. Alfred Stieglitz, 'The Flatiron' (photogravure 6⅝×3⁵⁄₁₆ inches), no date (Collection, The Museum of Modern Art, New York).

pre-war Paris paintings that stress the city are virtually always gay and, with the exception of those of a few politically-committed artists who will be discussed later, almost never hint at the existence of factories or of the industrial poor on the fringes of town.

New York was a very different city from Paris in 1900. It had few monuments from the past and, since it was growing by leaps and bounds, was rapidly becoming architecturally the most modern of cities. By 1900, the Brooklyn Bridge, much more prominent in the cityscape then than now, had been completed, a subway was being built, and the horizon of lower Broadway, already known as the 'Great White Way', was quickly becoming cluttered with skyscrapers. Just as Paris had come to be symbolized by its tree-lined boulevards, the Seine and its bridges, and the Eiffel Tower, so New York was also developing its characteristic symbols: the Brooklyn Bridge, the skyscrapers and the 'canyons' between them, and the bright lights of Broadway. However, in New York the severe overcrowding and poverty of hordes of European immigrants could not be overlooked [4].

Representational artists depicted New York in two major ways up to 1914. Such painters as Childe Hassam, Maurice Prendergast, and William Glackens, who had learned about Impressionism in Paris, painted lively images of New York's promenades and pleasure spots. Stieglitz, Edward Steichen, and Alvin Langdon Coburn, the major New York photographers of their generation, employed the soft focus then in vogue to blur New York's modern edges and humanized the new skyscrapers by capturing Impressionist climatic effects – in particular, snow (figure 4.2). Other artists, while also undergoing some French influences, recognized New York's modernity and chose to depict a wider range of subjects – and some of them absolutely banal – in a more realistic manner. The members of the Eight, a stylistically diverse group which included Prendergast and Glackens, were subjected to ridicule as the 'Ash Can School' for their preoccupation with the ordinary [5]. Under their brushes the ordinary nevertheless became picturesque, cheerful, and often positively pretty. John Sloan, the most prolific chronicler of New York among the Eight, was fascinated by daily life as glimpsed from rooftops, elevated trains, and apartment windows. His broad range of subject matter included crowded street scenes, unexpected happenings in the street, private moments in everyday life, child's play in drab back alleys, and the new look of the city traversed by elevated trains. George Bellows, not a member of the Eight, had similar interests, and he produced an image of the New York poor which tells a great deal about these realists' views of their metropolis. His 1913 work, 'Cliff Dwellers' (figure 4.3) depicts a neighbourhood of tenements jammed with life. Laundry hangs from above, people crowd the streets between drab apartment houses, housewives gossip or fan themselves in the gleaming sunlight, a group of immaculate-looking, well-behaved children is strongly lit by a ray of light. There is no mass here, but rather a collection of lively, picturesque individuals; nor is this a slum, but rather a sort of urban village. New York realists, unlike most of their Paris contemporaries, did recognize the industrial poor, the overcrowding, and the modernity of skyscrapers and subways, but they depicted these things with enjoyment, optimism, and in the soft-focus manner which blurs away the warts on the city's face [6].

German artists after Impressionism made a point of highlighting rather than minimizing the urban warts. Early-twentieth-century Berlin was quite different from Paris and New York, and there is an especially striking difference in the Germans' philosophical reactions to metropolitan life. True, the German Impressionists, Max Liebermann and Lovis Corinth, shared their French and American contemporaries' predilections for attractive slices of urban life [7]; and even the early Kandinsky, influenced by the Fauves, painted a gay, sun-filled

FIGURE 4.3. George Bellows, 'Cliff Dwellers',
1913. Oil on canvas, 39½×41½ inches
(Los Angeles County Museum of Art,
Los Angeles County Funds).

though indistinct view of Munich in 1908. But after about 1910, most artists in
Germany either ceased painting the metropolis altogether or else were among the
first visual artists to point to urban alienation.

The extent to which discomfort in the city is a phenomenon of the Northern, or
Protestant, countries would bear investigation. Robert Rosenblum has suggested
the existence since Romanticism of a Northern tradition in painting independent of
the mainstream Paris modernist tradition. The major non-Parisian characteristics
are an extremely emotional perception of nature and a mystical religiosity
expressed without the aid of traditional Christian iconography [8]. A massive
rejection of urban life by Northern artists would certainly be a logical accompani-
ment of their intense love of nature. It is clear, moreover, that the urban paintings
of the Berlin Expressionists, which will be discussed in a moment, were influenced
by the Oslo street scenes of Edvard Munch, which stress the individual's anxiety
and isolation within the urban crowd, and by James Ensor's claustrophobically-
packed, semi-Christian, semi-Socialist Brussels street scenes of the late 1890s. Since
Berlin is my present theme, I will confine myself here to a specific look at German
artists' relations with their capital city. (I include the pre-war Expressionists here,
rather than in the next section dealing with abstract art, because their canvases
remained insistently representational, however violent their colour, and however
distorted their form.)

The giant city was something new in Germany as, until 1870, the country had industrialized only to a moderate extent, and had had no central government. Cultural activity had been divided among the various courts according to each prince's desire or financial ability to patronize the arts. Berlin had little that was special to recommend it to the painters of 1900 except for its fast-growing status as a capital and cultural centre. As the capital of Prussia and, after 1871, of the German Empire, Berlin had grown exceedingly fast, and had also been industrialized rapidly along with the rest of Germany. The Brandenburg Gate and the nearby neighbourhood begun under Frederick the Great were the city's only outstanding landmarks. Modern artists positively loathed the bombastic new boulevards and gigantic monuments erected by the two Williams after unification [9].

Moreover, German thinkers of the turn-of-the-century were extremely wary of the metropolis [10]. Historians, philosophers, sociologists, and art critics pejoratively linked urban life, materialism, superficiality, rampant individualism, and hyper-intellectualism under the label 'civilization', to which they opposed the healthy values of 'culture', consisting of the spirituality, traditional folk life, and closeness to nature which they considered native to the German people, and which, they felt, was being submerged by imported mechanical industry and middle-class acquisitiveness. This criticism of modernity, labelled in various ways, had become very widespread in Germany around 1900 [11]; and I am convinced that elements of it are echoed in the works of the Berlin Expressionists, who made no secret of their mistrust of French modernism (despite the great deal they took from it), their intensely mystical feelings about nature, their insistence on showing their hand labour in their finished works, their search for a renewal of spirituality in non-Western folk cultures, and their discomfort in the city.

The Expressionist movement in painting began around 1905 in Dresden, which was then a medium-sized provincial city, rich in monuments from the past and open to attractive countryside. The young painters were a sort of artistic *Wandervögel*, who would hike through the countryside with their easels and tubes of intensest colours, sometimes taking along models who would pose nude for them in isolated spots. Their paintings mainly consisted, then and later, of strongly emotionalized depictions of nature and nudes; and they strongly favoured the woodcut, a medium which harked back to the pre-typographic era.

Around 1910 most of them moved to Berlin in order to take advantage of the greater opportunities for exhibition offered by the Secession movement and the interest of dealers and collectors in their work. While they enjoyed the colourful Berlin street life and the loose girls from the dancehalls, who often appear, clothed or nude, in their paintings, some of them considered urban daily life hateful and did not remain long in Berlin, while others settled in quiet, out-of-the-way neighbourhoods [12]. Most never depicted the city itself at all; for the others, Berlin paintings form a minute proportion of their output. Only Ernst Ludwig Kirchner depicted Berlin repeatedly, particularly in 1913–14, and then in works whose spatial distortions and indifferent or hostile figures are deliberately disturbing [13].

FIGURE 4.4. Ernst Ludwig Kirchner, 'Berlin Street Scene' (Potsdamer Platz), c.1913. Coloured chalk (courtesy of the Busch-Reisinger Museum, Harvard University).

Pedestrians in a crowd turn their backs to the viewer and their faces away from one another; streets curve or jut away from one another at radical angles, leaving a few lonely pedestrians stranded on precarious standing-spaces or lost in the concrete void of the street; absurdly dressed-up matrons loom larger than life over the rapidly-receding streets and buildings; pedestrians are now dwarfed by architecture, now dwarf it (figure 4.4). These paintings, like many of the critiques of 'civilization', present the metropolis as a place where human contact has become impossible, where anonymity and money reign. I know of no work of art outside Germany in this period which bears so intense a message about the city.

There is one other German painter who deserves mention here, and that is the eccentric Ludwig Meidner, who was a very peculiar Expressionist. Influenced by Van Gogh, Marx, and the Italian Futurists, he repeatedly painted scenes of apocalyptic urban destruction before 1914, but under the guise both of promoting social revolution and of embracing modern life. 'Let us paint what is close to us', he advised fellow artists in 1913, 'our city world! The tumultous streets, the elegance of iron suspension bridges, gasometers, which hang like mountains of white clouds, the shouting colouration of buses and fast locomotives, the waving telephone wires (are they not like songs?), the harlequinades of the publicity columns, and then the night . . . the big city night . . .' [14]. The meaning of his paintings, full of explosions, tiny figures seeking shelter, and barricades, is ostensibly that the present city must be destroyed before the true Socialist city can be built – but it is curious, and reminiscent of the Expressionists previously discussed, that when Meidner paints the new post-revolutionary order he winds up with an 'apocalyptic landscape' (figure 4.5) in which a blissful, newly-liberated man lies nude in nature before the ruins of a city.

Meidner, though no realist, brings me to the subject of one further realist mode of viewing the metropolis before the First World War. This is the work, dealing with Paris and Berlin, of several artists from various countries who were politically aware, if not active, before 1914, and who were concerned with achieving social justice for the poor [15]. This heterogeneous group of artists, not all of whom knew about each other, includes the Pointillist painters Georges Seurat, Paul Signac, and Maximilien Luce, who had anarchist leanings; the illustrators Théophile Steinlen and Heinrich Zille; the German realist painter Hans Baluschek; the Dutch painter Kees Van Dongen and Czech painter Frank Kupka, both of whom drew leftist caricatures before turning to modernism [16].

FIGURE 4.5. Ludwig Meidner, 'Revolution' (Apocalyptic Landscape), 1913. Oil on canvas (Nationalgalerie, Staatliche Museen Preussischer Kulturbesitz, West Berlin).

FIGURE 4.6. Théophile Alexandre Steinlen, 'There's nothing for anyone but dogs on this boulevard', from *Dans la vie*, Paris, 1890.

Il n'y en a que pour les chiens sur ce boulevard!

To all these artists – despite the great differences among them – the city was the scene of proletarian suffering. They represented it with full awareness of smoking factories, overcrowded and filthy tenements, the stunted lives and early deaths of the poor. And yet some of them also emphasized humour, bringing out the humanity and earthy naturalness of common folk. Here we find a backdrop of bleak streets, coal-blackened houses, sometimes with an undifferentiated human mass signalling the depersonalization of modern life, more often with picturesque individuals trying to cope with life in a slum, finding entertainment where they can, and philosophizing on their lot (figure 4.6). Or else, as with Seurat and many French caricaturists, there is an emphasis on satirizing the rich in their spendthrift enjoyment of the city [17].

These artists were critical of the metropolis, but they did not condemn it outright or dream it out of existence, any more than Marx dreamt the industrial system out of existence. Their political stance compelled them to register and reproduce what other artists screened out. As we shall see later on, adverse economic and political circumstances would compel later artists to view the metropolis in a similar light.

Abstract Art, 1910–1922: Cubism and Futurism

I mean to use the term 'abstract art' here in the broadest possible sense, to include not only the work of artists who aimed at totally non-objective styles (and who, as we shall see later on, often stopped short of a total excision of reality), but also that of artists such as the Cubists, the Futurists and the American Precisionists, whose goals in continuing to represent objects were highly intellectualized, or who represented objects less for their own sake than as examples of pure form. One might think that the work of these artists contains little more than fragments of the metropolis and that it would contribute little to our subject. On the contrary: the metropolis is at the origin of much of abstract art, and abstractionists have taken especial pains to represent it.

While there are major exceptions, such as the painting of Kandinsky, most abstract styles came into existence, beginning around 1910, in part as responses to the rapid industrial and urban transformation that had been going on in various countries for at least the previous fifty years. This is the case, first of all, because a machine, the camera, had provided a more accurate means than painting for recording visual reality, and artists now felt freed from any obligation to be copyists. Much more important, however, was an awakening on the part of many artists to their modern surroundings and a concern to find means of representation adequate to the look of modern engineering and the dynamism of the metropolis. The search for ways of representing modern life led artists to break up objects into various intersecting planes, in order to show multiple perspectives; to multiply images of the same object in order to suggest movement; and ultimately to leave reality itself behind in a search for images of pure mechanical form or pure dynamism [18].

As a part of this search, some of the first abstract artists attempted to paint the metropolis on a far vaster scale than the 'slices of life' provided by realists. In huge, highly-ambitious works, several artists attempted between 1910 and 1922 to render the essence of their cities through complex synthetic images blending observed fragments of urban space with popular symbolic representations. In the process of constructing them the human element often fell by the wayside; the metropolis of abstract art is more often than not a thing of stone, glass and iron, a thing of abstract forces and movements in which the artists take delight, but from which they have all but banished the human beings.

Picasso played with popular symbols of Paris and New York in two of the costumes he designed for *Parade,* the whimsical ballet of 1917 on which he collaborated with Jean Cocteau and Erik Satie [19]. His two sideshow 'managers' representing the two cities are walking Cubist sculptures; each city is defined by readily recognizable details: treetops, a moustache, a huge pipe, and the suggestion of an accordion for the Paris Manager; skyscrapers, a stovepipe hat, and a megaphone for the New York Manager. These costumes are humorous in the typical Picasso manner, and they transmit an enjoyment of the city that also appears in many other abstract works.

The early Cubists, mainly concerned with analysing objects in space and transposing views from various perspectives on to flat canvas, took from the city very small and private things, not always necessarily urban things, that served their purposes: the bottles, glasses and fruit on a café table; the juxtaposition of café table and guitarist or café table and newspaper; an accidental collage of publicity on an urban wall. By 1910 the so-called 'Orphists', Cubists with more dynamic interests, were out in the streets, using the Cubist method to study the refraction of light amid sky, streets, buildings and foliage; and the Italian Futurists, whose movement I am including here because it was launched from Paris and took Paris as its model metropolis, were depicting the urban scene as the prime example of everything modern and mobile.

In the work of Paris artists, the Eiffel Tower, that enormous but graceful mass of girders and rivets, became the symbol *par excellence* – and a combative one – for the beauty of the new technological age. Robert Delaunay included it in almost every painting he did from 1910 until the mid-1920s. He was the first to attempt a large-scale synthesis of a city, 'The City of Paris' of 1910–12, a gigantic Cubist frieze showing the Three Graces flanked by the Eiffel Tower and by the Seine with its bridges, barges and typical Parisian apartment houses. The nudes, who sport Cubist faces reminiscent of the 'Demoiselles d'Avignon' though rather less brutal than Picasso's, are not there as a bit of nostalgia for classical art (as is the beautiful nude in the 'masterpiece' of Zola's imaginary Impressionist, Claude Lantier), but rather to symbolize Paris's centuries-long tradition of art patronage and to show the classical in good company with technology and the metropolis. (That the presence of the Graces is not merely a bit of unexcised academicism is attested by Delaunay's inclusion of one of them atop the Pont de la Concorde in an Eiffel Tower painting of thirteen years later, 'La Tour' of 1925.)

Fernand Léger, too, had a life-long interest in the metropolis, beginning in the Cubist period with images of figures in a discomposed city of architectural fragments and foliage, or else mechanical forms. In the inter-war period he painted many works which blend fragments of girders, buildings, trees, railings, and bridges, along with monumental, often robot-like figures, in attempts to represent the city's multiplicity rather than any city in itself. Francis Picabia translated his enthusiasm for New York during a 1913 visit into huge non-representational canvases of mechanical forms. Other French and American artists inspired by Cubism were more modest in the scope of their paintings, but frequently represented fragments of the city or tried to suggest its dynamism. The New York painters, Max Weber and John Marin, adapted Cubism in very different ways to depict the colour and fast pace of Manhattan. All these artists were enraptured with their modern vision, but a few others had some doubts; the empty streets of Abraham Walkowitz's cubistic 'improvisations' on New York skyscrapers of 1915–16, and C. W. B. Nevinson's 'Soul of a Soul-less City', painted during the English Vorticist's trip to New York in 1919, refer to the claustrophobic effect of the skyscrapers and to the metropolis's loss of human scale [20].

In the 'Initial Manifesto of Futurism', launched from Paris in 1909, the poet Filippo Tommaso Marinetti, writing for a group of young Italian painters, proclaimed their shared artistic intentions:

We shall sing of the great crowds in the excitement of labour, pleasure and rebellion; of the multi-coloured and polyphonic surf of revolutions in modern capital cities; of the nocturnal vibrations of arsenals and workshops beneath their violent electric moons; of the greedy stations swallowing smoking snakes; of factories suspended from the clouds by their strings of smoke; of bridges leaping like gymnasts over the diabolical cutlery of sunbathed rivers . . . [21].

Contemporaneously with the Cubists and Orphists, they attempted to adapt static easel painting to the pace of the metropolis by suggesting movement, sound, and even smells with a tightly-packed fabric of repeating images and intersecting planes. Exalting many aspects of the modern city that are usually considered most worthy of criticism and which were carefully omitted by most of the Cubists – noise, smoke, crowds, traffic, rebellion – they painted crowded railway stations, moving trains, political riots, autos, street lights, pleasure spots, and the construction of the metropolis itself. One of the great works of Futurism is Gino Severini's 'Dynamic Hieroglyphic of the Bal Tabarin' of 1912, painted in Paris, which renders the press of dancers on a Montmartre dancefloor by a jumble of brightly-painted, fragmented images, with pieces of dresses, hairdos, glasses and tables, musical instruments, and lettering bouncing against one another in a syncopated rhythm which suggest both music and flashing signs. Perhaps the most ambitious Futurist painting is Umberto Boccioni's 'The City Rises' of 1911

FIGURE 4.7. Umberto Boccioni, study for 'The City Rises', 1910. Crayon and chalk. Sheet 23⅛×34⅛ inches (Collection, The Museum of Modern Art, New York [Mrs. Simon Guggenheim Fund]).

(figure 4.7), depicting the construction of a new metropolis – Milan, which in the Futurists' minds was becoming Italy's even more modern answer to Paris – by a literal image of horsepower amid the scaffolding of modern constructions, factory chimneys, bridges, tunnels and trams.

The most grandiose city painting of all in our period was done by an Italian who was influenced both by Delaunay and by Futurism, and who lived in New York: Joseph Stella. A middle-class immigrant to New York in 1896, Stella was torn all his life between the gentle countryside and antique traditions of his native village near Naples and the dynamism of the most modern city in the world. His work moves between these two poles, now hard-edged and modern in subject matter, now delicate and classically inspired, but he is famous mainly for his modernist representations of the Brooklyn Bridge as symbol of New York.

The Brooklyn Bridge was probably the most frequently depicted New York site between 1900 and 1940. It owes its appeal, I think, to the combination of its starkly modern network of steel cables and its graceful neo-Gothic stone pylons, a blending of old and new. Moreover, when seen from the Brooklyn side, it has a backdrop of Manhattan skyscrapers, another standard New York symbol. In drawings by C. W. B. Nevinson ('Looking Through Brooklyn Bridge', 1919–20) and Louis Lozowick ('Brooklyn Bridge', 1929) and also in one of Walker Evans's photographs of the bridge done in 1929, there is a realistic juxtaposition of cables and skyscrapers or cables and pylons reproduced as pure form [22]. The Cubist Albert Gleizes, however, much taken with the bridge while in New York during the First World War, went the abstractionist route and painted jumbles of cables, pylons, skyscrapers, mixed with solar reflections (and in one work with wavy forms suggesting a roller-coaster) which approach pure abstraction.

Stella almost certainly knew Gleizes's paintings, which were exhibited in New York [23], and they probably influenced him to paint the first of three ambitious Brooklyn Bridge works done over twenty years, in all three of which he balanced a legible depiction of the bridge, seen head-on from the Brooklyn side and symmetrically centred, with various abstract elements. The bridge, for him, was 'the shrine containing all the efforts of the new civilization of AMERICA . . .' [24], efforts characterized by electricity and steel, skyscrapers and bridges.

The second of these Brooklyn Bridge works forms part of Stella's attempt to sum up the entire city, 'New York Interpreted', painted between 1920 and 1922. This is an enormous work, 8¼ feet high in the centre and 22½ feet wide, consisting of five panels, which is deliberately suggestive of an altarpiece, with its central section higher than the rest, a symmetrical structure, and a predella which is both decorative and symbolic at the bottom of each section. The central panel, 'Skyscrapers', announces the analogy often made (and specifically made by Stella) between Manhattan's attenuated buildings and the heavenward flight of the Gothic cathedral; it is flanked by two semi-symmetrical, wildly-coloured panels representing the 'Great White Way' with its electric lights and flashing signs (figure

FIGURE 4.8. Joseph Stella, 'White Way', from 'New York Interpreted', 1922. Oil on canvas. 54×88¼ inches. (Collection of the Newark Museum, Felix Fuld Bequest).

FIGURE 4.9. Joseph Stella, 'The Bridge', from 'New York Interpreted', 1922. Oil on canvas. 54×88¼ inches. (Collection of the Newark Museum, Felix Fuld Bequest).

4.8), and then again by two outer panels, a brooding depiction of the Battery, 'The Port', on the far left and the Brooklyn Bridge on the far right (figure 4.9). The work evokes Italian religious art, medieval stained glass, and also musical polyphony, but it is painted in a hard-edged, abstract style and, consonant with the Futurists' rhetoric though not with their manner of representation, it proclaims the power of

FIGURE 4.10. Paul Citroën, 'Metropolis', 1923. Collage (Prentenkabinet, Kunsthistorisch Institut der Rijksuniversiteit te Leiden, by permission of the artist).

the metropolis and depicts the urban pulsations of light, noise and traffic. It thus both proclaims the city for itself and assimilates it into age-old artistic traditions.

On closer inspection this painting has an ambivalent meaning which is confirmed by Stella's several verbal statements about his feelings toward New York [25]. Here is what Stella says at his most depressed in a sort of prose poem directly referring to 'New York Interpreted':

> New York . . . monstrous dream, chimeric reality, Oriental delight, Shakespearian nightmare, unheard-of riches, frightful poverty. Gigantic jaw of irregular teeth, shiny black like a bulldozer, funereal gray, white and brilliant like a minaret in the sunlight, dull, cavernous black like Wall Street after dark. Clamorous with lights, strident with sounds – that's Broadway, the White Way – at night, blazing and mad with pleasure-seeking . . . The skyscrapers like bandages covering the sky, stifling our breath, life shabby and mean . . . sinister port where the energies drawn from all over the world become flabby and spent . . . with its dreadful, closed windows, barren of flowers [26].

Stella elsewhere referred to New York as a mixture of the spiritual and the crassly materialistic, and he repeatedly referred to his own discomfort in a city where the architecture cut out the sky. 'New York Interpreted' conveys the ambivalence of Stella's vision. Its lights are artificial, garish, yet grandiose, its darkness (as in 'The Port') menacing, yet enlivened with gay flashes of light. Above all, the space is ambiguous. Seeming, at first, to open out into a vast interior, it is actually uncomfortably shallow; with the exception of 'The Port', which is sombre, it has virtually no sky, and abstract elements, including one pylon in 'The Bridge', create prison bars on the surface of each panel, locking the observer out and the architecture in. Irma Jaffe has aptly termed this painting 'a prison-altar' [27].

I would like to evoke here one final abstract urban synthesis, this time mocking the modern city and packing all the dynamism of skyscrapers and traffic into a tiny format: Paul Citroën's witty Dadaist collage of 1923, 'Metropolis' (figure 4.10).

The New Realism of the 1920s

Immediately following the First World War there was a large-scale revival of interest in representation. Even many of the pre-war abstractionists either returned to realist styles or included more legible images in their abstract works. But Impressionism no longer had much influence on these new realist works. The new form now developed, styled 'Magical Realism' or 'New Objectivity' (*Neue Sachlichkeit*) by various critics, was, on the whole, sharp-focus; photographers of the time rejected the softening effects popular before the war, and painters emulated the extraordinary clarity that the lens was now giving to objects and, in a turn toward past art, the sharper-than-life quality of much Northern primitive and Italian *quattrocento* art. The new style was applied to many purposes, not all of which serve our look at the metropolis. Surrealism, for instance, inward-turned toward dreams, fantasies and myth, showed virtually no interest in the metropolis after De

Chirico's pre-war scenes of dreamlike urban voids. But it was applied primarily to the metropolis by a group of painters in Berlin and by a few others working in related styles in Paris and New York. The major characteristics of their works, other than the clarity of outline, are an interest in banal subjects (made to seem eerily important by minute attention to detail), an emphasis on accurate reproduction of objects, often a juxtaposition of incompatible but immaculately-represented objects, and an elimination of visible brushstroke which makes the images appear to be objectively 'caught' rather than deliberately chosen by the artist [28].

Berlin was a great cultural centre in the 1920s, but also an extremely troubled metropolis after the German defeat in the war and the ensuing revolutionary movements; and the Berlin realism is, among other things, a statement about these conditions, informed by political choice but also by the pre-war Expressionists' anti-urban bent. Wieland Schmied's list of the major motifs in European New Realist painting applies best to that of Berlin: 'The street as showplace of the metropolis, of the blossoming and humiliation of the human being, as place of confrontation, misery, loneliness, seduction. The world of publicity, the demi-monde of the whores. The cosmopolitanism of the boulevards and the poverty of the suburban quarters' [29]. While this realism rejects the individualistic outcry and gesture of the Expressionists, it perpetuates – this time in much more specific detail – their attack on 'civilization' (in the German understanding of the word circa 1900). It also displays an exacerbated ambiguity of feeling about the metropolis, because these realists were died-in-the-wool Berliners.

Let us look at yet one more grandiose work which, again in the guise of an altarpiece, aspires to sum up a city: Otto Dix's 'Big City Triptych' of 1927–28 (figure 4.11). In the central of three panels, 'high society', characterized by nearly featureless men in tuxedos and painted, overbearing women, dances frenetically but without enjoyment to the tunes of jazz in a hotly-lit, enclosed space; in the side panels, war cripples vie unsuccessfully for attention with the garishly-painted ladies of the street, who are scarcely distinguishable from the fine ladies at the dance.

The cheerlessness and scathing social satire of this and similar paintings resulted from Dix's and other young artists' experiences in the war, their resultant loss of respect for authority, their assignment of blame for the war to capitalism as well as the Prussian military machine, their turn, not formal in every case, to Communism in the wake of the Bolshevik revolution, and again their acute disillusionment over the savage suppression of Communists by the German democracy after 1918. But it also smacks of a traditional artistic interest in all the most extreme forms of human life which stood out from the metropolitan crowd – whores, transvestites, cripples, aristocrats, alcoholics, murderers, even artists and intellectuals.

The young George Grosz loved the idea of the metropolis; during the war he drew comic scenes of New York, where he had never been, replete with the usual

FIGURE 4.11. Otto Dix, 'Big City Triptych', 1927–28. Oil on wood (Galerie der Stadt Stuttgart).

symbols for that city. But he always had viciously satirical eyes for Berlin, and his satires heightened during the war into all-out attacks on the military and the comfortable war-enthusiasts at home. At war's end he became a Communist and worked to expose the evils of the city as dominated by capitalism. Rather than a strict realism, his style used Cubist and Futurist elements to depict a topsy-turvy city of fat capitalists, semi-nude women, robots, hypocritical preachers, firing squads for political dissenters, claustrophobia, and artificial light (since one of the besetting characteristics of the metropolis is that it lives at night) [30].

Max Beckmann, apolitical but profoundly disturbed by his wartime experiences as a volunteer orderly in a front hospital [31], set out after the war to expose the alienation and brutality spawned by the war, the war's loss, and by urban life in general. 'Precisely now', he wrote in 1918 '. . . I feel the need to remain among men. In the city. We [artists] must take part in all the misery that will come. We must abandon our hearts and nerves to the horrible cry of pain of the poor, betrayed people' [32]. His Berlin paintings and prints of the early 1920s combine Cubist influences with the New Realism in rendering alienation and pain, from the void of unpeopled streets, to crowded scenes of whores and cripples, to fantasies of excruciating torture (figure 4.12).

Along with Dix, Grosz and Beckmann, other Berlin realists of the period, such as Karl Hubbuch, Heinrich Davringhausen, Christian Schad, and the Flemish political illustrator Frans Masereel, exposed the metropolis as the place of crime, perversion, mechanization, hyper-intellectualism, and economic and sexual

FIGURE 4.12. Max Beckmann, 'The Night', 1918–19. Oil on
canvas (Kunstsammlung Nordrhein-Westfalen, Düsseldorf).

exploitation. In their paintings the metropolis appears as a mass of moderately-tall buildings (Berlin, of course, had no skyscrapers), sometimes in a wished-for state of collapse, sometimes impeccably ordered and seemingly indestructable; or as a messy street with paper posters, neon signs and disreputable-looking loiterers; or as a skyline seen through a café or bedroom window, or conversely, as a street offering views into bedrooms. It is full of people, sometimes in mobs, but they are caricatures, puppets with exaggerated physical characteristics but without personality. The inhabitants of these scenes are mass-men, decadents, or freaks, and they are offered no hope of redemption.

Many artists of the 1920s in other cities practised sharp-focus realism, but none that I know of in such a politicized or misanthropic vein. The fact that both Paris and New York were victors in the war is certainly relevant to this contrast. The realist works of those two cities, sharp-focus or not, study reality for its own sake (as in Georgia O'Keeffe's several paintings of skyscrapers which look like jewels in the neon-lit night or are cut by flares from the noontime sun); display cheerfully the urban sophistication the Berliners viewed so ambivalently (as in works by Raoul Dufy, Van Dongen, Lartigue, and Tamara de Lempicka); describe wistfully or satirize gently a moment in daily life (for example, in photographs by André Kertesz or the early paintings of Raphael Soyer and Reginald Marsh); or, in the wonderfully calm, almost minimal manner of an Edward Hopper, dwell tenderly on urban loneliness [33]. An especially apt comparison with Dix's triptych is Thomas Hart Benton's mural of 1930–31, 'City Activities', in the New School for Social Research [34], painted at a time when New York was facing economic crisis. It dwells, somewhat satirically perhaps, on such New York pastimes as movie-going, jazz, burlesque, boxing, and revivalist religion in the night-time ambience favoured by the Berlin artists and by Stella, but it is a populist celebration of America and of all the cultural delights the metropolis has to offer (figure 4.13).

FIGURE 4.13. Thomas Hart Benton, 'City Activities', detail, 1930–31. Mural (The New School for Social Research, New York City).

**Social Realism:
New York in the
1930s**

The 1929 stock market crash provided New York artists with a new perspective which led them to a more critical and politically-sophisticated view of their city. As unemployment, vagrancy, soup lines, and general misery grew, New York's streets teemed with a poverty they had not known since the height of immigration before 1914. And the plight of the poor seemed all the more poignant now that all America was threatened with destitution. The change in New York realist art within just a few years is dramatic. Painters and photographers suddenly forged a realism that did not prettify – though it was still often good-humoured – and that dwelt on the hunched shoulders of the Depression's victims, the indifferent faces of pedestrians, and the actual appearance of the city's brick walls.

Whether or not individual paintings of the time refer to the direct effects of the Depression, they depict a city which consists almost entirely of its inhabitants, shown with psychological insight and with reference to the misery of unemployment or the dehumanizing effects of job and commute, to the discomforts of the homeless or ill-housed, to the isolation of the individual amid the throng. Works by Raphael Soyer and Reginald Marsh depict vagrants in shelters or public parks,

FIGURE 4.14. Raphael Soyer, 'Office Girls', 1936. Oil on canvas (Collection of the Whitney Museum of American Art, New York).

breadlines, the blank or fatigued faces of pedestrians (figure 4.14), the rather sinister mixture of travellers and sleepers in the subway. Marsh also mocked the continuing pleasures of the rich and poked gentle fun at fashionable young ladies and at the mixture of bums, alcoholics and ordinary folk in busy neighbourhoods. Ben Shahn, in the late 1930s, emphasized the isolation of the ordinary person in a cityscape of blind façades and empty lots [35].

It is interesting to follow George Grosz's development after his arrival in New York, the city of his youthful dreams, in flight from Hitler in 1933. A panorama of Manhattan painted soon after [36] proclaims him joyously disarmed before the spectacle of skyscrapers and ships in the harbour. He continued to paint satirical social glimpses of crowded urban streets, now actually much like Marsh's, which had probably been influenced by the earlier Grosz. But for Grosz, who had problems gaining acceptance in New York because of his political reputation, the irony henceforth has more charm than bite.

The New Deal agencies that were set up, beginning in 1935, to provide work for destitute artists, the most important of which was the Works Projects Administration (WPA), institutionalized the sort of realism that had been forged *ad hoc* during the several previous years. Painters and sculptors worked on everything from giant murals in public buildings to mosaics in subway stations; the best American photographers of that generation were given the opportunity collectively to

FIGURE 4.15. Lewis W. Hine, 'Empire State Building', c.1930. Black and white photograph (International Museum of Photography, George Eastman House, Rochester, N.Y.).

produce a portrait of lower-class America. In New York, Berenice Abbott and Walker Evans continued the work of two great social photographers of the turn-of-the-century, Jacob Riis and Lewis W. Hine, who had thoroughly documented immigrant life. Hine was still active in 1930, and he made a series of photographs of construction workers on the Empire State Building, perched high above the city on girders, that are a tribute both to modern labour and to New York's continuing power to exhilarate (figure 4.15). Abbott's and Evans's New York photographs, whether or not produced under government projects, generally follow the painters' interest in the plight of ordinary people but also give attention to documenting the look of buildings and streets [37].

The government sponsorship also forged a 'heroic realist' style not really very different – class-consciousness and racism aside – from the Soviet- and Fascist-sponsored realism, or from public art in any Western country at the time. Here the tone is – has to be – patriotic and optimistic, and this art celebrates in monumental yet contemporary terms the constructor and forces of industry. One has only to compare a Max Weber painting of the 1930s with one of his earlier Cubist paintings to see the appeal of this new heroism for artists at the time [38]. The WPA murals create a myth of urban and rural dynamism and harmony in which there is brotherhood among all the inhabitants of the great melting pot.

Abstract Art Revisited, 1920–1945

Like the realism of the time, abstract art after the high-point of Cubism and Futurism was, as a rule, sharp-focus. It also tended to be small in scale and modest in scope: the New Realists had now assumed the task of depicting the city as a whole. Abstractionists henceforth depicted little chunks of the urban environment in a pristine style, or else transformed visual aspects of the city into totally abstract forms. In addition, a few artists began making art *out of* the city, which also means, *de facto*, about the city. I am thinking of Kurt Schwitters's witty collages of paper refuse furnished by the gutter, and of the *objets trouvés* of Marcel Duchamp, Man Ray and others, which would greatly influence post-World War Two sculptors.

The cityscape frequently appears in abstract art of the inter-war period through the unusual perspectives it provides from the height of its modern structures, or else upon those structures from the ground. The city is thus metamorphosed into sheer patterning and formal interplay. Already in 1912 Alvin Langdon Coburn had photographed the 'Octopus' in Central Park from a tall building, recording a picturesque pattern in the snow. In 1915 Paul Strand had photographed Wall Street in the slanting, late afternoon light as a powerful contrast of brilliant street with huge, shadowed windows, an impressive conjunction of canyon-street with massive modern architecture which dwarfs the pedestrians moving toward the source of light. Similar images were to become common in abstract art of the 1920s. The photographs of Laszlo Moholy-Nagy, Alexandr Rodchenko, Kertesz, and the young Walker Evans show this interest in seeing the city from an unaccustomed

FIGURE 4.16. Laszlo Moholy-Nagy, 'From the Radio Tower, Berlin, 1928', 1928. Silver print, 11⅜×8½ inches (Collection, The Museum of Modern Art, New York. Given anonymously).

angle or seeing patterns in the real world through perspectival distortions (figure 4.16). Delaunay's Eiffel Tower paintings of the 1920s are often colourful non-Cubist studies in perspective, in which the tower is seen at uncomfortable angles, from the close vicinity looking up, from under the legs, or from the sky looking down. And the Precisionists, including Charles Sheeler, Preston Dickinson and Niles Spencer, turned chunks of New York architecture, often seen from an unusual vantage point, into cool planar patterns [39].

I would like to suggest, finally, through three disparate examples chosen from many possible ones, that the metropolis looms large – behind the scenes, as it were – in the 'imagery' of non-representational art. It is the major subject in the work of Stuart Davis, an American artist much influenced by Cubism and Futurism, whose intensely-coloured works never ceased to 'represent' the movement, traffic, noise, and publicity of the metropolis while growing ever more abstract [40]. Over thirty years of his work, one can watch Davis's unified images of urban streets and signs of the 1920s progressively dissolve into a jumble of colourful, clashing forms and calligraphic elements that evoke the confusion and cacophony of Manhattan.

FIGURE 4.17. Mark Tobey, 'Broadway', c.1940. Tempera on masonite (Metropolitan Museum of Art, Arthur H. Hearn Fund, 1942).

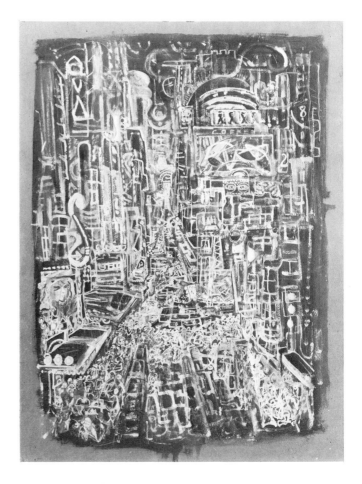

Exhibit two: Mark Tobey, the intensely private, mystical painter whose mature style consists of squiggles of white paint floated on a neutral, usually greyish, ground. Tobey's work largely originates, however, in a series of views of the 'Great White Way' and other intense urban streets, influenced by Stella but already much less colourful, that he did in the late 1930s and early 1940s (figure 4.17). The frenzied jumble of buildings, signs, theatre marquees, traffic and pedestrians in these works is painted in floating white outline – already Tobey's characteristic 'white writing'. Once again, one can follow the painter's development over ten years and see the forms become smaller, less distinct, and finally totally detached from visual reality [41].

My final example is Piet Mondrian, the great Dutch painter who represented nothing but rectangles and squares during the inter-war period, and who spent the final few years in his life, 1940–44, as a refugee in New York. There Mondrian's paintings, minimal though they remained, changed drastically, and it seems evident that the change is related to two things: his love, which had already developed in Europe but blossomed in New York, for the syncopated rhythms of boogie-woogie; and the Manhattan cityscape – the street grid, the rectangularity of the skyscrapers – and, perhaps, the syncopated rhythm of New York life as well [42]. Mondrian's last paintings, 'Broadway Boogie-Woogie' and 'Victory Boogie-woogie', contain a proliferation of tiny squares, a superposition of contrasting squares, and a complexity of grid which was new for him. The primary colours on a white ground – his trademark – are here made to flicker unevenly in a way that suggests music, dance, traffic, the Manhattan ground plan, or the look of skyscraper-façades with their rows of windows, so that New York is indisputably present in these works of utmost geometric purity.

With the arrival of Mondrian and other prominent European artists, New York became the centre of artistic innovation, and the architecture and crowds of Manhattan have continued to influence the canvases of the Abstract Expressionists, the images of many post-war photographers, and the explicitly satirical images of Pop Art. Despite our increased consciousness of the human misery and ecological disaster emanating from the metropolis, many of our artists continue to be fascinated by the 'place of the new'.

Conclusions

The metropolis provided artists with a new 'landscape', a variety of human subjects, a range of mechanical and industrial objects, and a concentration of movement and event which were new to art. Most artists – including hundreds of un-innovative ones I have not discussed here – chose to represent traditionally picturesque aspects of it, emphasizing famous sights and leisure occupations, in styles which range from straight realism to extreme *avant-garde* experimentation. While their dialogue with metropolitan modernity caused many artists to assert the need for radical pictorial innovation, it is surprising to see the extent to which modern artists strove to render the metropolis compatible with historical traditions of art, such as altar-pieces, nudes and primitive portraits. This denotes the artists' acceptance of modernity as 'art-worthy', but also demonstrates the continuity of Western art in the face of *avant-garde* revolutionary pretensions.

It is important to notice what is *absent* from modern urban depictions. Art has always sought out singularity, and never more than in the twentieth century, with its *avant-garde* ideology. Depictions of the metropolis – apart from relatively few by politically-committed artists – demonstrate this constant search for the imposing human figure or the arresting view, at the expense of the general. The mass of ordinary folk with their work, daily chores, and dreary suburban lodgings, are neglected. The historic or architecturally interesting urban centre is emphasized at the expense of the periphery, and moments of leisure – albeit becoming more accessible to the masses at the time – at the expense of work. There is considerable empathy with the metropolis's victims, but it is usually directed toward either the more traditional artisan poor, or else, more often, toward social pariahs – beggars, prostitutes, rag-pickers, clowns – who did stand out from the crowd, and with whom the artists identified out of their own, often rather genteel, urban poverty and their own preference for unsettled lifestyles. By many abstract artists the city is treated as a sort of new-fangled jewel, or a fugue of shapes, motions, and colour-intensities – that is, as a *thing*, without reference to the fact that humans live there and without questioning of what it is *like* to live there. The painters, and even the photographers who had of necessity to come closer to the reality they were capturing on film, rarely question the 'fairness to reality' of their own visual penchants, except in times of extreme political or economic crisis. In any case, that sort of questioning is precisely what the modern art revolution has taught us *not* to expect of them.

In a general way, though there are many exceptions, the more realist the art, the more it contains human figures, draws them in psychological depth, sees the metropolis as a human environment and criticizes it accordingly. The Socialist artists, in general, condemn the metropolis as the source of much suffering, but also look to a renewed, more salubrious city which will dispense to all the cultural benefits it has in plenty. Again, generally, and only with respect to the period covered here (I immediately think of the rousing counter-example furnished by the Abstract Expressionists of the 1950s), the more introverted the art, the more concerned with the individual reaction, the religious or the mystical, the less interest it displays in the metropolis or the more hostility it bears toward it. Here Gauguin, Van Gogh, the German Expressionists and the Surrealists are the prime examples.

What can we conclude about artists' reactions to each of our three cities? Paris was the least radically modernized of the three in our period, also the one with the longest history as a city of amusements, also the most beautiful in the traditional sense; and it is not surprising that Paris is the most universally loved by its painters, whether rendered realistically or with abstract concentration on its modern features. Apart from the works which dwell melancholically on the fate of those on the fringes of society, it is hard to find a critical or cheerless depiction of Paris between 1890 and 1945. Paris artists had few doubts about the city's *douceur de vivre*, and many esteemed ones wholeheartedly embraced its worldliness.

There *are* cheerful depictions of Berlin by Impressionists and more traditional painters, but none that I can find by the Expressionists or Magical Realists, Meidner's pro-modern panegyrics notwithstanding. Their radical criticism stems much less from actual observation of Berlin as a specific city than from rather abstract political and philosophical ideas about the evils of modern life, so that, while Berlin is indubitably present in their paintings as the 'scene of the crime', it is the crime which stands out in these works, not the scene of it.

New York, finally, set the model for the modern city, in its radically new skyscrapers and neon, its extraordinarily mixed population, and also in the boredom of its straight streets and unadorned brick buildings. The blending, in New York art, of European modernist trends with both the traditional American ideal of rural wholesomeness and America's new enthusiasm for its industrial might, produced a lot of exultation over New York's originality, but also many doubts about the effects of New York's pace and unnatural environment on its people. The many artists who loved the city – including, I think, many who were critical of it – did not look for a Paris-type *douceur de vivre*, which, in any case, it lacked, but rather embraced the brashness, energy, and fast-paced music of the city. The American ideals of hard work and wholesome living, as much as aesthetic satisfaction with the new, enter into many of the portraits of New York.

NOTES

1. For visual documentation beyond the illustrations presented here, see *Cityscape, 1910–39: Urban Themes in American, German and British Art* (1977–78). London: Arts Council of Great Britain; *Die Stadt: druckgraphische Zyklen des 19. und 20. Jahrhunderts* (1974). Bremen: Kunsthalle; *Paris vu par les maîtres, de Corot à Utrillo* (1961). Paris: Musèe Carnavalet; *Paris im Bild seiner Maler, 15.–20. Jahrhunderts* (1954). Mainz: Service des Relations Artistiques de la Direction Générale des Affaires Culturelles; *Panorama berlinois: Berlin vu par les peintres, 1750–1950* (1961). Paris: Galerie Creuze; Kuh, K. (ed.) (1956) *American Artists Paint the City*. Chicago: Art Institute; *The City in American Painting* (1973). Allentown, Pennsylvania: Art Museum; Lieberman, W.S. (ed.) (1968) *Manhattan Observed*. New York: Museum of Modern Art; and see further below.

2. Charles Baudelaire, Les foules, in *Petits poèmes en prose* (1861); Le peintre de la vie moderne, in *Curiosités esthétiques* (1860). The American realist, John Sloan, remarked late in life on his voyeurism that had been fully satisfied by New York (*John Sloan, 1871–1951* (1971). Washington DC: National Gallery of Art, p. 86).

3. Both artists painted a few pictures with Paris subjects, but mainly early in their careers.

4. An excellent compilation of historical images of New York is Kouwenhoven, J.A. (1953) *The Columbia Historical Portrait of New York*. Garden City, NY: Doubleday.

5. Goldin, A. (1973) The Eight's laissez faire revolution. *Art in America*, **61**, July–August, pp. 42–49. For illustrations of American art of this period, see Brown, J.D. (1977) *American Painting: From the Colonial Period to the Present*. New York: Rizzoli; Scott, D. (1975) *John Sloan*. New York: Watson-Guptill; Young, M.S. (1973) *The Paintings of George Bellows*. New York: Watson-Guptill.

6. On the images of New York in this period, see Corn, W.M. (1973) The new New York. *Art in America*, **61**, July–August, pp. 58–65; and Kuspit, D.B. (1977) Individual and mass identity in urban art: the New York case. *Art in America*, **65**, September, pp. 66–77. Corn deplores the fact that the New York realists did not create a style equal to their recognition of New York's radical modernity; Kuspit sees their softened, often humanized images of the city as the proof of their unwillingness to accept the city's modernity. I tend to think that these artists, obviously unaware of many of the urban problems that seem so blatant to us now, simply found their city picturesque and saw no inconsistency – especially before the Armory Show of 1913 – in depicting it in a traditional way. Despite the skyscrapers, many of which were themselves eclectic in style and highly

decorated, New York was quite an innocent city before 1914.

7. See *Max Liebermann in seiner Zeit* (1979). Berlin: Nationalgalerie.

8. Rosenblum, R. (1975) *Modern Painting and the Northern Romantic Tradition: Friedrich to Rothko*. New York: Harper and Row. *Cityscape, 1910–39, op. cit.* (see note 1) tends to bear out a similar rejection by English artists, but no one, to my knowledge, has ever directly posed the question.

9. Max Liebermann, a cosmopolitan Berliner if ever there was one, said he needed dark glasses to look at the Siegesallee, a wide boulevard lined with huge statues of Prussian rulers, which William II proudly inaugurated in 1901. Masur, G. (1971) *Imperial Berlin*. London: Routledge and Kegan Paul, p. 212.

10. Lees, A. (1979) Critics of urban society in Germany, 1854–1914. *Journal of the History of Ideas*, **40**, January–March, pp. 61–83.

11. A good discussion of German nationalist and antimodernist ideas as related to contemporary literature and art is Hamann, R. and Hermand, J. (1967) *Stilkunst um 1900*. Berlin: Akademie Verlag. See also Lees, *loc. cit.* (see note 10); Stern, F. (1961) *The Politics of Cultural Despair*. Berkeley and Los Angeles: University of California Press; and Mosse, G. (1964) *The Crisis of German Ideology: Intellectual Origins of the Third Reich*. London: Weidenfeld and Nicolson. The German sociologist, George Simmel, in an essay of 1903, The metropolis and mental life (in English in Levine, D.N. (ed.) (1971) *On Individuality and Social Forms*. Chicago: University of Chicago Press, pp. 324–39), credits the metropolis with a hypertrophy of intellectualism and individualism at the expense of emotion and interpersonal relations. Writers on visual images of the city have used Simmel's essay to diagnose portraits of urban alienation by artists of various nationalities (see *Cityscape, 1910–39, op. cit.* (see note 1), and Kuspit, *loc. cit.* (see note 6)). I am dubious about the applicability of Simmel's ideas to anything but the German context. While Simmel's is a far more reasoned and temperate look at the city than Ferdinand Tönnies's or Houston Stewart Chamberlain's, and while Emile Durkheim in France was also concerned about the possible evil effects of urban life on the individual (in *Suicide*, 1897), Simmel's thought on this subject nevertheless fits into a German national tend of thought, the likes of which did not exist elsewhere.

12. E. L. Kirchner wrote much later of the artistic stimulation provided by the city, but also stayed away after 1914 and expressed anti-urban sentiments in his Davos diary (Grisebach, L. (ed.) (1968) *E. L. Kirchners Davoser Tagebuch*. Cologne: DuMont.). Emil Nolde hated urban life, as he makes clear in letters and in his autobiography (*Briefe aus dem Jahren 1894–1926* (1927). Berlin: Furche-Kunstverlag; *Jahre der Kämpfe, 1902–1914*, 2nd edn (1958). Flensburg and Hamburg: Christian Wolff); he spent periods in Berlin for professional reasons, but stayed away as much as possible. Erich Heckel and Karl Schmidt-Rottluff settled in Berlin permanently, but in outlying areas of the city. The Munich Expressionists were even less in favour of urban life. Wassily Kandinsky and Franz Marc, in particular, chose to live far out in the country and depicted almost exclusively landscape and animals after 1910; Kandinsky's non-objective painting derived from views of landscape and horsemen. See also *Die andere Seite*, the 1909 antimodernist novel by Alfred Kubin, an Austrian Expressionist illustrator.

13. For illustrations of much of Kirchner's work, see Gordon, D.E. (1968) *Ernst Ludwig Kirchner*. Cambridge, Mass: Harvard University Press.

14. Einleitung zum Malen von Grosstadtbildern, reprinted in Schmidt, D. (ed.) (undated) *Manifeste Manifeste*. Dresden: VEB Verlag der Kunst, pp. 84–89. Author's translation.

15. I have discussed early-twentieth-century artists' relations with politics elsewhere: *Painters and Politics: The European Avant-Garde and Society, 1900–1925* (1976). New York: Elsevier.

16. For illustrations, see *ibid.*; Hamann and Hermand, *op. cit.* (see note 11); Jourdain, F. (1954) *Un grand imagier: Alexandre Steinlen*. Paris: Cercle de l'Art; Schumann, W. (1962) *Das grosse Zille-Album*. Hannover: Fackelträger Verlag.

17. John Sloan also sympathized with the Left and drew illustrations for the *New Masses*, but I detect no similar concern for the urban slums or any political message in his work.

18. Some artists have written about this search. See the manifestos of the Italian Futurists in

Gambillo, M.D. and Fiori, T. (eds) (1958, 1962) *Archivi del futurismo*, 2 vols. Rome: De Luca; Léger, F. (1973) *Functions of Painting*. New York: Viking; Delaunay, R. (1957) *Du cubisme à l'art abstrait*. Paris: S.E.V.P.E.N.; Mondrian, P. (1945) *Plastic Art and Pure Plastic Art*. New York: Wittenborn. Very helpful is Le Bot, M. (1973) *Peinture et machinisme*. Paris: Klincksieck, pp. 148–68.

19. Illustrated in Zervos, C. (1957) *Pablo Picasso*, Vol. 2. Paris: Cahiers d'Art, pp. 404–6.

20. For illustrations, see: Schmalenbach, W. (undated) *Fernand Léger*. New York: Abrams; *Francis Picabia* (1976). Paris: Centre National d'Art et de Culture Georges Pompidou; Werner, A. (1975) *Max Weber*. New York: Abrams; Gray, C. (ed.) (1970) *John Marin*. New York: Holt, Rinehart and Winston; *Cityscape, 1910–39*, op. cit. (see note 1).

21. Translation of 1912, quoted in Taylor, J.C. (1961) *Futurism*. New York: Museum of Modern Art, p. 124.

22. *Art of the Twenties* (1979). New York: Museum of Modern Art.

23. The best study of Stella is Jaffe, I.B. (1970) *Joseph Stella*. Cambridge, Mass: Harvard University Press.

24. Stella, J. (1929) The Brooklyn Bridge (a page of my life). *Transition*, **16–17**, June, p. 87.

25. See *ibid.*; Stella, J. (1960) Discovery of America: autobiographical notes. *Art News*, **59**, November, pp. 41–42, 64–67 (written in 1946); and two previously unpublished statements about New York, printed by Jaffe, *op. cit.*, pp. 77–78, 146–8 (see note 23), in Italian and partially in translation. The likely influence of this painting on Hart Crane's symbolic poem, 'The Bridge' is interestingly explored by Jaffe in *op. cit.* (see note 23), and in (1969) Joseph Stella and Hart Crane: the Brooklyn Bridge. *American Art Journal*, **2**, Fall, pp. 98–107.

26. Translation by Jaffe, *op. cit.*, pp. 77–78 (see note 23).

27. *Ibid.*, p. 80.

28. Schmied, W. (1977) Die neue Wirklichkeit – Surrealismus und Sachlichkeit, in *Tendenzen der 20er Jahre. 15. europäische Kunstausstellung*. Berlin: Dietrich Reimer, part 4, pp. 1–36.

29. *Ibid.*, p. 32. Author's translation.

30. For illustrations, see Hess, H. (1974) *George Grosz*. London: Studio Vista, 1974.

31. See Beckmann, M. (1916) *Briefe im Kriege*. Berlin: Bruno Cassirer.

32. Bekenntnis, reprinted in Schmidt, *op. cit.*, p. 140 (see note 14). Author's translation.

33. For illustrations, see *Georgia O'Keeffe* (1978). New York: Viking; *Tamara de Lempicka* (1978). Parma: Franco Maria Ricci; Goodrich, L. (1972) *Raphael Soyer*. New York: Abrams; Goodrich, L. (1972) *Reginald Marsh*. New York: Abrams; Goodrich, L. (1971) *Edward Hopper*. New York: Abrams.

34. For illustrations, see Baigell, M. (1974) *Thomas Hart Benton*. New York: Abrams.

35. For illustrations, see Lane, J.R. (1972) *Ben Shahn*. New York: Abrams.

36. And published, along with other paintings of New York, in *Fortune* (July, 1939), in honour of the New York World's Fair of that year.

37. For illustrations, see: Rosenblum, W. and N. (1977) *America and Lewis Hine*. New York: Aperture; *Walker Evans, First and Last* (1978). New York: Harper and Row; McCausland, E. (1939) *New York in the Thirties as Photographed by Berenice Abbott*. New York: Dover.

38. For illustrations, see Werner, *op. cit.* (see note 20).

39. For illustrations, see *Art of the Twenties, op. cit.* (see note 22); Dorival, B. (1975) *Robert Delaunay*. Brussels: Jacques Damase; *Charles Sheeler* (1968). Washington: Smithsonian Institution.

40. For illustrations, see Lane, J.R. (1978) *Stuart Davis: Art and Art Theory*. New York: Brooklyn Museum.

41. For illustrations, see Russell, Feininger, Cage and Gabo (1971) *Tobey*. Basle: Editions Beyeler; *Mark Tobey* (1961). Paris: Musée des Arts Décoratifs.

42. Welsh, R. (1966) Landscape into music: Mondrian's New York period. *Arts Magazine*, **40**, February, pp. 33–39; Masheck, J. (1974) Mondrian the New Yorker. *Artforum*, **13**, October, pp. 58–65.

Chapter 5

The Metropolis in Literature

PETER KEATING

ONE of the essays in H. G. Wells's collection of sociological prophecies, *Anticipations* (1901), is devoted to the 'probable diffusion of great cities'. Pointing out that never before in the history of mankind had there existed cities of one million inhabitants, Wells notes:

> There are now ten town aggregates having a population of over a million, nearly twenty that bid fair to reach that limit in the next decade, and a great number at or approaching a quarter of a million. We call these towns and cities, but, indeed, they are of a different order of things to the towns and cities of the eighteenth-century world [1].

Wells, of course, was not unique among novelists at the turn-of-the-century in recognizing this trend, and for sociologists and social reformers it would have been a fairly commonplace observation. But there certainly was something special about the seriousness with which Wells took this perception and what, imaginatively, he made of it. He recognized that the changes taking place in the structure of city life were not explicable simply in terms of gradual expansion, growth, and development, but represented a radical, fundamental shift in human society, and if that was correct, in human consciousness as well: 'These coming cities', he writes, 'will not be, in the old sense, cities at all; they will present a new and entirely different phase of human distribution' [2]. The word 'metropolis' Wells seems not to have used at this time, though he acknowledges that 'town' and 'city' will become terms as obsolete as 'mail coach' and that a new term will be required: 'urban region' he suggests might be suitable, drawing as it does on 'urban district', a term already in current administrative use [3].

As far as the novel is concerned – and I shall concentrate mainly on the novel – the importance of Wells's observations lies in his identification of these 'coming cities' as representative of entirely new phases of human society. If they are so new, then how is the novelist to deal with them? Do they raise questions, possibilities, types of psychological and social analysis which had hitherto not been explored by novelists? The town and the city – those terms to be made sociologically obsolete by the new kind of metropolis – had, after all, provided the subject matter of novels since the early eighteenth century, while the contrast between town and country is found centrally, in a wide variety of forms, throughout Western literature [4]. In the mid-Victorian period the success of novelists in dealing directly with contemporary city life was sometimes felt to threaten the relevance of poetry which seemed for a while unable to respond to changed social circumstances. Now the novel itself appeared threatened in a similar way, with modern cities grown so complex that new kinds of specialists were required to deal with them. Was it possible that the town planner, sociologist, and journalist were to take over from the novelist his traditional tasks of describing, evoking, and analysing city life? Or, to put the question in a slightly different way, was it possible for the novelist, with his traditional (and in some sense inviolable) emphasis on human relationships, to comprehend the new metropolitan experience? These issues are just part of what is deeply felt by writers at the turn-of-the-century as a state of cultural crisis; it is out of that sense of crisis that there emerges the modern movement in literature. The wider implications of this emergence cannot be discussed in this brief span. However, examination of some of the different ways that early modern writers responded to the challenge posed by the new metropolis can shed considerable light on the history of literature as well as on that of urbanization and planning.

Referring to American fiction, Blanche H. Gelfant has usefully divided the city novel into three main types: (1) the 'portrait', in which the city is revealed through the experiences of a single character, often a youth from the country; (2) the 'ecological', which centres on one unit of the city, perhaps a neighbourhood, street, or even house; (3) the 'synoptic', in which the city itself becomes the major protagonist [5]. All three of these types of city novel are to be found in the literature of 1890–1940. The 'portrait' and 'ecological' approaches are also common in the literature of much earlier periods, but the 'synoptic' novel is characteristic of the twentieth century (though when placed in a European context, as it needs to be, its development is far more complex than Gelfant's terms of reference allow). My concern here is with literary experiments which build towards the new, synoptic novel, and not, I must emphasize, with the generality of city life in fiction or with different portrayals of cities in literature.

Responses to the metropolis have to be seen in relation to nineteenth-century experience, as Wells so clearly understood. This is partly because of the special circumstances of London – with a population already rising above one million early in the nineteenth century – and partly because of the active imaginative interest shown in city life by early and mid-Victorian writers. Many of the attitudes and values, the human problems and states of mind that we tend to associate with the twentieth century, had already been given memorable expression and definition in fiction, most notably by Dickens in England and Zola in France. The key question then, as later, involved scale or scope. Throughout nineteenth-century fiction we find techniques being developed to convey a sense of the variety, complexity, and newness of the human problems caused by the massing of large numbers of people in the modern city.

As early as 1821, Pierce Egan in *Life in London,* a work that can in many senses be regarded as the archetype of the nineteenth-century city novel, had broken with the picaresque tradition of moving restlessly between town and country to offer his readers a *camera obscura* view of the metropolis. It was a method that promised to catch the bewildering variety of London life within a manageable and comprehensible frame:

> The EXTREMES in every point of view are daily to be met with in the Metropolis; from the most rigid persevering, never-tiring industry, down to laziness, which, in its consequences, frequently operates far worse than idleness. The greatest love of and contempt for money are equally conspicuous; and in no place are pleasure and business so much united as in London. The highest veneration for and practice of religion distinguishes the Metropolis, contrasted with the most horrid commission of crimes; and the *experience* of the oldest inhabitant scarcely renders him safe against the specious plans and artifices continually laid to entrap the most vigilant [6].

The vastness of the metropolitan world; the endless range of life it contains; the extremes of moral worth, social status, and material circumstances to be found in it – these make the metropolis not just part of the world but a world in its own right, each area of which is largely unknown to the inhabitants of other areas. Only the novelist or his surrogate guides – in this particular case, those mythical heroes of popular culture, Tom and Jerry – can comprehend the totality of the metropolitan experience; it is contained, held within the reflected image of the *camera obscura.*

Carlyle's remarkable description of the modern city in *Sartor Resartus* (1831) shares with Egan's an emphasis on extremes and contrasts existing side by side:

> The joyful and the sorrowful are there; men are dying there, men are being born; men are praying – on the other side of a brick partition, men are cursing; and around them all is the vast, void Night [7].

Here, as also with Egan, the point of view – the necessary way of comprehending the scale of the modern city – is from above, in this case Professor Teufelsdröckh's attic study. Carlyle's city is intended to be both archetypal – as its name, Weissnichtwo, indicates – and centrally modern in its structure and characteristics. Contrasts of extreme wealth and poverty are now given class significance; as darkness falls, those parts of Weissnichtwo dedicated to pleasure light up, reversing artificially the natural pattern of day and night; while the roads leading into the city are crowded with men and with produce:

A thousand carriages, and wains, and cars, come tumbling-in with Food, with young Rusticity, and other Raw Produce, inanimate or animate, and go tumbling out again with Produce manufactured. That living flood, pouring through these streets, of all qualities and ages, knowest thou whence it is coming, whither it is going? [8]

That sense of Weissnichtwo as the focal point of a nation, devouring the raw produce – human and non-human – and sending out in return manufactured 'produce' reveals an awareness of the functioning of a great city that goes far beyond Egan to anticipate the more sustained description of Les Halles that opens Zola's *Le ventre de Paris* (1873). And, as Carlyle's description gathers pace, other factors are added, satirically at times but with a clear social purpose:

Upwards of five-hundred-thousand two-legged animals without feathers lie round us, in horizontal positions; their heads all in nightcaps, and full of the foolishest dreams. Riot cries aloud, and staggers and swaggers in his rank dens of shame; and the Mother, with streaming hair, kneels over her pallid dying infant, whose cracked lips only her tears now moisten – all these heaped and huddled together, with nothing but a little carpentry and masonry between them – crammed in, like salted fish in their barrel – or weltering, shall I say, like an Egyptian pitcher of tamed vipers, each struggling to get its *head above* the others [9].

Already we have here a pressing awareness of numbers, of masses; each person or group of persons separated from others by fragile brick walls, isolated or 'alienated' by the artificial conditions of city life; we have the appeal to social conscience; the city as social, as human, problem; the city as the centre of radicalism and working-class discontent.

All of these concerns, with the significant exception of radical politics, are, of course, taken-up, expanded, humanized, and given new depths of meaning by Dickens. In his early work there is an exuberant delight in the city to set against its darker sides, a sense of it as known intimately and felt naturally by those who live in it, but this balance gradually changes and a key issue for Dickens becomes how people can survive at all in the city; from *Bleak House* (1853) onwards there is a shift of attention towards the need for the inhabitants of cities to learn how to understand or 'read' their environment:

It must be a strange state to be like Jo! To shuffle through the streets, unfamiliar with the shapes, and in utter darkness as to the meaning, of those mysterious symbols, so abundant over the shops, and at the corners of streets, and on the doors, and in the windows! To see people read, and to see people write, and to see the postman deliver letters, and not to have the least idea of all that language – to be, to every scrap of it, stone blind and dumb! [10]

This sense of unfamiliarity is not simply a matter of individual illiteracy. As the city grows larger and Dickens's apprehension of its complexities becomes profounder, more and more of the characters in his novels are lost and out of place. The people who seem most at home are the professionals, those whose 'job' it is to know their way around the city – the detective, lawyer, and doctor. No longer is the city seen as in any way 'natural'. In spite of this Dickens's novels are always structured upon the need to establish the inter-relatedness of city life, the urgent need to recognize the connections that *do* exist and *must* be traced between superficially disparate elements. Even the complex plots, coincidental meetings, and sometimes laboriously traced family trees, are so much more than legacies from the picaresque tradition; they are a view of life and a view of the modern city. These two elements are indivisible. As Raymond Williams has said of Dickens: 'It does not matter which way we put it: the experience of the city is the fictional method: or the fictional method is the experience of the city' [11].

A rather similar point can be made about Zola, though as he belongs to a slightly later period of the nineteenth century and draws upon very different literary and social traditions, his appeal for the inter-connectedness of life is made in the name of science rather than social cohesion or the human heart. The social range of his work – in a documentary sense – is also far wider than that of Dickens, and his ambition to portray the whole of mid-nineteenth-century France places him far closer than Dickens to the concerns and methods of the new school of empirical sociologists. So, whereas Dickens's insistence on the inter-relatedness of city life is structured within each novel (which means within the city), Zola's is within the whole Rougon-Macquart series, and Paris, his modern metropolis, is divided among several works [12]. The Paris of *L'assommoir* (1877) is not quite the same Paris we find in *La bête humaine* (1890) or *Le ventre de Paris* (1873). Already there is built into the novels a new kind of separation, and one that was to exert a considerable influence on later writers. Zola's cuts into society (and into the city) tend to be horizontal so that each class, group, or topographical area can be isolated and examined in its own terms – the railway workers in *La bête humaine*, courtesans in *Nana* – with connections between them being made across the novels. There is one moment in *Le ventre de Paris* that typifies this way of viewing the city. It is as Florent moves out of Les Halles on to a central road:

> As they emerged into the broad central way, he had the impression of some foreign town with its various districts, suburbs, villages, walks and streets, its squares and circuses, all tucked away under a roof one rainy day in the service of some gigantic joke [13].

That could almost be taken as Zola's ideal – a separate, complete, foreign town, with its own habits, language, way of life, its own kinds of complexity and variety, ready to be explored, documented, classified by the scientific novelist. It is within the span of Zola's career that we have the emergence of the empirical sociologist (and, indeed, the professional anthropologist as well) who, like the doctors, lawyers, and detectives of Dickens's later novels, are to make it their business to study such alien ways of life [14]. Dickens and Zola are our two greatest novelists of the city, and, in one phase of literature, the last novelists to feel that it was artistically possible to capture within a realistic mode the totality of city life.

Not, of course, that other novelists were not writing *about* the city; what disappears is a particular kind of nineteenth-century vision, the drive towards comprehension and cohesion. In England during the final decades of the nineteenth century there appeared a superb series of novels by George Gissing; a proliferation of novels and short stories that focus on the East End of London, and a light-hearted school of suburban fiction written mainly for the new mass-market periodicals [15]. In the early years of the twentieth century there is a significant movement out into the provinces, most notably by Arnold Bennett in his studies of the Potteries. In America at this time there are similar literatures of slum and suburban life, and, directly under the influence of French naturalism, the exposé or city-problem novel of writers such as Theodore Dreiser and Upton Sinclair [16]. There is certainly no absence of novelists writing about the city, but not with the originality and verve of Dickens or Zola. The fragmentation, and the division into schools and easily definable types, are themselves symptomatic of the challenge that the metropolis – the vast new aggregations that were to render obsolete the old 'towns' and 'cities' – was making to novelists.

To appreciate the full force of that challenge we must, I believe, consider a novelist not usually thought of in this context at all – Henry James; and we need to consider especially the way that James's theories of the novel – as well as his practice as a novelist – seems to deny that the modern city is possible as a subject for the novelist. The best way of doing this is to look at James's essay on Zola, first published in 1903.

James's criticism rests mainly on the materialism or 'coarseness' of Zola's art, though not necessarily on those aspects of the novels which made them so notorious in the late nineteenth century. In the characteristic language that can now sound so snobbish, James described Zola's scheme for the Rougon-Macquart novels in a labouring image: 'The pyramid had been planned and the site staked out, but the young builder stood there, in his sturdy strength, with no equipment save his two hands and, as we may say, his wheel-barrow and his trowel'. Of the final result of this artistic building project, he complains: 'It was the fortune, it was in a manner the doom, of *Les Rougon-Macquart* to deal with things almost always in gregarious form, to be a picture of *numbers*, of classes, crowds, confusions, movements, industries'. This, James argues, 'produces the effect of a mass of imagery in which shades are sacrificed, the effect of character and passion in the lump or by the ton'. James's approach to Zola can be summed up in one striking sentence: 'What the reader easily discerns in him is the sturdy resolution with which breadth and energy supply the place of penetration' [17]. The qualities which make Zola such a fine novelist of the modern city are, in fact, precisely those qualities which upset Henry James – the concern with crowds, the mass, confusions, movements, industries, breadth and energy, activity. They are distrusted not in their own right but because they stand in place of 'penetration'.

At the same time as the Zola essay, very similar issues are being argued out between James and H. G. Wells. The whole debate between them has been edited by Leon Edel and Gordon N. Ray, and here it can be summarized quickly. Referring specifically to *Anticipations*, James praises Wells's ingenuity, his adventurous imagination, and his wide-ranging speculation, but, as with Zola, James regards this kind of activity or energy as insufficient because it is not enough for Art. As James puts it: 'I think your reader asks himself too much "Where is *life* in all this, life as I feel it and know it?" ' [18] Over the years, Wells's answer is quite consistent. Life, for him, lies in ideas, in intellectual debate, in attempting to come to terms with what he calls this period of 'adventurous and insurgent thought, in an intellectual spring unprecedented in the world's history': For the world of 'pure technique' inhabited by James, for the 'dignity, finish, and perfection' of Art, Wells claims to have a 'natural horror'. If this is what art must be, then he would rather be a 'journalist', than an 'artist' [19].

James's influence on the theory of the novel and on professional literary criticism has been so great in this century that it is still fairly unusual to hear anything said in Wells's favour. The victory in their debate is generally reckoned to be entirely James's. And certainly the Jamesian tradition is important, especially for the way it enters the modernist movement through the novels of Virginia Woolf. The metropolis is not banished from this tradition; far from it. It becomes, rather, a major means of attaining the kind of intense 'penetration' sought by James, existing often only as it is seen, felt or experienced by the principal characters in novels like James's own *The Golden Bowl* (1904) or Woolf's *Mrs Dalloway* (1925). Both of these novels are, I would want to argue, important responses to the modern metropolis, but the metropolis as it saturates the awareness of a few minutely analysed individuals. Here for example, is a characteristic moment from *Mrs Dalloway*:

> I can't keep up with them, Peter Walsh thought, as they marched up Whitehall, and sure enough, on they marched, past him, past everyone, in their steady way, as if one will worked arms and legs uniformly, and life with its varieties, its irreticences, had been laid under a pavement of monuments and wreaths and drugged into a stiff yet staring corpse by discipline. One had to respect it; one might laugh; but one had to respect it, he thought. There they go, thought Peter Walsh, pausing at the edge of the pavement; and all the exalted statues, Nelson, Gordon, Havelock, the black, the spectacular images of great soldiers stood looking ahead of them, as if they too had made the great renunciation (Peter Walsh felt he, too, had made it the great renunciation), trampled under the same temptations, and achieved at length a marble stare [20].

There is no longer a dominant narrative voice or point of view, as there had been in a Dickens or a Zola novel, no one to attempt the comprehensive roof-top vision or a captured inclusiveness within a *camera obscura*. Virginia Woolf's West End of London here is only what Peter Walsh can make of it. When set against this tradition of refined consciousness, H. G. Wells can seem crude and abrasive, as he often is and as he himself knew.

Wells's approach to the literary problems posed by the metropolis was characteristic-ally speculative and fantastic. In the excitement of his perception that the nineteenth-century city was expanding so rapidly that it was likely to become a new social phenomenon representative of new kinds of social organization, he sets himself the task of portraying that phenomenon. In *When the Sleeper Wakes* (1899, revised as *The Sleeper Wakes*, 1910) all small towns and villages have disappeared, and throughout the world men are congregated in vast metropolises. As the awakened sleeper gazes on this new world he has 'a vision of city beyond city; cities on great plains, cities beside great rivers, vast cities along the sea margin, cities girdled by snowy mountains' [12]. These cities are reminiscent, as Wells points out at one point, of cities in the ancient world, except that protective walls have been replaced by giant glass domes. There are also obvious similarities with an earlier novel that had employed the narrative device of someone falling asleep in the nineteenth century and waking to find the urban world he once knew changed beyond recognition. Here is that futuristic view of Boston from Edward Bellamy's *Looking Backward* (1888):

> At my feet lay a great city. Miles of broad streets, shaded by trees and lined with fine buildings, for the most part not in continuous blocks but set in larger or smaller enclosures, stretched in every direction. Every quarter contained large open squares filled with trees, among which statues glistened and fountains flashed in the late afternoon sun. Public buildings of a colossal size and an architectural grandeur unparalleled in my day raised their stately piles on every side. Surely I had never seen this city nor one comparable to it before [22].

Like Wells, Bellamy placed his faith in the power of science to transform the material condition of mankind, but unlike Wells he believed it would be accompanied by a corresponding tranformation in man's moral nature. His futuristic Boston, although made possible by modern technology, looks much more like those monuments to Victorian municipal pride which, in turn, were modelled on idealized views of Athens and Rome. The glass-domed city of *When the Sleeper Wakes*, however, has none of this regressive piety. Giant wind vanes control the weather; movement within the city is either along multi-layered galleries or by 'moving ways', and the whole system of life is dependent on, and at the mercy of, modern energy sources: 'To live outside the range of the electric cables was', we are told, 'to live an isolated savage' [23]. Wells's city had nothing to do with the past:

> His first impression was of overwhelming architecture. The place into which he looked was an aisle of Titanic buildings, curving spaciously in either direction. Overhead mighty cantilevers sprang together across the huge width of the place, and a tracery of translucent material shut out the sky. Gigantic globes of cool white light shamed the pale sunbeams that filtered down through the girders and wires. Here and there a gossamer suspension bridge dotted with foot passengers flung across the chasm and the air was webbed with slender cables [24].

Here immediately we have an attempt to grasp the totality of the city of the kind we find in Dickens and Zola but expressed in quite different terms. We have also all of those qualities – of mass, energy, and social breadth – that James found so disturbing in Zola. James's fear that direct confrontation with the modern metropolis would eclipse the psychological penetration that he felt should be the main concern of the novelist is, clearly, confirmed; in its place we have Wells's compulsive speculation on how modern life must come to terms with its own mass identity. The criticism that can still be heard from orthodox (usually Jamesian) literary critics that Science Fiction does not count as Art because its characters lack psychological depth is actually recognized, and built into, the genre at its beginning. If Wells's type of speculative, prophetic fiction involved a conscious sacrifice of psychological depth – though not necessarily psychological accuracy, which is a different matter – in favour of ideas, it also demonstrated a new way of expressing the complexity of the metropolitan experience, and one that the twentieth century was to grasp eagerly. The fictional exploration of political issues, of 'mass politics', in the twentieth century turns increasingly away from the naturalistic tradition in favour of fabular and fantastic art, and Wells's demonstration in *When the Sleeper Wakes* that modern politics are inseparable from architectural change and technological transformations was to stand as a central influence [25].

Almost as soon as *When the Sleeper Wakes* was published, Wells's restless intellect had rejected the pessimistic picture it offered of giant, enclosed, glass-domed cities with populations of thirty millions linked by heli-ports across devastated countryside. In *Anticipations* he admits to having exaggerated the probable decline of rural life, and he offers a differential image of the modern city, though one expressed in equally imaginative terms:

> The star-shaped contour of the modern great city, thrusting out arms along every available railway line, knotted arms of which every knot marks a station, testify sufficiently to the relief of pressure thus afforded. Great towns before this century presented rounded contours and grew as a puff-ball swells; the modern Great City looks like something that has burst an intolerable envelope and splashed [26].

We can take our choice of images from the 'star-shape', 'puff-ball', or 'something that has burst an intolerable envelope and splashed', but it was the glass-domed city that was to haunt the imaginations of politically-minded novelists. It is directly present in Yevgeny Zamyatin's *We*, which was written in 1920 under the acknowledged influence of Wells, where the regimented masses live (without souls) in a green-walled city, with uncontrollable vegetation outside; inside, they are dominated by the symmetrical wonders of modern technology:

> I again saw all things as if I were seeing them for the very first time in my life – I saw the irrevocably straight streets, the ray-spurting glass of the roadways, the divine parallelepipedons of the transparent dwellings, the square harmony of our grey-blue ranks [27].

Continuing this same line of tradition is Aldous Huxley's *Brave New World* (1932). Here again we have a world of cities, containing within them all that it is presumed man needs to live, linked to each other by helicopters, and set apart from the 'reservations' for inferior beings situated in wilder, remote, non-regimented areas:

> The forest of Burham Beeches stretched like a great pool of darkness towards the bright shore of the western sky. Crimson at the horizon, the last of the sunset faded, through orange, upwards into yellow and a pale watery green. Northwards, beyond and above the trees, the Internal and External Secretions factory glared with a fierce electric brilliance from every window of its twenty storeys. Beneath them lay the buildings of the Golf Club – the huge lower-caste barracks and, on the other side of a dividing wall, the smaller houses reserved for Alpha and Beta members [28].

'Fantastic' is not an adequate description for this futuristic, or science-fiction, novel which develops from Wells. It takes its being from a speculative projection of contemporary social and political conditions, and an acute awareness of the metropolis, as the embodiment of modern political organization, lies at the heart of it. It draws on, contributes to, or embraces the visions of town planners and architects; it speculates on the problems of quantitative analysis being confronted by sociologists; it dramatizes the special political dangers of twentieth-century totalitarianism in its predominantly dystopian nature; and it retains the novelist's perennial concern with the individual within complex social structures. It is also a form of expression that is enormously, and immediately, visual, blending naturally with characteristic twentieth-century movements in painting, such as Cubism and Surrealism, as well as helping to inspire early cinematic techniques. Wells was not unduly sensitive about the uses made of his ideas. He was only too conscious that he himself had drawn freely on the work of many other writers, but when he saw Fritz Lang's *Metropolis* he could not resist pointing out how closely Lang's vision of metropolitan life related to that in *When the Sleeper Wakes*. Lang himself, of course, liked to say that a glimpse of the Manhattan skyline was the initial inspiration for his film [29]. The novel, reality, and cinema blend indistinguishably together in such experiences.

If the architectural descriptions of futuristic fiction suggest artistic connections with Cubism, the Jamesian tradition in the novel invites comparisons with Impressionism. When, in 1924, Virginia Woolf scornfully dismissed Arnold Bennett's claims to be considered seriously as a modern novelist, she did so in terms that recall irresistibly James's earlier rejection of Zola. Once again we find a concern with the limitations of naturalism, a conviction that materialistic description and analysis represent avoidance rather than revelation of character. Of the group of novelists, referred to collectively by Virginia Woolf as 'The Edwardians', she says:

They have laid an enormous stress upon the fabric of things. They have given us a house in the hope that we may be able to deduce the human beings who live there. To give them their due, they have made that house much better worth living in. But if you hold that novels are in the first place about people, and only in the second place about the house they live in, that is the wrong way to set about it [30].

The kind of distinction being made there is not one that Wells – who was included in Woolf's 'Edwardians' – could have accepted in his portrayal of the glass-domed metropolis of *When the Sleeper Wakes*, because, as we have seen, the problems of individual character were felt by him to be inextricably connected with the problem of the mass. For Woolf, moving further and further along of the line of character 'penetration', there seemed no longer any sense in trying for what she calls 'a complete and satisfactory presentment' of character. To achieve that end demanded a degree of social confidence no longer possible in the 1920s. A great new age of literature was about to emerge, but to understand it the reader would need to shed naturalism and brace himself to 'tolerate the spasmodic, the obscure, the fragmentary, the failure' [31].

In making that prediction Woolf had in mind not only her work, but that of T. S. Eliot and James Joyce, and it is precisely through these writers' confrontation with 'the spasmodic, the obscure, and the fragmentary', that the metropolis enters decisively into modern literature. In *The Waste Land* (1922) Eliot brutally rejected the nineteenth-century drive to contain imaginatively the organic totality of city life, evoking instead its unconnected units and creating great poetry out of imagistic fragments:

> Unreal City,
> Under the brown fog of a winter dawn,
> A crowd flowed over London Bridge, so many,
> I had not thought death had undone so many.
> Sighs, short and infrequent, were exhaled,
> And each man fixed his eyes before his feet.
> Flowed up the hill and down King William Street,
> To where Saint Mary Woolnoth kept the hours
> With a dead sound on the final stroke of nine.
> There I saw one I knew, and stopped him, crying: 'Stetson!
> You who were with me in the ships of Mylae!
> That corpse you planted last year in your garden,
> Has it begun to sprout? Will it bloom this year?' [32]

The city is 'unreal', deathly; a world of spiritual corpses, of non-communication, disconnections, fragments, sterility, and despair. The lifeless office workers walking across London Bridge are close, in some respects, to the concern with regimentation, the manipulation of the mass, that we find in the Wellsian science-fiction tradition. But whereas Wells – and, to a lesser extent Zamyatin and Huxley also – had recognized forces of energetic rebellion against authoritarianism, Eliot's vision is one of stultifying passivity. If we look back beyond Wells to the Victorians, then perhaps Dickens's *Dombey and Son* (1848) provides the most telling contrast with *The Waste Land*. The city of *Dombey* is commercial, mercantile and imperial, creating wealth and power but posing a threat to humanity that is held in check by Dickens's determination that it should be. Eliot's London is also commercial, mercantile and imperial, a centre of civilization, but no longer is there a corresponding artistic will to confront the threat to humanity. This civilization, like other great civilizations before it, is temporal and therefore unreal; its fragmented culture and enervated inhabitants merely announce its imminent collapse. There is no hope for it on earth, though there is just a hint that the City of God which is beyond the temporal, and therefore 'real', will survive:

> What is the city over the mountains
> Cracks and reforms and bursts in the violet air
> Falling towers
> Jerusalem Athens Alexandria
> Vienna London
> Unreal [33].

It is no doubt significant that London – the imperial capital of the nineteenth century – is given last in that listing of collapsing civilizations, and significant also that Eliot, like James fifty years earlier, had turned his back on America to establish a home in London. By the time of *The Waste Land* it was apparent that if London remained a grand imperial capital, it could not be accepted as the type of the modern metropolis; that title was already claimed by New York. Yet ironically, the literary city that was to exert the greatest influence on modernist fiction was not New York or London; nor was it Paris, Vienna, or Berlin, those metropolises that in other respects influence so deeply the modern movement. The new model was provided by Dublin, not because the city itself was in the vanguard of urban development – that was very far from the case – but because in *Ulysses* (1922) Joyce succeeded as no writer since Dickens had done in centering a novel entirely on urban experience, and he achieved this by means of revolutionary techniques which went beyond Eliot's fragmented images and Woolf's self-incarceration in the 'spasmodic, the obscure, the fragmentary', to establish a new kind of unity and wholeness. *Ulysses* remains, to the present day, the classic modernist novel.

In *Ulysses* Dublin is the world; the world is Dublin. Among the multiple meanings built into Joyce's Homeric parallels there is, first and foremost, the sense that cultural significance has changed so decisively that the journeying of Ulysses – from nation to nation, across land and sea – is now contained, without this ever appearing to be a matter of topographical restriction, within the modern city. The world inhabited by Leopold Bloom and Stephen Dedalus can be traversed, in a purely physical sense, within the space of twenty-four hours; the stages of their odyssey are marked by the everyday institutions of the urban world which exist to meet the spiritual and physical needs of modern man – the restaurant, bookshop, concert hall, necropolis, school, church, hospital, pub, library, house, home, or brothel, all linked by the interminable streets and tramways:

> Before Nelson's pillar trams slowed, shunted, changed trolley, started for Black-rock, Kingstown and Dalkey, Clonksea, Rathgar and Terenure, Palmerston park and upper Rathmines, Sandymount Green, Rathmines, Ringsend and Sandymount Tower, Harold's Cross. The hoarse Dublin United Tramway Company's timekeeper bawled them off:
> – Rathgar and Terenure!
> – Come on, Sandymount Green! [34]

Urban lists such as this carry with them no connotation – as they would, say, in Wells or Eliot – of the soul-destroying regimentation of mankind; for Joyce they express a Dickensian sense of wonder at the complexity and magic inherent in ordinary city life. The psychological penetration demanded by Henry James is certainly attained in *Ulysses* but it is placed at the service of a sensibility – Leopold Bloom's – that James would have regarded as distressingly inferior. Bloom's humanity – the 'divine' part of him, as Richard Ellmann rightly stresses [35] – is nurtured by, and is totally of, the modern city, so much so that his portrayal seems to mark a sharp break from the widespread disenchantment with city life that generally characterizes late nineteenth-century fiction. Bloom's understanding of the city streets and the humane sympathy he brings to that understanding are almost reminiscent of the kind of early Victorian urban confidence found in Sam Weller:

> The blind stripling tapped the curbstone and went on his way, drawing his cane back, feeling again.
>   Mr Bloom walked behind the eyeless feet, a flatcut suit of herringbone tweed. Poor young fellow! How on earth did he know that van was there? Must have felt it. See things in their foreheads perhaps. Kind of sense of volume. Weight. Would he feel it if something was removed? Feel a gap. Queer idea of Dublin he must have, tapping his way round by the stones [36].

This revitalization of humane feeling is an important part of Joyce's response to the modern city, especially when set against the more representative bland pessimism of Eliot, but there was loss for the reader as well. The Dickensian or Carlylean attempt to embrace the totality of city life was God-like in that it assumed the possibility of, literally and metaphorically, an all-encompassing view from above. The separate parts of the city, its variety, contrasts, and comparisons, were held, as we have seen, precariously in check by the novelist's role as a surrogate God; it gave meaning to his determination to prevent atomism, and also dictated the structure of his novels. This kind of possibility has gone entirely from *Ulysses*; the urban view comes to us through the alternating consciousness of Leopold Bloom and Stephen Dedalus, in itself an acknowledgement of a divided vision; and the overall structure of the book, the bringing into one those two consciousnesses, is imposed by the playful linguistic genius of a self-conscious artist. The characteristic nineteenth-century technique of sympathetic mediation between book and reader is replaced by an elaborate, intricate, highly-patterned artifice which can create artistic unity only by displacing as possible readers the great majority of people inhabiting its world. In *Ulysses* we have the curious case of a novel which endeavours to evoke the totality of city life, and in many respects succeeds triumphantly in doing just that, but which has within it no element of social conscience and no overt political dimension.

This is merely to say, perhaps, that Joyce's vision was unusually idiosyncratic or individualistic; certainly his kind of obsessive linguistic patterning was inimitable, and the immediate and wide-reaching influence he exerted on his contemporaries was primarily formalistic. The example of *Ulysses* demonstrated that the fragmented or atomistic nature of modern city life need not be expressed in artistic forms which were themselves fragmented. It was also clear that while Dublin had provided the inspiration for the fictional techniques which were to dominate modernist fiction, it could not stand as a type of the modern metropolis for anyone but Joyce. In the two most important city novels of the 1920s to continue the tradition established by *Ulysses* – John Dos Passos's *Manhattan Transfer* (1925) and Alfred Döblin's *Berlin-Alexanderplatz* (1929) – we find combined the inescapable influence of Eliot and Joyce, a resurgence of explicit social comment, and confrontation with the truly modern metropolis.

Both novels evoke concrete worlds intersected by streets and railways, trams and buses; vast conglomerations of people crammed anonymously together, following individual lives which, like the communications systems which are so lovingly described, cross constantly with little worthwhile contact or communication:

> On the Alexanderplatz they are tearing up the road bed for the underground. People walk on planks. The tram-cars pass over the square up Alexanderstrasse through Münzstrasse to the Rosenthaler Tor. To the right and left are streets. House follows house along the streets. They are full of men and women from cellar to garret. On the ground floor are shops [37].

> Steel, glass, tile, concrete will be the materials of the skyscrapers. Crammed on the narrow island the million-windowed buildings will jut glittering, pyramid on pyramid like the white cloudhead above a thunderstorm [38].

These two images (of Berlin in the first quotation and Manhattan in the second), while striving to break through to a new evocation of the metropolis, reveal at the same time the strength of what by the later 1920s was a very substantial and many-sided literary tradition. The presence of Dickens, of Wells, and of Joyce can all be detected as formative influences, though perhaps these two quotations are most reminiscent of Teufelsdröckh's attic view of Weissnichtwo in Carlyle's *Sartor*

Resartus, and it is not really surprising – in spite of the vast changes that have taken place in technology, communications, and urban scale – that this should be so. Teufelsdröckh had seen, as characteristic of the modern city, people 'heaped and huddled together, with nothing but a little carpentry and masonry between them – crammed in, like salted fish in their barrel' [39]. In a period of almost one hundred years that kind of problem had intensified but not changed fundamentally; it can still stand as a major appropriate image for the worlds of *Manhattan Transfer* and *Berlin-Alexanderplatz,* though not for *Ulysses.* For Dos Passos and Döblin, as for Carlyle, the basic drive is still to reach through the crammed urban mass to the individual.

Where both Döblin and Don Passos depart from tradition is in giving a different kind of emphasis to the relationship between the individual and the metropolis, with the city itself almost becoming a character or personality in its own right. It is this aspect of their work that has led critics to describe *Berlin-Alexanderplatz* as 'a symphony of big city life' and *Manhattan Transfer* as the type of 'synoptic' city novel [40]. Although both novelists clearly share this kind of aim, the methods they employ are quite dissimilar. Döblin uses an anti-hero, the criminal Franz Biberkopf, as the reader's guide to the shadier sides of Berlin life, drawing on age-old picaresque traditions to present a shifting tableau of a society that lacks moral stability or purpose; the expressionist technique is close to that of Döblin's contemporary, Bertold Brecht, who was to draw on eighteenth-century London for the setting of his greatest city drama, *Die Dreigroschenoper* (1929). Dos Passos denies himself the use of a centralizing character in order to follow phases of many lives and relationships, interspersing his story lines with snatches of popular songs and newspaper headlines, and relying on his evocation of Manhattan to hold his novel together. More than any other novelist of his time he is concerned with the contemporary, rather than futuristic, technology of the metropolis, and he combines a tough realism with a lyricism that at its best is closely related to Georgia O'Keeffe's paintings of New York. It is symptomatic of Dos Passos's methods that the analogies that come swiftest to mind are visual; Paul Citröen's photomontage *Metropolis* (1923) could well have been compiled as an illustration for the world portrayed in *Manhattan Transfer* [41]. There is, however, a much weaker side of Dos Passos that allows lyricism to fall too easily into 1890s aestheticism:

> Glowworm trains shuttle in the gloaming through the foggy looms of spiderweb bridges, elevators soar and drop in their shafts, harbor lights wink [42].

But that kind of sentimentality has its significance as well. It takes its place in a combination of qualities – social realism, narrative techniques developed from Joyce and Eliot, and an often cheap kind of Hollywood romanticism – that was to provide one of the most popular ways (in novels, films, and television) of portraying metropolitan life. As always in literary history, new literary forms build upon their predecessors before developing the confidence to break completely from them, and by the 1920s the novel was already giving way to film as the most popular form of narrative entertainment. The visual image was threatening to take over from the long primacy of the written word, and the experiments and innovations of the various writers discussed here were to be drawn on extensively in the new medium of cinema. It is also usually the case in literary history that when one narrative form gives way in popularity to another it does not die away but adapts to new circumstances, renewing itself by reasserting its commitment to basic human values, and this was to happen with the novel.

In Zamyatin's *We*, the rebel hero, trapped in a totalitarian State – symbolized by the glass-domed metropolis – thinks despairingly:

> Our poets no longer soar in the empyrean: they have come down to earth, they are striding side by side with us, keeping in step with the austere, mechanical March issuing from the Musical Factory: their lyre is the matutinal swishing of electrical tooth-brushes, and the awesome crackling of sparks in the Machine of the Benefactor [43].

That particular vision did not become reality. On the contrary, our modern 'poets' have been impressively loyal to the great traditions that descended to them and courageously innovative in their responses to the challenge posed by the modern metropolis. They have not yet succumbed to the non-human, as Zamyatin feared they might.

NOTES

1. Wells, H.G. (1901) *Anticipations*. London: Chapman and Hall, pp. 34–35.
2. *Ibid.*, p. 40.
3. *Ibid.*, p. 61.
4. See Williams, Raymond (1973) *The Country and the City*. London: Chatto and Windus.
5. Gelfant, Blanche H. (1954) *The American City Novel*. Norman: University of Oklahoma Press, p. 11.
6. Egan, Pierce (1869) *Life in London*. London: John Camden Hotten, p. 50.
7. Carlyle, Thomas (1896) *Sartor Resartus*. London: Chapman and Hall, p. 16.
8. *Ibid.*
9. *Ibid.*, p. 17.
10. Dickens, Charles (1971) *Bleak House*. Harmondsworth: Penguin Books, p. 274. On Dickens and London, see : Welsh, Alexander (1971) *The City of Dickens*. Oxford: Clarendon Press; Schwarzbach, F.S. (1979) *Dickens and the City*. London: Athlone Press; Collins, Philip (1973) Dickens and London, in Dyos, H.J. and Wolff, M. (eds.) *The Victorian City: Images and Reality* (2 vols). Routledge and Kegan Paul.
11. Williams, *op. cit.*, p. 154 (see note 4).
12. See Kranowski, Nathan (1968) *Paris dans les romans d'Emile Zola*. Paris: Presses Universitaires de France.
13. Zola, Emile (1955) *Savage Paris*, translated by David Hughes and Marie-Jacqueline Mason. London: Elek Books, p. 24.
14. See Keating, Peter (ed.) (1976) *Into Unknown England 1866–1913*. London: Fontana and Manchester University Press.

15. Two recent studies of Gissing emphasize the city aspect of his work: Poole, Adrian (1975) *Gissing in Context*. London: Macmillan; Goode, John (1978) *George Gissing: Ideology and Fiction*. London: Vision Press. For the portrayal of the East End of London in late-nineteenth-century fiction, see Keating, Peter (1971), *The Working Classes in Victorian Fiction*. London: Routledge and Kegan Paul.

16. For the city in American fiction at the turn of the century, see Taylor, W.F. (1942) *The Economic Novel in America*. Chapel Hill: University of North Carolina Press; Geismar, Maxwell (1954) *Rebels and Ancestors: The American Novel 1890–1915*. London: W. H. Allen; Rideout, Walter B. (1956) *The Radical Novel in the United States 1900–1954*. Cambridge, Mass: Harvard University Press.

17. James, Henry (1963) Emile Zola, in Shapira, Morris (ed.) *Henry James: Selected Literary Criticism*. Harmondsworth: Penguin Books, pp. 282–308.

18. Edel, Leon, and Ray, Gordon N. (eds.) (1959) *Henry James and H. G. Wells: A Record of Their Friendship, Their Debate on the Art of Fiction, and Their Quarrel*. London: Rupert Hart-Davies, p. 76.

19. *Ibid.*, pp. 147; 263–4.

20. Woolf, Virginia (1964) *Mrs Dalloway*. Harmondsworth: Penguin Books, pp. 57–58. For the London settings of Woolf's novels, see Brewster, Dorothy (1959) *Virginia Woolf's London*. London: George Allen and Unwin.

21. Wells, H.G. (n.d.) *The Sleeper Wakes*. London: Odhams Press, p. 106.

22. Bellamy, Edward (n.d.) *Looking Backward 2000–1887*. London: George Routledge, p. 30.

23. Wells, (n.d.) *op. cit.*, p. 105 (see note 21).

24. *Ibid.*, p. 36.

25. For a discussion of the relationship between politics and the fabular, see Wilding, Michael (1980) *Political Fictions*. London: Routledge and Kegan Paul. For some imaginative cities of the past, see Inch, Peter (1978) Fantastic cities. *Architectural Design*, **48**, (2–3). Jules Verne is influential on this aspect of science fiction. For general discussion of Verne see Allott, Kenneth (1940) *Jules Verne*. London: Cresset Press; Costello, Peter (1978) *Jules Verne: Inventor of Science Fiction*. London: Hodder and Stoughton.

There are some interesting observations on the way Verne saw fantastic cities within natural forms in Butor, Michel (1970) The Golden Age of Jules Verne. *Inventory*. Translated by Richard Howard. London: Jonathan Cape.

26. Wells (1901) *op. cit.*, p. 45 (see note 1).

27. Zamyatin, Yevgeny (1972) *We*. Translated by Bernard Guilbert Guerney. Harmondsworth: Penguin Books, p. 23.

28. Huxley, Aldous (1955) *Brave New World*. Harmondsworth: Penguin Books, p. 65.

29. Jensen, Paul M. (1969) *The Cinema of Fritz Lang*. London: Zwemmer, pp. 7, 59.

30. Woolf, Virginia (1966) Mr Bennett and Mrs Brown, in Woolf, Leonard (ed.) *Collected Essays*, vol. I. London: Chatto and Windus, p. 332.

31. *Ibid.*, p. 337.

32. Eliot, T.S. (1961) *Collected Poems 1909–62*. London: Faber and Faber, p. 65.

33. *Ibid.*, p. 77.

34. Joyce, James (1960) *Ulysses*. London: The Bodley Head, p. 147. For a photographic evocation of the world of *Ulysses*, see Quinn, Edward (1974) *James Joyce's Dublin*. London: Secker and Warburg.

35. Ellmann, Richard (1966) *James Joyce*. London: Oxford University Press, p. 372.

36. Joyce, James (1960) *Ulysses*. London: The Bodley Head, p. 231.

37. Döblin, Alfred (1974) *Alexanderplatz*. Translated by Eugene Jolas. London: Secker and Warburg, p. 105.

38. Dos Passos, John (1969) *Manhattan Transfer*. London: Sphere Books, p. 16.

39. Carlyle, Thomas (1896) *Sartor Resartus*, London: Chapman and Hall, p. 17.

40. Laqueuer, Walter (1974) *Weimar: A Cultural History 1918–1933*. London: Weidenfeld and Nicolson, p. 133; Gelfant, *op. cit.*, pp. 133–66 (see note 5).

41. For Paul Citroen's *Metropolis*, and related work, see Ades, Dawn (1976) *Photomontage*. London: Thames and Hudson.

42. Dos Passos, *op. cit.*, p. 267 (see note 38).

43. Zamyatin, *op. cit.*, p. 27 (see note 27).

Chapter 6

The Metropolis in the Cinema

ANTHONY SUTCLIFFE

'Sell your farm . . . come with me to the City.'
Sunrise, 1927 [1].

PETER Keating has already remarked (see above, p. 144) that between the two world wars the cinema took over from the novel as the principal artistic mirror of the big city and its life. In the early 1900s H. G. Wells thrilled the world with his vision of the high-technology cities of the future in *The Shape of Things to Come* and other novels (see above, pp. 136–8). Three decades later, H. G. Wells himself was enthused by the stunning realization of his towering cities, first of all in *Metropolis* (1927), and then in a number of variations, the most accomplished being *Things to Come* (1936) [2]. As the most comprehensive artistic experience yet invented, the cinema's power to suspend disbelief greatly surpasses that of the novel and indeed of the other art forms discussed in this volume. Moreover, it was entirely a creature of the period 1890–1940. Regular, commercial showings of moving pictures began in 1895. The addition of sound at the end of the 1920s gave the finishing touch to a technique which had already achieved a high degree of visual maturity, and paved the way towards the huge cinema audiences of the later 1930s when, in Britain, for instance, weekly cinema attendances were equal to half the total population of the country [3]. Sound gave a big fillip to the documentary movement, which did much to help the cinema achieve the peak of its persuasive power during the Second World War. The mass, by now almost captive, audiences survived into the late 1940s, but thereafter television, an inferior but more convenient artistic experience, took its toll. Meanwhile, few new cinematic techniques were added to the pre-1940 canon. Cinemascope and 3-D came and went; only by the wide screen and effective on-location sound recording was film-making permanently enhanced in the post-war era.

On the other hand, the cinema had big weaknesses as an interpretative medium for contemporary big-city life. Before 1914 its audience had been mainly working-class, but wartime news films helped to attract the middle classes as well. By 1918 a huge potential market existed and massive funds were attracted into film-making during the consumer boom of 1919–20. The very costly introduction of sound at the end of the 1920s bound the cinema even more closely to finance capital [4]. As audiences grew, larger and more ornate cinemas were built, reflecting the intensity of competition between the individual outlets and chains. By the 1930s it was no longer possible to make films, except the cheapest documentaries, which catered for minority tastes. With Hollywood leading the way, most feature films were aimed at a mass audience drawn broadly from the working and middle classes. Most productions, therefore, lulled more than they stimulated; efforts to educate the audience or to make it think were generally unpopular, while films which allowed ordinary people to escape their daily routine achieved great commercial success. From this perspective, it is possible to conclude that the cinema could have done little to form or even reflect popular attitudes towards the metropolis. However, the point is by no means beyond dispute. It can be argued, from a psycho-analytical standpoint, that films mirror, and to some extent stimulate, deep-seated or unconscious attitudes in individuals and even in whole national societies [5]. In other words, the products of Hollywood and other 'dream factories' can be subjected to a Freudian interpretation. Moreover, there is evidence to suggest that some members of inter-war audiences thought deeply about the films they saw, related them to their own worlds, and were to that extent influenced by them. The recollections of avid filmgoers collected by J. P. Mayer provide clear evidence of these processes [6].

A second weakness derives from the practical problems of portraying the reality of the metropolis on film. The film, like Peter Keating's novel (see above, p. 130) and the stage-play, is primarily a portrayal of personal relationships, of which the city can be no more than a container or a backdrop. A brief craze for 'city symphonies' in the later 1920s produced a handful of portraits of individual metropolises, and the rise of the documentary movement generated a number of short studies of urban problems towards the end of the following decade, culminating in two films bearing the same title, *The City*, in 1939 [7]. The rest of the thousands of films produced between 1918 and 1940 referred to the big city only indirectly or, more frequently, not at all.

These artistic discouragements were compounded by technical limitations. Location shooting in cities was difficult enough in the silent era owing to lighting problems and the bulk of the equipment. The directors of the Keystone Cops achieved it in the sunshine and semi-deserted suburbs of the Los Angeles conurbation, but elsewhere, and with more serious subjects, it was rarely attempted. Then, during the first two decades of the talkies, it became even harder to shoot on urban locations because the microphones picked up, and then distorted, the full range of city noises, drowning the voices of the actors. Meanwhile, changes in studio shooting had led to the widespread displacement of orthochromatic by panchromatic film after the latter's Hollywood adoption in 1927. The strength of panchromatic film lay in its sensitivity to the full range of colours, but it sacrificed depth of focus [8]. This was no great problem in the studio, but it

FIGURE 6.1. Publicity montage for *Berlin: die Symphonie einer Grossstadt* (1927). Curiously, none of the components of the montage was drawn from the film, but it conveys effectively the frenetic efforts of the 'city symphony' to comprehend the totality of metropolitan existence while time ticks remorselessly by (by courtesy of National Film Archive Stills Library).

FIGURE 6.2. On the set of *Sous les toits de Paris* at the Tobis studios at Epinay. Sound quality was very important in this musical film and René Clair (holding megaphone) mocked up a complete Paris street for the exterior shots. The trees of the studio grounds are visible on the right. The weather is clearly dry but chilly (by courtesy of National Film Archive Stills Library).

discouraged outside shooting, particularly in cities. The introduction from 1932 of back projection, a Hollywood invention developed for monster films, allowed outdoor scenes to be faked by the use of documentary footage [9], but the effect was never perfect and so was usually limited to street scenes viewed through the windows of 'moving' cars. Throughout the 1930s, therefore, exterior city shooting normally required the construction of special sets at considerable expense. Ironically, therefore, those final, post-1940 additions to cinematic technique, on-location recording and the wider screen, were precisely the ones which allowed the city film to come into its own. The first on-location crime thriller (*The Naked City*, 1948) and the first on-location musical (*On the Town*, 1949), both made dynamic and atmospheric use of their New York settings, and were immediately greeted as revolutionary. Hand-held cameras, growing respect for *cinéma-vérité* methods, the return of deep focus in the later 1950s when the screen was widened, *Shadows*, the *nouvelle vague* . . . all contributed to the rise of the cinematic metropolis to the point where, in 1979, Woody Allen could make *Manhattan*, an explicit attempt to relate human relationships to a distinctive urban environment, while Wim Wenders, shooting *Hammett* on location in Los Angeles, could tell a journalist:

> The city is present in every one of my films because it is the only context of existence that I know. It moulds the individual, imprints itself upon him, builds him up – and breaks him down – in its own image. People are different from city to city – someone from New York, for instance – you pick him up straightaway. It's something to do with the way he talks, his accent, what he does with his hands – just his attitude, maybe. Yes, you could say that the city is one of the characters in my films [10].

Before 1940, such sentiments were rarely expressed.

Discouraging though these limitations undoubtedly are, they are counter-balanced to some extent by the *implicit* presence of the giant city in pre-1940 films. The cinema has always been predominantly a phenomenon of the primate city, except in the United States where, as we have seen (see above, p. 5), the dominance of New York was attenuated by the presence of other huge cities elsewhere in that near-continent. When Hollywood sprang up as the main centre of North American film-making after World War One, it did so in a dusty outlier of Los Angeles where constant sunlight, cheap land and cheap labour were at first the main attractions. Outside North America, however, film-making moved into the giant cities or their surrounding regions in the early 1900s and never left them thereafter. The great strength of effective demand for the cinema in the teeming and prosperous national capitals meant that films were generally screened first there, so metropolitan taste exercised an important influence on the choice and treatment of topics, producing a degree of sophistication which reinforced provincial deference to the productions which eventually arrived from the big city. In the early 1900s public taste began to evolve from documentary scenes of daily life (of which city street-scenes were among the most popular) towards fictional films, which had to be made in specially-built studios by trained technicians and more or less competent actors. The necessary personnel, and various supporting services, could be secured most readily in the biggest cities, where the availability of alternative employment in the theatre and other media eased the qualms of those who were attracted to film-making but had doubts about the security of the careers which it offered. Once established in these ways, the link with the giant city was reinforced as time passed. In a primate city, directors, actors and writers could find the colourful social life which they craved and for which their growing earnings qualified them. Film publicity was best directed from a capital city. The primary artistic creators – directors, writers and composers – found their main inspiration there, in the cultural whirl which even the liveliest of provincial centres could not emulate. Meanwhile, the capital cities were the main source of the finance required by the producers. So, in Britain, Brighton lasted only a few years as the mecca of the British film industry. In France and Germany, sun-seeking migrations of studios to the Mediterranean coast and to Bavaria in the 1920s came to little. In more backward Japan, location in the capital was even more imperative; studios were built beside the electric commuter lines running into Tokyo because only the railway companies could supply abundant electricity at an attractive price [11]. Admittedly, high rents discouraged city-centre studios; instead, suburbs and, increasingly, towns and villages lying just outside the main built-up area where land was freely available for outside shooting, were preferred. Hitchcock's claustrophobic *The Lodger* (1926) was shot at the Gainsborough studios, Islington, but by the 1930s a high proportion of British films were being made at studios such as Elstree and Pinewood, within a radius of between ten and twenty miles from London [12]. The Berlin studios of Tempelhof and Neubabelsberg, built just before the First World War, remained in constant use thereafter [13]. In Paris, some of the most brilliant studios were in the dreariest suburbs such as Joinville and Billancourt, a setting which, as we shall see, may have had some influence on their products in the later 1930s.

The metropolitan siting of studios ensured that many stories of contemporary life such as lower-class or drawing-room comedies, and films of adventure, love and crime, were implicitly or explicitly set in the giant cities. Indeed, many Hollywood films were set in New York. However, the structure of the U.S. urban system was perhaps reflected in the fact that Chicago, New Orleans and San Francisco were more often the settings for American films than were Cologne, Lyons and Birmingham for European productions. They were also supplemented by an anonymous American big-city type, approximating to any one of a score of featureless industrial cities, referred to, when necessary, as Bigtown, Boom Town, Gulf City, or whatever. An implicit New York setting was usually characterized by opulent interiors, over-dressed actors, and a marked enhancement of the already high American words-per-minute rate, but cities outside New York were not normally portrayed as backward or quaint. In Europe, on the other hand, settings in big provincial cities were rare, and usually the occasion for a suave, sardonic appraisal of sullen or skittish regional oddities. Marcel Pagnol's trilogy of Marseilles harbour life wallowed in local colour and reduced the central love story to the near-ridiculous. *Love on the Dole*, that rare British excursion into the industrial Lancashire of the Depression, was marred by the absence of realistic exteriors and the highly diverse efforts of middle-class London actors to simulate northern accents. Mining films were rather more convincing, no doubt because their central dramas concentrated the minds of directors and actors more effectively. *The Stars Look Down* was perhaps the only non-patronizing British portrayal of provincial working-class life before 1940 and Pabst made a similar success of *Kameradschaft*. Mining films, however, were set in small or medium-sized towns, or even semi-rural areas like that portrayed by John Ford in *How Green Was My Valley*. Big-city stories, given the prevailing emphasis on the larger-than-life, were mostly located in one or other of two extreme milieus – the leisured, opulent (though somewhat neurotic) circles of the upper-middle class (for example *42nd Street*, 1933), or a Runyonesque, more or less criminal underworld (for example *Greek Street*, 1930). This concentration on untypical extremes may well have confirmed existing provincial impressions of metropolitan fecklessness, while reinforcing the provinces' general sense of inferiority to the capital. If it did so, it perhaps contributed to the political atmosphere in which the restriction or the dismantling of capital cities was so readily entertained after 1945. However, this is no doubt to claim too much for the cinema, at any rate before we have looked in more detail at some of its products.

Germany

Given the shortage of explicit portrayals of the giant city in the pre-1940 cinema, it is not surprising that there should be no obvious temporal pattern of development of this type of film. The rare examples are much too scattered for that. If there is any pattern, it is a spatial one, centred on Germany. In Germany, in the 1920s, the large city was quite close to the top of the film industry's agenda.

Andrew Lees has already shown (see above, pp. 71–3) that many Germans became unusually horrified or fascinated by the giant metropolis in the later nineteenth century. This interest sprang from the rapid grafting of dense and teeming cities, epitomized by Berlin, onto a previously somewhat backward society. A variety of problems were detected – such as moral degeneration and mental breakdown – which were not seen in such stark terms in other countries. The First World War, the abortive revolutions of 1918–19, the inflation and violence of the early 1920s, and continuing unemployment, all contributed to a tense atmosphere which did nothing to discourage the traditional German tendency to brood about the fate of the inner self in its unending struggle with an unfriendly world. Berlin, now unquestioned as Germany's dominant urban centre (see below,

p. 291), was the vortex both of these tensions and of the somewhat frenetic escapism which accompanied them. The German cinema, heavily concentrated in and around Berlin, could scarcely fail to reflect these concerns. Much purely escapist work was produced, but early post-war efforts in an extraordinarily bleak expressionist genre which had been pioneered before the war (for example *Der Student von Prag*, 1913) proved successful and were widely emulated through the early 1920s. Films of horror and the grotesque such as *Nosferatu* (1922) are not of direct concern to our theme, but audiences may well have been affected by the expressionist townscapes, usually studio-built, in which some of them were set. These distorted gables or blank facades implied that cities were inhuman, anonymous places in which unusual events occurred and which somehow threatened the innocent [14].

As, by definition, exercises in over-statement, these expressionist films were not infinitely repeatable. In the mid-1920s they gave way, on the bleaker side of the German cinema, to a social-documentary tendency, *Neue Sachlichkeit* (new realism), which echoed developments in the graphic arts and literature [15]. *Neue Sachlichkeit* showed a strong interest in the big city, while retaining a trace, and sometimes more than a trace, of expressionist techniques of presentation. This continuity was not surprising given that some of the leading expressionist directors moved straight into *Neue Sachlichkeit*. Rather more surprising, however, was that some of the most troglodytic of studio directors now evinced a desire to get out into the streets. The story is told of Carl Mayer, creator of the 'city symphony' genre, tiring of studio work and conceiving the idea for *Berlin: die Symphonie einer Grossstadt* while standing in the midst of Berlin traffic one day in 1925 [16]. Others used documentary shots in their films of city life, or constructed realistic, if still disconcertingly expressionistic, street sets at their studios, sometimes in the open air. There even emerged a distinct genre, beginning with Karl Grune's *Die Strasse* in 1923, in which the city street was the unifying element in the plot. In *Die Strasse*, a middle-aged man is tempted away from his bourgeois domestic milieu to taste the illicit pleasures of 'the street' at night. Tricked, robbed and thoroughly frightened, he returns to his wife the following morning. The street, and hence the city, is portrayed as a fascinating but sinister and dangerous place, deliberately contrasted with the tedious and conformist order of the hero's apartment. These qualities are expressed by contrasts of light and darkness, and moving shadows [17]. Admittedly, some of the 'street films' were no more than tangential evocations of the giant city. G. W. Pabst's *Die freudlose Gasse* (1925), for instance, followed the decline and fall of members of a down-at-heel middle-class family in inflation-hit Vienna. The 'joyless street' of the title was a narrow studio-built alley containing little more than a butcher's shop, and more evocative of a small, provincial town than the great metropolis. At the other extreme was *Berlin: die Symphonie einer Grossstadt* (1927). Though a documentary 'city symphony' rather than a 'street film', it attracted large audiences and its emphasis on street scenes, which recalled

FIGURE 6.3. *Berlin: die Symphonie einer Grossstadt* (1927): early morning shot
of workers leaving their suburban *Mietskasernen*. The gap-toothed
appearance of the street indicates the continuing effect of pre-1914 land
hoarding (by courtesy of National Film Archive Stills Library).

the early days of the cinema in the 1890s, almost certainly prolonged the 'street
film' genre. To make *Berlin*, thousands of feet of film were shot, much of it with
hidden cameras and ultra-sensitive film, to produce a kaleidoscopic view of Berlin
life during a twenty-four hour period. As edited by Walter Ruttman, the film
eschewed all social comment, but in portraying the density and vitality of big-city
existence the film managed to convey an impression of aimlessness and of the
sacrifice of individual freedom to an unrelenting city machine [18]. Similar points
were made in the fictional *Dirnentragödie* (1927), a story of prostitution, Joe May's
Asphalt (1929), and Lupu Pick's *Gassenhauer* (1931), a drama of unemployed street
musicians. Kracauer has even suggested that the street – and this meant, in effect,
the overcrowded Berlin street – had an irresistible attraction in Weimar Germany
[19]. However, although the street was certainly a focus of interest, it was the
proliferation of films about big-city poverty and degradation which really distinguished the German cinema in this period, for it ran strongly counter to the escapist
or sentimental tendencies of other national cinemas in the 1920s.

FIGURE 6.4. A carter struggles to raise his stricken horse, from *Berlin: die Symphonie einer Grossstadt* (1927). No symbolic significance can be attached to scenes such as this. It was one of many such chance events captured by extensive candid camera filming in the streets, and featured by Ruttman's editing purely because of its dramatic value (by courtesy of National Film Archive Stills Library).

As early as 1925, Gerhard Lamprecht directed *Die Verrufenen*, a study of Berlin slum life inspired by the socially-committed drawings of Heinrich Zille. Although it emphasized the golden hearts of the poor and their ability to rise above their tribulations, the depressing conditions of slum existence were realistically portrayed [20]. Then, in *Heimkehr* (1928), Joe May set a story of two soldiers demobilized in Berlin in 1918 against a series of gloomy cityscapes [21]. Towards the end of the decade some of these 'Zille films' began to carry an explicit political message, when certain Leftist directors began to take exception to the growing folksiness of the genre. Piel Jutzi's *Mutter Krausens Fahrt ins Glück* (1929) was set in the Berlin working-class district of Wedding. It included lengthy documentary shots of crowded, airless tenement blocks, and implied that there were only two ways out of the slum; either one turned on the gas like Mother Krausen, or militated for a better society as her daughter, under the influence of a young, socialist worker, decided to do. Explicit tribute was paid to Zille's environmental

FIGURE 6.5. *Der letzte Mann* (1924). The
hero, doorman at an exclusive hotel in
super-Berlin, is seen here in all his pride,
sheltered by the hotel awning and fawned
on by underlings, while harassed urbanites
hurry by in the rain. Note the expressionist
arrangement of lit windows in the facades
across the street (by courtesy of National
Film Archive Stills Library).

determinism. His celebrated remark that one can kill someone with a dwelling as
easily as with an axe was used to introduce the film, and a dialogue title made the
same point: 'It is not the girl's fault; the environment (*das Milljöh*) is to blame' [22].
Political commitment reached its zenith in *Kuhle Wampe* (1932), directed by Slatan
Dudow to a script by Bertold Brecht. Most of the action took place in a shanty town
on the edge of Berlin where unemployed workers discussed their lot and
encouraged one another, and from which they set out on fruitless forays into the
city to seek work [23]. Berlin was the obvious setting for such films because of its
status as the bastion of Social Democracy and the hope of Communism.

There was, of course, not to be much future in Germany for films like *Kuhle
Wampe*. Ironically, the slum films may well have contributed to the spread of the
anti-urban sentiments espoused by the National Socialist Party. The cumulative
effect of the films discussed so far was to establish competition, corruption,
conflict, and the contrast between riches and poverty as the normal context of daily
life in the big city. The point was reinforced even by films which did not fall readily
into the 'street' or 'Zille' categories. One of the finest German films of the period,
Friedrich Wilhelm Murnau's *Der letzte Mann* (1924), included both street and
tenement-block scenes, but rather than inveighing against poverty or urban crime,
it portrayed the city and its supporting economic and social system as an all-
embracing milieu within which the individual struggled and usually lost. To
emphasize the point, massive sets were constructed, including a broad commercial

street lined by tall facades, including the luxury hotel in which part of the action takes place, and a tenement courtyard [24]. The city was anonymous but it was implicitly Berlin, with the addition of a number of expressionistic skyscrapers which, as Lars Olof Larsson demonstrates (see below, p. 206), were the talk of Berlin at that time. The story of the fall from grace of an ageing hotel doorman, demoted to working in the basement lavatory, and derided by his tenement neighbours, persistently commented on the distortion of the lives of ordinary people by big-city conditions. After *Der letzte Mann,* Berlin was rarely portrayed in any but this pessimistic light. *Die Abenteuer eines Zehnmarkscheins* (1926) ended happily, but otherwise dwelt upon the unrelated lives which individuals lived in Berlin, linked only by the banknotes which circulated randomly among them [25]. Gerhard Lamprecht's *Emil und die Detektive* (1931) portrayed Berlin as a sunlit, cheerful place in which good, in the form of a gang of determined little boys, could triumph over an evil thief who had preyed on one of their number, recently arrived from the provinces. In the same year, however, Piel Jutzi's *Berlin-Alexanderplatz,* based on the novel by Alfred Döblin (see above, p. 142), was much more convincing in its evocation of a Berlin underworld [26]. 1931 also saw the release of Pabst's *Die Dreigroschener Oper,* based on Brecht's musical play. Although set in nineteenth-century London, its symbolic significance was lost on no one, and it very effectively complemented *Berlin-Alexanderplatz.* Indeed, Roger Manvell has suggested that Pabst was so keen to direct the film because it allowed him to recreate some of the slum atmosphere of his *Die freudlose Gasse* [27]. Finally, any suggestion that childish innocence could overcome urban dangers was contradicted in 1931 by Fritz Lang's *M.* This story of a child murderer was based on real events which had occurred in Düsseldorf, but the anonymous city in which Lang set the film was the epitome of the impersonal, uncaring, tension-ridden environment which Berlin had come to represent in the German cinema. Even the tenements were made to take some of the blame for the murder, with one of the characters lamenting the inability of working-class mothers to keep an eye on their children's play [28].

Lang used to relate that, while planning *M,* he incurred the distrust of a National Socialist official who assumed that the draft title, 'Murderers Amongst Us', presaged an exposé of his party's methods. According to another story, Lang was later offered the chance to become director of the German film industry under the Hitler regime. Lang refused the offer and immediately sailed for America. The stories sound too good to be entirely true, but they foreshadow the iron grip which the Nazis set on German film-making right from their accession to power in 1933. As a result, the big-city film disappeared almost overnight. Ambivalent though National-Socialist attitudes to the big city, and to Berlin in particular, undoubtedly were (see below, pp. 216, 309), the Party could at least ensure that the metropolis was kept out of the cinema. In one respect only was a Weimar tradition maintained, and then only for a while. This was the Berlin-set film of political struggle. Most obviously in *S. A. Mann Brandt* (1933) [29] but also in *Hans Westmar* and *Hitler Junge Quex*, Berlin was used as the backdrop for tales of noble beings triumphing over Communist riff-raff. However, in these answers to *Kuhle Wampe*, the Nazi cinema not surprisingly glossed over poverty and poor housing conditions in Berlin. The city became a neutral stage on which a struggle between 'right' and 'wrong' was fought out. The city's streets, far from being portrayed as gloomy corridors in which the individual lost his freedom or his sanity, became grandiose, animated, parade axes. The cinema thus foreshadowed the plans of Speer and his ilk (see below, pp. 216–18). However, once the doings of the Horst Wessels had been duly celebrated, this genre faded out, speeded on its way by the demotion of the S.A. in 1934. The overwhelmingly escapist character of Nazi cinema and the party's official anti-urban ideology allowed no place for big-city themes, even cheerful ones.

Russia and Japan

It is always tempting to dismiss National Socialism as an aberration yet, as Lars Olof Larsson suggests elsewhere in this volume, certain urban tendencies of the 1930s were apparently a function of totalitarian government rather than of specific political programmes (see below, pp. 216–18). It is not entirely surprising, therefore, to find that Soviet Russia had no place for big-city films either. On the contrary, Soviet filmographies suggest a predominance of rural themes between 1917 and 1940 [3]. A 'city symphony' was made about Moscow, and Mark Donskoi directed *In the Big City* (1929), the story of a young poet from the countryside whose talents are eroded in Moscow by easy success [31], but overall the giant city and its life were neglected. The cinema thus echoed the prevailing 'deurbanist' and 'disurbanist' tendencies which, much as in Germany, were contradicted in practice by the demands of industrial development, but which it was possible to honour on the silver screen without damaging the economy.

Such Soviet film-makers as chose to reveal a mind of their own did not normally get a chance to exercise their talents in exile, but German cineasts, already a very mobile group before 1933, were luckier. The National-Socialist takeover thus helped to export the Weimar interest in the city directly into other national cinemas. Of course, German influence had already been strong in the 1920s. The Japanese cinema, in particular, looked to Germany for technical and artistic inspiration from the expressionist period onwards. The Japanese version of 'new realism' produced a number of films about Tokyo slums with a 'street' emphasis, and there was a Tokyo 'city symphony' in 1929. Over the period as a whole, however, the Japanese emphasis on the individual and the domestic environment, combined with technical limitations, meant that it never came directly to grips with the big city [32]. The cinema may thus have reflected or protracted the somewhat blurred Japanese image of the metropolitan phenomenon discussed below by Shun-ichi J. Watanabe (see esp. pp. 403, 428).

United States

Where German influence really made its mark was in the United States. Hollywood had been rich and prestigious enough to attract German cineasts in the 1920s. One of the most distinguished was F. W. Murnau, whose brief Hollywood career was ended by a fatal car accident there in 1931 [33]. This tragic end might be regarded as the big city's revenge on the director, for Murnau had transported his German anti-urbanism to the United States, almost without modification. In *Sunrise* (1927) he brought to the screen a script by Carl Mayer based on the Hermann Sudermann novel, *Die Reise nach Tilsitt* [34]. He constructed a big, exterior city set – of the Bigtown, not the New York, variety – and used it as the setting for a confusing story, complicated by a commercially-imposed happy ending, of the corruption of rural innocence by the lure of urban excitement. *Sunrise* is widely considered to be one of the most beautiful films ever made, and the highlight is an inter-urban (long-distance tram) journey from Arcadia into the city which formalizes the contrast between bucolic purity and big-city frivolity. The exterior scenes echoed the German 'street' genre, with plenty of hurrying feet and scurrying traffic. Murnau went on to make another film about relationships between urban and rural people, *City Girl* (1929). Meanwhile, Josef von Sternberg was making a series of proto-gangster films set in depressing urban surroundings, most notably *The Docks of New York* (1927).

Until the Germans started work in Hollywood, the U.S. cinema had not been interested in the metropolis, except as a locale for Harold Lloyd antics and other slapstick. In the later 1920s, however, the German example was emulated with some vigour. The year 1928 saw Tod Browning's *The Big City*, Jack Conway's *While the City Sleeps*, Paul Fejos's *Lonesome*, and King Vidor's *The Crowd*. Vidor's was the first of a series of films in which he contrasted, with his usual degree of overstatement, the city and the country. In *The Crowd*, two young people of rural

FIGURE 6.6. *The Crowd* (1928). John and Mary discover that they are in love while returning on the subway from a Coney Island outing with a group of local children (from the MGM release 'The Crowd' © 1928 Metro-Goldwyn-Mayer Distributing Corporation. Copyright renewed 1956 by Loew's Incorporated).

FIGURE 6.7. *The Crowd* (1928). John and Mary, now married, watch in horror as their little boy is knocked down by a lorry outside their New York apartment (from the MGM release 'The Crowd' © 1928 Metro-Goldwyn-Mayer Distributing Corporation. Copyright renewed 1956 by Loew's Incorporated).

origin meet and fall in love during their early days in New York. They take up residence in a tenement, where gradually the hustle of city life takes its toll, ending with their little son being knocked down in the street before their eyes. Never afraid of stating the obvious, Vidor called his protagonists John and Mary to symbolize the innocence of American youth, and left his audience in no doubt that it was the city that gradually dragged them down [35]. Significantly, when Vidor pursued his theme with a study of rural life, *Our Daily Bread* (1934), his leading protagonists were again called John and Mary. Though a study of the hardships and injustices of rural life, *Our Daily Bread* demonstrated Vidor's confidence in the ability of decent country folk to overcome adversity by selfless cooperation and by standing together against the oppressive forces of big-city finance.

Vidor's simplistic view of the struggles of human existence inclined him to a crude anti-urbanism which set him apart from other Hollywood directors. In any case, the definitive arrival of sound in 1929 confirmed the credentials of the big city, as *par excellence* the home of noise, as a neutral or even positive setting for feature films. A never-ending series of musicals extolling, directly or indirectly, the excitements of New York began in 1929 with *The Broadway Melody* [36]. Most were studio-set and even stage-bound, but they made much use of decor and lighting symbolic of Manhattan.

The big city appeared in a less flattering light in the work of Charles Chaplin and Buster Keaton, which flourished in the sound era even though considerable continuity was maintained with the comic miming techniques of the 1920s. The beginnings of Chaplin's involvement with the big city coincided with the first musicals and gangster films. His *City Lights* (1930) and *Modern Times* (1935) were variations on the theme of the little man versus the big city which was also taken up by Buster Keaton in *Sidewalks of New York* (1931). This move to the metropolis probably reflected in part the exhaustion of the Hollywood and Beverly Hills locations which had been so extensively used by comics in the silent era. However, the element of mild social criticism in Chaplin's big-city films suggests that he and other creators of screen comedies were responding to the general shift of the American cinema towards metropolitan themes which had been under way since the later 1920s. The key contribution to that shift, however, was made not so much by the musical and the Chaplinesque comedy as by another new genre, the gangster film.

Though foreshadowed in the 1920s, the gangster film did not blossom until sound arrived. The constant prattling which marred so many run-of-the-mill American films in the 1930s actually contributed positively to the gangster films. After *Little Caesar, City Streets, The Public Enemy*, and *Scarface* had established them firmly in public affections, both in the United States and abroad, between 1930 and 1932, they held an impregnable position throughout the decade, their style and content influencing many stories of popular life which were not primarily devoted to the theme of crime. It was perfectly obvious that gangster films were set in an urban milieu, but the city (which in any case was Chicago more often than New York) was rarely more than a neutral background. The early gangster films stressed the evil or pathetic personality of the anti-hero rather than the urban environment from which he had emerged. Outdoor scenes were rare, and usually took place at night, which helped reduce the cost of studio sets [37].

In fact, by the mid-1930s the increasingly common choice of New York or Chicago as a setting for American films of contemporary life still had not shown the average cinemagoer very much of those cities. In most big-city films, such as *Go Into Your Dance*, an Al Jolson musical comedy of 1935, explicitly set in the show-business milieu of New York and Chicago, there were no exterior shots at all. It became customary to imply outside movement by beginning each interior scene with shots of the protagonists leaving lifts. George Stevens's *Swing Time*, a New York musical of 1936, was noted for the care which the director devoted to creating realistic street scenes in the studio, but the technique was too costly to secure widespread emulation [38]. Models and special effects were rarely used to simulate big-city exteriors, no doubt because they were considered more appropriate to films of fantasy. Films composed of successions of interior scenes certainly suggested the density of the New York environment, but they failed to convey anything of the scale or the physical functioning of the city. Suburban settings, moreover, were almost unknown, suggesting that apartment life was the norm.

In the later 1930s, however, a clear movement began towards the direct and realistic portrayal of the big-city slum. It was partly associated with Hollywood's growing interest in the social problems which had been exacerbated by the Depression, and to which public attention had been directed by the policies of the New Deal and by various sociological inquiries. This new American genre of the slum film echoed the German 'Zille' films of the later 1920s, particularly in its emphasis on environmental determinism. There was, however, a greater concentration on crime as a slum-generated problem than had been the case in Germany, no doubt because of the all-pervasive influence of the gangster film. One of the first purposive portrayals of New York as a bleak, unforgiving environment, generative of crime and general unhappiness, was *Winterset* (1936). Based on a Broadway play, its plot unfolded during a few night-time hours on a rainswept square under Brooklyn Bridge [39]. In the following year it was upstaged (literally as well as figuratively) by the biggest U.S. slum film of the period, *Dead End*. Based on another Broadway play, it was produced by Samuel Goldwyn and directed by

FIGURE 6.8. *Dead End* (1937). Note the highly stylized confrontation of the two gangsters (one of them played by Humphrey Bogart) and the admiring local youngsters. The heavily populated balconies contribute to the picturesque effect criticized by purists of the social realism school (courtesy of The Samuel Goldwyn Company).

William Wyler on one, huge set, representing a Lower East Side tenement street. In his earlier films Wyler had learned to use deep-focus interior shots to express social hierarchies [40], and he applied the same technique in the *Dead End* street, which had become temporarily a place of encounter for rich and poor owing to roadworks in an adjoining, fashionable thoroughfare. Wyler has been criticized for romanticizing poverty at the behest of Goldwyn [41], but *Dead End's* principal message was that the New York slums were full of decent people who deserved a better chance in life. In *Dead End* the gangster character, played by Humphrey Bogart, is unsympathetic and eventually meets his end at the hands of the hero, an unemployed architect(!). However, the gangster's mother and former mistress are portrayed as victims of the slum. In *Angels With Dirty Faces* (1938) the main message is that a big-city slum upbringing turns decent youngsters into criminals. In fact, in the later 1930s, the whole gangster genre turned away from the evil criminal genius towards the social origins of crime [42]. *Little Tough Guy* (1938) used much the same cast of boy actors as *Dead End*; Graham Greene, at that time a film critic, described its theme as 'the natural adolescent virtues decaying on the East Side under the iron ladder of the Elevated' [43]. The social roots of crime in the big city were also stressed in two more conventional gangster films, *The Roaring Twenties* (1939), and *City for Conquest* (1940).

Some of these studies were extremely persuasive, especially when child actors were used. Because tenement blocks, even when simulated in the studio, made good cinema, slum scenes were generally set in New York. Low-density working-class districts in other cities were less frequently portrayed and, *a fortiori*, the suburbs of New York and of other cities stayed completely out of the picture. Consequently, no alternative to the New York tenement slum was put before the cinemagoer except in *The City* (1939), a documentary call for planned green-belt

FIGURE 6.9. A New York street from *The City* (1939), a persuasive indictment of metropolitan congestion (courtesy of National Film Archive Stills Library).

towns commissioned by the Regional Plan Association of America. It was normally up to the viewer to envisage what might replace the slums (unless he made the connection with the Wellsian high-rise city glimpsed in science-fiction films); he could not fail to conclude, however, by the later 1930s, that big-city slums were an evil which ought to be removed.

Britain and France

So far we have almost completely ignored two national cinemas, those of Britain and France. We have done so for different reasons; British film-making was not very accomplished before 1940, whereas the French cinema did not have much to say about the giant city. However, both were very prone to influences radiating from the Berlin-Hollywood axis, and both had distinctive features which reflected their national urban realities.

The titles of some early, and deservedly forgotten, British films suggest an interest in metropolitan life – *London Pride* (1920), *The Road to London* (1921), *While London Sleeps* (1922) and *London Love* (1926) spring from the lists [44] – but the first really influential London film was Alfred Hitchcock's *The Lodger: A Story of the London Fog* (1926). Significantly, perhaps, Hitchcock had just returned from a period working in the German cinema, and Petley detects the influence of Murnau in *The Lodger* [45]. It included some interesting documentary shots of London traffic moving through darkened streets, and some on-location scenes, shot under real or simulated night conditions. It helped confirm London as the appropriate breeding ground for maniacs of Jack-the-Ripper lineage, and as the home of atmospheric, and also money-saving, fogs. These features were exploited by subsequent directors to an extent which it would be tedious even to begin to investigate, but the upshot was that cinematic London appeared even gloomier than the reality.

The sound era saw a number of films which embroidered Soho and theatreland themes in varying degrees of imitation of Hollywood products. *Piccadilly* (1929) was a story of exclusive night-club life but its emphasis on interiors and its self-conscious attempt to emulate Hollywood drew the following criticism: '. . . he might have been filming Timbuctoo for all the relation his picture bore to its title' [46]. Herbert Wilcox's lavish *London Melody* (1936) also managed neither to recreate Broadway excitement nor to portray a distinctive London environment. More effectively related to its milieu was *Greek Street* (1930), a story of colourful low life [47]. Soho and East End crime stories flourished thereafter, but portrayals of poverty were rare. Herbert Wilcox hit a mawkish note with his *London* (1927), the story of a Limehouse waif [48], and although slum and working-class studies were more common in the 1930s, sentiment generally prevailed over objectivity. In *St. Martin's Lane* (1938), Charles Laughton sought the best of both worlds, marrying slum life with theatreland via the adventures of a street entertainer. John Baxter's *Doss House* (1932) was a serious attempt to explore lower-class life, but was not emulated. The British cinema thus failed to produce any influential equivalents of the 'Zille' films and films of the *Dead End* type.

The almost complete invisibility of the London slums did not mean that the suburbs were favoured. Carol Reed's *Laburnum Grove* (1936), based on the J. B. Priestley play, tells the story of an apparently respectable suburbanite who is finally exposed as a counterfeiter; Graham Greene remarked at the time that 'suburbia . . . insinuates itself into every shot', but 'insinuates' is the word, given that the film consists entirely of interior scenes [49]. In fact, to see ordinary London life portrayed in the 1930s, we have to turn to the products of the expanding British documentary movement, with *So This is London* (1934), *Housing Problems* (1935), and *The Londoners* (1938), all three the work of Edgar Anstey. No London 'city symphony' ever reached the screen, however. In this regard it is significant that Carl Mayer, creator of *Berlin: die Symphonie einer Grossstadt,* moved to London in 1932 but was thwarted in his ambition to make a London equivalent because no one would produce his script [50].

Mayer died in 1944. Ironically, his last years saw the *Luftwaffe* exert a bigger influence on the cinematic portrayal of London than he had ever done. From 1940 British documentary film-makers found themselves required to produce propaganda films designed largely for transatlantic consumption. In the absence of uplifting military activity elsewhere, they focused on the dramatic events of the London blitz. For the first time, most notably in Humphrey Jennings's *London Can Take It* (1940), London became a film subject in its own right. Documentary, exterior-shot footage was now at a premium, and metropolitan symbols were used to the full. In *London Can Take It,* Jennings made much use of the unifying symbol of the dome of St. Paul's, and the soundtrack was backed by Vaughan Williams's *London Symphony.* London was portrayed as a powerful, permanent force, capable of coordinating and inspiring its citizens [51]. Subsequently, these documentary techniques and the theme of an eternal, indomitable metropolis were embodied in feature films, most noticeably in Sidney Gilliat's *Waterloo Road* (1945), with its influential combination of documentary and studio-shot street scenes [52]. Even the portrayal of London suburban life gained in realism and sense of environment in this wartime atmosphere, at any rate in David Lean's *This Happy Breed* (1944). The way now stretched clearly ahead to the London-set realism of the post-war cinema, in *It Always Rains on Sunday, The Blue Lamp,* and many more. However, that this exciting prospect should open up so quickly only serves to emphasize the significance of the discontinuity represented by the Second World War.

In its belated elevation to the status of film personage, London took on a role which Paris had played since the very origins of the cinema. However, Paris was not generally utilized to make people think. In the numerous boulevard comedies and stories of how the rich live, it was a smiling, sunlit backdrop; in the much rarer studies of lower-class life, it was quaint or quirky. So deep-seated was this tradition, in fact, that, years later, Claude Chabrol's *Les bonnes femmes* (1960) would be noted for its use of Paris as a lowering, doom-laden setting for a portmanteau story of the tragic futility of lower-middle-class life [53]. Only in early documentaries was Parisian poverty portrayed. In 1926 the Brazilian, Alberto Cavalcanti, made *Rien que les heures,* regarded by some as the prototype 'city symphony', and concentrating on the life of the poor districts [54]. Georges Lacombe's *La zone* (1928) was a unique study of suburban poverty, inspired by the typically Parisian phenomenon of the inter-war shanty-town (see below, p. 267) [55]. At the time, suburban squalor, even in Paris, could not qualify for picturesque treatment (though, thirty years later, even that obstacle would be overcome in René Clair's nostalgic and sentimental *Porte des Lilas*).

Paris as a fairy-tale city was developed explicitly by the mercurial, Paris-born René Clair in *Paris qui dort* (1923) and *Entr'acte* (1924), both of which included much externally shot footage. Ghostly or horrific events were featured in a series of variations on the 'Phantom of the Opera' theme, including René Clair's *Le fantôme du Moulin Rouge* (1924), but most had a light touch which distinguished them from the London variety. Stories of popular life were inaugurated by *Ménilmontant,* and *Paris,* both released in 1924, but they stressed the solid, sustaining qualities of working-class Parisian society rather than the tribulations of poverty or the harrowing effects of a high-density living environment. In this respect, they complemented cheerful stories of West End life such as *La Rue de la Paix* (1927) [56].

The onset of the sound era stopped directors like René Clair from shooting outside scenes, but it confirmed the sentimental bent of the Paris-set film. Clair set the pattern with his musically-enhanced extravaganza of sentiment, *Sous les toits de Paris* (1930). Using a big street set built in the open at the new Tobis studio at Epinay, he made great play of the multi-dimensional built form of Paris as the setting for a rich popular life [57]. In 1931 Clair made the same point in his even more wayward *Le million,* which begins with a tracking shot over a model of a Parisian roof- and chimney-scape. Significantly, when Clair essayed some mild criticism of modern industrial life in *A nous la liberté* (1931), he chose the setting of a large suburban factory (in any case not explicitly located in the Paris area) rather than a crowded city centre. In 1932 Clair returned to Parisian popular whimsy with *Le quatorze juillet.* The Parisian stereotype as the home of colourful characters was not seriously disturbed by the documentary movement. *Le Métro* (1934), by Georges Franju and Henri Langlois, was a serious attempt to portray an essential element of the functioning of the city, but *Village dans Paris* (1939) was a brief essay on the colourful life of Montmartre, directed by Pierre Harts but photographed by none other than . . . René Clair.

And yet, right at the end of our period, a curious and exciting fusion occurred of Parisian sentimentality and the idea of the hopeless struggle of man against the city which had lurked somewhere in the consciousness of French cineasts since it had taken visual shape in Germany in the 1920s. The main creators of this synthesis were Jean Renoir and Marcel Carné, who were entranced by the so-called 'poetic realism' which imbued the film scripts of the versatile poet, Jacques Prévert. The result was a set of city films, produced in 1938 and 1939, which were artistically the most impressive of the whole pre-1940 urban canon.

Jean Renoir, an admirer of Emile Zola and German expressionism, had taken to the dark and rainy world of the streets in three early films, *La chienne, La nuit du carrefour,* and *Boudu sauvé des eaux,* in 1931–32 [58]. *La chienne* included a murder by the hero in a tenement block which foreshadowed Carné's *Le jour se lève,* but by the time Carné came to this genre, Renoir himself had returned to it with his adaptation of a Zola story, *La bête humaine,* in 1938. The central theme of the plot was the havoc caused by the innate passions of a railway engine driver, and Renoir made great symbolic play of mighty locomotives careering along the rails. However, much documentary footage was shot in and around the Gare Saint-Lazare, and interior sets of railway workers' apartments were convincingly mocked up to look out onto the tracks outside the station. The Paris domestic scenes thus complemented the railway episodes in symbolizing the hero's imprisonment in a desperate pattern of events.

The tragic hero of *La bête humaine,* Lantier, was played by Jean Gabin. As an actor Gabin exuded a combination of virility and sensitivity for which he was much sought after. It was no coincidence, therefore, that he should reappear in other 'poetic realism' films. His presence emphasized that the city had trapped a heroic individual who in more propitious circumstances would have been capable of overcoming all obstacles. In Carné's *Quai des brumes* (1938), set in a bleak Le Havre, Gabin appeared in another exercise in the fatalistic implications of seedy urban environments and mass transport systems. In *Hôtel du Nord,* also released in 1938, Carné portrayed two hopeless lovers reduced to suicide in and around a grimy hotel in north-eastern Paris. Finally, in *Le jour se lève* (1939), he directed a story in which the hero, played by Gabin, is physically trapped for the entire film at the top of a grotesque block of workers' flats set in an anonymous industrial suburb [59]. All these films made extensive use of studio-built exteriors in which physical decrepitude was emphasized, with the fatalistic plots symbolized by single tram tracks running down the streets. Whereas American slum films of the later 1930s focused on underprivileged but malleable youngsters, Carné and Renoir concentrated on young adults unable to find happiness. The city was never explicitly blamed for their plight, but it was used as a physical expression of hopelessness, a definite end of the road.

Viewed objectively, these decors may be seen as reflecting the urban reality of France in the Depression. However, that factual significance was lost on the world-wide audiences which these films of 'poetic realism' secured among educated filmgoers. Instead, they carried the more general implication that the old world had come to a bitter end. Complete annihilation, or a completely new start, were the only alternatives. Soon, of course, the war would bring the world closer to both those solutions. Undoubtedly, the wartime and post-war determination to create completely new cities sprang from many influences other than those depressing

FIGURE 6.10. *Hôtel du Nord* (1938). As the Bastille Day street ball on the banks of the Canal Saint-Martin drags towards its close, the ill-fated lovers ascend the steps of a heaven bridge. The seedy implications of the ball contrasted with the carefree atmosphere of Clair's *Le quatorze juillet* (1932). The set, though consisting largely of a huge backdrop, was painstakingly realistic, the foreground, for instance, being closely modelled on an actual Canal Saint-Martin footbridge. Note the (probably last-minute) removal of gas lamps on the bridge to prevent their crowding the foreground (courtesy of National Film Archive Stills Library).

French city films. However, their insidious images may well have lurked inside the consciousness of many of those who set out after 1945 to create, at long last, the ideal city.

Science Fiction and the Vertical City

When Fritz Lang settled on *M* as the title of his study of a child murderer, he was aware no doubt of the implied connection with his earlier 'city' film, *Metropolis*. However, *Metropolis* was of less direct relevance to the big-city phenomenon than any of the films discussed so far. Set in the year 2000 or thereabouts, it was an extrapolation of existing tendencies in technology and class conflict, woven through with a strand of the occult. The 'city' of jostling skyscrapers with underground factories and workers' homes was merely a convenient expression of these political forces, which were more prominent in inter-war futurist literature than they had been in pre-1914 Wells, thanks to the work of Jack London, George Orwell, Aldous Huxley, and others. Lang had disappointed his father, a municipal architect-planner in Vienna, by not following him into the architectural profession [60], and, like at least one other thwarted Austrian architect, he appears to have sought compensation in manipulating models. However, there can be no doubt that *Metropolis* and other science-fiction films, in adopting Wells's 'domed city' alternative rather than the spreading, suburban city of *Anticipations* (see above, p. 137), tended to persuade the general public that the giant city of the future would be an apotheosis of Manhattan, rather than of Queens. That these future cities were incidental to exciting or even stupefying plots reinforced the potency of the image. In 1929, for instance, Gaumont's first British sound film, *High Treason*, set a story of political skulduggery in a high-rise London of 1949, using models and other special effects [61]. The film, *Things to Come,* was really about power and ideology rather than cities, but the special effects, unusually competent for a British-made film, not surprisingly concentrated on ultra-urban structures. The explanation is clearly not that film directors were committed urban prophets, but that the denser the urban environment, the more suitable a setting it is for exciting events. Even car chases, which are much easier to shoot in the open country or deserted suburbs, are at their most exciting in crowded city centres, as witness *The French Connection* (though *pace Bullitt*). Given that urban on-location shooting was so difficult before 1940, there was a strong temptation to turn to science-fiction because it justified the use of models and/or back projection. The same applied to exercises in fantasy such as *King Kong* (1933) and the *Batman, Superman* and *Flash Gordon* serials, which in their turn reflected a comic-book emphasis on multi-storey cities. In fact, one may reasonably presume that the flying abilities of these heroes were developed in the original comic-strips to facilitate a three-dimensional relationship with the skyscrapers of the New York location which (albeit thinly disguised as 'Metropolis' or 'Gotham City') pervaded these stories. To extend this discussion from science-fiction to children's reading and films would involve too disruptive a digression, but if we can assume that attitudes are largely formed in early childhood, it is not irrelevant to point out that the inter-war youngster could scarcely have failed to obtain the impression that 'city' meant a jumble of closely-packed skyscrapers. The persuasiveness of this image must have been even further enhanced when combined with a surrealistic as well as an expressionistic presentation, as it was, for instance, in the disconcerting *Betty Boop* cartoon films. These portrayals may well have helped convince the general public that 'cities of towers' were either excitingly desirable or a normal state of affairs, and, in the absence of cinematic studies of the suburbs, thus contributed to the worldwide breakthrough of tall building after 1945.

Conclusion

Siegfried Kracauer tells us that the function of the film is to 'confront us with our visible environment' [62]. As we have seen, the average filmgoer was not often confronted directly with the environment of the giant city before 1940. On the other hand, it was implicit in much of what he saw. Moreover, those occasional big-city scenes sometimes had the power to strike deep into the consciousness. Kracauer, again, relates that, in the first film he ever saw, one shot of a residential street made such an impact that the memory of it stayed with him throughout his life [63]. Might not then such elusive images, acting upon the emotions rather than the intellect, lie at the fountainhead of much of the planning of cities after 1945?

NOTES

1. The wording is quoted from the full scenario of *Sunrise* published in *L'Avant-Scène du Cinéma*, no. 148, June, 1974, p. 44. The year ascribed to film titles in this chapter is normally the year of release.
2. *Things to Come* was, of course, inspired directly by the Wells novel. Fritz Lang, director of *Metropolis*, claimed that the idea for his sky-scrapered upper city came to him when he first saw the Manhattan skyline from the deck of an approaching liner, but Wells, as Peter Keating has already pointed out (p. 138), regarded the film as a tribute to the persuasiveness of his own vision. Lang's view of the matter is discussed in Kracauer, Siegfried (1947) *From Caligari to Hitler: A Psychological History of the German Film*. Princeton: Princeton University Press, p. 149.
3. Thomson, David (1965) *England in the Twentieth Century*. Harmondsworth: Penguin, p. 182.
4. Dickinson, Thorold (1971) *A Discovery of Cinema*. London: Oxford University Press, pp. 8–9.
5. This viewpoint is predominantly associated with the work of Kracauer (*op.cit.*, passim [see note 2]) on the German cinema.
6. Mayer, J. P. (1948) *British Cinemas and Their Audiences*. London: Dennis Dobson.
7. The one was made by the G.P.O. film unit, and discussed traffic planning problems in London. The other, much better known, was made for the Regional Plan Association of America with the participation of Lewis Mumford, Pare Lorentz, Aaron Copland, and other leaders of the U.S. documentary and social-reform movements.
8. Dickinson, *op.cit.*, pp. 8, 13 (see note 4).
9. *Ibid.*, p. 61.
10. *L'Express*, 5–11 July 1980, p. 98 (author's translation). I am grateful to Anne-Marie Beslier for pointing out this reference, as well as introducing me, years ago, to that invaluable periodical, *L'Avant-Scène du Cinéma*.
11. Anderson, Joseph L. and Richie, Donald (1969) *The Japanese Film: Art and Industry*. Rutland, Vermont/Tokyo: Charles E. Tuttle Company, pp. 27–28. Filming presumably ceased during the morning and evening rush hours.
12. Low, Rachael (1971) *The History of the British Film, 1918–1929*. London: Allen and Unwin, pp. 168, 218–27; Betts, Ernest (1973) *The Film Business: A History of British Cinema 1896–1972*. Allen and Unwin, p. 108.
13. Kracauer, *op.cit.*, p. 17 (see note 2).
14. The important role of townscapes in German expressionism is emphasized in Eisner, Lotte H. (1969) *The Haunted Screen: Expressionism in the German Cinema and the Influence of Max Reinhardt*. London: Thames and Hudson.
15. See Kracauer, *op.cit.*, pp. 165–80 (see note 2).
16. *Ibid.*, p. 182.
17. Manvell, Roger and Fraenkel, Heinrich (1971) *The German Cinema*. London: Dent, p. 39; Kracauer, *op.cit.*, pp. 119–22 (see note 2).
18. Cf. Kracauer's views, *op.cit.*, pp. 182–6 (see note 2).
19. *Ibid.*, pp. 158–9.
20. *Ibid.*, p. 143; Monaco, Paul M. (1974) *Cinema and Society in France and Germany 1919–1929*. Unpublished Ph.D. thesis, Brandeis University, p. 264.
21. Monaco, *op.cit.*, pp. 267, 397–8 (see note 20).
22. Quoted in Plummer, Thomas *et al.* (1980) Conservative and revolutionary attitudes in Weimar film, in Hirschbach, Frank D. *et al.* (eds.) *Germany in the Twenties: The Artist as Social Critic*. Minneapolis: University of Minnesota, p. 81.
23. Manvell and Fraenkel, *op.cit.*, p. 62 (see note 17).
24. See the series of stills published in *L'Avant-Scène du Cinéma*, nos. 190–1, July–September, 1977.
25. Kracauer, *op.cit.*, p. 181 (see note 2).
26. *Ibid.*, p. 223.
27. Manvell, Roger (1973) *Masterworks of the German Cinema*. London: Lorrimer Publishing, p. 14.
28. The full scenario is published in *ibid.*, pp. 99–177.
29. Hull, David S. (1969) *Film in the Third Reich: A Study of the German Cinema 1933–1945*. Berkeley: University of California Press, p. 25.
30. See, for example, Birkos, Alexander S. (1976) *Soviet Cinema: Directors and Films*. Hampden, Conn.: Archon Books, pp. 127 ff.

31. *Ibid.*, p. 212.
32. For a full discussion of the Japanese cinema in the pre-1940 period, see Anderson and Richie, *op. cit.* (see note 11).
33. Manvell (1973), *op.cit.*, p. 16 (see note 27).
34. Dickinson, *op.cit.*, p. 289 (see note 4). A full scenario appears in *L'Avant-Scène du Cinéma*, no. 148, June 1974. Significantly, when Sudermann's novel was later brought to the screen, as *Die Reise nach Tilsitt* (1939), by that willing servant of National Socialism, Veit Harlan, the anti-urbanism of Murnau was completely effaced, and replaced by sheer sentiment (see Hull, *op.cit.*, pp. 153–4 (see note 29)).
35. I am grateful to Barbara Miller Lane for introducing me to *The Crowd*.
36. Kracauer, Siegfried (1961) *Nature of Film: The Redemption of Physical Reality*. London: Dennis Dobson, pp. 130, 147.
37. This interpretation draws heavily on MacArthur, Colin (1972) *Underworld USA*. London: Secker and Warburg, pp. 28–29.
38. Kracauer (1961), *op.cit.*, p. 147 (see note 36).
39. See Greene, Graham (1972) *The Pleasure-Dome*. London: Secker and Warburg, pp. 141–3.
40. *National Film Theatre*, May 1981, pp. 2–4.
41. *Ibid.*, p. 4; Petley, Julian (1978) *BFI Distribution Catalogue 1978*, pp. 119–20.
42. This judgement is drawn from Rotha, Paul and Griffith, Richard (1963) *The Film Till Now: A Survey of World Cinema*. London: Vision Press, p. 455, and MacArthur, *op.cit.*, p. 39 (see note 37).
43. Greene, *op.cit.*, pp. 198–9 (see note 39).
44. The most authoritative source is Low, Rachael (1971) *The History of the British Film, 1918–1929*. London: Allen and Unwin. The films mentioned appear on pp. 176, 401–2, 437, 477.
45. Petley, *op.cit.*, pp. 127–8 (see note 41).
46. Low, *op.cit.*, p. 190 (see note 12).
47. Discussed in Betts, Ernest (1973) *The Film Business: A History of British Cinema 1896–1972*. London: Allen and Unwin, p. 59.
48. Low, *op.cit.*, pp. 176, 401 (see note 12).
49. Greene, *op.cit.*, pp. 90–91 (see note 39).
50. Kracauer (1947) *op.cit.*, p. 246 (see note 2).
51. Petley, *op.cit.*, p. 8 (see note 41).
52. Betts, *op.cit.*, p. 206 (see note 12).
53. See Bellour, Raymond *et al.* (1966) *Dictionnaire du cinéma*. Paris: Editions Universitaires.
54. Manvell, Roger (1955) *The Film and the Public*. Harmondsworth: Penguin, pp. 38, 41.
55. Kracauer (1961), *op.cit.*, p. 180 (see note 36).
56. This judgement is derived almost entirely from the sensitive analyses of *Paris* and *La Rue de la Paix* provided by Monaco, *op.cit.*, pp. 249–50, 344–5 (see note 20).
57. See Armes, Roy (1976) *Film and Reality: An Historical Survey*. Harmondsworth: Penguin, p. 57.
58. This analysis leans heavily on Braudy, Leo (1977) *Jean Renoir: The World of his Films*. London: Robson Books.
59. Full scenario in *L'Avant-Scène du Cinéma*, no. 53, 1965. The debate over the actual location of the story, whether it be Paris or Amiens, is discussed on p. 42.
60. Eisner, Lotte (1976) *Fritz Lang*. London: Secker and Warburg, p. 9.
61. Low, *op.cit.*, pp. 174, 203 (see note 12).
62. Kracauer (1961) *op.cit.*, p. ix (see note 36).
63. *Ibid.*

Chapter 7

The Metropolis in Music

DAVID HAROLD COX and MICHAEL NASLAS

NO precise definition of the nature of this chapter is possible. Is it an essay? An observation of the image of the metropolis in music? A discussion on the nature of musical presentation? An analysis of the visual impact of music? The truth is that it is something of all these, without being precisely any one of them. The reader who is looking for profound, scholarly analyses may be disappointed. What he will find instead are fragments of ideas, rough outlines of thinking, suggestions that in many instances may lead to questions which are not clarified. To develop just some of the themes touched on in this chapter would have required a much greater length and, most probably, a different approach.

What we present here then is a dialogue between a Composer and a Listener. No doubt, there are instances of lack of balance, weak points, and gaps, but we did not intend to produce a treatise. Instead, we are suggesting that the device of the dialogue can usefully present the characteristic features of the metropolis, as portrayed and reflected in music. Our Composer is inspired by the metropolis and aware of contemporary trends – in his own music and in popular music. His counterpart – the Listener – is a person active in the fields of planning, architecture, and urban studies in general; he is attached to music, aware of the artistic trends in the eighteenth and nineteenth centuries, but slightly perplexed by the music of the twentieth-century composers.

All the elements necessary for a successful dialogue are present. Both the Composer and the Listener are determined to look for common ground. There is sincerity and mutual respect. The participants enter the dialogue as persons skilled in the art and practice of their respective fields, each ready to listen and learn. It is all this that makes the discussion a real dialogue, and not a search for an impossible synthesis.

The Dialogue

Why is the twentieth-century idiom so much more difficult to understand than the music of previous centuries?

Composer

The composer of today is influenced by a very different type of environment compared to that of his predecessor. The early lives of the great composers of the past were spent in small communities, ranging in size from very tiny villages (as with Haydn [1732–1809] and Dvorak [1841–1904]) to at most a town of a few thousand inhabitants (as with Mozart [1756–1791] and Beethoven [1770–1827]). In the twentieth century, however, many composers have been born and brought up in the big cities. It would be surprising if issues concerned with city life were not found in their music.

A composer is or should be an individual sensitive to sound. Sound is the raw material out of which music is formed. The sound-experiences composers encounter in their formative years are no longer the quiet peaceful sounds of country life, but the harsher, more aggressive sounds of the city: the hustle and bustle of crowds, the noise of traffic, of trains and of aeroplanes, the sounds of the docks, of the warehouse and of the factory. Many composers have been so influenced by this new range of sounds that they have sought to integrate them into their musical language, creating in sound a reflection of life in the scientific age. *Pacific 231* (1924) by Honegger (1892–1955), a depiction in sound of a train leaving a station, is one famous but rather simple example. Other composers have tried to explore the musical potential in these sounds in ways that have affected their style more radically, more fundamentally. It is this type of work that causes difficulty to the listener used to traditional classical music.

Listener

This is understandably the important social and historical factor, but what about music itself? It is a misapprehension to assume that the complex reality of the modern world prevents us from understanding twentieth-century music. I sometimes think how pleasantly comprehensible, for example, is Beethoven in his Sixth Symphony; how majestically he communicates with the listener in his pictorial suggestions. The impression of nature in this symphony is unmistakeably retained. The contemporary composer, however, prefers to use abstract means for concrete themes, so that it is impossible to comprehend his music.

Composer

Your comparison between the modern composer and Beethoven is rather misleading. There is no essential difference between them; the intention of both is characterized by an urge to work out a system of musical pictorial signs and use them in the process we call music. If we, for example, assume that the purpose of a composer is to portray the impressions of a visitor in the big city – as he strolls, listens to various street noises, and absorbs the atmosphere of the places of interest, then we also ought to suppose that there are composers who will not endeavour to represent in their music any definite scenery of the city – to the same extent to which Beethoven was not inclined to deal with any definite scenery of the countryside in his Sixth Symphony. We must be aware that these compositions are programmatic only in a general, non-imitative, pictorial way, so that the individual listener can read into the music, if he wants to, such visual features as his imagination pictures for him. In other words, in the absence of any firm commitment by the composer, the listener is free to choose.

Listener   But, nevertheless, a great number of compositions directly relate (in their titles) to particular places.

Composer   This remark gives me an opportunity to follow, almost directly, the previous point. It is true; one can certainly provide an elaborate description of a musical work devoted to, say, London, Paris, or New York. Some listeners will be keen, for example, to follow a melancholy tune, apparently played on the fiddle by the light of a gas-lamp – a tune rising to a passionate and emotional climax, bringing forth a deeply nostalgic picture of a particular part of the city; at some later point, other listeners will discover the river which flows calm and silent through the city; more precisely, it could be the daybreak by the ancient river that flows on as it always did – and always will; the city sleeps, and in the hushed stillness of the early morning the church bell is heard striking the half-hour; one feels the city gradually awakening and stretching its limbs at the first light of day; and suddenly the scene changes and the city bursts into life; in the streets there is the bustle and turmoil of morning traffic, a steady stream of people hurrying; the unexpected rhythmic changes and musical phrases combine to mirror the character of the most bustling spot in the city, musically portraying typical traffic congestion.

Listener   Yes, I frequently receive various visual experiences by following music; I can, for example, recognize particular buildings or streets, and furthermore become directly, almost physically, aware of the life of a big city and of its atmosphere. There are certain thematic suggestions in some compositions and I wonder how accurate they are.

Composer   Because of the imprecise nature of musical language – of sound – precise descriptions, or themes, are difficult to convey accurately. The sequence of events is chosen with a view to the musical principle of contrast, and could be associated with a considerable range of subject matter. It should be noted that music evokes the sense of a composer's own world-picture; it shows his ability to suggest and depict the life of a great city; it is picturesque rather than programmatic, though it may be said to move, sometimes, through a series of events in terms of a time-scale. Music naturally, inclines to absolute values, and, consequently, the purely musical interest takes over as mood follows mood in the development of a particular theme.

Listener   We know about the conception and existence of 'Programme Music'. I have been inclined to interpret this kind of music as being realistic, concentrating on real, practical, things, conveying the images of the everyday world that people know well; for instance, street scenes or historical objects. Yet you suggest that such a music, though programmatic, or picturesque, responds quite characteristically to the objective components of the visible world. In your words, it inclines to absolute values. How would you, in fact, define 'Programme Music'?

Composer

The conflict between the ideal of pure instrumental music as the supreme mode of expression on the one hand, and the strong literary orientation, required in order to describe, has been resolved in the conception of Programme Music. This is instrumental music associated with descriptive – or even narrative – subject matter, not by means of rhetorical-musical figures, or by imitation of natural sounds and movements, but by means of imaginative suggestion. Programme Music aims to absorb and transmute the imagined subject-matter (the big city in our case), taking it wholly into the music in such a way that the resulting composition, while it includes the 'Programme', nevertheless transcends it and is in a certain sense independent of it. Instrumental music thus becomes a vehicle for the utterance of thoughts which, though they may be hinted in words, are ultimately beyond the power of words to express. A number of leading composers have been interested in the life of a big city. They have published their compositions with descriptive titles or programmatic commentaries, not in order to explain or justify what they had written – they knew as well as anyone that a work of art has to be its own justification – but because the programme was part of the idea of the composition in the same way that the text is part of the idea of a song. One might say that the programme is no more than a faint mist about the structure, lending charm to the view but not obscuring the outlines. It avoids extremes of feeling and never allows the extra-musical inspiration to disturb the musical balance.

Listener

Nevertheless, the title often suggests a descriptive piece of music, thus leading the listener to describe the whole composition in words.

Composer

The title may suggest to some listeners a descriptive piece, but this is not necessarily the intention of the composer. The life of a metropolis, including the various sights and sounds, has suggested to the composer an attempt at musical expression; but it could be of no help to the listener to describe these sights and sounds in words. The music is intended to be self-expressive, and must stand or fall as absolute music. If listeners recognize particular buildings or streets, they ought to consider these as an accidental occurrence – like the singing of birds in Beethoven's Sixth Symphony – not essential to the music itself. The variety of emotional feeling – gaiety, nostalgia and humour, bustle and ceremony – pre-eminently represents a range of musical contrasts, tunes and rhythms. All these conjure the atmosphere of a metropolis, often haunting and mysteriously eloquent.

Listener	This means that the composer offers no programme, but an amusing pictorialization of a place.
Composer	This is true. The non-imitative and non-objective pictorial vocabulary predominates. This vocabulary, in spite of any help offered by the title, is very hard on any individual used to concrete guidelines. Through the combination of varied sounds, a new entity emerges with a totally distinct reality contained within it. This often implies the simultaneousness of the ambient, and, therefore, the scattering and fusion of details, freed from accepted logic, and independent from one another. The composition is the synthesis of what one knows and remembers and of what one has heard; an entity into which external things are incorporated by means of the atmosphere.
Listener	What is the meaning of this 'new entity', of this 'totally distinct reality'? What does the composer intend by creating this new reality? What does he want to communicate?
Composer	The immediate answer is that in his works, despite the incidental pictorial suggestions, he wishes to write absolute music. The main notion of art, which underlines the work of composing music – music devoted to the metropolis, in our case – could be defined as follows: since no artist can ever succeed in copying reality pure and simple by trying to reproduce its every trait, his purpose instead must be to represent the reality – the metropolis – with the means proper to music.

The composer is thus concerned with the conception and organization of an arrangement of sounds. He uses abstract means for a concrete theme – the theme of metropolis – in order to evoke a comprehension of the subject in the listener and keep him from thematic suggestions, so that it is possible with such means to demonstrate and exemplify rather than imitate or reproduce. |
| *Listener* | In spite of the number of, as you say, non-figurative and non-conventional forms, many examples show, nevertheless, how the impression of the metropolis is figuratively and realistically retained. |
| *Composer* | Yes, this impression is frequently clear and strong; it depends on the arrangement of, one might say, the sound areas, which do not in any way harm the spatial effects of the composition. These sound areas give the impression of a view on to a city with houses, streets, etc. They are used to show, say, the aggressive aspect of the metropolis, and thus to seize the listener's attention. It is a continuous study of form expressed in sounds by simultaneous contrasts. The composer is attempting to produce an architecture of sounds in the hope of creating, without using literary or descriptive anecdotes, a dynamic representation of his own image of the metropolis. |

Listener

What then, are these non-imitative, musically-autonomous means, which the composer employs in order to produce, as you say, the architectonic sound structure?

Composer

The primary aim of the composer is to create figurative impressions by employing melodies, harmonies, colours, rhythms, and formal principles, which, in one way or another, contribute to making a specifically musical language. One important element in that language is colour: colour not only in the narrow sense of timbre, but in the broader sense as rising from melodic, harmonic, and rhythmic factors as well. When the composer follows up his musical jesting with, for example, the sounds of traffic in the streets, it is scarcely his intention, as we have mentioned, to solve the riddle of authenticity. His primary aim is to create an image of the busy street by evoking moods through rich and varied colours. He does not seek to express a feeling or tell a story, but to evoke a mood, an atmosphere, with the help of suggestive titles and occasional reminiscences of natural sounds, rhythms, bits of melody, and the like. He relies on veiled allusions and images, matched by the strange harmonies, subdued colours, and restrained expressiveness of the music.

Listener

One might conclude that, in order to decipher what the composer is trying to communicate, the listener has to indulge in an extremely active exercise of perception. If I am interpreting your explanations correctly, the listener should be able to discover that a composition devoted to the theme of metropolis has ceased to relate directly to an external scene; that it is an architectonic sound structure which arouses one's sensibilities, corresponds to the emotions, and can radiate appropriately; that it accepts the city in the movement of its forces, and that it does not describe its unimportant aspects. Most importantly, the listener should be constantly aware of the separation of strictly imitative representation from musical elements. In order to remain within the bounds of musical means, to concentrate on rhythms, harmonies, colours, on a musical language, the listener's desire to experience music must be related to a specific perception. What are the essential characteristics of this kind of perception?

Composer

This perception is the kind proper to an individual who does not just listen to music in order to identify as many objects known before as possible – for example, streets and buildings in a particular city – but who is primarily concerned in listening to experience something of and about the nature of these objects – about the life and structure of the same city. Musical compositions are made exclusively for this kind of perception. For that reason they are 'a-scenic' and do not represent any situation or complex of situations. Whereas a 'realistic', 'scenic', form of perception is interested in practical things, the musical, artistic, perception concentrates on the sensuous cognition of the characteristics, qualities and conditions of various objects in the metropolis – and of the metropolis as a whole.

Hence musical 'pictures' do not cite the objects portrayed so as to evoke empathy and direct identification, or as practical objects with a use-value. They introduce them only as objects comprehensible in terms of an artistic perception. Whereas a 'realistic' presentation might be interested, for example, in portraying the logical aspects of man's connection with his immediate surrounding, music is interested in the lack of the same aspects. This discrepancy is one that the composer tries to transcend musically: by assembling a repertoire of forms specific to music, and by the devices of autonomous arrangements and organization. The composer begins to undo the objective world when he finds he can no longer take up a 'utility' attitude to objects and represent what he knows from just looking at them. Instead, he wants to bring listening and knowing together and to portray knowledge as if it were the process of testing, discriminating and recognizing objects, their characteristics and qualities.

Listener	How are these principles put into practice?
Composer	The first music to be inspired by metropolitan life was a kind of urban folk music: popular ballads written by the inhabitants about their cities. Many more examples, some justly famous, have been composed in this century. This type of piece was exploited by Kurt Weill (1900–1950) in *The Rise and Fall of the City of Mahogonny* (1929) to create a stage work containing a powerful social message. In this discussion however we are going to consider music in which the experience of city life is captured through the sound-material used, rather than works in which the nature of the experience explored is primarily conveyed by the text.
Listener	What were the first pieces of classical music to be inspired by the metropolis?
Composer	One of the earliest was *Paris, The Song of a Great City* by Delius (1862–1934), but at the same time and in the same place a composer called Gustave Charpentier (1860–1956) included two orchestral preludes in his opera *Louise* called *Paris s'éveille* and *Vers la cité lointaine.*
Listener	Is it known whether one composer influenced the other?
Composer	There is no evidence to suggest that this occurred. The first sketches for *Paris* date from 1897 when Delius was working on a piece called *Scènes parisiennes. Paris, The Song of a Great City* was completed in 1899 and received its first performance in Elberfeld in 1901. Charpentier's opera *Louise* was first performed in Paris at the Opéra-Comique in 1900 after Delius had finished his work. It seems most likely that the appearance of these two works at the same time was a coincidence; such coincidences are not uncommon in the history of music, where composers minds often follow similar paths at the same time. It is more probable that both

composers' inspiration originates in the move towards realism and naturalism evident in late nineteenth-century artistic trends in France, as found for example in Impressionist paintings like Monet: 'Boulevard des Capucines'; Renoir: 'Les Grands Boulevards'; and Pissarro: 'Avenue de L'Opéra'. Delius in particular was much closer to poets, painters and sculptors, than to other composers; while in Paris he met and later married an art student from Belgrade, Jelka Rosen.

Listener

A comparison of the works would indicate whether the same stimulus can produce different reactions from two composers.

Composer

Although both pieces clearly originate from the turn of the century there are considerable differences between them. Charpentier was the more conservative composer of the two so his music is harmonically much less adventurous. Other differences are more relevant to our subject. Charpentier's opera *Louise*, his best-known work, concerns the emotional development of a Parisian working-girl. In fact Charpentier founded a theatrical institution in Paris to give working-class girls like his Louise a chance to sing, to dance and to act. The opera is full of subsidiary characters that are typical Parisian figures: artists, philosophers, Bohemians, and street traders like chair-menders, rag-men and vendors of a wide variety of goods such as artichokes, carrots, green peas, potatoes, barrels, brooms and bird-food; all treated with sympathy, understanding and humour. The final score of the opera ends with the single word Paris on the lips of the chief protagonists – sung exultantly by Louise who, called by the city, goes off to find her lover, and sung with remorse by her father who having attempted to destroy his daughter's love is rejected by the city that he too really loves. The depth of feeling evident in the work shows Charpentier as a true Parisian, and understanding the city, its life and its people by being part of it and them. With Delius however, although he was a great Francophile and had lived in Paris from 1888 to 1897, the view he gives of the city is one, as it were, from the outside. The work begins with Paris as seen from afar and frequently concentrates on scenes of Parisian night-life that might be experienced by a visitor to the city. The composition of *Paris* comes at a point in Delius's life when he had already exchanged his love of the city for the country. In 1897 he finally settled permanently at Grez-sur-Loing near Fontainebleau. The Delian view of Paris is a very personal one – a recollection of the emotional impact that life in the city had made upon him. Philip Heseltine made this point when he wrote that, for Delius: 'Paris was not so much the capital city of France as a corner of his own soul, a chapter of his own memoirs' [1].

Listener

Indeed I have heard it said that Delius's Paris is unrecognizable to Parisians.

Composer

If there is any truth in that statement it is because of the heavy orchestration employed (Delius being influenced by the orchestral technique of Richard Strauss) to give many dark, sonorous textures that are not at all French in character. The rhythmic drive and vitality of the piece is also unexpected in a Nocturne. This characteristic originates in the depiction of the scenes of Parisian night-life also found in the poem which Delius wrote to preface the score.

> Mysterious city –
> City of pleasures,
> Of gay music and dancing,
> Of painted and beautiful women –
> Wondrous city,
> Unveiling but to those who
> Shunning day
> Live through the night
> And return home
> To the sound of awakening streets
> And the rising dawn.

One of Delius's aims may well have been to create a dramatic juxtaposition of mood between the raucous crowd scenes of Parisian night-life and the solitude of other parts of the empty city at night. He seems to come closest to evoking the real spirit of Paris in those sections that anticipate the more individual atmosphere of his later more famous works. At the opening, for example, or in the Adagio section where the violas give out a long haunting melody in their upper register, the orchestral sound loses its Germanic heaviness and becomes more French in its exploitation of colourful orchestral sonorities.

Charpentier's two pieces are not set in the darkness of the Parisian night but in a kind of half-light: at dawn (*Paris s'éveille*) and twilight (the stage direction for the scene following *Vers la cité lointaine*). The orchestral colours Charpentier uses, though still dark, are more delicately French than those of *Paris*. The play of light, rarely more dramatic than the situations Charpentier depicts, was a popular Impressionist subject with composers; since music is an art in time, it is able to capture gradual changes in character more effectively than a painting which is merely the representation of a single moment. Nevertheless the demands of musical logic can conflict with the demands of reality. Charpentier's depiction of dawn in *Paris s'éveille,* for example, returns after a substantial climax to the quiet mood and material of its opening. This creates a satisfactory musical shape but also gives the incorrect impression that no sooner has Paris woken up than it returns to sleep again. Delius turns this to his advantage, however, using the coming of day (see the final lines of Delius's poem) to bring *Paris* to a close on a harsh and banal climax that completely dissolves the nocturnal atmosphere that has hitherto pervaded the work.

Listener

Eighteenth- and nineteenth-century music is based on principles of balance and symmetry creating a satisfying musical shape. This must often be impossible to achieve if the subject-matter we are discussing is to be treated satisfactorily.

Composer	True, but in the twentieth century composers have in any case moved away from obvious patterns of symmetry that bring the listener back to his starting point towards more complex formal solutions that are more realistic. Many composers now reason that it is impossible to return exactly to a starting point; inevitably the experience that has been undergone colours one's concept of its origin. *Paris* is an early example of a piece which conceals the element of return to original material to preserve the effect of a continual progression of thought, and through its subject-matter achieves this more radical formal solution in an entirely logical manner.
Listener	Despite these differences between the two composers' treatment of the same subject, there must be some points of similarity.
Composer	Yes, one similarity is that both composers drew inspiration from the street cries of Paris. Delius's work opens with various thematic fragments representing different street cries being heard in the distance, and closes with their return as day approaches and its activities begin again. Charpentier's prelude *Paris s'éveille* also opens with a number of thematic fragments that are later identified as street cries by being associated with particular traders. Only one street cry is obviously common to both scores: the sound of the goatherd's flute in Montmartre, still a semi-rural area at that time. Delius has altered his material more radically, making it more instrumental in character, as the ideas have to form the basis of an extended orchestral work; Charpentier's material is more vocal in character but of course his ideas are going to be sung later in the opera.
	The strangest coincidence is the similar use of a very long pedal (a pedal is a sustained bass note over which harmony changes gradually build up suspense) at the start of *Paris* and at the start of *Vers la cité lointaine*. It is not so much the use of this device, a standard means of creating tension, that is coincidental as the fact that both composers chose the same note (D, two octaves below middle C) on which to base the distant rumble of the city.
Listener	The image of Paris at the turn of the century that is communicated by these works seems to me to be one of stark contrasts. The people have a great zest for life, overcoming the hardship and poverty of their existence by their love for the city in all its moods. Was the atmosphere of any other city caught by composers writing at this time?
Composer	In 1900 Elgar took inspiration from his experience of London life to write the overture *Cockaigne*, the work is subtitled *In London Town*. For Elgar his overture called to mind: 'all the good humour, jollity, and something deeper in the way of English good fellowship abiding still in our capital' [2].
	Unlike the works we have just discussed this general aim is achieved by the use of several themes with specific associations. The hustle and bustle of city life is

clearly heard in the opening theme which returns frequently during the work to provide a backcloth against which other themes are displayed. The concept of a 'Londoner' is represented by a broad nobilmente theme heard soon after the beginning of the work. There are also individual characters like a cockney street urchin whose relationship to his parent is established by the use of a diminution of the nobilmente theme. The lyrical second subject represents a pair of lovers. Typical London events are also portrayed: a solemn procession, and a blaring military band which approaches, passes and recedes into the distance. The demands of musical logic are satisfied in that all these themes return at the end of the work but in a different order designed to bring the piece to an exciting climax. The lovers theme, more confidently stated, appears earlier than would be conventionally expected with the recapitulation of a second subject, and is followed by the brass band making another bombastic appearance. Eventually the only theme left to reappear is the broad nobilmente theme representing the Londoner and, stated fortissimo on full orchestra, this ends the work in a blaze of Edwardian glory.

Listener

Elgar's music is associated in our minds with the pageantry and splendour of the great days of the British Empire. The atmosphere in London at the turn of the century that is revealed by *Cockaigne* is one of complete confidence and conviction. Yet in a work composed only a few years later, in 1914 – the *London* symphony of Vaughan-Williams (1872–1958) – the absolute certainty of *Cockaigne* is much less apparent. It is impossible to imagine a work like *Cockaigne* being written today.

Composer

A piece of music, like any work of art, though it may rise above its period and become valid for all time, still retains associations with the character of the age in which it originated. An excellent example of this is *Central Park in the Dark*, composed in 1906 by the American, Charles Ives (1874–1954). *Central Park in the Dark* is another piece inspired by life in the metropolis – this time New York. Throughout the work strings play slow chains of discords, very softly and with no temporal pulse. Into this background texture woodwind, brass, pianos and percussion interject sounds with man-made associations. Ives described the work as: 'a picture-in-sounds of the sounds of nature and of happenings that men would hear when sitting on a bench in Central Park on a hot summer night. The strings represent the night sounds and silent darkness – interrupted by sounds (the rest of the orchestra) from the Casino over the pond – of street singers coming up from the Circle singing in spots, the tunes of those days – of some "night owls" from Healy's whistling the latest or the Freshman March – the "occasional elevated", a street parade, or a "breakdown" in the distance – of newsboys crying "uxtries" – of pianolas having a ragtime war in the apartment house "over the garden wall", a street car and a street band join in the chorus – a fire engine, a cab horse runs away, lands "over the fence and out", the wayfarers shout – again the darkness is heard – an echo over the pond – and we walk home [3].

In the course of the piece it becomes evident that the sounds of man totally fail to disturb the tranquillity of nature. Although at times admirably courageous in their brashness and banality, man's interjections into the world of nature are transient and ephemeral – perhaps even desperate. This theme of Man against Nature was a fundamental part of the American experience in the nineteenth century. The impact of civilization upon nature was nowhere more evident than in the United States where cities like Chicago grew up within the memory of one generation. Ives portrayed man's struggle against nature by taking as his inspiration what was then one area of peace and calm (Central Park) amidst one of the world's most rapidly expanding cities (New York) and by creating dramatic contrasts between musical textures that were so far ahead of their time, they still seem radical today. Ives was as much an American pioneer as those who explored the uncharted lands of the West, but he was an explorer of new areas of sound. In *Central Park in the Dark* he used snatches of popular melodies of the time (including at one stage a jazz band) in a polytonal, polyrhythmic chaos that would seem self-indulgent were it not for the expressive purpose underlying the extravagant musical language. Although he made use of the popular musical idioms of his day, Ives transcends their banal origins by treating them in an unconventional and totally original manner to create a work of lasting significance in the intensity and power with which it deals with one aspect of mankind's experience.

Listener

The aural impact is such that one needs an awareness of the composer's intentions in order to rationalize the apparently chaotic nature of his musical language. *Central Park in the Dark* is clearly a product of the American experience of the metropolis, revealing a city whose inhabitants had experienced such rapid changes in their lifestyle, that they were forced to question the real significance of them. Compared to the other pieces we have discussed so far, this work shows more awareness of social issues; exploring, like other works by the composer, the isolation of the individual in modern society.

Composer

Ives was very sensitive about the human condition. He made his fortune in insurance, a business that aims to help people overcome life's difficulties. As a composer Ives was totally isolated, his works remained unperformed and unrecognized for many years. Nevertheless, *Central Park in the Dark* is a historically important work in that it illustrates the beginnings of a trend increasingly evident in the early twentieth century in which taking their inspiration from the metropolitan experience impels composers towards a more radical musical language.

In the second decade of this century a group of artists and composers known as the Futurists attempted to compose music using the actual sounds of the industrial environment. Futurism originated in Italy where it was led by the composer Francesco Pratella (1880–1955), whose works were written for conventional instruments, and by the artist Luigi Russolo (1855–1947), who invented a number of new instruments to reproduce the sounds of his music. From inside various rectangular wooden boxes with megaphones attached, machinery produced the sounds of:

> Thunderclappers, Exploders, Crashers, Splashers, Bellowers, Whistlers, Hissers, Snorters, Whisperers, Murmerers, Mutterers, Bustlers, Gurglers, Screamers, Screechers, Rustlers, Buzzers, Cracklers, Shouters, Shriekers, Groaners, Howlers, Laughers, Wheezers, and Sobbers [4].

Works written for this group of instruments, including Russolo's *The Awakening of a Great City* (1913) and *A Meeting of Motor Cars and Aeroplanes* (1913), were little more than a collection of noises. Indeed to judge from Russolo's manifesto, *The Art of Noise*, published in Milan in March 1913, nothing else was ever intended:

> Let us pass through a great modern capital, more attentive with our ears than with our eyes. An everchanging pleasure will gratify our sensibilities as we distinguish the gurglings of water, air and gas in the metal pipes, the snorting and growling of the motors, breathing with their indescribable suggestion of animal being, the pulsation of pistons, the screeching of mechanical saws, the noisy bumping of trams on their rails, the cracking of whips, the flapping of flags. We will find amusement in imagining the ideal orchestration of the swinging doors of shops, the buzzing of crowds, the varied hullaballoo of railway stations, forges, spinning works, electric generating stations and underground railways [5].

Listener

The music of the Futurist has not found a permanent place in the twentieth-century repertoire.

Composer

Overwhelmed by their range of sounds the Futurists failed to organize them into a harmonic and rhythmic order that would have formed the basis for lasting music. Their music functioned on a very superficial level as a pictorial depiction in sound of modern life. Music, however, being essentially a language without specific connotations, is most effective when suggesting those human emotions too complex to express in words. It was left to another composer to realize the potential in the new sounds the Futurists had pioneered in a more abstract language that did impose a harmonic and rhythmic order on such apparently unmusical ideas.

Edgard Varèse (1883–1965) was a French composer who knew Russolo and his work. In the 1920s, having just settled in the United States, Varèse began to use these new kinds of sound material within more logical patterns of musical thought. Varèse wrote for ensembles of conventional instruments (he favoured woodwind and brass rather then strings) with a much larger percussion section than had been usual, for the first time using instruments such as sirens. Sounds were linked by pitch relationships in a manner similar to, though not exactly the same as, traditional music. By the act of organizing these sounds into a logical sequence of ideas, Varèse hoped to transcend their trivial origins and create a new musical language that captured the spirit, rather than the reality, of the modern age. The process by which Varèse achieved this seems to have been at least partly subconscious, as the following anecdote concerning his reaction to the first performance of *Hyperprism* (1923) makes clear:

> In *Hyperprism* there is a re-iterated very shrill high C sharp and during the performance of the work it brought convulsive laughter out of the audience: but when the composer returned to his home that evening, and sat awake wondering, he heard from over the city (New York) somewhere a very familiar sound, a siren, and suddenly realized that he had been hearing it for many nights, over six months, during the time he composed *Hyperprism*, and that the tone was exactly a very shrill high C sharp [6].

The origins of Varèse's inspiration were all too apparent to his first audiences, many of whom reacted with great hostility to his new musical language, failing to appreciate the differences between Varèse's approach and that of the Futurists. Thus *Hyperprism* was described by one critic in the following terms: 'A trolley car gong, an automobile horn, and the rush of gutter water down a manhole' [7]. Similarly, the first performance of a large-scale orchestral work, *Amériques* (1920) in 1926 was described by another critic as:

> The progress of a terrible fire in one of our larger zoos. The animals sensed the conflagration before their keepers and set up awful howls and emitted cavernous groans. Suddenly the siren is heard in the distance. It grows louder and more piercing. The engines arrive. For twenty minutes the howling of the animals and the shrieks of the siren reach to the skies. There the piece ends without any resolution. One will never know what happened. Was the fire put out? Was the menagerie rescued? Mr. Varèse, like a true artist, doesn't commit himself [8].

Although labelled for a time as a Futurist composer, Varèse never thought of his music in the Futurist way. He sought to reproduce the sounds of his inner, not his outer, ear; the sounds of his imagination, sounds that, though influenced by his personal experience of city life, were sounds that no other ear had yet heard. In response to criticism of *Amériques* he described the work as: 'The portrayal of a mood in music, not a sound picture' [9].

An analysis of the score of *Amériques* shows how Varèse captured the mood of America, through a design the composer described as 'architectonic', comprising three successive sections, each an expansion of the previous one. Through this expansionist formal structure Varèse created an image in sound of the vitality and enterprise of American city life in the years before the Depression. In his works for small orchestra with percussion, *Hyperprism* and *Intégrales* (1926), Varèse continued to make use of the 'architectonic' principles of formal design found in *Amériques* with 'blocks' or 'areas' of sound that could be juxtaposed or even directly combined. At the opening of *Intégrales*, for example, there are two long textures composed of areas of brass, woodwind and percussion sound all revolving around each other in an aural equivalent of a geometric design. As the titles of his work often imply, Varèse was inspired by phenomena encountered in the world of science but he evolved methods of composition that enabled him to use his musical material in an abstract way.

Listener

The use of instruments like sirens is actually misleading since it conjures up precise images that the composer did not intend to convey.

Composer

Varèse used the curving pitches of the siren because it enabled him to explore the whole pitch range, not just those provided by the limiting system of equal temperament. He had a vision that ultimately science would provide composers with inventions that would offer new sounds for their use – sounds associated only with the scientific age. When technological developments like the invention of the tape recorder eventually made electronic music possible after the Second World War, Varèse was one of the first composers to realize a mature artistic conception in the new medium. In his electronic works *Déserts* (1954) and *Le poème électronique* (1957) Varèse made use of sounds of industrial origin which he had recorded in the Philadelphia area. Although the origins of these sounds are more obvious, Varèse still made use of them in an abstract way, placing the sounds within a logical musical structure that provides an artistic framework within which their emotional associations can be fully appreciated.

Listener

Déserts doesn't sound a very metropolitan title.

Composer

The deserts Varèse was referring to were not just those of sand, sea and space, but also those of empty city streets.

Listener

The use of actual industrial sounds makes the origin of the composer's inspiration in the metropolitan experience much more apparent, and obviates the necessity evident in some of our earlier examples for a programme to explain the composer's intentions. Electronic music enabled composers to work directly with sound – so that any sound at all could be made part of a musical composition should the composer wish it. This is the reverse of the music of previous centuries in which the sounds used were relatively narrow in range and specialized in production. Under the impact of twentieth-century life composers like Varèse completely transformed the language of their music.

Composer

In many of the artistic forms of the twentieth century Art has moved closer to Life. Music is no exception. We have seen from our study of musical works inspired by the metropolis how there has been an increasing trend towards a more realistic expression of human experience. Some composers have gone so far as to adopt a position that makes no distinction between their music and the sounds of everyday life. John Cage (b. 1912), one of the most well-known *avant-garde* composers of today, recalls a concert given by one of his pupils, Christian Wolff (b. 1934):

> One day when the windows were open, Christian Wolff played one of his pieces at the piano. Sounds of traffic, boathorns, were heard not only during the silences in the music, but, being louder, were more easily heard than the piano sounds themselves. Afterwards someone asked Christian Wolff to play the piece again with the windows closed. Christian Wolff said he'd be glad to but that it wasn't really necessary, since the sounds of the environment were in no sense an interruption of those of the music [10].

Listener

In the course of the twentieth century there have been many different responses to the impact of the metropolis upon composers. To what extent can all these be drawn together to produce anything of value for those interested in the history of the development of the metropolis?

Composer

While the reaction of one individual may not be typical of an era, it is true that the totality of artistic production reflects an age as a whole. It is a characteristic of the twentieth century that the intellectual turbulence of the time is reflected by many differing viewpoints; important contributions to the music of our century have been made by both conservative and radical figures. Compared with other art-forms musical language is imprecise, for the most part it depends on symbols – the sound of the oboe, for example, represents either joy or pain according to the nature of the material given to it. Because music appeals directly to the emotions it is not easy to put its significance and achievement into the precise language of words. Judgements, therefore, are a matter of interpretation. Nevertheless, there is overwhelming evidence of a reaction to twentieth-century life reflected in the development of forms of expression that are harsher, more dissonant, more unpredictable, more disturbing than the sound-material of the music of previous ages. Whereas dissonance used to be carefully prepared and resolved it is now the norm of musical expression and consonant sounds are those treated as exceptional. These trends cannot be wholly attributed to the rise of the metropolis. The function of musical composition has changed radically in this century. Composers have turned away from music as an entertainment art-form and created works more didactic in intent, works that aim to show us different sides of man's character. Frequently it has been the dark side of human nature that has been explored either through the psychology of the individual as in the Expressionist works of Arnold Schoenberg (1874–1951) in *Erwartung* (1909) or *Pierrot Lunaire* (1912), or through the violence of the collective group as in the *War Requiem* (1961) by Benjamin Britten (1913–1979) or the *Threnody for the Victims of Hiroshima* (1960) by Krzystof Pendereck (b. 1933).

A number of works with programmatic intentions provide specific examples of music consciously inspired by the metropolis. It is noticeable that during the twentieth century the style of these pieces changes from the rich lush textures of the late-nineteenth-century romanticism of Delius and Elgar, to a sparse, economical, astringent idiom, after exploring harsh, brutal sonorities combined with a powerful rhythmic drive. Composers were inspired by the sounds of the city to invent new sonorities that widened the expressive range of their music. The music they created was adventurous and challenging, continually pushing into the unknown as if in a search for a stable musical language that could never be attained. As well as reflecting an age of continual change and development, music captures the difficulty encountered in adjusting to these more rapid patterns of life. In so doing the music itself often became more difficult for its audience to understand, widening the gulf between the composer and the listener still further.

The record left us by the composers of the period provides a unique means of assessing the impact of the metropolis upon its inhabitants. A piece of music can give an insight into the emotional feelings of past generations that can help the historian to a correct interpretation of the facts he gains elsewhere. In so far as music captures and retains for all time the spirit of the age in which it was written, it opens up for the listener a wider view of life than his own. The listener can share the experience of past composers, understand the conflicts they portray and appreciate the realization of those conflicts they achieve. Life in the metropolis may have been hard but it was not unexciting and it stimulated composers to write many new and adventurous works that are worthy of our attention.

NOTES

1. Heseltine, Philip (1923) *Frederick Delius*. London: The Bodley Head, p. 131.
2. McVeagh, Diana M. (1955) *Edward Elgar*. London: Dent, p. 34. Letter from Elgar to Joseph Bennett, April 1901.
3. Ives, Charles (1973) *Central Park in the Dark*. New York: Boelke–Bomart Publications, p. 31.
4. Scholes, Percy (1970) *The Oxford Companion to Music*, 10th edn. London: Oxford University Press, p. 527.
5. *The Musical Times*, January 1914, p. 20.
6. See Rosenfeld, Paul (1924) *The Dial*. Scranton, Pennsylvania: Musical Chronicle.
7. Divertimento, in *The Nottingham Journal and Express*, 20 June 1924.
8. Chotzinoff, Samuel, in *The New York World*, 14 April 1926.
9. Varèse, Edgard, in *The Evening Bulletin* (Philadelphia), 12 April 1926.
10. Cage, John (1968) *A Year From Monday*. London: Calder and Boyers, p. 133.

Chapter 8

Metropolis Architecture

LARS OLOF LARSSON

Le problème d'architecture de la vieille Europe, lui répondis-je, c'est la grande ville moderne.
Le Corbusier, *L'urbanisme* (1925)

THIS discussion must begin with a question: what exactly is metropolis architecture? To make sense – and to restrict it to a compass commensurate with the length of this chapter – it obviously has to be defined as something more specific than just architecture in a metropolis or even architecture serving typical metropolitan demands, such as mass transport, warehousing and big offices. Thus, for the purpose of this analysis I will concentrate on plans, projects and buildings whose designers sought – or may have sought – to express a distinct metropolitan spirit, vague and elusive though that may appear. Now, unfortunately, but of course not surprisingly, few architects ever bothered to state that a design of theirs was meant to express such a spirit. Therefore we have to rely on our own analysis of the buildings, or, if we are lucky, on the judgements of informed or perceptive contemporaries. We are confronted with the problem of deciding how a certain style was understood fifty or more years ago. For instance, we may be tempted to conclude that certain realizations in the so-called International Style, or in Art Deco, express metropolitan feeling. But, in fact, they may reflect no more than changing fashions. We can seldom resolve these problems with any pretension of certainty as far as individual buildings are concerned. On the whole, however, it seems fair to assume that the design of a building in a radically modern style, serving typical metropolis functions, was meant to express a metropolitan spirit.

This solution raises a further question, however: what is a metropolis? The definition adopted in this volume is both too narrow and too broad for our subject. Not all large agglomerations create the necessary conditions for a metropolis architecture – the Ruhr district is a case in point. On the other hand, quite small cities may, in certain circumstances, foster a metropolitan feeling affecting their architecture. As is well known, cities like Copenhagen, Stockholm, Amsterdam or Stuttgart provide many examples of architecture from the 1920s and 1930s which match the metropolitan criteria discussed above. The absolute size of a city is obviously less important than the impression it made on residents or visitors, or – and this is very important – the ambition of a building promoter (such as a newspaper, a warehouse company, a hotel or whatever) to add a metropolitan flair to his project for reasons of publicity.

Without any doubt, the metropolis *par excellence* over the period 1890–1940 was New York. However, European opinions and projects will dominate our discussion. Europe was the source of the most influential writing about metropolis architecture and planning, and in the end European ideals even came to dominate the design of skyscrapers. Within Europe, a majority of the examples are taken from Berlin. This emphasis can be defended on fairly objective grounds. Berlin evolved within a few decades from a medium-sized *Residenzstadt*, dominated by the military and the bureaucracy, into an enormous, sprawling, overcrowded industrial city. Then came the shocks of the First World War and its immediate aftermath, with revolution in the streets of Berlin and the foundation of the Republic. Consequently, the experience of change, and the consciousness of the spirit and the problems of the new metropolitan phenomenon seem to have been stronger in Berlin than in most other cities. Berlin also became one of the most important centres of the new architecture, the International Style. In few other cities are the links between architectural style and political change so obvious as in Berlin [1].

Metropolis in Disorder

At the beginning of the twentieth century, discussion of the modern metropolis was conditioned by the effects of the rapid, uncontrolled growth of cities during the second half of the nineteenth century. Problems such as the miserable housing conditions of the lower classes, the proximity of noxious industries and living accommodation, inadequate transport and general overcrowding were often grouped together under the heading of 'metropolis problem'. These conditions were expressed aesthetically in the piecemeal appearance of the streets in which large, opulent buildings neighboured modest houses, or towering, blank fire-proof gables faced open countryside on the urban fringe. The lack of overall planning revealed by these conditions called out for reforms on a number of levels. In the field of architecture, what was described as an 'organic city' was sought.

'Organic' did not automatically mean 'ordered'. The disordered outskirts of large cities, notably Paris, were discovered by artists at the turn of the century. Ennobled by art, they became integrated into the image of Paris as propagated by international tourism. The vision of painters, and above all of the Impressionists, could open eyes to a certain beauty of the metropolis as a whole, despite all the ugliness of its individual buildings. A remarkable example of this effect is August Endell's *The Beauty of the Metropolis*, of 1908 [2]. Endell was a prominent German designer and architect, well aware of the needs and shortcomings of the modern city, but he opposed the widespread anti-urban ideology among his colleagues and described the specific beauties of the big city with poetic eloquence: 'My experience of French painting has opened up new horizons for me', he writes, 'has changed Berlin, my city, into a miracle . . .'. To most architects, however, sprawling suburbs remained symptoms of disorder and neglect.

Planning the Metropolis

It is clear from the nature of the metropolitan problem that the principal task was one of planning, rather than the designing of individual buildings. However, this emphasis by no means excluded the architect. On the contrary, practising architects and critics played a prominent part in the discussion of metropolitan problems from the turn of the century, reflecting not only their expanding professional self-consciousness but also the growing opinions that the planning of cities was part of the art of architecture, and that the metropolitan problem was partly an aesthetic one. On the whole, it was agreed that the task of the planner and architect was to bring order out of chaos, and that this new order ought to be discernible to the eye. This purpose, it would seem, was better served by uniformity of design than by artistic individualism. Le Corbusier summed up this sentiment: 'La grande ville, phénomène de force et mouvement, est aujourd'hui une catastrophe menaçante, pour n'avoir plus été animée d'un esprit de géométrie' [3].

Other contributions to this volume have emphasized the strength of anti-urban feelings, not least among intellectuals, during this period. Architects were no exception. To judge from the written evidence, few of them shared Endell's love of the metropolis. Of course, the written record can mislead. It is hardly surprising that the fight against slums and overcrowding should leave a richer documentation than the enjoyment of the pleasures of metropolitan life by individual architects. Certainly, such anti-urbanism as existed among architects did not discourage them from drawing up a large proportion of the numerous plans for large cities, many of them more or less utopian in character, which appeared between 1890 and 1940. Some of them are worth discussing here, if only from the viewpoint of architecture and aesthetics.

Otto Wagner

In 1911, Otto Wagner published his book, *Die Grossstadt* [4]. This was one of the most interesting contributions to the discussion of the metropolis to appear before the First World War. To Otto Wagner, a resident of imperial Vienna, the metropolis was a guarantee of democracy, thanks to the anonymity it offered its inhabitants. As a creation of industrial society, the structure and architecture of the metropolis ought both to conform to the needs of industry and to reflect its potential. In contrast to most other critics, Wagner saw no good in restricting the expansion of the big city. Fundamental to his conception of the city, therefore, was a structure allowing infinite growth. For Vienna he conceived a cellular plan consisting of

FIGURE 8.1. Perspective view of Wagner's treatment of
the XXIInd district of Vienna, one of the cells in his
proposed extension plan (Historisches Museum der
Stadt Wien).

districts separated from each other by broad boulevards. Each district was
envisaged as largely self-contained, and housing 100–150,000 people.

Equally fundamental to Wagner's conception of the metropolis were traffic and
mass public transport. Indeed, he had been entrusted with the design of the
architectural parts of the Vienna *Stadtbahn*, and tramways and railways played a
key part in his master plan. To ease traffic flow, the streets ought to be straight;
'busy people prefer straight lines', he wrote, in anticipation of Le Corbusier's
famous distinction between the 'chemin des ânes' and the 'chemin des hommes'
about a decade later [5].

Wagner's drawings of the model XXIInd district indicate what he wanted his new metropolis to look like. The uniformity of the buildings corresponded to the strict gridiron plan. However, it was also intended as an expression of anonymity and of a monumentality appropriate to modern conditions. 'By broadening the streets the architects of our time have raised uniformity to monumentality', Wagner wrote [6]. In fact, Wagner's approach might be summed up as an effort to ennoble the rationalist city planning of the late nineteenth century through art, and his schemes were certainly intended as a polemic against his famous compatriot, Camillo Sitte, whose ideas were very influential at the turn of the century and for many years thereafter [7]. Sitte's stress on enclosed spaces and modest volumes was of course at odds with Wagner's vision of a city of uniform architecture, open vistas and unlimited growth.

It is worth noting that Wagner, fascinated though he was by the traffic of the metropolis, did not try to express the movement and dynamics of metropolitan life in his architecture. His XXIInd district makes a static impression; the buildings are designed to be viewed from a standard frontal position, and they are certainly meant to be looked at closely, rather than glanced at hurriedly in passing. His designs for the *Stadtbahn* do little to live up to the idea of a metropolis architecture which we find in his later writing, even though they served important metropolitan functions. The vegetal decorative forms used in most of the structures are typically Art Nouveau; on the other hand, perhaps the use of stone slabs and glass in iron frames, as in the Karlsplatz station pavilions, was meant to convey an impression of industrialized production. More important from our point of view, however, is Wagner's Post Office Savings Bank of 1904–6. With a profusion of steel

FIGURE 8.2. Wagner's Post Office Savings Bank, Vienna, entrance hall. The visibly secured stone slabs were also repeated on the exterior.

elements and other smooth materials, and a design expressing the constructional aspects of the building (such as the covering of the walls with stone slabs fixed by visible nails), Wagner succeeded in creating a new architectural aesthetic. The building looks like an industrial product without losing its monumentality, even judged by academic standards.

Of Wagner's many apartment houses, only a few seem to correspond to his conception of metropolitan mass housing as 'conglomerations of cells', with long, uniform facades framing the streets. A good example, though, is his famous Maiolica house at the Wienzeile, of 1910. We can thus see how Wagner's conception of the metropolis contained many of the central ideas of the discussion of metropolis architecture in Europe. One was the synthesis of the technologically-practical and the aesthetic perspectives, and another was the stress laid on the solution of problems of traffic and growth. The long, unbroken block front epitomized the resolution of these issues. It was regarded both as an answer to the disconcerting variety of late-nineteenth-century urban architecture and as a means of encouraging traffic flow by reducing the number of intersections. By treating a block, or even a whole street, as an entity, rather than the individual building, architects hoped to bring order back into the chaotic city in both an aesthetic and a wider, social sense. This issue was of especial importance in German Werkbund circles, for instance [8]. In Stockholm, meanwhile, Sven Wallander's 1916 project for Kungsgatan, carried out after the war, provided a remarkable example of the treatment of a major street according to these principles. In Kungsgatan, ideas from Sitte and the Werkbund merged with the American theme of the skyscraper into a convincing image of a new level of urban design [9].

FIGURE 8.3. Wallander's project for a new street, Kungsgatan, Stockholm, 1916.

The City Beautiful

In 1909 Daniel H. Burnham published his famous Plan of Chicago [10]. Like Otto Wagner, Burnham accepted the metropolis, seeing no reason for restricting its growth. Both stressed the importance of the transport problem and suggested similar solutions. In contrast to Wagner, however, who conceived the city as a composition of cells of equal value, Burnham designed a strongly hierarchical structure composed around two crossing axes and bound together by broad diagonal streets. 'By doing so, a unified city, wherein each portion will have organic relation to all other portions, will result,' he wrote. The heart – or the head – of this organism was a civic centre crowned by an enormous domed building, a city hall which would have dominated the skyline of Chicago from afar [11].

Like Wagner, Burnham proposed uniform block fronts, but instead of using expressions like 'uniformity raised to the level of monumentality,' he wrote:

> Without attempting to search for formality, or to insist on uniformity of design on a large scale, there should be a constant display of teamwork, so to speak, on the part of the architects [12].

The Metropolis and the Deutscher Werkbund

This slight difference of vocabulary has much to tell us of the ways in which free enterprise Chicago and imperial Vienna affected the thoughts and feelings of their architects.

In contrast to Wagner, Burnham did not try to develop a new metropolitan aesthetic, either in the overall design or in the individual buildings. He used elements taken from Baron Haussmann's Paris to give his plan an organic unity, and the buildings represented in his perspectives remind us of the importance of the World's Columbian Exhibition of 1893 for the whole enterprise. Implicit in his plan was the objective of making Chicago as pleasant to live in as Paris, and the task of the beautifully painted views of parks and boulevards was to bring this point home to the reader.

The concentration of financial and industrial forces was early regarded as an essential characteristic of the metropolis. Big buildings representing and serving those forces dominated the central business districts and by the turn of the century their size and splendour were beginning to overshadow the traditional seats of power. For Karl Scheffler, an influential art critic active in Berlin and a member of the Deutscher Werkbund, it was a central idea, quite in tune with the general ideology of the Werkbund, that architects ought to pay regard to these facts by designing new city plans and a new architecture expressing the spirit of these forces and uniting them into an organic structure. In his book *Die Architektur der Grossstadt*, of 1913, Scheffler sketched the outlines of a metropolis according to his ideals [13]. The problem, according to Scheffler, was on the one hand to create living conditions favourable to family and social life through neighbourhood design, and on the other hand to make the central district a centre of 'world-wide business and industrial enterprise'. The solution was to be found in a new city structure. The centre of the city should function only as a business district and not tolerate any other functions, except some central cultural institutions like museums, theatres and the most important churches. Only the most valuable historical parts of the city were to be preserved. High-rise office buildings were largely to dominate this district, not only as a reflection of land values but also for ideal reasons; as Scheffler put it, 'the concentration of business life could never be strong enough'.

Scheffler further suggested a more localized division of functions, such as the concentration of all banks in one street. 'Through this large-scale architectural-commercial synthesis the concept of the guild, nowadays represented in the organization of great business corporations, would find its aesthetical expression. And at the same time the different parts of the city would once again set a specific character and an atmosphere of their own' [14]. Scheffler wanted to see the central district surrounded by a belt of large apartment houses, but most of the inhabitants were supposed to live in garden-city-like satellite towns. Overall, Scheffler sought a compromise between the traditional small town and the modern metropolis, an organized, clearly structured city where the forces he admired, big business and industry, could develop freely without damaging the living conditions of the inhabitants. Interestingly, and in contrast to Burnham's Chicago plan, no place for the traditional political powers is indicated in Scheffler's plan. High finance and concentrated industrial production are the new powers. In fact, Scheffler's toleration of industry in the city centre is, in a planning history perspective, the most surprising feature of his scheme.

Of course, Scheffler's picture of an ideal metropolis was a systemization of trends already visible at the beginning of the century. It was also, however, a popularization of ideas already current in the circles of Peter Behrens and the Werkbund. Indeed, Scheffler prophesied the emergence of a new international – or, at any rate, colonial – style of architecture. It was a *Weltnutzarchitektur*, conditioned by the working and thinking processes of the industrial world, an 'expression of the aesthetics of world-wide business and industrial enterprise'. In using the expression 'naturalistic classicism' to describe this style, Scheffler reminds us of the buildings designed by Peter Behrens for AEG and other big companies in the same period [15].

The classicism developed by Behrens in his factories, workers' housing projects and office buildings was no mere decoration as the new styles adopted in the previous century had been. Rather than a superficial application of art to vulgar necessity, it was a means of expressing, systematically, clearly, and in a purely architectural language, both the fundamental character of the plan and structure of the building and the organization of the work it was built for. Behrens's ambition, in short, was to create a style congruent with the organization of industrial society [16]. In 1914 he published a lecture, given at a meeting with the Werkbund, which

reads like an aesthetical complement to Scheffler's book [17]. In it he introduced the conception of movement into the discussion of metropolis architecture. He described rapid movement and hurry as characteristic of modern life. 'Hurry is the elementary basis of our work, but it has not yet become a cultural form mastered by art.' Thus the task was to recognize this new quality of life and to create the appropriate architecture for it. The streets ought to be broad and straight, not artificially curved to create picturesque corners, while prominent buildings should be sited at the focus of the street perspectives. The principle of movement also affected the design of the individual buildings. Moving rapidly through our great cities, we cannot take in the details of the buildings, wrote Behrens. The individual building no longer speaks for itself, and so simple, uniform surfaces and the creation of larger units by a serial addition of uniform elements are necessary. This approach naturally ruled out the use of ornament in city architecture, but Behrens did not suggest that buildings should adopt dynamic forms expressive of movement in themselves; instead, the fast movement of city life should be matched by a reduction of forms and a simple, clear layout. Although Behrens did not refer to the motor car, he appears to have had it in mind. If he did, his lecture might well be claimed as the first example of the influence of this new means of transport on the aesthetics of architecture and urbanism.

The principle of speedy movement and time-saving was also bound to affect the design of the big office building. In fact, it led to the final solution in the form of the tall office tower. And here, the circle was completed, for the high-rise building also came to be valued from the point of view of urban aesthetics. Only an ensemble of high buildings would dominate the skyline of a big city and suggest that the metropolis was one organic, architectural structure. Paradoxically, this organic ideal was influenced by the image of the walled town of old, of which the sprawling, twentieth-century city was the almost complete opposite. Most of the architects discussed here nevertheless argued as if the metropolis could still be conceived of as an organism or a potential work of art, capable of being comprehended by one man. Peter Behrens, for example, obviously formulated his ideas in opposition to Camillo Sitte, just as Otto Wagner had done. But, for all this, his mode of thinking – for instance, his view of the city as a single volume and of the street as a room – was clearly influenced by Sitte, or at least was part of the same tradition of thought.

Città Nuova

The above proposals for a new metropolis architecture all seem rather matter of fact and even conservative compared to Antonio Sant'Elia's designs for a *Città nuova*, first exhibited in 1914 in Milan [18]. Sant'Elia presented only fragments, not a plan for a whole city. These fragments summarized, however, the boldest fantasies of the period about future metropolitan life in a radical and artistically fascinating manner. Sant'Elia's starting point was a competition for a new railway station in Milan, but it seems fair to assume that, even without this stimulus, he would have concentrated upon transport and movement. In the most famous of his drawings, for instance, illustrating the Futurist manifesto of architecture, he chose to portray a street on three levels and a railway station, the whole topped by an airport.

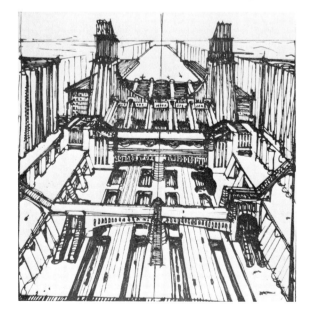

FIGURE 8.5. Antonio Sant'Elia, preparatory drawing for *Città nuova*, 1914.

In the *Città nuova* we find no disturbing elements of nature or human life. It is even impossible to figure out which is the ground level. The dimension of height is exploited not only for practical reasons but, above all apparently, as an expression of a new way of life. Sant'Elia imagined his futurist metropolis as a huge, restless and noisy place of work and movement, with no room left for leisure activities or just strolling around.

Some passages from the Futurist manifesto convey both his vision of the new city and the exalted sentiments which sustained it:

> We must invent and rebuild the Futurist city: it must be like an immense, tumultuous, lively, noble work site, dynamic in all its parts; and the Futurist house must be like an enormous machine. The lifts must not hide like lonely worms in the stair wells; the stairs, become useless, must be done away with and the lifts must climb like serpents of iron and glass up the house fronts. The house of concrete, glass and iron, without painting and without sculpture, enriched solely by the innate beauty of its lines and projections, extremely 'ugly' in its mechanical simplicity, high and wide, as prescribed by local government regulations, must rise on the edge of a tumultuous abyss: the street, which will no longer stretch like a foot-mat level with the porters' lodges, but will descend into the earth on several levels, will receive the metropolitan traffic and will be linked, for the necessary passage from one to the other, by metal walkways and immensely fast escalators [19].

The *Città nuova* was not an effort to solve the problems of the existing metropolis, nor to create better living conditions for its millions of inhabitants. In fact, Sant'Elia's designs solved no problems at all. They were a vision of what a new technology might achieve. They thus embodied an image of the industrial metropolis, and their importance for what might be called the iconography of the metropolis cannot be overstated.

Une Ville Contemporaine

The problem of providing food for the masses of the big cities during and after the First World War strengthened the already widespread hostility towards the metropolis. In the years around 1918 no metropolis utopias were published; proposals like Bruno Taut's *Die Auflösung der Städte* (the dissolution of the cities) are more typical for this period. The first pro-metropolitan utopia to be published after the war was Le Corbusier's *Ville contemporaine* of 1922, an ideal plan for a city of three million inhabitants [20]. Le Corbusier shared the general opinion of the existing city as an unorganic, chaotic structure. In his designs he portrayed a city possessing all the virtues the old metropolis lacked: fresh air, green parks and an easily read geometrical layout. By building skyscrapers Le Corbusier hoped to solve the problems of housing and traffic at one and the same time. They would reduce the need for transportation and leave large areas free for planting, sports grounds, and other amenities. This, however, required a plan which eliminated the nefarious effects of high-rise buildings as epitomized by New York.

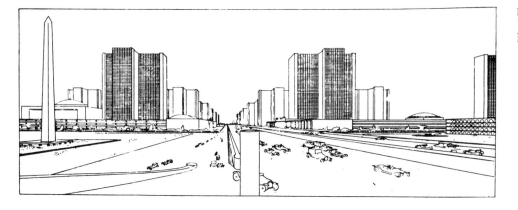

FIGURE 8.6. Le Corbusier, *Ville contemporaine* (from his *Urbanisme*, 1925).

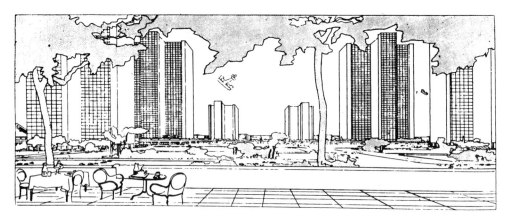

Le Corbusier's plan owes more to ideas formulated by architects active around the turn of the century than is generally admitted. Mutual reliance upon traditional French patterns may explain the similarities between the Le Corbusier plan and Burnham's plan for Chicago, but the location of a large park next to the skyscrapers is too reminiscent of Central Park in New York to be a coincidence. More important, however, is the similarity of the general structure of the plan to ideas propounded by Scheffler and Behrens. In 1910 Le Corbusier worked with Peter Behrens for five months and Werkbund ideas arguably exercised a strong influence on him. Sant'Elia's influence on Le Corbusier is more difficult to gauge. Much of the *Ville contemporaine* inevitably reminds us of the *Città nuova* but direct links between the two men are hard to establish.

From a purely architectural point of view, the most original elements in Le Corbusier's plan are the apartment houses. In combining two-storey apartments with spacious loggias in large blocks with hotel-like services such as restaurants, he put forward an inventive solution to some of the problems of metropolitan living.

More important for the future, however, was the totally new conception of urban space proposed by Le Corbusier. The streets were, at least in principle, separated from the buildings, thus doing away with the corridor street. In spite of the very high population density, the apartment houses were surrounded by trees and lawns. Le Corbusier referred to it as a vertical garden city, but this idyllic image depended on the omission of contradictory features; like all his contemporaries, Le Corbusier left the noise and air pollution caused by motor cars and aeroplanes out of his picture.

Le Corbusier subsequently improved his plan in many respects. In his *Plan Voisin* of 1925 he showed, with respect to central Paris, how his ideas could be applied to an existing city [21]. Five years later, with his Radiant City scheme, he solved the problem of giving the city a strict geometrical order without impeding its growth.

Ludwig Hilberseimer

In publishing his book, *Grossstadtarchitektur*, in 1927, Ludwig Hilberseimer provided a contribution to the discussion of the present and future metropolis which was surpassed in interest only by Le Corbusier's writings [22]. The two men agreed about the miserable state of the metropolis and the demands which a properly functioning metropolis should meet. Their solutions, however, were rather different; in fact, Hilberseimer's book was in part a criticism of, and an alternative to, Le Corbusier's ideas.

According to Hilberseimer, traffic problems could be solved by reducing or even eliminating the need for transport. He put forward a scheme for a city of huge slab blocks containing flats, with shops and workplaces in five-storey podia underneath them. This solution allowed people to take the lift to work, but of course it also required them to move house every time they changed jobs. Hilberseimer did not see this as a problem, however. He imagined future metropolitan man as a new kind of nomad, and he proposed the equipment of apartments on hotel-like lines to eliminate the need for private furniture. Residual transport was assured by an underground railway network, and pedestrian decks and bridges were provided to link the blocks at sixth-storey level.

Hilberseimer's scheme may be characterized as a city machine in which Sant'Elia's romantic fragments have been disciplined and integrated into a soberly calculated totality. It was, however, a totality from which elusive functions like social life and leisure-time activities were excluded. This obviously inhuman spirit set it more clearly apart from the *ville contemporaine* than a first glance at the drawings might suggest [23].

Ludwig Hilberseimer was more explicit about the political conditions necessary for the realization of his plan than was Le Corbusier. In his eyes the disorder of the existing city was a direct expression of capitalism. An ordered metropolis postulates an ordered society, or in other words, some kind of socialism, he

FIGURE 8.7. Ludwig Hilberseimer, scheme for metropolis architecture (from *Grossstadtarchitektur*, 1927).

argued. We might add that it was a socialist society which gave the architect unlimited power to have his plans executed. Hilberseimer epitomized a situation in which the ambitions of the architects and their honest belief in their vocation to solve the problems of the metropolis made them well aware of the shortcomings of parliamentary democracy and in some cases therefore sympathetic to totalitarian systems.

In his book Hilberseimer also discussed more tangible problems such as building types, traffic solutions and raw materials. He also reflected on a new aesthetic for metropolis architecture. In his treatment of big commercial buildings he was close to Peter Behrens, but he criticized the latter's use of a classicist vocabulary of style. He was also very critical of the verticality of Messel's famous Wertheim department store [24]. His ideal solution for the office building was Mies van der Rohe's project for a combination of reinforced concrete and glass, a design combining elegance and supreme logic. Although he went along with Behrens in seeing the tower as the logical solution for the office building, he also stressed the urban problems caused by skyscrapers and he did not accord them a high aesthetic value. To his mind, the best recent design for a skyscraper was also by Mies van der Rohe – his project for a tower of steel and glass, published in 1921.

In 1923, Mies van der Rohe, in his characteristically laconic style, had formulated his ideas about the office building, in a way of which Hilberseimer would certainly have approved:

The office building is a house of work, of organization, of clarity, of economy.

FIGURE 8.8. Mies van der Rohe, project for office building in concrete and glass, 1922.

Bright, wide workrooms, easy to oversee, undivided except as the organism of the undertaking is divided. The maximum effect with the minimum expenditure of means.

The materials are concrete, iron, glass.

Reinforced concrete buildings are by nature skeletal buildings. No noodles nor armoured turrets. A construction of girders that carry the weight, and walls that carry no weight. That is to say, buildings consisting of skin and bones [25].

It goes without saying that Mies had nothing positive to say about the architectural merits of the American skyscrapers built after the turn of the century. The application of historical styles to this new building type was of course entirely unacceptable to him. Hilberseimer took up this theme in 1927. Metropolis architecture ought to be an expression of metropolitan man's objective-collective sense of life. It should be characterized by economy and objectivity, with all forms reduced to their essentials. In creating it, the architect should be guided by the engineer, though this partnership need not exclude artistic quality or even refinement, as Mies van der Rohe's designs demonstrated.

Hilberseimer's book represents an extreme of functionalistic thinking. The city is seen as a machine, while its individual buildings primarily express the way in which they are constructed. The book ends with these words '. . . measure will reign, chaos will resolve itself – logic, clarity, mathematics, order'. Like Le Corbusier, Hilberseimer drew up plans for the renewal of an existing city; in his case, Berlin. And he too presented his ideas in photomontages contrasting the dark, untidy mess of the old city with the bright and clean order of the new, in a bird's-eye view which combined poetic strength and a fatal seductivity.

The Skyscraper

Architects and cartoonists alike were fascinated in the 1920s by the idea of solving the problems of overcrowding by exploiting the vertical dimension, in schemes incorporating skyscrapers or multi-level streets. The centre of high-rise building was of course New York. Under the impact of rapid economic growth after World War One, Manhattan was transformed into a jungle of skyscrapers. This combination of dynamic enterprise and apparent absence of planning produced a spectacle, at once fascinating and repulsive, which seems to have made an overwhelming impression on most visitors. Walter Rathenau is said to have called Manhattan an expression of dynamic energy, unique since the age of the Gothic cathedrals. The German architect, Bruno Möhring, who of course was well aware of the problems caused by the uncontrolled growth of high buildings, could not suppress his admiration. Interestingly, Möhring stood out against the general preference of his European contemporaries for uniformity of design by defending the unequal height of the skyscrapers. For him, the 'brave competition' to build the highest structure in the world gave life to the city. 'What a disaster if these office palaces were all of the same size (. . .) it would be unbearable to dwell in these canyons' [26]. Most European architects, however, were very critical of the American skyscraper. True, it was admired as a technical achievement and hailed as the herald of a new architecture, but its stylistic eclecticism and the local impact of uncontrolled skyscraper building were alike condemned [27].

Of great importance for the early history of the skyscraper in Europe were the debates surrounding two famous competitions. One was for a high-rise building at the Friedrichsstrasse station in Berlin in 1921/22, and the other for the Chicago Tribune tower in 1922 [28]. Political and economic conditions in Berlin and Germany in general at that time made the Friedrichsstrasse project especially interesting. To build a skyscraper right in the middle of the capital could equally well be regarded as an irresponsible adventure or as proof of the vitality of the new republic. The latter interpretation was emphasized with enthusiasm by Bruno Möhring in a report to the Prussian Academy of Architecture in 1920. Having been commissioned to investigate the scope for a skyscraper in this vicinity, Möhring presented an ambitious plan for several tall buildings [29]. He portrayed the skyscraper as an expression of the will to rise above 'simple necessity'. In this it was comparable to the medieval cathedral and a means of raising architecture to the level of true art. But a new business centre for Berlin, dominated by huge office buildings, might also show the world that the Germans were not a dying people: 'We have to make it manifest that Berlin will continue to be a metropolis'. Möhring also emphasized how much business time could be saved by skyscrapers, and he painted a seductive picture of clean, efficient American offices, in contrast with the old, cramped, dark and overcrowded business quarters of Berlin. In this presentation, the skyscraper became both a symbol of a new style of professional life and a means of improving the architectural appearance of the city. A business district dominated by high-rise buildings would give Berlin the crown (*Stadtkrone*) which it

FIGURE 8.9. Bruno Möhring, design for skyscraper opposite the Tiergarten, Berlin, 1920.

lacked, argued Möhring. He thus echoed the arguments put forward by Peter Behrens in 1914. However, in the design of the buildings, Möhring was very far from the pre-war ideals of Behrens.

Möhring illustrated his report with sketches of big office buildings on carefully-chosen sites in Berlin. Typical of his aesthetic ambitions was the huge building opposite the Tiergarten, straddling a proposed street connecting the old city with the western suburbs. The structure stands like a bridge tower or city gate, emphasizing the entrance to central Berlin. The motif of the street cutting through a big building, and thus indicating a new scale of construction, was one of the most typical elements of the iconography of the metropolis in the 1920s.

The Friedrichsstrasse competition entries ran the almost complete gamut of Central European approaches to high-rise design. There was great stylistic diversity, ranging from historicist compositions in brick to Mies van der Rohe's steel and glass tower. First prize was awarded to an expressionist design by J. Brahm and R. Kasteleiner, for which brick was patently the intended material. Second prize went to a project by the Luckhardt brothers and their associate, Hoffmann. This design incorporated the horizontal emphasis and rounded corners which were to flourish in the late 1920s. Only the whimsical, pavilion-like entrance hall, criticized by the jury, suggests its early date.

Nothing was built of all this, however. Berlin never got its *Stadtkrone* of office buildings. The application of expressionist styles, in brick, to large office buildings

FIGURE 8.10. Mies van der Rohe's Friedrichsstrasse competition entry.

can be better studied in Hamburg, where a large ensemble of big commercial buildings, designed by Fritz Höger and others, was constructed immediately after the inflation [30]. Ironically, the best-known of the Friedrichsstrasse entries today was one ignored by the jury at the time. This was Mies van der Rohe's steel and glass tower. Mies's design was, in fact, one of the few which appeared to be aiming at an aesthetic consonant with industrial building methods. Its glass surfaces would have made a strong contrast with the conventional stone buildings around it. In this design, Mies is said to have been inspired by seeing American skyscrapers under construction [31]. As we have already pointed out, steel frame construction was a popular symbol of progressive building technology, awaiting an adequate aesthetic expression. To cover the steel skeleton with brick or stone, suggesting traditional load-bearing walls, was regarded by progressive European architects as a betrayal of the very spirit of the construction. Thus a glass wall could be regarded as incorporating moral qualities. Of course, transparency also had an obvious aesthetic value. A glass building offered hitherto unknown opportunities to make use of light. In the day it would reflect the sunshine and at night it would stand as a body of light, an easily understood symbol of the progress of civilization and a denial of the tectonic principle in architecture.

The Chicago Tribune competition is generally notorious as a classic example of a completely wrong decision, amounting to a betrayal of the principle of progress in architecture. To achieve the newspaper's objective of building the 'most beautiful skyscraper in the world', a Gothic design by J. M. Howell and R. M. Hood was selected [32]. None of the numerous *avant-garde* entries from Europe was awarded a prize or even mentioned by the jury. Admittedly, the aesthetic solutions favoured were to some extent influenced by the building's function as an advertisement for the *Chicago Tribune*, but they were also, more generally, an expression of the City Beautiful ideology formulated in Burnham's Chicago plan. In choosing a Gothic design to stress verticality and height, the winning architects carried on a tradition of skyscraper design initiated by Cass Gilbert with his Woolworth building in New York in 1913. This approach ran contrary to the ideas which Hilberseimer and Le Corbusier were to formulate a few years later, and which were already visible in some of the European entries. On the other hand, it paralleled the ideas of the German expressionists of the early post-war years. Indeed, on a more general level, common roots may be found in the ideology of Henry van der Velde and his ilk. It was certainly felt in Chicago that it was more urgent to ennoble the forces of capital and business by art than to pay homage to them with an 'artless' design purporting to express the spirit of industrialization.

Richly decorated at ground level with statues, reliefs and inscriptions, the Chicago Tribune building calls the Gothic cathedrals explicitly to mind. This embellishment both enriches the visitor's confrontation with the building and, by a contrast of scale, stresses its enormous size. Similarly, Fritz Höger's Chile-house in Hamburg combines entertaining sculptural decoration at eye level with an enormous volume. From the point of view of those living and working in the city, this approach perhaps deserves rather less contempt than it has aroused in the rationalist camp of the International Style. The advertising function of the skyscraper may well have sometimes led architects into cheap overstatements of design, but it also resulted in some fascinatingly original, if not refined, buildings, like William Van Allen's Chrysler tower of 1928–30. It was not until later, around 1930, that the horizontality and decorative restraint of the International Style began to turn up, as for instance in the McGraw-Hill building. The work of R. M. Hood, the architect of the Chicago Tribune tower, this was a symmetrically composed tower of sober elegance. In his slightly earlier design for the Daily News building, in 1930, Hood had used vertically banded facades without a 'crown', reminiscent in some respects of the Gothic towers but much more abstract in composition. Banded facades recurred in the Rockefeller Center (1932) by Reinhard and Hofmeister and others. However, the importance of the Rockefeller Center lies less in its architecture than in its contribution to urban design. Here, for the first time, was created an ensemble of skyscrapers of different sizes grouped around a plaza. With its social content thus greatly enhanced in comparison with isolated towers, it had much in common with the European concept of the *Stadtkrone*. It was built too late to have any practical influence before the war, but it was to have a considerable impact in post-1945 urban renewal schemes.

Martin Wagner: Das Neue Berlin

In 1925 Martin Wagner was appointed *Stadtbaurat* (city architect and planning officer) for Berlin. He had close connections with many of the leading modernist architects and he aspired to transform Berlin into a truly modern metropolis. He summed up his ambitions in 'The new Berlin – metropolis Berlin', a short article published in his own journal, *Das Neue Berlin*. The new spirit of Berlin, wrote Wagner, was not the 'spirit of Potsdam' but a metropolitan spirit. This new spirit had to reshape the whole city. Central to his philosophy was the idea that the great economic value of new buildings constructed in Berlin should be reflected in their appearance, so that they conformed to the highest standards of 'metropolitan design'. Or, to use his own words, they should be imbued by 'einen weltstädtischen Spitzencharakter' [33].

This renewal of Berlin was begun with the extensive housing programme of the 1920s, but a parallel transformation of the business district was planned. Typical of the application of Wagner's approach were the plans for the Alexanderplatz from 1929 [34]. This was an important interchange for several underground lines and a surface railway line, as well as a junction of several important streets. It was made the subject of a competition in 1928–29. The Luckhardt brothers and their associate, L. Anker, supported by Martin Wagner, sought to reflect the unceasing traffic of the Alexanderplatz in curved facades and strip windows. The resulting hybrid of traffic-regulation machine and Sittesque piazza contrasted strongly with Mies van

FIGURE 8.11. Alexanderplatz design by Luckhardt and Anker, 1929.

FIGURE 8.12. Alexanderplatz design by Mies van der Rohe, 1929.

der Rohe's scheme, which was based on a fundamental distinction between street and architecture in the spirit of Le Corbusier. He placed box-like buildings of different sizes, only loosely connected with one another, around the roundabout. All sense of the Alexanderplatz as a volume of space was removed; instead, the buildings stood in open, unlimited space. In the end, however, a sober and less radical project by Peter Behrens was selected and partly carried out.

The idea of the modern metropolis as a focus of the dynamic forces of business and industry was more fully expressed in other buildings erected in Berlin in the 1920s and early 1930s. Erich Mendelsohn's reconstruction of the Mosse building in 1923 may be seen as the herald of a new era [35]. Here, Mendelsohn took a conventional, turn-of-the-century office palace and added top storeys and a corner architecture of demonstrative, dynamic elan – a rhetorical piece of commercial design. More convincing, perhaps, are the department stores Mendelsohn built for the Schocken company in Chemnitz and Stuttgart, or the Columbus-house at Potsdamer-Platz in Berlin (1931). In these buildings the denial of traditional tectonics, the smooth, resplendent surfaces, and above all the lavish display of light, express the new, optimistic metropolitan feeling of the 1920s. Nevertheless, it is probably true to say that rebuilding contributed more to the architectural transformation of the metropolis in the 1920s than did new building. Facades were replaced, or new shop fronts with large windows, and panels covered with tiles or marble slabs were forced into the old facades. These changes disturbed the traditional tectonics of the older streets, producing entirely new townscape images. Perhaps even more important was the introduction of the neon sign. As the profusion of fluorescent advertisements began to outshine the architecture behind,

FIGURE 8.13. Schocken department store in Chemnitz, by Erich Mendelsohn.

much effort was exerted by architects to domesticate this new element and make it an integral part of their creations [36].

Also in the category of specifically metropolitan features were facilities for entertainment and recreational activities such as sports and dancing. In the 1920s and 1930s many cinemas of architectural importance were built. Cinemas, admittedly, were seldom constructed as independent buildings and their main impact on the townscape was through their neon signs, posters and gigantic lettering. However, there were some notable exceptions [37]; Erich Mendelsohn's Universum cinema in Berlin, for instance, is the nucleus of a larger complex including shops, cafés and apartments. The result is an interesting composition, partly contrasting with the existing urban pattern and probably meant to express the new, dynamic spirit of the metropolis. The Titania palace by Schöffler, Schloenbach and Jacobi, also in Berlin, is a less distinguished piece of architecture, but the way in which it dominates a long street vista by the composition of its volumes and the use of artificial light to articulate the design makes it a good example of this type of building [38].

Metropolitan Housing

The greatest architectural achievement of the period, however, was in the field of housing. The enormous shortage of dwellings after the Great War made housing construction one of the most important social and political tasks of the time.

The political implications of housing construction were particularly important in the new republics of Germany and Austria, and also in Fascist Italy. Most architects believed that the garden city, or garden suburb, offered the ideal solution as far as living standards were concerned. Most, however, also recognized its impracticality in the face of a problem of such huge dimensions. Their ambition, therefore, was to find solutions combining the advantages of the garden city with a high density of population. The most adventurous thinking came from Soviet architects with their schemes for collectively organized apartment blocks, but little came of them. Much was written on this theme in the West as well, but only a few examples were built. Most proposals for large apartment blocks were thus more novel in their architecture than in their social organization.

As early as 1920 Bruno Möhring, the skyscraper advocate, suggested the building of huge apartment houses in a park-like setting, on lines similar to those proposed shortly afterwards by Le Corbusier, and finally realized in his *Unité d'habitation* [39]. In Berlin, a number of large housing estates were built during Martin Wagner's period of office, up to 1933. These were a convincing solution to the problem of reconciling the fundamental qualities of the garden city with a population density and architectural style appropriate to a metropolis [40]. Most notable are the large estates in Britz, designed by Wagner and Bruno Taut; in Zehlendorf, designed by Taut and others; and Siemensstadt, by Walter Gropius, Bartning and others. These can be compared with a smaller settlement, Linderhof,

FIGURE 8.14. Britz estate, Berlin, by Martin Wagner and Bruno Taut, 1925–27.

FIGURE 8.15. Apartment house by Otto Bartning in Siemensstadt, Berlin, 1929–31 (Photo: Eva Eriksson).

FIGURE 8.16. Staaken garden city, near Berlin, by Paul Schmitthenner, 1917 (Photo: Eva Eriksson).

designed by Martin Wagner immediately after the war in the style of the pre-war garden cities like Schmitthenner's Staaken. They suggest that Wagner adopted the new style of architecture in an effort to create a new kind of living environment, better suited to the industrial metropolis than his previous, arcadian ideal [41]. At least in this case we have a clear indication that contemporaries saw these radically modern houses, with their flat roofs and undecorated facades, as typically

FIGURE 8.17. Shopping centre in Römerstadt, Frankfurt-am-Main, by Ernst May, 1927–30 (Photo: Eva Eriksson).

metropolitan in spirit – though the distinction was not always drawn in favour of the new architecture. In some cases we can detect an effort to add metropolitan flair to the centres of these estates, as for instance in the so-called White City in Berlin by Otto Rudolf Salvisberg, or in Ernst May's Römerstadt at Frankfurt-am-Main.

Bruno Taut, however, never entirely deserted the garden-city conception of space. He therefore did not adopt the new orthodoxy of north-south oriented slabs and rows developed by the functionalists and propagated by Gropius, Hilberseimer and others. In Vienna, too, a distinctive solution was adopted [42]. Here, the municipality built big apartment complexes covering entire blocks, arranged around large courtyards. They were intended to function as largely independent communities, containing all necessary facilities. Their large size was an encouragement to monumental design, the most spectacular example being the Karl-Marx-Hof by Karl Ehn, completed in 1929. Of course, this monumentality carried a political message, which was reinforced by the big inscriptions on the facades, attributing them to the City of Vienna. The architecture symbolized their status as red strongholds in a socialist Vienna, yet remained bourgeois in spirit.

The Vienna blocks and the Berlin rows represented two very different solutions to the problems of metropolitan housing. The Viennese approach could be criticized – and indeed it was criticized at the time – for ignoring hygienic considerations such as exposure to sunlight. However, it retained a greater element of urbanity than did most German estates, and perhaps served human needs rather better than the uniform, scientifically-developed parallel rows of the International Style.

FIGURE 8.18.   Karl-Marx-Hof, Vienna, by Karl Ehn, 1927–29 (Photo: Fritz Wulz).

FIGURE 8.19.   Winarsky-Hof, Vienna, by Karl Ehn, 1924–25 (Photo: Fritz Wulz).

FIGURE 8.20.   Conversation in the Karl-Marx-Hof, Vienna (Photo: Fritz Wulz).

Metropolis under Dictatorship

The depression of the early 1930s put an end to almost all ambitious planning and architecture in most countries. When building activity started again, the political situation had changed in many countries, more often than not for the worse, as in Germany. Architects had to face a new cultural climate. The negative attitude towards the metropolis, important also in the 1920s but checked at that time by a prevalent optimism inspired by economic recovery, political change and the fascination of the perspectives opened up by the new technology, was now much stronger and to some degree, as in Germany, part of the official ideology. Nevertheless, a detailed master plan for a Berlin of ten million inhabitants was elaborated between 1937 and 1940 [43]. Designed by Albert Speer under the close supervision of Hitler, the plan was of course an instrument of political propaganda, conceived to demonstrate the power of Germany and at the same time to serve as an adequate setting for the military parades and political rallies which were an important means of self-representation of the Third Reich. It is worth noting, however, how deeply rooted the plan is in the traditions outlined above. Speer's Berlin may be understood as a last (?) effort to design a metropolis as if it were a work of art. In this sense, it represents a continuation of the tradition of Peter Behrens and the City Beautiful movement. Aesthetic considerations were especially prominent in the planning and architecture of the main axis, leading from the southern station to the *Stadtkrone* of Hitler's Berlin, the enormous domed hall. Each facade was separately designed to support the overall effect.

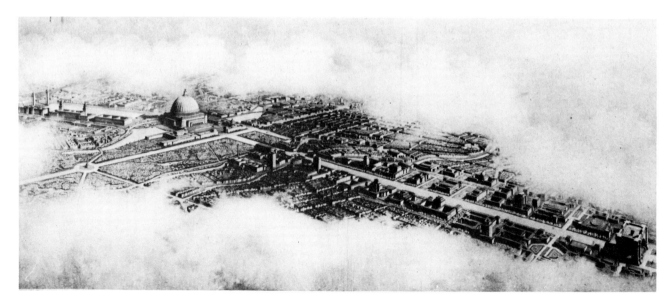

FIGURE 8.21. Master plan of Berlin, perspective of main axis, 1939.

FIGURE 8.22. Project for a square, Berlin, by Albert Speer.

This does not mean, however, that Speer ignored the planning ideas of functionalism and the Modern Movement. Like many of his contemporaries, he was influenced by the new view of the city which the aeroplane had opened up. Moreover, a comparison with the Athens Charter of 1930, the Modern Movement's planning manifesto, shows that Speer's plan conformed to the functionalist programme in its zoning, open spaces, separation of traffic from housing, and so on. These features were especially prominent in the big satellite town which Speer planned to the south of the city. Nevertheless, Speer clearly set out to design primarily an imperial capital, to which Berlin as a metropolitan centre of finance

FIGURE 8.23. Model of Speer's Berlin satellite, Südstadt.

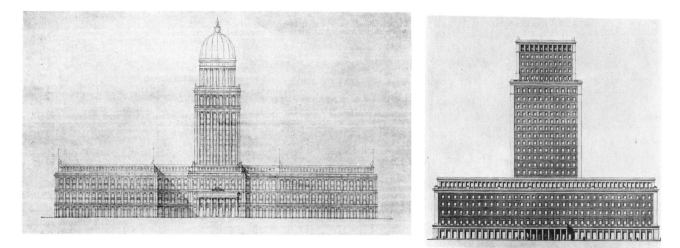

FIGURE 8.24. Project for the *Reichsversicherungsamt*, Berlin, by Cäsar Pinnau, c.1939 (competition entry).

FIGURE 8.25. Competition entry by Jäger for an office building on the main axis, c.1939.

and industry took second place. Thus Speer had no use for a modernist architecture expressive of economic dynamism and change. Required instead was an architecture which could transmit an impression of permanence without giving up the pretension of modernity. This dilemma is clearly illustrated in a number of skyscraper designs drawn up in connection with the plan.

Very little was built of Speer's plan. After the war, Hans Scharoun, one of the many architects out of favour during the Third Reich, was to draw up a new master plan treating Berlin as what it really was, an urban region and not an architectural body. Ironically, the Second World War created the physical conditions appropriate to the realization of Speer's plan, by destroying the old Berlin, while Germany's defeat swept away the whole of its political and ideological base. Outside Germany the discontinuity was not so sharp, but by the early 1950s it would be clear everywhere that modernism had triumphed. Thus the architectural uncertainties of the 1890–1940 period were resolved in an 'International Style' clearly expressive of the spirit of the modern metropolis.

NOTES

This chapter is dedicated to Erik Forssman.

1. Among the vast literature the following titles may be mentioned: Miller Lane, Barbara (1968) *Architecture and Politics in Germany 1918–1945.* Cambridge, Mass: Harvard University Press; Huse, Norbert (1975) *'Neues Bauen' 1918 bis 1933. Neue Architektur in der Wiemarer Republik.* Munich: H. Moos Verlag; Larsson, Lars Olof (1978) *Die Neugestaltung der Reichshauptstadt.* Stockholm: Almqvist & Wiksell.

2. Endell, August (1908) *Die Schönheit der grossen Stadt*. Stuttgart: Strecker and Schröder.

3. Le Corbusier (1925) *L'urbanisme*. Paris: Collection de 'L'Esprit nouveau', p. 24.

4. See also: Wagner, Otto (1914) *Die Baukunst unserer Zeit*. Vienna: Anton Schroll; Geretsegger, H. and Peintner, M. (1964) *Otto Wagner 1841–1918*. Salzburg: Residenzverlag, pp. 40 ff; Wulz, Fritz (1979) *Wien: En kulturpolitisk studie av en stad i förändring 1848–1934*. Stockholm: Almqvist & Wiksell, pp. 151 ff.

5. Wulz, F. (1979) *op.cit.*, p. 154 (see note 4); Le Corbusier (1925) *op.cit.*, (see note 3), heading of the first part, the 'Débat general'. As a motto to this part, he writes: 'L'homme marche droit parce qu'il a un but; il sait où il va, il a décidé d'aller quelque part et il y marche droit'.

6. Wagner, O. (1914) *op.cit.*, p. 3 (see note 4).

7. Sitte, Camillo (1965) (first German ed. 1889) *City Planning According to Artistic Principles* (Columbia University Studies in Art, History and Archaeology, No. 2). New York: Columbia University Press.

8. Behrendt, Walter Curt (1911) *Die einheitliche Blockfront als Raumelement im Stadtbau*. Berlin: Bruno Cassirer; Endell, A. (1914) Die Strasse als künstlerisches Gebilde. *Der Verkehr: Jahrbuch des deutschen Werkbundes*, pp. 18–23; Miller Lane, Barbara (1979), Changing attitudes to monumentality: an interpretation of European architecture and urban form 1880–1914, in *Growth and Transformation of the Modern City* (The Stockholm Conference, Sept. 1978, University of Stockholm). Stockholm: Swedish Council for Building Research, pp. 101 ff., and especially pp. 105 ff.

9. Wallander, Sven (1916), Nya Kungsgatan: förslag till gatans ordnande framlagt vid Samfundet S:t Eriks sammanträde den 26. nov. 1915. *S:t Eriks Årsbok, 1916*, pp. 1–11.

10 Burnham, Daniel H. and Bennett, Edward H. (1909, reprinted 1970) *Plan of Chicago*. New York: Da Capo Press.

11. *Ibid.*, pp. 100 and 116: 'The central administrative building as shown in the illustrations, is surmounted by a dome of impressive height, to be seen and felt by the people, to whom it should stand as the symbol of civic order and unity. Rising from the plain upon which Chicago rests, its effect may be compared to that of the dome of St. Peter's at Rome'.

12. *Ibid.*, p. 86.

13. Scheffler, Karl (1913) *Die Architektur der Grossstadt*. Berlin: Bruno Cassirer.

14. *Ibid.*, p. 14.

15. *Ibid.*, pp. 46 ff.

16. *Ibid.*, pp. 40 ff; Buddensieg, Tilmann and Rogge, Henning (1979) *Industriekultur: Peter Behrens und die AEG 1907–1914*. Berlin: Gebr. Mann Verlag, pp. 63 ff.

17. Behrens, Peter (1914) Einfluss von Zeit- und Raumnutzung auf moderne Formentwicklung. *Der Verkehr: Jahrbuch des deutschen Werkbundes, 1914*, pp. 7–10.

18. Caramel, Luciano and Longatti, Alterto (eds.) (1962) *Antonio Sant'Elia: Catalogo della mostra permanente*. Como: Villa Comunale dell'Olmo, pp. 57 ff. and no. 223 ff.

19. Conrads, Ulrich (ed.) (1970) *Programmes and Manifestos on 20th Century Architecture*. London: Lund Humphries, p. 36.

20. Le Corbusier (1925) *op.cit.*, (see note 3), pp. 157 ff; Fishman, Robert (1977) *Urban Utopias in the Twentieth Century*. New York: Basic Books, pp. 163 ff.

21. Le Corbusier (1925) *op.cit.*, pp. 262 ff (see note 3); Fishman, R. (1977) *loc.cit.* (see note 20).

22. Hilberseimer, Ludwig (1927) *Grossstadtarchitektur* (Die Baubücher, 3). Stuttgart: Julius Hoffmann. The scheme of a city of high-rise buildings was first published in 1925. Hilberseimer, L. (1926) *Grossstadtbauten*. Hanover: Merz, pp. 8 ff.

23. Cf. the clearsighted review of the two plans by Hugo Häring (1926) Zwei Städte. *Die Form*, I, pp. 172 ff., partly reprinted in *Tendenzen der zwanziger Jahre* (1977). Europäische Kunstausstellung: Berlin, part 2, p. 100.

24. Hilberseimer (1927) *op.cit.*, pp. 55 ff. (see note 22).

25. Conrads, U. *op.cit.*, pp. 74 ff. (see note 19).

26. Möhring, Bruno (1921) *Über die Vorzüge der Turmhäuser und die Voraussetzungen unter denen sie in Berlin gebaut werden können* (Vortrag in der Preussischen Akademie des Bauwesens am 22.12. 1920). Berlin, p. 6. On skyscraper architecture in New York see: Weisman, Winston (1970) A new view of skyscraper architecture, in Kaufmann, E., Jr. (ed.) *The Rise of an American Architecture*. London: Praeger, pp. 115 ff; and Robinson, Cervin and Haag Bletter, Rosemarie (1975) *Skyscraper Style: Art*

Deco New York. New York: Oxford University Press.

27. Representative of the reserved European attitude are the contributions in Gurlitt, C. (ed.) (1927) *Grosshaus und Citybildung* (fourth special number of *Stadtbaukunst alter und neuer Zeit*). See also *Wasmuths Monatshefte für Baukunst* (1928), pp. 136 ff. and 286 ff.

28. Paulsen, Friedrich (1922) *Ideenwettbewerb Hochhaus Bhf. Friedrichsstrasse* (second special number of *Stadtbaukunst alter und neuer Zeit*); Möhring, B. (1921) *op.cit.* (see note 26); *Tendenzen der zwanziger Jahre* (1977), part 2, pp. 74 ff; *The International Competition for a New Administration Building for the Chicago Tribune MCMXXII* (1923). Chicago: Chicago Tribune; Kruft, Hanno Walter (1981) Das Schönste Bürohaus der Welt. *Pantheon*, pp. 76–89.

29. Möhring, B. (1921) *op.cit.* (see note 26).

30. Marg, Anke and Volkwin (1974) *Hamburg: Bauen seit 1900*. Hamburg: Hans Christians Verlag, no. 106; Pehnt, Wolfgang (1973) *Architektur des Expressionismus*. Stuttgart: Verlag G. Hatje, p. 127.

31. Hilberseimer, L. (1927) *op.cit.*, p. 68 (see note 122). Le Corbusier (1925) *op.cit.*, p. 185 (see note 3), reproduces a photograph of an American frame construction, adding the following caption: Un building . . . on met du verre autour'.

32. See Kruft, H. W. (1981) *op.cit.* (see note 28).

33. Wagner, Martin (1929) Das Neue Berlin – die Weltstadt Berlin. *Das Neue Berlin*, I, pp. 4–5; Behrendt, W. C. (1929) Berlin wird Weltstadt-Metropole im Herzen Europas. *Das Neue Berlin*, I, pp. 98 ff.

34. Wagner, M. (1929) Das Formproblem eines Weltstadtplatzes: Wettbewerb des Verkehrs AG für eine Umbauung des Alexanderplatzes. *Das Neue Berlin*, I, pp. 33 ff. Mies van der Rohe's project was defended by L. Hilberseimer in *Das Neue Berlin*, I, pp. 39 ff. See also Huse, N. (1975) *op. cit.*, pp. 109 ff (see note 1); *Tendenzen der zwanziger Jahre* (1977), part 2, p. 104.

35. Huse, N. (1975), *op.cit.*, pp. 113 ff.

36. Cf. various articles in *Die Form*, I (1925/26), no. 7; II (1927), no. 2; III (1928), no. 9; IV (1929), nos. 4 and 9.

37. Sharp, Denis (1969) *The Picture Palace and Other Buildings for the Movie*. London: H. Evelyn. For Mendelsohn see Huse, N. (1975) *op.cit.*, p. 116 (see note 1).

38. Rave, Rolf and Knötel, Hans-Joachim (1968) *Bauen seit 1900 in Berlin*. Berlin: Verlag Kiepert, No. 91.

39. Möhring, B. (1921), *op.cit.*, pp. 18 ff (see note 26).

40. Miller Lane, B. (1968) *op.cit.*, *passim* (see note 1); Huse, N. (1975) *op.cit.*, pp. 87 ff (see note 1); Junghans, B. (1970) *Bruno Taut 1880–1938*. Berlin (East): Henschelverlag, pp. 61 ff.

41. Rave, R. and Knötel, H.-J. (1968) *op.cit.*, nos. 94, 79, 146 (see note 38).

42. Wulz, F. (1979) *op.cit.*, pp. 249 ff (see note 4); Linn, Björn (1974) *Storgårdskvarteret: ett bebyggelsemönsters bakgrund och karaktär*. Stockholm: Statens råd för byggforskning, pp. 167 ff.

43. Larsson, L. O. (1978), *op.cit.*, *passim* (see note 1).

Chapter 9

West End, East End:
London, 1890–1940

PATRICIA L. GARSIDE

THIS history of London in the half-century between 1890 and 1940 focuses upon a series of interlocking relationships between the city's several worlds – between the spheres of national and imperial capital, international clearing-house and industrial backwater, centre of conspicuous consumption and of potentially dangerous poverty. In fulfilling these multi-faceted roles, London came to exhibit some startling paradoxes. In the 1880s and 1890s, for example, the social, economic and political distance between the West End and the East End was revealed, not only through novels and tracts, but also through physical confrontation in strikes and demonstrations. In the Trafalgar Square riots of 1886 and 1887, and the 1889 London Dock Strike, the unemployed of the East End challenged the propertied and privileged West End in a social struggle that excited world attention.

During the same period, the ungovernability of London itself was contrasted with the successful management of vast imperial possessions abroad. Surveying London's want of democratically-elected institutions, one contemporary asked 'Is the capital of the British Empire to be the only space in that Empire in which the nation cannot speak through its local representatives?' London as a problem for and of government provides a major theme in this chapter. A subsidiary theme is the pride and animosity which London generated at the local, regional, national and international scales. Prescriptions and policies proposed for managing London reflected these ambivalent responses to its scale and complexity. The decades between 1890 and 1940 saw a sequence of formal and informal attempts to resolve the underlying issues of regionalism, centralism and localism in London government, of physical growth and economic diversity, of national parasitism and international leadership. In the early twentieth century, new technological developments, especially in engineering and communications, seemed to offer ways of resolving some of London's hitherto intractable problems. The fear remained however that the disease of London might merely be prolonged and not cured through the remedial measures offered by improved public services and

FIGURE 9.1.   London is Watching – 'All's Well', 1914 (GLC Photo Library).

the decentralization of some of the city's population and economic functions. Furthermore, as early as 1908, H. G. Wells expressed the ultimate technological solution to the London question in *The War in the Air:*

> No place is safe; no place is at peace. There is no place where a woman and her daughter can hide and be at peace. The war comes through the air, bombs drop in the night. Quiet people go out in the morning and see air-fleets passing overhead – dripping death – dripping death.

Zeppelins over London during World War I and the destruction of Ypres in 1918 reinforced this new and ominous message. Two decades later, in the 1930s, the debate about London's economic, social and strategic future still engaged public attention. On the one hand, the survival of London was being identified with the survival of the nation and its Empire. Rasmussen hymned London 'the Unique City', while economists debated the capital's contribution to the national income.

On the other hand, Spengler and Mumford predicted the collapse of 'overgrown' urban centres like London, victims of their own waste and corruption. Betjeman saw the prospect of aerial bombardment as a consummation to be wished — the welcome destruction of the unlovely and unloved:

> Come, friendly bombs, and fall on Slough
> It isn't fit for humans now,
> There isn't grass to graze a cow
> Swarm over, Death!

The diversity of the world of London, its internal differentiation, its juxtaposition of magnificence and decay, its uneasy relationship with its own regime and those of the provinces – all these domestic factors have been exacerbated by the vicissitudes of international politics and finance. Not surprisingly then, London and the London problem proved exceptionally difficult to conceptualize and to treat. The wide spectrum of responses to London in the period 1890–1940 must be recognized before answers can be suggested to another major issue – the means by which certain distinctive ideas for managing and controlling London came to be expressed, modified and finally institutionalized in planning policy in the decade after 1940.

London's Inheritance

Throughout its history, London has demonstrated an ability to combine turbulence with a fundamental orderliness. Despite the many occasions when the preconditions for disorder and disintegration undoubtedly existed, London's remarkable stability has been underpinned by her natural geological and geographical advantages at the lowest bridging point of the Thames with access to the chief trading routes of Europe. Roman London, originally without walls, seems not to have been established as a military fortress, but as a communication and commercial centre. Following Boadicea's attack in 61 AD, the city was walled, representing an enclave of comfort devoted to commerce and finance. Even after the Romans left, London's advantageous position soon reasserted itself. In the sixth century, according to Bede, London was once more 'a mart town of many nations which repaired thither by sea and land', even though Britain was exposed to attack from hostile tribes. Against the Danes, Alfred made London his bulwark, the fortifications of the city marking the limit of Danish territory. In the centuries that followed, London continued to assert its independence against the nascent monarchy and the church, and a pattern of symbiotic relationships grew up with these institutions and with the new centres growing up around, including Westminster, the seat of government. Paradoxically, London served these wider interests by maintaining its own territorial and administrative identity and its commercial prosperity.

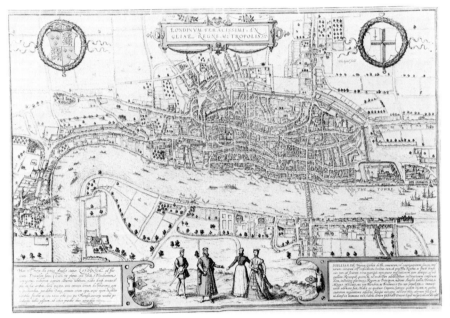

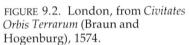

FIGURE 9.2. London, from *Civitates Orbis Terrarum* (Braun and Hogenburg), 1574.

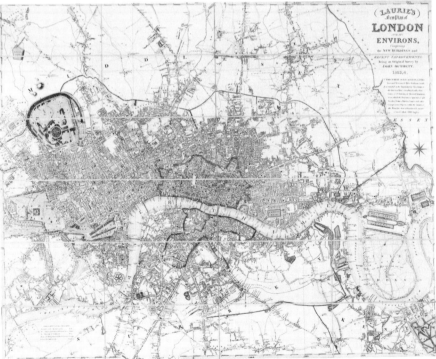

FIGURE 9.3. Laurie's New Plan of London, 1823–24 (Greater London Record Office).

These relationships and mutual interests came under increasing strain as London gained pre-eminence in the woollen trade from the end of the fourteenth century. London's commercial success brought far-reaching physical, social and political change, both to the City within the walls and to the surrounding districts. The sixteenth century represented a turning point and attempts were made to prevent and then to control the burgeoning suburbs outside the walls, and increasing densities within. The choice seemed stark – as Sir Josiah Child was later to express it: 'You must allow inmates (i.e. lodger families) or have a city of cottages'. The last attempt to prohibit inmates occurred in 1650, but thereafter City-suburban hostility increased. The independence and self-sufficiency of the City waned, especially after 1666, yet nevertheless sufficient of its ancient machinery of government remained to alleviate tensions and promote stability in London even in a century of rapid change and political upheaval.

By 1800, the built-up area of London had expanded to form a million-peopled city, though the population of the City's square mile had stabilized and would soon go into decline. London and Westminster were no longer separate, but formed 'one huge dragon of a town', with building surging away from the Thames to cover the fields to the north and west with courtly squares. The City itself was being redeveloped for commerce and a very different quarter was expanding in the East End in the wake of the first wave of dock building. London, indeed, seemed to stand on the verge of 'a new balanced completeness' benefiting its burgeoning imperial status. Despite its imperial function, London retained an essentially private and non-authoritarian character that was to delight Rasmussen more than a century later. The character of London building remained essentially a function of myriad individual decisions geared to prevailing market trends, rather than the result of 'empire-building' by kings or ministers, notwithstanding the successes of some landowner-led development schemes.

FIGURE 9.4. A view of London and Westminster from Islington, c.1820 (Greater London Record Office).

London in the Nineteenth Century: the Emergence of a World Metropolis

In the first half of the nineteenth century, London's hitherto undisputed position at the head of Britain's urban hierarchy faltered. Doubts about London's continued dominance derived on the one hand from the unprecedentedly rapid growth of provincial manufacturing centres, and on the other hand from the difficulty of understanding London's own new form and context. Though in relative terms London may have been growing more slowly than other British towns, in absolute terms, London's growth was still prodigious [1]. Confusion, rather than pride, however, was the predominant response to the continued expansion of a city that Cobbett had already dubbed in 1822 'the Great Wen'. The initial difficulty was one of perception rather than remedy; it was less a matter of dealing with the consequences and problems of London's growth than of *comprehending* its extent and significance. The way forward was suggested in the 1820s when the term 'metropolis' was first explicitly applied to London, to denote something more than a new urban form, a 'London as a whole, in contradistinction to the City' [2]. Until

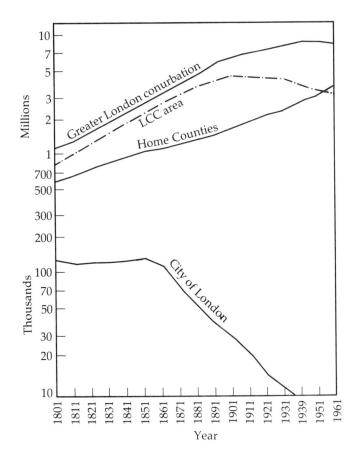

FIGURE 9.5. Population in London and surrounding areas, 1801–1961.

Source: Registrar General: OPCS.

Notes
All figures are approximations due to slight differences in the definitions of areas.
Greater London conurbation refers to the 1951 Census region.
Home Counties includes Kent, Essex, Hertfordshire and Surrey, excluding Greater London.

FIGURE 9.6. A scene near Temple Bar during the fog *(Illustrated London News*, 23 November 1844).

1851, however, London 'as a whole' defied definition even by cartography and the Census, and the favoured metropolitan image for novelists and journalists was that of mist and fog [3].

The provincial challenge to London was not simply a matter of relative physical size, but was related also to provincial claims to economic and political leadership. Although no attempt was made to classify the urban and rural components of the population before the 1851 Census, it has been calculated that in the period 1801–1851 it was the industrial towns of the North and North-West that had the highest rates of growth, with Liverpool, Manchester, Leeds, Sheffield and Newcastle the outstanding examples [4]. In each of the two decades from 1821 to 1841, these industrial centres increased their population by between 40 and 50 per cent [5]. Furthermore, towns like Manchester and Liverpool eclipsed London in some of the traditional industries such as textiles and established new lines of their own in national and international trade. 'Until the middle of the century,' observed a Frenchman in 1790, 'there was not one Birmingham trader who had direct relations with foreign centres; London merchants' warehouses had exported Birmingham goods. Now Russian or Spanish firms order what they want directly from Birmingham' [6]. London's influence was also modified as manufacturing towns began to exercise something of a metropolitan hold on the economies of their own regions.

Furthermore, commentators as diverse as Mrs Gaskell, Disraeli and Engels regarded Manchester rather than London as the symbol of 'modern life' which all students of society were required to understand [7]. After the Municipal Reform Act of 1835, provincial politics also came to the fore. With London excluded from the 1835 Act, the provincial centres and their new generation of vigorous local businessmen/politicians exhibited a marked political vitality – a commitment to civic pride and reform which the capital could not match. Political liberalism allied to religious non-conformity focused national attention on the energy of the provincial centres as well as on the problems which they had to face.

By 1890, however, London was able to claim once again the economic, political and cultural leadership of the nation. London's ability to regain her ascendant position was due above all to the reassertion and expansion of her national and international role in commerce and communications. In this process, the development of the railway system and public bureacracies at home, and the expansion of imperial possessions abroad, had a critical effect [8]. The significance of both railways and the Empire for London was, however, ambivalent; while serving to regenerate London's wealth and to remake London's physical structure, they also laid bare the extent of social distress in London, arousing parliamentary concern and labour militancy.

After 1840, the railways and steamships had ushered in a new era of world economic development in which London once more became a key focus of national and international communications. The enlarged role of London as the Empire's commercial stronghold and as the world financial capital transformed the functions and appearance of whole areas of the city. The City itself became 'one great depository and whole-time counting house', with London outstripping Liverpool in the volume of its trade, and Manchester in its claims to be the symbol of free trade [9]. In 1898, London's great warehouses were singled out by the American *Baedeker* as one of the city's great sights:

> Nothing will convey to the stranger a better idea of the vast activity and stupendous wealth of London than a visit to the warehouses, filled to overflowing with interminable stores of every kind of foreign and colonial products.

The opposition of the City authorities and the porters to the expansion of dock facilities had held up dock improvement until the powerful Committee of West Indies Merchants threatened to remove their trade from London. This threat was effective and the West India and London Docks were completed by 1806, to be followed quickly by the East India, Surrey and Commercial Docks, and by St Katherine's Dock, constructed in 1825–28. By the end of the nineteenth century every usable bend of the river between Woolwich and the Tower had been exploited for docks, jetties and warehouses [10]. Streets and bridges were also improved to cater for the additional traffic that was created. The scale of the increased activity in London's docks may be judged from the tonnages of ships handled. In 1820, the total tonnage engaged in foreign trade entering London was 777,858; in 1870, this had risen to over four million tons, and by 1901 to about ten million tons. Though dogged by intense rivalry between the dock companies, London had established itself as the world's major port by 1890, and with that, gained a position of extraordinary command over the whole British economy.

Just as the docks established London as an international emporium, the railways set London once more at the heart of the British communications system. The first terminal station in London opened at Euston Square in 1838, and by 1877 twelve more had been built on the periphery of London's central districts. The impact of railway and station building was essentially twofold; it increased commercial facilities and pressures at London's centre while providing the means, by the end of the century, for the separation of work and home through the suburbanization of the middle and upper-working classes. The physical and social impact of the railways in London has been well documented [11]. Rivalry between the companies extended to the grandeur of their terminal stations and hotels which, while adding significantly to London's leisure facilities, further decreased the number of its houses, especially those occupied by the working class. At the same time, the railway industry increased the demand for casual labour needing to live near work. Clearing away slums, 'shovelling out the poor', during their construction, the railways created the conditions for much worse slums in the immediate future.

Both the railways and the docks played an important part in that process of

FIGURE 9.7. Works of the Midland Railway terminus, Euston Road (*Illustrated London News*, 16 February 1868).

specialization of areas and segregation of functions which typified Victorian London [12]. Nowhere was this more apparent than in the divisions within and between London's East and West Ends. In the 'theatre of suburbs' to the west, the extension of the suburban railway system defined a careful gradation of social standing [13]. At the peak of the pyramid were Paddington and especially Bayswater – symbol of imperial London and the home of the colonial administrators, whom William Whiteley hoped to entice to his grand marble department store in Westbourne Grove. After 1880, residential estates for the lower-middle class followed the Metropolitan District Line (Fulham, Acton, Ealing) and the Great Western Railway (Hammersmith). Very few working men settled in West London before 1900 because of the absence of workmen's trains and trams. In the East End, however, the employment opportunities offered by the docks, railway workshops, clerical and gas industries combined with the cheap inner urban transport provided by the Great Eastern Railway and the trams to create working-men's districts with their own hierarchy and patterns of segregation [14]. While the 19,000 people who arrived early every morning at Liverpool Street by workmen's trains epitomized the 'respectable working class' of suburban dwellers in regular employment, the casual labourers of the East End came to represent the 'residuum', 'the unregenerate poor' who posed a threat to the economic and social stability of the capital especially at times of economic depression. The economic difficulties and social tensions of the 1880s culminated in the great dock strike of 1889 when it seemed that 'outcast London', the unalloyed degenerate casual labour force of the East End, might sack the West End and destroy civilization [15].

FIGURE 9.8. The workmen's train: early morning at Liverpool Street (GLC Photo Library).

The influx of poor East European Jewish immigrants in the last decades of the nineteenth century further heightened the connections already made between poverty, social alienation and potential revolution in the East End [16]. The East End was seen as a threat to social order at home and a source of weakness affecting the vitality and stability of the whole Empire. C. F. G. Masterman, writing in *The Heart of the Empire* (1901), re-emphasized the inter-relations between poverty and imperial expansion:

> The centre of Imperialism, as Lord Rosebery is never tired of reiterating, rests in London. With the perpetual lowering of the vitality of the Imperial Race in the great cities of the kingdom through overcrowding in room and in area, no amount of hectic, feverish activity on the confines of the Empire will be able to arrest the inevitable decline.

The fundamental question raised by London's continual physical expansion and the sharpening of its internal differentiation was the relationship between the constituent parts of the city and its totality. While the expansion of London's built-up area continued, the area of population decline at the centre increased [17]. London's suburban growth was not simply an outcome of commercial expansion at the centre, but increasingly took on a self-generating character. The building and servicing of the suburbs created employment and funds for reinvestment there; a lower-middle class originating in suburban commerce emerged – shopkeepers, clerks and teachers – whose peripherality in relation to London was economic and social and not merely spatial [18]. By the end of the nineteenth century London was no longer 'incomprehensible', but seemed rather to be ordering itself and sorting itself into recognizable units and areas as it grew.

Uncertainty remained, however, about whether London's continuing problems, especially in the East End and in housing, would be solved by this process, or whether the prognosis remained dire. H. G. Wells, an intense searcher for plan and order in London, expressed his hopes and fears through George Pondevero, the hero of his novel, *Tono Bungay*, published in 1909. Although George's first impressions of London had been of a 'smoke-stained house wilderness', he ultimately came to formulate 'a kind of theory of London' in which he described 'lines of an ordered structure out of which it has grown' and 'a process that is something more than confusion of casual accidents'. He adds, however, that this structure may never be shaped into a new and healthy order, but 'may be no more than a process of disease' [19]. The one certainty was that London was once more presenting reformers, politicians and novelists with major social and political issues, in a way that it had not done in the earlier part of the century.

In order to address the problems thrown up by London's growth in the nineteenth-century, some means for discovering the 'facts' had to be set in train. As Asa Briggs has pointed out, however, the public impact of any particular Victorian city depended 'not only upon the facts, but upon the imaginative power with which people arranged the facts in a pattern' [20]. The early statisticians and social scientists such as William Farr, Joseph Fletcher and Charles Booth provided some of the necessary 'facts', but more recent work has shown that they too applied analytical categories to their data which incorporated certain value judgements about the phenomena under investigation and implied certain remedies [21]. Remedies had also to be *adopted as policy* before they could have any effect on London and in this respect the structure of London government, its powers and its conception of practicable and legitimate policy must also be considered. Before 1880, the expansion and internal differentiation of London militated against any metropolitan political consciousness or local government reform. The radical Francis Place complained that London had

> no local or particular interest as a town, not even as to politics. Its several boroughs in this respect are like so many very popular places at a distance from one another and the inhabitants of any one of them know nothing, or next to nothing of the proceedings in any other, and not much indeed of those of their own [22].

Before 1855, London's elective local authorities – the vestries and the still powerfully independent City Corporation – were complemented by some 300 widely varying bodies deriving their powers from some 250 local Acts. The public health issue of the mid-nineteenth century finally brought about some changes, though the City itself maintained its anomalous position. The indirectly elected Metropolitan Board of Works was set up in 1855 with responsibility for 'the management of public works in which all have a common interest'. An uneasy compromise between the forces of localism and centralism in London, the mechanism of the MBW proved adequate only so long as London's primary problems were seen as physical and sanitary. The Board itself, steadily extending its range of activities through Joseph Bazalgette's system of intercepting sewers to other capital projects such as roads and bridges, demonstrated the scale of London's problems and the limitations of the existing governmental system [23]. What ultimately revolutionized the tenor of London politics, however, was the emergence of the housing question as *the* issue of the day, not only for Londoners, but for the nation and the Empire. In the 1880s, London's problems and politics merged with national concerns, and the meeting point was poverty and over-crowding in London housing. The Royal Commission on the Housing of the Working Classes (1884–85) focused essentially on the manifestations of these problems in London. The socio-economic and personal elements in the persistence of horrendous living conditions in London were examined rather than the purely physical or sanitary aspects. Lord Salisbury argued that because of its size and the need for so many of its inhabitants to dwell in the congested high-rental central sector, London 'stands by itself: it offers peculiar difficulties and requires special remedies' [24]. The debate over the Commission's report was long and bitter, involving as it did some acceptance that the 'laws' of supply and demand had broken down in London, and that some allocation of State resources was necessary to ensure the supply of working-class accommodation.

The 'new awareness and new era' in housing ushered in by the 1885 Housing Act was followed three years later by the setting up of the directly elected London County Council, which housing reformers hoped would be a new broom sweeping clean the capital by its vigorous enforcement of the housing acts. These expectations were boosted by the overwhelming victory of the Progressives (Liberals) in the first London County Council (LCC) elections, and by the 1890 Housing Act which consolidated and extended previous legislation to permit the Council to clear and rebuild slum areas (though such houses had to be sold within ten years) (Part I of Act) and also to acquire land compulsorily for the erection of working-class dwellings (Part III of the Act). Nevertheless, results before 1900 were disappointing, since despite continued attention to the housing question, both Progressives and the increasingly numerous Moderates (Conservatives) on the LCC showed a marked reluctance to embark on housing construction. This hiatus in London government in the 1890s represents a period when the severity of London's problems had been made manifest, but when the various remedies being envisaged were difficult to incorporate within existing governmental structures and accepted modes of political thought and action. Individual self-help solutions, notably movement to the suburbs, no longer seemed a universal panacea. So far as the working class was concerned there were two major difficulties. One was the uneven provision of transport by private enterprise, and here the LCC actively intervened to municipalize the tram system, though the equally unsatisfactory pattern of railway travel remained outside its orbit. The other, worrying, aspect was the character of late nineteenth-century suburban development itself – 'incontinent suburbia' as John Summerson later described it – formless, dreary and endless. For the middle classes, developments such as those at Bedford Park, Highbury New Park and Queens Park might offer rationally planned experiments in gracious suburban living, but the working classes often found in their suburbs 'all the misery, squalor, dirt and degradation which so tickle fashionable fancy with regard to the East End' [25]. Overnight, it seemed, such areas reproduced some of the worst physical features of the inner slums, though their main redeeming features remained low densities and purer air [26]. The suburban solution to London's problems faltered as the venue of that solution receded further and further from London's centre. 'Yesterday', wrote one commentator in 1901, '[the solution] lay in West Ham, in Streatham, Hackney and Tottenham: today it lies in East Ham, in Croydon, in Harrow: tomorrow it will be the belt of country lying beyond' [27]. Overcrowding in the older suburbs and in the central areas of London was seen to be increasing again as the shrinking stock of dwellings became inadequate for the numbers requiring to live there.

Some of the solutions offered were predicated on the virtue of non-government intervention. The university settlement movement, the various evangelical initiatives, and philanthropic housing, sought to redeem the morally and physically destitute by the 'enlightened action and generous friendship' of the nation's more fortunate 'choicest sons' [28]. While the 'new squires of the East End' tried to alleviate the area's problems by dispersing the 'classes' among the masses, the advocates of utopias and community experiments sought to organize 'incontinent suburbia' by dispersing the masses into model settlements under the aegis of enlightened landowners and reformers. Charles Booth advocated the removal of the shiftless 'residuum' to isolated 'colonies' as a means of restoring the well-being of the respectable working classes who remained in London. William Morris's more apocalyptic solution had London reborn 'small and white and clean' on the banks of the Thames: Ebenezer Howard's *Tomorrow: A Peaceful Path to Real Reform*, published in 1898, proposed a more socially harmonious solution. Howard sought to stimulate private owners and developers into creating counter-attractions to London through the promotion of garden cities. The irresistible appeal of combining the advantages of both town and country, Howard thought, would accomplish wholesale social reforms without radical social change.

Nevertheless, the gradual recognition of 'overcrowding' as a public and central, rather than a private and peripheral, element in the London housing question brought a fundamental challenge in Victorian beliefs. Overcrowding exposed above all the incompatibility of the free market in land with the free market in labour. Housing reformers showed that demand for land in London dictated high rents as certainly as demand for casual labour dictated low wages. Elimination of overcrowding therefore of necessity seemed to require some interference in the free market in the form of subsidy of either wages or rents, and in public additions to the housing stock [29]. The hiatus of the 1890s is to be explained by this spectre of 'State socialism' which accompanied discussions of housing reform and thereby threatened to remove public housing from the agenda of practical politics. The new housing powers granted in 1885 and 1890 were possible *because* means had been found of framing them in such a way as to prevent public housing from becoming a burden on public funds or a competitor with commercial building.

For all this, the fact remained that, by 1900, legislation had provided far wider housing powers than had previously been available. The LCC began its famous Boundary Street scheme in 1890, accompanied by thirteen other major slum clearance schemes. The Census of 1901 showed a reduction in overcrowding in the County of London during the previous decade, and in 1900 the LCC sought and was granted powers to acquire and develop land outside its boundaries for housing. The creation of the twenty-eight metropolitan borough councils in 1899 was followed a year later by the extension to them also of Part III powers under the 1890 Housing Act. Furthermore, the completion of the Metropolitan 'Inner Circle' Underground Railway in 1884, the City and South London Railway (the 'twopenny tube') to Stockwell in 1890, and the Central London line to Shepherds' Bush in 1900 suggested that London stood on the brink of another transport revolution which

FIGURE 9.9. The London County Council and the Metropolitan Boroughs.

1. City of London	16. Camberwell
2. Holborn	17. Lambeth
3. Finsbury	18. Battersea
4. Shoreditch	19. Chelsea
5. Bethnal Green	20. Kensington
6. Stepney	21. Paddington
7. Bermondsey	22. Hampstead
8. Southwark	23. Stoke Newington
9. City of Westminster	24. Woolwich
10. St. Marylebone	25. Greenwich
11. St. Pancras	26. Lewisham
12. Islington	27. Wandsworth
13. Hackney	28. Fulham
14. Poplar	29. Hammersmith
15. Deptford	

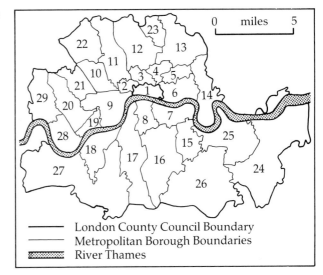

might yet provide the solution to the needs of a much larger and more populous city. For London, the new era of the twentieth century held out once more 'suggestions of indefinite and sometimes outrageous possibility, of hidden but magnificent meanings' [30]. The political and social upheavals of the 1880s had faded, and radical Socialist alternatives to the established order appeared something of a mirage. London no longer seemed likely to lead a 'social revolution', and the London of the Jubilees and of the Empire was apparently increasing its hold over its own internal affairs, as well as over those of the surrounding districts and the nation as a whole.

London 1900–1939: the New Urban Region

1900–1918

London entered upon the twentieth century in a far more confident and optimistic mood than could have been predicted even ten years previously. As the extremes of political views fell away – militant labour on the left and the 'cult of Empire' on the right – a less strident liberal reformism took its place, coupled with a more sober patriotism. Though London's physical expansion continued, reformers searched for ways of ordering growth rather than reversing it. By 1914, a new language had been forged to describe and define the phenomena of London, Patrick Geddes offering a new, sociological dimension to urban analysis, and coining a new word, 'conurbation', to articulate urban growth at the regional scale [31]. In 1900, the Empire ruled from London comprised over one-quarter of the world's land area and one-fifth of its population. In that year the Boer War was being waged, and the Unionists won a general election on the imperial war issue. On the night of 18 May 1900, London joined vast crowds all over Britain to celebrate the relief of Mafeking. The Boer War, however, seemed to exhaust imperial enthusiasm, and the Unionists' defeat in 1906 has been attributed to their over-insistence on imperialist policies [32]. By this time, the Empire in fact looked more secure than it had done for thirty years, both from external aggression and internal disaffection. Belligerence and expansionism, therefore, could give way to more peaceable activity – above all, the provision of stable, orderly administration. Trade, as ever, followed the flag, and after 1900 exports to the colonies increased once more following their depression in the 1880s and 1890s, and returns on colonial investments rose even more sharply. These changes had a number of far-reaching effects on London, 'the Heart of the Empire'. The importance of the revived export trades focused attention once more on the docks, where criticism of facilities and management led to the establishment of the Port of London Authority in 1909. The work of serving and administering the Empire generated further employment in the capital, heightening the quality and diversity of the labour market there. As well as 20,000 colonial administrators, and many more clerks and professional advisers, countless others were engaged indirectly at home in directing and supplying them, mostly from London. The rising income from invisible exports – insurance, banking and the rest – and from colonial investments was also channelled through London; as these 'invisibles' overtook 'visible exports' in importance, a kind of vicious circle was set up which starved domestic industry of capital as investment went elsewhere, while capital increasingly went elsewhere because British industry was lagging. Thus were sown some of the seeds of Britain's regional imbalance which was to become such an intractable problem after 1919.

London, however, benefited from the changing economic and political significance of the Empire in a number of ways. As a provider of services and a buoyant retail market, its economy prospered. The West End experienced for the first time 'the westward march of business', linked as it was by this time to the underground railway system. The building of the General Post Office in 1910 and the subsequent building of further telephone exchanges demonstrated the capital's importance in commerce and communications. The concentration in London society of the wealthy class who benefited directly from the profits of colonial investments ensured the continuance also of lavish entertainment and cultural facilties. Such amusements were still concentrated at the centre, and provided a glittering spectacle for entertainers, entertained, and onlookers alike. Nevertheless, the new mood of internationalism, order and rectitude found reflection architecturally in a reversion to classical styles after the chaos of Victorian eclecticism. Norman Shaw's 'coarsely classical' design for the new Gaiety Theatre, for example, was later described as being 'as gay as an elephant with its legs in the air' [33]. The classical columns of new stores such as Selfridges (1909) and Heals (1917) were felt to breed confidence in the consumer, while the dome, prominent at the Royal Academy of Music (1912) and the Victoria and Albert Museum (1909), was used to suggest

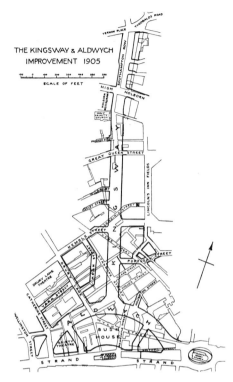

FIGURE 9.10. Kingsway and Aldwych Improvement, 1905 (GLC Photo Library).

FIGURE 9.11. Building plots along Kingsway, 1909 (GLC Photo Library).

FIGURE 9.12. 'God and Mammon', Kingsway, 1915 (GLC Photo Library).

moral worth and substance. Even the new hotels, the Waldorf (1909) and the slightly earlier Piccadilly, exuded a sombre monumentality reminiscent of some contemporary town hall. Perhaps it was the development of Kingsway, above all, with its massive Renaissance blocks, that symbolized both the new commercial London and the attempt to impose a degree of order and coherence on the previous exuberant anarchy of Victorian building.

The new economic and commercial development of Edwardian London reversed some of the social trends of the late nineteenth century, in particular by changing the relative access of the middle and working classes to living space in the centre and the suburbs. On the one hand, the continued redevelopment of the old urban core for commerce further reduced the supply of cheap residential accommodation, and overcrowding increased between 1901 and 1911 after the falls of the previous decade [34]. While the middle classes prospered, prices tended to outstrip the wages of working men, so that suburbanization for this group died away. In the decade before the First World War suburbanization became the sphere of social groups at the rank of clerk and above [35]. Many women in these more comfortable suburbs were also employed in clerical and professional work. Even the LCC was forced to recognize the trend by reassessing its suburban building programme after 1907 [36].

The new suburbs developed before the First World War were predominantly residential in character, containing few industrial establishments, as befitted their status as dwelling places for London's more senior clerks and executives. The resulting increase in commuting and in traffic congestion at the centre aroused considerable concern. Nevertheless, the multiplication of London's traffic problems did not seem to present an insoluble dilemma. The Royal Commission on London Traffic, established in 1903 'to inquire into the means of locomotion and transport in London', took comfort from American experience and concentrated on the improvements which could result from better coordination and control [37]. Some witnesses advocated ring roads to improve communications on London's outskirts, and to guide growth there, but the commission favoured a proposal to tackle the traffic problems of London's centre by means of parking restrictions and the construction of two cross-London double-deck avenues intersecting near the British Museum. The administrative, financial and aesthetic repercussions of such plans, however, were daunting, and the Board of Trade's London Traffic Branch, which succeeded the Royal Commission in 1907, concentrated instead on suburban bypasses, the Great Western and Eastern Avenues, and the North and South Circular Roads [38]. Again the predominant note was one of optimism – the swing away from the horse-drawn to motor traffic in the centre, for example, was described as 'distinctly beneficial', reducing both road maintenance and cleansing costs.

Since London transport was judged to suffer fundamentally from a want of coordination and planning, the question of an overall authority to supply these

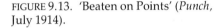

BEATEN ON POINTS

L.C.C. TRAM. "Hard lines on me!"
MOTOR-'BUS. "Yes, it's always hard lines with you, my boy. That's what's the matter; you can't side-step."

FIGURE 9.13. 'Beaten on Points' (*Punch*, July 1914).

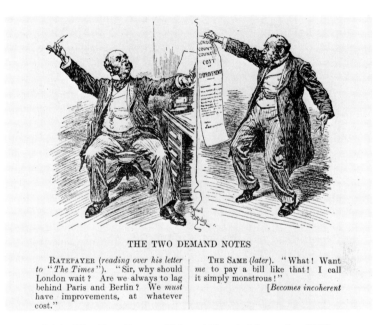

THE TWO DEMAND NOTES

RATEPAYER (*reading over his letter to "The Times"*). "Sir, why should London wait? Are we always to lag behind Paris and Berlin? We *must* have improvements, at whatever cost."

THE SAME (*later*). "What! Want *me* to pay a bill like that! I call it simply monstrous!"
[*Becomes incoherent*

FIGURE 9.14. 'The Two Demand Notes' (*Punch*, November 1905).

measures was bound to be considered. The Royal Commission recommended a London Traffic Board, but the suggestion was not implemented. This was partly because the private transport undertakings themselves attempted to secure their own internal unification. From 1909 onwards, Albert Stanley's Underground Group began to acquire control of trams, railways and bus services so that by 1918 only the Metropolitan Railway, the mainline railways and local authority (including LCC) tramway systems remained outside its control. Responsibility for roads remained unresolved, however, for although local authorities were sometimes unwilling to shoulder the cost of improvements, they bridled at relinquishing authority to a central body. The question was resolved by a series of conferences – the Greater London Arterial Roads Conferences 1913–1916 – which adopted the 'divide and rule' principle of splitting London into seven sections with the constituent local authorities working under a central government department, the Local Government Board. Thus the major lines of approach to many aspects of London's problems were set out – the *ad hoc* single-purpose body, the avoidance of governmental reform, the reliance on private endeavour, the shelving of the problems of central London, and the concentration on managing growth at the periphery.

Approaches to the housing question in many respects resembled discussions about London's transport and communications. Although the radical argument was still heard that eradication of poor housing required either the raising of working-class wages or the heavy subsidizing of rents and house construction, other, more moderate proposals gained in strength. The housing reform movement lost some of the impetus and urgency of former years as leadership passed from left-wing political organizations to the pragmatic and less radical labour groups coordinated by the Workmen's National Housing Council under Fred Knee. This Council, founded in 1898, lobbied ceaselessly for municipal enterprise in housing especially in the form of suburban estates. Though theoretically national in scope its executive council took a special interest in the affairs of London.

The Workmen's National Housing Council (WNHC) claimed that the LCC's decision to acquire sites for housing at Totterdown Fields, Norbury and Tottenham (White Hart Lane) was the result of its influence [39]. These three 'out-county' cottage estates totalled nearly 250 acres, and in 1905 the council purchased a further site at Old Oak, Hammersmith; all these acquisitions were of virgin suburban land, accessible by workmen's trains or tramways. Whether this policy arose directly from the influence of the WNHC is uncertain; certainly, the ruling Progressives at the LCC shared a commitment to municipal housing that stopped well short of any radical reorganization of the existing social fabric. After the Municipal Reform (Moderate) victory in the LCC elections of 1907, however, the emphasis on public housing diminished. Some undeveloped parts of the Norbury and White Hart Lane sites were sold, though the estates at Old Oak and Totterdown Fields were completed. Some re-emphasis on the 'residual' task of slum clearance emerged, but even this programme was wound down, and the Works Department abolished. The significance for London of the Liberal government's 1909 Housing and Town Planning Act was therefore limited; despite the Act's significant extension of housing powers and responsibilities, the LCC concluded that there was little in the Act that affected London [40].

Despite their lack of enthusiasm for a large suburban housing programme, the LCC Moderates adopted a Garden City model for their suburban building to a greater extent than their Progressive predecessors. The Old Oak Estate reflected these ideals in the picturesque character of its houses, with their steeply pitched roofs and gables, and by the set-backs and greens incorporated in the layout. Densities, however, were still high and the houses were small compared with those advocated by most reformers [41]. In private initiatives at Letchworth Garden City (1903) and at Hampstead Garden Suburb (1906), attempts were being made to carry out these ideas in a more complete form, but the slow growth of Letchworth reflected the difficulties of launching an entirely new town. Situated on agricultural land thirty-five miles north of London, capital and industry proved difficult to attract to the embryo garden city because of the site's lack of raw materials, energy supplies and consumer markets. Hampstead Garden Suburb, however, avoided these problems because of its proximity to, and continued reliance on, London's

FIGURE 9.15. Old Oak Common Lane, 1918 (GLC Photo Library).

labour and consumer markets. Despite the commitment of Garden City pioneers, and especially Raymond Unwin, to social as well as urban reconstruction, the early experience of the movement was scarcely encouraging in this respect. Events at Old Oak, Letchworth and Hampstead seemed to suggest that Garden City forms might not be viable in State housing [42], that the economic advantages of existing urban centres might prove irresistible, and that private co-partnership schemes might only be 'successful in helping those able to help themselves' [43].

An alternative solution to the problems of London's disordered and over-crowded growth was the 'architectural' approach to civic design which in America had found expression in the City Beautiful movement, and in Britain was supported by the Department of Civic Design founded at the University of Liverpool in 1909. Among the staff of the Department was Patrick Abercrombie, and he attempted to lead town planning away from the picturesque towards more formal design. Proposals for 'radial motorways' and parkway ringroads or boulevards for London echoed this conception and, in some cases, there was a direct stimulus from American and European practice [44]. Lord Meath, for example, after returning from a trip to America, proposed the linking of London's existing suburban parks and openland by 'broad sylvan avenues and approaches . . . a circle of green sward and trees' that should remain 'permanently inviolate' [45].

The alternatives of a return to village-like localism or an acceptance of ever-expanding urban centres found expression also in debates about the structure of London government. On the one hand, the newly-formed metropolitan borough councils provided new arenas for political loyalties as they equipped themselves with trappings of civic dignity. Among the Fabians, Hilaire Belloc preached the virtues of localism and the small community. H. G. Wells, however, scornfully dismissed such 'pink and golden dreams', and in a soberly titled contribution, 'The question of scientific administrative areas', delineated the process of 'delocalization' which he maintained was irreversibly underway in London [46]. A 'fundamental change in the scale of human relationships and human enterprises', Wells claimed, was being brought about by improvements in communication [47]:

> every tramway, every new two-penny tube, every improvement in your omnibus services, in your telephone services, in your organisation of credit increases the proportion of your local delocalised class, and sucks the ebbing blood from your old communities into the veins of the new [48].

The answer to this 'delocalization', Wells recommended, was to be found in the new 'mammoth municipalities' delimited by the natural watersheds of economic activity and movement between urban regions.

> My proposal would be to make a much greater area even than London County, and try to include within it the whole system of what I might call the London-centred population [49].

Wells's conception of, and proposals for, a new London region were accepted by the Fabian Society, and by Liberal/Progressive members of the LCC even though they were now in a minority on the Council. Progressives called for a new London authority for 'Greater London' – the area adopted by the 1881 Census with its boundaries reaching fifteen miles from Charing Cross, and coinciding with those of the Metropolitan Police District [50]. The scheme was condemned, however, as 'centralization gone mad' in Conservative circles, threatening as it did

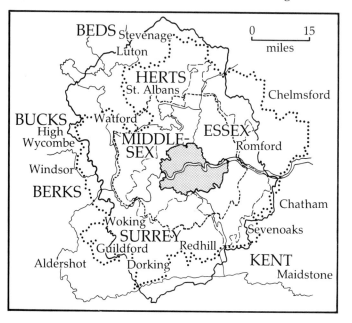

FIGURE 9.16. London's functional areas.

—————— London Passenger Transport Area
············· London and Home Counties Electricity District
– – – – – Metropolitan Water Board Area
- - - - - - - Metropolitan Police District
▨▨▨ Administrative County of London
—————— County Boundaries

not only the degree of local administration achieved by the establishment of the metropolitan borough councils, but also the authority of national government itself through the spectre of 'a new heptarchy' based on regional authorities throughout the country. Liberal members of suburban authorities around London were also hostile, and one Liberal MP advised the LCC to set its own internal house in order first, and especially to remedy the anomalous position of the City Corporation, before casting its eyes on the authorities of outer London [51].

By 1914, the question of whether priority should be given to the better administration of 'London proper', or to the reform and unification of the government of Greater London, appeared on the way to being resolved in favour of the latter. The outbreak of war only seemed to bring the prospect closer. In 1918, the Progressives, under the leadership of Scott Lidgett, entered into an electoral pact with the Municipal Reform (Moderate) Party on a platform of consolidating government in Greater London. Building on the new 'scientific understanding' of geographers, sociologists and political scientists, Scott Lidgett hoped peace would bring 'a new era in London government'. In 1919, the LCC called on the government to institute an enquiry to determine

> The particular services which should be brought under a single administration throughout Greater London; the area of Greater London which should be unified in respect of the administration of those services; the authority to which should be entrusted the administration of those services; and the relation of that authority to other local committees in the area [52].

This call, with its tacit rejection of the Metropolitan Police District as the only meaningful boundary for London, recognized the complex structure and nebulous extent that the city had now attained. London could no longer be regarded as coterminus with its built-up area; rather it was being realized that 'in a manner, all south-east England is a single urban community, for steam and electricity are changing our geographical conceptions' [53].

1919–1939

It has recently been argued that the ending of the First World War brought the issues of government and housing into a close and ideological relationship through the threats which arose to the established social and economic orders. 'Homes fit for heroes', built by local authorities with State subsidies along Garden City lines appeared to provide a peaceable way out [54]. The execution of such a programme for London presented unique problems, not least because of its physical size, and the fragmentation of its government. Nevertheless, political leaders in central government and in the surrounding authorities reacted very defensively to the LCC's continued insistence on an enquiry into London government. Despite Local Government Board pressure for joint action on London housing and the support for unified administration in the London region given by the government-appointed Committee on the Unhealthy Areas, political suspicions of the LCC's motives remained. The Cabinet agreed only to set up a Royal Commission under Viscount Ullswater to 'determine the facts'. Because of the known opposition to reform, the Cabinet agreed not to prejudice the question of whether London government should be changed. The Commission, therefore, was not asked to devise a scheme but

> to inquire and report, what, if any, alterations are needed in the local government of London and the surrounding districts, with a view to securing greater efficiency and economy in the administration of local government services and to reducing any inequalities which may exist in the distribution of local burdens as between different parts of the whole area [56].

The work of the Royal Commission was marked by the vehemence of suburban protests and the collapse of the LCC consensus on London government reform. Internal dissent in the LCC, particularly among the Conservative rank and file, re-emerged and was made public before the Commission. When the Commission produced its majority report in 1923, it recommended that no changes should be made, partly on the grounds that opposition to any extension of the LCC area was likely to be so extensive as to render proposals for change inoperable. Sir Herbert Jessel, a LCC councillor and a leading member of the London Municipal Society, spoke for the Conservative dissentients. In so doing, he anticipated the mechanisms and the atmosphere that were to mark London administration between the wars. In particular, he stressed the sufficiency of joint action between existing local authorities in dealing with problems such as 'overspill', and the hostility which prevailed to the role of the LCC in the wider region. 'London', he declared, 'is big enough as it is':

> What is wanted is not a great increase of the administrative area, which would make it unwieldy, but co-operation with outside bodies for all general purposes . . . Everything should be done to maintain the strength, authority and dignity of the Borough Councils. The County Council has not yet got over the infant stage of pride in its power [57].

London government, and the achievement of policy objectives, were thus made a matter of intricate diplomatic manoeuvring both within the Administrative County and beyond, which ensured that inter-governmental relations at local and regional level would have a considerable effect on the framing of metropolitan concerns and the management of metropolitan development.

Despite ebbing support for the idea of a regional London authority, the LCC itself was encouraged to develop a regional role in the sphere of housing, at least for a time during the Reconstruction period. The extent of London's housing need and the collapse of private building suggested to Hayes Fisher, President of the

Local Government Board from 1917, that the LCC must 'take the lead' in assessing and meeting London's housing requirements as a whole. In August 1918, a Greater London Conference was held at County Hall attended by delegates from ninety-two authorities; they resolved to cooperate on the basis of six sectional conferences along the lines already set out by the London Arterial Roads Conference. The LCC now began to suspect that leadership might pass out of its own hands to these sectional conferences or to some amalgamation of them. Addison, Hayes Fisher's successor at the Local Government Board, responded to the LCC's alarm by reminding the outer London authorities that the LCC alone had power to build houses outside its own area [58]. The LCC meanwhile adopted a programme of building 29,000 homes outside the Administrative County boundary.

It was the LCC's zeal in claiming hegemony over public housing in Greater London which more than anything else set the hostile tone of inter-governmental relations for the ensuing decade. The scale of LCC acquisitions in the surrounding counties did little to alleviate fears that the LCC's ultimate intent was their annexation. The most striking case was that of Becontree in Essex, where the LCC acquired 3000 acres in 1919 to rehouse 120,000 Londoners. Despite the intent to provide a green belt around Becontree, and to develop it along Garden City lines, the execution proved more commonplace. In 1931 it was described simply as 'the

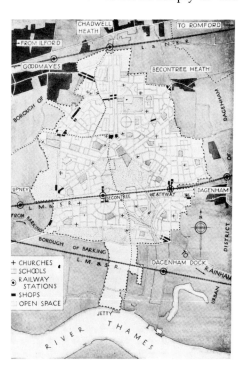

FIGURE 9.17. LCC plan for Becontree (from Gibbon and Bell, *History of the LCC*) (Macmillan Publishing Co.).

largest municipal housing estate in the world' [59]. The local resentment stirred by the 'LCC's Greater London colonies' was intense, and the prospect of the LCC acquiring some 1000 acres annually to maintain its out-county housing programme provoked images of 'inundation' in the suburbs [60]. Such a scale of acquisition presented problems for the LCC itself, and the search for sites became increasingly more difficult through a combination of economic and political factors. In the latter part of the 1920s, deteriorating relations with suburban authorities and the revival of private building forced a change of policy. In July 1928 the LCC decided to withdraw from the fray, and to concentrate on London's housing in the central area, within a radius of four miles from Charing Cross [61]. The victory of 'privatization' in Greater London may be judged from the fact that, in 1927, local authorities (including the LCC) provided 37 per cent of new housing there, but, ten years later, this proportion was less than a quarter. In other large cities of England the local authority contribution never fell below 50 per cent in the whole of the inter-war period [62]. During these twenty years, almost 175,000 new houses were built in Greater London, nearly 80 per cent of them by the private enterprise of very small builders [63]. Until the town planning legislation of the mid-1930s, the form, layout and siting of these houses was unregulated. Nevertheless, they did develop a recognizable character of their own – semi-detached and low-density, incorporating vernacular and 'modern' architectural motifs, and new standards of convenience and comfort [64].

The 'semi-detached' nature of London's suburbs extended to more than the predominant building form of the houses. Suburban living itself brought more than physical distance from 'London proper'. Employment and recreation no longer centred on the West End, but were generated locally through the development of suburban trading estates, cinemas and local clubs and societies. Increasing motor-car ownership helped to enhance the overlapping and intersecting private worlds of suburban dwellers. Though most roads still led to London, their influence was as much centrifugal as centripetal. This was certainly true for industry and commerce, since the flexibility of motor transport lessened the importance of a central location, and made possible the building of factories and warehouses along the arterial roads with no specific focal point. Almost half of all new factories employing more than twenty-three persons which opened in Greater London between 1932 and 1936 were located in the outer suburbs. Particularly favoured were the western approaches along the A40 to the Midlands, and the upper Lea Valley, at Enfield and Edmonton. The modern functional architecture of factories such as those for Hoover and Firestone, and the stylistic experimentation of suburban cinemas, symbolized the new economic and social worlds that were being created in outer London in the 1930s.

The myriad inter-relationships between the 'semi-detached' suburbs, central London and the Greater London region as a whole created new problems and intensified old ones. Inevitably the questions of public control, orderly develop-

FIGURE 9.18. Granada Cinema, Tooting – exterior (designers, Masey and Uren, 1931) (GLC Photo Library).

FIGURE 9.19. And interior (designer, T. Komisarjevsky, 1931) (GLC Photo Library).

ment and the coordination of competing interests were raised once more. In 1927, the London Council of Social Service lobbied the Prime Minister to look again at London, arguing that:

> the problem of housing the people in Greater London has now assumed very large proportions and it is closely interlaced with other questions such as the proper distribution of population, the provision and regulation of transport, the direction of new roads and bridges, the location of factories, the planning of suburban districts or satellite towns [65].

Coordination of these closely associated problems, however, remained voluntary and *ad hoc* following the report of the Ullswater Commission. Several of the outer London County and District Councils joined together under the encouragement of the Ministry of Health to prepare town-planning schemes and the Ministry of Transport was advised by a London and Home Counties Traffic Advisory Committee composed largely of local authority representatives. These piecemeal efforts, however, only served to emphasize the continuing lack of guidance at the regional level. Ambivalence about the LCC's role continued to deter moves in this direction:

WANTED—AN OPEN-AIR MINISTER

SPECULATIVE BUILDER (to London):
" It's your lungs I want".

FIGURE 9.20. 'It's Your Lungs I Want'
(*Punch*, December 1926).

FIGURE 9.21. Work begins on the South Circular Road, 1935 (GLC Photo
Library).

If the LCC were to take the lead in a regional movement, would it secure a whole-
hearted following from its neighbours? Would it be able to draw confidence from
those authorities whose independence it has been accused of threatening? On the
other hand, if the LCC were not able to take the lead, how could it enter into the
scheme in which it was a secondary party? [66].

Intervention by central government seemed to offer some degree of resolution to
the dilemma. Neville Chamberlain, Minister of Health, responded by setting up
the Greater London Regional Planning Committee in 1927. He hoped that by
getting the local authorities to work together and by providing them with
committed, experienced technical support under Raymond Unwin, they would be
able to make 'really sound and practical suggestions which will, if not solve, at any
rate go towards meeting, the difficulties' [67]. The basic problems, however,
remained. Before any plan which emerged could be implemented, the agreement
of some 126 local authorities had to be secured. Moreover, although the LCC
needed to be represented on each of the fourteen regional sub-committees because
of its wide-ranging influence, its representation was confined to the main steering
committee because of renewed nervousness about the Council's ambitions [68].
Despite Unwin's eloquent and elegant attempts to present 'an appropriate design

for urban growth' in GLRPC reports, its influence on contemporary developments was slight. Most significantly, the LCC offered the Committee scant support, dismissing the Second Report published in 1934 as 'useful . . . [but] it does not call for any action by the Council' [69].

The resistance of the LCC to considering the problems of Greater London as a whole increased during the 1930s because of growing social and political divisions between the County and the outer suburbs. The 1931 Census revealed the extent to which living conditions diverged between these two areas; overcrowding in central London was again on the increase, and borough Medical Officers of Health drew attention to some disturbing trends in infant mortality rates. Llewellyn Smith's *New Survey of London Life and Labour*, published in nine volumes between 1930 and 1935, revealed widespread general improvements in social conditions since Booth's report, but nevertheless showed half a million Londoners still living below a poverty line fixed in accordance with those used forty years earlier. Social polarization was, if anything, becoming more acute and the House of Lords heard that 'many interests were combining to cause the well-to-do and the poor to live apart in separate territories' [71]. The victories of the Labour Party in LCC and metropolitan borough elections in 1934 and 1937 both reflected and reinforced this social polarization. Herbert Morrison, Labour leader at the LCC, committed his party to a programme based on the objective, *Up With the Houses and Down With the Slums* [72]. Thereafter, the LCC's prime commitment was to slum clearance in inner areas, denigrating cottage estates as 'depressingly uniform' and 'of no practical use to most families living in slum conditions or in overcrowded conditions' [73]. Satellite towns were also dismissed from the realm of practical politics, even though Morrison and Lewis Silkin, chairman of the LCC Housing Committee, regarded them as 'a vision of the London of my dreams' [74]. The need to maintain the impetus and output of the Labour majority's slum clearance programme led to further stratification within the County itself. Opposition to the scale of the LCC's housing operations, not all of it derived from political differences among the metropolitan boroughs, led to a highly distorted pattern of public housing in the County. Not only did high-density flats become the norm, they also became highly localized. During the 1930s, almost half of the LCC's flats were located in just four of the twenty-eight metropolitan boroughs – Lambeth, Lewisham, Camberwell and Wandsworth [75]. Such a massive concentration of LCC housing served to introduce a further divisive element into London's social and political fabric.

The LCC's 'isolationist' stance caused a re-evaluation of its involvement in regional affairs. In 1936, the LCC suspended its financial contribution to the Greater London Regional Planning Committee and the Committee was dissolved. In its place, the Standing Conference on London Regional Planning was set up under the auspices of the Ministry of Health. Unlike its predecessor, it was not charged with making proposals for the planning of the region, but was to consider only those matters referred to it by the Greater London authorities or by the

Minister himself. Frederic Osborn, Garden City campaigner, condemned this weakening of regional planning:

> London spent on that [Greater London Regional Planning] Committee less than one-hundredth of a penny rate: and after a very few years the Committee was torpedoed and a copy of its Report was deposited in the British Museum along with Wren's plan. There is now a quite harmless Committee (The Standing Conference on London Regional Planning) which is guaranteed against any such bad habits of report and survey by a rule that it only speaks when it is spoken to – which is quite safe because no-one is likely to ask it any dangerous questions [76].

The plea, however, fell on deaf ears as the Labour LCC concentrated more and more on its own affairs. Prior to its defeat in 1934, the Municipal Reform Party had considered various schemes for drawing up a regional plan in cooperation with amenity societies, town planning groups and other local authorities. The incoming Labour majority, however, never pursued these proposals, but defined the County of London itself as the sole arena for LCC planning and reasserted the primary role of the Council's own officers and members in drawing up schemes [77]. The schemes which the LCC subsequently prepared were notable for their acceptance of the *status quo*, especially in respect of existing densities and land use. Challenged by Patrick Abercrombie to explain why LCC proposals had not been related to regional planning, Henry Berry, chairman of the LCC Town Planning Committee, responded by condeming Abercrombie's ideas as 'fascist' and 'un-British'. London local authorities, Berry went on, would continue to plan in their own way in response to their own electors without unwarranted 'dictation by any self-appointed body of experts, while at the same time we are perfectly willing and anxious to work with all outside authorities, duly elected' [78].

The nub of the dispute, Abercrombie and Berry were agreed, was 'a matter of the whole and not a question of the parts'. Berry, however, was not alone in considering that 'the whole' now raised seemingly insuperable practical, political and constitutional difficulties. Constant evidence of 'the mess London is in' served not to trigger action, but to promote the fear that effective organization and administration on the scale required would be 'beyond the ability of local government officers' [79]. That way lay the totalitarian temptation which appalled not only Berry but many supporters of planning in the 1930s [80]. As the ramifications of London's huge expansion went beyond the regional to the national scale, the temptation was to turn away from their enormity and complexity. In order to reduce the phenomenon of London to manageable proportions, the temptation was to redivide it into a number of constituent parts to be dealt with separately.

This reworking of the London problem was helped forward by developing the image of London as an organic machine whose malfunctionings might be remedied by selective surgery and engineering. London's road system and green belt are

FIGURE 9.22. County of London Town Planning Schemes, 1925–39.

Shaded areas show the schemes (1–18) completed or in preparation up to 1934.

Inset map shows the six divisions adopted under the general planning resolution of 1934. The City of London, the Temples and Lincoln's Inn were excluded from this resolution.

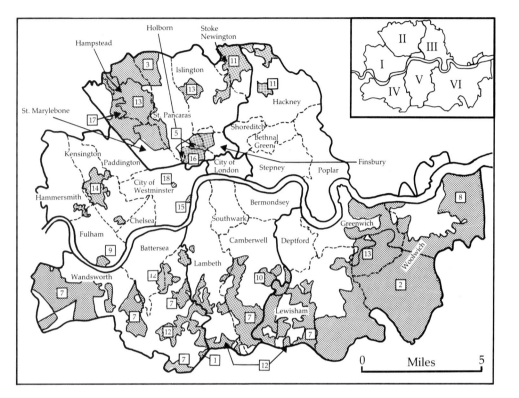

good examples of this change taking place first at conceptual and then at policy level. In his work for the Greater London Regional Planning Committee in the late 1920s and early 1930s, Raymond Unwin had stressed that the development of roads was not merely a matter of traffic efficiency, but was related also to economic, social and environmental questions. From 1934 onwards, however, the problems of London's traffic flow and residential and industrial 'ribbon development' along main roads were being dealt with in isolation from one another and without reference to any overall planning objectives. In 1935, the Restriction of Ribbon Development Act was passed, and Sir Leslie Hore-Belisha, Minister of Transport, appointed Sir Charles Bressey to undertake a survey of London highway developments 'in order to keep pace with the expansion of traffic'. Bressey was a notable contributor to pathological images of London. His primary concern was with 'centres of congestion' – which 'spots' would yield the most substantial measure of 'relief' if improved. Improvements would come, Bressey explained, by increasing the 'circulation' of traffic 'flow' by a series of fly-overs, by-passes and roundabouts, and by the provision of new 'arterial' roads. Such a simplistic engineering solution to London's traffic problems permitted the separation of the road question from town planning, architecture and even from the matter of Thames cross-river bridges. The concept of a green belt for London went through a similar metamorphosis and this time the prime instigators of change were Morrison and the LCC. Though this idea had a long history, it was Raymond Unwin in his Greater London Regional Planning Committee reports who gave the green belt its most thorough and comprehensive examination. Unwin explained that two approaches might be adopted; either a limited number of open spaces might be reserved to break up development that was in other respects uncontrolled, or, ideally, London's development might be planned so that 'units . . . spring up detached from the main mass of the town', each with a self-contained economic and social life and with 'the permanent reservation of belts of open space to prevent the units coalescing with one another or with the central mass' [81]. Unwin's proposals foundered because agreement between owners and local authorities was not forthcoming, and because they depended for their implementation on region-wide decisions and finance.

Morrison's proposal to offer £2,000,000 to assist local authorities around London to buy or preserve open space for public access seemed to cut through both administrative and financial difficulties. What was gained was the acquisition of some 14,000 acres of 'green belt' land by 1939, with provisional approval for 60,000 more [82]. There was no plan, however, because the LCC's role was purely reactive. Anxious to be above suspicion of renewed attempts at 'annexation', the LCC left the choice and subsequent maintenance of the land acquired to the out-County authorities themselves. No regional strategy and no regional planning authority was therefore required and the short-term effect of the scheme was to enhance the reputation of the LCC as a public-spirited and enterprising body. Though he regretted that his larger scheme was not being pursued, Unwin himself publicly thanked the LCC for its initiative [83]. William Davidge praised the Council's 'great work' in assisting the green belt around London which he said was 'a tribute to local government, the local county councils and the central body'.

Despite the contemporary and subsequent prominence given to the paradox of London's growth at a time when the manufacturing regions were severely depressed, attitudes to London in the 1930s were mixed. The desire to deal with its complex pattern of growth in a comprehensive manner and at a scale dictated by 'natural' boundaries had faltered largely because of the constitutional and political questions that were inevitably raised. By devising means to simplify the inter-relationships between population growth, physical expansion, industrial development and transport, some progress could be demonstrated. A semblance of order, coherence and control could be powerfully represented by carefully chosen imagery. Frank Pick, for example, could disguise the London Passenger Transport Board's opportunist and sometimes flagrant disregard for the regional impact of its operations by presenting them to the public in the supreme orderly simplicity of its tube map [84]. At the conceptual and practical level, the London authorities could claim that after decades of sterile debate London was being competently managed.

Even Llewellyn Smith was forced to admit that, despite the results of his social survey, the vitality of the city gave room for hope. Moreover, at the economic level, there was room for the view that London's growth had not been all loss. Though it was 'the fashion to deplore the size of London', *The Economist* asserted that in eonomic, if not in social terms, the continued growth of London had been a clear gain for the nation [85]. Not even the Royal Commission on the Distribution of the Industrial Population appointed in 1937, it went on, could make up its mind how to evaluate the economic contribution of London.

The argument against London was clinched, not on economic grounds, but by social and above all by strategic considerations. The social problems sprang from 'the monstrosity of a city that houses one-fifth of Britain's population on one one-hundred-and-twenty-seventh of Britain's land and calls upon a quarter of a million transport workers to move two and a half million people daily' [86]. The strategic problems were dramatically demonstrated at Guernica, and fear of aerial bombardment found expression in films, novels and science fiction of the 1930s [87]. Lewis Mumford left the implications for the metropolis in no doubt:

> For the first time in history, every region, every city, is open to attack – open and relatively helpless. The longer the frontier the greater the opening: the bigger the national capital, the more exposed to assault. *The task of modern civilisation is to live in a wall-less world.* At present, the nations are like people fleeing from a rainstorm, who take refuge behind the walls of ruin, forgetting that the roof itself has fallen down, and no matter how closely they huddle to the wall, they will be drenched from overhead. There is no alternative: no system of bombproof shelters, no mobilisation of fire-fighting apparatus, will avail as defence: the only possible answer is the certainty of equal aggression *by the same means* [88].

The Economist expressed the prospect for London in no less graphic, if more prosaic, terms, linking the expectation of confusion with prior concerns about the quality of London government and administration. Recalling that the 1888 reforms had come about because of a catastrophe, it warned that another 'compelling catastrophe' might be near:

> Reform may come as a result perhaps of aerial bombardment, discovering the fire hoses of one small area unfitted to the hydrants of another, or the good shelters of one district invaded by the scared inhabitants of another in which all defence duties have been neglected [89].

It was the contemplation of this 'abiding nightmare' that restored comprehensive planning and regional government to the centre of the London debate as the 1930s drew to a close.

War, Conflict and Consensus

William Robson's blueprint for the reform of London's 'present makeshift muddle', *The Government and Misgovernment of London,* was published in 1939. Robson advocated the setting up of a two-tier local government system, responsible for all existing services, and covering the 2419 square miles of the London Traffic Area – more than twenty times the area of the existing London County. This was followed in January 1940 by the publication of the report of the Barlow Commission, which advocated dispersal from congested urban centres, and the curtailment of the 'drift' of population and industry to London, above all because of its strategic dangers. The implication of the Barlow Commission's Majority Report was that the national problem would be solved if the London problem were tackled by dispersing the metropolis 'into properly planned smaller centres separated from one another by belts of open country within a radius of say 30 to 40 miles of Charing Cross' [90]. Dissension was apparent, however, in Minority Reports which advocated the need for national solutions, coordinated and controlled at national level. Robson's book and the Barlow Report are significant because they mark a readiness to contemplate the highly contentious issues of national and regional planning and administration. Yet their very contentiousness meant that there could be no certainty that the solutions advocated would be accepted by those concerned as legitimate and practical policy. The issue at stake was no less than the continuance of the established economic and political order. The swift appointment of the Uthwatt Committee on compensation and betterment, early in the war, raised once more the question of the relationship between public planning

FIGURE 9.23. The spectre of war – County Hall and Parliament, 1941 (*Evening News*).

and private ownership of land. The minority sections of the Barlow Report highlighted differences of opinion about the scale at which the problems of London had to be addressed and managed – local, regional or national. The relationship of the parts to the whole in the context of the County of London, the London region, the other major regions, and the nation, likewise remained unresolved. In the London region alone a choice could be made from several possibilities – the Garden City model, the complex of garden suburbs around a central city, the economic/ functional model set out by the MARS Group, the arterial/architectural mode of Bressey and the Royal Academy, the 'cosmetic approach' of the RIBA London Regional Reconstruction Committee and the realist/incremental approach of the LCC and the developers themselves. In finding a path through this nexus of contending claims, two factors above all demanded attention. One was the *pride* in London's ability to solve its own problems which derived from the achievement of the 1930s, and which was epitomized by the LCC's own Jubilee history, published in the same year as Robson's critique [91]. The second was the *power* of London institutions, whether elected, appointed or economic, to resist, ignore or modify whatever planning ideas gained the ascendancy. There is no doubt that the degree of consensus on London planning which was assembled and expressed during the war was impressive and unprecedented [92]. The subsequent fate of those ideas, however, depended on a consensus that was achieved not through confronting and resolving the inherent conflicts of interests, but by the 'tacit agreement to bury divisive conflicts' entered into by politicians, planners and administrators. The realization of Abercrombie's dream depended on government intervention in the structure of landownership and market values, in the extension of planning powers and in the structure of local, regional and national government. The post-war distortion of the dream was inevitable because these matters proved too contentious and too difficult to resolve, the existing structures of economic and political power remained unaltered, and the old principalities and powers of London – economic, social and political – reasserted their influence [93].

NOTES

1. Between 1801 and 1911 London's rate of growth fell below the national urban average. Nevertheless, London's population increased during this period from one to 6½ million – the greatest absolute growth of any city in England and Wales (information calculated from Mitchell, B.R. and Deane, P. (1962) *Abstract of British Historical Statistics*. London: Cambridge University Press).

2. Dyos, H.J. (1972) Greater and Greater London: notes on the metropolis and the provinces in the nineteenth and twentieth centuries, in Bromley, J.S. and Kossman, E.H. (eds.) *Britain and the Netherlands*. The Hague: Martinus Nijhoff.

3. Prior to the 1830s, 'London' was represented by cartographers as the ancient City 'with adjacent villages', or with 'the country 32 miles

from St. Paul's'. From 1830, the word 'metropolis' began to appear in map titles, and the 1851 Ordnance Map represented a turning point in the cartographic representation of London, providing not only factual information but 'a symbolic device which could be used to foster an awareness of an independent Metropolitan London'.

4. Law, C.M. (1967) The growth of urban population in England and Wales 1801–1911. *Transactions of the Institute of British Geographers*, **41**, pp. 125–43.

5. Briggs, Asa (1968) *Victorian Cities*. Harmondsworth: Pelican, p. 86.

6. Dyos, H.J. and Aldcroft, D.H. (1974) *British Transport*. Harmondsworth: Pelican, p. 114.

7. See Gaskell, Mrs., *North and South*; Disraeli, B., *Coningsby*, Engels, F., *The Condition of the Working Class in England*.

8. For example, between 1881 and 1901, the number of officers, clerks and messengers employed by central government in London more than doubled, from 46,000 to 100,000. See Marsh, D.C. (1965) *The Changing Social Structure of England and Wales 1871–1961*. London: Routledge and Kegan Paul, p. 112 ff.

9. Summerson, J. (1978) *Georgian London*. Harmondsworth: Peregrine, p. 291.

10. The Royal Victoria Docks were built in 1855, Millwall in 1868, the Royal Albert in 1880, and Tilbury in 1886.

11. In particular Dyos, H.J. (1955) Railways and housing in Victorian London. *Journal of Transport History*, **2**; Dyos, H.J. (1957) Some social costs of railway building in London. *Journal of Transport History*, **3**; Dyos, H.J. (1967) The slums of Victorian London. *Victorian Studies*, **11**; and Kellett, J.R. (1967) *The Impact of Railways on Victorian Cities*. London: Routledge and Kegan Paul.

12. This is the theme of Olsen, D.J. (1979) *The Growth of Victorian London*. Harmondsworth: Peregrine.

13. Reeder, D.A. (1968); A theatre of suburbs: some patterns of development in West London, 1801–1911, in Dyos, H.J. (ed.) *The Study of Urban History*. London: Edward Arnold.

14. Olsen, *op. cit.*, p. 320 (see note 12); Ashworth W. (1964) Types of social and economic development in suburban Essex, in Centre for Urban Studies Report no. 3, *London: Aspects of Change*. London: MacGibbon and Kee; Robbins, H. (1964) Transport lines and social divisions, in Centre for Urban Studies Report no. 3, *London: Aspects of Change*. London: MacGibbon and Kee.

15. Jones, G.S. (1976) *Outcast London*. Harmondsworth: Peregrine.

16. Fishman, W.J. (1975) *East End Jewish Radicals, 1875–1914*. London: Duckworth.

17. Wohl, A. (1977) *The Eternal Slum*. London: Edward Arnold, p. 285.

18. Reeder, *loc. cit.* (see note 13).

19. Quoted in Briggs, *op. cit.*, pp. 348–9 (see note 5).

20. *Ibid.*, p. 87.

21. Though Booth claimed that he started work with 'no preconceived ideas', his emphasis on dealing with 'the residuum' rather than with poverty in general is clearly expressed. In his conclusion to the first of seventeen volumes he wrote: 'In taking charge of the lives of the incapable, State Socialism finds its proper work, and by doing it completely, would relieve us of a serious danger . . . Thorough interference on the part of the State with the lives of a small fraction of the population would tend to make it possible, ultimately, to dispense with any socialistic interference in the lives of the rest.'

22. Quoted in Sheppard F. (1971) *London 1808–1870: The Infernal Wen*. London: Secker and Warburg, p. 319.

23. The Metropolitan Board of Works spent £7 million on street widening and £3 million on the Thames Embankment (Dyos and Aldcroft, *op. cit.*, p. 242 [see note 6]).

24. Quoted in Wohl, *op. cit.*, p. 244 (see note 17).

25. Pall Mall Gazette, How we do things in the suburbs, quoted in Dyos, H.J. (1961) *Victorian Suburb: A Study of the Growth of Camberwell*. Leicester: Leicester University Press, p. 62.

26. *Public Health*, **6** (1894), p. 327.

27. Lawrence, F.W. (1901) The housing problem, in Masterman, C.F.G. (ed.) *The Heart of the Empire*. London: Fisher Unwin, pp. 53–107.

28. Wohl, *op. cit.*, p. 215 (see note 17), quoting Rev. Montagu Butler.

29. The stages by which 'overcrowding' was recognized as the fundamental issue in London housing are discussed at length in Wohl, *op. cit.* (see note 17).

30. Wells, H.G., *Tono Bungay*, quoted in Briggs, *op. cit.*, p. 347 (see note 5).
31. Cherry, G. (1974) *The Evolution of British Town Planning*. London: Leonard Hill, p. 52.
32. Porter, B. (1975) *The Lion's Share*. London: Longmans, pp. 138–9, 178, 197–8.
33. Reilly, C.H. (1934) The architectural scene 1901–1934, *Architectural Review*, **65**, January–June, pp. 170–6.
34. In 1911, more than 758,000 Londoners, more than the population of Liverpool, Manchester or Birmingham, were officially overcrowded (Wohl, *op. cit.*, p. 301 [see note 17]).
35. See Ashworth, *loc. cit.* (see note 14).
36. This change in policy is discussed further below, pp. 240–1.
37. Greater London Council, Research Report No. 11 (1970) *London Road Plans 1900–1970*. London: GLC, pp. 7–8.
38. *Ibid.*, p. 10.
39. Workmen's National Housing Council. *Housing Journal*, 14 September, 1901.
40. LCC (1913) *Housing of the Working Classes 1855–1912*. London: LCC, pp. 19–21.
41. The density of the early LCC cottage estates was about twenty-five dwellings to the acre, as opposed to the eight to twelve of garden city developments (Cornes, J. [1905] *Modern Housing in Town and Country*, p. 7).
42. See Local Government Board (1913) *Memorandum with respect to provision and arrangement of houses for the working classes*. London.
43. *Housing Journal*, **69**, 1907, quoted in Swenarton, M. (1981) *Homes Fit For Heroes*. London: Heinemann, p. 11.
44. Wilson, H.W. (1902) Will London be suffocated? *National Review*, **37**, p. 598–609.
45. Lord Meath (1901) The green girdle around London. *The Sphere*, **6**, pp. 128–9.
46. Wells, H.G. (1903) The question of scientific administrative areas, published as an appendix to *Mankind in the Making*. London: Chapman and Hall.
47. Wells, H.G. (1934) *Experiment in Autobiography, Part II*. London: Victor Gollancz, pp 649–50.
48. Wells (1903) *loc. cit.* (see note 46).
49. *Ibid.*
50. The political aspects of proposals for London government reform are explored in Young, K. and Garside, P.L. (1982) *Metropolitan London: Politics and Urban Change, 1837–1981*. London: Edward Arnold, chapter 5.
51. Hemphill, F. (1907) *Reform of London Government*. London: Political Committee of the National Liberal Club, pp. 18–20.
52. LCC, Minutes of Proceedings, 28 October 1919.
53. Mackinder, H.J. (1907) *Britain and the British Seas*. Oxford: Clarendon Press, p. 258.
54. See Swenarton, *op. cit.* (see note 43).
55. Ministry of Health, Committee to Consider and Advise on the Principles to be Followed in Dealing with Unhealthy Areas (1920–21) *Reports*. London: HMSO. The episode is discussed more fully in Young and Garside *op. cit.* chapter 5 (see note 50).
56. Ministry of Health, Royal Commission on London Government (1923) *Report* (Cmd. 1830). London: HMSO.
57. *The Times*, 13 March 1927.
58. Letter from Ministry of Health to London authorities, 1 September 1919.
59. For the disenchantment with this early garden suburb vision, see Ashworth, W.A. (1954) *The Genesis of Modern British Town Planning*. London: Routledge and Kegan Paul, pp. 209–15.
60. Recent LCC housing progress, II. *Architect and Building News*, 20 January 1928, p. 124.
61. Dence, E.M. (1930) The present phase of the housing problem in London. *Public Administration*, **8**, p. 75.
62. Orr. J.P. (1937) Greater London housing campaign. *Builder*, **153**, p. 419.
63. Richardson, M.W. and Aldcroft, D.H. (1968) *Building in the British Economy Between the Wars*. London: Allen and Unwin, p. 33.
64. Detailed and illustrated in Jackson, A.A. (1973) *Semi-Detached London*. London: Allen and Unwin.
65. London Council of Social Service (1927) *A Royal Commission on the Housing of the Poor and the Regional Planning of London*. London: LCSS.
66. Adams, T. (1924–6) The planning of London. *Town Planning Review*, **11**, pp. 285–90.
67. *The Times*, 25 November 1927.
68. *Journal of the Royal Institute of British Architects* (1930) **37**, 196–7.
69. LCC Town Planning Committee Papers, 16 February 1934, item 33.
70. Smith, H.L. (ed.) (1930–35) *The New Survey of London Life and Labour*. London: King, P.S.

71. *The Times*, 23 March 1934.

72. Labour Party (1934) *Up With the Houses and Down with the Slums*.

73. Strauss, G.R. (1937) The LCC elections. *Labour Monthly*, January, p. 33.

74. Morrison, H. (1936) What I would like to do for London. *Evening Standard*, 9 January 1936.

75. In 1938–39, 76 per cent of LCC dwellings completed in that year were in the form of flats. In 1924–29, the proportion of flats was between five per cent and eight per cent. These figures are discussed in Young and Garside, *op. cit.*, chapter 7 (see note 50).

76. Osborn, F.J. (1938) London: an awful warning to Glasgow. *Journal of the Town Planning Institute*, **24**, p. 383.

77. These schemes and political attitudes are discussed in detail in Garside, P.L. (1979) Town Planning in London 1930–61: a Study of Pressures, Interests and Influences Affecting the Formation of Policy. Unpublished Ph.D. thesis, University of London.

78. Berry, H. (1937) Town planning the County of London. *Journal of the Town Planning Institute*, **23**, p. 366.

79. The LCC's Jubilee. *Economist*, 18 March 1939, p. 553.

80. On planning's search for acceptance in the 'middle ground' of British politics, see Marwick, A. (1964) Middle opinion in the 1930s: planning, progress and political agreement. *English Historical Review*, **79**, pp. 285–98.

81. Greater London Regional Planning Committee, *Second Report*, March 1933, p. 94.

82. *London Statistics*, 41 (1936–38). London: LCC, pp. 191–2.

83. Culpin, E.G. (1936) London's green belt. *Journal of the Town Planning Institute*, **22**, p. 266.

84. In 1943, Lord Justice Scott drew the attention of Minister of Town and Country Planning to the need to bring the London Passenger Transport Board under the control of the planning authorities. 'They deliberately made railways into pure country around London', Scott wrote, 'in order to create new traffic by creating vast new suburbs – which they called "metroland" in advance . . . at the same time, they left old industrial and over-populated districts of London very inadequately served . . . it is a striking case of development forced *against* national interest or balance.' Quoted in Donnison, D.V. and Soto, P. (1980) *The Good City*. London: Heinemann, p. 10.

85. Williams-Ellis, C. (1938) Can we scrap London? *Spectator*, 11 November, p. 804.

86. Why London? *Economist*, 18 February 1939, p. 333.

87. These manifestations of widely-shared fears are described in Bialer, U. (1974) Some Aspects of The Fear of Bombardment from the Air and the Making of British Defence and Foreign Policy. Unpublished Ph.D. thesis, University of London.

88. Quoted in The size of London. *Economist*, 13 August 1939, p. 313.

89. *Ibid.*

90. Royal Commission on the Distribution of the Industrial Population, *Minutes of Evidence*. London: HMSO, p. 100.

91. Gibbon, G. and Bell, R.W. (1939) *History of the London County Council 1889–1939*. London: Macmillan.

92. Donnison and Soto, *op. cit.*, chapters 1 and 2 (see note 84).

93. This process is described in Garside, *op. cit.* (see note 77).

Chapter 10

Paris, 1890–1940

NORMA EVENSON

VICTOR Hugo once remarked that Paris 'does not belong to a people, but to peoples. . . . the human race has a right to Paris. France, with sublime detachment, understands this' [1]. A century later, another Frenchman noted that, 'it is traditionally an honour for France to have known how to cultivate a city so open that one can consider oneself a Parisian, and be recognised as such, without the necessity of being French' [2]. To some observers, being the capital of France has long seemed too modest a destiny for Paris. The view of Napoleon that Paris should be regarded as the capital of Europe has continued to influence the thinking of many French urbanists, and it was recently suggested that Paris might be deemed the 'point of equilibrium' for the world [3].

Paris has been a big city since the Middle Ages, and continues to rank high in population among the world's urban agglomerations. Yet its uniqueness is based not on size, nor on the city's widely-acknowledged beauty, but on its exceptional breadth and balance of urban functions. Paris is not merely a French city, it is *the* French city. To some, it is virtually France itself. A French guidebook once explained; 'No other nation lives as completely, is expressed, summarized and centralized in its primary metropolis as France is in Paris. . . . Paris has taken everything, absorbed everything. It is in this centre that France lives; it is here where one can study its spirit and sense its heart. . . . The vitality of Paris is unrestrained. . . . Where does one find in Europe, and even in the world, an equal destiny and a dominance as strong?' [4]

That a single city should have such primacy has not always inspired enthusiasm among French urbanists, and Paris has sometimes been likened to a destructive cancer or a bloated parasite draining the nation of vitality and resources. It has been a focus of continual controversy, and efforts to restrict its growth can be found as far back as the sixteenth century, and as recently as the Paris regional plan of 1960. In spite of recurring proposals for decentralization, Paris remains, for better or worse, not only the largest metropolitan centre in France, but the unrivalled focus of political, economic and cultural life.

FIGURE 10.1. Central Paris in the 1970s, looking west from above the initial area of settlement, the Île de la Cité. The axis of the Champs-Elysées, passing through the Arc de Triomphe and continued by the Avenue de la Grande-Armée, stands out clearly, right of centre. The high-rise buildings which terminate it are the office centre of the Défense, first of the suburban tertiary employment centres planned, from the late 1950s, to decongest central Paris (La Documentation Française).

The City's Evolution

The Paris region in the river basin of the Seine attracted settlement as far back as the Lower Paleolithic period. By Neolithic times, the island later known as the Ile de la Cité formed the site of a village settlement. The future city was to get its name from a tribe called the Parisii, who controlled the island by 250 BC and who exploited toll bridges across the Seine at what had by then become the principal crossroads of northern Gaul. Although the site had certain economic advantages, the future of the city was to be determined more by its function as an administrative and institutional centre than by its inherent potential for commerce and industry. During Roman times, Paris functioned as a relatively prosperous, but modest settlement, serving as the junction between roads from the south and the Troyes-Rouen axis.

As the French nation began to take form during the Middle Ages, Paris gradually assumed primacy as the focus of the monarchy and as a centre for European diplomacy. Royal patronage was to provide a dominant force in shaping the physical fabric of the city as well as encouraging much of its economic activity. As the national capital, Paris received the continuing impress of monumental building, becoming the visual symbol of a government establishment which has remained one of the most centralized systems of administrative control in the world. As the government centre, it received a variety of institutions dependent on State patronage, becoming the site of the most important archives, libraries, museums and art collections.

The status of the city as an educational and intellectual centre was initially promoted by the presence of monasteries and, in the thirteenth century, by the foundation of the Collège de Sorbonne. The university was later to be supplemented by prestigious specialized schools for higher education, such as the *Ecole normale supérieure*. Official patronage, together with the growing presence of a prosperous and educated public, tended to perpetuate Paris as the centre for art, music, dance and the theatre. The city also became the centre for publishing and journalism, for medical institutions and scientific research.

The consolidation of government institutions in Paris was paralleled by the increasing development of the city as a trading and manufacturing area. By the thirteenth century, Paris had become a centre for international finance, and was to continue as the banking centre of France and headquarters of major commercial enterprises. Paris was noted for high-quality luxury goods, encouraged in the seventeenth century by such State industries as the Gobelins and the Savonnerie. As the industrial age evolved, Paris was given notable encouragement as a manufacturing district through the pattern of railroad construction. In 1842, it was made the cul-de-sac terminal of six converging national railroad lines. A historian once noted that 'ten other cities were situated more advantagously to shelter the metallurgical, mechanical and chemical industries. Paris had in its favour that it was artificially favoured at a decisive moment.' [5] Although central Paris would continue to house a variety of artisan industries, most manufacturing establishments tended to concentrate in the peripheral areas, with heavy industry emerging in the surrounding suburbs. As modern industry evolved, Paris remained in the forefront – the most complete and varied industrial centre in France, and the focus of innovation, research and the most highly skilled occupations.

Physically, Paris owes much to its history as a walled city. As the initial settlement on an island in the Seine expanded north and south across the river, the city came to be defined by a series of enclosures which both established a line of defence and marked the municipal boundaries. This containment tended to give

FIGURE 10.2. The Champs-Elysées, c.1900. This monumental, landscaped axis, gradually but single-mindedly developed between the seventeenth and the nineteenth centuries, provided the paradigm for improvements elsewhere in the city (Bibliothèque Nationale).

the city a compact form, and, as population grew, Paris was characterized by a high density of building. Although the rich favoured large houses with walled-in gardens, most of the populace came to be housed in multi-storey dwellings, and by the late eighteenth century, at least one tenement house of as many as ten storeys existed. By the mid-nineteenth century, apartment living was generally accepted as the norm, even by the affluent classes, and population densities rose as high as 1000 per hectare in slum districts.

During the reign of Louis XIV, new methods of warfare had rendered the Paris fortifications obsolete, and he ordered their demolition, replacing the old ramparts with a curving sequence of broad, landscaped streets, which came to be called the *grands boulevards*. The street pattern of Paris would continue to reflect the imprint of lines of defence.

It was also during the seventeenth century that Paris began to evidence a dramatic juxtaposition of urban scales. Beyond the dense pattern of accretive growth which had evolved within the old walls, the new dimension of Baroque ordering began to appear at the edge of the city. Under royal sponsorship, the Louvre-Tuileries complex was remodelled, and a long vista created through the extension of the Tuileries axis along the Champs-Elysées. Sharing a common aesthetic vision, the planners of Paris would continue to embellish this axis, creating an expansive composition of streets, landscaping and architecture destined to become the monumental symbol of the city. In the eighteenth century, the Place de la Concorde was created to link the Tuileries Gardens with the Champs-Elysées, and in the succeeding century, Napoleon would punctuate this axis with the Arc de Triomphe.

Although the defensive walls had been razed, Paris regained the image of an enclosed city in the later eighteenth century when a wall was erected to control the taxation of goods entering the city (*octroi*). The path of this tax barrier, like that of previous walls, was eventually incorporated into the street system. Following the defeat of Napoleon, Paris again became a fortified city through a new ring of military defences completed in 1845. Although generally ineffective as a military device, this fortification was not dismantled until after the First World War.

The centralization of governmental authority in Paris, begun under the monarchy, had been augmented by Napoleon. Withdrawing all vestiges of autonomy from the city, he took a strong personal interest in the development of Paris as a city reflective of the glory of his empire. Included in his achievements were such utilitarian public works as new markets, reconstruction of the river quays, new sewers and water sources, as well as ornamental embellishments like the Arc de Triomphe, the church of the Madeleine and the Rue de Rivoli. His military campaigns and eventual fall from power resulted in the interruption and abandonment of many of his projects. Later in the century, however, his nephew, Napoleon III, inspired by his uncle's intentions, was to subject Paris to the most comprehensive programme of urban redevelopment ever experienced by a major city.

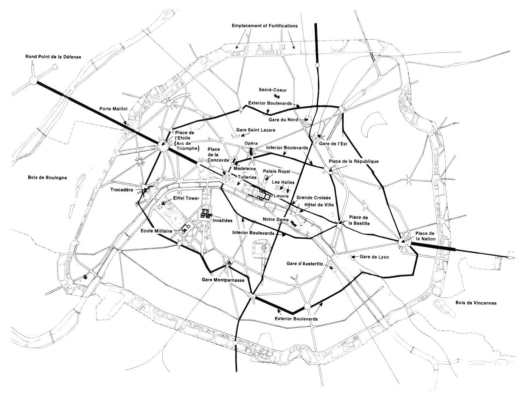

FIGURE 10.3. Major streets and principal monuments of Paris. Note the inner ring of the *grands boulevards* and their extension on the Left Bank, planned by Haussmann, and the middle ring following the *octroi* wall. The fortifications of the 1840s and their field of fire constitute the outer ring visible on this plan.

The Second Empire renovation of Paris remains a well-known chapter in the history of urban planning. Having established himself emperor in 1852, Napoleon III placed his virtually dictatorial powers behind a transformation of the French capital. Directing this work was an engineer, Georges Haussmann, who served as Prefect of the Seine between 1853 and 1870. Like many other programmes of urban works, the replanning of Paris clearly reflected the dominant influence of the national government. To many observers, however, the nineteenth-century renovation of Paris reflected also a growing influence of the bourgeoisie, who have been deemed its principal beneficiary. In the view of some, this alliance between powerful commercial interests and government authority has continued to be dominant in directing the evolution of Paris.

Much of Haussmann's work was directed toward the modernization of a Paris which, like most nineteenth-century cities, had been ill-equipped to accommodate the sudden growth of population which characterized the industrial age. Included in his programme were the creation of a new comprehensive sewer system, dramatic improvements in street lighting, vastly augmented water supplies, and the creation of extensive new park areas. City boundaries were extended outward to the line of the fortifications. Among the most conspicuous aspects of Haussmann's work was a network of new tree-lined avenues serving to facilitate traffic circulation and make the existing street pattern into a unified system. The large-scale demolitions entailed by these new streets remain among the most controversial aspects of Haussmann's work.

FIGURE 10.4. The Avenue de l'Opéra, c.1900. The completion of this, perhaps the most aesthetically convincing of the streets planned by Haussmann, in the late 1870s, symbolized the continuing credibility of the imperial conception of urban modernization under the Third Republic (photo: Ville de Paris).

The urban planning of the Second Empire has often been criticized as politically authoritarian, and reflective of an aesthetic insensitivity. Nevertheless, by the end of the nineteenth century, Paris had become a much-emulated model of urban beauty. The methods of Haussmann seemed, to many, to exemplify the scale of planning necessary for effective improvements in the modern city, and his achievements had a continuing international impact.

Although the Second Empire ended abruptly with the Franco-Prussian War and Commune, the planning concepts of this period persisted in the French capital. Haussmann's old assistant, Jean Alphand, served as Director of Works until his death in 1891. While neither political nor economic conditions permitted urban renovation at the scale of the Second Empire, Haussmann's plans provided the guidelines for future Parisian development.

Patterns of Growth, 1890–1940

In 1900, an American book on Paris informed its readers that 'the French people have created the cleanest, the healthiest, and the most beautiful city in the world' [6]. From the same epoch, however, one can find abundant testimony to the filth and stench of the streets, the squalour and pestilence of the slums, the shortage of open space, and the aesthetic horrors of contemporary architecture. Paris was by no means immune to the common range of urban problems, yet the highly subjective judgement that placed Paris far above other cities reflected a universal and continuing attitude toward the French capital.

By the 1890s, Paris had not only recovered from the destruction of the Franco-Prussian War and the upheavals of the Commune, but seemed in the midst of a glittering prosperity. Although the city retained its highly-visible links with the past, the dominant aspect was of a busy, sprawling modern metropolis. By the end of the century, the predominant character of the city had been established as both

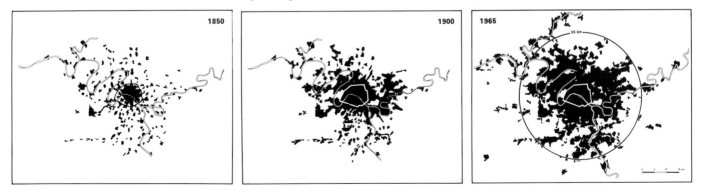

FIGURE 10.5. The built-up area of Paris and its region in 1850, 1900, and 1965, as portrayed in the *Schéma Directeur d'Aménagement et d'Urbanisme de la Région de Paris*.

the commercial and industrial centre, as well as the administrative and cultural focus of France. Surveys at the turn of the century indicated that industrial wages in Paris were virtually double those of the provinces, and this salary differential was to remain characteristic of the city. The advent of World War I served to enhance industrial expansion, as Paris became the centre of the armaments industry. Although the city was to be periodically affected by economic crises, the unmatched economic variety of Paris tended to assure a relative overall stability.

Gertrude Stein, who settled in Paris in 1903, once observed, 'Paris was where the twentieth century was' [7]. Paris had also been where the nineteenth century was, and the cultural dynamism of Parisian life continued unabated. Paris remained a magnet for the ambitious, for, no matter what one's occupation, reaching the top has usually meant residence in the capital.

Although Paris provided abundant rewards for the successful, there always remained a vast populace to whom it offered neither fame nor affluence. Beyond the glitter of the fashionable quarters was another Paris where the lights were not as bright. There were large districts disfigured by dilapidation and squalor, where the primitive living conditions of the poor were unaffected by the apparent modernity of the city.

Particularly noticeable was the contrast between Paris and its surrounding suburbs. While central Paris bore the imprint of a dominant urban order, the suburbs had grown haphazardly with a mixture of industry and some of the most wretched slums of the city. Huysmans, viewing this region from the ramparts of the Parisian fortifications, reported that 'along the horizon, against the sky, the round and square brick chimneys vomit clouds of boiling soot into the clouds, while below them, barely passing over the flat roofs of the workshops covered with tarpaper and tin, jets of white vapour escape, whistling, from thin iron tubes' [8]. To his eyes, the surburban fringe of Paris was a setting in which nature joined with the works of man to create a landscape of sadness and misery.

Deploring the living conditions of the outlying districts, an official report of 1908 noted that 'the suburbs are not sufficiently prepared to receive such a large and a rapid addition of new inhabitants; old villages, scattered here and there, have become in a few years large centres of population, which in an uninterrupted chain meet to form a disorderly mass like a single city spreading continuously from the centre, of which they form an extension. . . . Old country houses, lacking almost everything from the hygienic standpoint (drinking water, toilets, drainage, paving and maintenance of common courtyards) have received a number of occupants never foreseen in their original accommodations: a quantity of new housing has been constructed in complete freedom, without any regulation . . .' [9].

The evolution of nineteenth-century Paris had encompassed a continuous movement of residential population outward from the centre. Constantly increasing land values in the inner districts impelled the poorer classes toward the less-densely settled peripheral *arrondissements*. Because the fortified boundaries of the city provided a tax-collecting point for goods entering Paris, food and other products were usually cheaper in the suburbs than in the city. For this reason, the suburbs immediately surrounding the city sometimes became more populous than neighbourhoods directly inside the walls. Although a few fashionable suburbs developed outside Paris, affluent Parisians generally preferred the convenience and amenities of the city. The settlement of the suburbs became largely a working-class phenomenon.

A dramatic migration to the suburbs occurred during the 1920s. The influx of population inspired by the First World War had intensified the housing shortage within the city and, by 1921, Paris had achieved its highest-ever population of 2,906,472, while the suburbs housed 1,505,000. A decade later, in 1931, the city population had been reduced to 2,891,000, while the suburbs had grown to 2,016,000. This movement of residential population outward would continue to characterize the Paris region.

Suburban settlement was facilitated by the introduction of the eight-hour working day, which permitted increasing time for travel, and by the efforts of enterprising speculators, who acquired large tracts of cheap land, parcelled it into small lots, and sold the lots for modest weekly payments. The purchasers of these small suburban lots were usually too poor to employ commercial builders to construct their houses, and most built their own small dwellings from materials at hand. The new allotments quickly filled up with an assortment of constructions, including shanties of wood, plasterboard, tarpaper, and corrugated metal, accompanied by dwellings adapted from old trucks and wagons. Poor housing conditions in the suburban allotments were exacerbated by a lack of urban utilities. Existing legal provisions were inadequate to regulate the new districts, and punitive

FIGURE 10.6. A suburban *lotissement* at La Courneuve in the 1920s. The lack of street paving suggests the absence of underground services as well. Most of the constructions visible here would have been self-built by the purchasers of the plots (from *La Vie Urbaine*, no. 25, 1925).

FIGURE 10.7. An unidentified suburban settlement, photographed probably towards the end of the inter-war period. Some of these hutments might originally have been intended as weekend homes, but the serious Parisian housing shortage ensured that nearly all were permanently occupied. The nearest house has little girls playing obliviously on the doorstep while a suspicious mother keeps an eye on the photographer from the bottom left-hand pane of the door (H. Roger-Viollet).

sanctions for developers were virtually non-existent. Having no compulsion to do otherwise, land speculators sold the lots without streets, sewers, water supplies, drainage facilities, or gas and electrical installations.

Conditions in these suburban allotments became a major housing scandal, and the glaring contrast between the magnificence of Paris and the squalour of its outlying settlements was a subject of frequent comment. A senator observed: 'When one admires passionately the severe and grand lines of the architectural beauty of Paris, the spectacle of incoherence, anarchy, and ugliness presented by the greater part of the Parisian suburbs cannot but afflict us. Yes, the Parisian suburbs are a great stain of ugliness on the beautiful face of France' [10].

The inhabitants of the new suburban settlements found themselves socially isolated, exploited by the land proprietors, and often unable to obtain assistance from local governments. The local communes, in turn, saw themselves caught between the indifference of the land developers and the overwhelming demands of the hordes of new immigrants for services that the communes did not feel financially able to afford. The long struggle for improved conditions served to create a new political awareness among the settlers, and as the Communist Party began to gain strength during the 1920s, the consistent support of suburban voters gave the name 'red belt' to a circle of communities around Paris.

Assisting in the outward spread of urbanization was the expanding transportation system. Public transport in nineteenth century Paris had begun with the horse-drawn omnibus, which was supplemented in the 1850s by the horse-drawn tram. Mechanical traction began to appear on the tramway systems as early as the 1870s, with varied forms of electric traction being introduced in the 1890s. The tram lines were instrumental in linking the city with the inner suburbs, and served to encourage the trend toward working-class residence in the outskirts. Tramways often employed linked cars, sometimes including as many as five carriages in a single ensemble. The operation of transport lay in the hands of private conces-

FIGURE 10.8. The Place Saint-Michel, c.1900, showing horse-drawn omnibuses and trams, and an electric tram bound for the eastern suburbs. Though equipped with a trolley pole, it is here running on accumulators. Sustained objections to ugly overhead cables greatly restricted the contribution that electric tramways could make to transport in central Paris, and most of their mileage was in the outer districts and the suburbs (photo: RATP).

sionaries, and, by 1910, twelve tramway companies controlled more than a hundred lines in Paris and the suburbs. No attempt had been made either to coordinate routes or unify equipment and power systems. Both the horse-drawn omnibus and the horse-drawn tram, moreover, continued in use until 1913. The motor bus was first introduced in 1905, and gradually began to replace the slower, more cumbersome, trams. In 1929, the decision was made to replace all tramlines with buses, an aim which was accomplished by 1937.

While tramways and buslines served to connect the inner suburbs with Paris, large-scale commuting from the outer suburbs was facilitated by the development of suburban railroad lines. Towards the end of the century, there were systematic reductions in fares, and improvements in service, with electrification first appearing in 1900. Railroad commuting expanded rapidly during the 1920s, with the number of travellers reaching 363 million during 1931.

Compared with London, Paris was late in developing an underground rail system. Although such a system had been considered as early as the 1870s, construction was delayed through a dispute between the city and the national government over control of the system. Finally, in 1900, authority to develop the system was ceded to Paris, which constructed the new Métropolitain as a purely local system contained within the city boundaries. A few modest extensions into the suburbs were attempted in the 1930s, and the Ligne de Sceaux, a suburban rail line, was incorporated into the system in 1938.

In addition to various forms of street and rail transport, Paris was also served by a system of river steamers. At its height, during the 1890s, this system carried an average of 25 million people per year, and served a total of 42 million in the year of the 1900 exhibition. The number of passengers began to decline at this time, however, possibly because of the competition of the new Métro. Following a

FIGURE 10.9. *Métro* construction at the Place Saint-Michel in the early 1900s. Owing to the great depth of the line at this point, and the waterlogged subsoil, the Saint-Michel station was constructed on the surface and lowered into position. The vertical drum visible in the foreground is the bottom of the lift and staircase shaft. Most of the rest of the underground *Métro* was constructed without causing disturbance at the surface.

period of continuing deficits and decline in patronage, service was discontinued during the 1930s.

Between 1890 and 1940, the process of rapid modernization in Paris which had characterized the Second Empire appears to have slowed. Although the city retained its image as a centre of fashion and luxury, there were working-class districts in which living conditions had advanced little beyond those of nineteenth-century slums. Dwellings were often minuscule, and frequently lacked heat, running water, and adequate light and ventilation. Rising standards of hygiene only served to dramatize the gap between ideals and reality. While major epidemics had largely been brought under control by the end of the nineteenth century, tuberculosis had increased in virulence, remaining a major scourge until after the Second World War. The deteriorating slums of Paris, with their densely packed buildings, were considered an ideal breeding ground for the disease.

Whereas visitors to Paris in 1900 had frequently remarked on the cleanliness and modernity of the city, by 1940 they were more likely to report on the picturesque dilapidation of the buildings and the quaintness of the plumbing. Regulations dating from Haussmann's day required the periodic cleaning of facades, yet most buildings by 1940 carried a grimy patina of decades of soot. While Paris after dark was not without charm,. it might have been difficult to recall just why it had once been called the 'city of light'. The economic crisis of the 1930s depressed construction activity, and only one-fifth of what was needed to replace obsolescent housing stock was built at this time. A French journalist who had been fifteen in 1931 once recalled, 'someone of my age could have passed his entire youth without ever seeing a building under construction' [11].

While Paris retained its position as a historic centre, it had ceased to be a focus of urban innovation. Warning against complacency, a Parisian urbanist had

FIGURE 10.10. In an *îlot insalubre*. This is the Rue du Maure in the *îlot* 4 (later, 16) (Hôtel de Ville). Notorious in the nineteenth-century for its boarding houses packed with building workers, this district was among those singled out for special treatment, on account of its high tubercular mortality, before World War I. Little clearance or redevelopment was undertaken until the 1950s, however, and this photograph may well be of recent date (Préfecture de Paris).

FIGURE 10.11. An *îlot insalubre* of more recent construction, the *îlot* 6 in the industrial Faubourg Saint-Antoine (11th *arrondissement*). Large blocks crossed by interior courts and alleys, packed with housing and small-scale industry, remain typical of this area, which grew into its present over-built form between the late-eighteenth and the late-nineteenth centuries (Préfecture de Paris).

pointed out early in the century: 'It is not enough, in effect, to cry ''Paris, the City of Light, the Queen City!'', for Paris, by virtue of this proclamation alone, and without further effort, will never remain the first city of the world' [12].

Paris did not lack would-be Haussmanns, but there was no Napoleon III.

Public Planning Policy, 1890–1940

A government commission in 1913 described Paris at the time of Haussmann's retirement as 'a vast demolition site, momentarily abandoned, which it was necessary to continue' [13]. It was noted that 'the immense impetus given before 1870 has been continued through the uninterrupted effort of forty years, without, moreover, the end being near to attainment' [14]. Parisian planners continued to share with Haussmann the conviction that traffic circulation took high priority in

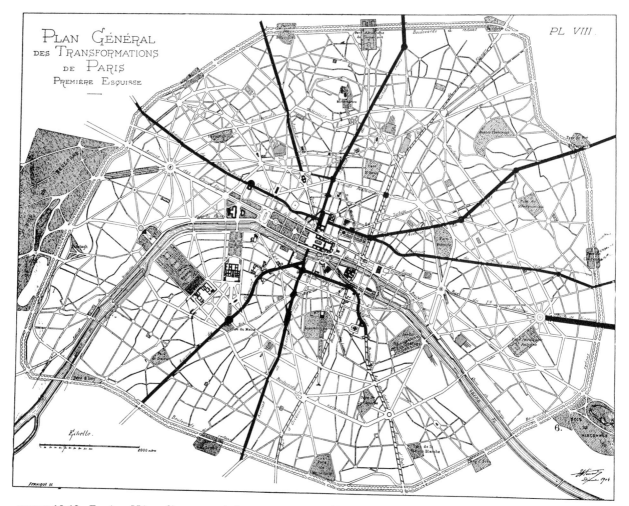

FIGURE 10.12. Eugène Hénard's proposals for new streets, published in his series of brochures, *Les transformations de Paris*, in 1905 and here reproduced in the *Proceedings of the American Institute of Architects*, vol. 39, 1905–6. Admirers of Hénard hailed their sinuosity, which allowed historic monuments to be avoided, as a major departure from the Haussmannic tradition, but critics pointed out that the widening of great lengths of existing streets which Hénard envisaged would have been even more disruptive of traditional Paris than the Second Empire's work.

Paris, and, as finances permitted, his projected street penetrations were realized, with the Boulevard Haussmann being completed as late as 1927. A growing conservatism, however, could be seen with regard to unrestricted demolition. The long, straight vistas of Haussmann's streets were attracting criticism on aesthetic grounds, and there was increasing reluctance to destroy buildings in the historic central districts in order to complete new traffic arteries. An official advised, 'let's guard ourselves against the fetishism of the straight penetration' [15]. Such projects as the extension of the Rue de Rennes through the Latin Quarter were eventually abandoned.

Although Haussmann's plan was to prove too ambitious for complete realization, various schemes were proposed for Paris which far exceeded his concepts in scope and destructiveness. A noteworthy series of planning studies for the city were produced independently between 1903 and 1909 by a government architect, Eugène Hénard. His suggestions included a new network of broad avenues penetrating into the heart of Paris. Although Parisian planners were unreceptive to his more radical concepts, they did adopt his proposal of the traffic roundabout (*carrefour à giration*). This system of directing traffic to circulate to the right in multiple intersections was first put into effect at the Place de l'Étoile in 1907. Hénard was also responsible for the creation of the Avenue Churchill, cut through at the time of the 1900 exhibition. The vista it created toward the Invalides has been deemed 'one of the last great moments in Parisian urbanism' [16].

As the automobile age advanced, suggestions even more sweeping than Hénard's appeared. The architect, Le Corbusier, produced his *Plan Voisin* for an exhibition in 1925. The scheme proposed the complete redevelopment of the centre of Paris into a district of skyscrapers. This was to be accompanied by a system of motor expressways cutting through the centre of the city. An admirer of Haussmann's scope of achievement, Le Corbusier repeatedly berated city officials

FIGURE 10.13. Eugène Hénard's design for a traffic roundabout with an underground pedestrian concourse, published at the same time as his scheme for new streets in Paris. This one would have been located at the point where his 'Avenue de Richelieu', descending from northern Paris, crossed the existing *grands boulevards*.

for their timidity and failure to match the scale of his operations. Toward the end of his life, he complained: 'Since 1922 (for the past 42 years) I have continued to work, in general and in detail, on the problem of Paris. Everything has been made public. The city council has never contacted me. It calls me "Barbarian"!' [17].

Because of limitations in political power and financial resources, government planning efforts between 1890 and 1940 tended to focus on limited, relatively short-range projects responding to immediately pressing needs, rather than on comprehensive long-range planning. In addition to programmes of street construction, there were attempts to improve sanitation and housing conditions within the city, and to consolidate and expand transportation systems.

The close of the century marked a strong interest in municipal hygiene and housing reform. The Prefect Eugène-René Poubelle, who served between 1883 and 1896, promoted sanitary improvements, and achieved immortality through the establishment of compulsory garbage bins [18]. He also instigated the *casier sanitaire*, a survey of Paris buildings based on their record of disease mortality. Housing studies conducted in Paris between 1894 and 1904 disclosed the existence of six specific districts with notably high tuberculosis mortality, and these centres

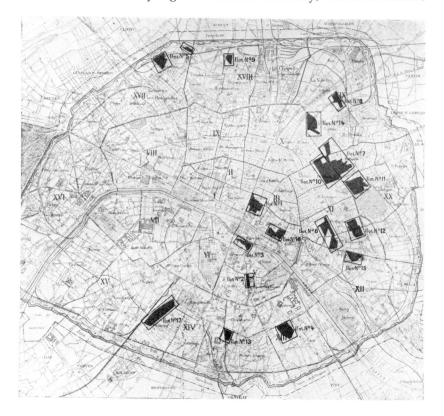

FIGURE 10.14. This plan shows the locations of the augmented list of *îlots insalubres* drawn up after World War I. Note the heavy concentration in the working-class districts of eastern Paris.

of pestilence were termed *îlots insalubres*. A second survey in 1919 disclosed seventeen such areas, including the six previously designated. The demolition of these enclaves, and their redevelopment, was to become a prime aim of Parisian planners for many years. It was believed that 'we must destroy the house, when it harbours the disease. Any palliative would be an illusion' [19]. Although limited efforts were made at clearing the *îlots insalubres*, beginning in the 1920s, financial and legal difficulties hampered accomplishment. Much to the chagrin of many planning officials, the *îlots* remained essentially intact on the eve of the Second World War.

The housing reform movement in France had inspired the enactment in 1894 of a law providing government assistance for housing. This was followed in 1912 by a law instituting public housing offices to construct low-cost dwellings. The Paris region was served in this respect by the Office Public des Habitations à Bon Marché de la Ville de Paris, and the Office Public des Habitations à Bon Marché de Département de la Seine.

The decentralist ideals of the Garden City movement led many planners to advocate the creation of new housing settlements outside Paris. True garden cities, however, were not attempted, and the so-called *cités-jardins* were intended merely as well-planned working-class housing projects within commuting distance of Paris. In the period between the wars, the Département de la Seine constructed sixteen such settlements. The earliest of these, begun shortly after the First World War, were strongly influenced in design by English prototypes. It was hoped to 'rival the beautiful creations which England offers us as models. If our neighbours have got ahead of us, it is up to us to catch up with them and to do as well as they' [20]. Picturesque cottage-style terrace houses were soon considered too costly, however, and the *cités-jardins* of the 1930s were characterized by three-to-five-storey apartment houses, and sometimes tower blocks.

FIGURE 10.15. The 'garden city' of Chatenay-Malabry, built in the suburbs by the regional H.B.M. office in the 1930s. Despite the high densities and the use of apartments, a commendable attempt has been made to retain the spirit of English low-density design (photo: N. Evenson).

FIGURE 10.16. The Paris fortifications, completed in the 1840s and here photographed probably in the later nineteenth century. The *glacis,* or field of fire, outside the walls would fill up with squatters' hutments to form the notorious *zone* by the 1920s (photo: Ville de Paris).

FIGURE 10.17. *Habitations à bon marché* built in the 1920s on the demolished fortifications, between the *boulevard extérieur,* visible on the right, and the *zone.* This solution, though heavily criticized as short-sighted both at the time and subsequently, was a response to the serious shortage of building land elsewhere in the municipal city of Paris (photo: N. Evenson).

A challenging opportunity for large-scale urban design in Paris came about through the acquisition and redevelopment of the ring of fortifications at the edge of the city. This line of battlements, accompanied by a wide band of open land, the *zone non aedificandi,* had long been obsolete as a military defence, and its annexation by the city had been discussed since the 1880s. Many urged that the area should be landscaped to give the congested capital much-needed parkland. The site was judged 'the last reserve of fresh air in our capital' [21]. The replanning of the fortifications would, it was hoped, help Paris regain its position as a leader in urban planning. 'France and the city of Paris owe it to themselves to catch up immediately the advance which has been lost' [22].

The fortifications were legally acquired by the city in 1919, and redevelopment proceeded during the 1920s and 1930s. Contrary to hopes, the emplacement was not developed according to a unified plan. The land was cleared and built upon in piecemeal fashion, with part of the area given over to institutional use, and part to low-cost housing. Large segments were simply sold to speculators. The redevelopment of the fortifications would long be invoked as a major planning failure in Paris, for what many had anticipated as a salubrious residential district, embodying abundant greenery and reflecting enlightened design concepts, had evolved into a dense wall of mediocrity encircling the city. According to the architect, Le Corbusier: 'Profit prevailed. Nothing, absolutely nothing was done in the public interest. No kind of advance for architecture, no kind of advance for city planning. This is a wasted adventure, but no one protests' [23].

In the years following the First World War, public transportation, which had initially been operated by private concessionaries, was gradually consolidated under government control. In 1921, all bus and tram lines were unified under a new organization, the Société des Transports en Commun de la Région Parisienne (STCRP), and placed directly under the control of the Départment de la Seine. The railroads were nationalized in 1938; and all private lines succeeded by the Société National des Chemins de Fer Français (SNCF). In the case of the Métro, the city had acquired the system as a matter of course, following the expiration of the twenty-five year contract which had been given to the Compagnie du Métropolitain de Paris in 1900.

While official planning activity centred on piecemeal public works, the desirability of comprehensive metropolitan planning for the Paris region was widely acknowledged by urbanists and officials. Although a unified administrative system for the Paris area would be delayed until the 1960s, a series of government-sponsored planning studies and competitions stressed the need for regional coordination. A study prepared in 1913 for the city of Paris recommended that, for planning purposes, Paris should be considered to include the Département de la Seine, which 'could provide the natural framework for a plan of extension' [24].

Following World War One, national legislation required that all cities of 10,000 or more prepare long-range plans for urban development. In Paris the new law inspired a municipal design competition in 1919, that included proposals for the Paris region. Contestants were 'advised to undertake their study with a large vision . . . and to include in their plans . . . everything that, in their conception, constitutes the Parisian agglomeration'. 'Paris and its surroundings', it was noted, 'have a community of relations, such that practically no economic or social problem can be envisaged or solved for Paris alone' [25].

The programme of the competition presupposed a continual expansion of the Paris region, and predicted that the regional population might reach fourteen million by 1961. The prize-winning plans strongly emphasized expanded transportation, including improved highways and suburban rail systems. A strong influence of the Garden city movement could also be seen in various proposals for systems of satellite towns.

The 1919 competition was merely a *concours d'idées* intended not for immediate realization, but as a stimulus for further reflection. The Paris region was not yet considered ready for political consolidation. Had the political climate been such as to permit the creation of a viable regional plan, however, 1919 would have been an excellent time to institute it. The succeeding decade was to mark a period of uncontrolled suburban expansion, and urbanists seeking to demonstrate the hazards of unplanned accretion could find ample support for their arguments in the jungle growth of the Paris region.

The first determined effort to develop a regional plan for Paris resulted in the so-called 'Prost plan', completed in 1934. This plan defined the Paris region as the area contained roughly within a circle with a radius of 35 kilometres measured from Notre Dame cathedral. Attempting to counteract the untrammelled growth of the region, the plan emphasized restrictions on development. According to the plan, each municipality was required to limit its zone of urbanization to the area for which the municipal budget could assure the complete provision of urban services for the next fifteen years. Urging the adoption of the plan, a government official maintained that 'it is the last occasion which offers itself to plan conveniently for greater Paris' [26]. Suburban municipalities, however, were generally unenthusiastic. It was noted that the scheme was less a plan for growth than a plan for nongrowth. Some saw it as a usurpation of local authority, and an attempt to restrict the vitality and future prosperity of the suburban communes.

The plan gradually gained government approval, however. It was accepted by decree in 1939, with certain reservations, and finally made law in 1941. Included in the modifications of the plan was a redefinition of the Paris region. Instead of being contained within a 35-kilometre radius of Notre Dame, the region was expanded to include all of the Départements of the Seine, Seine-et-Oise, and Seine-et-Marne, plus five cantons of the Département of Oise. The territory of the region was thus expanded from a proposed 512,000 hectares to 1,300,000.

The years between 1890 and 1940 marked a period when the ambitious aspirations of planners were met with frequent frustration. In the view of some,

FIGURE 10.18. The plan for the Paris region directed by Henri Prost and
published in 1934. The main emphasis was on open spaces and
communications, including a regional network of autoroutes.

Paris suffered from a chronic paralysis in attempting to meet the needs of a
growing metropolis. In 1929, the Directeur de l'Extension de Paris recalled the
planning competition for the Paris region held ten years previously:

Must I speak of the disappointment, the heartbreak which an administrator feels, who, having studied these projects, having lived during several weeks among mirages of a greater Paris, ordered, regulated, ventilated, sanitized, beautified, regains contact with reality and is confronted with the difficulties of the everyday, and the down to earth? . . . And when he sets to work, he finds himself faced with two insurmountable obstacles: shortage of money, crisis of housing. As to the financial dificulty, I shall limit myself to citing two figures: . . . from 1854 to 1871, Haussmann, the great model, spent 1,430 million francs on street openings and promenades, or, in round figures, 100 million per year. From 1871 to 1919, the annual expenditure was on the average less than 14 million, and since 1919 the devaluation of the franc and the financial and economic crisis have not permitted the undertaking of large works, except for the extension of the Boulevard Haussmann.

If, financially, the realization of a vast programme of street operations had been possible, how would the city of Paris have been able, without grave troubles, to demolish a considerable number of buildings? It would have been, in this Paris as full as an egg, to throw families out on the street, who, badly housed perhaps, would have been completely without shelter.

Planners were continually reminded, in the words of the same author, 'how far it is between the cup and lips, from the dream to the reality, to the hard and cruel reality' [27].

**The Sum of
Fifty Years**

As Paris grew from a walled city in the era of the horse and the railroad into a metropolis in the age of the automobile and the aeroplane, the development of the city was determined in part by government policies, and also by economic forces, and by that complex welter of private decisions which often defies analysis, but which, in the long run, may be the primary determinant of urban destiny. Whether or not Paris would have been a better city if it had, between 1890 and 1940, been comprehensively 'planned' is not certain. While one can find numerous complaints about the timidity and indecisiveness of municipal administrations of this period, one can find an equal number of complaints regarding the all-too-visible achievements of more decisive recent administrations. Paris has been the canvas on which many urbanists have painted their dreams, and in surveying the multitude of proposals that have been made for the redevelopment of the city, one does not always regret that they remained unrealized.

Looking at the street penetrations proposed by Eugène Hénard, one feels a certain relief that they were not taken seriously by city officials. Commenting on his suggestions, a government commission of 1913 observed: 'The Parisian street system can be improved, certainly, but one should guard against thinking that it is necessarily bad and that it must be remade from top to bottom. Moreover, in this matter, overly simple formulas are useless and dangerous' [28]. As to Le Corbusier's sweeping proposals for the centre of Paris, even people who respected his imagination and talent might have been appalled by the prospect of the city rebuilt according to his principles.

The upheavals of the Haussmann era may have inspired a natural reaction in the preservation movement that gained force toward the end of the century. The voices of those who advocated far-reaching urban renovation were continually countered by those who feared the destruction of the traditional urban fabric. Conflict inevitably arose over municipal proposals to raze the *îlots insalubres* as a public health measure. A preservationist maintained that there was 'no conception more false than the one envisaged in Paris, which condemns an entire quarter with the injurious epithet of *îlot insalubre*' [29]. Gertrude Stein once observed that 'we need the picturesque, the splendid, we need the air and space you get only in old quarters. It was Picasso who said the other day when they were talking about tearing down the insalubrious parts of Paris that it is only in the insalubrious quarters that there is sun and air and space' [30].

Public interest in questions of preservation had resulted in the foundation in 1884 of the Société des Amis des Monuments Parisiens. Although it was a private organization, the Société attracted the support of some civic officials, and in 1897 the Commission du Vieux Paris was created. This group served in an advisory capacity to the city administration, creating historic building inventories and

FIGURE 10.19. This photograph of the Rue de Rivoli shows some of the new attic storeys added after the relaxation of the building regulations in 1902. The public outcry which accompanied this rebuilding (as a result of which some of the offending additions were removed) epitomizes the highly conservative atmosphere in which Parisian architecture evolved between 1890 and 1940 (photo: N. Evenson).

making recommendations for preservation. It proved somewhat ineffectual, however, and a preservationist noted in 1943: 'It could only express its wishes. These wishes . . . were simply set aside as soon as a powerful interest came into play. And there were always interests in play. Who didn't have a municipal councillor up his sleeve?' [31].

An overall harmony in the architectural fabric of Paris had resulted from building regulations controlling height and surface decoration. Toward the end of the century, the rigidity of this code was challenged by many architects who considered it hampering to creative design as well as inimical to urban beauty. In consequence, a new building code was adopted in 1902, permitting more ornate facades as well as an increase in building height. Although the maximum cornice height remained at the traditional 20 metres, as many as three storeys could now be added to the attic level, giving a total height in some cases of 30 metres. Although such heights were modest in relation to what was technically possible, these so-called 'skyscrapers' were widely denounced by conservative critics for their deleterious impact on architectural harmony.

As the modern movement in architecture progressed, visionary proposals for inserting high-rise building into Paris continued to appear. Le Corbusier was not alone in believing that the French capital might benefit from such structures. Officialdom remained unconvinced, however, and following a lengthy reconsideration of building controls, a municipal commission concluded in 1930: 'In its general physiognomy, the city of Paris must conserve its own character, its discipline, its quality of order and measure. And so, without exception, buildings of excessive height, like those which provide the attraction of certain foreign cities, should be forbidden. . . . Reason dictates that Paris should be held to the same order of height as before' [32].

The architectural evolution of Paris was thus reflected in stylistic change, rather than in a notable alteration of building form. The ornate eclecticism and Art Nouveau of the turn-of-the-century gradually gave way to the simplification of the International Style and the stripped classicism of the 1930s. New structures appeared within the traditional street and block pattern, confined by relatively conservative building codes.

Although, during the preceding fifty years, drastic renovations in the Parisian urban fabric had been proposed in the name of traffic circulation, slum clearance, and modern design, Paris in 1940 had been far from revolutionized. The central city had remained remarkably stable in its physical form, with the most rapid change occurring in the burgeoning residential suburbs following World War One. To advocates of dynamic planning action, the period between 1890 and 1940 was characterized by stagnation and impotence. Municipal administrators were often criticized for their hesitancy in meeting the growing challenge of a modern metropolis. From our own vantage point, however, one may observe that 'he who hesitates is sometimes saved' [33].

1940 and After

The onset of the Second World War and German occupation, needless to say, brought a slow pace of urban reconstruction to a virtual halt. The war did not, however, put a stop to planning activity and, in some ways, encouraged it, as wartime legislation notably enhanced government power. Legislation in 1940 and 1941 created the Commissariat Technique à la Réconstruction Immobilière, charged with the establishment of reconstruction plans for towns suffering war damage. Also in 1941, the Délégation Générale à l'Équipement National was established to coordinate questions of urbanism and housing construction, while the Comité National d'Urbanisme was created to provide advice on urban problems.

It was wartime legislation that facilitated the complete annexation by Paris of the *zone non aedificandi* adjacent to the fortifications. Expropriation had proceeded slowly for twenty years, hampered by cumbersome legal processes. In 1940, however, the law was amended to permit direct requisition without lengthy court delays, and the grim days of the occupation were marked by a steady eviction of the *zone's* numerous squatter inhabitants. The new powers of requisition were also used to hasten acquisition of property in the *îlots insalubres*, although the acute housing shortage tended to deter immediate demolitions.

The interruption of construction necessitated by the war provided time for study and reflection, and the prevailing atmosphere of self-criticism promoted a desire to avoid the errors of the past. A national law of 1943 repeated the intentions of the 1919 legislation, requiring that a development plan be produced by all towns with a population of 10,000 or more, and by all communes forming part of urban agglomerations. It was considered particularly important that Paris have such a plan, and the Comité d'Aménagement de la Région Parisienne was created to serve as a consultative committee for its preparation.

Having been declared an open city at the time of the German invasion, Paris had been spared immediate physical damage, and the effects of the war years were to be computed largely in human terms. Some damage to buildings occurred, however, during the fighting which accompanied Allied entry into the city.

The years following 1945 encompassed accelerated activity in both planning and new construction. Government planning efforts in the city of Paris led to the establishment of a master plan in 1959, the Plan d'Urbanisme Directeur de Paris. This was followed in 1968 by the Schéma Directeur d'Aménagement et d'Urbanisme de la Ville de Paris. Both these documents were intended to establish general guidelines for the evolution of the city.

During the same years, steps were being taken to develop a regional plan. The Plan d'Aménagement et d'Organisation Générale de la Région Parisienne (PADOG) was approved by decree in 1960. This plan reflected a decentralist attitude among planners, and sought to restrain the untrammelled expansion of Paris. In an effort to counteract the dominance of the capital, preferential assistance for expansion was given to eight *métropoles d'équilibre* throughout France. The principles of the PADOG included a determination to stabilize the rate of population growth in Paris. Within the Paris region, the city was to be decongested in favour of the suburbs, where urban nodes were to be established. The District de la Région de Paris, as defined by the PADOG, included the Départements of the Seine, Seine-et-Marne, and Seine-et-Oise, an area comprising 12,070 square kilometres, 2.2 per cent of the territory of France.

As economic recovery advanced, government planners began to question the desirability of restricting Parisian growth, and references to Paris as the natural 'capital of Europe' arose frequently in arguments favouring expansion. It was believed by many that Paris should be considered within the context of an economically unified Europe, which placed 'Paris and its region in competition with other metropolises. . . . The role of the Paris region in comparison with the other regions in France can no longer be the same as before, and it must be defined in new terms' [34]. Paris was to be seen as part of a pattern of urbanization comprising a series of great centres forming an arc across northern Europe from London to Paris to Geneva by way of Rotterdam, the Ruhr, the Rhine, Basle and Zurich. Paris was deemed the only French city that could function at the scale of the other major European centres, and it was argued that to diminish its economic importance could only hurt France. In the vitality of Paris presumably lay the vitality of the nation.

A reconsideration of the PADOG scheme resulted in the development of a new regional plan, published in 1965 and called the Schéma Directeur d'Aménagement et d'Urbanisme de la Région de Paris. Far more ambitious in scope than the PADOG, which had projected development for a ten-year period, the Schéma Directeur incorporated projections to the year 2000. The Schéma did not seek to halt expansion, and assumed a regional population of fourteen million by the end of the century. The overall aim was to give order and coherence to future urbanization, seeking a balance of transport, employment, housing and urban services, and preventing the total obliteration of remaining open areas in the region.

The publication of the Schéma Directeur had been preceded by a political reorganization of the Paris region, in which the Départements of the Seine and Seine-et-Oise were reapportioned to create six new départments. These, together with the city of Paris and the existing Départment of Seine-et-Marne, comprised the District de la Région Parisienne, reconstituted in 1976 as the Région d'Île de France. Incorporated in the new plan were a series of 'new towns', conceived, not as small communities, but as urbanized regions tied to central Paris by rapid transport lines.

Post-war Paris has been subjected to a rapid physical redevelopment in which large complexes of high-rise building have become conspicuous in both the central city and suburbs. The automobile has also had a notable impact in the form of expressways, and an increasingly automobile-based pattern of regional settlement. While some have accepted the rapid pace of change as inevitable, others have bitterly regretted the transformation of a city which has long been a beloved part of the Western heritage. Apprehension about the future of Paris seems to reflect a fear that, in the speed of renovation, all sense of continuity with the past may be lost, and the richness of old Paris obliterated and even forgotten.

Conclusion

In retrospect, the period between 1890 and 1940 appears as a relative lull between two storms. Compared with the sweeping reconstruction of the Second Empire and the equally cataclysmic upheavals following the Second World War, the scope of planning activity during this fifty-year period seems modest indeed. One may note, however, the development of trends which set directions for future decades.

The years following 1890 marked an era of increasing consolidation between Paris and its suburbs. Both government policies and spontaneous development promoted the evolution of Paris into a metropolitan region characterized by long-distance commuting. Private initiative manifested in the creation of suburban housing allotments paralleled prevailing planning practices in providing housing outside the city. Expansion of transport lines, including tramways, bus lines and suburban railroads encouraged an increasingly dispersed pattern of settlement. The shift of population outward, seen so dramatically in the 1920s, has continued unabated into our own time.

The turn-of-the-century marked the emergence of government housing organizations, and a growing acceptance of governmental responsibility for the financing and construction of low-cost dwellings. The *cités-jardins* developed in the Parisian suburbs during the 1920s and 1930s were the forerunners of the *grands ensembles* of today. When housing officials decided to base the *cités-jardins* on apartment housing, including the use of tower blocks, the pattern was being set for the design of present-day housing complexes.

A concern for public health inspired the demarcation of pestilential districts, and these *îlots insalubres* have guided the location of much recent slum clearance. Although building height in Paris, between 1890 and 1940, was controlled by stringent regulation, a prophetic image of future Paris could be seen in the visionary schemes of certain modern architects. Such imagery created a receptivity to tall building in the minds of many planners, and strongly influenced post-World War Two decision-making with regard to building regulation and the nature of urban renewal projects.

The formation of a regional planning policy, which eventually resulted in the present-day political unification of the Paris region, together with its long-range plan, was evidenced in a series of studies, government competitions, and planning documents produced between 1890 and 1940. Of particular importance in this regard is the Prost Plan of 1934 which, with modifications, provided the basis for subsequent regional plans.

From the vantage point of 1965, a French historian observed that 'between

Haussmann and the most recent works of urbanism . . . there is nothing'. He went on to lament the 'lost opportunities and wasted talents' [35]. Yet if we think of the city itself, rather than what planners wanted to do with it, this period seems to embody a time of remarkable richness. The *Belle Epoque* seems to our eyes a golden age of opulence, and Paris of the 1920s a time of cultural efflorescence. Even in the years of the Depression, Paris still seemed a great and beautiful city, with its harmonious image intact. There is reputed to be an ancient Chinese curse: 'May you live in interesting times'. Perhaps there is an urban equivalent, such as: 'May you live in a period of significant development'. In the view of some, Paris might benefit from another period of 'nothing'.

NOTES

1. Hugo, Victor (1867) Reliquat de Paris, notes prepared for a Paris guide book. Reproduced in Hugo, *Paris*. Edition prepared by Hubert Juin. Paris: Livre Club du Libraire, p. 309.
2. Griotteray, Alain (1964) Exigences du destin de Paris. *Urbanisme*, **84**, p. 29.
3. Pilliet, Georges (1961) *L'avenir de Paris*. Paris: Hachette, p. 126.
4. Quoted in Gravier, Jean-François (1972) *Paris et le désert français en 1972*. Paris: Flammarion, p. 30.
5. Quoted in Flanc, Robert (1971) *Le scandale de Paris*. Paris: Grasset, p. 43.
6. Olivares, Jose de (1900) *Parisian Dream City*. St Louis: N.D. Thompson, pages unnumbered.
7. Stein, Gertrude (1940) *Paris, France*. New York: Scribner, p. 11.
8. Huysmans, Joris Karl (1955) *Croquis parisiens*. Paris: Mermod, p. 130. First published in 1880.
9. Sellier, Henri (1923) Les aspects nouveaux du problème de l'habitation dans les agglomérations urbaines. *La Vie Urbaine*, **19**, pp. 90–1.
10. Quoted in Bastié, Jean (1964) *La croissance de la banlieue parisienne*. Paris: Presses Universitaires de France, p. 285.
11. Giroud, Françoise (1972) *Si je mens*. Paris: Stock, p. 57.
12. Hénard, Èugene (1903) *Études sur les transformations de Paris. Fasicule 3: Les grands espaces libres: Les parcs et jardins de Paris et Londres*. Paris: Librairies-Imprimeries Réunis, p. 61.
13. Commission d'Extension de Paris, Préfecture du Département de la Seine (1913) *Considérations techniques préliminaires*. Paris: Chaux, p. 37.
14. *Ibid*.
15. Quoted in Léon, Paul (1947) *Histoire de la rue*. Paris: La Taille-Douce, p. 208.
16. Pons, Alain (1975) *2000 ans de Paris*. Paris: Arthaud, p. 167.
17. Le Corbusier (1967) *The Radiant City*. New York: Grossmann, Orion Press, p. 207.
18. The prefect's name was subsequently applied to the garbage bin, or *poubelle*.
19. Quoted in Sutcliffe, Anthony (1970) *The Autumn of Central Paris*. London: Edward Arnold, p. 110.
20. Société des Cités-Jardins da la Banlieue Parisienne (1914) Untitled brochure, pp. 10, 12.
21. Hénard, Eugène (1908) in *Musée Social: Mémoires et Documents*, no. 7. Paris: Musée Social, pp. 74–5.
22. *Ibid*.
23. Le Corbusier, *op.cit.*, p. 13 (see note 17).
24. Commission d'Extension de Paris, *op.cit.*, p. 47 (see note 13).
25. Préfecture du Departement de la Seine et la Ville de Paris (1919) *Programme du concours ouvert pour l'établissement du plan d'aménagement et d'extension de Paris*. Paris: Chaix, p. 4.

26. Quoted in Sellier, Henri and Brasseau, Paul (1935) Le plan d'aménagement de la région parisienne devant les corps élus. *Urbanisme*, **40**, October/November, p. 2.

27. Doumerc, Pierre (1929) Les résultats du concours d'urbanisme de 1920 ont dégagé des principes intéressants pour l'établissement du plan d'aménagement et d'extension de Paris. *L'Europe Nouvelle*, 8 June, pp. 733–4.

28. Quoted in Premier Ministre, Délégation Générale au District de la Région de Paris (1963) *Avant-projet de programme duodécennal pour la région de Paris*. Paris: Imprimerie Municipale, p. 10.

29. Pillement, Georges (1943) Démolitions présentes et futures. *Destinée de Paris*. Paris: Chêne, p. 96.

30. Stein, Gertrude (1940) *Paris, France*. New York: Scribner, pp. 17–18.

31. Pillement, Georges, *op.cit.*, p. 80 (see note 29).

32. Commission des Perspectives Monumentales (1930) *Rapport de la sous-commission chargée de la révision du décret du 13 août 1902*. p. 44.

33. Thurber, James (1952) *Fables for Our Time*. New York: Harper–Row.

34. Premier Minstre, *op.cit.*, p. 70 (see note 28).

35. Ragon, Michel (1965) *Paris, hier, aujourd'hui, demain*. Paris: Hachette, p. 12.

Chapter 11

Berlin, 1890–1940

HORST MATZERATH

THE German language, as Andrew Lees has already pointed out, (p. 67) is not immune to ambiguity when it comes to defining the distinction between the metropolis, or *Weltstadt,* and the run-of-the-mill large city (*Grossstadt*) [1]. We could well beat our brains out trying to establish whether the metropolitan qualities of Berlin within the German-speaking world were distinctively superior to those of Vienna, or even of Munich or Cologne. However, if post-1890 Berlin is compared to Paris or London, there can be no doubt that it merits its place among the leading world cities discussed in this volume. Indeed, in terms of rapid growth and vibrant atmosphere it rises above its European rivals, and shares something of the dynamism of New York evoked below by Kenneth T. Jackson. Perhaps we might wonder, much as R. A. French does in respect of Moscow (p. 355), how important a milestone is 1890 in the development of Berlin [2]. On the other hand, the outbreak of the Second World War definitely marks the end of a phase of development. However, there is a further parallel with Moscow in the presence of an important turning point at the end of the First World War – the establishment of Greater Berlin in 1920. Accordingly, the first section will deal with the general lines of development until 1890, the second with the period up to 1920 and the third with the development of Berlin in the period between the wars, up to 1939-40. The conclusion contains, aside from a summary, a discussion of the question of whether Berlin was able to preserve the character of a world city under the conditions of the post-war era.

The General Lines of Berlin's Development up to 1890

The history of Berlin up to 1890 cannot be conceived of as a unified period. Since the fifteenth century and especially since the seventeenth and eighteenth centuries, the development of the twin-city Berlin/Cölln (which had been founded in the thirteenth century) was connected with the rise of Brandenburg/Prussia. With the establishment of the Prussian monarchy (1701), Berlin finally became a capital and royal court. Having been converted into a fortified city at the end of the seventeenth century, it was beautified in the eighteenth century with self-glorifying buildings and expanded with planned suburbs. The royal court and the

FIGURE 11.1. The fortified town of Berlin in 1733. Although there are streets outside the rampart, this map accurately conveys the very small size of Berlin at this time.

army were the basis of the commercial economy. Manufacturing in particular was intensively promoted by the Prussian rulers (gold and silver, porcelain, iron and steel, foundries and gunpowder). The growing importance of Berlin as capital and royal court is reflected in the fact that Berlin's population grew between 1700 and 1800 from 29,000 to 172,000 [3]. At the same time, it was not only far behind London and Paris at the beginning of the nineteenth century, but also did not occupy a position of leadership among the German cities. The explanation lay in the political disunity of the Holy Roman Empire, which led to the polycentrism of the German city system, with a high degree of specialization.

The end of the Holy Roman Empire (1806) and the reorganization of Germany made Berlin after 1815 into the centre of a substantially expanded territory and allowed it to become, with Vienna, one of the two most important cities of the German Confederation. Partly on the basis of those manufactures which had been founded as a part of Berlin's function as capital and royal court, Berlin entered into an early phase of industrialization. The system of paved roads (*Chausseen*) – which was well developed by the standards of the rest of eastern and central Prussia – an extremely favourable position in the river system, with a connection to the Elbe and Oder [4], and a central position in the nascent railway system at the point of intersection of important German and European railway lines [5] made Berlin's geographical position unique in terms of transportation in the centre of Europe. The importance of Berlin's position was greatly increased by the founding of the German Customs Union (1834). These conditions made it possible, in spite of an unfavourable location with regard to supplies of primary resources, for a railroad

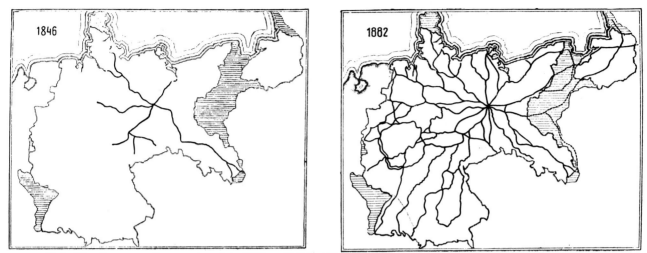

FIGURE 11.2. The German railway network in 1846 and 1882. Although industrial and commercial development in western Germany is reflected in the later map, Berlin remains the clear focus of the entire system.

industry to develop in Berlin, associated in particular with the name Borsig [6]. In this period, developments began which were to make Berlin into one of the leading machinery producers of Germany. The munitions industry stimulated the development of other industries. The chemical industry had its start comparatively early. The textile industry was pushed out of Berlin into the outlying areas; the garment industry began to take its place, stimulated by the production of uniforms [7]. New factors of development thus added to the city's function as capital and royal residence in the early phase of industrialization.

The industrial character of Berlin was further reinforced in the period 1850–1871, the era of the Industrial Revolution. The ranks of railway construction and machinery construction were joined by electrical engineering, the origins of which lay in the construction of telegraph installations and which was associated primarily with the name of Siemens [8].

The year 1871 ushered in a new era in Berlin's development. The territorial gains of the years 1864–1866 had already added to the importance of the Prussian capital. On top of that, Berlin became capital of the new German Empire after the Franco-Prussian War (1871). Berlin had thus finally become the political centre of Germany, and its preponderance among the cities of Germany became increasingly clear. Berlin's position as imperial capital was the basis for its rise as financial and commercial capital of Germany. Admittedly, Berlin already had some banks of more than mere regional importance, but now the banking system began to concentrate in Berlin. The big German banks set up important branches in the city

FIGURE 11.3. Berlin in 1850. The western districts of the city have been
clearly marked by the planned extensions carried out by the kings of
Prussia, principally in the eighteenth century. A more chaotic growth of
suburbs has taken place in the north and east, but the ordered street plan of
the Köpernicker Feld, to the south, under construction since the early 1840s,
both harks back to the older, Absolutist, traditions, and looks forward to the
Hobrecht plan.

or even moved their head offices there [9]. In the same way, the associations of
economic interest groups established their central offices in the capital and large
joint-stock companies relocated their main offices to Berlin. Berlin thus developed
into an important trade centre, not only for trade between eastern and western

Germany, but also on a European scale. The effect of all this was that Berlin took over part of the role of the old trade and banking centres, such as Frankfurt-am-Main, Hamburg, and Leipzig.

The development of Berlin as a leader in the intellectual and cultural sphere was not as clear [10]. Berlin of course had had the renowned Humboldt University since the beginning of the nineteenth century; the Technical University, which had been founded in 1879, developed in neighbouring Charlottenburg [11]; and numerous institutions for culture, research and education concentrated in Berlin. The theatre, museums, and libraries grew up, while the press, and with it, criticism, were centred in Berlin. At the same time, the importance of older cultural centres such as Munich, Dresden, Hamburg, Stuttgart or even Darmstadt, not to mention Vienna or Prague, remained undiminished, so that in the intellectual and cultural sphere the traditional German multi-polarity largely survived.

Table 11.1. The growth of Berlin's population 1709–1977.

	Old Berlin	Greater Berlin	Berlin (West)	Berlin (East)
1709	57,000	—	—	—
1750	113,000	—	—	—
1777	149,000	—	—	—
1800	172,000	—	—	—
1816	197,000	—	—	—
1840	330,000	—	—	—
1861	548,000	—	—	—
1871	826,000	(932,000)	—	—
1880	1,122,000	—	—	—
1885	1,315,000	(1,566,000)	—	—
1890	1,579,000	(1,960,000)	—	—
1900	1,889,000	(2,712,000)	—	—
1910	2,071,000	(3,734,000)	—	—
1919	1,907,000	(3,804,000)	—	—
1925	(1,971,000)	4,024,000	—	—
1933	—	4,243,000	—	—
1939	—	4,339,000	—	—
1950	—	(3,335,000)	2,145,000	1,190,000
1961	—	(3,244,000)	2,189,000	1,055,000
1970	—	(3,207,000)	2,122,000	1,085,000
1977	—	(3,056,000)	1,938,000	1,118,000

The growth of Berlin's functions is reflected in its population growth. Berlin had a population of only 197,000 in 1816, but by 1849 it had risen to 424,000; in 1871, 826,000; and Berlin's population doubled in the next twenty years, bringing it up to almost 1.6 million by 1890 [12]. The rate of population growth in this period was considerably higher than for comparable cities [13]. This rapid growth was based largely on immigration, especially from the eastern agricultural areas of Germany [14]. If the suburbs are included, the growth was even more spectacular; between 1871 and 1890 the population of the suburbs rose from 932,000 to nearly two million.

The seventeenth-century fortifications which surrounded the oldest parts of the city – Berlin, Kölln, Friedrichswerder and Neukölln – had been removed towards the end of the eighteenth century. Thereafter a customs wall was built further out. Until the 1840s it coincided with the municipal boundary, and it survived until 1867–68. Berlin's nineteenth-century growth was at first accommodated on unoccupied land within the city limits, especially in the south and east (Cöpenicker Feld, Stralauer Viertel), and partly on the basis of a network of new streets planned by the Prussian police-president in 1825. Later, however, largely unplanned settlements began growing outside the city gates, especially to the north, east and south. They included, aside from industrial plants, primarily workers' living quarters. This spatial growth led to extensions of the municipal area in 1841 and 1861. The second annexation incorporated the new, quickly-growing industrial suburbs of Moabit and Wedding [15].

Decisive for Berlin's physical development were the building code of 1853 and the Hobrecht Plan of 1858–62. The latter had striking similarities to Haussmann's

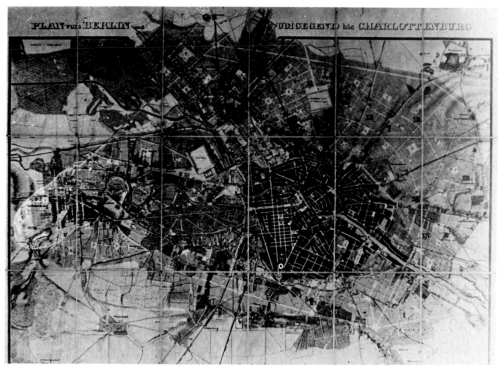

FIGURE 11.4. James Hobrecht's extension plan of 1862, showing the new districts which, it was envisaged, could accommodate a century of population growth (Landersarchiv Berlin).

plan for Paris. However, whereas Haussmann set out principally to reshape an already existing city, Hobrecht planned mainly for new peripheral growth, especially beyond the former walls. The Hobrecht Plan was based on broad, boulevard-like streets interspersed with large squares. An outer ring, still visible today in the form of the so-called *Generalszug* (Trautenau-, Kleist-, Bülow-, and Gneisenaustrasse), was intended to delimit the planned area. The grid of streets was largely systematic, with a view to dividing the peripheral area into very large blocks, up to 400 metres square. Hobrecht envisaged smaller streets to open up these blocks, but they were never built. Thus the vast areas behind the frontage buildings came to be filled up with factories, workshops, and low-grade tenements. The plan thus favoured the increasingly typical Berlin *Mietskaserne* (rental

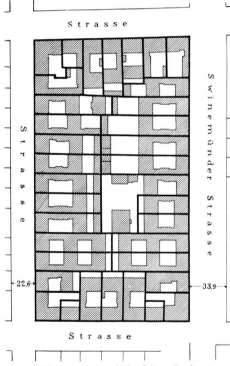

FIGURE 11.5. A typical block in a Berlin working-class district of the later nineteenth century. The interior courtyards were an economic response, conditioned by the building regulations, to the great depth of the sites. The open spaces in the middle of the block were, typically, occupied by light industry (from R. Eberstadt, *Handbuch des Wohnungswesens*, 1909).

FIGURE 11.6. This apartment house, photographed in 1937, stood in Köthenerstrasse, Kreuzberg, immediately to the south of the centre of the old city. The basement shops, reflecting heavy pressure on frontage land, were a feature of inner Berlin (Landesbildstelle Berlin).

FIGURE 11.7. Interior view of the front court of a nearby house in Köthenerstrasse (Landesbildstelle Berlin).

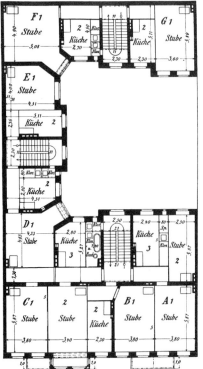

FIGURE 11.8. Plan of one of the upper storeys of a Berlin *Mietskaserne* of the end of the nineteenth century.

FIGURE 11.9. This photograph of *Mietskasernen* of recent construction was taken in the Wilmersdorferstrasse, Charlottenburg, in 1900. The sites awaiting development further along the street were typical of suburban Berlin, where the big land companies were often content to keep sites vacant for long periods until they could secure the required price (Landesbildstelle Berlin).

barracks), a four- or five-storey apartment house arranged around a courtyard, and often extended into the interior of the block by a series of back courtyards, with access to the street only from the first court [16].

The installation of a transportation system was of crucial importance for Berlin's development. Waterways were a major permissive factor in Berlin's growth. By the beginning of the nineteenth century Berlin was linked by navigable water to the Elbe and Oder, and via them to the North Sea and the Baltic. The river on which Berlin stood, the Spree, had been complemented further to the south by the *Landwehrkanal*, the two being linked by the *Luisenstädtische Kanal*. In the north, the *Spandauer Schifffahrtskanal* shortened the route to the Tegeler See. These and later cuts created a very dense system of waterways in and around Berlin. From the 1840s, this network was increasingly complemented by railways. At first, the radiating main lines terminated at unconnected stations, originally built at the periphery of the municipal area. In 1871, however, they were linked up by a belt railway running at a radius of about five kilometres from the centre of the city. Together with the waterways, this circular railway attracted an increasing number of factories and service installations such as warehouses and gasworks. In 1882 the line was supplemented by a metropolitan railway (*Stadtbahn*) which ran across the centre from east to west, much of it on a viaduct. Subsequently, a number of suburban lines were built, with the whole of the inner-urban system owned by the Prussian State. Berlin's omnibus system dated from 1846, when the first line was conceded to a private company. Numerous other companies followed, and later, tramway companies, one of the most important being the *Grosse Berliner Pferde-Eisenbahn AG*. In the 1880s the first experiments were made with steam and electric tramcars. However, as late as 1890 it still could not be said that Berlin possessed a mass-transport system.

Between 1871 and 1890, Berlin's suburbs began growing more quickly than Berlin itself [17]. Some of the growth occurred in the neighbouring towns of Charlottenburg and Spandau, but primarily in the directly adjacent rural districts (*Landgemeinden*) of Lichtenberg (with Boxhagen), Rixdorf/Neukölln, Schöneberg and Weissensee. These surrounding communities acquired an increasingly urban character as the Berlin building regulations, with their intensive land use, were applied to parts of the outlying areas [18]. Some of this peripheral development was guided by the Hobrecht Plan, which extended beyond the municipal boundary to the limits of the Berlin police district. Elsewhere, street systems were planned under the Prussian *Fluchtliniengesetz* (building lines law) of 1875.

Throughout these years, power was shared between the municipality of Berlin and the Prussian State. In deference to its size and importance, Berlin was removed from the province of Brandenburg in 1875 and placed under the direct supervision of the Minister of the Interior. Although the initiative of the municipality was thereby reinforced, the police-president, as a servant of the Prussian State, retained substantial powers. Previously he had been responsible for building regulations and street planning in Berlin, and although the latter was transferred to the municipality in 1875, changes in the building regulations in Berlin, as well as in the surrounding areas, continued to be subject to Prussian government approval.

By 1890 Berlin had developed the basic characteristics of a metropolis; it was, after London and Paris, the third-largest city in Europe, the capital of the newly-founded German Empire, the most important industrial centre in central and eastern Germany, a crossroads for the railway system and for domestic navigation, an important business centre, especially for banking, and one of the most important intellectual and cultural centres in the German-speaking world. The Berlin executive council (*Magistrat*) was thus perhaps entitled to its boast: 'With a speed unprecedented in Europe, our community has burst its bounds as a modest princely seat with an almost all-pervasive small-town character, and has suddenly become a world city which is an equal of the million-peopled cities which have traditionally been the focus of great events' [19].

Berlin from 1890–1920: Big City or Agglomeration?

The development of Berlin up to 1920 in many ways reveals a continuation and reinforcement of tendencies which were already present. With the growing political importance of the German Empire, the importance of Berlin as its capital also increased; industry expanded, especially the electrical industry, whose indisputable centre Berlin was in this era (Siemens, AEG, Bergmann) [20]. Banks and wholesale trade continued to be drawn to the capital. Meanwhile, publishing (Mosse, Scherl, Ullstein) and research institutes (among others, the *Physikalisch-Technische Reichsanstalt* and the *Kaiser-Wilhelm-Gesellschaft zur Förderung der Wissenschaften*) reinforced Berlin's character as an intellectual and cultural centre.

On the other hand, a revolutionary change in the physical structure of the city occurred after 1890, in the inter-related growth of outlying areas and structural change in the inner city. After 1890 the population growth of the municipal area, which was almost totally built-up, slowed, while the suburbs grew rapidly [21]. In around 1912, and thus before the outbreak of the war, the population in the municipal area began to decline, while the population of the outlying districts continued to grow [22]. Meanwhile, a number of suburbs had reached the size of large towns and had been granted the status of independent municipalities – Schöneberg in 1898, Rixdorf/Neukölln in 1899, Wilmersdorf in 1906, and Lichtenberg in 1907 [23]. In practical terms, however, their growth depended on the development of Berlin, with which they remained closely interconnected.

The peripheral growth corresponded to profound structural changes in the inner city, which was already regarded by contemporaries as in the process of evolving into a central business district (*City*) [24]. A number of tertiary functions grouped on particular streets; the government buildings were on Wilhelmstrasse, the banks of Behrenstrasse, the shops on Leipziger Strasse, the entertainment sector on Friedrichstrasse, newspapers around the Jerusalem Church, wholesale

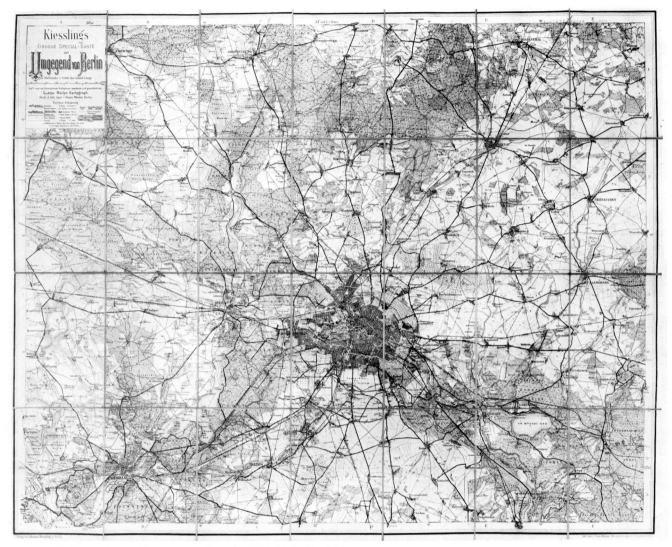

FIGURE 11.10. Berlin and its surroundings in 1890. Only the dark-grey areas
are fully built up. The extensive street networks on the periphery of Berlin
(shaded light-grey) and around nearby towns and villages have been
planned, under the Prussian *Fluchtliniengesetz* of 1875, to anticipate building
development.

clothing outlets on Hausvogteiplatz, and the so-called 'Ritterstrasse export-block'
in Luisenstadt [25].

    The building development of Berlin in this period was primarily a function of
the price of land, as well as of the developing building code. While the high price of

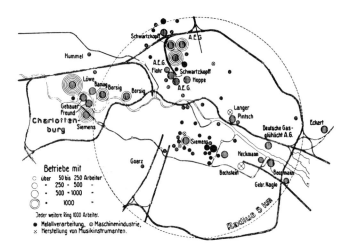

FIGURE 11.11. Locations of large engineering works within five kilometres of the centre of Berlin, and in Charlottenburg, in 1985.

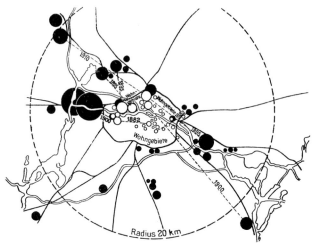

FIGURE 11.12. Movements of large industrial plants within a twenty-kilometre radius of central Berlin, 1890–1925. The white circles indicate abandoned locations, all of which were in the tightly-packed central districts bounded by the belt railway (*Ringbahn*).

land and high building rents made the western part of the city into a government and business district [26], heavy industry, with its considerable need for land, moved out to the city's periphery, and in some cases kept moving further and further out [27]. Borsig, for example, transferred its plants in 1898 from Chaussee-strasse in the north and Moabit in the west to Tegel, thus establishing the industrial district of Borsigwalde. The big industrial concentrations often attracted workers' housing areas, which clustered around the factories. Elsewhere, such as in Rixdorf/Neukölln, workers' residential areas developed on their own, to a large extent without industry [28]. In the western part of the city, residential areas grew up where the upper and upper-middle class lived, for example the villa colony of Grunewald. The bulk of the middle class lived primarily in the south-western portion of the city (Friedenau, Steglitz, and Lichterfelde).

The building regulations had only a limited impact on development in this period. The *Fluchtliniengesetz* allowed the municipalities to fix no more than the building lines, which meant that they could plan the street system, but not the use of private sites [29]. This latter was regulated by building ordinances (*Baupolizeiord-nungen*) issued by the Prussian State authorities. They laid down the type of building permitted, the maximum height, and the minimum dimensions of inner courtyards. In 1887 the Berlin police-president issued a new building code for the city which incorporated minor improvements but which, even after amendment in 1897, did not threaten the basic system of the *Mietskaserne* (although the maximum height of five storeys prevented the emergence of skyscrapers). However, in 1892 special building regulations were issued for the Berlin suburbs, which previously had conformed to the building code for the central city. They expanded the area zoned for four- and five-storey buildings, but at the same time they reduced the permitted densities in the outer suburbs, zoning part of their area for two-storey, detached houses [30].

The introduction of special regulations in the suburbs reflected a greater tendency towards suburbanization after 1890. The prerequisite for this decentralization was the mass-transit system which had been emerging before 1890 but which took clear shape thereafter. The main milestone was the introduction of fixed, standard fares on the belt railway, the *Stadtbahn*, and the suburban lines in the early 1890s [31]. The trams were finally electrified at the turn of the century and the buses were motorized soon afterwards [32]. In addition, Berlin followed the example of other metropolises by opening the first section of its underground system, in 1902. It was run by a private company, the *Gesellschaft für elektrische Hoch- und Untergrundbahnen*, founded in 1897 on the initiative of Siemens, and financed by the Deutsche Bank. The result, by the early 1900s, was an efficient transport system which permitted large-scale, long-distance commuting. In 1908 public transport usage in Berlin resembled that of London and Paris, while remaining inferior to that of American metropolitan districts such as Greater New York and Greater Boston. On the other hand, the Berlin system had many

FIGURE 11.13. Modernized Berlin transport at the Hallesches Tor in 1901. Note the electric trams, the *Hochbahn*, and an underground line under construction (Landesbildstelle Berlin).

FIGURE 11.14. The built-up area of Berlin in 1912. The hatching indicates the maximum height and site usage of buildings permitted in the various districts.

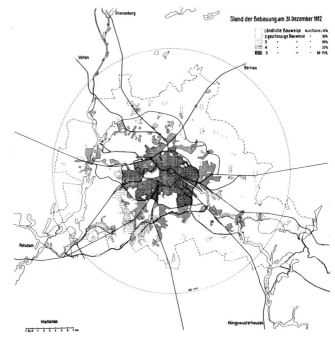

weaknesses. The multiplicity of companies hindered the coordination of the different systems and lines, and some suburbs were inadequately connected with the main network. In 1912, for instance, eight private and seven municipal tramway companies were operating in the Berlin area. Coordination was inadequate, being limited to the City of Berlin's efforts as a shareholder in the companies, and as the authority whose approval was required for the creation of new routes. All in all, the Berlin transport system exhibited both the advantages and disadvantages of capitalist competition, only slightly moderated by municipal activity.

These developments led to the progressive outward movement of the periphery, to a distance of 15–20 kilometres from the city centre. The suburbs nearest the city generally grew more quickly, but on the whole population growth did not follow a concentric pattern. Growth followed the transportation routes; industrial settlements tended to grow along waterways, so that the factories were concentrated in the south-eastern, north-western and western parts of the city. The suburbs often grew up around the already existing core of villages and estate-districts (*Gutsbezirke*), which are still clearly recognizable today.

Building development was strongly polarized between two very different types of organization. On the one hand, a number of large companies of private developers (*Terraingesellschaften* or *Bodengesellschaften*), supported by the big investment banks, bought large tracts of land, such as big private estates and government-owned land. After development, they sold the sites to private builders [33]. On the other hand, non-profit building companies and cooperatives constructed socially-oriented housing. In many of their estates and blocks, efforts were made to achieve a higher standard of living conditions through innovations in construction and equipment. This tradition was descended from Germany's first non-profit-making building company, the *Berliner gemeinnützige Baugesellschaft*, which had been founded in 1848. These organizations enjoyed cheap State finance and access to government or municipal land on favourable terms. At the same time, the imperial and Prussian governments built housing for their own employees in Berlin. However, this public and semi-public housing met only a small part of the total demand for good housing. One of the main explanations lay in the social composition of the municipal councils, which was heavily biased towards the property-owners. The Prussian three-class electoral system (*Dreiklassenwahlrecht*) favoured the propertied classes in general, and was reinforced by a specific legal requirement that houseowners should make up at least half of the membership of each municipal council.

The theory of urban planning reached its first peak in Germany between 1890 and 1920. Layout and street design continued to be influenced by Paris, while the technical infrastructure drew primarily on the British example. However, the rapid expansion of German towns and cities led to the progressive abandonment of these older foreign prototypes [34]. Intense discussion of the social, hygienic and aesthetic aspects of housing, and of the problem of workers' housing, led to the formulation of new principles. These ideas crystallized around the Garden City concept of Ebenezer Howard, which proved more influential in Germany than the similar idea set out by Theodor Fritsch in his book, *Die Stadt der Zukunft*, in 1896. Howard deeply impressed the younger generation of German architects, the result being the foundation of the very influential *Deutsche Gartenstadtgesellschaft* in 1902 [35]. The theory was put into effect – though in the form of the garden suburb rather than the garden city – in a series of influential settlements in the Berlin area, such as Staaken in 1913, and Lindenhof in 1918–19.

Rapid suburban growth caused ever-growing tensions between Berlin and the surrounding municipalities, rural districts, and communities. Attitudes changed over time. Until the 1890s the City of Berlin was opposed to extensions of its boundaries. Thereafter, however, the Prussian government and conservative interests in the Prussian parliament and the counties which neighboured the city were the main opponents of annexations. Some of the poorer suburbs, especially in the east, sought annexation in order to secure better communications and other services. Meanwhile, the richer western suburbs such as Charlottenburg and Grunewald opposed the idea. The Prussian government and the conservative forces were mainly motivated by fear of the growing threat from the Social Democrats, who were strongly supported in the Berlin area. The prosperous suburbs, on the other hand, wanted to preserve their low rates of local taxation.

These growing tensions motivated the search for a general solution for the whole area, which culminated in the semi-official Greater Berlin planning competition and exhibition of 1910–11. The competition brief required the submission of plans for the existing built-up area and the unsettled districts of the outer suburbs, as far as Potsdam. The main emphasis of the brief was on transport and open space, but entrants were not precluded from submitting detailed architectural schemes for housing, public buildings, and other elements of the environment. Many well-known architects and planners submitted entries. Their acceptance of the challenge to look well ahead in their thinking prompted a lively public debate, not only on Berlin's problems, but on urban planning in general. A number of specific projects were launched as a direct result of the competition, but the purely hypothetical character of the entries prevented their achieving a fundamental transformation of public policy.

Faced by increasingly serious problems, the Prussian government essayed a provisional solution in 1911, when it set up an inter-urban board, the *Zweckverband Gross-Berlin* [36]. It was composed of the municipalities of Berlin, Charlottenburg, Schöneberg, Neukölln, Wilmersdorf, Lichtenberg, Spandau, and the surrounding counties of Niederbarnim and Teltow, thus covering an area reaching to more than 40 kilometres from the city centre in the south and north and to nearly 20 kilometres in the west. Its competence was limited to transportation and land-use planning and building regulations. During its brief existence down to 1920, it was unable to fulfil its objectives, and it is doubtful whether a longer period of adjustment would have produced a happier result. So closely was the Berlin agglomeration by now interwoven that it is highly questionable whether an association of independent authorities (which worked well in the more loosely structured Ruhr region – see below) was the appropriate solution.

In the period between 1890 and 1920, the functions which gave Berlin its metropolitan character were reinforced. The disparity between Berlin and its international rivals, London and Paris, was reduced, while Berlin's precedence as the most important city of Germany became increasingly pronounced. The economic activity of Brandenburg, in particular, was increasingly concentrated in Berlin. On the other hand, a characteristic of this period was the fact that Berlin definitely broke out of the boundaries of the traditional city, so that an ever-growing antithesis between the official and the functional urban area developed. Centripetal tendencies in the form of the formation of a downtown business district and a centrifugal force which resulted in extensive suburban growth, with concomitant growing differentiation within the urban area, were the decisive characteristics of the metropolis of Berlin in this phase of development.

Greater Berlin, 1920–1940

The development of Berlin from 1920 to 1940 reflected the general contradictions of the period. On the one hand, the uniting of the separate municipalities to form

FIGURE 11.15. Changes in the Berlin municipal boundaries, culminating in the creation of Greater Berlin in 1920. Note that the city boundaries remained almost unaltered between 1861 and 1919, while extensive suburban growth occurred outside them. On the other hand, the boundaries of Greater Berlin included large tracts of open land, which greatly facilitated the planning task of the inter-war years.

Die Gebietsentwicklung von Berlin

Alt-Berlin — bis 1691 — bis 1802 — bis 1841 — bis 1861 — bis 1919 — 1920 eingemeindet

Greater Berlin laid the foundation for homogeneous development of the entire metropolitan area. On the other hand, all the political and social crises Germany went through in this period emerged with particular force in Berlin. The fundamental differences between the democratic system of the Weimar Republic and the Nazi dictatorship introduced an important element of discontinuity into this period.

The Greater Berlin Law of 1920 eliminated the tension between the official and functional urban areas, by merging eight municipalities, fifty-nine rural districts, and seven estate-districts to form an enlarged City of Berlin. It was a product of the new political circumstances in which, after the revolutionary events of 1918 and 1919, conservative influence was abolished and the Prussian government, now under Social Democratic influence, was able to pursue a more socially-oriented policy. In the Berlin case, the institutional solution adopted had been partially foreshadowed by administrative developments during the war, when the city of Berlin had exercised an enhanced influence over the outlying communities, particularly in the field of consumer supply. As in the enlarged Vienna, thirty years earlier, a two-tier executive was set up, consisting of a municipal administration with city-wide authority, and twenty district boards. The municipal administration thus had the task of welding into one urban unit the extremely densely populated area of the old city of Berlin, and the diverse suburbs. Real urban planning for Berlin thus dates from 1920 [37].

The Prussian Law on Housing Construction of 1918, the building ordinance which was based on it, and the zoning plan of 1925 provided a new legal basis on

FIGURE 11.16. Greater
Berlin zoning plan, 1925.

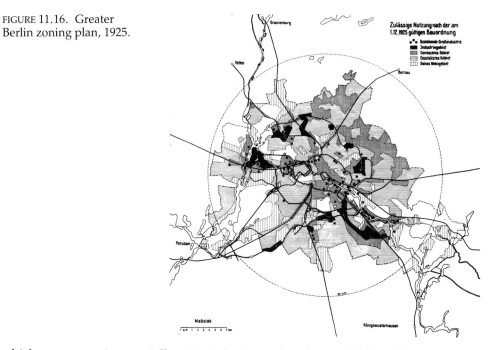

which a more active, socially-oriented urban planning could be elaborated. The
building ordinance of 1925 forbade the construction of back courts and thus meant
the definitive abandonment of the Berlin *Mietskaserne*. In addition, the Berlin
zoning plan of the same year fixed building forms and land uses throughout the
city. The plan distinguished between industrial, mixed, and residential areas. At
the same time, responsibility for zoning and building regulations was transferred
from the State-appointed police-president to the City of Berlin. The resulting
enhanced scope for coherent planning was reflected in the establishment of a
municipal department of urban planning in 1925, headed by the distinguished
planner, Martin Wagner.

The new planning code, the expansion of the city and the clearer social goals
gave a new generation of architects and planners the chance to put into action their
ideas for a new social orientation for house building. Garden City planning ideas
and Bauhaus design concepts, already partially formulated before the war, were
now carried further and put into effect. Architects such as the Taut brothers, the
Luckhardts, Gropius, Scharoun, Häring, Mendelsohn, Mies van der Rohe, Poelzig
and many others created exemplary architectural solutions to the problems of
constructing housing areas, large public and private buildings and single houses
[38]. Housing areas such as the Hufeisensiedlung in Britz, the Onkel-Tom-Siedlung
in Zehlendorf and the Weisse Stadt in Reinickendorf represented an attempt to tie
the new architectural ideas to the demands of standardization and rationalization

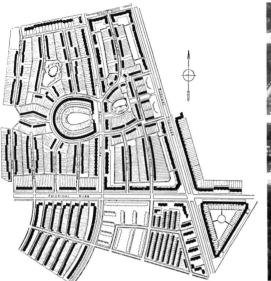

FIGURE 11.17.   Bruno Taut's plan for the Hufeisensiedlung, Britz.

FIGURE 11.18.   Aerial view of the Hufeisensiedlung (Landesbildstelle Berlin).

FIGURE 11.19.   Flats in the Onkel-Tom-Siedlung (Landesbildstelle Berlin).

of housing construction [39]. This building was carried out in particular by public-utility construction companies, which were supported by local authorities and the trades unions. The City of Berlin, for instance, held shares in fifteen limited liability companies, four housing associations, and four joint-stock companies, all of them engaged in building mass housing. Between 1924 and 1928 the bulk (61 per cent) of the nearly 87,000 new dwellings completed in Berlin were built by public-utility enterprises. Private enterprise built about one-third (35 per cent), with the remainder (four per cent) built by private owners. Much of the new housing, especially in the semi-public sector, was provided in large estates of low-rise, simply-built but not uniform, houses, intermingled with gardens, lawns and parks. Sometimes a rural, village-like appearance was secured, as a symbol of the improved living and hygienic conditions established in these new areas. At Siemensstadt the new concept was carried over, in the same impressive style, into the building of an industrial complex. Of course, Berlin shared in a European movement of architectural renewal in this period, but *das neue Bauen* found its most convincing expression, outside Amsterdam, in Berlin.

Parallel improvements were secured in the city's infrastructure [40]. The traffic

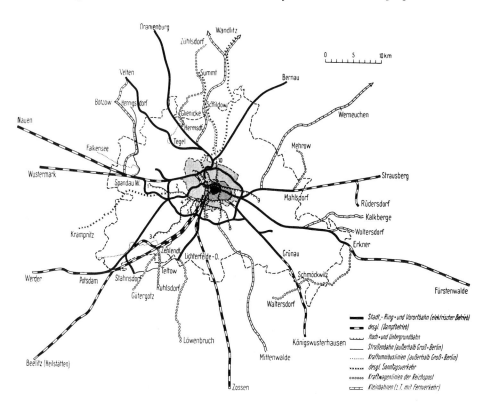

FIGURE 11.20. The Berlin area passenger transport network in 1932.

commissioner, Ernst Reuter (mayor of Berlin after the Second World War), combined the various transportation companies into the *Berliner Verkehrsgesellschaft* (BVG), conceived a unified system based on different means of transportation in which the underground system was to play a major role, and made the underground more efficient by introducing fixed, standard fares. The other public services (gas, water, electricity, refuse collection) were also united into municipal companies (with differing legal statuses) and services were expanded. These and other developments of City of Berlin services, such as swimming pools, sports facilities, parks and other open spaces, and cultural institutions, were, under the general characterization of 'municipal socialism', the subject of intense political debate in this era [41].

Under the Nazi dictatorship, Berlin's development was focused differently. No more big housing projects were begun, and smaller projects took the form of separate single-family houses and shared houses with gardens [42]. The new rulers, however, were only really interested in a self-glorifying, monumental architecture which was an expression of Hitler's personal interests. Hitler ordered special rebuilding projects for Berlin, Munich (the capital of the Nazi movement), Nuremburg (the city of the National Socialist Party rallies), and Hamburg. Albert Speer was given considerable special powers as Inspector General of Buildings for Berlin [43]. A section of the city, the Adolf-Hitler-Stadt, with buildings whose dimensions would have surpassed anything previously attempted, was to distinguish Berlin as the centre of a universal empire, pushing older metropolises such as Paris, London or Rome into the background. Speer's plans included an extensive network of roads, construction of which was begun, but the Adolf-Hitler-Stadt never got beyond the planning stage and only in the case of a few isolated public buildings (such as ministries, Nazi party buildings, and other government offices) was the fascist style of monumental simplicity put into reality.

The process of functional expansion of the city beyond its official boundaries did not end with the creation of Greater Berlin. The outward movement of industry again began to overstep the boundaries of the new official area at some points: to the north-west (Oranienburg, Velten, and Henningsdorf), to the south-west (Potsdam, Nowawes, and Teltow), and to the east and south-east (Königswusterhausen, Erkner, Rüdersdorf, Strausberg, and Finsterwalde). Satellite factory areas also developed (Eberswalde, Brandenburg, and Luckenwalde) [44]. Commuter traffic grew on the transit routes between the suburbs and the city centre. On the other hand, it became clear that the towns in the outlying areas had a good deal of trouble in developing high-level functions because of Berlin's preponderance [45].

The ties between Berlin and the surrounding areas again began to become very strong, and this led in 1929 to the establishment of the Provincial Planning Association for Central Brandenberg (*Landesplanungsverband Brandenburg-Mitte*). It brought together the authorities of the province of Brandenburg and the counties

FIGURE 11.21. Boundaries of regional planning associations in the Berlin area, 1929–37.

surrounding Berlin and, after 1934, the City of Berlin. The main responsibility of the Planning Association was to coordinate the activities of the various authorities with regard to the development of the periphery of the capital, but the association never achieved much of importance [46]. Speer's special powers put an end to the idea of coordinating the development of Berlin and the surrounding areas. Moreover, the association was disbanded in 1937 and its functions were transferred to a Provincial Planning Board for Brandenburg (*Landesplanungsgemeinschaft Brandenburg*).

In comparison with earlier population growth, Berlin grew very little between 1920 and 1939. The causes of this development lie less in another shift of population growth outwards than in the fact that the German population in general grew very slowly in this period, while Nazi armament policy favoured other locations. Berlin continued to be an important industrial centre, however, specializing in electricals, machinery construction, the garment industry, and banking [47]. Berlin was able to strengthen its position as a focal point of banking, the insurance business, wholesaling, and corporate head offices, despite the effects of the post-war crises, the hyper-inflation, and the Great Depression. As a part of the Nazi autarky policy, Berlin also became the centre of economic decision-making. The highway system, which was just beginning to be built, gave Berlin a central position in road transport; in air transport, which was also only starting to be developed, Berlin was second to Paris and on a par with London [48].

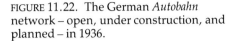

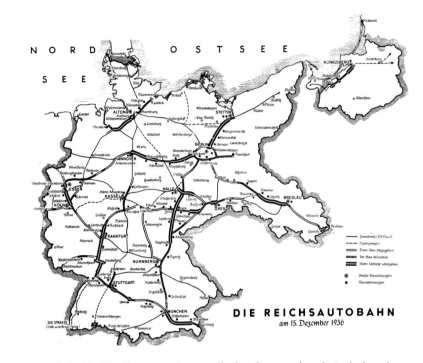

FIGURE 11.22. The German *Autobahn*
network – open, under construction, and
planned – in 1936.

DIE REICHSAUTOBAHN
am 15. Dezember 1936

Between 1918 and 1939, Berlin was above all the focus of political developments: the collapse of the Empire and the Revolution of 1919, the critical climax of
political conflicts which led to the failure of the Weimar Republic and the Nazi
seizure of power, and the system's self-portrayal in the 1936 Olympics, were
connected in a special way with Berlin, although Munich was in some ways a
counterpart to Berlin, especially in the 1930s. But above all, Berlin became in the
crisis-ridden 'Roaring Twenties' (*die goldenen zwanziger Jahre*) an intellectual and
cultural centre of European-wide stature, whether in the fields of theatre, film,
cabaret, art, architecture or literature. Neo-realism, expressionism and Dada were
admittedly not solely creations of Berlin. Nevertheless, they were very successful
in performances, exhibitions, and publications in Berlin and were diffused to a
broader public by the Berlin critics. However, it was precisely this intellectual
growth which was rooted out by National Socialism, which put in its place a
politically-dictated provincialism. For racial, political, or ideological reasons, the
most important artists and scholars of the German-speaking world were forced to
emigrate or were cowed into silence, a great loss for German culture and above all
for Berlin.

**Summary and
Perspective**

At the end of the 1930s, Berlin was in area and population one of the largest cities
of Europe, along with London and Paris, even if exact comparisons are nearly

impossible because of differences in the determination of the official boundaries of the city [49]. Berlin owed its importance above all to its role as capital and as the centre of an industrially-developed country. In its competition with other German cities, Berlin's superiority had become increasingly clear. In this regard, the inter-war period was the pinnacle of Berlin's development as a metropolis.

With the Second World War, Berlin's development as a world city was interrupted. Since then, it has become a negative example of the living conditions of a metropolis. The inner parts of the city were almost totally destroyed by the bombing raids and during the conquest of Berlin in the last phase of the war. At the end of the war, the city was divided into four sectors and was split into a western and an eastern portion in 1948. This division was sealed by the erection of the Wall. At first, the claim was made that Berlin was still the capital of a Germany that was to be reunited one day, but *de facto* the West finally gave up this claim. East Berlin was, on the other hand, declared capital of East Germany in violation of agreements made between the allied powers.

In its present form, Berlin is a unique phenomenon: an urban area which is divided by a line that is almost totally impenetrable, apart from a few crossing-points. West Berlin is thus no longer the centre of an important territorial state or

FIGURE 11.23. The ruins of Kreuzberg in 1945 (Landesbildstelle Berlin).

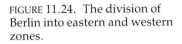

FIGURE 11.24. The division of Berlin into eastern and western zones.

economic area, but rather has a peripheral, insular character. It is no longer the centre of a large hinterland. All relations with the directly adjacent areas were cut off, so that West Berlin is no longer able to develop and expand outwards. Political conditions have also given Berlin a peripheral position and created the problem of guaranteeing the access routes politically and legally. These developments resulted in a considerable reduction of West Berlin's functions: the loss of its capital status, the weakening of its industrial character through the flight of numerous important companies, the loss of its identity as a financial centre and – though only to a certain degree – a lessening of its stature as the intellectual and cultural centre of Germany. In some respects, a state of affairs has reasserted itself in West Germany such as existed before Berlin's rise to the rank of a world city: a multipolarity in the city system with strong competition among the cities and the concentration of certain functions in particular cities (such as Bonn, Munich, Frankfurt-am-Main, and Hamburg).

These restrictions do not apply in East Berlin, the smaller part of the city, in which the old centre of Berlin lies. Nonetheless, it has not been able to develop into a true world city. East Berlin's claim to be the capital of East Germany was not really pushed until rather late in the game. The Communist authorities had great difficulty in repairing the damage done by the war and were rather hesitant in their development of a plan for the city. For a long time, Berlin's special political status strongly hindered the development of ties with the surrounding areas in the eastern sector of the city as well. In addition, new transportation systems had to be developed to by-pass the routes going through West Berlin. The 'capital of the German Democratic Republic' has thus basically remained just a part of a city and has not experienced any real prosperity.

FIGURE 11.25. The Berlin planning competition area (hatched), 1957, in its regional context. The competition was based on the assumption that a single Berlin region still existed, or might exist in a re-united Germany. Consequently, the results were wishful thinking rather than practical planning solutions.

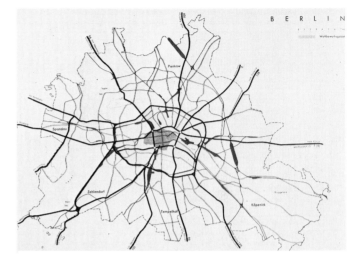

FIGURE 11.26. Land-use map of the Berlin area at the time of the 1957 competition. Again, political boundaries are ignored, creating a completely false impression of a single urban unit (Landesbildstelle Berlin).

Berlin is thus no longer a world city in the full sense of the term. The fact that West Berlin's population is decreasing and that East Berlin's is stagnating indicates that world city status has important practical implications. Berlin has, however, remained a world city in the sense that it is a unique phenomenon, a documentation of the contrast between East and West. It is a point that divides and unites two different systems, whose competition is reflected in the appearance of both Berlins. Particularly for West Berlin, this situation has been a challenge, which it has met with the help of the political and material support of the West German government, given in compensation for the disadvantages of Berlin's location. At the same time, the difficulties which Berlin has had in acquiring independent, self-sustaining functions are plain to be seen, Berlin cannot serve as a model for other big cities because of the exceptional nature of the conditions that keep Berlin alive. This basically just leaves Berlin with one field in which it can excel, a field which contributed earlier to Berlin's status and which will be increasingly important in a post-industrial society: scholarship and research, cultural institutions, and qualified services.

NOTES

1. On the discussion of the term 'Weltstadt' in Germany, see especially Schultze, J.H. (1959) Die Weltstadt als Objekt geographischer Forschung, in Zum Problem der Weltstadt. Festschrift zum 32. Dt. Geographentag in Berlin. Berlin: de Gruyter, pp. ix-xii, xvii-xx. Cf. also Sombart's development of the term 'Grossstadt' (1902), which already contained elements of the term 'metropolis': Sombart, W. (1902/1955) Der moderne Kapitalismus, vol. 3, part 1. Berlin: Duncker & Humblot, pp. 408–14.

2. General works on the development of Berlin: Dietrich, R. (ed.) (1960) Berlin: Neun Kapitel seiner Geschichte. Berlin: de Gruyter; Heimatchronik Berlin. Cologne: Archiv für Heimatpflege; Schinz, A. (1964) Berlin: Stadtschicksal und Städtebau. Brunswick: Westermann. On Berlin in the nineteenth century see: Thienel, I. (1973) Städtewachstum im Industrialisierungsprozess des 19. Jahrhunderts: das Berliner Beispiel. Berlin, New York: de Gruyter; Thienel, I. (1977) Verstädterung, städtische Infrastruktur und Stadtplanung: Berlin zwischen 1850 und 1914. Zeitschrift für Stadtgeschichte, Stadtsoziologie und Denkmalpflege, 4 (1), pp. 55–84; Zimm, A. (1959) Die Entwicklung des Industriestandortes Ber-

lin. Berlin: Dt. Verl. d. Wiss.; Wolters, R. (1978) Stadtmitte Berlin: Städtebauliche Entwicklungsphasen von den Anfägen bis zur Gegenwart. Tübingen: Wasmuth; Pfannschmidt, M. (1959) Probleme der Weltstadt Berlin, in Zum Problem der Weltstadt, Berlin: de Gruyter, pp. 1–16; Matzerath, H. and Ogura, K. (1975) Moderne Verstädterung in Deutschland und in Japan. Zeitschrift für Stadtgeschichte, Stadtsoziologie und Denkmalpflege, 2 (2), pp. 241–53. For further literature, see the bibliography in: Zopf, E. and Heinrich, G. (eds.) (1965) Berlin-Bibliographie. Berlin: de Gruyter; Scholz, U. and Stromeyer, R. (eds.) (1973) Berlin-Bibliographie (1961–66). Berlin: de Gruyter.

3. Dietrich,R. (1960) Berlin und die Hohenzollern, in Dietrich, op. cit., pp. 109–10 (see note 2).

4. Natzschka, W. (1971) Berlin und seine Wasserstrassen. Berlin: Duncker & Humblot.

5. (1896) Berlin und seine Eisenbahnen, 2 vols. Berlin: Springer.

6. On the industrialization of Berlin see: Büsch, O. (ed.) (1971), Untersuchengen zur Geschichte der frühen Industrialisierung vornehmlich im Wirtschaftsraum Berlin/Brandenburg. Berlin: Colloquium; Büsch, O. (1971) Industrialisierung und

Gewerbe im Raum Berlin/Brandenburg. Berlin: Colloquium; Baar, L. (1966) *Die Berliner Industrie in der industriellen Revolution.* Berlin: Akademie-Verlag; Doogs, K. (1928) *Dier Berliner Maschinen-industrie und ihre Produktionsbedingungen seit ihrer Entstehung.* Berlin: Springer; Wiedfeldt, O. (1898) *Statistische Studien zur Entwicklungsgeschichte der Berliner Industrie von 1720–1890.* Leipzig: Duncker & Humblot.

7. Krengel, J. (1978) Das Wachstum der Berliner Bekleidungsindustrie vor dem Ersten Weltkrieg. *Jahrbuch für die Geschichte Mittel- und Ostdeutschlands,* **27**, pp. 206–38.

8. Kocka, J. (1969) *Unternehmensverwaltung und Angestelltenschaft am Beispiel Siemens 1847–1914.* Stuttgart: Klett.

9. Dietrich, R. (1960) Berlins Weg zur Industrie- und Handelsstadt, in Dietrich, *op. cit.,* pp. 185–6 (see note 2).

10. Masur, G. (1970) *Imperial Berlin.* New York: Basic Books, p. 153.

11. Rürup, R. (1979) *Wissenschaft und Gesellschaft: Beiträge zur Geschichte der Technischen Universität Berlin 1879–1979,* 2 vols. Berlin, Heidelberg, New York: Springer.

12. *Statistisches Jahrbuch der Stadt Berlin,* **33** (1916), pp. 3–4.

13. Berlin grew more rapidly in this period than Paris or Vienna, but also more quickly than German cities such as Hamburg, Munich or Dresden. Only new industrial cities in the centres of heavy industry (Rhein/Ruhr, Saar, Upper Silesia) showed greater growth tendencies.

14. Köllmann, W. (1959) Industrialisierung, Binnenwanderung und soziale Frage. *Vierteljahrschrift für Sozial- und Wirtschaftsgeschichte,* **46** (1), pp. 63, 66. Cf. also Obermann, K. (1971) Du rôle et du caractère des migrations internes vers Berlin de 1815 à 1875. *Annales de démographie historique,* pp. 133–59.

15. On the development of Moabit, see Thienel (1973) *op. cit.,* pp. 175–238 (see note 2).

16. On the importance of the Hobrecht Plan, see the polemic: Hegemann, W. (1930, 1963) *Das steinerne Berlin: Geschichte der grössten Mietskasernenstadt der Welt.* Berlin, Frankfurt/M., Vienna: Ullstein, pp. 207–33. On the architectural development of Berlin, see: Architekten-Verein zu Berlin (1877) *Berlin und seine Bauten.* Berlin:

the Verein. Compare also the 2nd edition of 1895. Cf. also Fassbinder, H. (1975) *Berliner Arbeiterviertel 1800–1918.* Berlin: Verlag für Studium der Arbeiterbewegung; Geist, J.F. and Kürvers, H. (1980) *Das Berliner Mietshaus, 1740 bis 1862.* Munich: Prestel.

17. Zimm, *op. cit.,* p. 81 (see note 2).

18. On the development of the Berlin building code see: Jaeckel, O. (1964) Die Bauordnungen für Berlin und die ehemaligen Vororte von Berlin, in *Berlin und seine Bauten,* part 2, Berlin, Munich: Wilhelm Ernst & Sohn, pp. 10–28.

19. *Verwaltungsbericht des Magistrats zu Berlin pro 1876,* p. 3. In 1896, on the occasion of the trade exhibition – according to Masur a turning-point in the history of the city – the Kaiser wrote: 'The glory of the Parisian robs the Berliners of their sleep. Berlin is a great city, a world city (perhaps?)', cited in: Masur, *op. cit.,* pp. 125–6 (see note 10). On the evaluation of Berlin, which oscillated between exaltation and self-doubt, see also: Herzfeld, H. (1952) Berlin als Kaiserstadt und Reichshauptstadt, in Das Hauptstadtproblem, pp. 141–5. Also: Sagave, P.-P. (1971) *1871 Berlin, Paris, Reichshauptstadt und Hauptstadt der Welt.* Frankfurt/Main, Berlin, Vienna: Propyläen, pp. 27–28.

20. On the development of Berlin as an industrial location in this period, see especially Zimm, *op. cit.,* pp. 85–103 (see note 2). Berlin's character as an industrial city was contested by Sombart, W. (1902, 1955) *Der moderne Kapitalismus,* vol. 3, part 1. Berlin: Duncker & Humblot, pp. 411–14. On the development of the electro-industry, see: Czada, P. (1969) *Die Berliner Elektroindustrie in der Weimarer Zeit.* Berlin: Colloquium, pp. 38–57.

21. Certain parts of the city had passed the peak in the development of their population as early as 1867–75. On the development of the individual suburbs between 1871 and 1991, see: Leyden, F. (1933) *Gross-Berlin: Geographie der Weltstadt.* Breslau: F. Hirt, pp. 207–10.

22. Statistisches Amt der Stadt Berlin (1928) *Berlinswirtschaftliche Verflechtung,* Berlin: Grunert, p. 11.

23. Leyden, *loc. cit.* (see note 21). In 1919, Charlottenburg had a population of 323,000; Neukölln, 262,000; Schöneberg, 175,000; Lichtenberg, 145,000; and Wilmersdorf, 139,000.

24. See especially Schott, S. (1912) *Die grossstädtischen Agglomerationen des Deutschen Reiches 1871–1910*. Breslau: Korn. On the formation of Berlin's central business district see: (1932) *Berliner Wirtschaftsberichte* (**17/18**), pp. 150–3, 159–62; Krause, R. (1958) *Die Berliner City*. Berlin: Duncker and Humblot.
25. Schinz, *op. cit.*, pp. 167–70 (see note 2).
26. Voigt, P. (1901) *Grundrente und Bodenfrage in Berlin und seinen Vororten*, part 1. Jena: G. Fischer; Reich, E. (1912) *Der Wohnungsmarkt in Berlin von 1840 bis 1910*. Leipzig: Duncker & Humblot.
27. See especially Heiligenthal, R. (1928/9) *Berliner Städtebaustudien*. Berlin-Halensee: author, pp. 1–8.
28. See especially Thienel (1973) *op. cit.*, pp. 175–238 (see note 2).
29. On the development of the building code and of urban planning, see: Albers, G. (1967) Vom Fluchtlinienplan zum Stadtentwicklungsplan. *Archiv für Kommunalwissenschaften*, **6**(2), pp. 192–211; Hartog, R. (1962) *Stadterweiterungen im 19. Jahrhundert*. Stuttgart: Kohlhammer.
30. Jaeckel, *op. cit.*, pp. 10 ff (see note 18).
31. *Berlin und seine Eisenbahnen*, vol. 2, pp. 75–95 (see note 5).
32. Möller, P. (1906) Berlin und sein Verkehr, in Berliner Bezirksverein deutscher Ingenieure (ed.) *Ingenieurwerke in und bei Berlin*. Berlin: Sittenfeld, pp. 13–32; Reichhardt, H.D. (1974) *Die Strassenbahnen Berlins*. Düsseldorf: Alba; Erbe, M. (1972) Probleme der Berliner Verkehrsplanung und Verkehrsentwicklung seit 1871, in *Aus Theorie und Praxis der Geschichtswissenschaft*. Festschrift für H. Herzfeld. Berlin, New York: de Gruyter, pp. 209–35.
33. On the role of the *Boden- and Terraingesellschaften* see: Hegemann, W. (1911) *Der Städtebau nach den Ergebnissen der allgemeinen Städtebauausstellung in Berlin*, part 1. Berlin: Wasmuth, p. 31. Cf. also the description of available construction sites in (1908) *Die Berliner Vororte: ein Handbuch*. Berlin: Baedeker and Moeller.
34. See the pioneer work: Baumeister, R. (1876) *Stadterweiterungen in technischer, baupolizeilicher und wirtschaftlicher Beziehung*. Berlin: Ernst & Korn. See also the later works of Sitte, Stübben, Heiligenthal, Hegemann, Wolf, and Eberstadt.
35. On the influence of the garden city idea see especially: Hartmann: K. (1976) *Deutsche Gartenstadtbewegung: Kultur und Gesellschaftsreform*. Munich: Moos. For related developments in architecture, see: Posener, J. (1979) *Berlin auf dem Weg zu einer neuen Architektur: das Zeitalter Wilhelms II*. Munich: Prestel.
36. Takàts, E. (1933) *Der Verband Gross-Berlin vom 19. Juli 1911 bis 1. Okt. 1920*. Cologne: Kölner Studentenburse (university thesis).
37. Matzerath, H. and Thienel, I. (1977) Stadtentwicklung, Stadtplanung, Stadtentwicklungsplanung. Probleme im 19. und 20. Jahrhundert am Beispiel der Stadt Berlin. *Die Verwaltung*, **10** (2). See also Werner, F. (1976) *Stadtplanung Berlin, Part 1, 1800–1960*. Berlin: Kiepert.
38. See especially (1970) *Berlin und seine Bauten*, Part 4. Berlin, Munich, Düsseldorf: W. Ernst. See also (1977) *Tendenzen der Zwanziger Jahre: 15. Europäische Kunstausstellung Berlin 1977*. Berlin: D. Reimer, vol. 1, pp. 26–41.
39. Lane, B.M. (1968) *Architecture and Politics in Germany 1918–1945*. Cambridge, Mass: Harvard University Press, pp. 57–124.
40. Büsch, O. (1960) *Geschichte der Berliner Kommunalwirtschaft in der Weimarer Epoche*. Berlin: de Gruyter.
41. Böhret, C. (1966) *Aktionen gegen die 'kalte Sozialisierung' 1926–1930*. Berlin: Duncker & Humblot.
42. Teut, A. (1967) *Architektur im Dritten Reich 1933–1945*. Berlin, Frankfurt/M., Vienna: Ullstein.
43. On Nazi construction policy in Berlin, see, apart from Werner, *op. cit.* (see note 37), especially: Thies, J. (1976) *Architektur der Weltherrschaft: Die 'Endziele' Hitlers*. Düsseldorf: Droste; Petsch, J. (1976) *Baukunst und Stadtplanung im Dritten Reich*. Munich, Vienna: Hauser; Dülffer, J., Thies, J. and Henke, J. (1978) *Hitlers Städte*. Cologne: Böhlau; Larsson, L.O. (1978) *Die Neugestaltung der Reichshauptstadt*. Stuttgart: Hatje.
44. Pfannschmidt, M. (1937) *Die Industriesiedlung in Berlin und in der Mark Brandenburg*. Stuttgart, Berlin: Kohlhammer, pp. 69–96.
45. Wiebel, E. (1954) *Die Städte am Rande Berlins*. Remagen: Verlag der Bundesanstalt für Landeskunde.
46. Pfannschmidt, M. (1970) Landesplanung

Brandenburg-Berlin-Mitte, in *Raumordnung und Landesplanung in 20. Jahrhundert.* Hanover: Jänecke.

47. Pfannschmidt (1937), *op. cit.,* pp. 21–61 (see note 44); Zimm, *op. cit.,* pp. 122–209 (see note 2).

48. Gerlach, E. (1953) Berlin im deutschen und europäischen Verkehr, in Institut für Raumforschung (ed.), *Die unzerstörbare Stadt.* Cologne; Berlin: Heymann, pp. 103–5.

49. See especially Bergmann, K. (1970) *Agrarromantik und Grossstadtfeindschaft.* Meisenheim-am-Glan: Hain.

Chapter 12

The Capital of Capitalism: the New York Metropolitan Region, 1890–1940

KENNETH T. JACKSON

THE southern tip of present-day Manhattan Island was already a centuries-old Indian trading post in 1524, when Giovanni da Verrazano, an Italian in the employ of France, became the first known white man to sail up the narrows into the lower bay [1]. It was a natural site for a city. Located at the point (40 degrees north latitude and 74 degrees west longitude) where the Hudson and Passaic Rivers mingle with the waters of the Atlantic Ocean and Long Island Sound, Manhattan was surrounded by the finest harbour in the western hemisphere and was ice-free in all seasons [2]. Not until Henry Hudson's visit in 1609, however, did the possibilities of the location become known to the Dutch, who established a fort (later New Amsterdam) there in 1624 and made it the centre of their West India Company operations on the North American continent [3]. Forty years later, on 2 September 1664, the English captured the city without loss of life and renamed it New York. The city then gave its name to the colony, which after independence became the 'Empire State', as George Washington had foreseen [4].

Because the earlier settlements at St. Augustine (1565), Jamestown (1607), and Plymouth (1620) either disappeared altogether, as at Jamestown, or declined into insignificance, New York stands as the oldest major city in what is now the United States [5]. It was outdistanced, however, between 1630 and 1740 by Boston (founded in 1630) and between 1690 and 1800 by Philadelphia (founded in 1682). Soon after the winning of national independence, New York began to surpass its rivals. By 1789, it was the leading city in the coasting trade. It exceeded Philadelphia in total tonnage in 1794, in the value of imports in 1796, and in exports in 1797. And early in the nineteenth century, the city on the Hudson emerged as the largest metropolis in the New World. There were four main reasons for this [6].

First, at the end of the war of 1812, British merchants and manufacturers chose New York as the site for well-publicized auctions to dispose of the large quantities of goods which had accumulated on British docks. This circumstance gave Manhattan businessmen an important advantage over Boston and Philadelphia in recovering from the earlier naval blockade.

Secondly, New York had a central location between the intensively-developed and heavily-populated New England and Chesapeake regions, and in addition, possessed an all-water, low-level route to the Great Lakes and the interior of the continent. This potential was realized with the opening of the Erie Canal between Albany and Buffalo in 1825. By most measures this was the most ambitious and successful public works project in the nation before the Inter-state Highway Act of 1956.

Thirdly, New York businessmen placed less importance on family connections, religion, and social class and more emphasis on risk-taking than did their counterparts in Boston and Philadelphia. New Yorkers organized the first chamber of commerce in 1768, and in 1817 they introduced to the United States the then novel idea of regularly scheduled shipping services [7].

Fourthly, because of its central location and thriving port, New York had become the central place in the circulation of commercial and political information in North America as early as the 1780s. As historical geographer Allan Pred has shown, New York entrepreneurs took advantage of the easy and quick availability of the latest business news, and by 1850 had developed the largest American collection of firms capable of providing technical and professional information and services [8].

The city's major advantages reinforced one another, and by mid-century New

Table 12.1.   Population of the city of New York and the New York metropolitan region, 1790–1970.

Year	City limits	Metro area (thousands)*
1790	33,131	49.4
1850	515,547	696.1
1860	813,660	1,174.8
1870	942,292	1,478.1
1880	1,164,673	1,911.7
1890	1,441,216	2,507.4
1900	3,437,202	5,048.8
1910	4,766,883	7,049.0
1920	5,620,048	8,490.6
1930	6,930,446	10,859.3
1940	7,454,995	11,660.8
1950	7,891,957	12,912.0
1960	7,781,984	17,624.3
1970	7,894,862	19,061.8

* The Metropolitan Region is defined as the area within the present limits of the City of New York for the period 1790–1890, as the New York-New Jersey Standard Consolidated Area (seventeen Counties) for the period 1900–1950, and as the Regional Plan Study Area (thirty-one Counties) for the period 1960–1970.

Source: United States Bureau of the Census.

York was the pre-eminent port of entry for European immigrants to the New World. By 1890, the island of Manhattan had 1.4 million residents (Brooklyn and the immediate environs included another 1.1 million) and was the unchallenged centre of American enterprise. By every criterion – from population to industrial production to bank deposits to wholesale trade – the Empire City ranked first in the nation. But unlike London, Paris, Berlin, Tokyo, Vienna, and other world cities which had grown to substantial size by the end of the nineteenth century, New York was not the capital of a nation, a region, or even of a single state [9].

Throughout the first three centuries of Gotham's history, the cornerstone of its growth was commerce, and the backbone of its economy remained at the water's edge, from which the city crawled ashore, multiplied, waxed rich, and became an entrepot of power and culture. Its protected waterways were ideal for ocean-going vessels and for smaller canal boats. From 1820 until 1960, when Rotterdam overtook it, the Port of New York ranked as the world's busiest, and the value of its trade regularly exceeded that of Boston, Philadelphia, and Baltimore combined. Between 1830 and 1906, the harbour annually handled between 37 per cent and 71 per cent by value of the nation's foreign trade, a proportion more than triple that of its nearest competitor. Newcomers were awed by the vast traffic of tramp steamers, sailing vessels, barges, and ferries. Ramshackle docks and piers loomed mile after mile up the Hudson and East Rivers, along the shallow New Jersey and Staten Island shores, and from Greenpoint to Red Hook in Brooklyn. Behind the docks stretched acres of warehouses and storage tanks, coal dumps and stone yards, sugar mills and breweries, and dry docks and ship chandlers. And dominating the harbour were two man-made structures which were completed within a few years of each other in the 1880s: the Statue of Liberty and the Brooklyn Bridge [10].

The Transformation of the Metropolis, 1890–1940

Limited to the 22 square miles (5700 hectares) of the island of Manhattan for the first 250 years of its existence, the City of New York gained a beachhead on the mainland of the United States in 1874, when it annexed the southern edge of Westchester County [11]. The great expansion of its boundaries came in 1898, however, when Kings, Queens, Richmond, and additional parts (to become known as the Bronx) of Westchester County were added to the corporate limits of the city [12]. The new area of 299 square miles (327 square miles including water) included not only Brooklyn, then the nation's third largest city, but also substantial tracts of open land for future development. Of the five counties which came together to form the expanded City of New York, New York County (Manhattan) and Richmond County (Staten Island) were entirely surrounded by water, while Kings County (Brooklyn) and Queens County were both on Long Island [13].

The years between the consolidation of 1898 and the end of World War Two represented a kind of 'golden age' for New York. It contained the largest

Table 12.2. Population of the fifteen largest metropolitan areas in the world, 1890, 1940, and 1980 (in millions).

	1890		1940		1980	
1.	London	4.2	NEW YORK	11.7	NEW YORK	20.4
2.	NEW YORK	2.7	London	8.7	Tokyo	20.0
3.	Paris	2.4	Tokyo	7.1	Mexico City	15.0
4.	Canton	1.6	Paris	4.9	Sao Paulo	13.5
5.	Berlin	1.6	Chicago	4.5	Shanghai	13.4
6.	Vienna	1.3	Berlin	4.3	Los Angeles	11.7
7.	Tokyo	1.2	Moscow	4.1	Peking	10.7
8.	Chicago	1.1	Shanghai	3.5	Rio de Janeiro	10.7
9.	Philadelphia	1.1	Osaka	3.4	London	10.3
10.	St. Petersburg	1.0	Leningrad	3.2	Buenos Aires	10.1
11.	Constantinople	0.9	Los Angeles	2.9	Paris	9.9
12.	Calcutta	0.9	Philadelphia	2.9	Osaka	9.5
13.	Moscow	0.8	Buenos Aires	2.4	Dusseldorf	9.3
14.	Bombay	0.8	Boston	2.4	Calcutta	8.8
15.	Rio de Janeiro	0.8	Detroit	2.3	Seoul	8.5

Sources: For 1890: Adna F. Weber, *The Growth of Cities in the Nineteenth Century* (New York: Columbia University Press, 1899), p. 450; *The World Almanac and Bureau of Information* (New York: Copyright Press, 1891), p. 242; and United States Census for 1890 and 1940.

For 1940: *The World Almanac and Book of Facts for 1942* (New York: New York World Telegram, 1942), pp. 274, 431, 464, and 596; and United States Census for 1940.

For 1980: *United Nations Fund for Population Activities Annual Report, 1980.*

concentrations of architects, bankers, lawyers, consulting engineers, industrial designers, and corporate officials on the continent. By the turn of the century, the Wall Street law firm had become a national institution, and investment bankers like J. P. Morgan, the Seligman brothers, and August Belmont had become legendary figures. And as national corporations took shape, New York became the headquarters city for American industry. In 1895, the metropolis contained 298 mercantile and manufacturing firms worth more than one million dollars, more than Chicago, Philadelphia, Boston, San Francisco, Baltimore, and St. Louis combined [14].

Nowhere else were the symbols of wealth and power so abundant – even the streets were representative of the entrepreneur – Madison Avenue was for advertising, Seventh Avenue for fashion, Fifth Avenue for elegant shops, Wall Street for investment banking. Manhattan became a kind of Main Street to the nation, and the 'robber barons' of American industry, including those like John D. Rockefeller, Andrew Carnegie, and F. W. Woolworth who had started their empires elsewhere, hastened to move to the giant city as if to ratify their national significance. According to an 1892 survey, New York and Brooklyn contained 1265 millionaires, or 30 per cent of the extreme wealth holders in the United States. Another 15 per cent lived in the nearby suburbs [15].

Although it was not the national capital, New York also assumed a cultural dominance by the turn of the century that equalled its role in finance and industry. The hub of communications, Gotham swept past Boston as the centre of book and magazine publishing, and when the new science of telecommunications developed in the 1920s, New York became the home of the major radio and television networks. Broadway emerged as the focus of American theatre, while the Metropolitan Opera (after 1890), the Metropolitan Museum of Art (after 1880), and the New York City Ballet (after 1945) set a standard of excellence matched only in Europe. Artists congregated in Greenwich Village, and America's foremost writers made their homes in the city. In sports, New York was also pre-eminent: Yankee Stadium provided a showcase for heroes like Babe Ruth and Lou Gehrig, and Madison Square Garden became the nation's foremost indoor sports arena. By 1940, with a city population of more than seven million and a metropolitan population of more than eleven million, New York had become the world's largest and richest city [16].

The American metropolis was particularly unusual in the extraordinary heterogeneity of its citizenry [17]. Between 1880 and 1919, more than 23 million Europeans emigrated to the United States; about 17 million of them disembarked in New York. No one knows how many remained in Gotham, but as early as 1880 more than half the city's working population was foreign-born, providing New York with the largest immigrant labour force on earth. Half a century later, the city still contained two million foreign born (including 517,000 Russians and 430,000 Italians) and an even larger number of persons of foreign parentage. Travellers often described walking for blocks without hearing a word of English spoken. Neighbourhoods changed from one ethnic group to another, and New York itself remained a hodge-podge of nationalities. In his famous study, *How the Other Half Lives*, Scandinavian-born journalist Jacob Riis tried to explain this immense variety in 1890 [18]:

> A map of the city, colored to designate nationalities, would show more stripes than on the skin of a zebra, and more colors than any rainbow. The city on such a map would fall into great halves, green for the Irish prevailing in the West Side tenement districts, and blue for the Germans on the East Side. But intermingled with these ground colors would be an odd variety of tints that would give the whole the appearance of an extraordinary crazy-quilt . . . the red of the Italian would be seen forcing its way northward along the line of Mulberry Street to the quarter of the French purple on Bleeker Street and South Fifth Avenue, to lose itself and reappear, after a lapse of miles, in the 'Little Italy' of Harlem, east of Second Avenue.

The black proportion of the New York population, which reached 20 per cent in the colonial period and declined to less than 2 per cent in the 1870s, began a slow rise in the 1880s as newcomers from the coastal states of the Old South began moving north. In contrast to the white ethnic groups, however, Afro-Americans experienced increasing discrimination as their numbers rose. Instead of the slow dispersal that characterized the residential patterns of white immigrants, blacks encountered increasing ghettoization. The largest concentration developed in central Harlem, where blacks began to move as early as 1905 after speculative overbuilding by real estate developers made available to Negroes apartments intended for white occupancy. By 1925, the Jewish population previously resident in the area was in full exodus, and by 1930 Harlem had the reputation as the largest 'black city' in the world [19].

The competition of blacks and of white ethnic groups for residential space in New York was particularly acute because of the extraordinary concentration of economic activity and of population in a small area. In 1911, Edward Ewing Pratt published a careful analysis of *Industrial Causes of Congestion of Population in New York City*. Arguing that far too many businesses and manufacturing concerns were locating in lower Manhattan and adjacent sections of Brooklyn, Pratt presented detailed density and journey-to-work statistics that suggested that the spatial patterns of the region made a decent life impossible for most workers [20].

Pratt's meticulous research was reinforced by the visual impressions of casual observers. The concentration of large buildings, the volume of both pedestrian and vehicular traffic, and the general absence of open space (Central Park being the notable exception) were common observations. Soon after the development of the skyscraper in Chicago in the 1880s, New York assumed the vertical shape that has distinguished it ever since. The specialization and differentiation of the Manhattan business district led to rising land costs and in many commercial sections buildings of less than six storeys had practically disappeared by 1930. The very tallest behemoths, especially the Woolworth Building, the Chrysler Building, and the Empire State Building, which set new records for height, attracted the most attention. As late as 1974, New York City contained as many buildings of sixty storeys as the rest of the world combined [21]. Precise floor area calculations are difficult to compute, and are generally unavailable for the period before 1940, but in 1967 Manhattan contained about twice as much non-residential floor space as any other central business district on earth. In fact, a single square mile (259 hectares) in midtown Manhattan contained 16 million square metres of office space, or half again as much as the Chicago Loop or the entire 10 square mile area of central London [22].

The extraordinary concentration of commercial and manufacturing activity, as Pratt recognized, exacerbated the housing crisis. Overcrowding, a problem ever since the original Dutch settlers huddled together below Wall Street for protection against Indians, reached frightening proportions between 1870 and 1920. For the middle class, the preferred dwelling type was the single-family brownstone, a large row-house with a front facade faced in the plentiful local stone which gave the structure its name. Because of the great expense of Manhattan real estate, it was typically built on a standard 25 by 100 foot lot. After 1870, however, even this space became too expensive. As Charles Wingate wrote in 1885:

New York is distinctively a city without homes. Two-thirds of its population live in tenements, and the remainder either occupy palatial but cheerless brownstone fronts on Murray Hill and its vicinity, or board. The rich and poor are increasing, while the great middle class of thrifty and intelligent people are being crowded into the suburbs [23].

The poorest immigrants settled on the Lower East Side of Manhattan, where rents were cheapest and unskilled and semi-skilled employment was concentrated. As population increased, attics and cellars were rented, homes were partitioned for multiple occupancy, and shacks were put up on back lots. Next, landlords tore these structures down and put up four- or five-storey tenements. These buildings were 80–90 feet long (and thus occupied 80 to 90 per cent of the lot) and held about twenty families, exclusive of boarders [24].

But tenement overcrowding had only begun to approach its limits. An innovation in design called the 'dumbbell' caused the housing situation to reach horrifying proportions. In 1879, a magazine called *The Plumber and Sanitary Engineer* held a contest for the best plan combining maximum safety for the tenant with maximum profit for the landowner on the standard 25 by 100 foot lot. The judges selected the 'dumbbell' design from about two hundred entries because it provided every room with a window. An indentation on each side of the structure 2½ feet in depth and 50 feet in length gave it the shape of a dumbbell when it adjoined a tenement of similar design [25]. When the winning proposal was announced, the *New York Times* expressed scepticism: 'If the prize plans are the best offered, which we can hardly believe, they simply demonstrate the problem is insoluble' [26].

A dumbbell stood six storeys high, covered 90 per cent of its lot, and contained eighty-four small rooms. It housed about 300 people. The poor tenants usually took in relatives or boarders, causing further overcrowding (bedrooms averaged about 7 by 8 feet). Hailed by contemporaries for the light and ventilation provided by the air shaft and for the seemingly adequate toilet facilities (two per floor), the dumbbell idea caught on quickly, aided by an 1879 New York City housing law that required a window in every room in new buildings. By 1903, more than two-thirds of the 3.5 million people in the city lived in tenements [27].

Table 12.3.   Gross population density per square mile of the five boroughs of the City of New York, 1880–1970.

Borough	1880	1910	1940	1970
New York (Manhattan)	52,940	105,979	85,906	69,965
Kings (Brooklyn)	8,564	23,348	38,547	37,531
Bronx	1,268	10,512	34,017	35,066
Queens	524	2,630	12,015	18,293
Richmond (Staten Island)	672	1,482	3,008	5,120

Source: Calculations from United States Bureau of the Census.

FIGURE 12.1. The southern edge of Harlem on 14 March 1934. This photograph was taken from 111th Street looking north up Seventh Avenue. These substantial apartment buildings were originally erected for a middle-class clientele, but by the date of this picture the neighbourhood was overwhelmingly black (Municipal Archives of the City of New York).

The dumbbell produced unbelievably congested neighbourhoods. At the turn of the century, the average density of the Lower East Side was more than 1000 per hectare (260,000 per square mile), and in certain immigrant precincts it exceeded 3000 per hectare, a concentration that has perhaps never been matched [28]. In 1900, the Charity Organization Society sponsored a conference, organized by the reformer Lawrence Veiller, on the ideal form of workers' housing. One of the exhibition's architectural models was designed to show that the 1879 legislation had only aggravated conditions. This model of a 'typical dumbbell' tenement neighbourhood depicted a Lower East Side block which housed four thousand persons on a plot of about one hectare [29].

Pressured by the Charity Organization Society, the New York State Legislature created a new Tenement House Commission in 1900. With Robert DeForest as chairman and Veiller as secretary, the commission published in 1903 the most complete analysis of the tenement problem completed to date. An even more important result of the group's work was the passage of the Tenement House Law of 1901, which set the national standard for housing legislation in the United States and which remains the basis for low-rise housing design in New York City in 1983. But even in 1914, one-sixth of the city's total population still lived on the Lower East Side on only one-eighty-second of the city's land area. And Manhattan remained the most intensely developed piece of real estate in the United States. In 1950, when the population density of Los Angeles was 4391 per square mile, of Philadelphia 16,059 per square mile, and of Chicago 16,165 per square mile, the figure for Manhattan was 86,730, and for all of New York City 26,395 per square mile [30].

FIGURE 12.2. This 1931 photograph of Seventh Avenue looking north from 33rd Street gives some indication of the traffic congestion in Manhattan even during the Great Depression (Municipal Archives of the City of New York).

FIGURE 12.3. Allen Street on the Lower East Side of Manhattan on 20 February 1928. Easily the widest north-south thoroughfare in the neighbourhood, Allen Street was less congested than Rivington, Hester, Orchard, Henry and other notoriously overcrowded tenement blocks in the Jewish quarter. Notice the elevated track on the opposite side of the street (Municipal Archives of the City of New York).

FIGURE 12.4. Looking east on East New York Avenue between New York and Brooklyn
Avenues on 22 August 1924. This block, which was only a short distance from Ebbets Field
and Prospect Park and which is now the site of Lefferts Hospital, illustrates the broad streets
and general absence of automotive traffic in the outer boroughs during the 1920s. Note also
the absence of front gardens (Municipal Archives of the City of New York).

While the problem of overcrowding was at its worst and while Edward Ewing
Pratt was writing *Industrial Causes of Congestion of Population in New York City*, a
process of metropolitan deconcentration was underway. The population of
Manhattan reached a peak of 2.3 million in 1910. By 1940, it had declined to 1.9
million, and by 1980 to 1.2 million. The outlying boroughs and suburbs exhibited a
strong contrary pattern. Brooklyn, a thriving city in its own right before
consolidation, grew from 1.2 million in 1890 to 2.7 million in 1940. But the most
startling changes came in the Bronx and in Queens. Scarcely developed at all and
containing only 89,000 inhabitants in 1890, the Bronx was covered with six- and
eight-storey apartments south of Fordham Road by 1940, when its population
reached 1.4 million. Queens blossomed from less than 100,000 in 1890 to 1.3 million
in 1940. On a city-wide basis, as table 12.4 indicates, about one-half the population
in 1905 lived within four miles of City Hall; by 1925, the percentage in this area was
below 30 [31].

FIGURE 12.5. Because the Williamsburg section of Brooklyn was adjacent to the East River and thus easily accessible from Manhattan, the neighbourhood was largely built up by the beginning of the twentieth century. This photograph of Johnson Avenue, looking east from Graham Avenue, reveals a mixture of uses and of building materials within a single block. Note the trolley tracks and the fire escapes, which were required by the building law of 1901 (Municipal Archives of the City of New York).

Table 12.4. The percentage of population in the city of New York living in specified mileage zones, 1905–1925.

Zone	1905	1910	1915	1920	1925
0–4 miles	53.76	46.16	39.95	36.55	29.45
4–8 miles	35.90	40.39	41.58	42.94	44.88
8–12 miles	8.55	11.90	16.55	18.16	22.13
12+ miles	1.44	1.55	1.92	1.99	3.54

Source: Regional Plan Committee, *Regional Survey*, Vol. 2, p. 100.

The decentralizing trend was even more apparent on the fringes of the New York Metropolitan Region, where affluent citizenry followed the American dream of a single-family house surrounded by a lawn. Moving away from the row houses and apartment buildings typical of the city, they chose the more verdant and bucolic surroundings of Westchester County and New Jersey. The very rich – families like the Morgans, Vanderbilts, Fricks, Whitneys, Woolworths, and Phippses – built great manor houses on the rolling North Shore of Long Island, well beyond the corporate limits of the city. Usually set on 25 hectares or more and equipped with every luxury that Western civilization could provide, these European style edifices often resounded to horses' hooves and the bay of the hounds. F. Scott Fitzgerald caught one aspect of this sumptuous life style in *The Great Gatsby* [32].

FIGURE 12.6. Putting down the infrastructure of the city. This photograph near Bath Avenue in the Bensonhurst section of Brooklyn was taken on 15 July 1924. The laying of sewers, which was financed by the general revenues of the city, was necessary for residential development in the twentieth century and was one of many examples of official encouragement of peripheral growth (Municipal Archives of the City of New York).

The suburban shift accelerated after World War Two, aided by a national mania for the motorcar and by federal policies favouring private transportation. By 1970, more than 2200 square miles had been urbanized, about five times the area urbanized in 1920 for a population only twice as large [33]. Because the suburbanites rejected annexation into a Greater New York City, as happened in London, political balkanization became a major problem. In 1960, political scientist Robert C. Wood could identify more than 1400 separate governments and taxing authorities in the immediate area [34].

Employment followed the same sort of deconcentrating trend. As late as 1920, about 70 per cent of the people and 80 per cent of the jobs in the New York-New Jersey Standard Consolidated Area were in the four main boroughs of New York City or in Newark and Jersey City. Most of the others worked in satellite cities that were well served by rail lines like Yonkers, White Plains, Paterson, and Passaic. By 1970, more than half the employment and the population in the New York Metropolitan Region (NYMR) was outside the old urban core [35].

The Transportation Network

The outward movement of people and jobs proceeded more quickly in New York than in most other world cities because the NYMR extensively adopted every new development in transportation technology, because the United States government adopted housing policies favouring suburbanization, and because land was cheaper in North America (including the New York suburbs) than in Europe or Japan [36]. New Yorkers had regularly scheduled steam ferries to Brooklyn in 1817, omnibus service on Broadway in 1829, and a rudimentary horse-drawn streetcar in 1832, but the main developments involved the application of mechanical power to ground transport. Between 1890 and 1940, three separate modes – steam railroads, elevated and subterranean rapid transit lines, and electric streetcars – gave the region a public transportation system without equal, whether measured by riders per capita, total ridership, route mileage, track mileage, or capital investment [37].

Commuter travel by steam railroad in North America began in 1837 when the New York and Harlem Railroad offered regular service to 125th Street, a stop that is now in the centre of Harlem but which was then about six miles north of the built-up area. Additions to this line reached central Westchester County by 1844, and the *New York Tribune* predicted that 'the line of this road will be nearly one continuous village by 1860'. Meanwhile, the New York and New Haven Railroad along Long Island Sound reached New Haven in 1843, and the Harlem River toward Albany reached Peekskill in 1849. In 1855, an English observer, W. E. Baxter, noted that suburban villas were 'springing up like mushrooms on spots which five years ago were part of the dense and tangled forest; and the value of property everywhere, but especially along the various lines of railroad, has increased in a ratio almost incredible' [38].

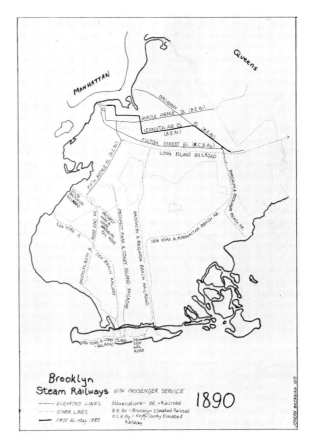

FIGURE 12.7. Brooklyn steam passenger routes, 1890.

Just as the northbound railroad opened up Westchester County (including what would later become the Bronx) so did other lines enable former Manhattanites to commute from other directions. To the south five separate railroads cut through Brooklyn toward Coney Island by 1890. To the east, the New York and Flushing Railroad was devoted to short-haul traffic and was unabashedly the instrument of real estate speculators. By bringing villages in what is now Queens within one hour of the city in the late 1850s, it caused an influx into Newton, Maspeth, and Flushing [39]. Across the Hudson River, Jersey City was the focus of a combined ferry-railroad system which enabled commuters to get from South Orange and other towns west of Newark to Manhattan [40].

With the introduction of electric locomotives after the turn of the century more than 1000 trains per day were available for commuter service. New facilities became necessary. Between 1904 and 1910, a terminal complex of unprecedented proportions, Pennsylvania Station, rose from a four-block square hole between 32nd and 34th Streets on the west side. And just a few years later, the almost equally elegant and gargantuan Grand Central Station was made more efficient by dividing its sixty-seven tracks between two underground levels. Moreover, electrification allowed the railroad to fill in the open cut that had been Park Avenue north of 42nd Street, transforming the thoroughfare into one of the most fashionable in the nation. Meanwhile, a score of office buildings and hotels were constructed adjacent to the terminal. The result was a technological marvel. As architectural editor Douglas Haskell has written [41]:

> The brilliant breakthrough of the Grand Central Terminal project came of the fact that there, during the first decade of our century, New York brought together her two major achievements – concentrated building and swift urban transportation – into a single, interrelated, planned operation. The event was majestically fantastic. It stood at the pinnacle of creative effort. Here was compounded the great movement of urban 'futurism' . . .

The great railroad stations and the commuters they served had their greatest impact upon the burgeoning suburban ring. Within the city itself the dominant influence was the rapid transit system, which was made up of both elevated (called 'Els') and underground (called subways) trains. The elevated was the older mode, its first line having opened in 1870 [42]. Faster and more capital intensive than the horsecars with which it initially competed, the 'El' was noisy, unsightly, and dirty, even after electrification began to replace the small steam engines after 1901. But it had a profound influence upon population growth in the outer boroughs. The Third Avenue 'El', for example, was the major route by which second generation immigrants entered the Bronx [43].

The underground in New York became necessary because the elevated structures were themselves an impediment to the smooth flow of traffic. After many fits and starts, including a single-car subway between Warren and Murray

12.8. On the narrow streets of lower Manhattan, the elevated structures almost completely shut out the sunlight. This 1930 photograph of the intersection of Allen and Broome Streets illustrates the visual dominance of the rapid transit system (Municipal Archives of the City of New York).

FIGURE 12.9. Brooklyn subway and elevated lines, 1920.

Streets that operated on a pneumatic tube principle in 1870 [44], the Rapid Transit Act of 1891 became the plan under which the subway system was initiated. It did not allow for municipal ownership. After many court battles questioning the liabilities of both city and private companies and the property rights of private citizens, the Rapid Transit Subway Construction Company entered into contract with the city in 1902 [45].

Manhattan's first subway opened in 1904, long after London (1863) and shortly after Glasgow (1886), Budapest (1896), Boston (1897), Paris (1900), and Berlin (1902). Although not the oldest, the New York system was important for two reasons: its immense size and its technological innovation. Gotham's competing transit companies built new lines and extended old ones with unmatched vigour, and by 1937 the region had 308 route miles (and more than 700 track miles) of rapid transit service and was handling 4.2 million passengers per day, exclusive of bus and streetcar patronage [46]. As designed by Chief Engineer William Barclay Parsons, New York's underground was the first in the world with a fully integrated express and local system. Parsons chose the cut-and-cover method of digging, and his subway became a model for the construction of rapid transit elsewhere [47].

Overcrowding began on the first day of operation, when the *New York Tribune* announced 'the birth of the subway crush', and within one year the Interborough Rapid Transit (IRT) Company's first line (up Park Avenue to Grand Central Station, across 42nd Street to Times Square, and up Broadway to 242nd Street) was carrying 600,000 passengers per day (1.2 million by 1914). Such a vast ridership along only a single route surpassed every prediction, but it failed to provide the expected relief for the congested surface railways. As Charles M. Higgins noted in 1905, the streetcars were still 'crowded and jammed with passengers, inside and out, not like cattle cars, as this would not be allowed by law in a car of cattle, pigs, or sheep, but more like a basket of fish or other dead freight' [48]. In the same year, the *Street Railway Journal* editorialized about the problem:

> One of the most interesting features of opening new transit lines for service in the densely populated districts of large cities is the effect of these additional facilities upon the volume of traffic within the tributary region. It has long been recognized that a permanent solution of the rapid transit problem in a growing city cannot be secured by the development of a single route of high speed service. New facilities not only open up additional avenues of travel and thereby can – and often do – relieve congestion existing upon other lines; they apparently create traffic, which sooner or later grows to a volume that requires additional means of transportation to be furnished [49].

As the example of Brooklyn illustrates, the rapid transit paths tended to follow the tracks of the earlier steam railroads. Some measure of the importance of the subways and elevateds in the spatial ordering of the metropolis may be inferred from the fact that in 1905 every neighbourhood with a population density exceeding 250 per hectare, except the Lower East Side, was within 250 metres of a rapid transit line. And by 1925, about 86 per cent of New York's population lived in the 97 square miles served by subways or elevateds. The remaining 14 per cent was spread over 202 square miles [50].

Because New York had such an extensive transit network above and below the ground, the electric streetcar had a less decisive impact upon Gotham than on most other major cities of the world. The NYMR did possess an extensive trolley system (in Manhattan the streetcar typically received its power from a third rail rather than from the overhead 'troller' which was typical in the outer boroughs), but the streetcar tracks did not radiate out from the core as was common in American cities. They complemented and ran perpendicular to the rapid transit lines, affording a type of lateral supplement to the more important subways and elevateds. As the *Street Railway Journal* noted on 10 February 1906: 'The street railway lines in the borough of the Bronx were laid out primarily as feeders to the elevated roads and the subway'. Nevertheless, the tram was an efficient method of transport, and the city suffered when Mayor Fiorello LaGuardia cooperated with National City Lines (and its sponsor, General Motors) in the replacement of the electric streetcar system by General Motors buses in the 1930s [51].

FIGURE 12.10. Trolley tracks on Bath Avenue, looking north from Bay 26th Street, in the Bensonhurst section of Brooklyn, on 8 September 1920. As was typically the case in the New York Metropolitan Region, this trolley service operated as a feeder to the West End Rapid Transit Line into Manhattan (Municipal Archives of the City of New York).

The spread of the city was also made possible by a spidery web of more than a dozen bridges and an invisible tether of tunnels. The Brooklyn Bridge was acclaimed the eighth wonder of the world when it opened in 1883, but it was later eclipsed, at least in terms of size, by the Triborough Bridge, which linked Manhattan, Queens, and the Bronx with four separate spans in 1936; by the George Washington Bridge, which became the world's longest suspension structure when it opened in 1931; and by the Verrazano-Narrows Bridge, which assumed that title in 1964. Other major connectors included the Williamsburg Bridge, the Manhattan Bridge, the Outerbridge, the Queensboro Bridge, and the Goethals Bridge, as well as the Brooklyn-Battery, Hudson, and Lincoln Tunnels. All exemplified an important difference between New York and other world cities – the waterways around Manhattan were broad, and the structures which spanned them were gargantuan, quite unlike the charming, human-scale bridges of Paris, London, Rome, and Berlin [52].

FIGURE 12.11. Aerial view looking north-west from Queens across upper Manhattan. In the foreground is Hell Gate, the junction of the East River, the Harlem River, and Long Island Sound. At the top of this 1930s photograph is the Hudson River and the new George Washington Bridge to New Jersey. The white line is the proposed route of the East River Drive (now called Franklin D. Roosevelt Drive) along the eastern edge of upper Manhattan. The structures in white are portions of the immense Triborough Bridge complex, which was opened by Robert Moses in 1936 (Municipal Archives of the City of New York).

Public Planning Policy

The most important planning decision ever reached in New York came in 1811, when a special commission imposed a gridiron street layout upon the entire island of Manhattan above Houston Street. The straight, right-angled system simplified the problems of surveying, minimized legal disputes over lot boundaries, maximized the number of lots that fronted the thoroughfare, and stamped New York City with a standard 25 by 100 foot plot. As John Randel candidly admitted when he submitted the plan, it facilitated 'buying, selling, and improving real estate' [53].

The next general plan was the New York City Improvement Plan of 1907. The proposal had its genesis in 1894, when the Municipal Art Society was founded to promote decorative amenities in the city. Whatever else Gotham had become by the end of the nineteenth century, it was not beautiful, and the pages of the journal, *Municipal Affairs,* were crowded with suggestions to remedy its ugliness – artistic street signs, diagonal avenues, more attractive open spaces. In 1902, stimulated by publicity surrounding the Senate Park Commission's mandate to rebuild a monumental Washington, Manhattan Borough President Jacob A. Cantor joined with Mayor Seth Low and the *New York Times* to ask the Municipal Art Society to convene a temporary conference on planning. The report of this conference, submitted on 11 January 1903, contained recommendations about freight terminals and dock systems as well as civic centres and monuments [54].

Impressed by the report, Mayor Low pushed through a bill that year establishing a commission to prepare a 'comprehensive plan for the beautifying and development of this municipality'. But Low lost the subsequent mayoralty election to George B. McClellan, Jr, who appointed his own political favourites to the first New York Public Improvement Commission. This group issued a preliminary report in 1904 and a more elaborate one in January, 1907. In addition to calling for more open spaces and more attractive vistas, it stressed the need for tying the metropolis together. In 1907, there were no tunnels or bridges across the Hudson River and few connections across the Harlem and East Rivers north of 14th Street. The 1907 plan recommended more bridges, a more rational interconnecting street system among the boroughs, and a more uniform method of pier construction and organization. Mayor McClellan was unenthusiastic about the report, however, and it received little support.

The leadership of the planning effort in the New York Metropolitan Region was then assumed by Charles Dyer Norton, an insurance executive. A former president of the Commercial Club of Chicago, he had worked closely with Daniel Burnham in designing and winning approval of the ambitious 1909 plan for that city. In 1911, Norton became vice-president of the First National Bank in New York and almost immediately set about the business of preparing a similar document for the nation's largest urbanized area. Collaborating with Manhattan Borough President George McAneny, Norton helped establish a Committee on the City Plan (made up of the five borough presidents) in 1914.

One result of the McAneny-Norton collaboration was the passage of the first comprehensive zoning law in the United States. Prior to 1916, many American cities, including New York, had regulated the construction and height of structures, but none followed the German practice of limiting the general *usage* of land. The New York ordinance was passed after a group of Fifth Avenue merchants became concerned over 'the gathering together of factory operatives at the noon hour on Fifth Avenue'. Immigrant garment workers were eating lunch from brown paper bags within sight of patrons of the nation's most expensive shops. The solution was a zoning law that pushed the garment district west of Seventh Avenue, well away from the fashionable emporiums of Fifth Avenue. Theoretically, the 1916 measure was designed to protect the interests of all citizens by limiting land speculation and congestion. In actuality, it restricted development only slightly because much more land was zoned for commercial and high-density residential use than could ever have been employed for such purposes. In 1945, the entire population of the United States could have been legally housed in New York City if all property had been developed to its maximum allowable use [55].

Norton was not satisfied with the Committee on the City Plan or the 1916 zoning law, and he and McAneny pushed hard to create a private pressure organization such as that which had been so successful with the 1909 Plan of Chicago. Believing that the Metropolis would never reach its potential until a document worthy of a great world city was prepared, Norton said: 'No plan of New York will command recognition unless it includes all the area in which New Yorkers earn their livelihood and make their homes. From City Hall a circle must be swung which will include the Atlantic Highlands and Princeton; the lovely Jersey Hills back of Morristown and Tuxedo; the incomparable Hudson as far as Newburgh; the Westchester lakes and ridges, to Bridgeport and beyond – all of Long Island' [56].

In 1921, the Russell Sage Foundation adopted the project, which was launched with appropriate fanfare the following year as the Committee on the Plan of New York and Its Environs [57]. During the 1920s, it sponsored a ten-volume *Regional Survey of New York and Its Environs*, directed by Professors Robert Murray Haig and Roswell G. McCrea of Columbia University. The study was completed in 1929 (a second was issued in 1968), and the Regional Plan Association (RPA) was legally incorporated to foster it. The first metropolitan planning agency to be formed in the United States, the RPA should not be confused with the Regional Planning Association of America (RPAA), with which it was often in disagreement [58].

The RPA's first important report, *Planning the New York Region: An Outline of the Organization, Scope and Progress of the Regional Plan*, was put together by Thomas Adams, a Scottish surveyor who had been the first president of the British Town Planning Institute and, earlier, first secretary of the Garden City Association which had promoted Letchworth. Adams came to Canada in 1914 as a consultant to the Commission of Conservation and moved to New York in 1923. Writing in 1927, he proposed broad programmes for decentralizing manufacturing and commercial establishments and coordinating them with available housing, and he predicted that: 'Wide radial highways with adequate connecting roads will facilitate a rational degree of dispersal and closer contiguity of industry and residence'. Good roads, he said, would create more viable neighbourhoods, improve downtown property values, and shorten the average journey-to-work. A half-century of experience has shown that expressways accomplished none of those goals [59].

The RPA recommended 470 separate projects and put together a permanent staff to see that they were accomplished. RPA generally opposed the low-density suburban sprawl, disregard for the landscape, and automobile-oriented transportation policy that had become typical of American urbanized areas by 1930. It adopted the novel notion of government subsidies for public transportation, it supported the concept of residential open space, and it lobbied for zoning ordinances in outlying communities [60]. It took a prominent role in the planning and location of the three most important New York area airports. Somewhat incongruously, it also advocated compact downtowns and business clustering while promoting an arterial highway network. Between the two world wars, the RPA exercised the dominant influence in American planning circles, and even critics like Lewis Mumford conceded that it broke new ground [61].

The Regional Plan Association, however, was and is a private pressure group. The city itself had no official mechanism for proposing alternative courses of action. This is not to suggest that the Mayor, the City Council, and the Board of Estimate did not make planning decisions in a variety of ways between 1811 and 1938. The placement of public schools, the opening of streets, the laying of sewers and sidewalks, the extension of power lines, the construction of bridges and tunnels, and most importantly, the granting of franchises to transportation companies for service on particular routes, all affected land use and development. And the power to regulate building use, as represented by the zoning law of 1916, involved public officials in decisions affecting the pattern of future development. But prior to the Great Depression, no city agency was responsible for the systematic collection of planning data or for the preparation of policy proposals [62].

The legislative shift came in 1936 with the adoption of a new charter which created a New York City Planning Commission 'to guide and to influence the city in its development and future growth'. This mandate, which took effect in 1938, could scarcely have been more ambitious or far-reaching. And the seven-member commission, through the instrumentality of overlapping eight-year terms, seemed secure from overt political influence. But the City Planning Commission (CPC) had no organized constituency. When attacked by special-interest groups it often had to back down. Mayor LaGuardia slowly withdrew his support, and by 1945 the CPC had reduced its functions to those specifically required in the charter: (1) the preparation and maintenance of a master plan (an injunction sometimes not followed); (2) the submission of zoning regulations to the powerful Board of Estimate; and (3) the proposal of an annual capital budget.

Although the CPC exhibited solid growth in terms of personnel and expenditures, its effectiveness was limited before the end of World War Two and did not improve thereafter. In 1969, under Chairman Donald H. Elliott, the commission produced what was to have been the master plan for urban development in the five boroughs of New York City. But neighbourhoods fought the imposition of a grandiose scheme, and by 1975 the emerging fiscal plight of the city stripped the CPC of its significance. The commission gradually lost its control over what, when, and where the city would build, as the critical decisions on budgeting, zoning, and land use were largely shifted to other city agencies or to the community boards. Perhaps Wallace S. Sayre and Herbert Kaufman were correct: 'The enduring enigma about the City Planning Commission is not its failure to realize the aspirations of its creators but rather how it has survived at all' [63].

Robert Moses

In 1941, the Regional Plan Association proudly noted the completion or the official commitment to more than half of the 470 specific recommendations of the 1929 plan. But the most important, such as the proposed trunk line railroad system, were not even being seriously discussed, and many of the improvements which had been made were the works of a single-minded genius. The protean agent of the huge public works project, Robert Moses was the greatest builder in American history and as powerful a non-elected public official as the United States has yet produced. Indeed, he was active and influential, until his death in 1981 at the age of 93, as an expert in the art of expediting the construction of immense structures [64].

Between 1924 and 1968, Moses conceived and executed public works costing $27 billion (before post-Vietnam War inflation). His was the dominant planning influence during these years in the city and state of New York, an arena and a period that included Governor Alfred E. Smith, Mayor Fiorello LaGuardia, Governor and President Franklin D. Roosevelt, Governor W. Averell Harriman, Senator Robert F. Wagner, Governor Herbert H. Lehman, Governor Thomas E. Dewey, Mayor John V. Lindsay, and Governor Nelson Rockefeller, not to mention the sachems of Tammany Hall or the bankers of Wall Street. Indeed, in the field of public works, Moses's impact was as great as the rest of them combined. In addition to improving the 3522 hectares of parks which already existed in the city in 1930, Moses increased the number of neighbourhood playgrounds from 119 to 374, planted 2½ million trees, and opened Jones Beach and Orchard Beach in his first decade as Park Commissioner. Moses was responsible for virtually every parkway, expressway, and public housing complex in the metropolitan region, as well as the Brooklyn-Battery Tunnel (he had planned a bridge there instead); the Henry Hudson, Bronx-Whitestone, Cross Bay, Throgs Neck, Verrazano Narrows, Marine Parkway, and Triborough Bridges; Lincoln Center for the Performing Arts; Shea

FIGURE 12.12. One of the many park improvements of Robert Moses, this park at the junction of East 84th Street and the East River is illustrative of the well-kept public spaces that were characteristic of New York in the 1930s. The northern tip of Welfare Island (now called Roosevelt Island) is visible at the centre of this photograph, while the Triborough Bridge is partially visible at the top of the picture. Note the ferry slips on the Queens side of the East River (Municipal Archives of the City of New York).

Stadium; and both the 1939 and 1964 World's Fairs. As Robert Caro noted in 1974:

> Other great builders left their mark on physical New York. But the achievement of even the greatest – a Zeckendorf or a Helmsley or a Winston or a Lefrak, the Rockefellers of Rockefeller Center – is dwarfed by the achievement of Robert Moses . . . He was a shaper not of sections of a city but of a *city*. He was, for the greatest city in the Western world, the entire city shaper, the only city shaper. In sheer physical impact on New York and the entire New York metropolitan region, he is comparable not to the works of any man or group of men . . . In the shaping of New York, Robert Moses was comparable only to some elemental force of nature [65].

Long Island is a particularly important case in point. Although the rich families of the North Shore were determined to keep their extravagant world for themselves, Moses began in the 1920s to build a series of parkways – first the Northern State, later the Southern State, Wantagh State, Cross Island, and Bethpage State Parkways – across the length and breadth of Nassau County. Moses intended that his roads be passports to recreation: Sunday drives to the country or holiday trips to the seashore. Instead, the new automobile right-of-ways had their greatest impact on the weekday journey-to-work. The Southern State Parkway, for example, gave motorists an east-west route across Long Island without a single traffic light or intersection. Designed to bring bathers to Jones Beach, it found its heaviest use as a commuter road to Manhattan. By 1957, it was notorious as one of the most heavily-travelled highways in the world [66].

Robert Moses did not even pretend to follow the advice of planners; he built projects according to his vision of the metropolis, not according to the Regional Plan [67]. In 1931, when the RPA opposed his proposal for the Northern State Parkway, Moses dismissed the Regional Plan as visionary and its drafters as irresponsible. In 1938, after another clash, Moses spoke more bluntly: 'The fact of the matter is that they do not know what they are talking about and that there is no talent on the Regional Plan at the moment worth listening to or bothering about' [68].

Moses was a creative thinker. In the 1930s, for example, the waterfront along the Upper West Side of Manhattan was a six-mile long wasteland. Although called Riverside Park, the area was scarred by four parallel tracks of the New York Central Railroad, as well as by rotting timbers, mounds of untreated garbage, and tar-paper squatter settlements. Ten years later, the area had been transformed – the railroad tracks were covered with tennis courts and lawns and promenades and playgrounds, and the nations's first controlled-access parkway within a major city [69] stretched northward from 72nd Street beyond the George Washington Bridge all the way to Riverdale in the Bronx. Moses liked to tell of his dreams for the West Side as early as 1911, and how even as a powerless young man he had envisaged the clean-up of the defaced shore. Perhaps he did not know of the plans prepared by the city in 1911 for covering the tracks, building a depressed highway, and landscaping the park [70].

Moses left his mark not only on New York, but on the entire nation. Many of the designers and administrators of the Bureau of Public Roads and later the Interstate Highway system had originally been trained as 'Moses men', and they remained disciples of their former chief. Lewis Mumford, a consistent opponent of

FIGURE 12.13. Looking south along the West Side Highway (now the Henry Hudson Parkway) and the Hudson River toward the George Washington Bridge and the New Jersey Palisades in 1938. The first urban expressway to be built in the United States, this immense highway project stretched from the southern tip of Manhattan to Westchester County, where it merged with the Saw Mill River Parkway. With Inwood Hill on one side and the broad expanse of the Hudson River on the other, this photograph illustrates the natural beauty of Manhattan.

the big roads philosophy, has written that: 'In the twentieth century the influence of Robert Moses on the cities of America was greater than that of any other person' [71]. As was said of Sir Christopher Wren in St. Paul's Cathedral, London: *Si monumentum requiris, circumspice* – If you would see his monument, look about you.

The Public Authority

Robert Moses's power bases were the Triborough Bridge and Tunnel Authority and the New York State Power Authority. Such quasi-governmental agencies were created by the state legislators to perform functions beyond the capacity of any municipality. The system seemed an efficient way to construct bridges, build water systems, and operate harbours, but critics insisted that the agencies were responsible more to their bondholders than to the public. The first special function district in New York was the Metropolitan Police District in 1857 (abolished in 1870). The Palisades Interstate Park Commission (1900), the Passaic Valley Sewage Commission (1907), the New Jersey District Water Supply Commission (1907), and the Port of New York Authority (1921) followed.

The most important of these units from a planning and land-use perspective was the Port of New York Authority (PNYA). It was created to deal with the fact that in 1920 about 90 per cent of the docking facilities in the harbour were located in New York City, but all the railroads terminated in New Jersey. The irony bordered on the incredible. The world's busiest harbour was not designed for direct rail-water shipment. Boxcars had to be loaded on and off flat, open barges with railroad tracks which shuffled back and forth across the Hudson and East Rivers. There was no fee for the service despite repeated lawsuits by New Jersey interests 'to separate lighterage from the New York rate for freight stopping in New Jersey and not requiring lighterage'. These overlapping and conflicting movements added to the cost of doing business in the metropolitan region [72].

The Port of New York Authority prepared a comprehensive report on the problems of a shipping industry troubled by the congestion of traffic in the harbour and by the competition of ports which had constructed modern terminal facilities. The PNYA rebuilt many of the piers in Brooklyn and Manhattan, and it attempted to integrate harbour transportation. On balance, however, it failed to resolve the basic problems, such as the lack of a direct freight line linking Brooklyn docks either with the other boroughs or New Jersey. It did almost nothing to halt the deterioration of public transit after 1920, concentrating instead on building bridges to serve automotive traffic. The ill-advised policies and programmes of the Port Authority culminated with the completion in 1974 of the twin 110-storey towers of the World Trade Center. This monstrosity added 10 million square feet of office space (more than four times as much as the Empire State Building and as much as in the total inventory of moderate-sized cities) to a temporarily glutted commercial space market, thus reducing the city's tax base even while diverting public funds

FIGURE 12.14. Lighterage in the Port of New York. A small barge loaded with boxcars is shuttled between the railroad yards in New Jersey and the Brooklyn docks (Photo: author).

from transit projects which would more adequately have furthered the objectives which the PNYA was designed to advance [73].

While the neglect of the waterfront by political and Port Authority administrators contributed to the decline of Manhattan shipping, this neglect served only to aggravate a trend that had its origin in new methods of materials handling. Until almost the beginning of World War Two, freight unloading techniques had remained essentially unchanged, in terms of basic concept, from the methods that had been used from the earliest days of maritime trade. Vessels had become larger and tools for transference more sophisticated, but the process of unloading still involved the movement of individual boxes, crates, barrels, and bundles by men and machines. Perishable goods rested on docks until trucks picked them up, and the theft of merchandise was a frequent occurrence. Then, in the 1930s, a wide variety of containerization methods were introduced in both the shipping and railroad industries. Seatrain Lines, operating primarily between New York and the Gulf of Mexico, stacked ships full of railroad cars, which were lifted by giant cranes directly on to railroad tracks. A later development was 'piggy-back' shipment, which used the trailer section of a truck as the main container unit. The efficiencies of the new methods required large areas of clear land space to back up the unloading operations at the pier. The necessary plots of hundreds of hectares were simply unavailable within the tight confines of New York City [74].

Garden Cities and Garden Suburbs

Although New York has a generally undistinguished record in city and regional planning, smaller-scale projects in the metropolitan area have had a much greater influence. At least six utopian communities (exclusive of commercial areas like Rockefeller Center) are particularly significant in the history of American planning:

1.   The nation's first picturesque suburb was developed in 1853 in the eastern foothills of New Jersey's Orange Mountains, just twenty-one kilometres (thirteen miles) by rail from Manhattan. Llewellyn S. Haskell, a prosperous drug merchant, accumulated 162 hectares (400 acres), and Alexander Jackson Davis, the most prolific architect of his generation, introduced two features – the curvilinear road and a natural open area at the centre – which were unprecedented in human experience. Known as Llewellyn Park, the community became a haven for the well-to-do and provided an environment free from the nuisances of city life.

2.   The most ambitious planned suburb in nineteenth-century North America was the brainchild of Alexander T. Stewart, a Scottish immigrant whose elaborate dry goods emporium on Broadway is usually regarded as the world's first department store (1846). In collaboration with his long-time architect, John Kellum, Stewart purchased almost 3000 hectares of the common lands of the Town of Hempstead, a rural Long Island community about 32 kilometres east of the city, and proceeded to build a carefully landscaped suburb of wide street and generous lots. Garden City was unusual, however, in that Stewart refused to sell any property, choosing instead to rent the houses at annual leases of about $350. The affluent businessmen who could afford such rents did not accept the leasing idea, however, and Garden City remained sparsely settled until the more traditional ownership arrangement was adopted after 1900.

3.   Forest Hills Gardens in Queens was also a development for the affluent. The Russell Sage Foundation purchased the land in 1906–1910 with the intention of building housing for the working classes. Grosvenor Atterbury was hired as architect, and Frederick Law Olmstead, Jr as landscape architect. Together they designed a garden suburb, replete with winding streets, Tudor houses, and a beautifully scaled central Greenway, of such quality that it quickly became one of New York's choicest residential enclaves. Only fifteen minutes via the Long Island Railroad from the centre of Manhattan, Forest Hills Gardens remains a textbook example of exquisite site planning.

4.   Three of the great names in the twentieth-century utopian housing – Clarence Stein, Henry Wright, and Alexander Bing – worked together on Sunnyside Gardens, a 1200 unit garden-apartment complex on 23 hectares of undeveloped land in Queens. Constructed between 1924 and 1928, the low-rise buildings provide small private gardens and much larger inner courtyards for communal use. The project was intended as an American test, on a very limited basis, of the Garden City theories of Ebenezer Howard, and it was successful in providing low-density living at modest cost.

5.   After the success with Sunnyside Gardens, Alexander Bing's City Housing

Corporation purchased a tract of farmland in 1928 in Fairlawn, New Jersey (near what is now the George Washington Bridge). Radburn was to be a community of 25,000 persons, but the Great Depression intervened, and only 408 houses had been built when the community went bankrupt. But the side plan was prophetic, grouping houses tightly around cul-de-sacs, providing huge, common lawns throughout the town, and separating automobile traffic from pedestrians through a system of attractive bridges and underpasses.

6.   Parkchester is the best high-rise housing complex in the New York Metropolitan Region. Built by the Metropolitan Life Insurance Company between 1938 and 1942, it is a gigantic complex of red brick towers housing a total of 40,000 residents. Parkchester features a large and well-maintained open space, known as the 'oval', at the centre, as well as attractive shopping streets that provided some of the first decentralized department stores in the United States. According to Paul Goldberger, 'the whole place stands as a reminder that it is possible to build housing on a mass scale and not lose touch with what we like to call the human values' [75].

The New York Metropolitan Region Since 1940

The New York Metropolitan Region peaked in wealth and population, relative to the rest of the country, in about 1940. In some respects World War Two brought short-term prosperity to the area. The Brooklyn Navy Yard operated around the clock, its 90,000 workers producing warships and merchant vessels. The Bush Terminal Complex functioned as the trans-shipment point for most of the military hardware headed for Europe. Nearby cities like Bridgeport and Newark were centres of munitions manufacture, and Long Island factories contributed thousands of warplanes to the Allied cause. Moreover, World War Two hastened the trend toward Wall Street hegemony in the financial markets of the world [76].

But trends established between 1939 and 1945 undermined the position of New York and the entire North-East. Unlike Great Britain (the Barlow Report of 1939), the Soviet Union (the Moscow Master Plan of 1935), Japan (the Capital Region Development Act of 1956), or France (the policy of industrial decentralization since 1949), the United States never adopted a formal policy to limit the size of the largest city. But the federal government's financial aid formulas for welfare, which paid a smaller percentage of Gotham's expenditures than of Mississippi; for transportation, which emphasized the automobile and the controlled-access highway and which paid a smaller portion of New York's public transportation costs than of smaller cities; and for water, which made possible vast irrigation projects in the West and which paid for new sewer systems even while denying assistance for the repair of New York's ageing, underground pipes; were more effective in limiting New York's growth than anything adopted by other national governments. And because New York was not a national or state capital, as was the case with most other world metropolises, it did not profit from the increase in the size of bureaucracies which accompanied the post-war years. Finally, with the expansion of the military establishment after the beginning of the Korean War, the Soviet detonation of a nuclear device and the concentration of defence installations and arms procurement in the South and West, the city suffered a relative decline in population and prestige [77].

The great metropolis remained in a class by itself, however. Although the same deconcentrating trend that was evident throughout the nation continued in the NYMR, the legal city contained almost seven million inhabitants in 1980 [78], more than twice as many as any rival. Together with the twenty-six other counties which make up what the Regional Plan Association defines as the metropolitan region, New York housed in 1980 about 9 per cent of the national population on about one-five-hundredth of the land area of the contiguous forty-eight states. It stood at the very centre of 'Megalopolis', the urbanized north-eastern seaboard that contained fifty-one million people, stretched from Washington to Boston, and accounted for 22 per cent of the population of the United States on 1.4 per cent of the area. As the French geographer, Jean Gottmann, noted in 1961: 'No other section has a comparable role within the nation of a comparable importance in the world. Here has been developed a kind of supremacy, in politics, in economics, and possibly even in cultural activities, seldom before attained by an area of this size' [79].

Conclusion

New York's most important period of change and development occurred between 1890 and 1940. In the former year, the metropolis was still a mercantile city, with a largely German, Irish, and American-born population engaged in activities appropriate to a major entrepot of trade. By 1940, Greater New York was the corporate centre of American industry, even as its own manufacturing sector declined in relative importance. Between 1890 and 1940, more than 90 per cent of the river crossings, the entire subway system, and more than half of the residential housing in Manhattan, Brooklyn, and the Bronx were constructed. By 1940, the mass-transit and park systems were in place, and most of the neighbourhoods had assumed the physical shape – and sometimes the ethnic composition – that would characterize them until the present day. The building of a parkway and arterial highway system that would later be copied throughout the United States was well underway. Taken together, the new facilities created a circulatory network which united the New York Metropolitan Region into an interdependent economic colossus. Finally, the consolidation of the five boroughs into one great city came in 1898, and there remains scant prospect that further adjustments in the corporate boundaries of the metropolis will be made.

The physical planning of the region was mixed. Practically every office and residential structure was built for private profit, and in the major exception, public housing, a bland skyscraper architecture combined with ghetto locations to create an environment only slightly better than the tenements which previously sheltered the poor. No landmarks legislation existed to protect important structures from the wrecker's ball. Its monotonous gridiron layout and tendency to concentrate the better residential and commercial districts, rather than to disperse them as in Paris or London, suggest that New York favoured size and newness at the expense of the human scale and informal social interaction that make life in a great city bearable.

With all of its problems, however, New York still commands the loyalty of most of its inhabitants. Its population is more heterogeneous, its atmosphere more tolerant, and its pace much quicker than its competitors, just as its reliance upon the automobile is much less, and its dependence upon mass transit much greater, than in other American cities. Gotham is the architectural pacesetter of the world. It is a real city, the quintessential city, whose buses and subways operate around the clock. In New York, one can dine *after* an evening at the theatre, find booksellers and grocers open at midnight, and read local newspapers in a dozen languages. New York is not relaxed, or pleasant, or clean, or particularly beautiful, although along its wide and brimming harbour the eye can be rewarded with scapes of land and sea that impose a wonderment on the mind. As E. B. White noted:

> New York will bestow the gift of loneliness and the gift of privacy . . . New York is peculiarly constructed to absorb almost anything that comes along without inflicting the event on its inhabitants, so that every event is, in a sense, optional, and the inhabitant is in the happy position of being able to choose his spectacle and so conserve his soul.

NOTES

1. Vikings and Norsemen probably visited the area in the eleventh century, but their names have been lost to us.
2. The best book on the geography and early history of New York is actually a six-volume effort: Stokes, I. N. Phelps (1928) *The Iconography of Manhattan Island*. New York: Robert Dowd and Company.
3. The first four buildings on Manhattan Island were constructed in 1613 by Adrian Block, whose ship caught fire, forcing him to build shelter. Henry Hudson was English, but he was working for the Dutch East India Company, which later spawned the Dutch West India Company.
4. New York was named in honour of the Duke of York, brother of King Charles II of England. The term 'Gotham'; used often in this chapter, was first applied to New York by Washington Irving in *Salmagundi* (1807–1808). The 'wise men' of Gotham (England) were traditionally noted for their stupidity. The term 'Big Apple' derives from jazz musicians in the 1920s, who regarded any engagement as an 'apple' and one in New York City as a 'big apple'.
5. Other older American cities outside the United States are Santo Domingo (1493), Buenos Aires (1580), and Quebec City (1608).
6. The best volume on the growth of New York before the Civil War is: Albion, Robert G. (1939) *The Rise of New York Port, 1815–1860*. New York: Charles Scribner's Sons, pp. 3–87. See also:

Luke, Myron H. (1953) *The Port of New York, 1800–1810*. New York: New York University Press.

7. On the peculiar entrepreneurial spirit in New York as contrasted with more conservative Boston, see: Jaher, Fred C. (1968) The Boston Brahmins in the age of industrial capitalism, in Jaher, Fred C. (ed.) *The Age of Industrialism in America*. New York: The Free Press, pp. 188–262.

8. New York City was the capital of the United States between 1789 and 1791, but the government moved to Philadelphia and then to Washington. In 1900, the total deposits in Gotham Banks were approximately the same as those of the rest of the country combined. Pred, Allan R. (1973) *Urban Growth and the Circulation of Information: The United States System of Cities, 1790–1840*. Cambridge: MIT Press.

9. Fein, Albert (1976) Centennial New York, 1876, in Klein, Milton M. (ed.) *New York: The Centennial Years, 1676–1976*. Port Washington: Kennikat Press, pp. 73–120.

10. The best study of the late nineteenth-century metropolis is Hammack, David C. (1982) *Power and Society: Great New York at the Turn of the Century*. New York: Russell Sage Foundation.

11. The 1874 land addition was initially termed the 'Annexed District' and for administrative purposes was a part of New York County. After a larger piece of Westchester County became part of New York City in 1898, the mainland portion of the city became Bronx County.

12. Kaplan, Barry J. (1979) Andrew J. Green and the creation of a planning rationale: the formation of Greater New York City, 1865–1890. *Urbanism Past and Present*, **8**, pp. 32–41.

13. Because New York City has intermittently expanded into the surrounding waterways using landfill, the area of the city has grown slightly over the years even in the absence of political annexation. A forthcoming Columbia University Ph.D. dissertation in urban planning by Ann Buttenwieser is the most exhaustive analysis of this process.

14. The city's business centre of gravity shifted northward during this period, especially in terms of retail trade, from 14th Street in 1870, to 23rd Street in 1890, to 34th Street in 1920, and to 42nd street in 1940.

15. In 1930, when about 25 per cent of all American millionaires made their home in New York City, the per capita income of New York State was about 60 per cent higher than the national average.

16. Although New York surpassed Boston in population and economic importance about 1750, it was not until about 1880 that Gotham clearly eclipsed the Massachusetts capital in publishing and the arts.

17. Even before 1650, when eighteen separate languages were spoken in Manhattan, New York (New Amsterdam) was unusual in the New World because of the ethnic mix. The Dutch and French Huguenots predominated in the seventeenth century, with the English not becoming numerically dominant until after 1700. Archdeacon, Thomas J. (1976) *New York City, 1664–1710: Conquest and Change*. New York: Columbia University Press.

18. Kessner, Thomas (1976) *The Golden Door: The Jews and Italians of New York City*. New York: Oxford University Press; Riis, Jacob (1890) *How the Other Half Lives: Studies Among the Tenements of New York*. New York: Hill and Wang.

19. The black residential distribution in New York did not follow the familiar pattern established in Chicago, Detroit, Philadelphia, and other northern cities in which the ghetto expanded from an inner-city core. In New York, the black community moved from Five Points to Greenwich Village to the Tenderloin and to San Juan Hill before focusing on Harlem after World War One, Osofsky, Gilbert (1966) *Harlem: The Making of a Negro Ghetto, 1890–1930*. New York: Harper and Row; Gurock, Jeffrey S. (1979) *When Harlem Was Jewish, 1870–1930*. New York: Columbia University Press; Huggins, Nathan Irving (1971) *Harlem Renaissance*. New York: Oxford University Press.

20. Pratt, Edward Ewing (1911) *Industrial Causes of Congestion of Population in New York City*. New York: Columbia University Press. In 1920, for example, New York City had only 365,963 dwellings for 1,278,341 families, while Philadelphia had 352,944 dwellings for only 402,946 families. Moreover, the renting habit has always been stronger in Gotham than elsewhere in the United States. Only 6 per cent of New Yorkers owned their homes in 1890;

only 12 per cent in 1920. Both figures were less than one-third of the national average.

21. Even at lower heights Manhattan has traditionally dominated the nation. In 1929, New York contained 188 of the 377 American buildings that were at least 200 feet high.

22. The New York estimates are from the 1969 City Plan and from various publications of the Regional Plan Association, especially Pushkarev, Boris S. (1969) The Atlantic urban seaboard: development issues and strategies. *Regional Plan News*, **90,** p. 15. The London figures are from Hall, Peter (1966) *The World Cities.* New York: World University Library, pp. 30–58.

23. Wingate, Charles (1885) The moral side of the tenement house problem. *The Catholic World, 41,* p. 160.

24. Lubove, Roy (1963) *The Progressives and the Slums: Tenement House Reform in New York.* Pittsburgh: University of Pittsburgh Press; Rischin, Moses (1962) *The Promised City: New York's Jews, 1870–1914.* Cambridge: Harvard University Press, pp. 76–94.

25. Because the airshaft was often used as a convenient garbage dump, tenants typically kept their windows shut to keep out the stench.

26. Even the most liberal of American housing reformers in the nineteenth century, such as Alfred T. White, insisted that it was necessary for investors to make a profit on dwellings for the working class.

27. Before 1840, the word 'tenement' in American usage referred to any building housing three or more families. By 1880, the word came to mean a crowded, lower-status apartment building. DeForest, Robert W. and Veiller, Lawrence (eds.) (1903) *The Tenement House Problem,* 2 vols. New York: The Macmillan Company, vol. 1, p. 94; vol. 2, p. 78.

28. In 1910, the number of people in Wards 7 and 10 reached 542,000, and the average block density was 867. There is a report of a post-World War Two density of 840,000 per square mile in a section of Bombay, but the district under consideration was itself less than one square mile in area. Hoselitz, Bert F. (1962) A survey of the literature on urbanization in India, in Turner, Roy (ed.) *India's Urban Future.* Berkeley: University of California Press, p. 427;

New York State Tenement House Commission (1895) *Report of 1894.* Albany: Legislative Document no. 37, 17 January 1895, p. 11.

29. Ford, James (1936) *Slums and Housing,* 2 vols. Cambridge: Harvard University Press, vol. 2, plates 10A, 10B, 10D, and 10E.

30. These figures understate the degree of crowding in New York because so much of the land area was either completely undeveloped in 1950 (eastern Queens and most of Staten Island) or given over to commercial and business functions (about half of Manhattan south of 59th Street). A tedious, administrative history of municipal attempts to regulate residential density is Comer, John P. (1942) *New York City Building Control.* New York: Columbia University Press.

31. Lockwood, Charles (1976) *Manhattan Moves Uptown.* Boston: Houghton-Mifflin Company; Moore, Deborah Dash (1980) *At Home in America: Second Generation New York Jews.* New York: Columbia University Press. For a more general treatment of this process, see Jackson, Kenneth T. (1975) Urban deconcentration in the nineteenth century: A statistical inquiry, in Schnore, Leo F. (ed.) *The New Urban History: Quantitative Explorations by American Historians.* Princeton: Princeton University Press, pp. 110–42.

32. Jackson, Kenneth T. (1973) The Crabgrass Frontier: 150 years of suburban growth in America, in Mohl, Raymond A. and Richardson, James F. (eds) *The Urban Experience: Themes in American History.* Belmont, California: Wadsworth Publishing Company, pp. 196–221.

33. Urbanized in this sense means fully developed. The figures do not include non-agricultural lands which were not yet in the process of conversion to residential or commercial use. Farm land is similarly excluded.

34. Wood, Robert C. (1961) *1400 Governments: The Political Economy of the New York Metropolitan Region.* Cambridge: Harvard University Press; Jackson, Kenneth T. (1972) Metropolitan government versus suburban autonomy: politics on the Crabgrass Frontier, in Jackson, Kenneth T. and Schultz, Stanley K. (eds.), *Cities in American History.* New York: Alfred A. Knopf, Inc., p. 442–62.

35. Pushkarev, *loc. cit.,* p. 15 (see note 22); Griffin,

John I. (1956) *Industrial Location in the New York Area*. New York: City College of New York Press.

36. Jackson, Kenneth T. (1980) Race, ethnicity, and real estate appraisal: the Home Owners Loan Corporation and the Federal Housing Administration. *Journal of Urban History*, **6**, pp. 419–52.

37. New York's rapid transit supremacy has eroded since 1945, when the various lines occasionally serviced as many as eight million passengers in a single day. In 1981, it averaged about four million fares per weekday, or about the same as Moscow, Tokyo, and Paris. The London Underground operated over more route miles in 1980 than the New York Subway (252 to 231), but the British system daily accommodated only about 60 per cent as many passengers. There is no adequate history of the New York transit system. The better studies include: Carman, Harry James (1919) *The Street Surface Railway Franchises of New York City*. New York: Columbia University Studies in History, Economics, and Public Law; Walker, James Blaine (1918) *Fifty Years of Rapid Transit in New York, 1864–1917*. New York: The Law Printing Company; Cudahy, Brian J. (1979) *Under the Sidewalks of New York: The Story of the Greatest Subway System in the World*. Brattleboro, Vermont: The Stephen Crane Press; Fischler, Stan (1976) *Uptown, Downtown: A Trip Through Time on New York's Subways*. New York: Hawthorne Books. The best comparative study is: McKay, John P. (1976) *Tramways and Trolleys: The Rise of Urban Mass Transport in Europe*. Princeton: Princeton University Press. The number of rides per capita per year in New York was 274 in 1904 and 343 in 1914.

38. Greene, Joseph Warren (1926) New York City's first railroad: the New York and Harlem, 1832–1867. *New-York Historical Society Quarterly Bulletin*, **9**, pp. 107–123.

39. Smith, Mildred H. (1958) *Early History of the Long Island Railroad*. Uniondale, NY: Salisbury Printers, pp. 2–9.

40. Spann, Edward K. (1981) *The New Metropolis: New York City, 1840–1857*. New York: Columbia University Press.

41. Quoted from Condit, Carl W. (1981) *The Port of New York: A History of the Rail and Terminal System from the Electrification of Grand Central Terminal*. Chicago: University of Chicago Press. See also, Condit, Carl W. (1980) *The Port of New York: A History of the Rail and Terminal System From the Beginnings to Pennsylvania Station*. Chicago: University of Chicago Press.

42. Tarr, Joel A. (1973) Transportation planning in 1875. *High Speed Ground Transportation*, **7**, pp. 265–88.

43. Reeves, William Fullerton (1936) *The First Elevated Railroads in Manhattan and the Bronx of the City of New York*. New York: New-York Historical Society.

44. The mini-subway was the brainchild of Alfred Ely Beach, who encountered financial obstacles and abandoned the project in the 1870s.

45. Interborough Rapid Transit Company (1904) *The New York Subway*. New York: McGraw Publishing Company, pp. 15–21.

46. Cudahy, *op. cit.*, pp. vii–viii (see note 37).

47. Hood, Clifton (1981) William Barclay Parsons. *American Public Works Association Reporter*, **48**, pp. 4–5.

48. Higgins, Charles M. (1905) *City Transit Evils: Their Causes and Cure*. Brooklyn: publisher not stated, pp. 7–8.

49. The rapid transit problem. *Street Railway Journal*, 18 March 1905, p. 501. See also, Turner, Daniel L. (1926) Is there a vicious circle of transit development and city congestion? *National Municipal Review*, June, p. 322.

50. The best examination of the influence of transportation on land development in the New York area is: Schoenebaum, Eleanora (1976) Emerging neighborhoods: the development of Brooklyn's fringe areas, 1850–1930 (Ph.D. dissertation, Columbia University). A useful earlier study is: Spengler, Edwin H. (1930) *Land Values in New York in Relation to Transit Facilities*. New York: Columbia University Press.

51. Snell, Bradford C. (1974) *American Ground Transportation: A Proposal for Restructuring the Automobile, Truck, Bus, and Rail Industries*. Washington: Government Printing Office.

52. The Humber Bridge in Great Britain has recently become the longest suspension structure in the world.

53. Schuyler, David (1979) Public Landscapes and American Urban Culture, 1800–1870: Rural Cemeteries, City Parks, and Suburbs. Ph.D.

dissertation, Columbia University, pp. 221–2.

54. Kantor, Harvey A. (1971) The City Beautiful in New York. *The New-York Historical Society Quarterly*, **57**, pp. 149–71; Kantor, Harvey A. (1971) Modern Urban Planning in New York City: Origins and Evolution. Ph.D. dissertation, New York University.

55. Commission on Building Districts and Restrictions (1916) *Final Report, 2 June 1916*. New York: Board of Estimate and Apportionment Committee on the City Plan; Makielski, Stanislaw J. (1966) *The Politics of Zoning: The New York Experience*. New York: Columbia University Press.

56. Regional Plan Association (1979) *Annual Report*, p. 3.

57. The Russell Sage Foundation was the legacy of a major stockholder of the Metropolitan Elevated Company, the premier firm in Manhattan after 1881.

58. Lewis Mumford, for example, who favoured small-scale human environments, was a bitter critic of the 1929 Regional Plan.

59. Adams, Thomas (1927) *Planning the New York Region: An Outline of the Organization, Scope and Progress of the Regional Plan*. New York: Regional Plan Association, pp. 28–29.

60. The RPA supported Sunnyside Gardens, Radburn, and Parkchester, which are discussed later in this chapter.

61. Hays, Forbes B. (1965) *Community Leadership: The Regional Plan Association of New York*. New York: Columbia University Press.

62. Most other American cities hired outside consultants to prepare city plans, but few had permanent city planning commissions in the 1930s.

63. Sayre, Wallace S. and Kaufman, Herbert (1960) *Governing New York City: Politics in the Metropolis*. New York: Russell Sage Foundation, pp. 379–81.

64. Until his death in 1981, Robert Moses continued to report for work regularly at the Triborough Bridge and Tunnel authority, where he was a consultant.

65. Caro, Robert A. (1974) *The Power Broker: Robert Moses and the Fall of New York*. New York: Alfred A. Knopf, Inc., pp. 1–25.

66. Moses lost very few confrontations. In his struggle for a bridge between Brooklyn and the financial district he failed only because of the intervention of the War Department, and by implication, his enemy, President Franklin D. Roosevelt. For another side of the story, see Moses, Robert (1970) *Public Works: A Dangerous Trade*. New York: McGraw-Hill Book Company.

67. Moses was of course planning the metropolis, but not according to the dictates of the city agency charged with that responsibility.

68. *New York Times*, 2 July 1938; Hays, *op.cit.*, pp. 63–65 (see note 61).

69. The first controlled-access highway of any type was the Bronx River Parkway, constructed between 1906 and 1923 between Bruckner Boulevard in the Bronx and White Plains.

70. *Real Estate Record and Builders Guide*, 23 September 1911, pp. 415–16; Caro, *op.cit.*, pp. 65–67 and 525–34 (see note 65).

71. Caro, *op.cit.*, p. 12 (see note 65).

72. New York City Writers' Project (1941) *A Maritime History of New York*. Garden City: Doubleday, Doran and Company; Griffin, John I. (1959) *The Port of New York*. New York: Arco Publishing Company; Rush, Thomas E. (1920) *The Port of New York*. New York: Doubleday, Page and Company.

73. Under pressure from both New York and New Jersey, the Port Authority did take over rapid transit lines running under the Hudson River, but the PATH network, as it is called, represents only a small fraction of the public transportation needs in the region.

74. Chinitz, Benjamin (1960) *Freight and the Metropolis*. Cambridge: Harvard University Press. See also, Report of Engineering Department, Port of New York Authority (23 January 1948) *Development of New York City Piers*. New York: PANY; Black, William N. (1891) *The Crippled Commerce of New York*. New York: W. K. Farrington Company.

75. *New York Times*, 17 April 1981.

76. The Brooklyn Navy Yard and the Bush Army Terminal Complex were both closed by the Department of Defense between 1968 and 1978, and their functions were transferred to southern states.

77. The best work on this subject is: Lotchin, Roger W. (1979) The city and the sword: San

Francisco and the rise of the metropolitan-military complex. *Journal of American History,* March.

78. Because many illegal aliens reside in New York, informed observers estimate that the official census population understakes the actual total by at least one million persons in the metropolitan area. In 1981, the city brought suit against the Census Bureau alleging that computer checks indicated that 8 per cent of the individuals on welfare were not counted in the census.

79. The twenty-six counties outside the city in the NYMR include Nassau, Suffolk, Rockland, Westchester, Orange, Dutchess, Putnam, Sullivan, and Ulster Counties in New York State; Hudson, Essex, Union, Passaic, Bergen, Ocean, Monmouth, Middlesex, Somerset, Morris, Mercer, Hunterdon, Warren, and Sussex Counties in New Jersey; and Fairfield, New Haven, and Litchfield Counties in Connecticut. The quote is from: Gottman, Jean (1961) *Megalopolis: The Urbanized Northeastern Seaboard of the United States.* New York: The Twentieth Century Fund.

Chapter 13

Moscow, the Socialist Metropolis

R. A. FRENCH

ALL cities are unique phenomena, however hard geographers seek for common patterns; all periods are arbitrarily defined, however earnestly historians identify turning points. For Moscow, the period 1890 to 1940 may well have less significance in its progression to metropolitan status than it does for other metropolitan areas of the world. The year 1890 came in the middle of the city's first phase of rapid industrialization, the year 1940 in the middle of its second phase. Only after 1940 did Moscow achieve a metropolitan rank comparable to that of the other very largest cities, such as London or New York, either in terms of its population and spatial extent or in terms of its worldwide significance. One can regard its arrival in this select company of cities as being symbolized by the creation of Greater Moscow in 1960.

It is true that in the very middle of the half century in question there occurred what is probably the most significant event in Moscow's history, the 1917 Revolution. However, the socio-economic forces, particularly industrialization, which culminated in the Revolution, began long before 1890; by then Marx had been dead for seven years. Nevertheless the Revolution did set in train the processes which have helped to give the city its present character. Moscow is not just *a* metropolis, it is *the* socialist metropolis; as the pioneer, it has been both the exemplar for all Soviet urban places of any size and, in no small measure, the model for other capitals of the socialist world.

The Rise of Moscow

It has frequently been suggested that Moscow was destined for importance from its very origin, thanks to its central position in the great plain of European Russia and thanks to the protecting swamps of the Meshchera lowland, which shielded it from Tatar onslaughts [1]. In fact, when Yuriy Dolgorukiy founded Moscow in 1147, it was merely a minor western outpost of the important princedom of Vladimir and any environmental advantages of its location applied with equal force to Vladimir, Grand Princely capital and seat of the Orthodox Metropolitan before Moscow. Rather, Moscow's acquisition of more significant central-place functions was due to the energy, cunning and unscrupulousness of its early princes, who in the dark ages after the Tatar invasion of 1237–1240 used a skilful mixture of diplomacy, force and the support of the Tatars to achieve supremacy over the neighbouring princedoms. The removal of the Orthodox Patriarch to Moscow in 1326, the defeat of the Tatars at Kulikovo by Dmitri Donskoy in 1380, the assumption of the title of Tsar of All the Russias by Ivan III in the fifteenth century and the capture of the Tatar khanates of Kazan and Astrakhan in 1552–1556 by Ivan the Terrible, all marked stages in Moscow's development into the capital, the ultimate central place, in the single unified country of Russia. In consequence the fifteenth and sixteenth centuries saw a steady growth in the international links of Moscow, including those with Elizabethan England. The emergence of Moscow as the undisputed centre of all the Russias can be regarded as the first critical phase in its metropolitan evolution. Its importance was enhanced by the nature of the ruling regime: there are no central places quite as central as the seats of autocracies, whatever form that autocracy may outwardly assume.

The development of Moscow's capital function was parallelled by its physical growth. The original fortified enclosure, the Kremlin, was gradually divested of functions other than defence and authority (both temporal and spiritual), as craft manufacture, trading, and the residences of merchants, artisans and labourers moved into a trading quarter to the east, known as the Kitay Gorod. This, too, was walled in time, but the growing town spread outside it into new artisan suburbs – the semi-circle of the Belyy Gorod or White Town. The Belyy Gorod was also

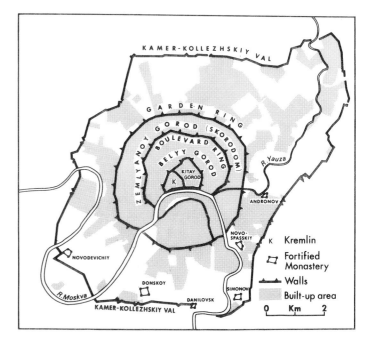

FIGURE 13.1. Stages in the early growth of Moscow; built-up area as in the 1830s.

walled in the sixteenth century, but by then Moscow was expanding still further out into a ring of newer suburbs, called the Zemlyanoy Gorod or Earthen Town, which in 1592 was also protected by an earthen bank and palisade (figure 13.1). The sixteenth-century fortifications around the White and Earthen Towns were later replaced by wide circular avenues, the Boulevard and Garden Rings. The broad Garden Ring today, with its underpasses and flyovers, serves both as an inner motorway and as the approximate limit of the central city core. Thus the cellular stages of Moscow's medieval expansion have left an imprint on the appearance and plan of the inner city and indeed were the beginnings of Moscow's characteristic 'ring and radial' pattern of structure. In the seventeenth century, Moscow's capital and trading functions were joined by an industrial one, as factory manufacture began to crystallize out of the artisan craft production of the city's many suburbs [2]. The pre-eminence of metal-working and textile production, which then developed, has remained a trait of Moscow's industrial profile to the present day.

The opening of the eighteenth century brought a major setback in Moscow's development, when in 1703 Peter the Great founded his Baltic 'window on Europe', St. Petersburg; in 1712 he made it his capital. Many of Moscow's craftsmen were transferred there to assist in the building of St. Petersburg. Members of the nobility were compelled to erect houses in St. Petersburg; they and their servants, together with many of the merchants, craftsmen and shopkeepers dependent on their patronage, all moved to the new capital. For a time Moscow's growth was halted and its population briefly declined [3].

That loss of its capital function should affect Moscow adversely is not surprising; what is perhaps remarkable was the city's resilience and speed of recovery. Even during Peter's reign, the population began to increase again as new factory industry appeared, first through State action and then through private enterprise. By Peter's death there were thirty-two factories, employing some 5500 workers. Nor was Moscow's recovery confined to its industrial life. It remained a strong contender as the principal cultural centre of the country, with Russia's first university founded by Lomonosov in 1755. In 1742 the expansion of Moscow far beyond its old, medieval limits of the Earthen Town was recognized by the establishment of new city bounds, the Kamer-Kollezhskiy *Val*, or Wall, so doubling the official area to 7100 ha (figure 13.1). It was to remain the official boundary until the end of the nineteenth century. Unlike the earlier walls, the *Val* was not a defensive work, but a customs barrier, where at each gate tolls were levied on incoming goods.

The eighteenth century witnessed the beginnings of conscious planning in Moscow [4]. In 1762 a Commission for the Construction of St. Petersburg and Moscow was established and in 1773 it began work in Moscow, producing the city's first master plan two years later. The plan, with grandiose concepts of wide squares and boulevards, was never accomplished but the classical revival in architecture of this period embellished Moscow with many of its finest buildings, the individual splendour of which could rival the planned magnificence of St. Petersburg [5]. During this century, Moscow remained the larger of the two principal cities, but St. Petersburg moved into first place in 1812, when Napoleon's invasion and the consequent, devastating fire brought disaster to Moscow. Over 70 per cent of the buildings were destroyed. The population, which had been 275,000 in 1811, fell to a few thousand in 1812 and not until 1827 did the number of inhabitants surpass its previous level (table 13.1; figure 13.2) [6]. The very immensity of destruction led to the first implementation of large-scale city planning. The Commission for the Building of the City of Moscow, with O. I. Bove as its chief architect, was set up in 1813 and worked until 1843. It drew up a plan, making use of features from the defunct 1775 plan; among its achievements was the opening up of squares near the Kremlin including enlargement of the Red Square. The Moskva was embanked, the Neglinnaya river north of the Kremlin was converted into an underground culvert, and the lines of the old fortifications were widened into broad boulevards. The rebuilding of housing, however, was left to individuals. Within two years, 90 per cent of the lost houses were replaced, but it was largely an unplanned and unsupervised process, which produced everything from palaces to wooden shacks and which did little to modify the pre-existing layout.

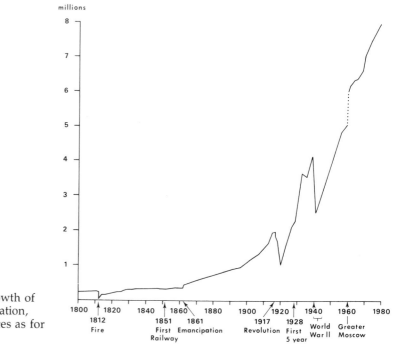

FIGURE 13.2. Growth of Moscow's population, 1800–1980. Sources as for table 13.1.

Table 13.1.   Growth of Moscow's population.

Date	Population	Source	Date	Population	Source
c.1400	20–30,000	S	1919	1,550,000	
c.1500	30-40,000	S	Aug 28 1920	1,027,000	V
1701	c.200,000		1921	1,148,000	K
c.1720	140-150,000	S	1922	1,278,000	K
1785	188,700	R	Mar 15 1923	1,543,000	
1811	275,281	IM	1925	1,744,000	K
1812	251,000	V	Dec 17 1926	2,025,900	Census
Jan 1814	161,986	IM	Jan 1 1929	2,313,900	IM
Aug 1814	170,424	IM	1930	2,469,000	K
1816	166,515	IM	1933	3,663,300	IM
1822	234,000	IM	1934	3,613,000	K
1825	241,500		1936	3,550,000	V
1827	278,305	IM	Jan 17 1939	4,182,916	Census
1829	303,599	IM	1940	4,536,000	K
1830	305,631	IM	Dec 1 1941	2,500,000	IM
1833	312,462	IM	1956	4,839,000	TsSU
1835	335,800	R	Jan 15 1959	5,045,905	Census
1840	347,224	IM	*Aug 1960	6,046,000	TsSU
1847	353,300	R	Jan 1 1961	6,208,000	TsSU
1848	349,987	IM	Jan 1 1962	6,296,000	TsSU
1852	336,538	IM	Jan 1 1963	6,354,000	TsSU
1858	377,800	R	July 1 1964	6,408,000	TsSU
1862	377,833	IM	July 1 1965	6,443,000	TsSU
1863	462,500	R	Jan 1 1966	6,463,000	TsSU
1864	364,000	S	July 1 1966	6,482,000	TsSU
Jan 12 1871	590,469	IM	Jan 1 1967	6,507,000	TsSU
Jan 24 1882	753,469	IM	July 1 1968	6,590,000	TsSU
1892	911,000	IM	Jan 1 1969	6,642,000	TsSU
Jan 28 1897	978,537	Census	Jan 15 1970	7,061,008	Census
Jan 31 1902	1,175,673	IM	Jan 1 1971	7,188,000	TsSU
Feb 1 1907	1,346,749	IM	Jan 1 1972	7,229,000	TsSU
Mar 6 1912	1,617,700	IM	Jan 1 1973	7,410,000	TsSU
1914	1,762,700	R	Jan 1 1974	7,528,000	TsSU
Nov 1915	1,984,000	V	Jan 1 1975	7,632,000	TsSU
Feb 1 1917	2,017,173	IM	Jan 1 1976	7,734,000	TsSU
Sept 1917	1,854,000	V	Jan 1 1977	7,818,000	TsSU
Apr 21 1918	1,716,000	V	Jan 1 1978	7,909,000	TsSU
			Jan 17 1979	8,011,000	Census

* Formation of Greater Moscow

Sources: S   Saushkin, Yu.G. (1964) Moskva. Moscow: Mysl'.
R   Rashin, A.G. (1956) Naseleniye Rossii za 100 Let. Moscow: Gos. Stat. Izd.
IM   Istoriya Moskvy (1954–59), 3–6.
V   Vydro, M.Ya. (1976) Naseleniye Moskvy. Moscow: Statistika.
K   Kerblay, M.B. (ed.) (1968) Les grandes villes du monde: Moscou.
TsSU   Statistical yearbooks published by Tsentral'noye Statisticheskoye Upravleniye.

Early Industrialization   At the same time as Moscow was gradually recovering from the effects of 1812, the city was experiencing a quickening tempo of industrialization. The Industrial Revolution had come late and slowly to Russia, but the first half of the nineteenth century saw Moscow's factory industry steadily growing with a clear predominance of textile manufacture. The opening of the Moscow stock exchange in 1837 may have given some stimulus. Much more significant was the opening in 1851 of the railway to St. Petersburg, Russia's first commercial line. This opening may be fairly taken as symbolic of the start of 'take-off' in Moscow's industrial development. During the 1860s the city was linked by radiating railways to Nizhniy Novgorod (modern Gor'kiy) with its world-famous fair; to Yaroslavl, also on the Volga; to Ryazan and the grain lands beyond and in 1869 to the Donbass coalfield; and finally, in 1870, was opened the trunk route westwards to Smolensk, Warsaw and Berlin. Moscow was now connected to the energy resources of the coalfield, to the grain supplies of the Black Earth region; its factories had rapid access to all the vast market of European Russia.

At the same time, the Emancipation of Serfs in 1861 commenced the process of freeing the peasantry from the bonds tying them to their villages. Initially, the heavy incidence of redemption payments to their former lords made it difficult for most peasants to leave their villages, but slowly at first and then in an ever-rising tide they began to move into the towns and into Moscow in particular. As figure 13.2 indicates, the rate of population growth accelerated after the early 1860s and this was almost wholly due to in-migration. One consequence was a marked preponderance of males in the population, an imbalance which persisted throughout the nineteenth century. From about 350,000 at mid-century, Moscow's population increased steadily to 911,000 in 1892.

Together with the greater availability of manpower went greater use of steam. In 1853 only thirty-one plants were employing steam power; by 1890 there were over 250. Correspondingly there was a marked increase in the average size of factory. The new industry and accompanying housing were spilling out beyond the limits of the Kamer-Kollezhskiy *Val*, especially to the east, but the built-up area was still very compact. Development of public transport was tardy. Only after 1872 were the first horse-tram lines constructed and the network's growth was painfully slow. Moreover, the fares of 5 kopecks per stage 'inside' and 3 kopecks 'on top' were still too high for most workers. The great majority had to walk to work. As a result the density of housing and of occupation of housing increased rapidly.

As important to Moscow's metropolitan development as the rise of industry in the city itself, was the evolution in Moscow's neighbourhood of the first Russian region of manufacture – the Central Industrial Region. This comprised a triangular area, stretching east and north-east of Moscow to the Volga and south as far as Tula, with some two dozen or more towns. The textile industry in all its branches dominated the region and naturally was closely linked to Moscow's own textile industry. As also in Moscow, metal-working and engineering were rapidly

FIGURE 13.3. Moscow in the 1880s; Okhotnyy Ryad (now Prospekt Marksa), immediately north of the Kremlin in the central business district (Photo Tass).

FIGURE 13.3. Moscow in the 1880s; Okhotnyy Ryad (now Prospekt Marksa), immediately north of the Kremlin in the central business district (Photo Tass).

growing, not only in such early centres of iron-making as Tula, but also in towns like Kolomna with its locomotive works. In all, the Central Industrial Region possessed 20.9 per cent of all factories in the Russian Empire, but they accounted for 38.1 per cent of production by value and employed 47.3 per cent of the work force in manufacturing [7].

Hand in hand with Moscow's industrial growth went expansion of its trading and commercial functions, not least as the focus of a prospering manufacturing region (figure 13.3). Gohstand has calculated that some 97,000 people in 1882 were engaged in trade, with a further 26,000 employed in providing accommodation, food and drink. This represented some 16 per cent of the city's population, a share still maintained in 1897 [8].

1890 and After

If the first phase of Moscow's metropolitan history was its emergence as the early capital, the second phase was its development as a major focus of industry and this stage had already been reached by 1890. The decade following 1890 was one of remarkable industrial boom. In particular, heavy engineering and machine-tool making flourished, although textile manufacture held on to first place. The number of factory employees reached 99,000 in 1900, while at the same time, the average size of plant was steadily becoming larger.

The expanding industries encouraged, and were encouraged by, another surge in the building of the railway network in the 1890s and the opening years of the twentieth century, which ended with Moscow at the centre of a spider's web of lines radiating out to all parts of European Russia and beginning to push out into the Asiatic parts of the Empire. By the time that the railway-building era was over Moscow had been given an unrivalled nodality, unrivalled even by St. Petersburg. In subsequent growth to metropolitan size and status, there can be no question that Moscow's position as national railway focus had considerable relevance, as it still does; in the 1970s about a tenth of the total freight turnover of the USSR was handled in the Moscow marshalling yards.

The spreading rail net, with all iron roads leading to the Third Rome, facilitated the ever-rising flood of migrants into Moscow. By the time of the first modern census of Russia in 1897, Moscow's 978,537 inhabitants represented eight per cent of national urban population. If the built-up suburbs adjacent to the official Kamer-Kollezhskiy boundary are included, the metropolitan area was already over the million mark. About three-quarters of the population had been born outside Moscow and seven out of ten were classified as peasants [9]. The imbalance between the sexes was still almost as marked in the 1870s, with women making up only 43 per cent of Muscovites.

The early 1900s were a period of economic recession for Russia in general, culminating in the disaster of the Russo-Japanese war and the 1905 revolution, during which an insurrection took place in the Presnya district of Moscow. Thereafter growth was resumed, notably in the metal-processing industries, which overtook the traditional front-runner, textiles. In contrast, the role of the textile industry in employment over the period declined absolutely and proportionately [10]. Nevertheless overall industrial production rose rapidly and, as it did so, the population continued to swell. On the eve of the Revolution of 1917 Moscow had doubled in size over twenty years and passed the 2,000,000 mark. Moreover, as more women migrated into the city to join the menfolk who had preceded them in search of work, the previous sex disproportion was evened out; in 1917 there were 982 women to every 1000 men.

The bulk of the incoming migrants were crowded into existing houses or into the appalling 'doss-houses', which mushroomed in the poorer areas of the city. Although public transport had made advances with the coming of the electric tram after 1895, the network of track was still very limited. This kept most of the population within walking distance of their place of work, with consequent overcrowding. On average there were nine persons per apartment, as against 3.6 in Berlin, 4.2 in Vienna and 2.7 in Paris [11]. Some flats had fifteen or more persons in them. In all some 70 per cent of Muscovites lived in the doss-houses, in overcrowded flats, in cellars or in sub-basements [12]. The health risks of such conditions were exacerbated by the very poor level of service provision by the town authorities. Even in 1913, a quarter of Moscow's dwellings were without piped water supplies or sanitation [13]. Outbreaks of disease, particularly cholera, smallpox and typhus, occurred almost annually.

If at one end of the scale, Moscow's slums were proliferating and breeding revolution, at the other end civic wealth was making its mark on the appearance of the city. Many banking, insurance and other financial and trading organizations set up their offices. Commercial success and municipal pride were reflected in the 'revivalist' architectural fantasies of the Moscow Duma building (now the Lenin Museum), the Tretyakov Art Gallery and the Upper Trading Rows on Red Square (now the GUM department store), among others (figure 13.4). Rich merchants built stylistic extravagances, such as those now serving as the House of Friendship and the French embassy. The relatively thriving commercial situation is indicated as much by these status symbols, as by the fact that in 1912 the city budget was larger than that of St. Petersburg, although the capital on the Baltic was some 10 per cent larger in population (figure 13.5) [14].

FIGURE 13.4. Building of the present USSR State Bank, Ulitsa Neglinnaya, built in the 1890s and designed by K. Bykovskiy (Photo Tass).

FIGURE 13.5. Kuznetskiy Most today; in the heart of the pre-Revolutionary central business district (Photo Tass).

Revolutionary Moscow

The onset of the First World War initially accelerated Moscow's growth, as industry geared itself to the war effort and as refugees and wounded poured into the city. But the outbreak of the Revolution in 1917 and the Civil War which followed it led to yet another major hiatus in development. Little enough structural damage resulted from the fighting, but the turmoil, the flight of upper- and middle-class citizens, the uncounted deaths through starvation and disease and, above all, the exodus of many hundred thousands of Muscovites back to their villages of family origin in search of food, all resulted in halving the population by 1920. Manufacturing came almost to a complete halt.

However, if the short-run effects of revolution on Moscow were wholly negative, the events of 1917 were, of course, the most important occurrence in the whole history of the city's acquisition of world metropolitan standing. In the first place, Moscow regained its former role as capital, when in March 1918 Lenin and the government moved there from St. Petersburg. Its formal designation as capital was confirmed at the First Congress of Soviets in 1922. Secondly, the Revolution brought into existence the first state in the world to try to organize itself on Marxist principles. Thus the Revolution simultaneously set in motion the processes of capital function and socialist exemplification, which together with the older process of industrialization have made Moscow a metropolis and which has given it its peculiar characteristics.

Nevertheless, the beginnings of a new era for Moscow were slow and exceptionally difficult. The socialist regime certainly made some immediate impact. The large houses of the bourgeoisie and aristocracy were sub-divided into dwellings for workers from overcrowded slums. Pre-revolutionary spatial distinctions of class or income groups were very largely swept away. But for the time being the principal concerns were survival and then recovery. The introduction by Lenin of the New Economic Policy, allowing private enterprise on a limited scale, temporarily put the fulfilment of socialist ideals into the background, but it did permit the rapid restoration of the city economy. By the 1926 census, the pre-Revolutionary population size had been regained and industry had once more started up.

Meanwhile people had begun to think about what the success of the communist revolution should mean in urban terms. The 1920s and early 1930s were a period of intense intellectual excitement and creativity on all fronts, and town planning was no exception. Indeed town planning and architecture were indissolubly linked with other aspects of the visual arts. Often artists and architects embraced each others' roles, particularly in the group of constructivists headed by Tatlin and Rodchenko, who were as much concerned with architecture as with sculpture and with urban design as with painting. For them the dawn of a new society had to be appropriately reflected in revolutionary art form, in new approaches to the use of materials and in concern with the fitness of town and building forms to the new social structures they envisaged emerging. Other architects from abroad, including Le Corbusier, were attracted by the exciting opportunities.

While expressions of the revolutionary era in the form of a limited number of individual buildings were being added to the urban landscape, some at least of the past was being destroyed. Some slum areas were cleared, but the shortage of living space as the population expanded past its previous level, meant that very little renewal was possible. Rather, it was historic buildings, especially churches which suffered. Although the Department for Museums and the Preservation of Ancient and Artistic Monuments, under the art historian I. Ye. Grabar, had considerable success in the years after 1917 in preserving and restoring historic buildings, by the late 1920s more and more of them were being pulled down, including the huge Spasskiy Cathedral [15]. The destruction began to die away in the later 1930s, although neglect and disrepair continued until the rising influx of tourists in the 1970s (and above all, the approach of the 1980 Olympic Games) caused a massive and widespread programme of restoration and reconstruction.

Other than the scattered buildings of forward-looking architects, the 1920s saw relatively minor changes to the appearance of Moscow. There was little redevelopment or expansion. But many were thinking about the future. The constructivists and others were full of plans for the capital of the new, planned society. Two opposed schools of thought had already evolved in pre-Revolutionary times. On the one hand were the classical planners; this view stressed urban living and from there went on to communal living, as exemplified in the schemes of L. Sabsovich and I. Leonidov. On the other side were the disurbanists, or deurbanists, who derived their thinking in large measure from Ebenezer Howard and the Garden City ideas developed in England. The Russian branch of the Society of Garden Cities, founded in St. Petersburg in 1913, had lapsed in 1918, but was refounded in 1922 [16]. The deurbanists' ideas went beyond the Garden City to the total disintegration of towns and even distribution of population along roads, which would provide access by vehicle to spaced-out work centres, as in the 'Green Town' plan for Moscow devised by M. Ginzburg and M. Barshch in 1930 [17]. In 1923 an actual, if small, beginning of deurbanization was made in laying out the Sokol suburb of cottages, designed by N. V. Markovnikov; some of the cottages still survive [18].

Other views and plans for the focus of the new social order were intermediate between the extreme positions of deurbanists and communal urbanists. The eclectic A. V. Shchusev, designer of Lenin's Mausoleum on the Red Square, envisaged a rebuilt Moscow core, combining preservation of many of the historic buildings with abundant greenery, but his scheme made little allowance for growth [19]. Much more in keeping with present-day ideas of regional planning was the

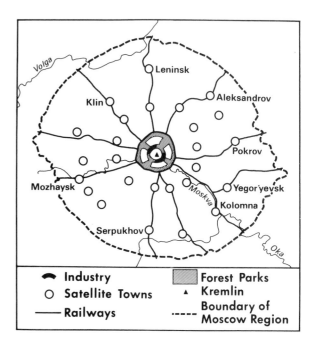

FIGURE 13.6. The Shestakov scheme for the development of Moscow and its region.

1925 proposal of S. S. Shestakov, whose scheme embraced the whole of Moscow Oblast and a double ring of satellite towns around the city itself. These satellites maintained the historic structure of concentric rings and radial routes on a vastly larger scale; Greater Moscow was envisaged as the largest city in the world. Within the city itself large forest-parks would separate the areas designated for residence and for industry (figure 13.6) [20].

Shestakov's plan, in some degree a compromise between urbanists and deurbanists, may well have influenced the constructivist N. A. Milyutin, who propounded the use of green belts to separate work and residence, but in long, parallel belts – his concept of the linear city [21]. Although Milyutin himself was chiefly concerned with completely new towns, his linear city theme of parallel strips of residence and industry separated by a green belt was adapted for Moscow by N. Ladovskiy, who envisaged Moscow growing 'open-endedly' from its circular historic core in a north-westerly direction along the axis of the Leningrad Prospect and Leningrad Chausee. This road axis would be a service zone, flanked by housing areas either side, which in turn would have belts of industry beyond them, giving way finally to outer zones of agricultural activity (figure 13.7) [22].

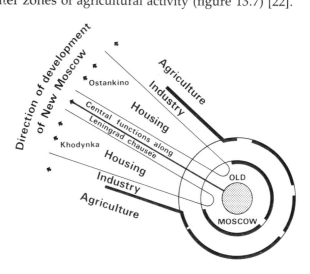

FIGURE 13.7. Ladovskiy's linear scheme for the development of Moscow.

Exciting, even visionary, as were many of these early ideas on the way that a socialist metropolis should be designed, in practice little or nothing was achieved. Some aspects of the linear city concept have survived in subsequent town planning, notably the idea of separating work and home by green belts, yet keeping them within walking distance of each other. Perhaps one can see Shestakov's forest-parks in current concepts of 'green wedges' penetrating deep into the city core. The communal ideas of Sabsovich and Leonidov were developed by S. G. Strumilin into his 'micro-region' (*mikrorayon*), or housing neighbourhood with its appropriate services [23]. Although the aspects of communal living and break-up of family life envisaged by Strumilin have never materialized, the microregion as the basic spatial unit of town planning has remained the dominant feature of Moscow's more recent development, as it has in every Soviet town of any size.

Meanwhile, as the period of the New Economic Policy came to an end and the Stalinist regime took ever firmer hold, the planning hopes and ideals of the 1920s were crushed. The revolutionary architecture and plans of the constructivists, their allies and their rivals petered out in the early 1930s and in 1936 were officially condemned as 'formalist'. Kaganovich uncompromisingly told the 1931 Plenum of the Party Central Committee that all existing towns were now 'socialist', since the socialist revolution had taken them over [24]; it followed that utopian ideas of Sotsgorod, Socialist City, were unnecessary. Indeed utopianism became one of the derogatory words of Soviet terminology. The reality behind the change in attitude was the total, over-riding priority given by Stalin to industrialization through the early plan period, which lasted from the inception of the First Five Year Plan in 1928 until the German invasion of 1941 brought the Third Five Year Plan to a premature end, and which was then resumed after the war.

Moscow under the Command Economy

In the fulfilment of the aims of the plans for the USSR as a whole, the already existing industrial base of Moscow (like that of Leningrad) was essential as one of the principal springboards. Thus, despite the resolution passed at the 1931 Plenum of the Central Committee to suspend all new industrial development in Moscow, in fact under pressure from the powerful industrial ministries, the city's industries were vastly enlarged and reinforced by new plants. The weight of new growth was in heavy and producer-goods industries, to supply the needs of industrialization in the city itself, in the Central Industrial Region and throughout the country. Engineering established a commanding lead among Moscow's industries. Enterprises already established were enlarged and transformed out of all recognition, for example the 'Hammer and Sickle' steel works and the Likhachev Vehicle Works. The latter became the largest plant in Moscow and with its associated housing for its employees it formed a new district on the south-eastern outskirts. Other factories were wholly new, such as the ball-bearings plant and the Kalibr and Frezer precision instrument factories [25]. The industrial profile was greatly widened within the metal-working and engineering groups of industries. It is difficult to think of any other major city outside the Soviet Union, let alone a metropolis, where the growth of heavy industry began to play a significant part at such a late stage in its development

The huge industrial upsurge during the 1928–1941 period attracted a greater flood of incoming labour than ever before. In the thirteen years between the 1926 Census and that of 1939, Moscow doubled in size to 4,183,000 at an average growth rate of over 8 per cent per annum. This increase was achieved in spite of the efforts made to restrict the inflow in the 1930s by imposing a residence permit requirement and by the passportization of all Soviet urban dwellers. However, the attempt to check Moscow's growth was not entirely without effect and between 1933 and 1936 there was even a small absolute decrease [26], although one may well suspect that this was principally a result of the purges. To some extent Moscow's phenomenal rate of growth can be attributed to the needs of its capital role and employment in government offices. To some extent also, the very difficult conditions of life in the Soviet Union made Moscow, as the show town with fewest shortages, an attractive focus. But the basic reason was the imperative requirement of industrialization, which ignored all limitation on in-migration.

To industry went almost all the limited available capital. Infrastructure did not receive anywhere near an adequate share and the populace had no priority at all, whether in housing, food supply or consumer goods. Not even the work of government was reflected to any extent in new building in the mid- and late 1930s. Because so little housing was constructed, the massive influx of people was accommodated in ever more appalling conditions of overcrowding, which rivalled anything seen before the Revolution. Within the Garden Ring population densities reached 1000 persons per hectare, 259,000 per square mile [27]. The official city boundary was several times adjusted, but the rather minor changes lagged behind urban growth. The 228 km^2 of 1917 were increased to 234 in 1926, 285 in 1933 and 294 km^2 in 1938 [28]. The increasing discrepancy was mirrored by the growing share of the population of the agglomeration, which lived in the suburbs beyond the city boundary, 15 per cent in 1926, but 27 per cent in 1939 [29].

Although the idealistic and futuristic plans were now rejected as formalist or utopian, Moscow did in fact adopt a long-term development plan. Its compilation was ordered at the 1931 Party Plenum of the Central Committee, where it was stated that the growth of urban infrastructure was lagging behind population increase and that the lack of a guiding plan was 'abnormal' [30]. On 10 July 1935 a 'General Plan for the Reconstruction of Moscow' was formally approved. Its aims were 'to build and create high-quality structures for workers in order that the construction of the capital of the USSR and the architectural setting of the capital should fully reflect the grandeur and beauty of the socialist epoch' [31]. It called for the building of 15,000,000 m^2 of housing over a ten-year period and, at the same time, a limitation of the city's size to 5,000,000 inhabitants. Densities in inner Moscow would be reduced to 400 persons per hectare. City limits would be enlarged to cover 60,000 ha [32].

In practice the shortage of capital and the obsessive concern with industrialization meant that the 1935 Plan was largely a dead letter. Some central area improvements took place, notably the widening of Gor'kiy Street and the creation near the Kremlin of Manezh Square (now Square of the 50th Anniversary of the October Revolution). The Moskva and Yauza rivers were given some 35 km of granite embankments. But the principal consequences of the 1935 Plan were in the sphere of communications. First, with the large-scale use of penal labour, the Moscow-Volga Canal was cut, linking the city directly northwards to the Volga by a waterway capable of taking sea-going ships. The canal at the Moscow end became an axis for the location of new industries.

The second achievement in transport of the 1930s was the construction of the first stages of the Metro, Moscow's underground railway. Intra-urban public transport had improved relatively slowly in the 1920s. Tramway lines, which totalled 388 km in length in 1925, grew by only 20 km in the next three years, although the number of passengers carried per year climbed from 394 to 611 millions. By 1928 the bus fleet was only 163, carrying some 50,000,000 passengers a year. In the 1930s there was some improvement. By 1934 the length of tram routes had reached 532 km and in 1933 the first trolleybus service began operating [33]. Even so, more was needed in the face of the enormous population increase and the ever more complex mesh of journeys to work, as more and more factories were set up. In 1935 the first 11.6 km of Metro line were opened to public service, running from Sokol'niki to Park Kul'tury. Further work increased the length of lines to 26 km by 1938. The elaborately ornate and differing designs of the stations, with unstinting use of marble (in part stripped from the cemeteries of Moscow), statuary, stained glass and chandeliers, were intended to make a strong impression on the beholder. Whether or not one has aesthetic reservations, no one can doubt their success in making such an impression.

The most grandiose plan of all in the 1930s to signal Moscow's position as the communist metropolis was for a gigantic, towering Palace of Soviets, topped by a 75 m statue of Lenin, on the site of the Spasskiy Cathedral. The project never got beyond the drawing board and its designated site is today occupied by a vast open-air swimming pool. It might well be considered, therefore, that the 'palaces' of the Metro were the first real, conscious expressions of Moscow as the capital and centre of world communism.

Certainly by 1940 there was little else to mark a new grandeur. With over four million inhabitants, Moscow was one of the world's largest cities and undoubtedly one of the fastest growing, but its function was still primarily industrial. It seems unlikely that in any other major capital of the developed world at that time was the tertiary sector weaker. In 1940 industry engaged 43.7 per cent of total employment in Moscow [34]. Nevertheless the capital importance of the city must not be undervalued. In functional terms it had by then established several levels of central-place operation:

1.   as centre of a major urban agglomeration, with a central city in a suburban zone containing a large group of satellite towns, a degree of daily commuting, a green belt for amenity and an area of intensive market gardening for the urban citizenry;

2.   as centre of the Central Industrial Region, with considerable and growing industrial linkages;

3.   as focus of European Russia, to all of which it was connected by an excellent radial network of railways, backed up by rather less efficient waterways and roads, and to which Moscow was the major supplier of a wide range of engineering and textile products and from which the city derived its fuel and energy supplies;

4.   as capital of the Soviet Union, for which it provided the ultimate, highly-centralized node of planning, decision-taking and administration, and which it served as the outstanding focus of publication, education, research and design and as supplier of a number of specialized manufactures.

The Emergent Metropolis

No more than 1890, can the year 1940 be seen as any kind of turning point, still less as the end of an era. The momentous events of the previous fifty years were the progressive outcome of earlier historical processes. The most individualistic aspects of planning history – the theories and imagination of the 1920s projects – had faded leaving almost no mark on the city and little enough on later planning thought. As in 1890, Moscow in 1940 found itself in the midst of intensive industrial growth, although the city was already in the shadow of the Second World War, which was to be the latest in its 800-year sequence of catastrophes. The German invasion of 1941 reached to the very outskirts of Moscow; today a monument marking the limit of their advance is passed by visitors driving in from Moscow's international airport at Sheremet'yevo. Over 210 major factories were evacuated eastwards with their personnel; by 1942 industrial production was one-third of the pre-war level [35]. Many government departments, together with foreign embassies, were evacuated to Kuybyshev. By December 1941 Moscow's population was little over half its pre-war size and the remaining half were busy making and manning defences. Nevertheless, although a setback in the short term, the Second World War might well be regarded as the final factor in making Moscow the type of metropolis that it is today. The allied victory not only left the USSR clearly the second most powerful country in the world, but also made it the leader of a group of socialist countries. Moscow in 1941 was the inward-looking capital of the Soviet Union, of 'socialism in one country'; in 1945 it was the capital of the communist world. If, since then, some of the socialist countries have rejected Soviet leadership, the position of Moscow has remained that of a world metropolis, rather than simply a national one. To the four levels of central-place function in 1940, post-war Moscow has added an international regional level as the centre of the Warsaw Pact and CMEA countries and a world level as the seat of a government, which controls or influences most of the communist block, which sits on the United Nations Security Council as a permanent member with power of veto, and which has a final say in the events and developments of the world as a

FIGURE 13.8. Building of the Moscow City Council, Ulitsa Gor'kogo, as reconstructed in 1945 by Chechulin (Photo Tass).

FIGURE 13.9. Stalin period skyscraper on Ploschad' Vosstaniya; in the background, the television tower at Ostankino (Photo Tass).

whole. It is thus in the post-war period that one finds the blossoming of Moscow into a world-scale metropolis (figure 13.8).

However, in 1945 there was still much time to go before the city's geography began to reflect the status it had achieved. The first post-war Five Year Plan from 1946 to 1950 was concerned almost exclusively with the task of reconstructing the country's badly battered economy. Even so the aim of making Moscow into the show-piece of communism was not forgotten. Indeed, Stalin's megalomania gave its own special character to the city's development. The 'cult of personality' has left a mark on the visible – and invisible – fabric of Moscow as vividly clear as that of the Orthodox church in medieval times. Below ground, the building of the Metro continued; indeed, it had not ceased even in the war years. Above ground, the ponderously over-ornate architectural reflection of 'socialist realism', often known as the 'Stalinesque' style, culminated in the seven tall, 'wedding-cake', sky-scrapers. Vast sums were spent on a limited and quite inadequate number of buildings, whether public or residential, in a policy that was officially condemned once Stalin was safely dead (figure 13.9) [36].

The obsession with grandeur meant that by the death of Stalin in 1953 the overcrowding of the existing stock of housing was worse than it had been before the war. In 1926 there were 5.7 m^2 of living space [37] per capita in Moscow (as against the official planning norm of 9 m^2); in 1956 the space had shrunk to 4.8 m^2 per head [38]. Khrushchev on achieving power was faced with the same problem on a national scale and in 1957 put into operation a crash building programme, which has never since really slackened pace. Since 1961, 1,921,500 flats have been completed [39], although one must remember that over the same period the population has grown by 1,803,000. Already in the late 1950s new suburbs of housing were appearing all round the periphery of the built-up area, with blocks of flats usually aligned in strict rectilinear patterns, mainly built of brick, and five storeys high to avoid installing lifts, which were mandatory for taller buildings. Each apartment house was grouped in a quarter, which in turn formed part of a microregion. Microregions were grouped into a residential district. In theory, each microregion was provided with all services required on a weekly or daily basis – food shops, hairdressers, laundry, a club or cinema, kindergarten and school. In practice, the service provision often trailed long after the completion of the housing, a deficiency still frequently apparent. Similarly there has often been a prolonged time lag before adequate transport services to the new microregion have been organized. In consequence, the population served by the facilities of a microregion, or group of microregions, is often far greater than the optimum size sought by the planners, originally some 2000–2500 persons [40]. In fact, the term 'microregion' has come to be used very loosely for urban residential sections of widely varying size and level of service provision.

Greater Moscow

The sudden and very large-scale extension of Moscow's built-up area in the late 1950s was acknowledged in the creation of Greater Moscow in 1960. The new boundary was set at the Orbital Motorway (figure 13.10), thereby including within Moscow five of its satellite towns – Tushino, Babushkin, Perovo, Lyublino and Kuntsevo – as well as twelve urban districts and about 150 villages. Beyond the Orbital Motorway lies the surrounding Forest-Park Zone, an amenity green belt administratively subordinate to the Moscow city authorities (figure 13.10). Although over two dozen satellite towns already existed in the Forest-Park Zone, their expansion was now severely restricted and new industry was prohibited. As a result, new developments were pushed out into a more distant suburban ring, beyond the Forest-Park Zone, where accelerated growth began to take place.

The establishment of Greater Moscow and its green belt created the framework

FIGURE 13.10. Greater
Moscow and its Forest-Park
Zone.

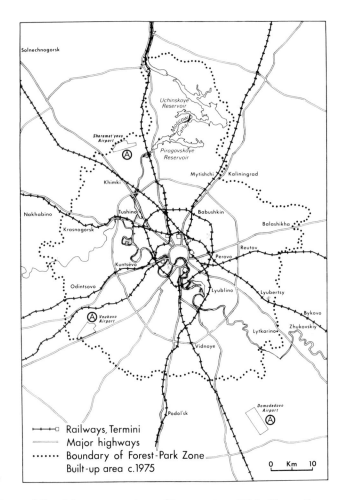

for the subsequent evolution of the Moscow metropolitan region [41]. Since then
the city has continued to expand its built-up area rapidly as the massive housing
programme rolls on. The building of five-storey, brick apartment blocks has given
way to ever greater use of prefabrication and standardization, in huge, monotonous series of microregions, while since the early 1970s more and more high-rise
towers have added a major new element to the skyline (table 13.2).

The outward sprawl to a very large extent was on an *ad hoc* basis, with new
microregions being established where they could be built most quickly and
cheaply. Often they were, and are, distant from places of employment. Yet
notwithstanding all edicts to the contrary, new industry has still been coming into
Moscow, such as the Khomotron factory which produces colour television tubes
[42]. Equally, the removal of environmentally undesirable enterprises out of the

Table 13.2. Percentage of total living space in buildings of different height.

No. of storeys	1966	1967	1970	1971	1972	1973	1974	1975	1976	1977	1978	1979
1–4	28.4	25.7	19.0	16.9	15.0	13.0	11.4	10.1	9.0	8.2	7.6	6.8
5	43.9	44.3	40.6	39.3	37.8	36.6	35.4	34.1	33.0	32.1	31.2	30.3
6–8	16.4	15.6	13.5	12.9	12.3	11.9	11.5	11.1	10.7	10.4	10.2	9.8
9	7.0	8.9	16.8	19.6	21.8	23.6	24.9	26.1	26.9	27.3	27.6	27.9
10–14	} 4.3	} 5.5	}10.1	10.5	11.8	13.4	15.0	16.5	17.4	18.1	18.8	19.5
15 and over				0.8	1.3	1.5	1.8	2.1	3.0	3.9	4.6	5.7

Sources: Moskva v Tsifrakh, 1966–70 (1972); 1971–5 (1976); 1979 (1979). Moscow: Statistika.

Table 13.3. Employment structure in Moscow.

	1940	1960	1965	1969	1970	1971	1972	1973	1974	1975	1976	1977	1978
Industry	43.7	36.4	33.2	31.0	30.3	29.6	28.9	28.5	28.1	27.8	27.6	27.4	27.0
Transport	9.9	8.9	8.4	8.1	8.1	8.1	7.9	8.0	8.0	8.0	8.0	8.1	8.1
Post and telecommunications	0.1	1.4	1.5	1.4	1.4	1.4	1.5	1.5	1.5	1.5	1.5	1.5	1.5
Building, including construction research and design	7.0	10.2	8.9	9.3	9.7	10.0	10.3	10.3	10.2	10.1	9.9	10.0	10.1
Retailing trade and catering	9.2	8.0	8.7	9.0	9.0	9.0	8.9	8.9	8.8	8.9	8.8	8.9	9.1
Housing and services	6.9	5.7	5.0	5.0	5.1	5.2	5.1	5.0	5.0	4.9	4.9	4.7	4.7
Health and social welfare	3.3	4.4	4.3	4.6	4.5	4.6	4.7	4.7	4.9	5.0	5.1	5.2	5.2
Education	3.3	5.3	5.7	6.0	6.0	6.0	6.0	6.0	6.1	6.1	6.1	6.2	6.3
Arts	0.8	0.6	0.6	0.5	0.5	0.5	0.5	0.5	0.5	0.5	0.5	0.6	0.6
Science	4.8	12.4	17.0	17.5	17.6	17.8	18.2	18.5	19.0	19.0	19.1	19.2	19.2
Finance	0.6	0.4	0.5	0.4	0.5	0.4	0.5	0.5	0.5	0.5	0.5	0.5	0.5
Government	7.3	3.2	3.7	4.6	4.7	4.7	4.8	4.8	4.9	5.0	5.0	5.0	4.9
Other	3.1	3.1	2.5	2.6	2.6	2.7	2.7	2.8	2.5	2.7	3.0	2.7	2.8

Sources: Moskva v Tsifrakh, 1966–70 (1972); 1971–75 (1976); 1917–77 (1977); 1978 (1978); 1979 (1979). Moscow: Statistika.

city has gone very slowly, although some divisions of the Likhachev Vehicle works have been shifted, bus-making to Likino-Dulevo and dumper truck production to Mytishchi. Large, heavy industry plants still remain, even in central areas. Nevertheless, Moscow's employment structure has changed considerably in post-war years, reflecting its burgeoning capital and metropolitan roles. By 1978 industry was occupying only 27 per cent of the labour force (table 13.3). Correspondingly education, scientific research, technology and design have become major employers.

Despite the 1935 master plan, the growth of socialist Moscow has been sub-optimal in practice. Pragmatic responses have been made to urgent needs; speed and economy perforce won the day over ideals. As a consequence a new plan was badly needed to channel the great expansion. In 1960 the Council of Ministers initiated preparatory work and research for a new plan. The capital should be 'planned to develop in correspondence with the general tasks of communist construction in our country and with the concept of Moscow as the principal political and administrative centre, the largest industrial node, the city of outstanding international and historical-revolutionary significance, the focus of science, art and culture' [43]. In 1971 a General Plan for the Development of Moscow was officially approved by the Central Committee of the Party and the Council of Ministers of the USSR. If the promulgation of Greater Moscow set up the framework, the 1971 Genplan laid down the future form of the metropolis, as it should develop for the remainder of the twentieth century [44].

The plan, for the first time since the Shestakov project of 1925, regards Moscow as a metropolis with a closely integrated metropolitan region. It seeks to hold the city's population at eight million and divert growth to outer parts of Moscow Oblast in more distant 'expanded' towns, although one may have reservations about the success of such a policy in view of the 1979 Census, which shows the city as already over eight million [45], and in view of the 1970s growth rate of 100,000 per year, with under a fifth of this attributable to natural increase [46].

Considerable emphasis is placed on improving the environment, with extensions of the forest-park zone, with the establishment of 'green wedges' of park and forest penetrating deep into the heart of the built-up area [47], and with improved control of air and water pollution. Already great efforts have been made in combatting the previously high pollution levels, with visible effects.

The city is to be structured on a new, polycentric basis, with eight development zones each of roughly a million inhabitants and each having its own zonal centre. Apart from special, occasional needs of service or entertainment provided by the all-city centre, a single zone will normally meet all requirements of residence, work and services. Each zone will be made up of three or four regions of 250,000–400,000 people with regional subcentres. These will be subdivided into 'living regions' of 30–37,000 population, which in turn will consist of groupings of microregions. Appropriate services at each level will reduce travel to a minimum. Land is to be used more intensively by more and higher tower blocks. Functional separation of land uses at the microlevel is to be made sharper, dividing industry from housing by open space, but the types of land use will be interspersed over the city area to minimize journeys to work. Each of sixty-five productive zones throughout the city will provide a local nucleus of employment. Massive expenditure on public transport will augment the Metro network by extended radials and a new, outer ring line, to achieve a maximum journey-to-work time of 30–35 minutes.

Conclusion

There is still a long way to go to the shining Moscow of the future and how far the Genplan goals will be achieved or how they will be modified remains to be seen. The year 1980, which put Moscow on display for the Olympic Games, is not an

FIGURE 13.11. Central Moscow and the Kremlin; right, the Rossiya Hotel, 1960s; left rear, Prospekt Kalinina, 1960s; centre rear, Stalin period skyscraper on Ploshchad' Vosstaniya (Photo Tass).

inappropriate moment to review the city's past and to assess any particular significance to it of the period 1890–1940 (figure 13.11). Clearly any half-century which includes 1917 is a period of prime importance in Moscow's development, but the given span sits awkwardly with the stages in the city's progress.

These stages, which are marked sometimes by sudden events or transitions to the next stage, sometimes by gradual evolutions, begin with Moscow's early role as capital, which was then largely (but never wholly) usurped by St. Petersburg. From the late seventeenth century dates the process of industrialization, which reached 'take-off' and very rapid expansion about the middle of the nineteenth century. This development, with its concomitant growth of an increasingly dissatisfied urban proletariat, eventually brought about the Revolution of 1917.

To present-day Soviet Marxists 'urban culture stands out as an important stimulus in the field of ideology and world outlook' [48]. Moscow therefore assumed not just political and cultural pre-eminence, but also a moral leadership. The city, in the eyes of those planning its future, should reflect the superiority of Marxist-Leninist ideology. From the utopian dreams of the 1920s, through the 1935 master plan to the 1971 General Plan, this has remained the objective. In practice, however, more pragmatic and often less desirable policies have been imposed by the realities of the times, war, Stalinism and, above all, forced industrialization. If there is any particular legacy of the 1917–1940 period it is an industrial one, although the process of industrial development continued unabated for long after 1940. Other processes of the Soviet period up to 1940, which have contributed to the character of this socialist metropolis, have remained operative to the present. These include the restriction on in-migration, which if far from fully effective in attaining its goals, has certainly prevented Moscow from growing even faster than it actually has; they include also the inefficiency and conflict of an unwieldly bureaucracy and divided responsibilities which have so often hampered the municipal authorities in achieving their aims for the city. It is in the continuing processes, both positive and negative, of a socialist metropolis that understanding of Moscow's development since 1917 must lie. As the capital of a huge country and as a great industrial centre, Moscow would in any case have become a significant metropolis; but its particular world consequence and its form and appearance owe most to the political system deriving from the Revolution, which in turn resulted from a prolonged period of social and economic developments. In the historical unfolding of these processes, perhaps 1917 alone stands out as date of key significance.

NOTES

1. This view was recently reiterated in: Lappo, G., Chikishev, A. and Bekker, A. (1976) *Moscow Capital of the Soviet Union*. Moscow: Progress, p. 65.
2. For industrial development in Moscow before 1917 see, for example, Saushkin, Yu.G. (1964) *Moskva*. Moscow: Mysl'; Livshits, R.S. (1955) *Razmeshcheniye Promyshlennosti v Dorevolyutsionnoy Rossii*. Moscow: Izd. AN SSSR; and particularly the six-volume *Istoriya Moskvy* (1954–59). Moscow: Izd. AN SSSR.
3. Saushkin, *op. cit.*, pp. 76–77 (see note 2).
4. For a full account, see Sytin, P.V. (1950) *Istoriya Planirovki i Zastroyki Moskvy*, vol. 1. Moscow: Muzey Istorii i Rekonstruktsii Moskvy.
5. Berton, K. (1977) *Moscow: an Architectural History*. London: Studio Vista.
6. *Istoriya Moskvy*, 3 (1954) *Period Razlozheniya Krepostnogo Stroya*. Moscow: Izd. AN SSSR, p. 162.
7. Livshits, *op. cit.*, p. 150 (see note 2).
8. Gohstand, R. (1977) The shaping of Moscow by nineteenth-century trade, in Hamm, M.F. (ed.) *The City in Russian History*. Lexington: University Press of Kentucky, p. 166.
9. Saushkin, *op. cit.*, p. 79 (see note 2).
10. Vodarskiy, Ye.Ye. (1973) *Naseleniye Rossii za 400 Let (XVI-nachalo XXvv.)*. Moscow: Prosveshcheniye, p. 139.
11. Bater, James H. (1980) *The Soviet City: Ideal and*

Reality. London: Edward Arnold, p. 18.

12. Saushkin, *op. cit.*, pp. 160–1 (see note 2).
13. Bater, *loc. cit.* (see note 11).
14. Bater, James H. (1976) *St. Petersburg: Industrialization and Change*. London: Edward Arnold, p. 361.
15. Berton, *op. cit.*, pp. 198–202 (see note 5).
16. Starr, S. Frederick (1977) The revival and schism of urban planning in twentieth-century Russia, in Hamm, M.F. (ed.) *The City in Russian History*. Lexington: University Press of Kentucky, pp. 232–6.
17. Bliznakov, M. (1977) Urban planning in the USSR: integrative theories, in Hamm, M.F. (ed.) *The City in Russian History*. Lexington: University Press of Kentucky, pp. 244–51.
18. Miliutin, N.A. (1974) *Sotsgorod: the Problem of Building Socialist Cities*. Cambridge, Mass.: The MIT Press, pp. 5–7.
19. Kirillov, V.V. (1976) Idei rekonstruktsii Moskvy v proyektakh 20-kh –nachala 30-kh godov XXvv., in Yanin, V.L. (ed.) *Russkiy Gorod (Istoriko-Metodologicheskiy Ocherk)*. Moscow: Izd. Moskovskogo Universiteta, pp. 215–17.
20. *Ibid.*, p. 218.
21. Miliutin, *op. cit.* (see note 18).
22. French, R.A. and Hamilton, F.E. Ian (1979) Is there a socialist city? in French, R.A. and Hamilton, F.E. Ian (eds.) *The Socialist City: Spatial Structure and Urban Policy*. Chichester: Wiley, p. 10.
23. See Frolic, M.B. (1964) The Soviet City. *Town Planning Review*, **34**, pp. 285–7.
24. Bliznakov, *op. cit.*, p. 252 (see note 17).
25. See, for example, Skobeyev, D.A. (1961) Promyshlennost' Moskvy. *Voprosy Geografii*, 51.
26. Vydro, M.Ya. (1976) *Naseleniye Moskvy*. Moscow: Statistika, p. 13.
27. *Istoriya Moskvy*, **6** (2) (1959) *Period Postroyeniya Sotsializma (1917g. – iyun' 1941g.)*. Moscow: Izd. AN SSSR, p. 44.
28. Kerblay, M.B. (ed.) (1968) Les grandes villes du monde: Moscou. *Notes et Etudes Documentaires*, no. 3493, Paris: Secretariat Général du Gouvernement, p. 19.
29. Strogina, M.L. (1970) *Sotsial'no-ekonomicheskiye Problemy Razvitiya Bol'shikh Gorodov v SSSR*. Moscow: Nauka, p. 52.
30. Saushkin, *op. cit.*, pp. 156–7 (see note 2).
31. *Istoriya Moskvy*, **6** (2) (1959) *op. cit*, p. 44 (see note 27).

32. Yevstratov, N.F. and Matveyev, S.M. (1967) Razvitiye i rekonstruktsiya Moskvy v perspektive. *Izvestiya Akademii Nauk: Seriya Geograficheskaya*, **5**, p. 63.
33. *Istoriya Moskvy*. **6** (2) (1959) *op. cit.*, pp. 12, 29 (see note 27).
34. *Moskva v Tsifrakh 1917–1977gg.* (1977). Moscow: Statistika, p. 79.
35. Saushkin, *op. cit.*, p. 113 (see note 2).
36. See, for example, Il'in, M.A. (1963) *Moskva*. Moscow: Izd. Isskustvo, p. 364.
37. In Soviet calculations, 'living' space measures only reception and bed rooms and is roughly two-thirds of the 'useful' space figure, which includes bathrooms, kitchens, corridors, etc.
38. Bater (1980) *op. cit.*, p. 100 (see note 11).
39. *Moskva v Tsifrakh (1966–1970gg)* (1972). Moscow: Statistika pp. 51–2; *Moskva v Tsifrakh 1979* (1979). Moscow: Statistika, p. 75.
40. Frolic, *op. cit.*, p. 287 (see note 23).
41. Hamilton, F.E. Ian (1976) *The Moscow City Region*. Oxford: Oxford University Press, p. 41.
42. Lappo *et al.*, *op, cit.*, p. 74 (see note 1).
43. Barkhin, M.G. (1974) *Gorod 1945–1970: Praktika, Proyekty, Teoriya*. Moscow: Stroyizdat, p. 144.
44. Promyslov, V. (1972) Osnovnyye printsipy sovremennogo gradostroitel'stva i razvitiya gorodov v interesakh ikh zhiteley, in *Urbanistica Contemporalis*. Budapest: Aedes Scientiarum Hungaricae, pp. 391–2.
45. *O Predvaritel'nykh Itogakh Vsesoyuznoy Perepisi Naseleniya 1979 goda* (1979). Moscow: Statistika, p. 11.
46. French, R.A. (1979) The individuality of the Soviet city, in French, R.A. and Hamilton, F.E. Ian, *op. cit.*, p. 78 (see note 22).
47. Shaw, Denis J.B. (1979) Recreation and the Soviet city, in French, R.A. and Hamilton, F.E. Ian, *op. cit.*, pp. 119–43 (see note 22).
48. Kogan, L.B. (1976) Gorodskaya kul'tura i prostranstvo: problema 'tsentral'nosti', in Kogan, L.B. (ed.), *Razvitiye Gorodskoy Kul'tury i Formirovaniye Prostranstvennoy Sredy*. Moscow: TsNIIP Gradostroitel'stva, p. 6.

Chapter 14

The Ruhr: Centralization versus Decentralization in a Region of Cities

JÜRGEN REULECKE

IN this volume the Ruhr has to stand comparison with London, Paris, Berlin, New York, Tokyo and Moscow. Certainly, the Ruhr is one of the world's biggest industrial agglomerations, and to many visitors it looks like one huge city. However, the Ruhr cannot be regarded as a metropolis in the strict sense of the term, or not at any rate if we define a 'metropolis' as a gigantic, self-contained, hierarchically-structured and centrally-administered urban unit from which specifically urban influences radiate into its hinterland. The Ruhr has no centre and no unified administration. Even today, the region is divided up by ancient territorial and traditional boundaries. Important decisions affecting the planning of land uses, communications, and industrial and other economic development, are made outside the region. Düsseldorf is the main external location of power, but Arnsberg and Münster are also important. Basically, the Ruhr is a high-ranking but extremely decentralized urban area which can lay claim, at best, to only a handful of metropolitan characteristics [1]. It is an urban association, a city of cities, or an urban realm. To this extent, the Ruhr exemplifies the observation that giant conurbations do not have to develop into unified metropolises [2]. The process of urban growth permits other solutions.

This is not to say, however, that there has never been any chance of making a metropolis out of the Ruhr. During the course of the last eighty years the idea of removing the autonomy of the individual cities and creating a *Weltstadt Ruhr* (Ruhr metropolis) in their place has often been discussed. Indeed, various partial steps have been taken in this direction, the most important being the establishment of the *Siedlungsverband Ruhrkohlenbezirk* (SVR) in 1920. However, the centrifugal forces have won out – at any rate in the latest stage of the Ruhr's development that we are now going through – over the centripetal, integrating ones. Today, the only administrative institution acting for the Ruhr as a whole is a federation of local authorities known as the *Kommunalverband Ruhr*. Its responsibilities extend no further than environmental conservation, refuse disposal, mapping, recreational areas, and publicity. This body's loose organization and limited powers contrast

FIGURE 14.1. The middle Ruhr region in 1857 (from H. G. Steinberg, *Sozialräumliche Entwicklung und Gliederung des Ruhrgebiets*, 1967). Note the northward movement of the coalfield, as indicated by the envisaged deep mines in the upper part of the plan.

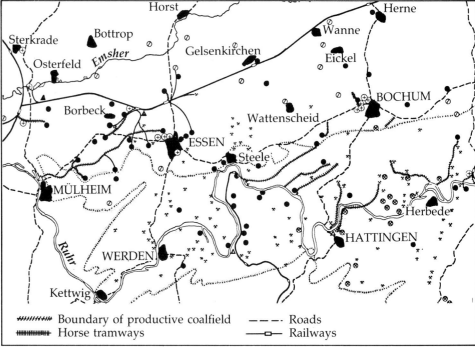

● Deep mines
⊘ Planned deep mines
⤬ Other coal mines
⊗ Iron ore mines
▲ Blast furnaces
⊗ Other mining sites

Boundary of productive coalfield —— Roads
Horse tramways —□— Railways

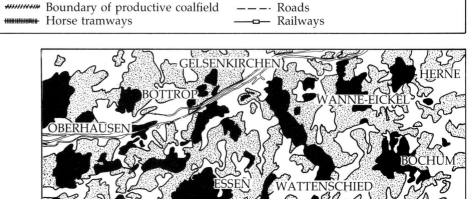

FIGURE 14.2. The middle Ruhr region in 1957 (from Steinberg [see note 4]).

built-up area in 1890   built-up area in 1957

strikingly with its constituency – eleven cities with a total population of around 3.6 million spread over 1680 square kilometres (2170 people to the square kilometre), and four districts (*Kreise*) with some 1.8 million inhabitants on just under 2800 square kilometres (650 to the square kilometre). The whole agglomeration thus contains nearly 5.5 million residents [3].

The other cities in this volume grew outwards, in that their cores came increasingly to dominate surrounding areas, threw out suburbs or incorporated existing settlements nearby, and constantly took on new functions and responsibilities. In the Ruhr an opposite evolution took place. Growth occurred simultaneously in a number of settlements, which burst their boundaries and grew into one another, producing a growing impression of a gigantic patchwork carpet. It came to look sometimes as though the whole area from Duisburg to Dortmund would be built up or in industrial use within a few years.

Origins and Growth

Although mining and metalworking were early established in the Ruhr, the real take-off phase did not occur until the 1840s and 1850s [4]. Outcropping coal had been mined on the slopes of the Ruhr valley since the Middle Ages. Systematic mining began in the late eighteenth century, with the coal shipped out along an improved River Ruhr, which at that time was the most heavily trafficked waterway in Germany. However, there was no question as yet of the beginnings of an industrialization process in the Ruhr, which contrasted in this respect with the neighbouring textile region to the south, along the Wupper valley. The decisive forward step came in the 1840s, when it became technically possible to sink shafts through the 600 metres of marl which covered the seams to the north of the Ruhr, and deep mining got underway. The zone of real industrial progress now switched north from the Ruhr valley to the parallel line of the Hellweg, an ancient trade route running from the Rhine to Middle Germany via Essen, Dortmund and Soest. From now on, the heavy industries became the key leading sector of German industrialization, with textiles sinking into a subsidiary role. This leap from a pre-industrial to a proto-industrial stage in the Ruhr was linked partly to political changes arising from the abortive 1848 revolution, but much more important was the rapid extension of the west German railway network which coincided with the beginnings of deep mining [5]. Railway growth provided a challenging opportunity to which the region responded in a number of important ways. For instance, efforts to produce coke from the bituminous coal won from the deep mines were successful at the end of the 1840s. Thus the final foundations were laid for the development of efficient blast furnaces and consequently of large iron, steel and engineering works. At the same time, the Ruhr urbanization process began.

Large-scale environmental planning was completely absent from the development of this Hellweg zone, as indeed it was from a third growth strip, the Emscher zone, opened up from the late 1860s by the continued northward spread of

FIGURE 14.3. The area of
the *Siedlungsverband
Ruhrkohlenbezirk* (SVR) from
W. Brepohl, *Industrievolk im
Wandel von der agraren zur
industriellen Daseinform
dargestellt am Ruhrgebiet*
(1957).

I   Ruhrzone
II   Hellwegzone
III Emscherzone
IV   Vestïche zone
V   Lippezone

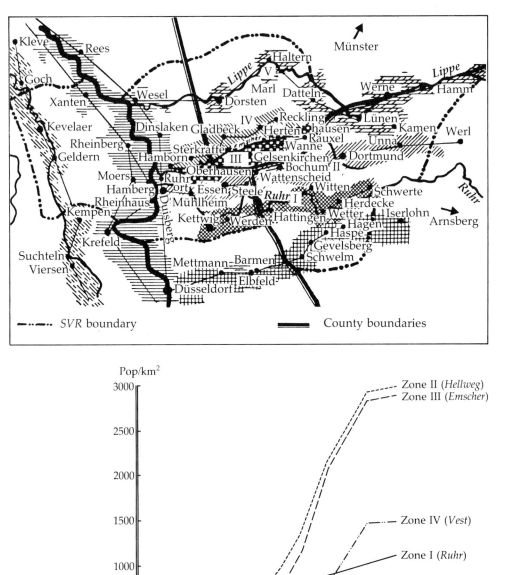

FIGURE 14.4. Increasing population densities
in the five Ruhr zones, 1820–1940 (based on
figures cited in P. Wiel, *Wirtschaftsgeschichte des
Ruhrgebiets: Tatsachen und Zahlen*, 1970).

coalmining. The characteristics of this early industrial concentration were dictated solely by the profit-oriented location decisions of individual owners, and subsequently of public companies, partly financed by foreign capital [6]. There were no large towns at first; until the middle of the nineteenth century the old-established Hellweg towns remained small, decayed communities, centres of handicrafts and semi-rural pursuits with virtually no central-place functions [7]. Their populations ranged between four and eight thousand, at a time when the textile towns of Elberfeld and Barmen, in the Wuppertal region to the south, had reached around 80,000 inhabitants. Meanwhile, the established villages in the Emscher marshes had between 500 and 1000 inhabitants each. The big collieries and iron works were established on the fringes of these small towns and villages so that, at first, their location was almost a rural one

Clearly, the region's existing population could not provide the labour force which this rapid industrial growth required. From the 1840s to the end of the 1860s, a first wave of migration brought 50,000 people into the Ruhr. It was, as yet, short-distance migration from nearby agricultural districts and former areas of domestic industry, where poverty now threatened. From early on, the employers started to provide housing for some at least of their workers, but such 'planning' as this involved did not extend further than the needs of the industrial concerns. Workers' colonies were built as close as possible to the works, since residence in such settlements linked the workers more closely to the enterprise, aided discipline, and discouraged rapid labour turnover. Furthermore, the colonies helped to integrate new arrivals from agricultural areas into an industrial style of life and work [8].

At first, the indigenous élites in the old Hellweg towns took a sceptical view of this industrial revolution. In the end, however, they integrated with the new, industrial, middle and upper classes. In the town councils, they exercised a growing influence on the continuing physical expansion of industry, to such an extent that some of their actions verged on planning [9]. These efforts were, however, confined to the individual towns. They did not relate to the industrial region as a whole, which was still gradually pushing northwards. Indeed, in the third zone, the Emscher strip, matters were completely different. So sparsely settled was this area at first that for a long time the industrialists found no established structures, or interests other than their own, to worry about. There was no upper class there, and apart from a few prosperous townfolk, and rural craftsmen, there was almost no middle class either [10]. In any case, during the last thirty years of the century these indigenous interests were drowned in a mighty wave of in-migration from the east, and notably from East Prussia. During the period of high industrialization some 800,000 migrants came into the Ruhr from the east [11]. They settled predominantly in the newly-developing northern part of the coalfield, which meant the northern districts of the Hellweg zone, but even more the Emscher zone and, from the turn of the century, a fourth zone – the Vestisch zone – where mining had meanwhile been opened up. There were a few model colonies in which the mine owners provided their workers with a small house, a garden and a stable. Most of the new arrivals, however, ended up in hideous, poorly equipped, and overcrowded housing which was thrown up in the shortest possible time with complete disregard for the pre-existing environment. Whereas, by the end of the century, some kind of urban infrastructure was beginning to emerge in the Hellweg towns, in the newer zones it was completely absent, so that there existed, in extreme cases, settlements of up to 100,000 inhabitants with the legal status of a village. By now, the Ruhr was regarded throughout Germany as a 'coalscuttle', an area of grime, noise and lowering skies. This image was based principally on the jagged landscape of winding towers, spoil-heaps, colliery buildings, criss-crossing transport lines and straggling housing areas which typified the Emscher zone [12].

It should be clear by now that at the end of the nineteenth century the Ruhr region lacked a unitary structure and did not even possess a single, dominating urban core. At best, the Hellweg strip might be regarded as a core *area*, but certainly no more than this. The situation was further complicated by the fact that between the cities of Essen and Bochum there ran, from north to south, the historic boundary between the Rhineland and Westphalia. When the whole region was handed over to Prussia at the Congress of Vienna, this boundary remained in existence, to the extent that the western part of the future Ruhr region was included in the Düsseldorf county (*Regierungsbezirk*) of the newly-created province of the Rhineland, whereas the eastern part was incorporated into the province of Westphalia. To add to the confusion, the eastern area was further divided between two Westphalian counties. The Gelsenkirchen-Recklinghausen area became part of the county of Münster, while the remainder, a larger area, was made part of the county of Arnsberg [13]. These administrative boundaries remain very significant today, as we shall see. In the second half of the nineteenth century, all three county presidents kept a jealous eye on the soaring economic significance of the Ruhr region, with a view to protecting their established interests and influence. However, their rivalry was paralleled by competition between the eastern and western Hellweg towns. Particularly prominent were Essen, which saw itself as 'the heart of the coalfield', and Dortmund, which clung to its proud tradition as a one-time free imperial city. Moreover, it was not without importance that the Protestant and Catholic churches of the Ruhr were organized from centres outside the region, their institutions conforming to the traditional boundaries. Particularly significant, however, was the fact that important economic decisions affecting the Ruhr were not made locally but in more distant cities. Düsseldorf was the main one, but Cologne and Berlin also had their say, because interested banks, and the head offices of numerous public companies active in the Ruhr, were located there.

Planning before 1914   Though fragmentation was the dominant feature of the Ruhr, early indications of a move towards comprehensive planning are to be noted before 1914. The size and density of the contribution required, in certain respects, a degree of cooperation which surpassed the individual concerns and local authorities, if only to ensure the Ruhr's continued economic growth. It was not only a question of industrial alliances, the most important of which was the Rhine-Westphalian Coal Syndicate, founded in 1893 [14]. Even more important were the mixed-economy companies and associations which were set up from the 1890s to provide important regional services like electricity and water on an organized basis [15]. These concerns emerged from a number of early agreements between neighbouring towns for the joint running of tram services. In 1899, for instance, the Rhine-Westphalian Electricity Company (RWE) was founded, with its head offices in Essen. At first this was a predominantly private company, but various towns were represented on its supervisory council. Gradually, they acquired shares in order to strengthen their influence over regional energy supplies [16]. More directly concerned with public welfare were two associations founded at about this time by municipal and private interests, the Ruhr Valley Barrage Association and the Emscher Association. The former worked from 1899 to maintain the purity of the Ruhr and to secure additional water supplies [17]. The Emscher Association secured the drainage of the whole of the middle Ruhr by building purification plants and upgrading the Emscher as the region's main outfall river into the Rhine [18]. For all this, however, cooperation between local authorities remained generally limited until 1910.

The main stimulus for the first – and only – assessment of the general situation of the Ruhr, and above all for the developing recognition that some kind of comprehensive, long-term planning was necessary, came just before the First World War. Its sources were the International Town Planning Exhibition held at Berlin in 1910, and, perhaps even more important, a similar exhibition held at Düsseldorf in the same year. Both exhibitions gave the public an impression of the objectives and the potential of modern town planning, as opened up by the work of Camillo Sitte, Ebenezer Howard, and others [19]. They demonstrated that artistic and human considerations ought to be decisive in the future planning of large cities, and that urban areas which in the past had often grown in an utterly anarchic manner might be transformed into organic units with inner districts of a clearly urban character, separate industrial areas, and green-flecked residential districts. Such calls for a transformation of German's cities had in fact been made since the turn of the century. They reflected a deep-seated determination to discredit the widespread pessimistic critique of large cities current in Germany at that time [20], and to put forward the large city, reconstructed on modern lines, as the 'pathbreaker of progress', or the home of a 'new man' [21]. The obviously harmful effects of the previous development of large cities could be remedied by purposeful planning and a pooling of efforts.

One result of the Berlin exhibition was an attempt to develop a unified planning concept of the Greater Berlin region and to use it as the foundation for the creation of a modern metropolis [22]. The Düsseldorf town planning exhibition also started senior administrators and politicians thinking about a Ruhr region which had grown up almost spontaneously, but which had now reached a point where there was no longer any denying that a number of extremely damaging features were present which, in the long term, could undermine the whole region. The Düsseldorf county president, Francis Kruse, was among those influenced in this way, and he took the initiative by drafting a plan for a 'national park' to cover the whole of the Rhine-Westphalian industrial area, with a view to conserving and, as far as possible, extending all the surviving stretches of agricultural land and forest [23]. A committee was set up, under the chairmanship of *Oberbürgermeister* Lehr of Duisburg, to finalize the details of the plan. Its remit was to draw up a programme for the system of green belts which would progressively be created throughout the industrial area. However, Kruse's authority was limited to the industrial areas which lay in Düsseldorf county, and the committee likewise had to restrict its attention to the area west of the old boundary between the Rhineland and Westphalia.

In the light of these difficulties, Robert Schmidt, deputy mayor of Essen with special responsibility for town planning, was given the task of carrying out a factual inquiry and writing a memorandum on the basis of its results [24]. Schmidt's Essen experience had given him an unsurpassed knowledge of the planning problems of the coalfield. In the past he had been particularly critical of the municipal boundaries of the Ruhr towns, which coincided with the limits of their planning authority and so acted like fetters, making any broader vision absolutely impossible. Certainly, all the larger Ruhr cities had extended their boundaries to include suburban communities, sometimes against bitter opposition, in order to give themselves greater freedom of action. Recently, however, this expansion had reached the point where, within the densifying regional settlement pattern, the large cities were rubbing shoulders with one another and were competing to extend their spheres of influence. Therefore, right from the start of his investigation in 1912, Schmidt regarded it as only a first step on the path towards a 'perfect big-city organism, fully conforming to the conditions of modern life', embracing the whole of the Ruhr region, including the Westphalian sector [26]. His analysis and prognosis led him, together with certain other observers, to the position where he expected to see the urbanized area of the Ruhr 'form one single, continuous city within a few decades' [27]. He thus started a debate which would rumble on for sixty years, until 1970 or thereabouts, over a meaningful 'integration of the whole Rhine-Westphalian industrial region' either through the establishment of one, huge 'Ruhr metropolis' (*Weltstadt Ruhr*), or by the creation of a new country or a federation of municipalities [28]. To this end, Schmidt drew up a 'general plan of the built-up area' (*Generalsiedelungsplan*) which virtually ignored the existing administrative boundaries. Of course, he expected opposition and counter-arguments, but he evaded them with the observation that in 'the age of the airship and the bird's-eye view [it was] no longer permissible' to argue from the worm's-eye view [29]. He wanted the State to intervene, since only the State could put right 'this deplorable state of affairs in the interests of the community' – a state of affairs which had arisen as the result of the previously tolerated profit-making ability of one interest group at the expense of another, the industrial workforce [30]. In the hideously depressing industrial areas with their shocking housing conditions, especially in the north of the Ruhr, 'it is possible to produce neither contented workers nor loyal citizens' [31].

Reactions to Robert Schmidt's sweeping opinions were predictable. They provided an early indication of the battle lines around which the later dispute over the 'Ruhr metropolis' would be carried on. Some were unsympathetic to the social criticism which underlay Schmidt's ideas, and which combined environmental planning and social-reform considerations in a single, contentious political issue. The Düsseldorf county president was more positive, but he rightly saw that any adoption of Schmidt's plans would have far-reaching consequences for the whole administrative structure of the Ruhr and that some venerable boundaries would have to be erased [32]. He utterly rejected the idea of giving such a shock to the existing order. For their part, the mayors of the big Ruhr cities were afraid of seeing their independence considerably reduced – and this was at a time when Prussian mayors ruled their cities like minor princes [33]. They also saw little point in the further discussion of Schmidt's ideas, the more so as the Zweckverband Gross-Berlins, a federation of local authorities imposed on the Berlin area by the Prussian government in 1912, had been rent by internal disputes and had quickly become a cautionary tale rather than an example to be followed.

This, then, was the situation on the eve of the First World War. Robert Schmidt's reflections marked him out as an outstanding authority on the long-term planning of large cities but they had almost as little practical effect as the social-scientific research which was being carried out in the early 1900s into the morphological, sociological, psychological and biological characteristics of large urban areas [34]. Indeed, Schmidt's memorandum would doubtless have mouldered in some obscure archive if he had not submitted it as a thesis at the Technical Highschool in Aachen.

When the war came it created new barriers between the cities of the Ruhr and their immediate surroundings. The cities vied with one another in their efforts to ease the deteriorating lot of their lower- and middle-class residents, principally by bulk purchases of food and domestic fuel, in order to counter growing war-weariness [35]. War conditions thus deepened the gulf between rich and poor, between town and country, and between those who profited from the war and those who suffered by it [36]. Moreover, divisions between neighbouring cities in the Ruhr were reinforced.

The Siedlungsverband Ruhrkohlenbezirk

At first sight it may seem surprising that despite the desolate prospects for Ruhr planning on the eve of the war, the return of peace was soon followed, on 5 May 1920, by the Prussian government's establishment of the Siedlungsverband Ruhrkohlenbezirk (federation of urban areas in the Ruhr mining district) (SVR). The SVR was statutorily entrusted with a series of important planning and executive powers. Later, this innovation would come to be regarded as the most significant 'organizational step towards a unified Ruhr agglomeration' [37]. It must be emphasized, however, that it was only the absolutely exceptional circumstances which marked the early days of the Weimar Republic that allowed the SVR to be set up. The reparations programme made it necessary for the German government to ensure the regular delivery of large quantities of coal over a long period [38]. Ruhr production was severely hampered by the effects of the wasteful exploitation of the mines during the war, lack of maintenance, and the departure of some 150,000 miners of Polish origin. It was decided to fill this latter gap by bringing in an equivalent number of miners from elsewhere in Germany, principally from Upper Silesia. With their families, they totalled some 600,000 people. None of the Ruhr cities wanted, or was in a position, to tackle this massive transfer problem. In the autumn of 1919, Hans Luther, *Oberbürgermeister* of Essen (and a future German Chancellor), working closely with Robert Schmidt, took up the idea of a special association of local authorities which would assume responsibility for the reception and settlement of the expected newcomers [39]. The exceptional character of the problem was reflected in the name, Siedlungsverband Ruhrkohlenbezirk. After various meetings between Ruhr municipal leaders, Robert Schmidt was given the task of drawing up the necessary legislative instrument. He used the opportunity greatly to extend the powers of the proposed federation, in ways which corresponded to his pre-1914 thinking. These included involvement in house-building, participation in the preparation of local street- and building-plans, the planning of the main features of the regional transport network, economic planning, and the direction of the entire open-space programme.

Schmidt's bill was drawn up in the winter of 1919/20. As time now pressed, it was voted *nem.con.*, and with only minor amendments, by the Prussian parliament in early May 1920. Parliament thus ignored the protests of many Ruhr towns about the infringement of their planning powers, Schmidt having made it rather too clear that in the future 'part of the sovereignty of the individual authorities [would have to be] transferred to the union of authorities' [40]. At first, the SVR covered seventeen municipalities and eleven rural districts; this meant a total of 346 local authorities with some 3,600,000 inhabitants spread over an area of 3840 square kilometres. Between 1920 and 1929 further areas were added, extending the SVR's responsibilities to an area of 4571 square kilometres and 4,200,000 people [41]. It included not only the urbanized core areas, but also the surrounding rural districts which looked towards the Ruhr. The SVR's assembly of the 200 members functioned almost as a regional parliament. Half the members were representatives of the participating city and rural district councils. The other half was composed of equal numbers of employer and worker representatives – a most interesting innovation. The seventeen-member executive committee was similarly constituted, with the director of the SVR taking the seventeenth seat [42].

From 1920 onwards the whole environmental development of the Ruhr was closely linked to the SVR's planning policy. Within a few years a far-reaching system of environmental planning was in operation. As ever, the county administrations, the municipalities, and local chambers of commerce and industry continued to complain about it. However, their opposition was offset by the admiration of urban scientists and planners both in Germany and abroad, who cited the SVR as an admirable example for other heavily populated regions [43]. However, the fact that the SVR's competence extended deep into the rural areas around the industrial core makes clear that the Prussian legislature did not intend it to be regarded as a first step towards a 'Ruhr metropolis'. Instead, it was a superior planning authority for an otherwise polycentric region. The surrounding rural areas were included partly because it was assumed that some of them, such as the Lippe zone, would sooner or later be swallowed up by the expansion of the industrial area, and partly to secure housing land and, even more important, recreational space for the growing population of the Ruhr. In this respect the Prussian government's approach to the Ruhr differed from its policy in the Berlin area, where in 1920 it finally converted the union of neighbouring urban authorities into a single city administration for Greater Berlin. In the Ruhr, the State, acting in a hurry under the pressure of economic and political circumstances, had set up a most unusual intermediate tier of government, drawing powers not only from the municipalities and districts but also from the superior county and provincial administrations, without any alteration of the existing local government units and boundaries [44]. Consequently, grounds for tension and conflict were built into the system from the start. In fact, the SVR could survive only as long as it had the support of the Prussian government.

Robert Schmidt was chosen as the first president of the SVR, and he held the position until 1932. Thanks to the support of the State, he was able to pursue an aggressive policy right from the start. The SVR's terms of reference incorporated the expression *Siedlungstätigkeit* (development activity). Schmidt interpreted this remit very broadly. Basically, he strove 'to shape the whole settlement structure of the Ruhr so that it reflects the stage that our civilization has currently reached' [45]. This meant drawing up an 'overall master plan, which seeks to equate the interests of industry, both above ground and below, with the demands of public health'. The implementation of such a plan, together with its associated land-use plans [46], thus involved far more than the simple technical control of building development, and bore heavily on economic, cultural and social conditions [47]. Schmidt thus merits recognition as a pioneer of comprehensive environmental planning in Germany.

The first task was to secure all the open land which was currently of importance or which might acquire importance in the future. There were two objectives here. One was to extend the existing residential and recreational areas, and other stretches of open space, while preventing residential development in areas blighted by industry. The other was to create so-called *Verkehrsbänder* (communications corridors) to permit rapid movement by motor vehicle, tram or local train throughout the whole of the Ruhr [48]. At that time, the road and railway network was in such an uncoordinated state, owing to the fragmentation of local government, that it used to be said that a journey from Essen to the Rhine took up so much of the traveller's time that his philosophical education would benefit greatly from it [49]. Subsequently all the arterial roads and the main radial roads of the urban areas were removed from the responsibility of the local authorities and classified according to their regional importance. This was done so that the first-class roads could meet at specially designated intersections from which second- and third-class roads could also branch off. The SVR estimated that the road network which the Ruhr would ultimately require would total 1660 kilometres, some 770 kilometres of which still remained to be built [50]. Most important of all, planning started on the sorely needed east–west motorway, the so-called 'Ruhrschnellweg', which was seen as the most effective means of easing the

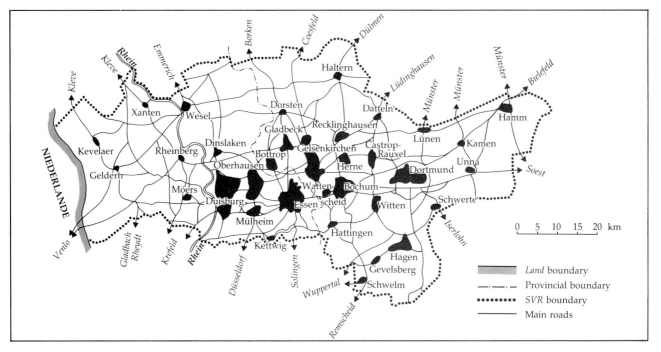

FIGURE 14.5. Main roads in the SVR area, c.1930.

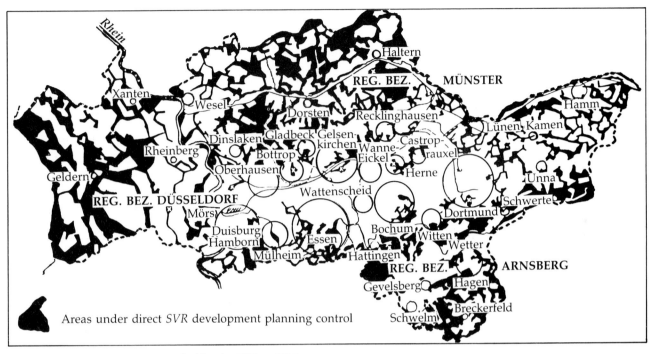

FIGURE 14.6. Open spaces controlled by the SVR, c.1930.

pressures generated by the growing volume of motor traffic in the area. At the same time, the SVR undertook the improvement of the canal system, promoted the unification of the dense but highly fragmented tram and bus network, pursued plans for an expressway system from Cologne and Düsseldorf across the Ruhr to Dortmund, and participated in the construction of three civil airfields at Düsseldorf-Lohausen, between Essen and Mülheim, and near Dortmund.

The 'communications corridors' were not only intended to secure the smooth and rapid movement of goods and labour, including commuters; they were also to link the residential districts to the inner cities and, even more importantly, to the recreational zones which lay just outside the industrial area. After transport planning, the securing of these recreational zones was the second main area of activity on which the SVR embarked in the 1920s. It secured development control powers over an increasing area of open land. At the same time, it acquired a number of large forests, and supported the municipalities in their purchases of open land. Further, it organized a programme of planting for disused spoil heaps, canal and river banks, and railway lines, and laid out footpaths. Later, it went on to establish country parks [51].

For Robert Schmidt, all these efforts were 'civilizing work of the highest quality, helping to bridge the gap between the classes and serving the common good' [52].

The social-reform overtones of his appraisal of the 'economic and cultural significance' [53] of the SVR linked back directly to his pre-war thinking. In one respect, however, he made a break with his past. His experiences in the establishment and the early development of the SVR had persuaded him to set aside all ideas of working towards one huge 'Ruhr metropolis'. Instead, he now looked forward to the creation of a *Grosskreis* (super-county) as the optimal settlement form for the Ruhr. By *Grosskreis* he understood an entity which would exercise many of the functions of a large city authority; for instance it would direct economic planning for the whole of the Ruhr, would conserve and enhance its productive unity with particular respect to taxation revenues, and, above all, would provide central finance for all activities which surpassed the boundaries of the component local authorities. However, it would function, 'not in the form of a compact, concentric and radially developed city', but 'in a scattered form emerging naturally from the actual requirements of the whole area' [54]. Schmidt returned to these ideas, despite strong protests from a number of Ruhr mayors, in the later 1920s when there was discussion of a reform of local government boundaries within the industrial core. Schmidt knew that his super-county idea had so far been a failure, so he proposed an interim solution in the form of a division of the industrial zone into four spheres of interest (*Interessenscheiben*) centred on large cities: West (Duisburg), Middle (Essen), Mark (Bochum), and East (Dortmund) [55]. These should be surrounded, he felt, by enlarged, and more powerful, districts. Schmidt echoed the Prussian government in rejecting the idea of a single, giant city from Duisburg to Dortmund, even though it had once again secured support in some quarters. According to Schmidt, the region was 'now much too large to be administered as a single city' [56]. In contrast to Greater Berlin, the Ruhr region should be composed of a large number of independent authorities, none of which should occupy so focal a position that it could act as a centre for a 'Ruhr metropolis' [57]. Instead, Schmidt saw the Hellweg cities as 'mature urban units' which could jointly take over leading positions, in association with nearby medium-sized towns, within spheres of interest which had expanded from south to north over the years [58]. In the long term, Schmidt hoped that the serious structural deficiencies of the Emscher zone would be overcome by its association with the well-equipped Hellweg cities.

The law of 29 July 1929 on local government reorganization in the Rhine-Westphalian industrial area incorporated a number of Schmidt's proposals. For instance, the boundaries of the districts were altered so that they no longer penetrated into the industrial core. The number of local authorities in the SVR area, which on the eve of the law had numbered twenty municipalities and nine districts, was reduced to seventeen of the former and five of the latter. On the other hand, there was very little north-south linking of districts developed in different phases of the Ruhr's growth, and in those cases where it was undertaken, it mostly had a southward emphasis, with the Hellweg zone being linked to the Ruhr valley rather than to the Emscher zone [59]. A number of municipal boundary extensions and mergers of municipalities were included, but the Prussian government showed no inclination to Schmidt's idea of creating a number of dominant centres within the Ruhr. On the contrary, strong political motives directed it towards a policy of decentralization. This point was emphasized in the preamble to the law, which pointed out that growing communities reinforced feelings of local patriotism among their residents, and that from a political point of view these sentiments were well worth encouraging. This was because, the preamble went on, local patriotism was 'an important pre-condition of cooperation in the tasks of the local community, and of even greater significance for the awakening, encouragement and development of a sense of civic responsibility' [60]. There was an echo of the earlier thinking of Freiherr vom Stein and Rudolf Gneist in the importance attached to direct involvement by the citizens in local government, as a defence against the growing power of paid officials in large cities, and the consequent exclusion of the public from the decision-making process. The idea of a Ruhr metropolis had no chance in this atmosphere [61]. Schmidt criticized the concessions made to these powerful political considerations. Nevertheless, he welcomed the reorganization, for all its deficiencies, as an opportunity to 'carry through a consistent and beneficial reconstruction of Germany's most important industrial region' [62]. He was encouraged in this view by the fact that the law explicitly confirmed the powers of the SVR and extended its boundaries.

The Triumph of Decentralization, 1929–79

For all Schmidt's optimism, there were plenty of signs that the future would not favour a further integration of the Ruhr region. State advocacy of decentralization was accompanied by a growing uneasiness, shared by the county presidents and certain municipal leaders, about the increasingly pervasive role of the SVR. In the more heated political atmosphere which set in from the early 1930s the SVR found itself subject to criticisms of growing severity. Robert Schmidt was particularly in the firing line, partly because he attracted politically-motivated attacks [63], and when he came to the end of his term of office in 1932 his presidency was not renewed. The resulting power vacuum within the SVR was a gift to the National Socialists. Only a few weeks after Hitler came to power the vacant post was filled by a State commissioner, whose task it was to draw up a re-agrarianization programme for the Ruhr, to break up big concentrations of industry, and ultimately to wind up a SVR which found little favour in Nazi circles [64]. For Germany's new rulers the Ruhr was a 'great storm-centre', and apparently a prime example of the kind of 'unhealthy concentration' singled out by Hitler in his attacks on the large city [65]. In *Mein Kampf*, Hitler had contrasted what he claimed to be the cold, rational tyranny of the large city, and its associated lack of *Kultur*, with the emotional links which bound the *Führer* to his followers. These bonds could not develop in the monotonous, soulless environment of the big city. Instead, Hitler called for towns of individual character, small and distinctive enough to be comprehended by their citizens. As for the physical arrangement of these towns, he wanted to see the 'whole townscape dominated by monuments', a reference to the distinctive 'symbols of the age' which were to be stamped upon them [66].

Experience soon convinced the State commissioner, Justus Dillgardt, that the SVR ought to be retained [67]. However, he wanted to use it as a means of implementing National Socialist policy for the distribution of population and economic activity. He saw a contrast between a Ruhr in which the concentration of population presented a political threat, further exacerbated by the dilution of its racial purity by Polish immigration [68], and the numerous thinly-populated regions of Germany 'in which a racial-cultural [völkisch] renewal could take place' [69]. It was not simply, therefore, a question of using town-planning powers to disperse the Ruhr industries; in addition, numerous workers – and, if possible, all footloose industries as well – would have to be relocated in the 'distant rural surroundings'. This resettlement would, it was hoped, halt the flight from the land and eradicate unemployment. For those workers who remained in the Ruhr, allotments would be provided. These would allow Ruhr workers to devote some of their time to work 'on their own land', and, in addition, they would help to reduce the amount spent on unemployment relief [70]. In this way, so the new planners believed, the Ruhr could gradually regain its original rural character. 'We need more than just a housing policy, we need a *settlement* policy', was thus the new motto [71]. As for those who could not be moved out of the coalfield, the official line was that they should use their half-acre to 'win their own share of Germany's great cultural heritage by the sweat of their own brows' [72].

As it happened, the population of the Ruhr nearly stagnated in the 1930s. However, further research would be needed to establish whether this was a result of National Socialist settlement policy or of structural weaknesses exacerbated by the world economic crisis. On the whole, the latter explanation seems more likely in view of the general failure of National Socialist policies to influence population mobility [73]. However, there can be no doubt that many SVR initiatives which did not conform to National Socialist objectives were abandoned. Even when continuity from Robert Schmidt's time was maintained, as for instance in sustained efforts to solve the communications problem, all long-term planning was pushed on one side until the outbreak of the war, and thereafter the urgent, day-to-day considerations of wartime ruled it completely out of the question [74]. The SVR ended up participating in a decentralization of industry made necessary by strategic rather than political considerations. It played an especially important part in the building of air-raid shelters and joined in the evacuation to rural areas of that part of the Ruhr population which was not required for the war effort.

Thus the SVR survived the Third Reich. The end of the war saw a return to an administrative situation which approximated to that prevailing before 1933, and immediately the SVR was able to take part in reconstruction and the formulation of long-term planning guidelines. In 1950 the *Land* government of North Rhine–Westphalia passed a law transferring the direction of environmental planning in the SVR area from the county presidents to the SVR itself. This function was confirmed by further legislation passed in the early 1960s. At the same time, however, a sometimes heated debate sprang up about a general reform of Ruhr government, involving the replacement of the SVR by an independent regional government. Finally, in 1968, the SVR president called for the creation of a 'Metropolis of the Ruhr' (*Weltstadt Ruhrgebiet*) [76]. This lively and controversial interest in a new planning strategy developed against the background of the coal crisis. In many districts of the Ruhr, collieries were closing because coal could no longer compete with much cheaper oil. Then, in 1967, the Federal Republic ran into its first general economic crisis, which marked the end of the German 'economic miracle' and threw the structural problems of the Ruhr into stronger relief. Ruhr local government reform was the subject of numerous plans and discussions in the early 1970s, and finally, in 1974, the *Land* government came to the conclusion that the best way of resolving the Ruhr's problems would be to dissolve the SVR and hand over its planning powers to the three county presidents. However, there had been some talk of replacing the SVR by a more loosely organized, less powerful organization, and it was this solution which was adopted by the law of 1 October 1979 which wound up the SVR but set up the Kommunalverband Ruhr (association of Ruhr authorities) in its place. Thus the Ruhr is further away, in 1983, from becoming a unified metropolis, than at any time in the last sixty years.

Conclusion

Taking the Ruhr urbanization process as a whole, the conclusion is unavoidable that the centrifugal forces have proved stronger than the centripetal ones, at any rate from an administrative point of view. The most powerful institution of integration, the SVR, could not maintain its position against pressure from the higher levels of government, particularly when the structural crisis of an overpopulated Ruhr became an increasingly threatening political issue owing to its exceptionally high unemployment. Indeed, these unresolved structural problems weighed heavily throughout the period, in the sense that the industrial composition of the Ruhr has always been dangerously narrow, while historic social-overhead deficiencies have continued to affect the area until the present day. The Emscher zone, in particular, remains backward in many important respects, and major differences persist between the north and the south of the industrial core in the provision of numerous tangible and intangible goods and services to the population [77]. On the other hand, it has to be admitted that – and not least owing to the efforts of the SVR – there has been much success in establishing the unity of the Ruhr in the eyes of its residents. Today it is perfectly possible to speak of a 'people of the Ruhr', with its own inherent characteristics and dialect [78]. A number of recent studies have shown that these people's communal loyalties are centred on their immediate neighbourhood. This means that very often they are attached to some small town or village surviving from the pre-industrial or proto-industrial periods, rather than to one of the much-enlarged cities. Their broader loyalty is to the region. Clearly, the melting-pot effect of the 'coalscuttle' and the common 'regional experience' of the last three generations have made their mark, and there has been no lack of foci for a common Ruhr consciousness. The well-known Schalke 04 football club is a case in point [79].

To that extent, the visitor is right in his impression that, however fragmented the administrative structure, he is in 'in effect, the biggest city in Germany' [80]. Admittedly, the Ruhr's deficiencies and unbalanced structure make it a very unusual metropolis in comparison with some of the others discussed in this volume. On the other hand, however, it has a right to be considered as the prototype of the 'polycentric metropolis' which the future may have in store [81]. Only time will tell whether the new swing of the pendulum towards 'black gold' will regenerate a move towards centralization in the Ruhr, or whether the loose association of powerful cities will persist.

NOTES

1. See auf der Heide, Ulrich (1977) *Städtetypen und Städtevergesellschaftungen im rheinisch-westfälischen Raum*. Köln: Selbstverlag im Wirtschafts- und Sozialgeographischen Institut der Universität Köln.
2. Compare, for instance, the Geddes-influenced development model in Mumford, Lewis (1938) *The Culture of Cities*. New York: Harcourt, Brace & World, Inc., esp. pp. 283 ff.
3. The figures relate to 1979 and are taken from the brochure, *Wechsel auf die Zukunft*, published by the Kommunalverband Ruhrgebiet, April 1980, Essen.
4. For a good overview of Ruhr history, see Först, Walter (ed.) (1967) *Rheinisch-westfälische Rückblende*. Köln/Berlin: Grote'sche Verlagsbuchhandlung, and especially the following contributions – Köllmann, Wolfgang: Von rheinisch-westfälischer Wirtschaft (pp. 127–71); Croon, Helmuth: Vom Werden des Ruhrgebiets (pp. 175–226); and Steinberg, Heinz Günter: Zur Sozialgeschichte des Reviers (pp. 229–74).
5. See Fremdling, Rainer (1975) *Eisenbahnen und deutsches Wirtschaftswachstum 1840–1879*. Dort-

mund: Ardey-Verlag GmbH; also Steitz, Walter (1974) *Die Entstehung der Köln-Mindener Eisenbahngesellschaft*, Köln: Rheinisch-Westfälisches Wirtschaftsarchiv.
6. Ipsen, Gunther (1956) Stadt (IV) Neuzeit, in *Handwörterbuch der Sozialwissenschaften*, vol. 9, Stuttgart etc., pp. 786–800.
7. On this point see Croon, *loc. cit.*, pp. 188–9 (see note 4).
8. For further discussion of the Ruhr housing problem, see Brüggemeier, Franz J. and Niethammer, Lutz (1978) Schlafgänger, Schnapskasinos und schwerindustrielle Kolonie: Aspekte der Arbeiterwohnungsfrage im Ruhrgebiet vor dem Ersten Weltkrieg, in Reulecke, Jürgen and Weber, Wolfhard (eds.) *Fabrik, Familie, Feierabend: Beiträge zur Sozialgeschichte des Alltags im Industriezeitalter*. Wuppertal: Peter Hammer Verlag, pp. 135–75.
9. Croon, Helmuth (1958) Die Stadtvertretungen in Krefeld und Bochum im 19. Jahrhundert, in Dietrich, R. and Oestreich, G. (eds.) *Forschungen zu Stadt und Verfassung*. Berlin, pp. 289–306.
10. Brepohl, Wilhelm (1957) *Industrievolk im*

Wandel von der agraren zur industriellen Daseinsform, dargestellt am Ruhrgebiet. Tübingen: J. C. B. Mohr (Paul Siebeck). esp. p. 20.

11. For internal migration and its significance for the growth of the Ruhr region, see Köllmann, Wolfgang (1974) *Bevölkerung in der industriellen Revolution.* Göttingen: Vandenhoeck & Ruprecht.

12. Brepohl, *op. cit.,* p. 21 (see note 10).

13. For the history of local boundaries in the Ruhr, see Wiel, Paul (1970) *Wirtschaftsgeschichte des Ruhrgebiets: Tatsachen und Zahlen.* Essen: Siedlungsverband Ruhrkohlenbezirk, esp. pp. 2 ff.

14. On this point see Schunder, Friedrich (1959) *Tradition und Fortschritt: Hundert Jahre Gemeinschaftsarbeit im Ruhrbergbau.* Stuttgart: W. Kohlhammer Verlag, esp. pp. 210 ff.

15. Schnur, Roman (1970) Entwicklung der Rechtsgrundlagen und der Organisation des SVR, in *Siedlungsverband Ruhrkohlenbezirk 1920-1970.* Essen: Siedlungsverband Ruhrkohlenbezirk, p. 10.

16. Fischer, Wolfram (1965) *Herz des Reviers: 125 Jahre Wirtschaftsgeschichte des Industrie- und Handelskammerbezirks Essen/Mülheim/Oberhausen.* Essen: Verlag Richard Bracht GmbH, p. 363.

17. Schnur, *loc. cit.,* p. 10 (see note 15).

18. Emschergenossenschaft (ed.) (1925) *25 Jahre Emschergenossenschaft 1900-1925.* Essen: Emschergenossenschaft.

19. See Steinberg, Heinz G. (1968) Geschichte des Siedlungsverbandes Ruhrkohlenbezirk. *Die Verwaltung: Zeitschrift für Verwaltungswissenschaft,* **1**, pp. 165-83; see also Pfeil, Elisabeth (1972) *Grossstadtforschung: Entwicklung und gegenwärtiger Stand,* 2nd edn. Hannover: Gebrüder Jänecke Verlag; also Lees, Andrew (1975) Debates about the Big City in Germany, 1890-1914. *Societas,* **5**, pp. 31-47.

20. Bergmann, Klaus (1970) *Agrarromantik und Grossstadtfeindschaft,* Meisenheim/Glan: Verlag Anton Hain.

21. Pfeil, *op. cit.,* p. 59 (see note 19).

22. Thienel, Ingrid (1977) Verstädterung, städtische Infrastruktur und Stadtplanung: Berlin zwischen 1850 and 1914. *Zeitschrift für Stadtgeschichte, Stadtsoziologie und Denkmalpflege,* **4**, pp. 55-84, esp. p. 74.

23. Steinberg (1967), *loc. cit.,* p. 167 (see note 19);

also Knopp, Gisbert (1974) *Die preussische Verwaltung des Regierungsbezirks Düsseldorf in den Jahren 1899-1919.* Köln/Berlin: Grote'sche Verlagsbuchhandlung, p. 249.

24. For Schmidt, see Steinhauer, Gerhard (1967) *Robert Schmidt: Lebensbild eines grossen Ordners.* Köln/Opladen: Westdeutscher Verlag.

25. Petermann, Hans (1912) *Die Eingemeindungen der kreisfreien Städte des rheinisch-westfälischen Industriebezirks.* Dortmund: Verlag Fr. Wilh. Ruhfus; for a general discussion of the boundary extension question, see Matzerath, Horst (1978) Städtewachstum und Eingemeindungen im 19. Jahrhundert, in Reulecke, Jürgen (ed.) *Die deutsche Stadt im Industriezeitalter.* Wuppertal: Peter Hammer Verlag, pp 67-89.

26. Schmidt, Robert (1912) *Denkschrift betreffend Grundsätze zur Aufstellung eines General- Siedelungsplanes für den Regierungsbezirk Düsseldorf (rechtsrheinisch).* Essen, p. 2.

27. *Ibid.,* p. 102.

28. Petermann, *op. cit.,* p. 153 (see note 25).

29. Schmidt, *op. cit.,* p. 92 (see note 26).

30. *Ibid.,* p. 91.

31. *Ibid.,* p. 30.

32. Steinberg (1967), *loc. cit.,* pp. 168-9 (see note 19).

33. On the role of the *Oberbürgermeister* in Prussia, see Hofmann, Wolfgang (1974) *Zwischen Rathaus und Reichskanzlei: Die Oberbürgermeister in der Kommunal- und Staatspolitik des Deutschen Reiches von 1890 bis 1933.* Stuttgart etc.: Verlag W. Kohlhammer.

34. See Pfeil, *op. cit.,* pp. 61-62 (see note 19).

35. See Reulecke, Jürgen (1975) Städtische Finanzprobleme und Kriegswohlfahrtspflege in Ersten Weltkrieg unter besonderer Berücksichtigung der Stadt Barmen. *Zeitschrift für Stadtgeschichte, Stadtsoziologie und Denkmalpflege,* **2**, pp. 48-79.

36. Compare Kocka, Jürgen (1978) *Klassengesellschaft im Krieg: Deutsche Sozialgeschichte 1914-1918,* 2nd edn. Göttingen: Vandenhoeck & Ruprecht.

37. So SVR director Neufang put it in 1968. Quoted from *Westdeutsche Allgemeine Zeitung,* 12 June 1968.

38. See Schnur, *loc. cit.,* p. 11 (see note 15).

39. *Ibid.,* pp. 11-12; Steinberg, *loc. cit.,* p. 171 (see note 19).

40. These words come from Schmidt's memories of the early days of the SVR; Schmidt, Robert (1931) Die Aufgaben des Siedlungsverbandes Ruhrkohlenbezirk, in Brüggemann, Heinrich (ed.) *Verkehr und Industrie*. Berlin: Reichsbund Deutscher Technik, p. 70.
41. Figures from Steinberg, *loc. cit.*, p. 173 (see note 26).
42. Schnur, *loc. cit.*, p. 14 (see note 15).
43. A number of these encomiums were printed as an appendix to the half-century celebration volume of the SVR, *Siedlungsverband Ruhrkohlenbezirk 1920–1970*. Essen: SVR, 1970, pp. 139–42.
44. Schnur, *loc. cit.*, pp. 14–15 (see note 15); see also Froriep, Siegfried (1970) Gemeinschaftsarbeit im Siedlungsverband Ruhrkohlenbezirk, in the same volume, pp. 134–5.
45. Quoted from a report by Robert Schmidt in 1932, under the title 'Die volkswirtschaftliche und kulturtechnische Bedeutung des Ruhrsiedlungsverbandes' (SVR Archives, Essen). p. 11. The following quotation comes from Robert Schmidt's article (1921) Das Verkehrswesen im Rahmen des Siedlungsverbandes Ruhrkohlenbezirk. *Wirtschaftliche Nachrichten aus dem Ruhrbezirk*, 15 January 1921, pp. 86–87.
46. See Schmidt, Robert (1928) Grosskreis und Grossstadt, eine Frage der Überlegenheit der Siedlungsform. *Deutsche Bauzeitung*, no. 1929, p. 138.
47. Steinberg (1967), *loc. cit.*, p. 172 (see note 19).
48. Linden, Walter (1970) Verkehr und Verkehrsaufgaben im Ruhrgebiet, in *Siedlungsverband Ruhrkohlenbezirk 1920–1970, op. cit.*, pp. 49–75 (see note 43).
49. Quoted from Schmidt (1921a), *loc. cit.*, p. 89 (see note 45).
50. Steinhauer, *op. cit.*, p. 23 (see note 24); by 1926 the SVR had managed to establish 425 kilometres of communications corridors, which have remained of significant importance down to the present day (see Steinberg (1967), *loc. cit.*, p. 175 [see note 19]).
51. Cf. Pflug, W. (1970) Landespflege durch den Siedlungsverband Ruhrkohlenbezirk, in *Siedlungsverband Ruhrkohlenbezirk 1920–1970, op. cit.*, pp. 77–112 (see note 43); in 1923 36.8 per cent of the SVR area was unbuilt land under SVR control. By 1932 this proportion had risen to 39 per cent, and by 1966, to 54.3 per cent (*ibid.*, p. 87).
52. Schmidt (1921), *loc. cit.*, p. 89 (see note 45). This conception set Schmidt firmly in the ranks of the social-reforming town planners of the Weimar Republic, who were leading the movement from *aesthetic* to *social* planning. See Rublack, Hans-Christoph (1979) Städtebau und Sozialreform: Fritz Schumacher. *Die alte Stadt. Zeitschrift für Stadtgeschichte, Stadtsoziologie und Denkmalpflege*, **6**, pp. 136–55.
53. See the title of Schmidt's 1932 paper cited in note 45.
54. Schmidt (1928), *loc. cit.*, p. 138 (see note 46).
55. See Schmidt, Robert (1928) Gutachten über die Kommunale Neuregelung im Ruhrkohlenbezirk, in *Preussischer Landtag: Sammlung der Drucksachen*, 3. Wahlperiode, 1. Tagung 1928/29, Drucksache 2042, pp. 1376–95, esp. p. 1381.
56. *Ibid.*, p. 1382.
57. *Ibid*, 2. Wahlperiode, 1. Tagung 1925, Drucksache 1612, p. 3110.
58. Schmidt (1928), *loc. cit.*, p. 1382 (see note 55).
59. Schmidt, Robert (1929) Das Gesetz über die kommunale Neugliederung des rhein.-westf. Industriegebiets vom 29. Juli 1929 und der Siedlungsverband. *Rhein und Ruhr. Wirtschaftszeitung*, **10** (32), pp. 1041–7.
60. *Preussischer Landtag*, 3. Wahlperiode 1. Tagung 1928/29, Drucksache 2042, p. 1345.
61. *Ibid.*; similar ideas can be found, for instance, in C. Perry's neighbourhood unit conception, which was taken up by many architects and planners in the late 1920s. See Pfeil, *op. cit.*, pp. 343 ff (see note 19).
62. Schmidt (1929), *loc. cit.*, p. 1047 (see note 59).
63. Steinhauer, *op. cit.*, p. 27 (see note 24).
64. Steinberg (1967), *loc. cit.*, pp. 178–9 (see note 19).
65. On this point, see the SVR brochure of 1934, *Die Siedlungsfrage im Ruhrgebiet*, esp. p. 8.
66. Hitler, Adolf (1938) *Mein Kampf*, 330–334th edn. Munich: Zentralverlag der NSDAP, pp. 288 ff.; see also Bergmann, *op. cit.*, esp. Chapter 3 (see note 20); Petsch, Joachim (1976) *Baukunst und Stadtplanung im Dritten Reich*, Munich/Vienna: Carl Hanser Verlag; also Thies, Jochen (1978) Nationalsozialistische Städteplanung: 'Die Führerstädte'. *Die alte Stadt*, **5**, pp. 23–38.
67. Steinberg (1967), *loc. cit.*, p. 179 (see note 19); see also the memorandum by Dillgardt, Justus

(1935) *Das Ruhrgebiet fordert die Erhaltung des Siedlungsverbandes.* Essen: Siedlungsverband Ruhrkohlenbezirk.

68. The strong Communist presence in city councils at the end of the Weimar Republic, especially in the Emscher zone, is discussed in Herlemann, Beatrix (1977) *Kommunalpolitik der KPD im Ruhrgebiet 1924–1933.* Wuppertal: Peter Hammer Verlag.

69. SVR (1934), *op. cit.*, p. 9 (see note 65).

70. *Ibid.*, p. 37.

71. *Ibid.*, pp. 36–37.

72. *Ibid.*, p. 51.

73. Matzerath, Horst (1978) Nationalsozialistische Kommunalpolitik: Anspruch und Realität, *Die alte Stadt*, **5**, pp. 1–22, esp. p. 18.

74. Steinberg (1967), *loc. cit.*, p. 182 (see note 19).

75. Schnur, *loc. cit.*, p. 21 (see note 15).

76. See note 37; also, Weltstadt Ruhr: das Ende einer Utopie. *Ruhrwirtschaft*, **11**, 1970, p. 404.

77. For further discussions of this problem, see Landwehrmann, Friedrich (1980) *Europas Revier: das Ruhrgebiet gestern, heute, morgen.* Düsseldorf: Droste Verlag.

78. Brepohl, *op. cit.* (see note 10).

79. Cf. esp. Gehrmann, Siegfried (1978) Fussball in einer Industrieregion: das Beispiel F. C. Schalke 04, in Reulecke and Weber, *op. cit.*, pp. 377–98 (see note 8).

80. See e.g. Schneider, Wolf (1960) *Überall ist Babylon: die Stadt als Schicksal des Menschen von Ur bis Utopia.* Düsseldorf: Econ Verlag, p. 356.

81. Froriep, *loc. cit.*, p. 135 (see note 44).

Chapter 15

Metropolitanism as a Way of Life: the Case of Tokyo, 1868–1930

SHUN-ICHI J. WATANABE

URBAN planning, which seems to dominate the contemporary Western World, is the product of the socio-historical conditions of late-nineteenth-century Europe and America. Nowhere is this more true than in the attitudes towards the planning of the metropolis. By the 1890s, the ever-growing metropolis was seen not only as an inescapable phenomenon but also as a menace to the physical, social, and even political welfare of the people living there. It was to tackle the 'metropolitan problem' that urban planning was institutionalized as a social system, and thus it acquired a hereditary, built-in 'anti-metropolitan' bias. This early planning system was the most strongly supported by the then emerging middle-class who, with increasing political power, wanted to move out into a suburbia previously open only to the more affluent classes [1]. It is ironic that modern Western urban planning is so deeply biased by an anti-urban ideology.

A sharp contrast is presented by Japanese planning, to which the anti-urban or anti-metropolitan bias is virtually alien. Pioneering Japanese planners, with a strong urban tradition and centralized planning powers, tried to foster the metropolis rather than to discourage it as the British did or to dismantle it as did the Americans. Japan is one of those rare cases in which the metropolis is still alive and doing well at the functional as well as the ideological level.

With this contrast in mind, a general history of Tokyo's metropolitan development is presented as a case study for international comparison [2]. The uniquely individual character of the Japanese planning system can be understood through a study of the attitudes of modern Japanese planning to metropolitan development and its effects thereon, and by identifying the socio-historical factors determining these attitudes and effects.

Although neither Japan nor Tokyo has thus far established authoritatively the historical subdivisions of its planning history, five major periods can be identified: Pre-Modern (until 1868), Meiji (1868–1912), Taisho-Early Showa (1912–30), War-time (1930–45), and Post-War [3]. This periodization differs from that commonly applied to Western countries, which complicates international comparison.

For instance, in the 1890s, when the metropolis began to be questioned in Western countries, modern Tokyo's population was still no larger than the peak population reached by Edo in feudal times. It was not until the early 1900s that Tokyo began to grow beyond Edo's urban area into suburbs, and this factor was not acknowledged in the planning context until as late as the 1910s. Accordingly our main focus will be on the Taisho-Early Showa period, roughly corresponding to the 1910s and 1920s, when Tokyo's suburbanization, now proceeding apace, was related to Japan's emerging planning system. With this period as the core, a detailed analysis will be devoted to tracing the historical background back into the Meiji and pre-Meiji periods, and there will be a briefer examination of the 1930s.

Castle Town Edo, 1590–1868

For nearly a century, centring on the year 1600, feudal Japan was the scene of the building of castle towns all over the country; an episode referred to by Henry Smith as 'one of the world's great efforts in the planned construction of new cities' [4]. The outstanding achievement was the building of Edo by the new Shogun, Tokugawa Ieyasu. As soon as he moved into a small fishing village with a castle facing the swamp of Tokyo Bay in 1590, Tokugawa started a massive engineering project to level the hills and to fill the marsh in order to create a castle town of his own. In little over a century, the once isolated village became a thriving urban complex with a population of well over a million – an event unrivalled in the world's urban history. This pre-modern experience of living in and administering a large city had a major influence on Japan's modern attitude towards the metropolis.

Edo's phenomenal growth was the result of the *sankin-kotai* system, under which provincial lords (*daimyō*) were required to spend alternate years in residence in Edo. They had to maintain a huge retinue of their vassals in Edo as well as in their fiefs. These warriors (*samurai*), together with Tokugawa's own subjects, amounted to well over half a million. To support these consumers, many commoners moved into Edo and became merchants, artisans and miscellaneous labourers, totalling another half a million or more. In fact, Edo was the political and consumption centre of pre-modern Japan, in contrast to Kyoto as the imperial capital and cultural centre, and Osaka as the trade centre.

Edo, though the largest of the castle towns, was typical. The town itself was not enclosed by fortifications although the castle proper was defended by deep moats, thick walls, and stout gates. Its administrative boundaries (*shubiki*) extended four to six kilometres from the castle, but the actual periphery was blurred by the continued sprawl of Edo into the surrounding rural area. The far-flung urban periphery soon became the limit of the mature urban area. The concept of 'suburbia', as an entity distinct from the 'urban' or the 'rural', was alien to the people of Edo as, to some degree, it still is to contemporary Japanese.

The physical structure of Edo, like other castle towns, was characterized by strict segregation of land into three major areas: namely, the warriors' district, the

FIGURE 15.1. The urban structure of Edo in 1800, showing the extensive sprawl and the segregation into distinct social areas (source: see note 21) (reproduced by permission of Princeton University Press).

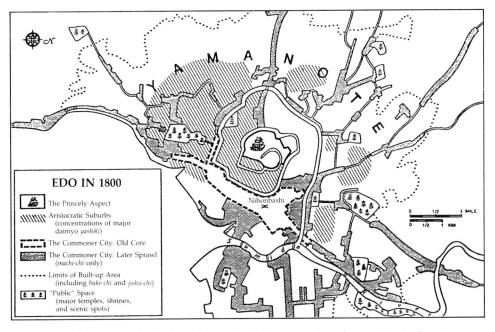

EDO IN 1800

The Princely Aspect

Aristocratic Suburbs (concentrations of major daimyo *yashiki*)

The Commoner City: Old Core

The Commoner City: Later Sprawl (*machi-chi* only)

Limits of Built-up Area (including *buke-chi* and *jisha-chi*)

"Public" Space (major temples, shrines, and scenic spots)

commoners' area, and the temples and shrines quarter (figure 15.1). Centring on the imposing Edo Castle, the warriors' area, with its thousands of estates connected by irregular streets, stretched over the hills to the south, west, and north of the town, the area generally called *yamanote*. It occupied 60 to 70 per cent of the urban area. The eastern lowland, with Nihonbashi as its centre, was laid out on a regular grid plan for commoners, where they lived and conducted their commercial and artisan activities. Over a thousand Buddhist temples and Shinto shrines were either situated in strategic locations or scattered over the urbanized areas. The commoners' and temple-shrine areas each occupied a further 15 to 20 per cent of the land. The population density is estimated as 600 people per hectare in the commoners' quarters and 140 in the *samurai* area [5], while the temple-shrine area was practically uninhabited. It follows then that the basic structure of Edo was composed of the over-populated commoners' area and the low-density warriors' district located side by side. Another characteristic of Edo is what Kawazoe calls the 'garden-mosaic city', as almost all the warrior estates, temples, and shrines had beautifully landscaped gardens with artificial mountains and ponds [6].

The Shogunate government was primarily concerned about defence. The commoners' area was subdivided with barriers and checkpoints at every major intersection, while the numerous T-intersections of the streets in the warriors' area helped to deny through-access to any rebellious forces. This mode is in sharp contrast to baroque planning which reflects aggression rather than defence, and results in long, broad avenues suited to parades and martial display [7].

FIGURE 15.2. Population growth of Tokyo since 1600, compared principally with London (source: see note 22) (reproduced by permission of Princeton University Press).

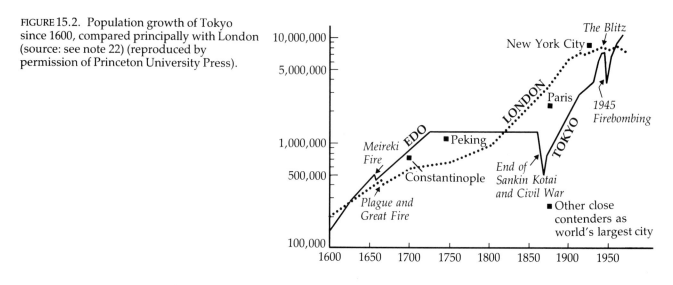

Fire was another problem. The density of wooden houses in the commoners' area made it particularly vulnerable to fire. During slightly less than three centuries under Shogunate rule, over two hundred major fires erupted in Edo. The worst was the Meireki Fire of 1657, in which over 100,000 lives were lost and the majority of the urban area was destroyed. Fire prevention measures taken after the fire included the relocation of *samurai* estates, temples and shrines, and the widening of streets in order to create fire zones. However, the houses remained basically wooden structures. This marks a sharp contrast to the measures taken after the London Fire of 1666. To commoners, fire was more or less an annual event. They were resigned to the regular loss of their property and quickly rebuilt their homes after fires. Hence, the Japanese traditionally regarded the land, not the house, as the only secure property.

Throughout almost the whole of the seventeenth and eighteenth centuries, Edo was the world's largest city, surpassing London (figure 15.2). In the eighteenth century, its population stabilized at well above the million mark, a situation which lasted until the Meiji Restoration in 1868. By the mid-nineteenth century, only London, growing rapidly owing to industrialization, had surpassed it among the world's leading cities.

Meiji Tokyo, 1868–1912

From Edo to Tokyo

Modern Japan originated with the Meiji Restoration. In 1867, the Tokugawa Shogunate returned political power to the Court and the following year the Meiji Emperor moved from Kyoto to Edo, which was renamed Tokyo and became the seat of the new government. The period of slightly less than half a century following the Restoration is known as the Meiji period. With the official slogan of 'a wealthy nation and a strong army' (*fukoku kyōhei*), the government strenuously sought to create administrative and social institutions based on Western models. The primary attention of public policy, however, was directed to rural society and its economy, as Japan was basically still an agricultural society. The urban concern of the Meiji government was discernible only in the nation's new capital.

The fall of the feudal system caused the exodus of the warrior class from Tokyo. Their former estates were deserted, with many converted to the cultivation of tea and mulberry fields. Most land passed into the hands of the Meiji government and became sites of government buildings and military installations. Some of the land was divided into small landholdings which were sold on the open market.

The *samurai* exodus and the civil war that followed the Restoration caused a decline in the population of commoners as well. Thus the total population decreased by nearly half a million, a figure nearly half that of Edo's peak population. The history of Meiji Tokyo is that of a city re-approaching and then surpassing Castle Town Edo in terms of population, urban area, and urban structure.

The economic base of Meiji Tokyo was government, although commercial and industrial functions were gradually strengthened over the years. As the centre of political power, the city attracted many ambitious youths from all over the country. It also became practically the only information channel through which Western civilization poured into the nation. The name 'Tokyo' was the symbol of progress and the city, the symbol of hope.

Tokyo's initial growth far surpassed that of early Edo, at an average annual rate of 30,000 or more. In the mid-1880s, the population for the wards area (equal to the later City of Tokyo) passed one million. And, when it approached the two million figure at the end of the Meiji era, first-generation immigrants were regarded as accounting for half that total.

This growing capital was not given strong local autonomy, not because the central government overlooked Tokyo's importance but precisely because a special importance was attached to it. After the Restoration the former Edo area was divided into fifteen wards, and was incorporated into the Prefecture of Tokyo, together with its rural hinterlands. Its governor was appointed from among the Home Ministry bureaucrats by the minister. In 1888, the national Municipality Act created the City of Tokyo, but this status involved nothing more than the election of a group of city councillors. Tokyo did not have a mayor, elected or appointed, officials, or even a city hall of its own. The prefectural governor carried out all mayoral duties from his own office. It was not until 1898 that the citizens of Tokyo finally obtained their own elected mayor. However, the municipal administration continued to be strictly controlled by the national government. This tradition of national control of Tokyo has been one of the strongest warps of Tokyo's history. To the government leaders, 'Tokyo was the State'. This tradition made it easy for the government to co-ordinate the interests of the various municipalities in the Tokyo region, and may explain why, in its later process of metropolitan growth, Tokyo did not face the serious conflicts with surrounding municipalities that Western large cities did.

Urban Problems and Policies

The immediate urban problem faced by the Meiji government was fire, which it inherited from Edo. The new government, for instance, was greeted with a massive fire which deprived 50,000 people of 3000 houses on 95 hectares of land in the downtown area in 1872. This led to the government's reconstruction prog-ramme of the Ginza Brick Quarters, to be described below. In 1881, the prefectural government issued an order restricting the use of hazardous building and roofing materials. Within a decade, the regular and devastating fires that had been habitual for three centuries were almost completely eradicated.

If this was a success story of solving Edo's problems by 'completing' Edo, as Fujimori puts it [8], the more challenging problem facing Meiji leaders was how to build a modern city by 'destroying' Edo. The urban structure of the former castle town was completely inadequate for modern use. Their strategy for the capital was radical surgery of the urban structure, not for the entire area but for certain areas or functions of crucial importance. The actual urban tactics, however, varied according to the needs and ideas of the leaders. Fujimori identifies three major groups of leaders, each with a distinct ideology and approach; namely (1) 'Europeanizationists', (2) entrepreneurs, and (3) Home Ministry bureaucrats [9].

The first group, composed of influential political leaders, including Inoue Kaoru and Mishima Michitsune, shared the idea that Tokyo should in no way appear inferior to European capitals. They tried to import and transplant Victorian London or Haussmann's Paris on to Edo's soil. They viewed the city as a structural form in terms of Western architectural concepts. Tokyo's modern (that is, European) appearance (but not necessarily function) would help them succeed in their long-term project of revising the unequal treaty with the Western countries.

One example was the redevelopment project after the fire of 1872, known as the Ginza Brick Quarters Project (*Ginza renga-gai keikaku*), 1872–77. Its primary purpose was to create a 'little Europe', or showcase of Western civilization, in the middle of Tokyo, although it answered valid fire-prevention and slum clearance needs as well. The site was a strategic location, surrounded by the Imperial Palace and government buildings to the west, by Nihonbashi, or Edo's downtown centre to the north, by a foreign concession to the east, and by Shinbashi Station (the railway terminal which connected Tokyo with Yokohama and, indirectly, Europe and America) to the south. Thomas Waters, an English engineer, prepared a plan for 993 brick buildings of two storeys with 9.5 hectares of floor space, one-third of which were actually built in subsequent years. The streets were paved with bricks and were separated into driveways and sidewalks, the first of their kind in Japan.

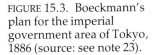

FIGURE 15.3. Boeckmann's plan for the imperial government area of Tokyo, 1886 (source: see note 23).

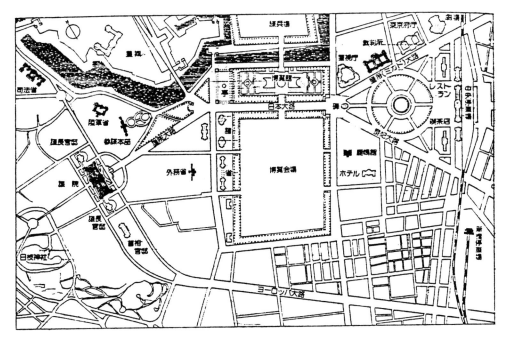

Horse tramcars and, later, electric streetcars rattled along; gas lanterns and, later, electric lights shone in the streets. Modern shops dealt in imported goods; newspaper companies began to cluster in the area. By the late 1870s, Ginza took the place of traditional Nihonbashi and became Tokyo's new commercial centre.

Another example was a project for a vast government centre at Hibiya, south of the Imperial Palace, now known as the Government Block Project (*kanchō shūchū keikaku*), 1885–88. British and German architects prepared several plans, among which Boeckmann's was the most famous. His plan envisaged a grand seat for the Imperial government in a dramatic baroque style (figure 15.3). None of these plans was ever implemented as Inoue, the initiator of the project as Foreign Minister, fell from power in 1887. In fact, the project was turned down by the Home Ministry, which did not approve of such heavy expenditure and wanted to deprive the Foreign Ministry of its absolute planning powers. Subsequently, this line of urban thought was gradually weakened as the 'European fever' began to fade around 1890.

The second group, the private entrepreneurs, had emerged by 1880 and included such men as Shibusawa Eiichi and Masuda Takashi. This group considered Tokyo as the home of its activities in manufacturing and business, and was eager that the economic base of Tokyo should become industrial and commercial, as well as governmental. In 1879, Taguchi Ukichi, a liberal critic, proposed to make Tokyo an international business centre in the Far East by building Tokyo Port. His proposal was accepted by Governor Matsuda Michiyuki and was incorporated in his plan for Tokyo, which later evolved into the Municipal Improvement (*shiku kaisei*) Programme. Shibusawa and Masuda sat on the planning committee for the programme, representing emerging business interests, and succeeded in obtaining the allocation of the Marunouchi area for office use. Although their plea for a new port was never accepted by the government, their concepts were often reflected in later government policies.

Thirdly, the Home Ministry politicians and bureaucrats, such as Yamagata Aritomo and Yoshikaya Akimasa, envisaged modern Tokyo in terms of its function, rather than its appearance. It was their conviction that the urban structure of Castle Town Edo needed radical surgery, in which they were assisted by the ministry's technocrats in civil and sanitary engineering. In 1888, they were successful in enacting the Tokyo Municipal Improvement Act after some twelve

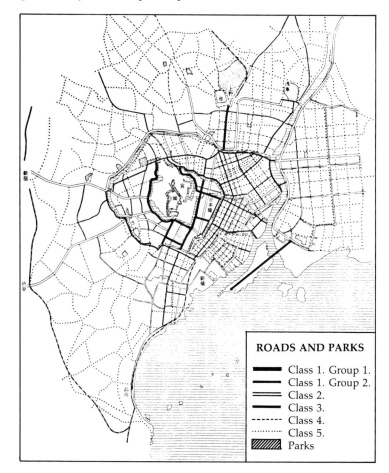

FIGURE 15.4. The Tokyo Municipal Improvement Plan of 1889 (source: see note 24).

ROADS AND PARKS

━━━ Class 1. Group 1.
──── Class 1. Group 2.
════ Class 2.
──── Class 3.
------ Class 4.
·········· Class 5.
▨▨▨ Parks

years of preparation. The plan, approved by the government in the following year, included the building or improvement of 315 streets, thirty-four rivers and moats, one elevated railway, many bridges, forty-nine parks, eight markets, five crematoria, and six cemeteries. Great efforts were mounted to build a network of major streets in the already built-up area (figure 15.4) and to facilitate waterworks for the prevention of epidemics. The planning committee discussed land-use control and building regulations but did not incorporate them into the plan. The curtailed and revised plan was practically completed by 1918. Japanese planners tend to consider the programme as Japan's first modern planning. In modern terms, however, it was no more than a large-scale, fairly systematic public works programme. The 1888 Act concentrated on urban infrastructures, and housing and environment were totally ignored. The Act also established the pattern under which the national government held the responsibility for planning and the municipal government (with some national subsidies) for the expenses of public works. This planning system was appropriate to the highly centralized power which produced it, and it had an immense impact on all subsequent planning concepts.

Changing Urban Structure
By around 1890, Tokyo had recovered Edo's peak population, but it was not until about fifteen years later that Tokyo expanded beyond Edo's urban boundary. These twin milestones are doubly significant. First, suburbanization finally started in Meiji Tokyo half a century or more later than in Western capitals. Second, the Tokyo urban area came to be more densely populated than that of Edo. The overpopulated inner city and expanding suburbia, however, were not to be related in urban policy until the Taisho era. Nevertheless, Meiji Tokyo was gradually changing the urban structure of Edo and preparing for the full-scale metropolitan development of later years.

The change may be roughly summarized as the diversification of Tokyo into three major areas. First, Edo's *samurai* district, located in the western area of hills, was turned into residences for the upper and white-collar classes, an area generally known as *yamanote*. Second, areas for government, business, and retail activities appeared in the traditional downtown and its vicinity. Third, merchants, artisans, and labourers found their places of work and homes in the downtown and its eastern periphery of marshy lowland, forming the area called *shitamachi*. Thus, Meiji Tokyo more or less determined the urban structure of contemporary Tokyo. All this change, however, was scarcely the product of overall planning but of the interaction of topography, existing land uses, transportation systems, and piecemeal government decisions. Moreover, such conscious urban concern as existed was exclusively directed towards the urban area, rather than the periphery.

Nihonbashi, Edo's commercial centre and the starting point for the national milestone system of Shogunate Japan, began to flourish as a 'downtown' in early Meiji days. In the 1870s and 1880s, Meiji Tokyo's new establishments such as banks, insurance companies, the stock exchange and the Chamber of Commerce were built to the east of Nihonbashi, forming the first business quarter of its kind. Fujimori names it 'Shibusawa Business District', as many of these establishments had some connection with the activities of the entrepreneur Shibusawa, who even built his Venetian-style mansion in the district [10].

The office district, however, needed a more central location. In 1890, the Mitsubishi Company bought 35 hectares of land in Marunouchi, east of the Imperial Palace and adjoining the future site of Tokyo Central Station. The area had formerly been occupied by warrior estates. After the Restoration, it had become a military parade ground and finally just a weed-covered wasteland. Mitsubishi planned to turn this wasteland into Japan's 'Lombard Street'. Four years later, the first office building was completed in accordance with the blueprints designed by Josiah Conder, a resident British architect. In the 1890s, many offices moved in from the 'Shibusawa Business District'. By 1914, when the Tokyo Central Station opened, there were over twenty of Mitsubishi's brick-clad office buildings, popularly known as 'little London' (*itchō Rondon*).

Thus, traditional Nihonbashi was somewhat left behind in the rapid march of Tokyo's modernization. It lost the retail function to Ginza, as previously described, and the office function to 'Shibusawa Business District' and then to Marunouchi. Wholesale businesses, however, remained in Nihonbashi and even expanded both northward and eastward. There, they mingled with small shops, family factories, labourers' lodging houses, artisans' tenements, slums, temples and shrines, and formed an area called *shitamachi* with a distinct atmosphere more or less equivalent to London's East End.

The Meiji government fostered the establishment of industries necessary for the construction of a modern capital. It built, for instance, model factories for the bricks, cement, glass and iron needed for building the modern capital. Private entrepreneurs gradually increased and took over these factories. The Russo-Japanese War (1904–5) provided the momentum for Japanese capitalism to establish itself. Small factories began to pop up all over the city, as there was little restriction upon them. Larger factories began to appear in the paddy fields and marsh lands of Kōtō Delta eastward beyond the Sumida River, where inexpensive land, abundant water, rail and water transport, and cheap labour were available and dumping waste was possible. For the same reasons, factories were sited on the low land upstream of the Sumida and Arakawa Rivers north of Tokyo. All these areas, extending to the future Tokyo-Yokohama Industrial Belt along the Bay, were to form a crescent circling central Tokyo on its eastern periphery.

Meiji Tokyo did not have adequate industry to absorb all the immigrants pouring into the city. Many of them lived in slums and had only marginal occupations, working as day labourers, coolies, rickshaw drivers, peddlars, and street artists. In addition to the old Edo slums, new slum areas appeared almost everywhere, although favoured locations were marshlands, sea and river shores, and the neighbourhoods of isolation hospitals, crematoria and cemeteries. At the end of the 1880s, there were at least seventy major slums; the worst was Samegabashi where some 5000 people lived in 1400 shacks [11]. These slums, which were a serious social problem, were as over-populated, insanitary, and vulnerable to fires and epidemics as those in other countries, but there were also some differences. First, Tokyo's slums were simple low-rise wooden structures which were easy to replace, typifying the traditional concept that houses were not permanent. Second, the slums were often converted to more profitable uses, as land prices went up, or into better or safer functions after the frequent fires. Thus, land inflation and fire served as important 'self-purifying agents'. Displaced slum-dwellers were forced to find cheaper land, creating new slums scattered all over the urban periphery. At the same time, marginal labourers in the slums slowly found factory work as industries gradually expanded at the end of the Meiji Period. In brief, therefore, Tokyo's slums failed to become a major social issue which would have prompted the institutionalization of urban planning, as happened in Britain.

Meiji society created not only the poor and distressed but also the rich and privileged, including new peers, powerful politicians, élite bureaucrats, rich merchants, and successful entrepreneurs. Some lived in the downtown area as Shibusawa did, but most built their mansions on the former warriors' estates further out in the urban area. According to Ishizuka, fifty landowners held 3.3 hectares or more of urban land in 1878, while by 1906 the figure had risen to 108 [12]. Their ideal residence was a mansion with a grand appearance situated in a large, landscaped estate – in a word, in the *samurai* style with a European flavour. Some of these people moved to the periphery, not for the pursuit of suburban life, but to obtain larger estates. Even in the middle of the downtown, a large estate secluded by walls provided its master with a satisfactory pastoral atmosphere. In a sense, it was 'private suburbia' within the confines of the urban area.

Following the late 1890s, there gradually emerged a new middle class, consisting of low-rank public servants, company employees, schoolteachers and other minor professionals. They were the forerunners of the white-collar class who were to be called 'salary men' in the Taisho era. They were mostly an immigrant population of nuclear families, and, in order to meet their housing needs, single-family, low-rent detached houses began to appear, especially on the urban periphery. As we have seen, the periphery was the location of new slums. Thus, suburbia was not developed as the new and sought-after housing area for the middle class, as it was in the Western countries, but as an inferior substitute for the urban area. It was the least desirable housing alternative.

To sum up, Meiji Tokyo, in its primitive stage of suburbanization, had 'private suburbia' and 'sub (i.e. inferior)-urbia' but it possessed little of the Western suburban phenomenon. To see such a concept grow on Japanese soil, one has to wait until the Taisho era, when the affluent middle-class begins to emerge.

All these changes in urban structure were strongly influenced by the development of urban transport systems. Meiji Tokyo saw its intra-urban transport change from the Edo-type *kago* (the Japanese palanquin), to the rickshaw (1869), the omnibus coach (1869), the horse tramcar (1882), and finally to the electric tramcar (1903), although the people's main mode of travel was still walking. Reflecting poor road conditions, the motor car was a rarity. In 1909, there were only sixty-two registered cars, mostly imported, which ran at the legal speed limit of 16 kilometres per hour. When the City of Tokyo bought the streetcar system from private enterprise in 1911, the 190-kilometre network carried 580,000 passengers daily, and was the major means of intra-urban transport for the Tokyo citizens.

On the other hand, three inter-urban railways, owned by the government by the late Meiji Period, basically determined the direction and tempo of the suburbanization that would take place later. First, Japan's earliest railway was laid down between Shinbashi (Tokyo's terminal) and Yokohama in 1872. The result was the connection of Tokyo with its southern hinterland. Second, the Yamanote line was built in 1885 specifically to transport silk exports from the northern Kanto Plain to Yokohama. Running one to one-and-a-half kilometres west of Tokyo's urban fringe, the line opened stations which were to become important terminals for suburban railways in following years. Third, the Chūō line, which was opened in 1889, ran directly westward into a flat, rural area of fields and woods. It served as Tokyo's first suburban railway. Thus, all the necessary conditions for Tokyo's suburbanization seemed to be present at the end of the Meiji Period.

Urban Problems of the Industrial Metropolis
The Taisho-Early Showa Period covers the entire Taisho Era (1912–26) and the first five years of Showa (1926–30). This period, which could also include the Russo-Japanese War years (1904–5), is generally identified as 'democratic Taisho' in contrast with 'nationalistic Meiji' and 'militaristic Showa'. The Japanese economy started to expand after the Russo-Japanese War and grew dramatically during World War One. Rapid industrialization and urbanization brought to Tokyo drastic social change and the enormous problems of an industrial metropolis.

The development of energy and transportation gave modern factories great freedom of location. They began to concentrate in Tokyo, where an ample supply of labour and consumers existed. During and after the war, large-scale factories intensified the existing trend in industrial location by creating the Tokyo-Yokohama Industrial Belt along the Tokyo Bay. Thus emerged an industrial crescent surrounding present-day downtown Tokyo and stretching over 50 kilometres into three prefectures. At the same time, smaller factories popped up everywhere in the built-up area and even in the expanding western suburbs, causing such environmental problems in terms of air, water and noise pollution. In order to combat these problems, land-use control through zoning would be institutionalized, as we shall see.

In step with industrial development, commerce and business rapidly expanded. In 1922, 12 per cent of the nation's companies and 39 per cent of their capital were concentrated in the Prefecture of Tokyo. About 70 per cent of companies located in the prefecture in 1925 had been established as recently as 1918–22. These companies sought office space in the Marunouchi area and its vicinity. The retail centre was in the Nihonbashi-Ginza area. The modernized Mitsukoshi department store was built in Nihonbashi in 1914, with a bronze lion sitting at its entrance, a replica of the original in Trafalgar Square. Government buildings expanded from Ōtemachi into the Hibiya and Kasumigaseki areas. The highlight of the construction boom was the building of the long-awaited National Diet Building from 1920. Tokyo's central business district, its diversified functions reflecting the thriving metropolis, was thus taking shape.

The drastic social change that typified Taisho Tokyo threw up new kinds of social classes. One was the urban labouring class. In fact, in the Taisho Era, factory workers also emerged as a distinct social class. The number of factory workers in Tokyo Prefecture increased from 100,000 in 1914 to 178,000 five years later. Most of them lived in slums, rooms and lodging houses of inferior quality in the vicinity of their factories. Suburban living and long-distance commuting were unknown to them. Socialism, which had been introduced from the industrial nations of the West in the late Meiji period, gradually spread among these workers. Together with other classes at the bottom of the social scale, they were often involved in urban unrest such as mass riots, labour troubles, and socialist demonstrations. The tramway system was a constant target of vengeance in the urban riots.

The other emerging class was that of the white-collar worker, who engaged in such expanding fields as business, government, education, and other service industries. The first national census in 1920 revealed that about 15 per cent of the prefectural population fell into this category. The majority of the middle class, however, had to live on modest incomes and were often called 'the well-dressed poor' (Yōfuku saimin). Nearly 90 per cent of them lived in rented houses, averaging 40 square metres in floor space. They had little choice but to live in the peripheral municipalities and had to commute to the city by surburban railways and trams. For the better-off middle class, private builders began to undertake residential development, albeit on a small scale, in the former samurai district as well as on peripheral agricultural land.

By the beginning of the Taisho Period, the major issues of utilities management and ownership, which had bothered Meiji city officials, had largely been resolved. But the increasing urban population and its demand for better municipal services had now risen to such a degree that everybody, both in the City Hall and in the streets, agreed that the shortage of urban facilities was Tokyo's most crucial urban problem. Almost all the streets that the Municipal Improvement Programme had left untouched were unpaved and completely unfit for vehicular traffic. They were like paddy fields on rainy days and turned into a desert with accompanying clouds of dust in dry periods. The trams, as the main means of transport for the masses, were always full and their services inadequate. Government railway tracks were still awaiting construction through the built-up area to complete the loop and through-services. Water and electricity services, although available in the city area, did not cover the growing suburbs. Sewage was the least developed service of all; the ultra-modern Marunouchi Building, equipped with flush toilets, was not connected to the sewer system at all and depended upon the regular visits of night-soil men. In order to respond to increasing social unrest, the necessity arose for such facilities as free lodgings, employment agencies, open markets, sanatoria and so on. In addition, the expanding urban area needed to secure lands for future crematoria, cemeteries and large-scale parks. All these problems required a far more ambitious and comprehensive treatment than in the past; only a completely new approach to municipal management seemed capable of resolving them.

Tokyo's problems were direct concerns of the city officials as well as challenges to the Home Ministry bureaucrats. In fact, the characteristics of Japan's pre-war urban policies were largely attributable to the Home Ministry, which was responsible not only for planning, building, and housing but also local government, police and other domestic administration.

The bureaucrats regarded themselves as 'enlightened' by the experience of the advanced Western nations, where the Industrial Revolution had brought socialism and democracy which, they thought, would threaten the monarch. They sought to prevent such trouble by introducing the 'social policy' approach from Bismarckian Germany in the late Meiji period [13]. The Local Improvement Movement after the Russo-Japanese War was one of the early efforts that the Home Ministry devised for rural Japan. The Ministry bureaucrats even introduced, in this connection, the British Garden City idea to Japan, though without really understanding its essence because they were overly obsessed with rural improvement [14]. Thereafter, however, they increasingly had to shift their attention from rural to urban, or even metropolitan, Japan. Urban policies became one of the most important domestic issues in the Taisho Era. The problem was not only a matter of inconvenient urban living but also one of threatened internal security, as typified by urban unrest. In contrast to those of Western countries, where citizens and professionals worked hard and with a fair degree of altruism for urban improvement, Japanese urban policies were thus under the strong leadership and control of the Home Ministry bureaucrats.

Emerging 'City Planning'
The Municipal Improvement Programme was in a sense 'Meiji's urban planning', but none of the dictionaries of the day listed the word 'urban planning' (*toshi keikaku*). In fact, this Japanese word (and so the concept) was created and popularized in early Taisho as the translation of the English 'town planning',

American 'city planning', and German 'Städtebau'. Japan's encounter with 'town planning' took place in the architectural profession [15].

In April 1910, a letter from the Royal Institute of British Architects arrived at the Institute of Japanese Architects, announcing a 'Town Planning Conference' to be held in London the same year. Nobody in Japan seemed to have known of the British Town Planning Act of 1909 nor to have understood exactly what 'town planning' meant, but the Japanese architects decided to send a representative to the conference. The Institute's journal, in referring to the conference over several issues, changed the word from 'town planning' (untranslated), to *taun puranningu* (transliteration), and then to *shigai haichi-keikaku* (literally, built-up area layout planning).

As this translation suggests, the architects tended to understand 'town planning' as the layout or site planning of part of the urban area as a means of adding beauty to the townscape. This understanding perhaps reflects the piecemeal approach of the 1909 Act and the civic design approach of the British architectural profession. To Japanese architects, 'town planning' was just large-scale architecture. The planner's job was to draw blueprints for it. Such a naive, optimistic view seems to have hindered them from broadening their activities into general urban planning, which was more heavily dependent upon administration and politics.

In 1913, the Institute submitted a proposed housing and building ordinance to the city of Tokyo after six and a half years of study. The proposal, however, did not reflect the impact of 'town planning' but was concerned solely with technical aspects of building regulations. The city left the proposal untouched for a long period, although the architects worked for its adoption.

In 1913, Seki Hajime, Osaka's noted deputy mayor and ex-professor of municipal management, coined the expression *toshi keikaku* (city planning). Three years later, Osaka architect Kataoka Yasushi, whose main information source was the writings of Nelson P. Lewis, started to propagate *toshi keikaku*, and to campaign for its enactment. It was mostly due to his efforts that the word (though not necessarily the concept) was accepted among architects and subsequently the Home Ministry bureaucrats.

Kataoka's target was Home Minister Gotō Shimpei who, as an official of long experience, had experienced planning administration in Taiwan and Manchuria and who, as a 'scientific politician', saw planning's potential for municipal management. The government soon decided to institutionalize a planning system of general applicability. The Home Ministry bureaucrats, who became aware of the RIBA conference later than the architects, tended to understand 'town planning' as municipal management of urban facilities and services, although they regarded the national government as having a greater role than 'unreliable' municipalities. However, they regarded planning as broader in scope than the Municipal Improvement Programme, which had now come to be seen as the mere building and broadening of streets. In 1918, the Home Ministry established a City Planning Section with Ikeda Hiroshi as its chief. He was to draft the City Planning Act and the Urban Building Act, both enacted in 1919.

Behind the City Planning Act was an idea that Ikeda earnestly advocated. It may be called the 'organic city theory' (*toshi yūkitai setsu*), which saw the city as a kind of organism and so insisted that the 'real city' should be planned as a whole, and not fragmented into individual municipalities separated by 'arbitrary' boundaries. This view reflected the metropolitan reality of Tokyo, where suburbanization was taking place beyond the city limits and the large-scale comprehensive management of facilities and services was desperately needed.

Under the strong leadership of the Home Ministry, Tokyo was provided with a Prefectural Planning Committee responsible for the long-range comprehensive planning of the 'real city'. The logical conclusion of the 'organic city theory' was thus a metropolitan planning system with centralized planning power and, in consequence, the removal of planning initiative from the municipal level.

The City Planning Act provided, at least theoretically, a fairly comprehensive planning system incorporating such new techniques as zoning, building-line control, compulsory purchase and site consolidation. The basic framework, however, was that of the traditional Municipal Improvement Programme. The new system was designed to deal with all kinds of important facilities but, in practice, such public works as road construction remained the central concern.

The Urban Building Act provided zoning and other land-use controls and the legal bases for building regulation. But land-use control in particular was unpopular among the citizenry (though building regulation was more readily tolerated). People could not understand why such control should be imposed when they built their own houses on their own land. They simply did not recognize that such restrictions would result in the enhancement of their property values. In Western countries, where land-use control was used to preserve property values in the newly developed suburbs, zoning controls could be fairly strict. In Japan, however, land-use control applied not to suburbia but to the inner city where the standard had to be kept low in order to reduce the number of possible non-conforming uses. It was not until 1929 that most of Tokyo's suburbs were covered by zoning control (figure 15.8). Thus, the total system set up by the two Acts crystallized into public works, on the one hand, and building regulations on the other, with the intermediate land-use control practically nullified. This marks a sharp contrast with the West, where urban planning traditionally centres around land-use control.

The number of cities which the Planning Act affected rose from six in 1919 to thirty-one in 1923, and exceeded one hundred in 1931. An amendment in 1933 made it applicable to the smaller towns (*machi*) and villages (*mura*). Thus, for all its defects, it became the cornerstone of Japanese planning, a position which it would retain for half a century after its first enactment.

Capital Reconstruction Programme, 1923–30

The City Planning Act, which became effective in January 1920, preceded the Tokyo earthquake by only three years and nine months. In December, the City of Tokyo elected Gotō as mayor. Assisted by three deputy mayors, all ex-Home Ministry bureaucrats including Ikeda, Mayor Gotō prepared a plan for capital expenditure for the next ten to fifteen years. This was commonly called the '800 Million Yen Plan' of 'Big-Talker' Gotō. Although the plan failed to secure any official status, some of its basic principles were realized in the designation of the planning area and in the reconstruction programme after the earthquake.

In April 1922 the government announced the designation of the city-planning area for Tokyo, or the area which was to be treated as a whole for the purpose of Tokyo's planning. The designated area, with a radius of 16 kilometres, or one-hours' travel from Tokyo Station, covered eighty-four suburban and rural municipalities as well as the City of Tokyo (figure 15.5). This area, 6.7 times larger than the city proper, exactly embodied the concept of the 'real city', covering as it did a metropolis which continued to expand beyond established municipal jurisdictions. Indeed its appropriateness would be confirmed by the adoption of the whole area as the expanded City of Tokyo ten years later.

FIGURE 15.5. The Tokyo city-planning area, 1922.

FIGURE 15.6. Area devastated by fire after the Tokyo earthquake, 1923 (source: see note 25).

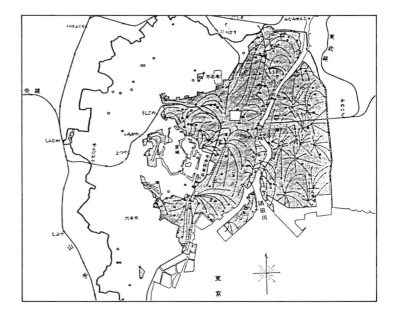

Around midday on 1 September 1923, a formidable earthquake (magnitude 7.9) devastated Japan's capital and its environs. In Tokyo City, nearly 70,000 persons (or 3 per cent) were killed or presumed dead, and almost 1.4 million people (or 61 per cent) lost their homes. The earthquake and the fire it spawned levelled most of central and eastern Tokyo (figure 15.6). The calamity was the first great trial for modern Tokyo. Some agrarianists and moralists even saw it as a heavenly punishment for sybaritic urbanites. Their criticisms, however, tended to be aimed at popular lifestyles, rather than Tokyo's great size as such. A strongly hostile analysis of the modern city in Japan in the decade after the earthquake hardly existed, as Smith points out [16].

Five days after the earthquake, the newly-appointed Home Minister Gotō proposed four basic principles for the reconstruction of Tokyo: (1) rejection of the transfer of the capital to another site; (2) a reconstruction programme costing three billion yen; (3) application of the latest Western planning; and (4) a determined stance with respect to the landowners. The Reconstruction Agency was immediately established in order to carry out the reconstruction programme for Tokyo and Yokohama. The Agency (and its successor, the Bureau) spent 690 million yen during the following seven and a half years, ending with the fiscal year 1930. It should be noted that the three-year-old Tokyo and Yokohama planning powers were transferred to the Reconstruction Agency – a further example of the constantly recurring direct control of planning by the central government.

The reconstruction programme concentrated heavily upon street building and site consolidation, which secured 54 per cent and 15 per cent respectively of the total expenditure. Tamaki Toyojirō, himself an Agency planner, maintained that the completely destroyed *shitamachi* area was replanned into commercial, industrial and warehouse districts, and so an ideal street system, consisting of 52 major routes and 122 auxiliary routes, was laid out on an ambitious scale [17].

The Special City Planning Act was enacted to enable the Agency to apply the site consolidation technique to the ruined area. In the consolidation process, land-owners had to surrender up to 10 per cent of their land for new streets and other public purposes. Some 200,000 buildings had to be removed to new sites. Citizens and, in particular, landowners were bitterly opposed to the land consolidation programme for the first few years, but gradually came to cooperate with it. The consolidation programme, which covered over 3600 hectares of land in the central area and included the acquisition of 440 hectares of new streets without compensation, is considered one of the most valuable achievements of Japanese planning. Overall, the capital reconstruction programme achieved a radical surgery of Edo's urban structure which not only fitted it for its modern functions but to some extent paved the way towards the future. At the same time, however, the post-earthquake experience reinforced the traditional concept of planning as the building of urban facilities by the central government and as a response to extraordinary events. The concept of planning as a routine tool for municipal management was as yet hardly discernible.

The earthquake and the subsequent reconstruction were full of interesting dramas. Minister Gotō was obviously one of the key actors, and another was Charles A. Beard, a noted American scholar of history and public administration. When the earthquake struck Tokyo, Beard, who had just returned to the United States from his first visit to Japan at Gotō's invitation, sent a telegram to Gotō, saying: 'Lay out new streets, forbid building within street lines, unify railway stations'. Gotō invited Beard to return to Tokyo and asked for his recommenda-tions on the reconstruction programme. In the final memorandum submitted to Gotō, Beard stressed the need for the integration of street planning with metropolitan planning, for strict land-use controls, and for improving the financing of planning [18]. As a dedicated municipal reformer and director of the New York Bureau of Municipal Research, Beard insisted on the scientific management of the the city. Gotō shared his scientific and apolitical stance. But the difference between the two gradually became more obvious. Beard's position reflected that of the emerging middle class which had obtained political power in the Progressive Era, whereas Gotō had only a limited political base and his apoliticism meant government control not by politicians but by bureaucrats. During the forty days of his second stay, Beard was unable to secure the acceptance of his recommenda-tions. In November, he left Tokyo filled with restrained disappointment.

The official adoption of the zoning regulation was considerably delayed, until 1925 (figure 15.7). The area covered by the zoning was only slightly larger than the city proper, which meant that zoning neither limited nor protected the developing

FIGURE 15.7. Tokyo zoning map, 1925 (source: see note 26).

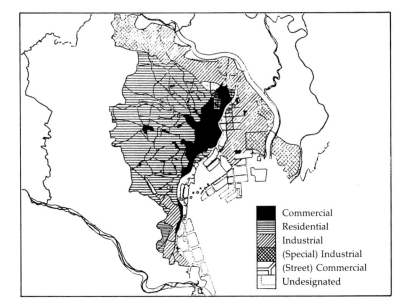

Commercial
Residential
Industrial
(Special) Industrial
(Street) Commercial
Undesignated

suburbia and the rural land beyond. Indeed, the growing part of the 'real city' was left to its natural growth, and only the mature part was placed under land-use control. Even there, the zoning tended to follow existing trends rather than prescribe for future use. The planners designated the eastern industrial area (37 per cent of the zoned area) as industrial, the traditional *shitamachi* and major commercial streets (15 per cent) as commercial, and the *yamanote* area (45 per cent) as residential. About 3 per cent of the area, between the commercial and the industrial districts, was zoned as 'undesignated', with a view to precise designation after the future trend in land use had emerged.

This 1925 zoning seems to have determined the urban structure of later Tokyo. How successful, then, can the zoning be adjudged to have been? The answer would depend on the definition of planning adopted. If it is defined, as in the West, as directing a future course of development, the Tokyo zoning was a failure, whereas if planning is something that should conform to the market trend, it may be considered a success.

Suburbanization in Full Swing

In the Taisho Era, housing construction became more active in the rural areas outside Tokyo City. Population growth accelerated in these areas, especially after the earthquake. In the decade 1920–30, the population of Tokyo City decreased, due to the disaster, from 2.2 to 2.1 million, whereas five peripheral counties (*gun*) grew from 1.2 to 2.9 million in population. Suburban Ebara County saw particularly rapid growth, quintupling its population in ten years. Thus sub-urbanization went into full swing.

Rapid suburbanization brought two sets of problems. The central city had to maintain various urban facilities and services for daily commuters who did not pay taxes to the city. On the other hand, the suburban municipalities that had to provide schools and other facilities for the increasing population had insufficient financial capacity and their powers of zoning control were very limited. Indeed, it was this lack of planning control that encouraged suburbanization in Japan, whereas the accelerated suburban expansion of the 1920s in America was securely based on strong zoning powers.

The emerging suburbanites were mostly white-collar 'salarymen' who commuted to the central business district. The 1930 census, for instance, showed 308,000 people commuting from suburbia to the city and 35,000 people in the other direction. The commuters relied upon suburban railways and government lines (shōsen). The trains operated only within the city area. Buses carried an increasing number of passengers both in the suburban and inner areas in the 1920s.

Suburban railways made rapid strides in the 1920s. The lines extended westwards and southwards from terminals at stations on the government's Yamanote line. Landowners along the suburban lines, who expected a rise in their property values, were generally cooperative in selling part of their holdings and became stockholders. The railway companies had unique policies in several ways. First, they built or encouraged residential development, schools, and recreation grounds so as to secure an adequate number of passengers. Second, the companies often attracted potential residents by waiving or discounting their railfares for a certain period of time. Third, they appealed to the suburban image of tranquillity and a modern life style for the middle class and emphasized the suburban home (that is, land rather than the house upon it) as a valuable property.

Garden City Japanese Style
The largest, and perhaps the most interesting, suburban developer in the Taisho Period was Den-en Toshi Company Ltd., Japan's only 'garden city' Company [19].

In 1915, a group of agricultural landlords in rural Ebara County asked Shibusawa Eiichi for his assistance in developing their land. Three years later, Shibusawa and other leading entrepreneurs founded the Den-en Toshi company Ltd. The promoters formally designated it as a property company and saw its clients as middle- (but in fact, upper-middle-) class people to whom suburban life was a dream. The company prospectus publicized the development of Den-en Toshi (Garden City) as an ideal residence for middle-class families who were suffering from inconvenient living, unhealthy conditions and moral dangers in the overcrowded and dusty capital city.

The company acquired 150 hectares of agricultural land in Ebara County. It extended in an irregular shape over six rural jurisdictions, with its nearest corner about two kilometres away from the urban fringe of expanding Tokyo. The company used the site consolidation technique and laid out lots, open spaces, streets, railway lines and stations. As Den-en Toshi was an island in the middle of agricultural fields, the company arranged for water and electricity to be supplied, and relied upon the government for public services. In order to connect Den-en Toshi with stations on government lines, the company created its subsidiary suburban railway.

Den-en Toshi Company grouped the acquired land into three separate areas and began selling residential lots in the first area Senzoku, in 1922. About 80 per cent of the total lots were contracted for within the first ten days. The sale took place even before the first train ran and proved that suburban living appealed to the middle class. The second area, Ōōkayama, became the campus of the present-day Tokyo Institute of Technology, and the third area, Tamagawadai, was developed before and after the earthquake as a garden suburb, which has become one of the most prestigious residential areas in Tokyo. In all these transactions, the company succeeded in selling land for seven to ten times what it had originally paid.

It was up to the purchaser to build his house upon the lot which was the general practice of the time and, to some degree, is still so today. Since the area lacked statutory land-use control, the company designated the use of the lots it sold. Most were designated as residential, and the remainder as neighbourhood-commercial. The sale contract was accompanied by an agreement incorporating specified building and land-use controls the precision of which far exceeded that of statutory regulations effective in the built-up area. The agreement, though lacking all legal basis, was long respected by the upper-middle-class residents, who recognized that it protected their lifestyle and property. In the history of Japanese urban development, this was a rare outcome.

In the middle of the severe depression after World War One, Den-en Toshi Company was a miracle. It kept paying 10 per cent dividends and once, in 1927, a 20 per cent special dividend was declared. Its commercial success was partly due to the impact of the Great Earthquake. Indeed, the company managers were convinced that the disaster proved the validity of the Garden City idea, as it offered safety to potential customers still living in the city area.

In conclusion, the case of Den-en Toshi Company suggests some interesting lessons in respect of suburban issues. First, the company built a garden suburb and called it a garden city. Unlike the British Garden City advocates, who tended to denounce the large city, Den-en Toshi accepted, and even made use of, the metropolis. Den-en Toshi residents did not try to, and in any case could not, incorporate themselves into a municipality to protect their interests as American suburbanites did. Second, the Den-en Toshi Company was one of the earliest examples in Japan of a planned suburban community in which residential amenities were deliberately, and successfully, included to attract purchasers. Whereas statutory city planning was mostly concerned with urban facilities within the built-up area, this private company built a 'garden city' in suburbia to an environmental standard that 'city planning' could not attain. Ironically, the two were totally unrelated. Third, the Den-en Toshi experience demonstrated that the combination of land development and railway business had a great potential. This combination became a typical pattern for large-scale suburban development which lasted until recently. Thus, in Japan betterment value is often recouped by developer-railway companies, rather than by the community.

Epilogue

Before concluding, a brief look forward to wartime and post-war Tokyo is necessary. The wartime period covers the fifteen years from 1930 to the end of the Pacific War (1941–45), in which all national policies were directed toward the preparation and execution of the war.

Outstanding among planning issues around 1930 was the question of how to deal with disorderly suburban sprawl, to which city planning control did not extend. One of the steps taken was the expansion of the zoning area to cover most of the Tokyo City Planning Area in 1929 (figure 15.8). The other was administrative reorganization. In 1932, Tokyo City annexed eighty-two peripheral municipalities and became 'Greater Tokyo City'. The new city area was more or less that of Tokyo's planning area, and roughly corresponds to the present-day Tokyo Ward Area. In 1943, the long-awaited merger of the City and the Prefecture of Tokyo took

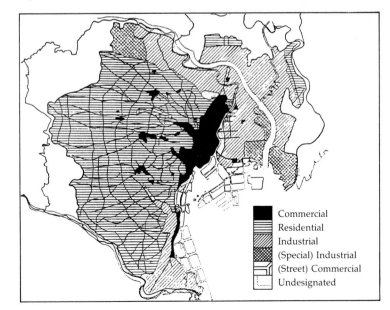

FIGURE 15.8. Zoning map for Tokyo built-up area, 1929 (source: see note 27).

place. The newly-created Tokyo-to, however, was a disappointment to reformers because it was even more closely controlled by the national government than in the past.

Another important development was the move towards limiting metropolitan growth and even towards decentralizing the metropolitan population. This idea was yet another Western import, whose origin can be traced back to the international conferences held in Gothenburg in 1923 and in Amsterdam in the following year. Iinuma Kazumi (Issei), who attended the Gothenburg conference and later became the Home Ministry's Planning Section chief, constantly advocated the planned dispersal of metropolitan concentrations into small- and medium-sized cities in the name of regional planning [20].

In subsequent years, Iinuma's idealistic argument found a realistic basis in the need for decentralization as a wartime measure. Possible air attacks on Tokyo became a serious concern among planners around 1938. Two years later, the Home Ministry announced planning policies for air defence measures. As an increasing number of citizens were bombed out near the end of the war, the government undertook a compulsory evacuation programme. Tokyo's population declined sharply from 6.6 million to 2.5 million in sixteen months from February 1944. Thus, Tokyo achieved the dispersal of its population and industries, but through war rather than planning. In the spring of 1945, the great fire-bomb raids reduced Tokyo to ruins.

In August 1945, Tokyo started to rise again from the midst of destruction which covered more than double the area razed by the earthquake and fire disaster two

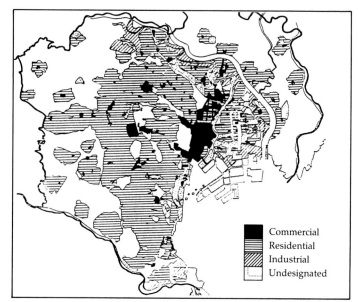

FIGURE 15.9. Tokyo zoning map, 1946, showing undesignated, or 'greenbelt', land (source: see note 28).

Commercial
Residential
Industrial
Undesignated

decades before. Soon waves of evacuees, repatriates, and other jobless surged back to the destroyed capital. Thus the Meiji-old, nay Edo-old tradition of quick rebuilding was revived. However, in contrast to past reconstruction episodes, the expanding metropolis was countered by the decentralization argument that had been developed since the early Showa period. The decentralization theme materialized in post-war Tokyo's 'greenbelt' plan, which was another replica of a British original (figure 15.9).

From the late 1950s to the early 1970s, the Japanese economy grew dramatically. So did Tokyo's economy and population, followed by building booms, suburban expansion, traffic congestion, housing shortages, and environmental disruption. Professionals and laymen alike argued over what to do with this giant metropolis. While all these somewhat idealistic discussions went on, the urban reality never stopped evolving. The urban front crossed the ineffective 'greenbelt' around 1960 and further invaded the adjoining prefectures. Ten years later, a star-shaped metropolis, about 80 kilometres across, was observable on the Kantō Plain.

To sum up, the history of Edo-Tokyo has been in a sense one of reconstruction. Burnt downtown Edo was repeatedly rebuilt; *samurai* estates were redeveloped into Meiji's residential districts; old Tokyo, ruined first by the earthquake and then by bombing, was replaced each time by a new Tokyo. Indeed, most of downtown Tokyo was built anew twice in less than a generation. In all these instances, people considered Edo-Tokyo as worthy of being rebuilt and regarded the enlarged city as more or less desirable. In this sense, therefore, 'metropolitanism' has been affirmed as a value and a way of life to which the residents of Edo-Tokyo have been consistently loyal.

This preference marks a distinct contrast to the attitudes of Western planning. British planning, for instance, traditionally sought to limit the size of the metropolis and to build small settlements such as 'garden cities' and new towns away from it. American planning is generally indifferent to the size of the metropolis as long as its suburbia can keep its identity and independence. To put it another way, Britons hate the large city whereas Americans dislike the central city. Despite these subtle distinctions, planning in both countries shares some characteristics: namely, (1) an anti-urban tradition as a cultural factor; (2) suburbia-central city dichotomy as an ecological factor; and (3) local autonomy as a political factor.

In Japanese planning, at least until 1945, all these factors took different forms. First, the city, especially the large city, has been the ideal place to live in. Tokyo has often been described as 'over-crowded' but rarely as 'overgrown'. Second, modern Tokyo has been successful in building a well functioning central business district connected with an expanding suburbia by efficient rail transport systems, whereas suburbia, a potential opponent of the central city, has not remained a distinct and separate entity. On the contrary, each new suburban zone has eventually developed into a mature urban part of the inner city. Third, strong national government and weak local autonomy have been a constant feature in Japan, and this has facilitated inter-municipal coordination.

While British planners are proud of their massive council housing and American planners confident of their strict land-use controls, Japan has followed a system of minimum intervention combined with intermittent trouble-shooting. These weak regulatory powers and the related insufficient financial provisions have been a constant source of frustration to Japanese planners. However, the result has been an ever-growing economy and a thriving metropolis. Indeed, Tokyo is one of the few metropolises among those in advanced nations in which entrepreneurs continue to invest in the central business district, where private railway companies operate efficient services for profit, and where one finds neither a huge slum like Harlem nor a vacant building like Centre Point.

Tokyo has surely succeeded in making a metropolis for modern business, but how about the metropolis for modern living? Here enormous problems stack up, partly due to the unfavourable results of the boom period of the 1960s and partly due to people's changing values in the 1970s. Soaring land prices, a threatened residential environment, and municipal finance in deficit are just a few factors. Some advocate that decentralization and strong local autonomy are needed to solve these problems; others still insist on urban renewal, not to revitalize Tokyo, but to utilize Tokyo's potential to its maximum. Should Tokyo abandon or enrich its traditional metropolitanism? This is the precise point at which the contemporary history of Tokyo's, and Japan's, planning stands today.

NOTES

1. For the American case, see Watanabe, S.J. (1977) *America Toshikeikaku to Community Rinen* (American Urban Planning and the Community Ideal). Tokyo: Gihōdō.
2. For material on Tokyo's planning history, we owe a great deal to: Ishizuka, H. (1977) *Tokyo no Shakai Keizaishi: Shihonshugi to Toshimondai* (The Economic and Social History of Tokyo: Its Capitalism and Urban Problems). Tokyo: Kinokuniya; Smith, H.D., II (1978) Tokyo as an idea: an exploration of Japanese urban thought until 1945. *Journal of Japanese Studies*, **4**, (1), pp. 45–80; Smith, H.D., II (1979) Tokyo and London: comparative conceptions of the city, in Craig, A. (ed.) *Japan: A Comparative View*. Princeton: Princeton University Press, pp. 49–99; Tokyo Hyakunenshi Henshū Iinkai (ed.) (1979) *Tokyo Hyakunenshi* (Tokyo's Hundred Year History), 6 vols. Tokyo: Gyōsei; Fujimori, T. (1979) *Meiji-ki ni okeru Toshikeikaku no Rekishiteki Kenkyū* (Historical Study of Urban Planning in the Meiji Period). Doctoral dissertation; Tokyo Saikaihatsu Kenkyū Iinkai (1979) *Daitoshiken ni okeru Sōgōteki Kankyō Seibi no tame no Toshi Saikaihatsu no Hitsuyōsei to Kanōsei ni kansuru Chōsa Hōkokusho* (A Report on the Necessity and Feasibility of Urban Redevelopment for Comprehensive Environmental Improvement of the Metropolitan Area), Report & Data book. Tokyo: Shakai Kaihatsu Sōgō Kenkyūjo.
3. Meiji, Taisho, and Showa represent three successive emperors of modern Japan, the present Showa Era starting in 1926.
4. Smith (1979), *loc.cit.*, p. 64, n. 23 (see note 2).

Also see Tamaki, T. (1974) *Nihon Toshi Seiritsu-shi: Toshi Kensetsu Shiryō Shūsei* (An Urban History of Japan: Collection of Data on City Construction). Tokyo: Rikōgakusha.

5. Based on the figures given by Ishizuka, *op.cit.*, pp. 37–38 (see note 2).

6. Kawazoe, N. (1979) *Tokyo no Gen-Fūkei: Toshi to Den-en to no Kōryū* (Tokyo's Original Landscape: Interactions between the City and the Country). Tokyo: NHK, pp. 98–170.

7. Smith (1979), *loc.cit.*, p. 43 (see note 2).

8. Fujimori, *op.cit.*, p. 43 (see note 2).

9. The following analysis draws heavily on the themes developed in Fujimori, *op.cit.* (see note 2).

10. Fujimori, *op.cit.*, p. 95 (see note 2).

11. Ishizuka, *op.cit.*, pp. 129–30 (see note 2).

12. These figures for land indicate the total area of their landholdings, and not the size of individual estates. See Ishizuka, *op.cit.*, pp. 115–16 (see note 2).

13. Pyle, K.B. (1973) The technology of Japanese nationalism: the Local Improvement Movement, 1900–1918. *Journal of Asian Studies*, **33**, (1), pp. 51–65; Pyle, K.B. (1974) Advantage of followership: German economics and Japanese bureaucrats, 1890–1925. *Journal of Japanese Studies*, **1** (1), pp. 127–64.

14. Watanabe, S.J. (1978) Nihonteki den-entoshiron no kenkyu (2): Naimushō chihōkyoku yūshi hen *Den-entoshi* (Meiji 40 nen) o megutte (Upon the Home Ministry (ed.), *Garden City* (1907): The study of the garden city Japanese style [2]). *Nihon Toshikeikakugakkai Gakujutsu Kenkyū Happyōkai Ronbunshū* (Proceedings of the Annual Conference of the City Planning Institute of Japan), **13**, pp. 283–8.

15. Watanabe, S.J. (1980) Toshikeikaku no yōgo no seiritsu katei ni kansuru kenkyū (Historical analysis of the formative process of the word *toshikeikaku*). *Nihon Toshikeikakugakkai Gakujutsu Kankyū Happyōkai Ronbunshū*, **15**, pp. 19–24.

16. Smith (1978), *loc.cit.*, p. 72 (see note 2).

17. Tamaki, T. (1972) Kantōdaishinsai to fukkō jigyō (Kanto earthquake and reconstruction program), in Nihon Kenchiku Gakkai (ed.) *Kindai Nihon Kenchiku-gaku Hattatsu-shi* (History of Architectural Studies in Modern Japan). Tokyo: Maruzen, pp. 1014–31.

18. Beard, C.A. (1923) *Memorandum Relative to the Reconstruction of Tokyo*. Tokyo: The Tokyo Institute for Municipal Research.

19. Watanabe, S.J. (1980) Garden city Japanese style: the case of Den-en Toshi Company Ltd., 1918–28, in Cherry, G.E. (ed.) *Shaping an Urban World*. London: Mansell, pp. 129–43.

20. Iinuma, K. (1927) *Toshi Keikaku no Riron to Hōsei* (Theory and Legislation of City Planning). Tokyo: Ryōshofukyūkai.

21. Smith (1979), p. 66 (see note 2).

22. Smith (1979), p. 51 (see note 2).

23. Fujimori, T. (1978) Ende Boeckmann niyoru kanchō shūchū keikaku no kenkyū, 3 (Study of government block project by Ende & Boeckmann), *Nihon Kenchiku Gakkai Ronbun Hōkokushū*, no. 273, p. 146.

24. Kawakami, H. (1977) Tokyo city improvement program, 1884–1918. Unpublished paper presented at the First International Conference on the History of Urban and Regional Planning, London, 1977, Fig. 3.

25. Tokyo Saikaihatsu Kenkyū Iinkai (1979), Data book, p. 39.

26. Konno, A. & Hirose, M. (1959) Tokyo-to ni okeru yōto chiiki shitei no hensen (Tokyo's zoning changes, 1923–59). *Toshi Keikaku*, **29**, p. 26.

27. *Ibid.*, p. 28.

28. *Ibid.*, p. 31.

Chapter 16

Postscript: Metropolis 1940–1990

PETER HALL

PERHAPS the irony of history is that metropolitan planners always fight the last war. In the 1920s and 1930s, they waged battle against the evils of nineteenth-century industrialism just as the market was showing a way out into the suburbs. It was the same after World War Two. The war – at least in some countries – belatedly made the idea of planning respectable, at any rate to the establishment of the day; and that in turn allowed not merely the production of plans, but also the development of administrative machinery that might permit their realization. But the immediate result was perverse. In the 1950s and 1960s, the age that now comes to be seen as the golden age of dynamic capitalism, planners sought to impose a steady-state view of the city derived from the stagnant 1930s. In the 1970s, as growth flagged, they produced plans for metropolitan expansion. Only belatedly, during the 1980s, are they coming to terms with a new reality of metropolitan decline.

They had one excuse: after 1945, the pace of change was unprecedentedly and unexpectedly rapid. In the golden years of the late 1950s and the 1960s, planning had to cope simultaneously with every kind of growth. Metropolitan populations rose, as birth rates – contrary to all the demographers' confident predictions – went up. A growing service economy needed more and more people – especially women – to work in the offices that the property development industry was only too anxious to provide in the urban cores. A boom in demand for consumer durables meant investment in new factories and warehouses at the urban periphery and in new and satellite towns. Economic growth in turn brought rapidly increasing household incomes and demand for new homes, new equipment to put in them, and more cars to drive around in. And these last in particular brought an acute need for urban reconstruction to provide new roads, new parking garages, new forms of shopping and entertainment. As cities proved incapable of adjusting completely to the demands of a car-based population, more and more people voted with their wheels, transferring themselves to suburbia and exurbia. And local political pressures in the cities themselves led to huge slum clearance programmes, which rehoused urban populations in new landscapes of glass and steel and concrete.

It was the same story in each of the great metropolitan centres of the capitalist world. These were the years of London's Property Boom [1], when developers like Joe Levy and Harry Hyams became part of popular folklore; in Paris the earth movers began to scoop out the ground for La Défense and Maine-Montparnasse and Fronts de Seine; Midtown Manhattan was transformed by such masters of the Modern Movement as Mies van der Rohe, and by their lesser followers. A little further out, in the inner residential areas, public agencies worked to renew ageing and outworn infrastructure, often with too much haste and too little forethought. Le Corbusier's spirit triumphed in London's Roehampton and in hundreds of less inspired imitations. Prefabricated construction, first used in the Soviet Union and Scandinavia, was sold to city councils over-eager to rehouse their working-class populations. The highway engineers produced bewildering mathematical models to prove the absolute necessity for vast urban motorway programmes: three orbitals, plus associated radials, at a cost in 1970 of £2000 million for London; the Boulevard Périphérque and two outer motorways, plus expressways on both banks of the Seine, for Paris; an Expressway through the heart of Lower Manhattan. And the reality of the coming age of universal motorization, so it plausibly seemed, would demand more: wholesale reconstruction of large parts of London and other British cities, according to the 1963 Buchanan report [2], so as to combine mobility with civilized urban living.

No sooner had planners got to grips with this new reality, than the reality itself changed. By 1965, metropolitan planning everywhere was attuned to the idea of growth. The plans of that period – alike in London, Paris, the Dutch Randstad, Copenhagen, Stockholm, New York – were all centrally concerned with the task of accommodating large numbers of new people at the periphery of the metropolis, while simultaneously reconstructing the urban cores. The irony was that, precisely at this time, powerful voices were being raised against the wholesale change that would be entailed. Citizens revolted against motorway construction and large-scale urban renewal to accommodate the car. Conservationists demanded a more sympathetic treatment of the urban fabric, which would eschew brutal surgery and would conserve the best of what already existed. Ecologists called for a more resource-conserving, pollution-conscious style of planning. London abandoned its motorway plans altogether, and scrapped the plan for the comprehensive reconstruction of Covent Garden, substituting rehabilitation; after the spectacular collapse of a systems-built tower block in East London in 1968 [3], it (and the rest of Britain) moved away from high-rise construction altogether. Paris, already far gone in completion of the Périphérique, scrapped the Left-Bank Expressway; New York similarly shelved its Manhattan Expressway. To be sure, there were significant differences between one city and another; those that espoused the bulldozer treatment earliest, and those most tightly controlled by a central technocracy (Paris, Tokyo), maintained the grand style of the 1960s for longer than did London or New York.

At the same time, people continued to leave the cities – leaving them open, at last, to the threat of actual depopulation and de-industrialization. And by the mid-1970s the threat had become a reality. The Age of Conservation gave way to the Age of Contraction. Now, clearly, the problem of the cities was not just the flight of people; it was the flight of capital. For whatever reason, the traditional activities of the city – manufacturing and wholesale trade – began to die there. Some plants moved out; some others rationalized, substituting capital for labour and throwing many thousands out of work; many gave up the ghost altogether. The inner city, it increasingly seemed, was the last place where any rational entrepreneur would conduct this kind of business. And there were ominous signs that other kinds of business – the big headquarters offices – might be following suit in the flight from the city.

It seemed ironic that, so relatively recently, everyone worried about metropolitan overgrowth; growth of any kind might now be worth holding on to.

London: Abercrombie and After

London provides the first and archetypal case. Abercrombie's twin plans of 1943–44 – the first, with Forshaw, for the inner Victorian area of London, the second for the entire conurbation and its surrounding region [4] – were based on the principle of what Douglas Hart has called ordering change [5]. The great city was seen as an organism, which like a plant could be trained to grow in an orderly and seemly way. Instead of the anarchic and ungainly sprawls that had characterized the 1920s and 1930s, physical elements controlled by the planner – major highways and green spaces – would be used to define the boundaries of residential neighbourhood and finally of the whole urban mass. The metropolis would thus have a clear size, shape and internal structure. Radial and ring roads, running for the most part as free-flow arterials through park strips, would define and separate London's historic urban villages. The innermost ring would define the outer edge of the central business district; the second ring would follow the approximate boundary between inner Victorian London and outer Georgian London. Two outer rings, one at the very edge of the urban mass, the other running as a parkway through the green belt, would help emphasize the sharp break between London town and London country.

All was thus to be neat, sharp, defined. Within the physical shells thus provided, there was to be a massive and rapid redistribution of people: over one million people would lose their homes through slum clearance and lower-density redevelopment of the inner areas, to be rehoused in new towns and expansions of old towns on the far side of the green belt. But here, again, the paramount emphasis was on clear physical division between town and country. Gerald Dix has drawn attention to Abercrombie's own early effort in regional planning for Dublin, in 1922, which in some striking details seems to anticipate the Greater London Plan [6]. And in all his work Abercrombie clearly recognizes a debt to

Howard's Social City and to a host of interpretations by Howard's followers, such as Arthur Crow's 1910 scheme for Ten Cities of Health, Purdom's 1921 plan for Satellite Cities and Unwin's regional plans of 1929–33. Howard's own ideas, as John Rockey has stressed [7], owe much to earlier utopian schemes for social reconstruction, notably Robert Pemberton's neglected 1854 plan, *The Happy Colony*, and G. J. Ouseley's *Palingenesia or the Earth's New Birth*, published in 1884.

Still, like Howard's own work, the Abercrombie Plan was a unique combination of proposals. What underlay it was a philosophical assumption that planning could lead to a harmonious steady state. Unplanned growth and change in themselves were positively bad, for they would lead to rapid obsolescence of buildings and land uses. But the containment of the urban area, through a green belt, could arrest this process – an idea that Abercrombie developed fully not in his London plan, but in the less celebrated plan he produced for the West Midlands four years later [8]. It could do so because the total population level would remain nearly static – the received demographic wisdom after World War Two, as it was just before it [9] – and because controls on industrial location – as recommended by Abercrombie in his historic minority report to the Report of the Royal Commission on the Distribution of the Industrial Population in 1940, and as enacted in the Distribution of Industry Act 1945 – would effectively halt the process of net migration from depressed north to prosperous south.

Perhaps such a static view of planning might have been possible, had not the British people and British industry proved so obdurately uncooperative. They continued to move from Britain's relatively depressed north to its relatively undepressed south, and to compound this error the people started unexpectedly to reproduce on a quite remarkable scale. When Abercrombie had sat on the historic Barlow Commission in 1937–40, the expectation was that birth rates would remain at a low level of around 15 per thousand and that the population of Great Britain, 46 million in 1937, would be between 44 and 49 million by 1971. In fact the birth rate increased steadily from 1955 to a peak of 18.6 in 1964, and the actual 1971 population was nearly 54 million [10]. What made this ironic was that the date of the upturn in the birth rate, 1955, was also the year when simultaneously the British government enjoined local authorities to resume their slum-clearance programmes and to press on with the establishment of green belts around the major urban agglomerations [11]. And not only this: the same mid-1950s years marked the relaxation by a Conservative government of the tight regional planning controls that had been operated by the previous Labour administration – thus undermining the neat assumptions about migration, and the associated idea that the overall population of the region could be maintained at a constant level.

Rising birth rates and a relaxed regional policy gave an arithmetic that did not work; something had to give, and it was the fundamental Abercrombie assumption of planning for a fixed future state. The history of British planning from 1960 to

1970 is one of uncertain and reluctant movement towards a fluid, growth-oriented style of regional planning which could adapt to changes in demographic assumptions. Three major plans for South East England – the *South East Study* of 1964, the *Strategy for the South East* of 1967 and the *Strategic Plan for the South East* of 1970 [12] – mark successive points along this road; two further reports, the *Development of the South East Strategic Plan* of 1976 and the *Government Response* of 1978 [13], represent a bewildered attempt to adjust the plans to the facts of a falling birth rate coupled with a rapid out-migration from London. Five reports in fourteen years signify not merely long-drawn-out political conflicts over policies, but also the uncertainty that planners had to face.

These plans owe much to two senior central-governmental planners, Sir Wilfred Burns and Geoffrey Powell. Building on the Abercrombie plans of a generation before, they helped fundamentally to reshape the London region. The 1964 *Study* proposed new cities and major expansions at distances from London that would put them effectively outside the capital's commuter field; the 1970 *Plan* developed these further into major and medium growth areas, the former to be planned agglomerations of up to a million and a half people. Essentially then these plans re-projected Abercrombie's ideas on to a larger screen and with a variable focus. In the last resort, this essential continuity may be more important than the element of change. Essentially conservative and evolutionary, British regional planning reacted to change by continuing to stress the Howardian virtues of the new town and the green backcloth. Garden city might have become planned agglomeration – but even this was clearly presaged in Howard's own concept of Social City. The fact is that the 1970 *Plan*, with its clear distinction between growth areas and restraint areas and with its strategic highway net, belongs to the same tradition as Abercrombie, Unwin, Purdom and Howard.

But there is an important difference. What resembled Abercrombie in these plans was the continued emphasis on discrete, relatively self-contained urban places as independent counter-magnets to the metropolis, albeit on a scale never contemplated by Abercrombie or Howard. What was different was the built-in flexibility that would allow a growth area to be inflated or deflated in response to changing present reality and future forecasts. And this new emphasis became ever more evident during the late 1970s and early 1980s. It did so by necessity; for, by then, the history of British planning had taken yet another of its ironic twists. As the birth rate fell after 1965, so it ought to have reopened up the prospect of a return to Abercrombie's steady state. But from the late 1960s onward, it emerged that the outward movement of people from London was failing to stop at the magic point when, according to Abercrombie and all the official planners who had interpreted him, it should have done. As late as 1970 the *Strategic Plan* could assume that the population of the Greater London conurbation, then some 7.5 million, would stabilize at about 7 million. But it did not. The people, cussedly, continued to move out, and so did their employers; by the 1981 Census Greater

London's population was down to 6.7 million, with a prospect of a further fall to less than 6 million by the early 1990s.

The causes of the flight were complex. But one of the most evident – and, to planners, most alarming – was the contraction in the economic base of the metropolis. In the five years from 1971 to 1976 alone, manufacturing employment fell by 30 per cent; modest increases in service employment failed to compensate [14]. Thus the whole nature of the London problem, as perceived by the planners, turned itself inside out. For over thirty years, from the Barlow inquiry at the end of the 1930s to the Greater London Development Plan at the end of the 1960s, they had been obsessed with the what saw as London's overgrowth; suddenly, all too suddenly, they were faced with the problem of its decline. This was disorientating in the extreme, for other features of the metropolitan problem remained much as before. There was rioting on the streets of Brixton – and of Wood Green and Acton – in the summer of 1981. But there had been riots in Trafalgar Square a hundred years before, on Bloody Sunday in 1887. There was unemployment once again in East and South London; but there had been unemployment, and basic poverty, when Charles Booth began his great inquiry into the life and labour of the people in London a century before that. The difference lay solely in this: that in Victorian London poverty, squalor and despair went hand-in-hand with a dynamic economy. Now, it seemed, the economic mainspring was broken; and London's planners, long attuned to the idea of controlling and constraining growth, had next to no idea of how to encourage it.

Tokyo: The Metropolis Uncontainable

In another great metropolis, Tokyo, a direct attempt was made to import an Abercrombie-style package – and it failed. Perhaps there, however, the whole exercise was doomed to failure from the start. Abercrombie's own ideas were developed against a background of sluggish demographic growth. London's growth, which seemed such a threat during the 1930s, took it merely from 6.5 million in 1921 to 8.5 million in 1939. In contrast, Tokyo's population – 6.9 million in 1942 and only 3 million after wartime bombing and evacuation – leapt to 7.4 million in 1953 and to 11.4 million in 1960. The similarity lay in the fact that, in both cases, natural increase contributed little to the result; the two cities grew because their economies were strong and because they attracted migrants from other parts of the country. But Tokyo's growth rate – 329,000 a year in the second half of the 1950s, 237,000 a year in the first half of the 1960s – was of a quite different order from interwar London's.

Yet the chosen remedy was the same. The National Capital Region Development Law of 1956 defined a built-up area stretching for an average of about 10 miles from Tokyo Central Station, and including also the neighbouring cities of Yokohama, Kawasaki and Kawaguchi. Beyond this developed area, a green belt zone some 7–10 miles wide was to stop further suburban sprawl. To absorb the consequent development pressures, a third zone between 17 and 45 miles from the centre would contain satellite towns. The parallel with the Abercrombie 1944 plan was precise – and so even was the legislative consequence. Just as the British had followed the 1944 plan with the 1945 Distribution of Industry Act and the 1946 New Towns Act, so the Japanese followed their 1956 measure with the 1958 Law for Town Development in the National Capital Region and then with the 1959 Law Restricting Industrial and Educational Establishments in the Built-Up Area within the National Capital Region. Thus the Japanese armed themselves with a plan and with the means – regulation of industry and public money for the development of new towns – to bring it all about [15].

The only problem was that it did not work; the rate of growth simply proved unmanageable. In 1965 the Census showed that in ten years the so-called Green Belt ring had added more than two million to its population. The Japanese authorities, recognizing defeat, simply tore up the plans. In the same year, 1965, they amended the National Capital Region Development Law, abandoning the Green Belt and substituting a suburban development area extending 30 miles and more from the centre. The satellites were to remain, but no longer with that title. The only surviving trace of the original plan was a notion that the new suburban development areas – including the former satellites – would be separated from each other, and from the old Tokyo, by some form of open park strip. In 1968 a revised basic City Planning Law tried to codify this concept by distinguishing urban promotion areas, with infrastructure, from urban control areas, without it. But significantly, the latter were at the far periphery where there would be least pressure for development anyway. The conclusion is impossible to resist: the Tokyo planners had unconditionally surrendered. The amended laws were an elaborate exercise in face-saving: city planning was now a recipe for free-for-all land development on a vast scale.

This saga poses the obvious question: can policies of metropolitan containment work effectively at all in a truly dynamic metropolis? Perhaps Abercrombie-style planning could work for a city like London only because London, and Britain generally – despite British preconceptions – were growing only sluggishly. But, as already seen, British-style planning did prove capable of intelligent adaptation to growth during the 1960s. The difference rather is this: the British machine could adapt because in fact it was steering a delicate course between a set of pressures – for rapid commercial land development – and a planning idea that coincided with another set of pressures – to continue to contain growth in the interests of preserving a traditional way of life. The 1970 Plan for South East England was in fact an historic compromise between these two sets of interests and pressures; it allowed rapid development of a few relatively small areas in order to guarantee continued tranquillity in the rest. But in a truly dynamic economy like Japan's in the 1950s and 1960s, there simply was no real constituency for conservation. Containment policies were the artificial brainchildren of a few planners who had absorbed western ideas. Consequently, as soon as real battle was joined, they proved impotent.

The Metropolis of Communism: Moscow under the 1935 plan

It was perhaps understandable that the planners of dynamic capitalist Tokyo should find themselves haplessly grappling with the consequences of uncontrollable urban growth. What was more surprising, perhaps, was that their counterparts in socialist Moscow should find themselves almost overwhelmed by the same forces.

Moscow, under Stalin's 1935 Plan – at that point a city of 3.66 million – was supposed to reach its 'ultimate' population of 5 million and thereafter stabilize. And, just as in Abercrombie's prescription for London, this was to be achieved by cutting net immigration into the city to zero; communist planning like capitalist planning could make that happen. But, as already seen in Chapter 2, Moscow was four-fifths of the way to this target after only four years, at the Census of 1939 [16]. The war brought relief of an unexpected nature, as people and jobs were evacuated eastwards; and afterwards, perhaps mercifully, the Soviet Union did not take another Census until 1959. That showed the population already to be just over the 5 million target; but it was itself a mere statistical artefact, for in the following year nearly a million more people were added as the city was extended to include suburban areas that had been developing outside it. By the 1970 Census Moscow had reached a total of 7,061,000. Particularly interesting was the fact that, only a year before, the official population estimate had given a total 400,000 lower, indicating that the official machine could not keep up with reality [17].

What all this illustrates is that in a modern industrial state, under whatever politico-economic prescription, no bureaucratic edict can control the complexity of individual and organized group behaviour. Moscow grew because people wanted to be there for education or for employment, and because powerful interests – industrial, research, bureaucratic – in effect overruled the Moscow city planners. These interests wanted to be in Moscow and to grow there because they felt that outside it their position would be weakened. This conflict became quite specific during the 1960s. In 1965 the Moscow planners submitted a plan that called for the city's ultimate population to be limited to between 6.6 and 6.8 million, to be enforced through an immediate halt on new industrial construction. This was strenuously opposed by the economic planning bodies of Gosstroi and Gosplan but was finally upheld by the Council of Ministers of the USSR; the draft plan, published in 1966, was approved 1971 [18]. But, as so often, reality was different; the 1970 Census showed the population to be already 7.1 million; that for 1979 showed it to be 8.0 million.

But even these 8 million were only part of the reality. Moscow in the 1960s and 1970s was just one component of a huge and complex metropolitan region, which already contained a total of 9 million people by 1960 and some 10.7 million by 1970.

Virtually all the growth in this period was in the *goroda-sputniki* (satellite towns), closely linked to Moscow by commuting and other ties. They were developed as part of the 1935 plan to draw off growth from the city itself, and so can be regarded as a planned creation. At any rate, the attempt to limit the city's growth did not apply to the *sputniki:* Soviet planners were not obsessed, as their western European counterparts so often were, by the need to redress regional imbalances between centre and periphery.

The 1971 plan for the city of Moscow, as finally approved, accepted the then level of population as the basis for stabilization – a vain hope in the event – and thence for planned contraction: 7.4 million people were to be reduced to only 6.5 million by the year 2000. But, conversely, a 1973 regional plan allowed for the population of the satellite zone to expand in the same period by nearly 2 million – and for that of the zone further out to grow by a similar amount, with a planned decentralization of no fewer than 1000 factory units from the city itself. The entire regional population was thus to grow by no less than 3 million in just over twenty-five years. Soviet, like British, planning was forced to recognize the reality of metropolitan growth.

The difference lies elsewhere. If the Soviet planning technocracy was weak in competition with the rival industrial bureaucracies, it was immeasurably strong in relation to the voice of the consumer. Perhaps, the people might have preferred the old two-storey Moscow; perhaps, they did not need or want the twelve-lane highways much too big for their traffic; perhaps, they did not much like life fourteen storeys up in the air. No one asked them; the planners pursued their own prejudices without benefit of popular feedback. It would be easy, too easy, to blame this simply on the system. The fact is that centralized bureaucratic provision flourishes on brute shortage: when people live two to a room, any kind of apartment seems good. Soviet housing managers never experienced what their British counterparts – first in the decaying provincial cities, then in London – began to discover from the end of the 1960s: the problem of the unlettable estate. The priority – alike in Moscow and in London and Paris in the 1960s – was to build fast and think afterwards. In London and in Paris, the thinking came soon enough. In Moscow, apparently, it is still to happen.

Paris: The Plan Disinhibited

It was historically just that Paris should be the metropolis where planning finally shed its deepest inhibitions. French planners had never fully shared the fundamental Anglo-Teutonic-American belief that the great metropolis was sinful. True, Le Corbusier in the late 1930s had come to share that belief, but this was a belated and perhaps superficial conversion; for him Paris was the soul and the glory of France and, like the *Roi Soleil* and Haussmann, he believed that the planner should be concerned to remake it so as the better to convey that image. In the period from the seventeenth to the nineteenth centuries, that image was expressed in the city monumental. Translated into twentieth-century terms, as Le Corbusier grasped as early as 1922, it meant the marriage of the city monumental and the city technocratic.

Le Corbusier's great disappointment was never to be allowed to realize that dream. And for nearly twenty years after World War Two, despite the beginnings of a French economic miracle engendered by a new union of public planning and private initiative, Paris appeared to be still sunk in its inter-war stagnation. The built stock and the infrastructure of the historic city continued to age in a way that charmed visitors but depressed the ordinary resident. The îlots insalubres remained as decaying tenements or as holes in the ground [19]. Outside the historic fortifications, the suburbs remained as chaotic, ill-planned and ill-serviced as they had in the 1930s. The response of planning, as in the regional plan of 1960, was to try to contain the further growth of the metropolis in pure Abercrombie fashion while providing no compensating new towns outside; instead, the plan stressed the reconstruction of the suburbs to make them into genuine centres for services and culture, plus far-distant counter-magnets 100 or more miles away.

But then came De Gaulle. Having extricated France from the Algerian debacle and secured its leading role in the Common Market, De Gaulle consciously sought a Paris that would symbolize the new France: a Paris that would be dynamic, expanding, modern, and technologically at the leading edge. This was an age when Jean-Jacques Servan-Schreiber could publish a best-seller called Le Défi Américain: a central French objective must be to challenge American technological and economic superiority, and Paris must play a leading role in that enterprise. Logically, De Gaulle appointed as regional prefect (Delégué au District de la Région de Paris) one of his right-hand men in Algeria, Paul Delouvrier, and told him to rewrite the plan.

The result was the 1965 Schéma Directeur for the Paris region, a plan that marked a radical break with European tradition. True, the celebrated 1948 Finger Plan for Copenhagen and the 1952 Markelius plan for Stockholm were earlier examples of planning for orderly metropolitan growth, in which urban development was consciously related to the expansion of the transportation network, and they may have served as explicit models to the Parisian planners. But there was no comparison in scale. Copenhagen and Stockholm were among the smaller European capitals – the Copenhagen plan provided for an eventual population of around 1.5 million, Stockholm's for around 1.2 million [20] – and in both it was possible to plan for an integrated metropolis with a strong centre. In contrast, the Parisian planners were dealing with a population that was expected to expand from 9 to 14 million between 1965 and the year 2000; a scale at which, despite the long tradition of centralization of the city, it would be necessary to think of a different kind of urban structure. Further, to cope with the demand of the population for better housing conditions and more open space, the plan had to think of doubling the total built-up area – a daunting prospect.

The first, stopgap response of the Parisian planners of the early 1960s had been a series of gigantic housing estates (*grands ensembles*), hastily-planned and hastily-built at the edge of the agglomeration and often lacking in proper transportation or services. Already, by the time of the *Schéma Directeur*, they were generating complaints; later these became a flood [21]. The response of the planners of 1965 was interesting; it was to borrow the British notion of the new town, but to turn it into something curiously French. Just as, earlier, Henri Sellier had developed garden cities that were part of the fabric of the agglomeration itself, so these latter-day new towns were consciously planned as enlargements of the urban mass. To emphasize the fact, they were to be linked to it both by new motorways and by a totally new express rail rapid transit system – a complete contrast with the London new towns of 1945–50, which were deliberately developed outside London's commuter field at that time.

Paris was thus to be transformed from a monocentric to a polycentric city: several of the new towns were to become prefectures for new *départements*, created as part of De Gaulle's administrative reorganization of 1964. But there was to be no doubt that, in the new planetary order, Paris was still to be the sun. It was to decentralize those functions inappropriate to its role as world city, but only to reinforce the latter. Further, throughout the whole agglomeration the main emphasis was to be on a cataclysmic modernization of the whole stock of homes, factories, offices, schools, hospitals, libraries, roads, public transport – literally the entire urban fabric. Some parts of this gigantic scheme were taken over bodily, where appropriate, from earlier plans – as with the gigantic decentralized office, apartment and shopping complex at La Défense, which had even anteceded the 1960 plan, or the schemes to 'revertebrate' some of the older suburbs such as Créteil, or the schemes for new motorways and a completely new rapid transit system (the Réseau Express Regional, or RER). But what was new and audacious about the 1965 plan was the way in which all these elements, new and old, were melded into an integrated scheme for the total reconstruction of a city region. In this sense the plan compares with Abercrombie's vision twenty-one years earlier for London. What was different was the relative lack of concern about the continued growth of the metropolis. It was going to happen anyway, argued the White Paper (*Livre Blanc*) that preceded the plan [22]; it might as well happen in an orderly way.

Metropolises Manqués: Berlin and Rhine-Ruhr

One of the great metropolitan cities of this book is today a ghost. As the world knows, Berlin has been cut in half administratively since 1948 and physically since 1961. West Berlin, a little more than half of the old city, is surrounded by foreign territory and is separated by 110 miles from its economic, social, political and cultural contacts in the Federal Republic. The *Autobahn* signs proudly proclaim East Berlin *Hauptstadt der DDR*, but is a peripheral capital for a nation whose demographic, economic and cultural weight is overwhelmingly concentrated at its southern periphery. The historic centre of the German *Reichshauptstadt* – the complex of administrative buildings gathered around the original medieval settlements of Berlin and Cölln – is a relatively deserted area of East Berlin, in the shadow of the wall; both West and East Berlin have now developed quite separate city centres, the first around the Kaiser Wilhelm Gedächtniskirche and the Kurfürstendamm, the second along the Frankfurter Allee.

Not only is each of these Berlins a shadow metropolis; it is also a stagnant or a declining metropolis. West Berlin, kept buoyant on subsidies from the Federal Republic, has lost virtually all its former administrative role and a substantial part of its industry. The subsidies go to support two major universities and a vigorous cultural life; in this respect, and in the range of entertainment and the sophistication of its intellectual life, Berlin retains an echo of its past. But its position is different even from that of the most obvious parallel case: Vienna after 1919. Then, Vienna ceased to be the capital of a great land empire and became capital of a fairly small European state. But at least it was still unambiguously the chief city for a nation of 7 million people, and – despite its peripheral position – a major centre of communications. Further, until World War Two a substantial tributary area of its former empire, especially in Czechoslovakia, still used it as employment, shopping and cultural centre: trams carried commuters from Bratislava to the centre of the city, across what is now the Iron Curtain. The accident of history deprived West Berlin, at a stroke, of any such role.

If West Berlin thus lost, which cities were the gainers? It is commonplace to say that after World War Two Germany reverted, more or less effortlessly, to the spatial organization that had characterized it before the ascendancy of Prussia and the unification of the country. In place of an imposed centralization, a natural federalism; in place of a strong national capital, a series of provincial centres of government and of culture. Today Bonn and Düsseldorf, Frankfurt and Stuttgart, Munich and Hamburg, all lay claim to vigorous independent life. The first two of these cities, further, belong to a single polycentric agglomeration of vast size; the Rhine-Ruhr region, which with some 10 million people is one of the twenty greatest metropolitan areas of the world. Yet a doubt remains. The heart of Rhine-Ruhr is an overwhelmingly industrial region with no pretension to the status of a great city; the two cities that could lay claim to the title are on its western periphery, and neither numbers as much as a million people. The fact is that Germany is a nation that gets by without a true metropolis. It has strong provincial capitals, with all the strengths and weaknesses such a status implies: a greater diffusion of independent intellectual, political and cultural life, without any of the excitements of the metropolis. And in West Berlin it retains nostalgic shadows, from the 1920s, of what it has lost.

The Non-Plan Metropolis: New York in the 1950s and 1960s

There was, finally, one great world city where the writ of the planners never truly ran at all. That might be thought an exaggeration; New York City did have its Planning Commission, the three states of New York, New Jersey and Connecticut did establish a joint Tri-State Planning Committee, and the Regional Plan Association continued to work on plans for an even wider area stretching up to 50 miles from Manhattan. What New York lacked was any notion of an attempt to control and guide its development through draconian planning powers, such as first London and then Paris had employed.

The Regional Plan Association, significantly, had been established as long ago as 1922, as part of that historic regional planning process that Mumford had condemned. During the 1950s and 1960s it continued to work as it had worked in the 1930s, to encourage good planning by cooperation among the myriad of authorities in their own best interests. And, recognizing its own status as a voluntary and unofficial body, it did not hesitate to do what Mumford had precisely attacked it for: advocate positive land development as the tool of good regional planning. During the mid-1960s, for instance, it called for a bold new regional design to house the 11 million extra people that were then expected in the region, and that might consume as much space as the 19 million already there. To that end it advocated a positive plan for the development of sub-centres, some nearer in, some farther out, which would make the region less monocentric than traditionally it had been; coupled with an improved transportation system that would tie these centres effectively together [23]. Following this, in the late 1960s it devoted much of its energies to a plan for the development of one such sub-regional centre at Jamaica in the borough of Queens [24]: a plan that would closely resemble what the French were doing at La Défense and the Japanese at Shinjuku. It spent no time at all on advocating ambitious plans for green belts (though it did advocate reservation of land for an Appalachian regional park) or for new towns, simply because in the political circumstances such plans would have had no chance of realization.

In a sense it did not have to worry. New York by the early 1970s, contrary to the optimistic predictions of a few years earlier, was already a metropolis in decline. Not merely the city itself, but also the whole wide region around it – however defined – were by then slowly losing people. As in London, manufacturing industry and traditional goods-handling services were massively contracting; the growth of the new white-collar jobs was failing to compensate. The new problem was how to regenerate the city's economy – a task to which the growth-oriented Regional Plan Association was perhaps more temperamentally-suited than the control-oriented statutory land-use planners of London. But whether either group had any positive ideas remained to be seen.

Towards Nekropolis   It was in a sense appropriate that New York should be the first great metropolis to face the spectre of decline. Lewis Mumford in the 1930s had written *The Culture of Cities* [25] there; there can be no doubt that he had his native city in mind when he wrote of the coming transition from Megalopolis, the overgrown giant city, to Nekropolis, the city of death. At that time, the vision still seemed fanciful. Forty years later, it seemed less so. The population and employment figures plainly spelt out the message that America's major urban areas were stagnating; growth was transferring itself to the smaller cities in the more rural parts of the nation; geographers were writing about a clean break with the 200-year-long trend of migration from farm and small town to metropolis [26]. Economic activities of all kinds, it seemed, no longer required the immediate, dense, face-to-face contacts that – as recently as the 1950s, in the classic Harvard account of the New York regional economy [27] – had provided the basis for metropolitan agglomeration. Convenient access by car and truck to the highway system, space to expand, and a congenial physical and social environment now suggested almost any location but the older, denser, bigger central city. Thus technological and economic forces were taking entrepreneurs in the newer, expanding activities far away, while social forces – residential preferences, fear of crime, the search for a better environment – took the people away too; and the two sets of forces reinforced each other, as pools of skilled labour and consumer markets contracted in inner cities and burgeoned in the exurbs and the smaller towns.

It seems that this fate befell the great cities of the Anglo-American world some time before it affected the others. Indeed, until the end of the 1960s London's planners continued to promote outward movement, confident that Canute-like they could stop the tide at the magic point when the city's population reached their predetermined target of some 7 million. But already by the early 1970s, the new reality was making itself felt and the central government was appointing consultants to analyse the plight of the English inner cities; they reported in 1977, and the government began to pump money into London and other British cities in a vain attempt to stem the tide. Over on the European mainland, it was just becoming evident in the contraction of artisan industry in eastern Paris, in the decline of the leading Dutch cities, in the belated recognition of pockets of deprivation in Berlin and Frankfurt.

The final irony is that the planners had again fought the last war. Just as they had so earnestly desired, the metropolis was solving its old problems by thinning out; the people and their jobs were returning to arcadian cities in the countryside. Yet somehow, the result was not as benign as they had hoped or expected. Like Fitzgerald's tragic figure – symbolically, an exurban escapee from New York – they constantly sought the orgastic future but were borne back ceaselessly into the past.

NOTES

1. See Marriott, O. (1967) *The Property Boom*. London: Hamish Hamilton.
2. G.B. Steering Group (1963) *Traffic in Towns: A Study of the Long Term Problems of Traffic in Urban Areas*. London: HMSO.
3. For an account of this transition, see Esher, L. (1981) *A Broken Wave: The Rebuilding of England 1940–1980*. London: Allen Lane.
4. Abercrombie, P. and Forshaw, J.H. (1943) *County of London Plan*. London: London County Council; Abercrombie, P. (1945) *Greater London Plan 1944*. London: HMSO.
5. Hart, D.A. (1976) *Strategic Planning in London: The Rise and Fall of the Primary Road Network*. Oxford: Pergamon, Chapter 3.
6. Dix, G. (1978) Little plans and noble diagrams. *Town Planning Review*, **49**, pp. 331–2.
7. Rockey, J. (1983) From vision to reality: Victorian ideal cities and model towns in the genesis of Ebenezer Howard's garden city. *Town Planning Review*, **54**, pp. 92–3, 98.
8. Abercrombie, P., and Jackson H. (1948) *West Midlands Plan*. London: Ministry of Town and Country Planning, para. 4.1 (12).
9. See Royal Commission on Population (1949) *Report*. London: HMSO.
10. Dix, *loc. cit.*, p. 344 (see note 6).
11. Hall, P., *et al* (1973) *The Containment of Urban England*. London: George Allen and Unwin, Volume 1, p. 605; Volume 2, p. 57.
12. Ministry of Housing and Local Government (1964) *The South East Study 1961–1981*. London: HMSO: South East Economic Planning Council (1967) *Strategy for the South East*. London: HMSO; Joint Plan Team (1970) *Strategic Plan for the South East*. London: HMSO.
13. South East Joint Plan Team (1976) *Strategy for the South East: 1976 Review*. London: HMSO; Department of the Environment (1978) *Strategic Plan for the South East: Review; Government Statement*. London: HMSO.
14. Standing Conference for London and South East Regional Planning (1981) *Development Trends in the South East Regional Planning (1981) The First Report of the Regional Monitoring Group (SC1467R)*. London: The Standing Conference.
15. Hall, P. (1977) *The World Cities* (2nd edn). London: Weidenfeld and Nicolson, pp. 233–5.
16. See above, Chapter 2.
17. Hall (1977), *op. cit.*, p. 151 (see note 15).
18. Frolic, B.M. (1975) Moscow: the socialist alternative, in Eldredge, H.W. (ed.) *World Capitals: Towards Guided Urbanization*. New York: Anchor Press/Doubleday, p. 276. Cf. Pallot, J. and Shaw, D.J.B. (1981) *Planning in the Soviet Union*. London: Croom Helm, p. 222; Huzinec, G.A. (1978) The impact of industrial decision-making upon the Soviet urban hierarchy. *Urban Studies*, **15**, pp. 144–5.
19. Evenson, N. (1979) *Paris: A Century of Change, 1878–1978*. New Haven and London: Yale University Press, p. 216.
20. Hall, P. (1967) Planning for urban growth: metropolitan area plans and their implications for South-East England. *Regional Studies*, **1**, pp. 103, 107.
21. Evenson, *op. cit.*, pp. 245–51 (see note 19).
22. Premier Ministre: Délégation Générale au District de la Région de Paris (1963) *Avant-Projet de Programme Duodécennal pour la Région de Paris*. Paris: Imprimerie Municipale.
23. Regional Plan Association (1967) *The Region's Growth*. New York: The Association.
24. Regional Plan Association (1968) *Jamaica Center*. New York: The Association.
25. Mumford, L. (1938) *The Culture of Cities*. London: Secker and Warburg.
26. Vining, D.R. and Kontuly, T. (1977) Increasing returns to scale in city size in the face of an impending decline in the size of large cities: Which is the bogus fact? *Environment and Planning, A*, **9**, pp. 59–62; Vining, D.R., Strauss, A. (1977) A demonstration that the current deconcentration of population in the United States is a clean break with the past. *Environment and Planning, A*. **9**, pp. 751–58.
27. Cf. especially Hoover, E.M., and Vernon, R. (1959) *Anatomy of a Metropolis: The Changing Distribution of People and Jobs Within the New York Metropolitan Region*. Cambridge, Mass.: Harvard University Press.

Index